The Reading Process
the teacher and the learner

The Reading Process
the teacher and the learner
fourth edition

Miles V. Zintz
University of New Mexico

Zelda R. Maggart
University of New Mexico

wcb
Wm. C. Brown Publishers
Dubuque, Iowa

Book Team

T. Greg Bell   *Editor*
Sandra E. Schmidt   *Developmental Editor*
Kevin P. Campbell   *Production Editor*
Catherine Dinsmore   *Designer*
Mavis M. Oeth   *Permissions Editor*
Faye M. Schilling   *Visual Research Editor*

wcb group

Wm. C. Brown   *Chairman of the Board*
Mark C. Falb   *President and Chief Executive Officer*

wcb

Wm. C. Brown Publishers, College Division

Lawrence E. Cremer   *President*
James L. Romig   *Vice-President, Production Development*
David Wm. Smith   *Vice-President, Marketing*
David A. Corona   *Vice-President, Production and Design*
E. F. Jogerst   *Vice-President, Cost Analyst*
Marcia H. Stout   *Marketing Manager*
Linda M. Galarowicz   *Director of Marketing Research*
William A. Moss   *Production Editorial Manager*
Marilyn A. Phelps   *Manager of Design*
Mary M. Heller   *Visual Research Manager*

Photo credits

Cover image by Carol Anthony

Southwest Cooperative Educational Laboratory: pp. 11, 21, 73, 126, 161, 162, 196, 266, 315, 417

Photo David Woodward/Courtesy of University of New Mexico Photo Service: pp. 50, 105, 136, 247, 331, 354

Ray Garduno/Courtesy of Albuquerque Public Schools: pp. 122, 174, 187, 219, 225, 227 (top and bottom), 248, 321, 351, 378, 418, 490, 503

Printed in the United States of America
10   9   8   7

To Mary Hatley Zintz
and
Harley B. Maggart

Contents

Tables

Table of Figures

Table of Tables

Table of *From Theory to Practice* Activities

Preface

In today's world, reading is the major avenue to learning, and the educational system operates with learning to read as its highest priority. Yet, it is often reported that the schools are not meeting this priority. The primary purpose of this text is to help students become successful teachers of reading in the classroom. Because the differences in learning and achievement are so great among children, all teachers must learn to measure the success of their teaching and to apply diagnostic, adaptive, and prescriptive measures early and continuously during the school year. We hope that this text will help teachers to become *diagnostic teachers of reading* every day from the first day of school.

What Are the Issues?

The controversy about choice of method leaves each of us with the responsibility of doing his or her best to make wise choices about how to teach boys and girls to read. There are several viewpoints:

1. One could start with the isolated pieces of language and put them together in reading. The result is a phonics approach, which teaches the names of letters and the sounds of phonemes and combines them into isolated words. There can be no denying that many children have learned to read by this practice.
2. One could start by memorizing a limited vocabulary of selected words without any attention, at first, to letters. People who follow this approach would argue that one can learn "ball" as "one piece of language," which can be identified as easily as "b," "a," and "l" can be learned separately.
3. One could start by encouraging boys and girls to enrich and extend their oral language use and to become able to tell stories in sequence. This approach leads to allowing children to dictate their own stories, which become the first reading material in which they identify their

words. The belief is that if these children identify their own words, then motivation to read will be much greater, and the task of reading will seem much more relevant to them.

4. One could accept the point of view that all children will "arrive" at this state of optimum readiness for reading when their language, thinking, and motivation give them the confidence that they can read. In this approach, the teacher will allow one or more children in this optimum state of readiness to *try* to read. Perhaps the teacher or another adult will read the story to the child or children. Then one child will try to reconstruct the story in the "book language" that the teacher has used to read it.

Many teachers will find that they are expected to use a basal reader. Upon inspection, they may find that the basal reader actually is a tool for carrying out one or more of the four approaches to reading just described. It is important that teachers recognize the theoretical perspectives of the writers of these books. Clearly, these schools of thought are so divergent that there will not soon be a "meeting of the minds" about how to teach beginners to read. There will also continue to be controversy about how to teach various groups of children, some of whom are in regular classes while others are in special settings. These include bilingual children, children with special learning problems, the gifted, children with limited English proficiency, and children with reading problems. In this text, we have tried to present all of these points of view on teaching methods, as well as a perspective on children with special needs, so that the teacher who is free to do so can select his or her preference and use it to meet the needs of the students. For those who work in a system where one method has been established for the entire school, we encourage the teacher to utilize that method while seeking ways to enrich the teaching *eclectically* by borrowing from other avenues to learning.

How To Study This Text

Each chapter begins with a cognitive map (structured overview) that points out the chapter's key concepts. We believe this cognitive map will help students prepare to read the chapter and integrate its subsections. You may look back after reading the chapter to see if you agree with our organization that makes the chapter a unit. We have included a brief list of technical terminology at the beginning of each chapter, and we believe that some familiarity with these words will make reading the book much easier. The monograph *A Dictionary of Reading* (International Reading Association, 1981) will provide formal definitions beyond those given in the text. We have also included guide questions at the beginning of each chapter that are answered in the text. If students can discuss these questions with confidence, we believe they will have understood the content.

There are fifty activities for students to complete as they study the text. Called *From Theory to Practice,* these constitute a good set of assignments for the course. Time available, maturity of students, and overall course planning will determine how you will use these activities. You may find that some can provide the bases for written assignments, while others can be used for class or group discussions. These *From Theory to Practice* activities are set off from the regular text.

The chapter summaries are brief restatements of the significant ideas presented. Students may use the chapter summaries to review what they have read, and to find out if they need to refer back to parts of the chapter.

Philosophical Approach

We believe that reading is an integral part of communication and that learning to read builds on the abilities of boys and girls to receive and express language. Studies of how young children acquire language and how they move from speaking to writing reveal our need to study linguistics. To this end, we have included chapter 3, "Linguistic Foundations for Reading Instruction." Reading requires language comprehension, semantic processing, unique types of language behavior, and reorganization of schemata stored in memory; the teacher must understand these concepts.

We believe that the affective component of learning is very important. Permanent interest in reading and in the development of critical and evaluative skills is as much a product of affect as of cognition. Failure to understand and to act upon this principle can destroy motivation, ingenuity, and creativity, and can seriously complicate further reading instruction.

Because our nation has accommodated millions of boys and girls for whom English is a second language, we now have made the teaching of reading more complex. Those students with *limited English proficiency* need a great deal of enriched oral language development to make reading a rewarding experience. *All* classroom teachers should know something about the techniques for teaching English as a second language. Such teaching must be systematic, sequenced, and relevant to the child.

Chapter Outline

This text is organized into six parts: (1) Overview; (2) A Good Beginning; (3) Facilitating Instruction in the Classroom; (4) The Skills of Reading; (5) Provision for All the Children; and (6) Evaluation.

Part 1: Overview. While psychological foundations (chapter 2) and linguistics (chapter 3) are basic to the understanding of the content of the text, there may be readers who have previously studied this content and are able to review the material quickly.

In this edition of the text, the informal reading inventory has been placed in the overview in chapter 4. We believe that students of reading must learn how to listen to children when they read. So, in this text, the IRI serves genuine purposes at two levels. Very early in the course, each student needs to learn to identify the facets of oral and silent reading that determine success or failure. The first student activity is intended to demonstrate the complexity of knowing "how to listen" when someone reads. The second purpose is to help teachers become able to identify and analyze readers' miscues and to provide learning experiences based on that information. The IRI is also the most important evaluative instrument for the student to be able to use at the end of the course. Perhaps the activity at the end of chapter 4 needs to be redone at the end of the semester. A sample IRI is provided in Appendix 2 to make it easier to carry out the activity.

Part 2: A Good Beginning.　　These chapters offer teachers techniques to assess readiness for reading and to teach beginning reading. A child's readiness for reading encompasses language skills, listening skills, attention, motivation, and some understanding of what the reading process is and how it works. Introduction to formal reading should be gauged by the success of learners in their attempts at reading activities. It is important to "follow the child's lead" in introducing formal reading.

Part 3: Facilitating Instruction in the Classroom.　　The learning environment deserves its fair share of the teacher's attention. To facilitate learning, classroom management requires grouping for reading instruction, provisions for interaction, and parent-teacher-child cooperation.

Part 4: The Skills of Reading.　　Strategies to meet each child's learning needs become the focus of attention in part 4. Chapters 9 through 14 present techniques for teaching word recognition, the skills of comprehension, study skills, use of reading skills in reading expository materials, critical reading, oral reading, and the building of permanent reading habits.

In this edition, chapter 10, "The Skills of Comprehension," has been rewritten to develop the meaning of comprehension and to describe methods of teaching to help children read with good understanding. Comprehending written discourse can be made easier by: (1) extending all students' experiences so that concepts in textbooks will be meaningful; (2) teaching such aspects of comprehension as inference, metaphor, and anaphora; and (3) learning to recognize writing patterns used in textbooks—such patterns as sequence, effect-cause, and generalizing. Teachers need to view oral reading as both a tool and a goal. As a tool, it helps the classroom teacher to continually evaluate a child's developmental reading skills, and as a goal it will serve most people as an important skill for life.

Part 5: Provision for All the Children.　　The gifted, the retarded, the bilingual, the gifted bilingual, and the child with a specific learning disability—each one may function in his or her own way in the regular classroom if an adequate individualized educational program (IEP) is prepared. Teachers need to be prepared for the presence of children with special needs—sometimes those being mainstreamed from special education classrooms—becoming fully functioning members of their classes. It is at this juncture that a good diagnostic program, one that evolves from an eclectic approach, will be most necessary. For one, a teacher-pupil planned individualized reading program; for another, a structured program to teach skills and review them; and for yet another, basal lessons to provide long periods of practice on plateaus of learning. In any case, during the busy day, the decision-maker and programmer (the classroom teacher) will need the patience of Job.

Part 6: Evaluation in the Reading Program. The text emphasizes both the informal and the formal types of evaluation used by the classroom teacher. Teacher judgment, when it is based on careful observation and the use of informal evaluation, is probably the most valid assessment of a child's learning in the school.

The text concludes with a reaffirmation of the importance of reading in the elementary school curriculum. Additional guides are offered to show how *each teacher* can increase the functional reading ability *each child* brings to the classroom. This is what diagnostic teaching is all about.

Diagnostic teaching is a methodology that requires that the teacher ascertain the level of functional skills and abilities of *each child* in the classroom. It will never be possible for all the children in a group to learn the same thing at the same time with the same amount of practice. To teach diagnostically, teachers must utilize important psychological concepts:

1. The varying innate abilities of children in all skills, abilities, and appreciations.
2. The role of practice in learning.
3. The importance of motivation for efficient learning.
4. Development of understanding.
5. Transfer of learning where common elements exist.
6. The problem of forgetting.

Finally, diagnostic teaching provides for every child's learning needs, whether the child is linguistically different, culturally different, gifted, retarded, emotionally disturbed, or neurologically impaired.

The references at the end of each chapter offer extensive reading in any phase of the program that a teacher may find especially meaningful or necessary in day-to-day work.

We would like to thank the following reviewers for their valuable assistance with this revision: Beverley L. Zakaluk, University of Manitoba; Lauren Leslie, Marquette University; and Jean M. Casey, California State University, Long Beach and the University of Southern California.

Miles V. Zintz
Zelda R. Maggart

The Overview

Part

Chapter 1 defines reading as a continuous developmental process. Chapter 2 then discusses the psychological foundations on which learning is based. Chapter 3 contains information about the phenomenon of language and language acquisition—that is, how children learn to talk. Teachers should have some understanding of what linguistics—the scientific study of language—teaches about the nature of language before they begin helping children develop reading skills.

Chapter 4, "The Informal Reading Inventory," is presented as a part of the overview of the text. We believe students of the teaching of reading must very early in the course (1) listen to many children read; (2) learn what to listen for when children do read; and (3) develop an ability to make value judgments about the individual child's performance in oral and silent reading.

What Is Reading?

A Cognitive Map: What Is Reading?

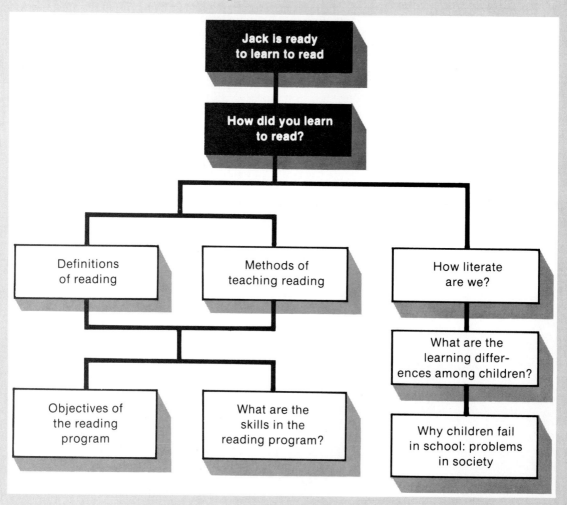

1

Guide Questions

1. Contrast bottom-up and top-down theories of the reading process.

2. Compare phonics, skills-based, and language-experience approaches to teaching reading.

3. What is reading?

4. Describe the various social factors that are influences on the learning-to-read process.

5. What is meant by the statement that "as children go through school, differences among them grow greater and greater"?

6. What are the major objectives of the reading program?

Terminology

basal reader

bottom-up approaches

language-experience approach

phonics approach

reading process

skills approach

top-down approaches

Jack is in the first grade. He is a happy little boy who happened to be born into a comfortable, middle-class family early in May. He had one brother and no sisters. When Jack was born, his father was past thirty and already a junior executive. Often, he brought his briefcase home and worked at a desk in the extra bedroom. Jack's mother had graduated from a two-year college course with an A.A. degree and then worked for a few years as a secretary in a large telephone company office before she married. Jack's father was a very curious, interested, "always learning" kind of man who read a great deal. His mother read too, usually about subjects that would give her practical hints. When Jack was an infant, his mother spent all her time with him while his father was at work. They laughed and played, and she *talked to him* a great deal. By the time he was able to walk around a bit, his mother was pregnant a second time. During her pregnancy, she continued to spend a great deal of time *talking to Jack.* When he was eleven months old he was saying *mama, daddy, go, come,* and a few other words in clearly intelligible language. Jack's mother explained to him that she would be going to the hospital when his little brother was born. When that time arrived, his grandmother came and lived in the house and assumed full responsibility during the mother's absence.

The grandmother bought books of the *Baby's First Book* variety and shared them with Jack. By the time Jack was eighteen months old, his mother was holding him on her lap reading *Mother Goose* to him for relatively long periods of time in the afternoon while his brother slept, or in the evening while they waited for Daddy to come home. By the time Jack was three, he was "demanding" a story hour at bedtime and using language confidently in complicated sentence structures. His growth in language skills was constant, and as he developed a *broad vocabulary* he could deal with concepts and problem solving. He learned to *listen,* to *observe,* and to like books.

Even though the state in which he lived did not provide kindergarten classes for five-year-olds, Jack enjoyed many of the experiences of kindergartners with his mother and brother sixteen months younger. He learned how to *sequence ideas,* how to *explain* simply and carefully, teaching his little brother many things big boys had already mastered.

Jack entered first grade with *highly developed verbal* skills. He could *listen well with understanding* and *understand* many of the *simple jokes* his mother and father told largely for his benefit. He went most *willingly* to *school* because he felt he was getting very grown up by the time he was *six years and four months old.* When he asked his mother about words, she had always answered his questions. He usually recognized his own, his father's, and his mother's names on letters that came in the mail. He could distinguish many of his books by the pictures on the covers, but he was probably also noticing distinguishing features in the titles, too. By the time he entered school, Jack and his brother had a library of nearly 200 books, mostly of the variety picked up in the supermarket.

Needless to add, Jack entered first grade *confident and secure*. He was anxious to learn to read. With a teacher who was gentle, understanding, and efficient in the teaching of reading, he would probably read by almost any method. Fortunately, the teacher did know that all children grow at different rates, have varying needs for emotional response and security, and have different levels of mastery of language as a communication process. The teacher encouraged all the children to talk, to discuss, to explain, and to have fun at school. By the end of one month, the teacher had divided the class into groups—those who were ready for formal reading, those who needed readiness activities and a gradual introduction to formal reading, and those who would not show a great deal of interest in the printed word for several months.

The teacher continued to study the children carefully. She discussed them with her supervisor and, as problems in their learning arose, referred them to the school nurse, the school psychologist, or the school social worker. But her goal was to keep everybody learning something.

When Jack dictated an especially good experience story, she encouraged him to take it home and read it to his father and mother. When he finished each of the preprimers, she encouraged him to carry them home and read aloud to whichever *parent* would *really listen*.

Phonics, spelling, and writing developed naturally and smoothly for Jack. His manuscript writing was very legible almost from the beginning. Jack will finish first grade able to read fluently and smoothly from books more difficult than first grade readers. He may have read stories in a first-semester, second grade book or many trade books of interest to him. Also he will have written (dictated) at least one book of stories which will have been bound together with a table of contents and with his name visibly displayed on the cover distinguishing him as the author.

How fortunate Jack was to have six excellent *years of readiness* for the academic job of going to school!

Now contrast Jack's successes with the problems confronting Ernesto.

Ernesto is in the fifth grade. His grandparents speak only Spanish, and his parents learned Spanish first at home but attended only English language schools. They were never taught the structure of English as a second language and never learned to speak it confidently. As a result, Ernesto and all his brothers and sisters have difficulty with English syntax and vocabulary. While they use the superficial everyday expressions "Good morning, Miss Smith" or "How're things?" with ease, they lack both ability and confidence to compose essays in class or give good oral reports. Similarly, Ernesto neither studied Spanish nor learned to read or write it.

Consequently, in fifth grade Ernesto has confidence and understanding with the sound patterns of commonly used Spanish vernacular and he gets along with the minimum amount of English language. He is illiterate in Spanish and considerably substandard for fifth grade in reading and writing English. He is well on his way to leaving school neither monolingual nor bilingual. As Knowlton said, "He may graduate from high school illiterate in two languages!"[1]

Jack and Ernesto represent only two of the innumerable children any classroom teacher in the elementary school must be prepared to meet and guide through a school year. While all children are like each other in more ways than they are different, it is the understanding and acceptance of the degrees of difference that enable each child to grow.

Of course, the school could have provided a quite different curriculum for Ernesto. More and more schools today would be able to offer a child like Ernesto some options in first grade:

1. A language specialist in the school system could determine whether *English* or *Spanish* was his primary language. If it was Spanish, he could be encouraged to develop it through oral language usage to the level of reading readiness and then learn to read in Spanish first. At the same time he could be learning English systematically and efficiently as a second language. However, if his primary language was English, he could be encouraged to develop it further through oral language usage to the level of prereading competence and then learn to read in English first. At the same time he could be learning Spanish systematically and efficiently as a second language. In either event, he could be proud of being a bilingual/bicultural person in our pluralistic society.

2. If a school does not provide regular instruction in a child's primary language, an extended period of time would be allotted for him to master English for the formal reading necessary for success in the school grades. Even though certified teachers of the child's primary language may not be available, the school would be responsible for providing opportunity for the child to use and extend his knowledge and understanding of it orally as another language.

3. Because the school is concerned that a child's self-concept be strengthened and not destroyed, it provides a variety of programs in which children of minority groups are encouraged to appreciate their language and culture. Children learn that their extended families are integral parts of the community. The school bolsters their self-concept and thus makes them feel important as persons. Chapter 15 is devoted to this topic.

What Is Reading? Is reading pronouncing words correctly? Is reading getting ideas from printed pages? Here are some definitions:

Reading is decoding written words so that they can be produced orally.
Reading is understanding the language of the author of a printed passage.
Reading is the ability to anticipate meaning in lines of print so that the reader is not concerned with the mechanical details but with grasping ideas from groups of words that convey meaning.

Reading encompasses all of these things. The differences in current reading programs in use today lie mainly in the relative importance assigned to each of these three definitions.

Harste states that both teachers and students hold a particular and identifiable theoretical orientation toward the process of reading and reading instruction, whether or not it is implicitly stated. Even teachers who claim to hold no theoretical orientation on approaches to teaching reading demonstrate a consistent theoretical orientation in their definitions of reading and their choices of instructional approaches and materials:[2]

If a teacher emphasizes word recognition, students are likely to view reading as a process of word identification.

If a teacher emphasizes phonics, students are likely to view reading primarily as a process of decoding words.

If a teacher guides the students in extracting a message from a passage, much freer thought about ideas and meanings prevails.

Two major theoretical orientations that have stimulated much debate in the field of reading are the *top-down* and *bottom-up* approaches. An understanding of these two philosophies enables a teacher to make informed instructional choices about methods, materials, and instructional techniques.

Deford suggests that the two philosophies differ primarily in the way language is viewed.[3] The bottom-up theory views language as systematic and mechanistic. Reading is composed of discrete parts that can be separated for units of instruction. The top-down theory, which might be termed "organismic," views language as systems that are interrelated and interdependent. The reading act is a total process that cannot be broken down into parts without distorting the process. With the top-down theory, the whole is thought to be greater than the sum of its parts.

Burke[4] suggests that the reading models described by Singer and Ruddell[5] can be organized into three major clusters along a continuum of language. These same models can be categorized according to the top-down/bottom-up orientations to reading. Models that focus on smaller-than-word units (Gough)[6] and on word units (LaBerge)[7] can be seen as bottom-up approaches. Those models that focus on larger units can be seen as top-down approaches. In this context, bottom-up theory clearly includes phonics and skill-oriented approaches to reading. Top-down theory is represented by the whole-language approach to reading.

Phonics Approaches

A phonics approach will clearly be concerned with decoding. Emphasis will be on the mastery of sound-symbol correspondences, with less attention given to meaning. One underlying assumption is that if the words are pronounced, then meaning will automatically follow. Letters and letter clusters are introduced and then followed by short words that utilize the letters learned. Content is limited to those words that conform to the phonics generalizations introduced up to that point. Those few needed function words for which the phonics have not yet been learned are learned as sight words; however, learning them is not emphasized.

When children encounter difficulty with an unknown word, they are encouraged to "sound it out." McCracken and Walcutt advocate this approach.[8] They believe that reading is essentially a process of mechanically decoding words.

Programs strongly oriented to a phonics approach for identifying words have proved unsuccessful in motivating children strongly enough to want to continue to learn to read. Recent attempts to construct preprimers that use no more than twelve, fifteen, or twenty different words have only provided further evidence that this is not a way to motivate children to learn to read. Savage's example of teaching spelling patterns in rigidly controlled sentences using the ridiculous "Flick the tick off the chick with a thick stick, Nick," exemplifies the possible extremes in such sentence composition.[9]

Without alert, innovative teachers, the newer reading programs in use may allow too much time for teaching beginners the names of letters, severely controlled vocabularies, and other artificial ways of encouraging the work of decoding.

The belief in a bottom-up approach to reading instruction has existed for many years. Robinson, in a review of the history of reading instruction, described phonics methods in use during the period from 1776 to 1840 in the United States.[10] By the beginning of the twentieth century "there were loud voices raised against an overdose of phonics, since there appeared to be many poor readers in the upper grades who had been raised on strong phonics programs."[11] Despite the outcry, phonics remained the dominant approach for instructional materials.

An incident from 1947 demonstrates the philosophical approach to reading just described.

> A rural county superintendent of schools was explaining to a small group of teachers that she was very proud of her kindergarten phonics program. "Why," she said, "before the end of the kindergarten year, every one of my five-year-olds can spell *shrapnel*." The teachers looked at each other wondering *why* a five-year-old boy living on a farm near Clarinda, Iowa, who couldn't read yet would need to spell *shrapnel*.

This superintendent would undoubtedly have agreed with Rudolf Flesch,[12] who says:

> To contend that most English words are not phonetic is a blatant lie. Recent computer studies show that only about 2½ percent of all English words aren't spelled according to phonic rules. There are about 180 of these rules, and most children can learn them all in a matter of months in first grade. At that point, a child can read and understand about 24,000 words, which is the number of words that most first graders have in their speaking and listening vocabularies.[13]

In a discussion of "Look-and- Say" books that present the phonograms "or" and "ar" with only three examples for children, Flesch states:

> In a phonics-first text the children would get about a hundred "ar" words and a hundred "or" words to practice on until the pronunciations of "ar" and "or" are firmly fixed in their subconscious minds.[14]

Teachers may contrast Flesch's statement with Sterl Artley's comment that "sounding out the word is cumbersome, time consuming, and unnecessary. Like the appendix, its usefulness is a vestige of the past."[15]

Skills Approach

The skills approach also represents a bottom-up approach and emphasizes word identification, that is, instant recognition of sight words. Meaning is recognized to the extent that words are always introduced in context rather than in isolation. In the beginning, the emphasis is on word recognition, not meaning. Later, the emphasis is on learning how to exercise a skill in reading rather than on reading to learn and understand.

Skills such as sight words, structural analysis, comprehension skills, study skills, and interpretive and creative reading skills are seen as distinct units that can be taught in isolation. Phonics is also included in the skills program, but without a major focus. The skills approach is apt to present (1) the letter symbols (graphophonics), (2) syntax (the grammar of the language), and (3) semantics (meaning) as three discrete units extracted from the total process of reading.

Basal Reader

The materials most commonly associated with the skills approach are the basal readers found in almost every school in America.

It is estimated that approximately 90 percent of the schools in the United States use *a basal reader series* as the primary curriculum requirement to teach boys and girls to read. Basals will be described later in the text; suffice it to say here that we are talking about each child at each grade level having a *reader,* which is his or her textbook for that year for learning how to read. Basal readers are organized to: (1) provide carefully sequenced presentation of decoding and word recognition skills; (2) provide for teaching the skills of reading all through the elementary grades; and (3) facilitate growth in independent learning and the application of reading abilities in content area learning.

Basal readers have been heavily criticized as being shallow, repetitive, and uninteresting. They are said to present only the life of the middle-class child in the urban world. While these arguments were more nearly true two decades ago, significant changes were made in basal readers during the sixties and seventies. Guthrie reminds us that a basal series analyzed recently contained many more authored than non-authored stories and many authored poems.[16] One reader contained fifteen narrative and nine expository passages—topics of the stories included images on the moon, life on Kilimanjaro, communication among astronauts, dreams of gnomes, and a child thief who is brought to justice.

Bettelheim's claims that basals are bland, colorless, overshadowed by the theme of playfulness, and most uninteresting to children are simply exaggerated and not based on a careful analysis of the facts.[17]

Language-Experience Approach

A sentence meaning approach reflects the top-down orientation. The major focus is on meaning. There can be no reading without meaning. The reader must *actively participate* to create his meaning from the printed symbols, using both visual and non-visual cues. Meaning does not automatically result from word identification. It is further true that exact identification of every word is not necessary and should *not* be expected in the beginning. The act of reading is a process of hypothesis testing, and miscues are to be expected. The meaning sought is much more in the *mind* of the reader than it is in the print visible to the *eye*.

Children need not start with simple sentences prepared for them by a "strange" author. If they are allowed to dictate their own stories, the materials need not be limited by vocabulary or knowledge of phonics. Children will develop strategies for predicting, sampling, confirming, and integrating all of the cue systems into meaning. The use of familiar stories, rhymes, etc., helps children to learn predicting strategies.

Knowledge of phonics is necessary, but extensive phonics instruction is not. Exposed to rich oral language use, children learn phonics generalizations and can apply them without extensive instruction.

When the reader encounters an unknown word, the task is to think about what word would make sense in that context. He or she is not interrupted to correct an error or to receive help identifying a word, unless the help is requested. The reader learns to read by reading. Reading, like language, is acquired rather than taught.

The rationale of this "language-experience" approach is that children need to learn how the process of reading works by seeing that what they can express in their own vernacular can be recorded for them and that it means what they said when they first thought of it. Allen, author of language-experience materials, said, "Children who write, read! They have to read!" He continues:

> To children who have experienced authorship many times, reading is not lessons, worksheets, practice exercises, or a time each day in a time schedule (perhaps to dread). It is the continuous discovery of stepping-stones to a lifetime of enjoyment of books. It results in the conceptualizations:
>
> > What I can think about, I can say.
> > What I can say, I can write.
> > What I can write, I can read.
> > I can read what I can write and what other people have written for me to read.[18]

There is basic psychological value in having first or second graders use their own vocabulary and sentence structure in preparing a great deal of their reading material during the beginning of the reading program. If the reading program ended here, they would not be mature readers. Reading must take children into new areas of life and experience that are provided for their enjoyment through the writing of other people. Of course, children need all the clues they can be given in order to help them anticipate meaning in all they read.

Beyond this, children require a great deal of easy reading practice, just as in learning analogous skills, such as how to play the piano, or how to use another language fluently. As they refine their decoding skills through a great deal of

Books of familiar stories help children to learn predicting strategies.

interesting reading practice, more of the words they encounter in print become sight words. What happens is that by using the analytical skills they have learned and the context of what they are reading, they can immediately identify the necessary word to complete the meaning in a sentence or paragraph.

Reading is a process of thinking, evaluating, judging, imagining, reasoning, and problem solving. It is necessary, however, to distinguish between the tasks of learning how to read as young children do it and of daily reading as mature readers do it. Teachers must provide children with learning opportunities that allow them to sense from the very beginning that reading produces meaning and that reading and writing are only extensions of the listening and speaking that the children have been doing for some years.

Reading materials for children just learning to read must be structured to allow them to anticipate and acquire meaning from context from the very first lessons. This has been explained by Burke as a process by which children utilize the grammar of their language to express ideas personal and important to them. They are not being bogged down with the sound-symbol relationships of letters until there is need for them, and then only after they have understood how the process of reading works.[19] (See figure 1.1.) This emphasis is based on the point of view that children bring to school a fully developed language and possess all the skills of thinking, reasoning, problem solving, and imagining in oral language. Instead of supposing that they do not know any words to read with, teachers must recognize that they know thousands of words, but not in their written form. By using a child's own experiences, conversation, and ability to explain events, teachers can write this language for the child to read. Seeing the written form

Figure 1.1
Meaning must always
be the center of the
reading task. Every
lesson should be
figuratively like a
wedge that reaches to
the center as in the
diagram.

From Carolyn L. Burke,
"The Language Process:
Systems or Systematic," in
*Language and Learning To
Read,* ed. Richard E.
Hodges and E. Hugh
Rudorf (Boston: Houghton
Mifflin, 1972), p. 26.
Reprinted by permission.

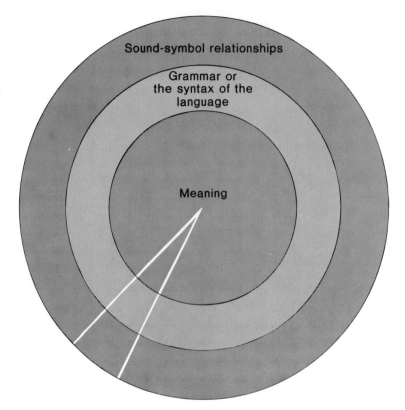

Sound-symbol relationships

Grammar or
the syntax of the
language

Meaning

of their own language and hearing it read back, children understand that the written words are an extension of their spoken language. This language-experience approach to beginning reading is the logical way to extend the child's listening and speaking skills to include reading and writing. As the avenue to formal reading for all children, the language-experience approach will be discussed more fully in a later chapter.

When children read at an appropriate level of difficulty, three kinds of *feedback* help them decide how accurately they are anticipating meaning. First, the printed word must correspond to an idea or concept they already know. They will reject any nonsense word and accept one that makes sense. Second, they will know whether or not a pronunciation of a printed word fits the syntax of a sentence spoken correctly in their own vernacular. If a noun is needed but an oral reader supplies an adjective or a verb, it will be rejected immediately because it does not fit the syntax. Third, children will be continually testing the appropriateness of meaning of a sentence the way they have read it and reject any words that do not make sense in the context of the passage. So, the reader's (or listener's) knowledge of words, grammar, and semantic correctness provides not only feedback for what is being read but enables one to anticipate, to some degree, what is going to be read next.[20]

The language-experience approach helps the child make the transition from oral to written language. A child's own story or sentence dictated to a teacher is a part of the child's experience, so the teacher need not be concerned about the child's comprehension. The child's task is only to decode the message that already belongs to him. A child whose language is already rich in concepts, vocabulary, and imagination has the potential for "writing" many stories before reading stories written by others. If the language-experience approach is used, the first 75 to 100 written words children learn may be from their own repertoire of language rather than arbitrary choices of the authors of a series of readers. With this personal sight vocabulary, a child can read comfortably after developing an understanding of what the reading process is and how it works.

Naturally, young children soon exhaust their own realm of experience, and extension of their learning depends upon reading what others have written about other places and other experiences. Then it is time for children to begin acquisition of all the word recognition skills that will make them independent readers and all the evaluation skills necessary for making valid judgments about the worth of what is read.

In conclusion, it can be said that the top-down approach is not so much a contradiction of the bottom-up approach as it is an extension. Reading, as seen by the total language approach, encompasses those aspects identified by the bottom-up approaches, but it treats them as means rather than ends in themselves. Reading must be practiced and learned as a total process, not studied as bits and pieces of that process.

Reading Defined
Horn defined reading in this way:

> . . . reading includes those processes that are involved in approaching, perfecting, and maintaining meaning through the use of the printed page. Since there are many such processes, and since each one varies in degree, the term must be elastic enough to apply to all the varieties and gradations of reading involved in the use of books.[21]

Horn, further, analyzed communication through reading as follows:

> The author does not really convey ideas to the reader; he merely stimulates him to construct them out of his own experience. If the concept is already in the reader's mind, the task is relatively easy, but if, as is usually the case in school, it is new to the reader, its construction more nearly approaches problem-solving than simple association.[22]

Gates pointed out that reading is more than a mental activity; emotional responses are also required:

> . . . the child does more than understand and contemplate; his emotions are stirred; his attitudes and purposes are modified; indeed, his innermost being is involved. . . . The reading program should, therefore, make provision for exerting an influence upon the development of the most wholesome dynamic and emotional adjustments.[23]

Strang, McCullough and Traxler identified the purposeful nature of the reading process:

Reading is more than seeing words clearly, more than pronouncing printed words correctly, more than recognizing the meaning of isolated words. Reading requires you to think, feel, and imagine. Effective reading is purposeful. The use one makes of his reading largely determines what he reads, why he reads, and how he reads.[24]

More recently, Goodman has defined reading in terms of the cognitive strategies employed by the reader. He wrote:

Reading is a sampling, selecting, predicting, comparing, and confirming activity in which the reader selects a sample of useful graphic cues based on what he sees and what he expects to see.[25]

Gray identified four steps in the reading act: perception, comprehension, reaction, and integration.[26] Perception is the ability to pronounce the word as a meaningful unit. Comprehension is the ability to make individual words evoke useful ideas as they are read in context. Reaction requires judgmental action and a feeling about what the author has said. Integration, the final step, is the ability to assimilate the idea or concept into one's background of experience so that it is useful as a part of the total experience of the individual. Of course these four steps are completely interdependent for the meaningful use of reading as a tool in the solution of problems. (See figure 1.2.)

Piaget concerned himself for decades with the study of how children build their own logical thought processes. The children's cognitive development is determined by their own active structuring of their environments as they live in and respond to them. They use only those aspects of the world that make sense to them. As new input adds to their thinking (assimilation), their patterns of thinking are modified by accommodation.

Lavatelli states it this way:

Intelligence grows through the twin processes of assimilation and accommodation. In the process of assimilation, the child incorporates new elements from his experiences into existing structures; in the process of accommodation, existing structures change to accommodate to the new inputs. Experiences should be planned to allow opportunities for assimilation and accommodation.[27]

The processes of assimilation and accommodation provide a basis for Gray's four-step model of reading. Integration, the final and summary step, permits application of the Piagetian processes to the reading act. In this step, ideas gained during the act of reading are assimilated into the reader's cognitive structure. The cognitive structure is also changed in some degree to accommodate the new information.

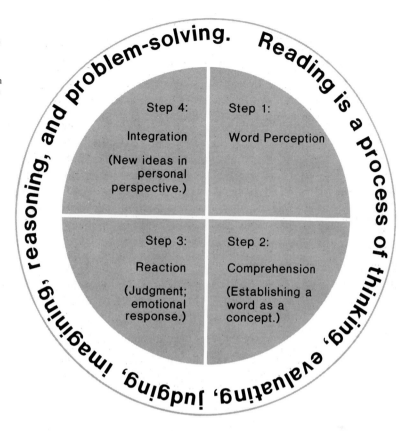

Figure 1.2
Gray's definition of reading as a four-step process.

This diagram is adapted from one written in Spanish in an unpublished language bulletin prepared for elementary teachers by Señora Coñsuelo de Escorcia, Tegucigalpa, Honduras, Ministry of Education.

Reading is a process of thinking, evaluating, judging, imagining, reasoning, and problem-solving.

Step 4:
Integration
(New ideas in personal perspective.)

Step 1:
Word Perception

Step 3:
Reaction
(Judgment; emotional response.)

Step 2:
Comprehension
(Establishing a word as a concept.)

In this text, reading is defined as the process by which the graphic symbols are translated into meaningful sound symbols in the reader's experience. *Meaning* is the key: learning to read necessitates mastery of all the linguistic clues that facilitate anticipation of meaning in a line of print.

Ability to anticipate meaning in context is stressed in order to emphasize what reading is *not*. Reading is *not* being concerned with the mechanical details; it is, rather, being concerned with perception of chunks of language that convey meaning. The main difference between the "learning how to read" process of beginners and the reading of mature readers is that beginners must give some attention to the mediating process of pronouncing words for so long as they are internalizing the nature of the process. Successful transition to mature reading depends upon the richness of a person's language, the ability to function with and extend one's language, and the ability to solve problems with language. A section in chapter 6 is devoted to extending oral language competence because this is a primary requisite to the language acquisition necessary for facile reading.

Literacy in Today's World

Most people who become teachers in the United States have probably been fortunate enough throughout their lives to live in an environment where reading is encouraged, respected, and expected. They have developed sufficiently mature reading habits to succeed in general education courses in college. In this environment it is easy to overlook the fact that many people in this country grow up and live out their lives without learning to read.

An individual can scarcely survive in present-day society without reading skill. To participate fully, a person needs to have achieved a high level of literacy. Appreciation of the extent and seriousness of illiteracy is evidenced by special reading programs in the schools, general reading clinics, and numerous programs funded by federal grants since 1965, such as Right to Read and the National Reading Program.

Holloway has recorded the extent of failure or deficiency of reading skill in the United States: "In 1971, there were some eighteen million adults who were considered functionally illiterate and seven million elementary and secondary school children who had reading deficiencies sufficient to cause a problem in the schools."[28]

An assessment of seventeen-year-olds in 1974 continued to emphasize the fact that many young people graduate from high school each year unable to assimilate the reading materials they encounter in life outside the school, such as road signs, advertisements, blank forms, and maps.[29]

Carl Rowan wrote:

Adult illiteracy takes a devastating toll. Unemployment, poverty, alienation are all part of its legacy. One study found that half of the unemployed 16-to-21-year-olds in major cities were functionally illiterate. A large percentage of welfare recipients—over half in some surveys—read at grade-school levels. Chief Justice Warren E. Burger has noted that "the percentage of inmates in all institutions who cannot read or write is staggering."[30]

Chall has written:

We consider that any adult is at a disadvantage when he cannot read a serious newspaper like the *New York Times,* a news magazine such as *Time* or *Newsweek,* the Federal income tax forms and instructions, and the bold and fine print on a house or apartment lease. The approximate readability level of these documents is estimated to be about twelfth grade reading level . . . it will take all our ingenuity as scientists, as teachers, as clinicians, and as administrators to bring this level of literacy about, for we are not now achieving it, even when the average educational attainment is twelfth grade.[31]

Studies surveying populations in adult basic education programs show evidence that the person over twenty-five who attended school for seven years is apt to perform on an achievement test at about the fourth grade level. If school attendance was for four years, the person is likely to perform nearer to the second grade level.

It is obvious that current efforts of federal agencies are long overdue if the adult population is to acquire minimum literacy skills.

Societal Problems that May Cause School Failure

Teachers need to be aware of certain trends or forces in society that will affect the success children have in learning to read and in establishing permanent reading habits. Trying to teach children to read without an awareness of these factors will surely lead to discouragement for both teachers and students.

High on the list of present trends affecting classroom learning is the changing structure of the family. Teachers cannot assume that all of their students come from a two-parent family in which the mother works at home.

Disrupted Family Life

Twenty-nine million children have mothers who work outside the home; only one in sixteen American families is a two-parent family in which the mother stays at home to care for the children.[32] In addition, the significant adults in many children's lives have been people other than mothers and fathers. One is led to ask what the future role of mothers is to be, and what are the added responsibilities of fathers in two-career families.

Single-parent families are becoming ever more common. In the past, children have usually lived with their mothers after divorces. Now fathers frequently have custody of children. Hammond stated that of the children born in 1978, 50 percent will live part of their young lives in single-parent homes. The stigma formerly associated with divorce has lessened, due to its frequency, but its harm to children has not decreased in the least.[33]

As more and more children are born to unwed mothers, this family form will become increasingly common in the schools. In growing numbers, these mothers are teenagers, ill equipped by any standards to prepare children for successful introductions to literacy.

In contrast, there also appears to be a trend toward older parents in another segment of the population. At one time, only one out of five women age 24 to 29 was childless; now more than 50 percent of that group has no children. Because women will be older when they bear children, their children will probably have fewer siblings. Frequently, children of these marriages will enjoy the relative security of homes where jobs and economic security are already established and where obtaining basic needs are not matters of daily concern.[34]

Children Out of School

Many other conditions affect children and their learning negatively. Teachers, most of whom never experienced such conditions, may be totally unaware of the problems and stresses competing for attention with school tasks.

> The Children's Defense Fund reported in *Children Out of School in America* (1974) that two million school-age children were not in school in the United States. . . . Far greater numbers of children are technically in school but benefit little or not at all. Sooner or later, they become frustrated and drop out. . . . They are non-English-speaking children who sit uncomprehendingly . . . they are learning disabled children whose problems have not been diagnosed or have been misdiagnosed . . . they are poor White or Black children in rural areas or inner cities who are labeled dumb and expected to graduate from high school reading at an elementary level . . . they are children whose clothes are inadequate or who don't have money for textbooks, fees, or transportation . . . they are pregnant, too bright, or not bright enough.[35]
>
> Hunger is chronic . . . many are anemic; many have worms; most are malnourished. From 500,000 to 750,00 children in the United States live away from their families.[36]

Cultural and Language Differences

There is a growing awareness of the impact that children's cultures have on their school learning. Educators are beginning to sense that much instructional effort has been useless if not detrimental. An understanding of the effects of culture and community expectations on school learning is beginning to lead away from the wholesale use of such terms as lazy, dumb, unmotivated, and troublesome.

Much of the knowledge that is imparted in schools is discontinuous with the social and cultural reality that children experience outside of school. This is particularly true of ethnic minority children who are linguistically and culturally different and whose background of knowledge and experiences goes unrecognized in the symbolic world of school learning. School knowledge, therefore, has to be analyzed for its congruence and its appropriateness with the child's family, community, and culture.[37]

An important aspect for reading teachers is a community or culture's view of language, of the relationships between first and second languages, and of the purposes of reading instruction. Some knowledge in this area is becoming available to teachers. Heath noted that all normal individuals can learn to read satisfactorily, provided that the school takes note of the role that literacy plays in the community and culture, that the need for literacy within the cultural setting is established, and that those already literate within the community are involved in the process of teaching literacy.[38]

The success of literacy efforts will be limited to some extent by any limitations placed on available reading materials. Censorship is a problem for schools and libraries, and would-be censors seem to spring from many sources at unpredictable times. The American Library Association has prepared a *Bill of Rights* supporting free access to reading materials in whatever ways possible, while at the same time avoiding endorsement of specific ideas. It is important that teachers and other school personnel give strong support to the effort to prevent censorship of reading materials.[39]

One of the objectives of reading instruction is to lay the groundwork for life-long reading habits in boys and girls when they are going through school. To build such habits, to instill constructive attitudes, and to ensure that students' efforts are successful are *sacred trusts of classroom teachers*. This extends far beyond knowledge of the reading process itself to include knowledge of and respect for the children and their communities.

This brief discussion suggests that there are many factors at work in a child's life that may predispose him or her to failure at school. We have designed figure 1.3 to summarize the depth of the problem of school failure. There are six sets of community factors that largely determine what the curriculum of the school will be. These are the psychological, sociological, economic, political, religio-cultural, and linguistic factors. Many times it must seem to the teacher that political factors, or economic factors, are rated more highly than the welfare of children in the determination of the school's curriculum.

Inside that hexagon there is also a circle of social problems that parent and child must "live with" even before the child appears at school. There are children from disrupted families, children in poor physical health, anxious children, children whose values at home are in conflict with values in school, runaway children and children not in school, abused children, and those with limited English proficiency in English-speaking schools. All of these extremely difficult child welfare problems are predispositions to failure in our present school system.

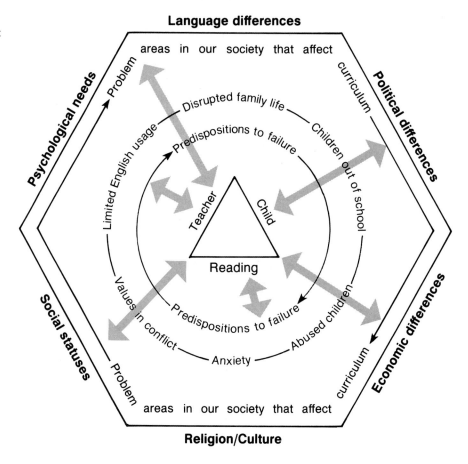

Figure 1.3
Societal problems that cause children to fail.

It becomes clear, then, that the inner triangle in which teacher and child focus on the meaningful and pleasurable reading experience may not be the environment in which the child is able to succeed. The extraneous factors may impinge so severely on the child's whole affective life that chances of success are minimal no matter how carefully the teacher plans the child's instruction.

Differences among Children

Such expressions as "all children are different" and "no two are alike" have become trite through verbalization but not through day-by-day teacher performance in the classroom. Children vary greatly in physical, mental, emotional, and social characteristics. Teachers are admonished at every turn to recognize that children grow at different rates in all these characteristics.

Of course, children who have a vision or hearing impairment, a neurological handicap, poor general health, insufficient sleep or rest, a substandard living environment, a speech impediment, emotional upsets, inadequate language readiness for reading, or long absences from school are apt to have difficulty beyond

Teachers need to put into practice the generalization that "no two children are alike."

that experienced by other children in learning to read. But the differences in normal children under normal circumstances are what teachers need to understand and plan for in their everyday work.

Since no two children can learn the same thing in the same amount of time with the same amount of practice, there can be no arbitrary standards for what constitutes first grade or fifth grade in the elementary school.

As children progress through the grades in public schools, the range of individual differences on various traits will become greater and greater, not less and less. It follows that twelve-year-olds will vary more within their age group than will six-year-olds. What happens to the range of IQs within a group will demonstrate this point. The IQ—intelligence quotient—is the arithmetic relationship between a child's chronological age and measured mental age, and it is assumed to remain relatively stable for any individual. Therefore, if the range of IQs in a given class of six-year-olds is 75 to 125, the mental ages will vary from four and a half years (4.5/6 = IQ 75) to seven and a half years (7.5/6 = IQ 125). The same group when twelve-year-olds will have mental ages varying from nine years (9/12 = IQ 75) to fifteen years (15/12 = IQ 125). And when fifteen-year-olds, they will have mental ages varying from eleven years and three months (11.25/15 = IQ 75) to eighteen years and nine months (18.75/15 = IQ 125).

Even though the limitations of tests that yield IQ scores are generally recognized, almost every school uses the scores as an index of general learning ability. Such a measure always demonstrates a wide range of ability among children.

The real problems in trying to teach six-, seven-, and eight-year-olds arise from the children's specific strengths and weaknesses when they are confronted with the complicated four-faceted process of learning how to read the printed word: (1) mastering a basic sight vocabulary, (2) learning phonic and structural analysis skills, (3) developing comprehension skills, and (4) getting lots of easy practice. Obviously, most teachers sufficiently understand their job, because the great majority of children do learn to read with encouraging degrees of success.

Perhaps *too much* emphasis has been placed on the techniques of teaching reading and *not enough* upon the peculiar nature of the child who does not learn what he is taught. Different methods as currently used probably do not account for the extreme range of differences in children's learning. But the idiosyncrasies of children vary extremely. Teachers, then, need to be constantly evaluating the individual *child* as well as the specific techniques used to help that child learn to read.

The Skills of Reading

It has been estimated that nearly 90 percent of a child's school day is spent on reading and writing activities. This amount of time is certainly not necessary and probably not desirable, but it is the way most classrooms are operating. This fact emphasizes that reading is not taught or practiced only during a scheduled reading class. It is taught all day long in some form. Actually, often reading is not taught at all but, more accurately, is assigned and tested. The fact that 10 to 15 percent of boys and girls have problems with reading in school may be due in greater measure to inadequate teaching than to failure to learn. No teacher can deny this charge until both sides of the issue are competently examined.

One classroom was observed where the sixth grade had been divided into three subgroups for reading: high second grade level, easy fourth level, and easy fifth level. Yet, all the sixth graders were assigned the same spelling word list of sixth grade words for regular spelling, and each member of the class was issued a sixth grade geography book adjudged to be too difficult for more than half a class in which the achievement normally fits the sixth grade achievement level. Can even the top subgroup, reading at easy fifth grade level, read with any degree of understanding a sixth grade geography book that is likely to be written at a more difficult reader level than a sixth grade reader?

It has been said that the teachers in the primary grades teach children how to read, while in later grades teachers assign reading for the children to learn the content of the course of study. This idea is not true, and teachers must be very careful to discredit it. Of course, in the first year and perhaps most of the second, children have to develop a great deal of decoding ability so they can pronounce or recognize words for the reading process. They must learn how to phrase, punctuate, and make proper uses of inflection. However, students should be improving these very same skills all the way through secondary school in a comprehensive reading program.

On the other hand, children during their very first reading lessons are going to find the primary emphasis given to "getting the idea" or "finding the meaning in the story" even while the decoding process is being learned (and no reading can happen unless the child can pronounce the words). Teaching that reading is a process of deriving meaning through interpretation of printed symbols must be given primary emphasis. Just as reading for meaning is important during the initial reading program, it remains the primary reason for reading throughout one's life. Consequently, one learns to read and reads to learn as two concurrent processes all the way through school.

Reading skills at different levels are often broken down in the following way:

A. Developmental: The how-to-read skills
   1. Word recognition skills
   2. Comprehension skills
   3. Study skills
B. Functional reading
   1. Location activities
   2. Specific skills for study/comprehension
   3. Selection and organization
   4. Summarizing
   5. Providing for remembering
C. Recreational reading
   1. Reading as a "free time" activity
   2. Locating books of interest in the library
   3. Developing tastes for a variety of reading material
   4. Giving pleasure to others through oral reading
   5. Fixing permanent habits of reading every day

Objectives of the Reading Program

The objective of teaching reading is to make each person as literate, in the broadest sense, as possible. Four levels of mastery are necessary: (1) mastering the skills necessary to decode the written word so that it is immediately pronounceable and meaningful; (2) mastering the skills necessary to comprehend so that the reader demands meaning from the passage being read; (3) developing the abilities necessary to think about and evaluate the validity or usefulness of what one reads; and (4) developing a lifelong habit of relying on reading to gather information, to substantiate one's thinking, to solve new problems, or to entertain oneself. All teachers undoubtedly have some general purposes similar to these four as global purposes of teaching.

A good school reading program would be based on the following principles:

1. Reading is communicating. So are listening, speaking, and writing. All these skills should develop in an integrated, interdependent manner in the school.
2. All school personnel teach reading; overtly or covertly, they demonstrate its value.
3. Reading development takes place within the framework of total child development.
4. Each child grows at his or her own rate and needs to follow a well worked out program from kindergarten through all the school years.

5. The reading program (a) teaches how to read, (b) provides for much reading practice, and (c) encourages both functional and recreational reading in a very wide range of interests and levels of difficulty.
6. The reading program provides other avenues for communicating learning for nonreaders and provides diagnostic and prescriptive services for those who can profitably use them.

Summary

Reading is the process by which graphic symbols are translated into meaningful sound symbols in the reader's experience. Meaning is the key: learning to read requires mastery of all the linguistic clues that help one to anticipate meaning in a line of print.

The reading act as practiced by mature readers may be thought of as a four-step process: perception, comprehension, reaction, and integration.

Learning to read is a complicated developmental process that large numbers of children do not master, although most do to some degree of proficiency. Children need to grow into reading. They do this by extending their communication skills from well-developed listening and speaking skills to reading and writing. The language-experience method of beginning reading means that children's own ideas and concepts are presented in their own words, which they learn to read first.

For Further Reading

Clay, Marie. "What is Reading?" Chapter 1 in *Reading: The Patterning of Complex Behaviour*. 2d ed. Auckland, New Zealand: Heinemann, 1979.

Heilman, Arthur. "Principles of Reading Instruction." Chapter 1 in *Principles and Practices of Teaching Reading*. 5th ed. Columbus, Ohio: Charles E. Merrill, 1981.

Hodges, Richard E., and E. Hugh Rudorf, eds. *Language and Learning to Read: What Teachers Should Know About Language*. Boston: Houghton Mifflin, 1972.

Smith, Frank. *Understanding Reading*. 3d ed. New York: Holt, Rinehart and Winston, 1982.

Smith, Nila B., and H. Alan Robinson. "Thought, Language, and Reading." Chapter 1 in *Reading Instruction for Today's Children*. 2d ed. Englewood Cliffs, N.J.: Prentice-Hall, 1980.

Zintz, Miles. "An Overview of the Reading Process." Chapter 1 in *Corrective Reading*. 4th ed. Dubuque, Iowa: Wm. C. Brown, 1981.

Notes

1. Clark S. Knowlton, "Spanish-American Schools in the 1970's," *Newsletter*, General Department of Mission Strategy and Evangelism, Board of National Missions, United Presbyterian Church in the U.S.A., 475 Riverside Drive, New York, N.Y. 10027 (July 1969), p. 4.
2. Jerome C. Harste and Carolyn Burke, "Toward a Socio-Linguistic Model of Reading Comprehension," *Viewpoints in Teaching and Learning* 54 (July 1978): 43.

3. Diane Deford, "A Validation Study of an Instrument to Determine a Teacher's Theoretical Orientation to Reading" (Dissertation, School of Education, Indiana University, 1979).

4. Carolyn L. Burke, "The Language Process: Systems or Systematic," in *Language and Learning to Read,* ed. Richard E. Hodges and E. Hugh Rudorf (Boston: Houghton Mifflin, 1972), pp. 25–27.

5. Harry Singer and Robert Ruddell, eds., *Theoretical Models and Processes of Reading,* 2d ed. (Newark, Del.: International Reading Assn., 1976).

6. Philip Gough, "One Second of Reading," in Singer and Ruddell, *Theoretical Models and Processes of Reading,* pp. 509–35.

7. David LaBerge and S. Jay Samuels, "Toward a Theory of Automatic Processing in Reading," in Singer and Ruddell, *Theoretical Models and Processes of Reading,* pp. 548–79.

8. Charles Walcutt et al., *Teaching Reading: A Phonic/Linguistic Approach to Developmental Reading* (New York: Macmillan, 1974).

9. John Savage, ed., *Linguistics for Teachers: Selected Readings* (Chicago: Science Research Associates, 1973), p. 216.

10. H. Alan Robinson, ed., *Reading and Writing Instruction in the United States: Historical Trends* (Newark, Del.: International Reading Assn., 1977).

11. Ibid., p. 49.

12. Rudolph Flesch, *Why Johnny Still Can't Read: A New Look at the Scandal of Our Schools* (New York: Harper & Row, 1981).

13. Rudolph Flesch interview, "Pro and Con: Teach Reading Old-Fashioned Way?" *U.S. News and World Report* 92 (April 1982): 69.

14. Flesch, *Why Johnny Still Can't Read,* p. 77.

15. A. Sterl Artley, "Phonics Revisited," *Language Arts* 54 (February 1977): 121–26.

16. John T. Guthrie, "Is Bettelheim Believable?" *The Reading Teacher* 35 (April 1982): 879.

17. Guthrie, "Is Bettelheim Believable?" 878–80. Evaluation of Bruno Bettelheim and Karen Zelan, "Why Children Don't Like to Read," *Atlantic Monthly* (November 1981), pp. 25–31.

18. Roach Van Allen and Claryce Allen, *An Introduction to a Language Experience Program, Level I* (Chicago: Encyclopaedia Britannica Press, 1966), p. 21.

19. Burke, "The Language Process," p. 26.

20. Bradford Arthur, *Teaching English to Speakers of English* (New York: Harcourt Brace Jovanovich, 1973), pp. 43–45.

21. Ernest Horn, *Methods of Instruction in the Social Studies* (New York: Charles Scribner's Sons, 1937), p. 152.

22. Ibid., p. 154.

23. Arthur I. Gates, "Character and Purposes of the Yearbook," *Reading in the Elementary School,* 48th Yearbook of the National Society for the Study of Education, ed. Nelson B. Henry (Chicago: University of Chicago Press, 1949), p. 3.

24. Ruth Strang, Constance McCullough, and Arthur E. Traxler, *The Improvement of Reading,* 4th ed. (New York: McGraw-Hill, 1967), p. 8.

25. Kenneth Goodman, "Reading," in *A Dictionary of Reading and Related Terms,* ed. Theodore L. Harris and Richard E. Hodges (Newark, Del.: International Reading Assn., 1981), p. 265.

26. William S. Gray, *On Their Own in Reading* (Chicago: Scott, Foresman, 1948), pp. 35–37.
27. Celia Stendler Lavatelli, *Piaget's Theory Applied to an Early Childhood Curriculum* (Cambridge: American Science and Engineering, 1970), p. 48.
28. Ruth Love Holloway, *Right to Read: The First Four Years* (Washington, D.C.: U.S. Office of Education, 1974), p. 2.
29. "Functional Literacy—Basic Reading Performance," a newsletter of The National Right to Read, National Assessment of Educational Programs, Denver, Colorado, 1975.
30. Carl T. Rowan and David M. Mazie, "Johnny's Parents Can't Read Either," *The Reader's Digest* 110 (January 1977): 153.
31. Jeanne S. Chall, *Reading and Development,* keynote address, International Reading Association, 1975 (Newark, Del.: International Reading Assn., 1976), pp. 5–6.
32. Marian Edelman, "Justice for Children Everywhere," (Special Feature of the International Year of the Child), *Today's Education* 68 (February–March 1979): 41.
33. Janice Hammond, "Children, Divorce and You," *Learning* 9 (February 1981): 83.
34. Harold Shane, "Forecast for the 80's," *Today's Education* 68 (April–May 1979): 62ff.
35. Edelman, "Justice for Children Everywhere," p. 41 ff.
36. Ibid.
37. Leroy Ortiz and Catherine Loughlin, "Building Personally and Culturally Relevant Curriculum with Children: A Point of View" (Unpublished paper, University of New Mexico, July 1980).
38. Shirley Brice Heath, "The Functions and Uses of Literacy," *Journal of Communication* 30 (Winter 1980): 123–33.
39. American Library Association, "The Freedom to Read," *Bill of Rights* (Chicago: American Library Association, 1972).

Psychological Foundations for Reading Instruction

A Cognitive Map: Psychological Foundations for Reading Instruction

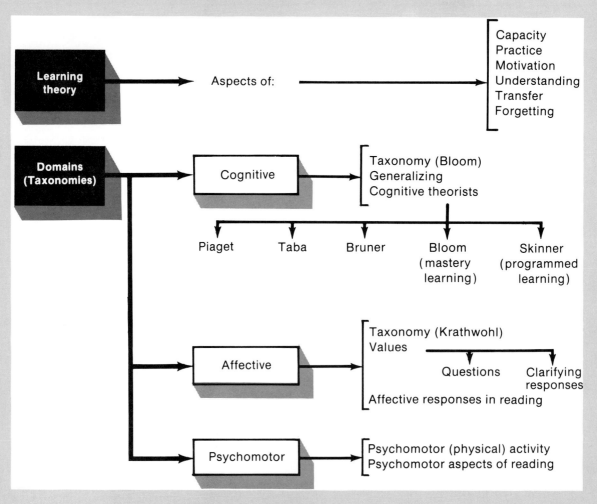

2

Guide Questions

1. What range of reading ability should a teacher expect to find in a third grade class? In a sixth grade class?

2. How can a teacher's knowledge of *the hierarchy of human needs* help her or him to motivate reading?

3. What is the significance of *feedback?*

4. What are the steps in learning to generalize?

5. What do teachers need to do about helping students clarify values?

6. Relate Bloom's taxonomy in the cognitive domain to "levels" of reading skill.

Terminology

affective domain

cognitive domain

concept

cone of experience

feedback

generalization

hierarchy of needs

instructional plan

learning theory

level of aspiration

mastery learning

normal distribution

process vs. content

psychomotor domain

range of achievement

valuing process

Each classroom teacher is confronted with problems of classroom management, of motivation of learning, and of connecting this year's work with the previous and following year's work. Within the class, the teacher must expect to find the normal range of abilities in intellectual, physical, emotional, and social development.

There are a number of principles of learning that the teacher needs to understand, accept, and use in interpreting the school success of individual children.

> When the teacher and child meet, a major part of the teacher's armament must be a knowledge of the principles of learning. Many normal children learn readily in spite of the repeated violations of learning principles. . . . By sharpening our awareness of some of these principles, as applied to teaching children, . . . we can anticipate broader adherence to them. . . .
>
> Some of these major principles of learning include *overlearning, ordering,* and *sizing* (programming) of new material, *rewarding* only *desired responses, frequent review,* and avoidance of interference and negative transfer.[1] [Italics added.]

Gagné discusses eight types of learning and defines them briefly as follows.[2] Each definition is followed by a suggestion of its application to reading instruction.

1. *Signal learning.* Learning to make a general, diffuse response to a signal. Except that this kind of learning may underlie higher types of learning, it has little immediate application to learning to read.
2. *Stimulus response.* A precise response to a discriminated stimulus. This type of learning may be used in learning sounds and simple words.
3. *Chaining.* A chain of two or more stimulus-response connections. Chaining leads to the association of letters with the sounds they represent and to the speaking or reading of predictable phrases and sentences.
4. *Verbal association.* Learning of verbal chains. The children learn words, creating chains of words they can read.
5. *Multiple discrimination.* Even with n different responses to x different stimuli, the learners do discriminate. Children are able to identify and read words of increasingly similar appearances.
6. *Concept formation.* Acquiring ability to respond to entire classes of objects or events with proper identification. In reading, children develop concepts about the reading process and use reading to acquire concepts about the world around them.
7. *Principle learning.* Chaining of two or more concepts. Readers chain the concept of the one-to-one relationship between the spoken and written words with the concept of left-to-right directionality of print to permit efficient reading. Reading also permits the learners to chain concepts from the environment to permit the learning of principles.

8. *Problem-solving.* Using thinking to combine principles to obtain new solutions. Critical and creative reading and reading in the content fields often require problem-solving by readers.

Rohwer proposes three instructional phases that compliment Gagné's learning principles.[3] In the *planning* phase, conditions to promote prerequisite learning are identified. These include ways to stimulate the recall of relevant, previously learned discriminations and strategies for presenting the concept to be learned in a variety of ways. The second phase, *implementing instruction,* is characterized by promotion of the ability to generalize responses, to stimulate recall of earlier related learnings, to deliver needed feedback, and to encourage transfer through the development of adequate learning hierarchies. The final phase, *evaluating instruction,* is the time when instructors gain feedback on their instructional efforts as well as information about what students have learned.

According to Hilgard, learning theory might be expected to answer questions one might ask about learning in everyday life. Any theory, then, may be appraised in terms of its attention to measuring.[4]

1. *Capacity.* What are the limits of learning? How is learning measured? What is the range of individual differences?
2. *Practice.* What is the role of practice in learning? Practice causes improvement in efficiency in performance only when the conditions of learning are suited to the one who is practicing.
3. *Motivation.* How important are drives and incentives? What about rewards and punishments? Or intrinsic vs. extrinsic motives?
4. *Understanding.* What is the place of insight? Or a hierarchy of steps leading to generalizations?
5. *Transfer.* Does learning one thing help you in learning something else?
6. *Forgetting.* What happens when we remember? When we forget?

This chapter discusses such elements of learning theory as capacity, practice, motivation, understanding, transfer, and forgetting as they relate to reading. These observations lead to principles of programmed learning, of helping children learn to generalize and of taking into account the affective, the cognitive, and the psychomotor domains in the education of children.

Elements of Learning Theory

Capacity

The normal bell-shaped curve of distribution has become well-known. It represents the range, the extent, and the distribution of a skill or trait. This concept that the distribution of any given attribute, skill, or ability falls normally around a central or average value is an important one.

For example, if we were to administer a standardized reading test to one hundred fifth graders at mid-year, we would find out something about their similarities and their differences. Since the average fifth grader at mid-year is expected to earn a grade score of 5.5 on the reading test, most of the scores would

Figure 2.1
Areas under the
normal curve. (The
Greek letter σ is the
statistical
representation for
standard deviation.)

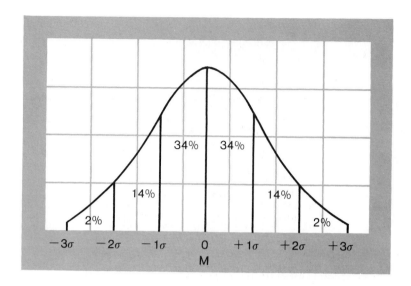

be close to that one. Some would earn scores below the 5.5 level, while others would earn scores well above. If one were to plot this information on graph paper and generalize it to a curved line (see figure 2.1), the graphed points would tend to cluster around a central value, resulting in the normal curve.

Intelligence, problem-solving abilities, length of time required to memorize nonsense syllables, or scores on a vocabulary test constitute skills and abilities that also fall in a *normal distribution* when a large unselected group is measured.

Statistically, the area under a normal curve can be divided into three equal deviations from the median or center. The standard deviation represents a given distance (in points) on the baseline that corresponds to arbitrarily predetermined *areas* for each standard deviation. One standard deviation encompasses 34 percent below or 34 percent above the median; two standard deviations encompass an additional 14 percent above or below the median; and three standard deviations include the additional 2 percent on either side. This tells a teacher that if there is a random distribution, 68 cases in 100 lie within one standard deviation above and one standard deviation below the median; 28 cases are in the second standard deviation, 14 above and 14 below the median; and 4 are in the third, 2 above and 2 below the median. (See figure 2.1.)

When the median is defined, half the class will perform above the median, and half the class will perform below the median. To try to get a class to perform in such a way that everyone is average or better is to deny the existence of this spread of abilities.

This interpretation becomes meaningful when the arithmetic average (mean) or the position of the middle child in a distribution (median) gives a value for the *typical* or *average* level of performance.

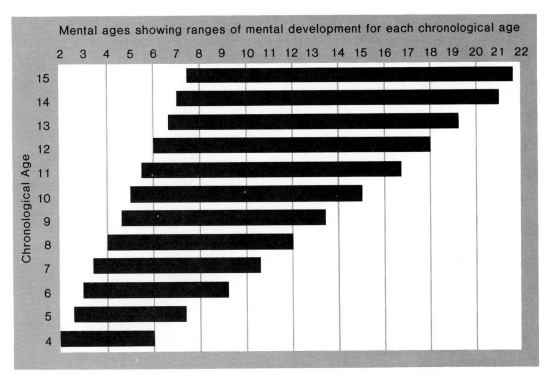

Figure 2.2
Variations of general learning abilities in relation to chronological ages.

The range of differences in achievement in reading and arithmetic get wider with good teaching. For each teacher this means that the children taught should become more different in achievement, *not more alike,* during a year of instruction.

Some children grow faster academically; some children show average growth; and other children grow more slowly academically. Figure 2.2 shows the increasing spread of general learning abilities associated with chronological age range from four to fifteen years.

The *Wechsler Intelligence Scale for Children* is a common individually administered intelligence test in schools and children's clinics. It has been standardized so that a score of 100 is *normal* for any given chronological age. In other words, if a child of ten earns a full scale IQ score of 100, this represents normal or average intelligence and ranks him or her at the median, or the 50th percentile, in the distribution. Since the standard deviation for this test is 15, two standard deviations (a range from 70 IQ to 130 IQ) include 96 percent of the total sample tested, as indicated in table 2.1. This corresponds to the normal curve of distribution already discussed. About 50 percent of all the people of a given age test between 90 and 110. This is called the normal intelligence range. (See table 2.1.)

Table 2.1 Intelligence classification for WISC IQs.

IQ Ranges	Classification	Percent in Each Group
130–	very superior	2
120–129	superior	7
110–119	bright normal	16
90–109	average	50
80–89	dull normal	16
70–79	borderline	7
69 below	mental defective	2
		100

From Henry E. Garrett, *Testing for Teachers,* 2d ed. (New York: American Book Co., © 1965), p. 75. Reprinted by permission.

The Spread of Differences

The longer a group of children the same age attends school, the *more different* they become. Teachers may expect to find that in classes of unselected children (heterogeneous groups) the range of reading achievement measured by a standardized test will be, on the average, three years at the end of grade two, four years at the end of grade three, five years at the end of grade four, six years at the end of grade five, and seven years at the end of grade six.

Many factors in the child's total growth and development contribute to these differences in achievement. Figure 2.3 shows that differences in school learning are attributable to constitutional, intellectual, environmental, educational, and emotional factors.

Knowing that children are all different from each other, and that the longer the children attend school the greater the range of difference becomes in all types of skills, abilities, interests, and ambitions, teachers cannot rely on teaching any *one* thing to all members of a class. Consequently, any teacher who accepts the facts about the way children grow, develop, learn, and satisfy their curiosities must be searching for ways to manage the classroom so that each child has an opportunity to continue learning.

Figure 2.4 illustrates why it is impossible for the classroom teacher today to think of a group of boys and girls as "doing fourth grade work" or "doing second grade work." The boxes labeled "Conventional Grade Competence" represent the narrow limit of what may be thought of as appropriate to that grade, while the shaded horizontal bars show the *range* of achievement in general knowledge to be *expected* in any single grade. The appalling dilemma of the sixth grade teacher who tries to teach only the content of "the sixth grade textbooks" is obvious because the group probably has an achievement range spanning almost eight years.

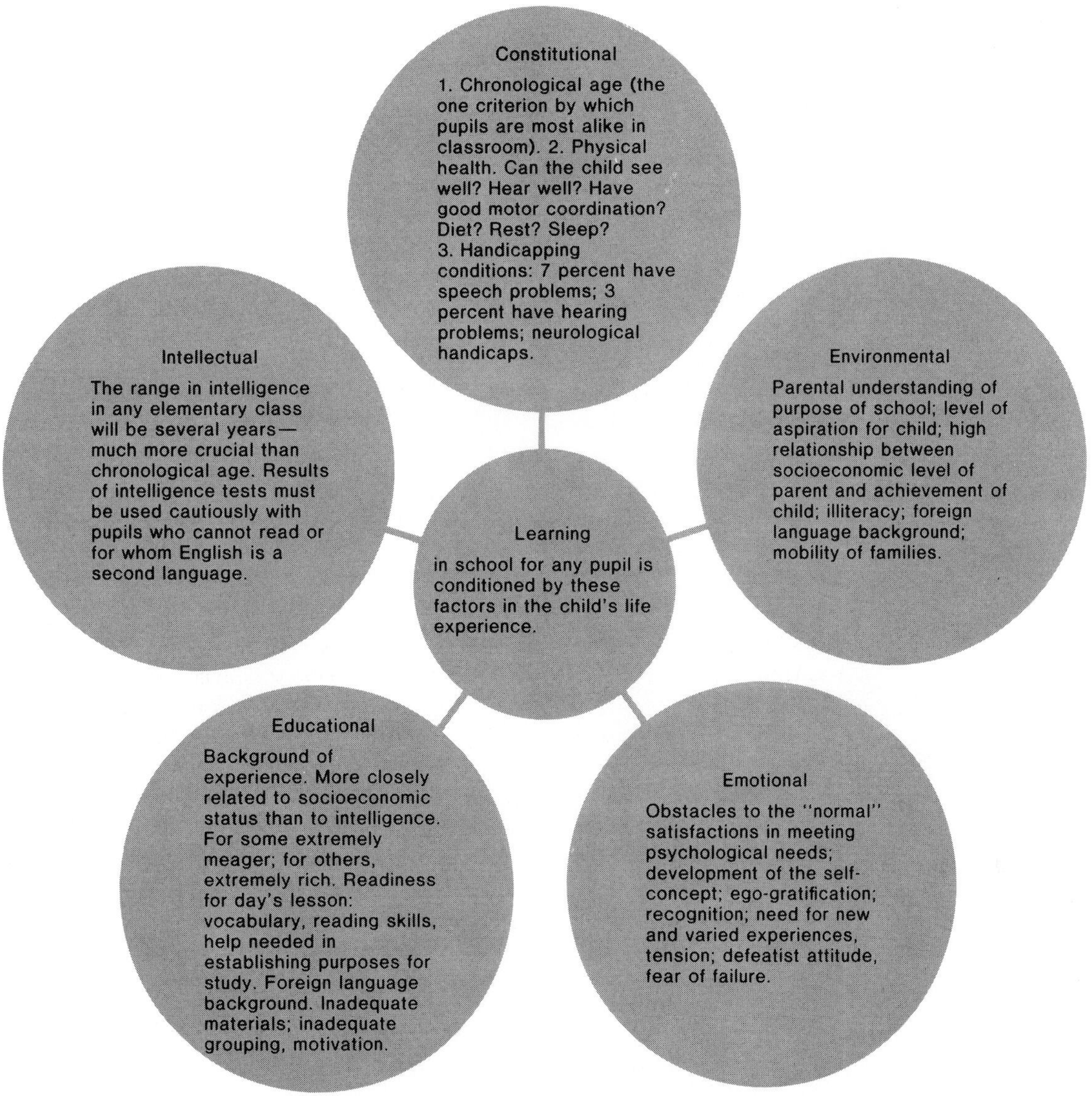

Constitutional

1. Chronological age (the one criterion by which pupils are most alike in classroom). 2. Physical health. Can the child see well? Hear well? Have good motor coordination? Diet? Rest? Sleep? 3. Handicapping conditions: 7 percent have speech problems; 3 percent have hearing problems; neurological handicaps.

Intellectual

The range in intelligence in any elementary class will be several years—much more crucial than chronological age. Results of intelligence tests must be used cautiously with pupils who cannot read or for whom English is a second language.

Environmental

Parental understanding of purpose of school; level of aspiration for child; high relationship between socioeconomic level of parent and achievement of child; illiteracy; foreign language background; mobility of families.

Learning

in school for any pupil is conditioned by these factors in the child's life experience.

Educational

Background of experience. More closely related to socioeconomic status than to intelligence. For some extremely meager; for others, extremely rich. Readiness for day's lesson: vocabulary, reading skills, help needed in establishing purposes for study. Foreign language background. Inadequate materials; inadequate grouping, motivation.

Emotional

Obstacles to the "normal" satisfactions in meeting psychological needs; development of the self-concept; ego-gratification; recognition; need for new and varied experiences, tension; defeatist attitude, fear of failure.

Figure 2.3
Factors in the range of individual differences.

From Miles V. Zintz, *Corrective Reading,* 3d ed., published by Wm. C. Brown Publishers, Dubuque, Iowa. Copyright © 1977, p. 44. Reprinted by permission.

Figure 2.4
Range of achievement
in general knowledge
among elementary
school children at
indicated grade levels.

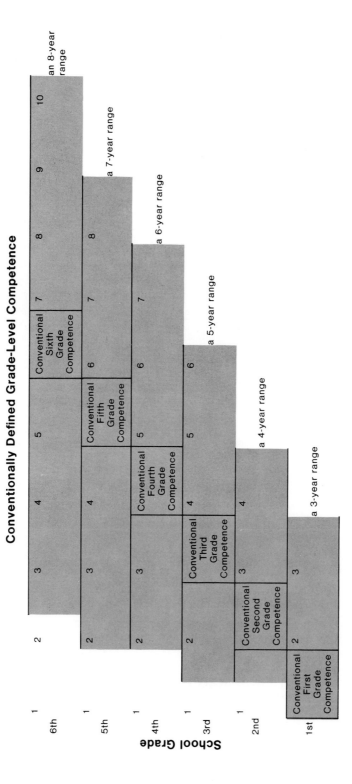

Conventionally Defined Grade-Level Competence

From Theory to Practice 2.1
Meeting Reading Needs of Individuals

The existence of a range of reading abilities within a class cannot and should not be prevented; it must be recognized, and instructional plans must be made. Shown here is a set of instructional level reading scores, months of reading growth since last year, ages (in years and months), and other relevant information for a group of ten members of a fourth grade class. The information was taken at the beginning of the school year. After you have studied the data, participate in a discussion in which you develop instructional plans for these children. The plan developed should provide maximum attention to individual needs, yet be realistic for the teacher.

Student	Instruc. Level	Months of Growth in Reading	Age	Other Comments
Art	4.6	.9	8–10	Auditory handicap; loves horses and math
Marlene	1.9	.1	9–10	Pre-delinquent behaviors
Josie	4.1	1.1	9–0	Likes TV detective shows; bilingual Spanish and English
Carol	4.0	?	9–1	Collects stamps; new in school
Bob	3.8	.7	8–11	In Cub Scouts; helps father in sporting goods store
Jon	4.2	1.1	10–1	Absent often; loves fishing
Kenneth	7.1	1.8	8–10	Very shy; stamp collector
Bernice	2.8	.3	9–3	One of eleven children; poor health
Cathy	4.2	2.0	9–6	Competitive; likes sports
Karen	5.0	1.0	9–1	Declares no interests; mother recently left family

Practice

Practice (drill) provides the circumstances for conditions of learning to operate. For effective practice, essential conditions include motivation, immediate knowledge of results, distributed practice, elimination of error. This suggests, then, that drills in classroom instruction should be at the point of error, spirited, of short duration and filled with meaning and purpose.

What a student practices must be meaningful *to that student*. In reading instruction, drills should feature materials that are relevant to the students' experiences. If teachers follow the suggestions made here, they will not drill children on words in isolation, for instance, and will avoid drills that cause language to be fragmented into nonsense.

To stay motivated, children must have some expectations of success. They cannot seriously compete if they feel they cannot win. Evaluations that signify merit and identify strengths should be given to all students. Responding to children from this perspective is an especially important strategy when working with the lowest achievers in class.

Immediate knowledge of results shows a child whether or not he or she is successful; such feedback is a strong motivational factor. Feedback may be intrinsic; the learners obtain knowledge of the results by their own actions. When the teacher provides the information, it is called extrinsic feedback. Both forms are effective in promoting learning.[5]

Distributed vs. Massed Practice

Ebbinghaus demonstrated that with any considerable number of repetitions of an act, a planned distribution of repetitions over a period of time is decidedly more advantageous than the massing of them at a single time. More short practice periods return greater dividends than fewer long ones.

Teachers need to be aware of the importance of *distribution of exposure* to concepts and generalizations to be taught. Summarizing at the end of the class period, reviewing each lesson on succeeding days, and helping students write summarizing statements are important in this exposure of learning. This evidence should be used by teachers to reduce the amount of procrastinating and cramming students do for tests.

For the drill included in any subject, such as spelling, handwriting, and overlearning arithmetic algorithms, the principles of distributed practice in shorter periods apply. Short, lively, motivated drills on basic sight words, consonant blend sounds, most common prefixes, or responding with synonyms or antonyms will be very profitable in the reading program.

Motivation

No learning takes place without a motive. Motives are conditions within the organism that cause it to seek satisfaction of need. The basis for the condition is obscure, generally speaking, since the real motivation a given student has for a specific learning objective may not be the same as the teacher suspects it to be. An intrinsic motive to learn something may not be as strong as the extrinsic motive the student established at home, or as strong as the many psychological needs apart from the student's intellectual growth.

Motivating students is a complex, involved process for teachers and often leaves them baffled when their plans go awry. Since there will be no one way to motivate every child, the teacher must seek ways to cause each student to set his own goals, both immediate and mediate.

The relation of education to the level of motivation in the society is more direct than most people recognize. The goals a young person sets are very heavily affected by adult expectations. The educational system provides the young person with a sense of what society expects in the way of performance. If it is lax in its demands, then the student will believe that such are the expectations of society. If the educational system expects much, the young person will probably have high expectations for himself or herself.

When the United States Office of Education completed a three-year study of methods of teaching reading in the first grade, where thousands of teachers used dozens of approaches, the one big generalization to be drawn was that a *good teacher,* not a special twist in methodology, was the variable that exercised most control over teaching success.

Students respect the teacher who is honest with them, the teacher who works for them, sits in on class projects as an advisor, and listens to problems and keeps them confidential.

Teachers of the highest achieving groups are positive in their approach to teaching. They encourage responses even when those responses aren't exactly what the teacher had in mind. They explore content with the students at many thinking levels.[6] Good teachers try different approaches. They allow children to demonstrate why they think they are right, and praise them for their effort. Good teachers ask open-ended questions so that there is no pat answer such as reciting "a fact." However, the kinds of questions teachers ask affect the classroom climate in ways other than providing occasions for praising a student.

The effective teacher understands that there are many bases for motivation: (1) mastery motives—desire to excel, desire to succeed, desire to overcome difficulties; (2) social approval motives—desire for approval, desire for self-esteem, desire for attention; (3) conformity motives—desire to conform, desire to avoid censure.

Motivation should:

1. Include success experiences so the student has feelings of personal worth and security.
2. Be greater in school if the school curriculum emphasizes social utility with considerable emphasis on the usefulness, here and now, of what it teaches. In addition to school being a preparation for future life, it is more importantly preparation for life here and now; and the result of learning to live here and now prepares one to live in an undefinable future.
3. Include methodology to reinforce self-expression and self-esteem in *all* boys and girls.
4. Maximize competition with one's own past record and minimize competition among members of a class.

Intrinsic vs. Extrinsic Motivation

When young children enter school, much of their motivation may be teacher- or adult-generated. Elementary teachers are using extrinsic motivation when one hears them say: "You'd like to do that for Miss Brown, wouldn't you?" or "Mr. Wilson would like you to finish that before you go out to play."

Figure 2.5
Growth in intrinsic
motivations; acquiring
the desire to learn.

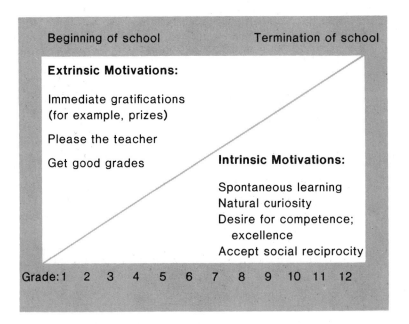

One of the goals of education in a free society is that the value of learning becomes its own reward. The extent to which the school achieves this goal will determine how successfully students are intrinsically motivated to achieve self-realization. Motivation for learning may be diagrammed as in figure 2.5, largely extrinsic in first grade and largely intrinsic in twelfth.

The hierarchy of needs described by Maslow leads to the conclusion that the well-integrated personality on the top step in the hierarchy has a curiosity about life, the future, and the unknown that is satisfied through a need to know and to understand.

Physiological needs, safety, love and belonging, esteem, and self-actualization needs must be met to some degree before man explores his need to know and understand. When a more basic need is fairly well satisfied, the next higher order need emerges and serves as an active motivator of behavior (see figure 2.6).[7]

Maslow concluded:

These basic goals are related to each other, being arranged in a hierarchy of prepotency. This means that the most prepotent goal will monopolize consciousness and will tend of itself to organize the recruitment of the various capacities of the organism. The less prepotent needs are minimized, even forgotten or denied. But when a need is fairly well satisfied, the next prepotent (higher) need emerges, in turn, to dominate the conscious life and to serve as the center of organization of behavior, since gratified needs are not active motivators.

Figure 2.6
Hierarchy and
prepotency of needs.

Based on Hierarchy of
Needs, *Motivation and
Personality,* 2d ed.
Copyright 1970, Abraham
H. Maslow, Harper &
Row, and from Herbert J.
Klausmeier and William
Goodwin, *Learning and
Human Abilities*:
Educational Psychology,
4th ed., Copyright © 1961,
1975, by Herbert J.
Klausmeier. By permission
of Harper & Row,
Publishers, Inc.

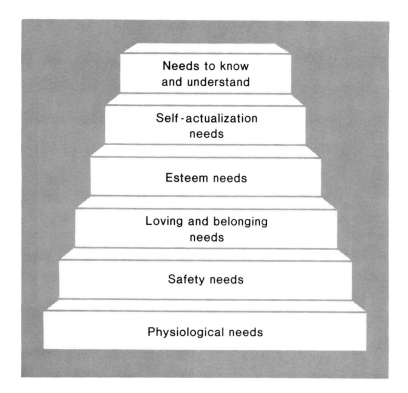

Thus man is a perpetually wanting animal. Ordinarily the satisfaction of these wants is not altogether mutually exclusive, but only tends to be. The average member of our society is most often partially satisfied and partially unsatisfied in all of his wants. The hierarchy principle is usually empirically observed in terms of increasing percentages of non-satisfaction as we go up the hierarchy. Reversals of the average order of the hierarchy are sometimes observed. Also it has been observed that an individual may permanently lose the higher wants in the hierarchy under special conditions. There are not only ordinary multiple motivations for usual behavior, but in addition many determinants other than motives.[8]

*Rewards and
Punishments*

Praise works better than blame, rewards work better than punishments, and children need to experience more successes than failures. Teachers can support children's efforts to learn by pointing out what has been done well even though many things have been done poorly. Calling attention to what has been done correctly will ultimately be more effective than myriads of glowing red marks signifying failure.

Children's fear of failure can be traumatic enough to hinder their ability to function in a learning situation. Children who perceive that they are likely to fail on any particular task will stop trying to succeed. Their classmates who sense that they are succeeding on their tasks tend to hold high expectations of success on later tasks. The old saying, "Nothing succeeds like success," is certainly true. Jucknat has graphed the effects of success and failure on children's levels of aspiration (figure 2.7).

Understanding

Learning progresses from the concrete to the abstract. Dale's cone of experience shows the importance of concrete, direct experiences and the difficulty of conceptualizing from only abstract verbal symbols (see figure 2.8).

Dale divides the cone of experience into activities of doing, observing someone else do something, and interpreting abstract visual or verbal symbols.

A. Activities of action. The child is a participant in the learning process.
 1. Direct experience with a purpose. Experiences that involve the senses: touch, smell, sight, hearing, taste. For example, preparation of a meal in class or construction of a piece of furniture.

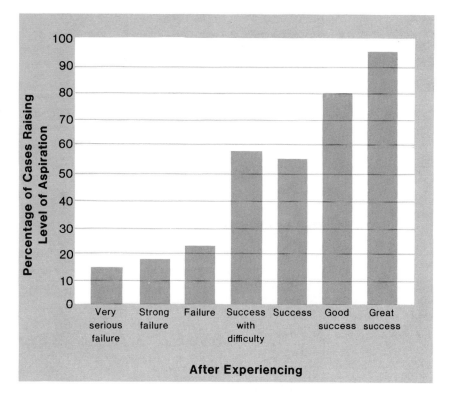

Figure 2.7
Effects of failure and success on level of aspiration.

From James M. Sawrey and Charles W. Telford, *Educational Psychology* (Boston, Mass.: Allyn & Bacon, 1958), p. 356. After M. Jucknat, *Psychol. Forsh.,* 1937, pp. 22, 89. Reprinted by permission.

(Chart axis labels: Percentage of Cases Raising Level of Aspiration — vertical axis 0 to 100. Horizontal axis "After Experiencing": Very serious failure, Strong failure, Failure, Success with difficulty, Success, Good success, Great success.)

2. Contrived experiences. A method that simplifies the details. For example, a model or a small reproduction.
3. Dramatization. Participating in a drama.

B. Activities of observation. The child only observes someone else doing the action.

4. Demonstration. Performed by the teacher.
5. Excursions away from the school. For example, to the dairy or to the store.
6. Exhibitions. Collections of things in the experiences of children: stamps, coins, dolls, etc.
7. Educational motion pictures.
8. Vertical picture files, photos, the radio, records.

C. Abstract representations.

9. Visual symbols. Charts, graphs, maps, diagrams, etc. Each is only a representation of an idea.
10. Verbal symbols. A word, an idea, a concept, a scientific principle, a formula. In each case, completely abstract.

Intellectual life functions primarily on a very high level of abstraction or symbolization. The point is that children need much experience at concrete levels before they can solve abstract questions and problems with good comprehension.

Figure 2.8
Cone of experience.

From *Audio-visual
Methods in Teaching,* 3d
ed., by Edgar Dale.
© Copyright 1946, 1954,
1969 by Holt, Rinehart and
Winston, Inc. Reprinted by
permission of Holt,
Rinehart and Winston,
CBS College Publishing.

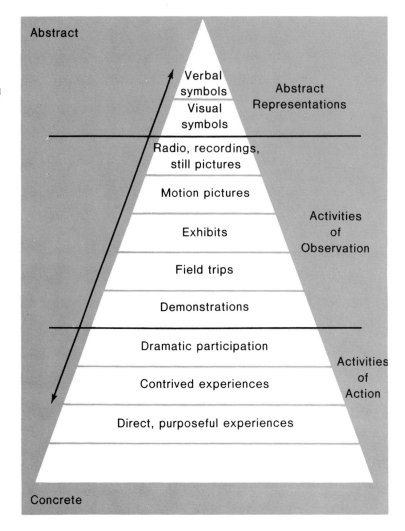

Moffett provides another way of organizing ideas that is similar to Dale's.[9] He proposes that individuals encode their knowledge at three levels: (1) conceptualization, (2) verbalization, and (3) literacy. First, children encode experiences as concepts. Since they are having experiences continually, concepts grow in number and complexity. At the verbalization level, thoughts are encoded into speech. The process may also be reversed. Finally, at the literacy level, oral language is encoded as writing. Writing may be decoded to speech, in a reverse process.

Well-planned reading lessons are consistent with the ideas represented in Dale's cone of experience and Moffett's levels of coding. Unfortunately, too many lessons begin at the highest levels of these models.

Suppose a middle grade teacher planned to teach a story in the basal reader that concerned living two hundred years ago. The wise teacher's lesson plans might call for roleplaying of some aspects of pioneer life. Perhaps some objects used by people of those days, such as garments, could be obtained for the children to use in the roleplaying. Perhaps on the following day the teacher might show a movie about pioneer life. Since there are many films on this topic, the teacher would have selected one that included some concepts to be read about later in the readers. Finally, the class would be ready to read the story. In preparation for the story, several pictures relating directly to the text would be available for display and discussion. The children might do some drawings of their impressions of pioneer life. At last the class would be ready to read, perhaps after brainstorming about words and phrases that class members predict would be in the story. The teacher would then have guided the children through a series of experiences, from the concrete to the most abstract.

Process vs. Content   To enhance understanding in the school life of the child, the curriculum of the school should be based more on *process* than on *content*. When teachers are aware of how the cognitive processes of children develop and therefore understand the necessity of putting new learning to work in order for it to be remembered, they are apt to see much that is objectionable in the traditional classroom. Such teaching emphasized factual recall, parroting back explanations to the teacher, and performing on tests that require much regurgitation of factual information at the simple recall level. To point up the differences, *process* methodology is contrasted here with *content* methodology.

Process Methodology	**Content Methodology**
Learning to think clearly to solve problems.	Careful memorizing of teacher's lecture notes.
Learning to categorize the *relevant* and the *irrelevant* in a problem situation.	Depending on the teacher to decide what is important.
Learning by discovery—learning by inductive methods is more valuable than learning what the teacher says.	Relying on information learned from teachers, books, and parents.
Experimenting with, testing, and integrating subject matter information.	Studying each subject as a small isolated body of necessary information.
Evaluating—using the evidence—and accepting or rejecting the results.	Accepting the judgment of teachers and textbooks as unquestioned authority.
Emphasizing *how* to read, study, think, and learn.	Emphasizing *what* to read, study, think, and learn.
Free discussion and small group work to search for answers to the "larger" questions.	Recitation in class.

Children must learn a great deal of factual information *to use* how-to-think situations. One should not make a dichotomy of "Do we teach children *what* to think or *how* to think?" since without the *what* it will not be possible to do the *how*.

Transfer of Training

Transfer of training is exhibited when the learner is able to make use of learning in circumstances that are different from the situation in which the learning initially took place. Transfer is a necessary factor in all growth in learning. Transfer is absolutely necessary in the extension of any generalized skill taught in the elementary school, such as reading, writing, and arithmetic. Thorndike explained the concept of transfer in this way: ". . . a change in one function alters any other only insofar as the two functions have as factors identical elements."[10]

The theory of identical elements explains an important condition in the probability of transfer. Judd advanced the theory of generalized training to explain the likelihood of transfer. His position was that the ability to generalize, understand, or abstract enhanced transfer.[11]

Ellis listed principles of transfer that include:[12]

1. *Overall task similarity.* Transfer of training is greatest when the training conditions are highly similar to those of the ultimate testing conditions.
2. *Stimulus similarity.* When a task requires the learner to make the same response to new but similar stimuli, positive transfer increases with increasing stimulus similarity.
3. *Learning-to-learn.* Cumulative practice in learning a series of related tasks or problems leads to increased facility in learning how to learn.
4. *Insight.* Insight, defined behaviorally as the rapid solution of problems, appears to develop as a result of extensive practice in solving similar or related classes of problems.

5. *Amount of practice on the original task.* The greater the amount of practice on the original task, the greater the likelihood of positive transfer.
6. *Understanding and transfer.* Transfer is greater if the learner understands the general rules or principles that are appropriate in solving the problems.

Applying Ellis's principles of transfer to reading, we can identify some appropriate and inappropriate practices. When students need practice, the tasks they engage in should be similar to the *real* task of reading print for meaning. Focusing attention on isolated elements and words is not sufficiently similar to the behaviors required to read sentences, paragraphs, and stories to guarantee transfer. It is often found that children know many isolated skills, but are unable to apply them without suggestions from the teacher.

Children may be guided into building generalizations about print that will help them learn how to learn. They become, in effect, independent learners. Children who are guided to learn discrete facts or bits of information about print and reading will have a harder time building any sort of generalizations. They will fail to see how to group all the individual pieces of information into useful patterns.

Forgetting

The most widely cited historical study of forgetting is that of Ebbinghaus, first published in 1885. He reported that 66.3 percent of what one learns is forgotten within twenty-four hours. The conditions surrounding this fact are important. He was his own subject, his materials were nonsense syllables, and his criterion was two errorless repetitions. The Ebbinghaus curve of forgetting is reproduced in figure 2.9.

The importance of review to reduce the high rate of forgetting has been recognized for a long time. Reviewing very soon after learning and then reviewing several times at spaced intervals will help to minimize forgetting.

The practical bearing of the results obtained on education in general is that when associations have once been formed they should be recalled before an interval so long has elapsed that the original associations have lost their 'color' and cannot be recalled in the same 'shape', time, and order. In general it was found that the most economical method for keeping material once memorized from disappearing, was to review the material whenever it started to 'fade.' Here also the intervals were found to be, roughly speaking, in arithmetical proportion. For similar reasons the student is advised to review his 'lecture notes' shortly after taking them, and if possible, to review them again the evening of the same day. Then the lapse of a week or two does not make so much difference. When once he has forgotten so much that the various associations originally made have vanished, a considerable portion of the material is irretrievably lost.[13]

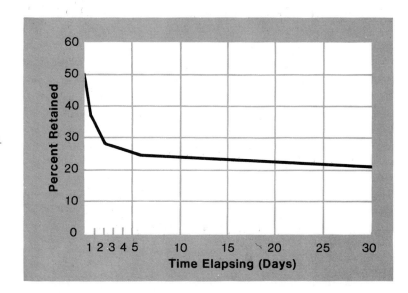

Figure 2.9
Curve of retention (Ebbinghaus) for nonsense syllables after various time intervals.

From Henry E. Garrett, *Great Experiments in Psychology* (New York: Appleton-Century-Crofts, Copyright © 1941), p. 273. Reprinted by permission.

Studies of retention show the importance of immediate recall and spaced review in helping students remember. Rules for remembering are:

1. Material is easy to remember in proportion as it is meaningful.
2. Material is easier to remember if it gets well organized in the individual's mind.
3. Outlining, summarizing, or taking good notes are aids to remembering.
4. An active intention to recall is an aid to remembering.
5. A single reading is rarely enough. Reviewing and re-reading are necessary for remembering any length of time.
6. Recall must be selective. One must sift out the main points.
7. Immediately after reading, one should reflect on what has been read and recite important points to oneself.
8. What we learn and never review is gradually forgotten. What we want to remember must be refreshed from time to time by review.[14]

The Cognitive Domain

Human learning is frequently divided into three large areas, called domains. They are the *cognitive, affective,* and *psychomotor* domains. This division is useful to remember when planning learning experiences, since it helps teachers prepare a balanced educational "diet" for children. We are reminded that there are knowing and feeling aspects to all learning, as well as psychomotor ones. In practice, however, one would not plan and teach a lesson that was entirely in one domain or the other. People function in all three areas simultaneously and continuously.

Cognition is knowing. Knowing utilizes a hierarchy of abilities: the ability to recall facts; the ability to use factual information for solving problems; and the application of problem-solving abilities in new situations. Concrete knowledge, abstract thinking, reflection, application, and deriving generalizations are all processes in cognition.

Knowledge may be specific bits of information, terminology, methods of dealing with specific information, awareness of the arbitrary conventions of social behavior, classifying or categorizing, or stating principles and generalizations.

Intellectual skills and abilities are utilized in putting knowledge to work. Included are skills and abilities in comprehension, translation (paraphrasing, interpreting figures of speech), interpretation, application, analysis, synthesis, and evaluation.

In this frame of reference, *comprehension* is the ability to understand the idea being communicated by the speaker or writer. *Translation* is the listener's ability to paraphrase the ideas into his or her own thought patterns. Figures of speech have to be understood. Translation includes the ability to summarize the important points or *interpret* data reported in a study.

Application requires the ability to use a rule, a method, or a generalization in a new situation. *Critical analysis* includes ability to separate fact from opinion, to evaluate supporting evidence, to understand the relationships between ideas, and to see through persuasion, advertising, or propaganda.

Synthesis is the ability to assemble ideas into an integrated unit.

Evaluation requires the ability to establish or accept criteria for judgment and to use them objectively.

Bloom's categories of thinking include:

1. *Knowledge* (memory). The student recalls or recognizes information.
2. *Comprehension.* The student knows and can use the material without sensing its fullest meaning. Comprehension is further divided into:
   a. *Translation.* The student changes information into a different symbolic form or language (paraphrases).
   b. *Interpretation.* The student discovers relationships among facts, generalizations, definitions, values, and skills.
   c. *Extrapolation.* The student utilizes given information to make predictions consistent with the original facts.
3. *Application.* The student solves a lifelike problem that requires the identification of the issue and the selection and use of appropriate generalizations and skills. This is a step at which many readers fail. They have many skills and other bits of information, but cannot ally them as needed.
4. *Analysis.* The student solves a problem in the light of conscious knowledge of the parts and forms of thinking.
5. *Synthesis.* The student solves a problem that requires original, creative thinking.
6. *Evaluation.* The student makes a judgment of good or bad, right or wrong, according to standards he or she designates.[15]

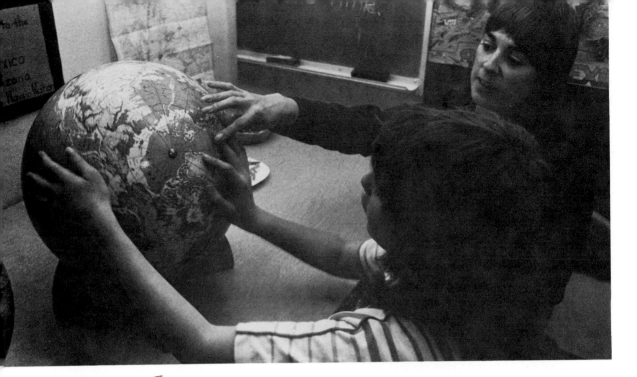

"Hands-on" experiences, carefully guided by teachers, help children to grow in their ability to make useful generalizations.

Figure 2.10
Accumulative perceptual experiences grow into concepts.

From Asahel D. Woodruff, *Basic Concepts of Teaching.* Con. ed. (San Francisco, Calif.: Chandler Publishing Co., Copyright © 1961), p. 184. Reprinted by permission.

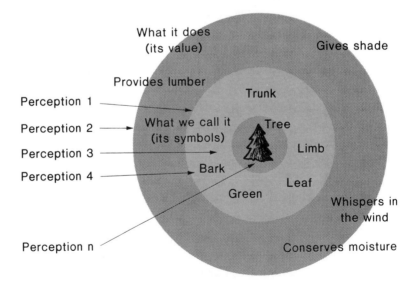

Perception 1
Perception 2
Perception 3
Perception 4
Perception n

What it does (its value)
Gives shade
Provides lumber
Trunk
What we call it (its symbols)
Tree
Limb
Bark
Leaf
Green
Whispers in the wind
Conserves moisture

Learning to Generalize

A generalization is a statement or principle that encompasses the common characteristics of a cluster of ideas or individual statements. Teachers should help students to generalize their knowledge in a given subject. Sanders has pointed out that in a fourth grade geography book, the generalization "Life in the desert is difficult" is not stated directly but is clearly implied in such subordinate information as: (1) the home is crude and the family moves frequently; (2) medical help is not available; (3) life is close to nature and often dependent on the caprice of nature; (4) transportation is by foot or animal.[16]

This development of generalizations from the students in the class is an inductive method of teaching. By analyzing their own experiences and forming concepts that are meaningful and useful to them, children can accumulate descriptive information to allow them to arrive at a generalized statement.

Woodruff illustrated how this process works in developing an extended understanding of the concept "tree." This process utilizes perception, conceptualization, thinking, evaluating, and selecting the contributing components to the generalization (see figure 2.10).

The most immediate perceptions about "tree" include its parts, its color, and the shade it casts. Some of the abstract ideas learned later may be that trees rustle in the wind, conserve moisture, and are either evergreen or deciduous. Accumulation of all these perceptual experiences leads to concept formation and generalizing.

In understanding many elementary concepts about weather and its components, children grow toward the ability to draw generalizations about weather and climate. This is illustrated in figure 2.11, which shows Woodruff's diagram of a major concept developed from many supporting concepts.[17]

Finally, one can construct a conceptual model based on many individual, miscellaneous experiences, grouped into simple facts or ideas contributing to broader concepts and finally leading to a generalization.

The way perceptions lead to conceptualizations, which lead to generalizations, is further discussed in chapter 10, "Comprehension Skills."

A number of writers have made significant contributions to the understanding of the cognitive domain and its implications for reading instruction. Of course, none of them considered the domain alone, since the domains do not exist alone. However, their contributions have the greatest impact on the study of cognition.

Jean Piaget, a Swiss psychologist known for his work in cognitive psychology, has contributed several ideas that are crucial to successful reading instruction. He identified four periods of intellectual growth: the sensorimotor, preoperational, concrete operational, and formal operational. The second and third periods are the ones in which children are most likely to be during initial reading instruction.

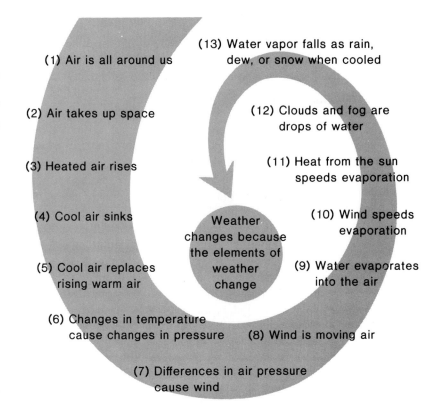

Figure 2.11
A major concept and some supporting concepts.

From Asahel D. Woodruff, *Basic Concepts of Teaching.* Con. ed. (San Francisco, Calif.: Chandler Publishing Co., Copyright © 1961), p. 184. Reprinted by permission.

(1) Air is all around us

(2) Air takes up space

(3) Heated air rises

(4) Cool air sinks

(5) Cool air replaces rising warm air

(6) Changes in temperature cause changes in pressure

(7) Differences in air pressure cause wind

(8) Wind is moving air

(9) Water evaporates into the air

(10) Wind speeds evaporation

(11) Heat from the sun speeds evaporation

(12) Clouds and fog are drops of water

(13) Water vapor falls as rain, dew, or snow when cooled

Weather changes because the elements of weather change

Since, in the preoperational stage, children are intuitive thinkers, the abilities to conserve, to think reversibly, and to de-center are beyond their range of thought. It is of questionable value to require children to convert sounds to letters and to deal with frequent transformations. Raven and Salzer wrote:

> In presenting the young reader with upper- and lower-case letters, different type faces, manuscript and cursive writing, variations in the rendering of particular alphabet letters, and all of these in many different combinations and contexts, those responsible for initial reading instruction constantly expose children to transformed situations and expect them to isolate the single common attribute which is the key to solving the problem.[18]

Piaget contends that children must create their own rules; therefore, a rule-based program must create difficulties. Even if children memorize the rules, they often have trouble in their application.

Young children are avid oral language users. Teachers should take advantage of this. Children's reading should grow out of the events close to their own experiences. This will minimize the problems just described. With stories from their own experiences and a whole-language approach by the teachers, children can begin to have successful experiences with print.

Concrete operational children are capable of learning to read formally. They can perform all the mental operations required to interact with print. They can read widely, but Raven and Salzer suggest:

> . . . reading activities during the concrete-operational period would provide increased emphasis on developing logical operations by including opportunities to combine sentence and word elements, associate elements in different ways, establish correspondence or identity among elements, and would encourage students to transform the order of elements and observe the differences produced.[19]

The concrete operational child will probably work best with these suggestions if the reading materials relate to ideas about which first-hand information is available.

Hilda Taba is remembered for her work in curriculum and particularly in the social studies. In these frameworks, she identifies four areas to be emphasized.[20] They are basic knowledge, thinking, attitudes and feelings, and skills. These are four areas that should also be remembered when planning reading instruction. Taba presents a highly structured set of strategies for promoting concept development. These strategies are organized into three steps: (1) concept formation through listing, grouping, and labeling ideas; (2) interpretation of data through differentiating and relating ideas and making inferences; and (3) application of principles by predicting consequences and explaining and verifying predictions. These are all useful strategies in guiding the reading of unfamiliar materials.[21]

Bruner writes about the need to make reading an active enterprise.[22] He notes that reading, of all the language forms, is apt to be the most passive, the one during which the user is most likely to go to sleep. He notes the power of language, including reading, to serve as a tool for organizing and reorganizing experience. He also points out that reading and writing are second-order abstractions; they stand in relation to oral language as algebra does to arithmetic. Because of their abstract nature, he suggests that they create an opportunity for the learner to become aware of the power and creative potential of language. Bruner's comments direct the teacher to encourage reading as an active process, to utilize language with children for creative purposes, and to employ the abstractness of language as a tool for study rather than as a handicap.

Mastery Learning

Mastery learning is a concept predicated upon the belief that students should be given assignments with predetermined criteria of achievement and then should not be permitted to move to another task until those criteria are met. For example, *mastery* could be arbitrarily defined as scoring 90 percent correct on a criterion-referenced test of the material to be learned. Each learner uses as much time as he or she needs to master the assignment. Benjamin Bloom has helped educators to understand the processes and implications of mastery learning. He suggests that the sources of mastery are the student's prerequisite cognitive learnings, the attitude brought by the student to the task, and the quality of instruction.[23]

Bloom identified four elements of good teaching:[24]

1. *Giving the student adequate motivational cues.* This is the way the teacher presents and explains the assignment. Whether or not the student can use the cues depends on the breadth of the student's background and the variety of enriching materials accessible to him or her.
2. *Reinforcement of the student's successes.* A skillful teacher knows what would be a reward for a given student.
3. *Involvement of the student in the learning process.* The extent to which a student actively participates is a good index of the quality of learning taking place.
4. *Giving the student immediate feedback* with necessary correction is the ingredient that makes the first three elements work over an extended period.

While one may not teach in a school in which the formal elements of mastery learning are employed, ideas may be taken from the concept. For example, with learning centers in the classroom, with adequate informal diagnosis of *entering behaviors,* and with attention to the attitudes toward tasks, teachers will be able to incorporate a great deal of mastery learning for their students in the course of study. Students who need more time can take it. Fast learners can either move more quickly to enrichment activities or take time to be peer teachers and work with their own classmates in learning activities.

Skinner is often associated with programmed learning as a means of teaching reading. He wrote:

. . . reading can also be most effectively taught with instrumental help. A pupil can learn to distinguish among letters and groups of letters in an alphabet simply as visual patterns. . . . He can be taught to identify arbitrary correspondences in a more complex type of stimulus control which is within reach of the same device. . . . The same device can teach correspondences between words and the properties of objects. . . . Traditional ways of teaching reading establish all these repertoires, but they do so indirectly and, alas, inefficiently.[25]

Programmed learning uses the following learning principles:

1. Easy steps.
2. Continuous response at each step of the way.
3. Immediate knowledge of results.
4. Progressing at individual rates.
5. Elimination of error.
6. Repetitive practice.

These principles are some of the most fundamental for promoting learning. Individualized lessons that are paced to the tempo and maturity of the individual student and which provide immediate feedback about correct and incorrect responses are the types of lessons conscientious teachers have been dreaming about for a long time. The greatest difficulties have arisen in the quality of programs; it has been easier to produce *programs* than to produce *high quality* programs with adequate content that conforms to the principles.

An example of programmed reading based on these principles that has been successfully used is the following:

Sullivan, M. W., and Cynthia Buchanan. *Programmed Reading*. 3d ed. New York: Webster Division, McGraw-Hill, 1973. A series of 23 student response booklets to teach reading skills from readiness through grade three level.

Traditional materials with comparable objectives are:

Science Research Associates. *Junior Reading for Understanding Laboratory*. 259 East Erie Street, Chicago, Ill. 60611: Science Research Associates, 1963.
Anderson, Donald G. *New Practice Readers*. 2d ed. New York: Webster Division, McGraw-Hill, 1978. A series of eight workbooks, A–G, with graded difficulty from 2.0 to 6.8.
McCall, William A., and Lelah Mae Crabbs. *Standard Test Lessons in Reading*. New York: Teachers College Press, 1979. Provides six levels, from grade three through high school.

The Affective Domain

In the primary grades, most children develop the attitude that reading is something to be valued. Some develop a preference for reading over some other school activity. A few—far too few—develop a real commitment to reading. In any event, reading as a value develops from the accumulation of many experiences over a long period of time. Accumulated experience produces many values that each individual must organize into a personal value hierarchy. The end result is character in a person.

Krathwohl's outline of the development of values within the affective domain is as follows:[26]

A. Receiving
   1. Awareness
   2. Willingness to receive
   3. Selective attention
B. Responding
   1. Acquiescence in responding
   2. Willingness to respond
   3. Satisfaction in response
C. Valuing
   1. Acceptance of a value
   2. Preference for a value
   3. Commitment to a value
D. Organization
   1. Conceptualization of a value
   2. Organization of a value system
E. Characterization by a value
   1. Generalized set
   2. Characterization

Krathwohl et al.[27] have indicated ways in which the cognitive and affective domains interact, overlap, or follow parallel steps:

Cognitive	Affective
The cognitive continuum begins with the student's *recall* and *recognition* of knowledge;	The affective continuum begins with the student's merely *receiving* stimuli and giving them passive attention and then more active attention;
it extends through *comprehension* of the knowledge;	the student responds to stimuli on request, willingly, and with satisfaction;
skill in *application* of the knowledge comprehended;	the student values the phenomenon or activity and voluntarily responds and seeks out ways to respond;
skill in *analysis* of situations involving this knowledge; skill in *synthesis* of this knowledge into new organizations;	the student *conceptualizes* each value responded to;
skill in *evaluation* in this area of knowledge in order to judge the value of material and methods for given purposes.	the student organizes the values into systems and finally into a single whole, a *characterization* of the individual.

Values and Teaching

Raths et al. have defined values as those elements that show how a person has decided to use his or her life.

Values are based on three processes: choosing, prizing, and acting. One chooses freely from alternatives after thoughtful consideration of the consequences of each alternative. One prizes and cherishes one's choices, is happy with them, and is willing to affirm the choices publicly. One does something with the choice, does it repeatedly, in some pattern in his life. These criteria of valuing about one's beliefs, attitudes, activities, and feelings are based on self-directed behavior.[28]

Teachers recognize that in any group of children, individual behavior varies widely. Some children seem to know clearly what they value, while others are apathetic, flighty, uncertain, or inconsistent. Or there may be drifters, overconformers, overdissenters, or roleplayers. Children who are unclear about their values may be said to lack a clarity of relationship to society.[29]

Teachers need to know and use a number of neutral clarifying responses to help children strengthen their choices and deepen their commitment to values.[30]

Neutral questions that help to clarify responses include:

Is this something that you prize?
Are you *glad* about that?
How did you feel when that happened?

Have you felt this way for a long time?

Did you *have* to choose that; was it a *free* choice?

Do you *do* anything about that idea?

Would you really *do* that or are you just talking?

What are some good things about that notion?

What other possibilities are there?

Is that very important to you?

Would you do the same thing over again?

Would you like to tell others about your idea?[31]

The Affective Response to Reading

One of the surest ways to help a child develop a permanent attachment for reading is to ensure *an affective response* to the reading world. The child who lives the experience of the mongoose in its struggle to kill the cobra in Kipling's *Jungle Book;* the boy or girl who reads Laura Ingalls Wilder's *Little House on the Prairie, On the Banks of Plum Creek,* or *The Long Winter* is sure to develop strong empathy for Laura, her sisters, and her father and mother during their pioneer struggles as farmers in the Midwest. Several other examples from children's literature that emphasize affective response can be cited. Booker T. Washington's autobiography, *Up From Slavery,* has one recurring central theme—the struggle for education. First, his own, then his brother's, then the Indians', and finally his own people's. Interest, attitude, value, commitment, an organized value system, and a complete philosophy of life are exemplified.[32]

Elizabeth Yates, in her Newbery Medal Book *Amos Fortune, Free Man,* shows how Amos throughout his life learned to treasure freedom and education most of all. All that he earned as a free man helped others buy freedom. Freedom became the characterization of Amos as an *ultimate value.*[33]

In Doris Gates's *Blue Willow,* Janie never wanted to have to move again. She wanted to stay in one place, have a friend, and go to school. But because her father was a migrant worker, she had no friends and she did not attend school. If she could stay in one place, she could have friends to play with happily, like the children she had observed so many times as her family drove through towns between jobs. When the story ends, Janie's father gets a regular job and they will not have to move.[34]

Boys and girls find *Charlotte's Web* very sad when Charlotte explains to Wilbur, the pig, that she is going to die. Even though her babies do hatch, and Fern, the little girl, realizes she is getting too old to come to the barn to talk to the animals, it is very sad because Charlotte dies.[35]

When Travis must go out and shoot Old Yeller because he has rabies, the reader is as emotionally involved as Travis is.[36]

By the time Billy has succeeded in training his pair of coon hounds so they are the best hunting dogs around, the reader feels the same sadness Billy feels when the male of the pair is wounded and dies and the female dies of a broken heart.[37]

Cavanah creates a strong affective response to the inherent drive for learning held by young Abe when she tells how he learned *grammar:*

One morning when Abe Lincoln was having breakfast at Mentor Graham's house, he said,
"I have a notion to study English grammar."
"If you expect to go before the public, I think it would be the best thing to do."
"If I had a grammar I would commence now."
Mentor thought for a moment. "There's no one in town who owns a grammar," he said finally, "but Mr. Vaner out in the country has one. He might lend you his copy."
Abe got up from the table and walked six miles to the Vaner farm. When he returned, he carried an open book in his hands. He was studying grammar as he walked.[38]

Other books that will have value in developing the attachment for reading that is based on emotional response include Eleanor Estes' *The Hundred Dresses,* Esther Forbes's *Johnny Tremain,* Marguerite de Angeli's *Yonie Wondernose,* Joseph Krumbold's *And Now Miguel,* Jade Snow Wong's *Fifth Chinese Daughter,* William H. Armstrong's *Sounder,* Jean George's *Julie of the Wolves,* Laurence Yep's *Dragonwings,* Jane Wagner's *J.T.,* John Gunther's *Death Be Not Proud,* or Margaret Craven's *I Heard the Owl Call My Name.*[39]

Dora V. Smith, in her Kappa Delta Pi lecture, emphasized the importance of reading in sharing experiences in these words:

Books such as these help young people the world over to share their experiences one with the other—to discover the ways in which they are very much alike and the ways in which they are different and therefore capable of making a unique contribution to the world's life. Truly the arts of communication are making possible the miracle of shared living.[40]

The Psychomotor Domain

The psychomotor domain encompasses such activities as muscular or motor skill, manipulation of materials and/or objects, or any act that requires a neuromuscular coordination. The following types of activities would be most common in elementary school physical education programs:

Dances and rhythms: fundamental movements and traditional and creative dances
Activities on equipment: jungle gym, ladder, rings, bars, swings, slides, seesaws
Games: dodge ball, circle tag, endball, ring toss
Classroom games: Simon says
Team sports: softball, soccer, touch football, volleyball
Stunts and tumbling
Calisthenics

Figure 2.12
Relative use of motor
and perceptual
components for
different skills.

From Herbert J.
Klausmeier and William
Goodwin, *Learning and
Human Abilities:
Educational Psychology,*
4th ed. Copyright © 1961,
1975 by Herbert J.
Klausmeier. By permission
of Harper & Row,
Publishers, Inc.

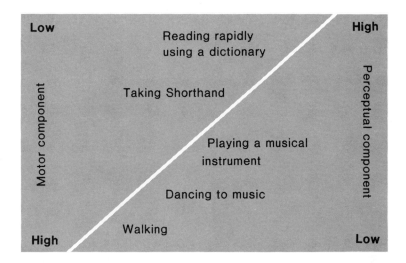

Psychomotor objectives emphasize some muscular or motor skill, some manipulation of material and objects, or some act that requires a neuromuscular coordination. Few such objectives are stated in education except for handwriting, physical education, and perhaps trades' skills, technical courses, and special education.

The classroom teacher could easily test some areas of psychomotor abilities in six-year-olds entering the formal reading program in order to locate areas of potential difficulty before the child fails in academic skills. The way certain skills develop as children master motor and perceptual components is illustrated in figure 2.12. These skills include the following abilities:

Distinguish the right from the left hand and copy letters, numbers, and designs correctly.

Sense (understand) the position of one's body in space.

Perceive figure-ground relationships, finding outline birds or squirrels in large pictures, recognizing what an object must be in terms of the things around it that are easily identified.

Summary

Some general principles based on learning theory are:

1. No learning takes place without a motive. Motivation, from childhood to maturity, moves from greater to lesser *extrinsic* motivation and from lesser to greater *intrinsic* motivation.
2. Active participation in learning is better than passive reception of learning.
3. Material is more easily learned and remembered according to how well it is meaningfully understood by the learner.

4. Praise works better than blame; reward works better than punishment.
5. Generally, brighter people learn some things less bright people do not.
6. Once crucial facts have been understood, they must be overlearned to reduce loss by forgetting. Memorization is important after understanding is established.
7. Immediate knowledge of results aids learning.
8. Distributed practice is better than massed practice.
9. Nothing succeeds like success.
10. Provision for each child to grow at his or her own rate is necessary.

Educational psychologists have evolved many valuable generalizations about children and how they learn. The following principles of programming are based on some of the most important generalizations.

1. Easy steps
2. Continuous response at each step
3. Immediate knowledge of results
4. Progressing at completely individual rates
5. Elimination of error
6. Repetitive practice

For Further Reading

Ausubel, David P. "The Role and Scope of Educational Psychology." Chapter 1 in *Educational Psychology: A Cognitive View,* pp. 3–34. New York: Holt, Rinehart and Winston, 1968.

Beyer, Barry. "Concepts and Inquiry Teaching." Chapter 6 in *Inquiry in the Social Studies Classroom: A Strategy for Teaching,* pp. 111–30. Columbus, Ohio: Charles E. Merrill, 1971. The chapter suggested is an excellent statement and explanation of the development of concepts, and is valuable to any academic area. There are practical suggestions for working at concept development, as well as clearly defined theoretical notions.

Duckworth, Eleanor. "The Having of Wonderful Ideas." In *Piaget in the Classroom,* ed. Milton Schwebel and Jane Raph, pp. 258–77. New York: Basic Books, 1973. The author makes some powerful interpretations of Piaget's theories as they apply to schools, curriculum, children, and literacy.

Elkind, David. *Children and Adolescents: Interpretive Essays on Jean Piaget.* New York: Oxford University Press, 1974.

Hughes, Marie. "The Child As a Person." *Teem Exchange* 3 (Fall 1975): 2–5, 10–11.

Rowe, Mary Budd. "Wait, Wait, Wait . . ." *School Science and Mathematics* 78 (March 1978): 207–16. This excellent article focuses on questioning and thinking in the classroom. The author proposes lengthening the teacher "wait time" after a question is posed to increase classroom thinking.

Smith, Frank. *Comprehension and Learning: A Conceptual Framework for Teachers.* New York: Holt, Rinehart and Winston, 1975.

Notes

1. Barbara Bateman, "Learning Disabilities—Yesterday, Today, and Tomorrow," *Exceptional Children* 31 (December 1964): 176.
2. From Robert M. Gagné, *The Conditions of Learning,* 2d ed., New York: Holt, Rinehart and Winston. Copyright © 1970, pp. 35–62, *passim.* Reprinted by permission.
3. William Rohwer, Jr. et al., *Understanding Intellectual Development* (Hinsdale, Ill.: The Dryden Press, 1974), pp. 85–100.
4. Ernest Hilgard, *Theories of Learning,* 4th ed. (New York: Appleton-Century-Crofts, 1974).
5. John DeCecco, *The Psychology of Learning and Instruction: Educational Psychology* (Englewood Cliffs, N.J.: Prentice-Hall, 1968), pp. 290–91.
6. See Norris M. Sanders, *Classroom Questions: What Kinds?* (New York: Harper & Row, 1966), and Frank J. Guszak, "Teachers' Questions and Levels of Reading Comprehension," in *Perspectives in Reading: The Evaluation of Children's Reading Achievement* (Newark, Del.: International Reading Association, 1967), pp. 97–109.
7. Herbert J. Klausmeier and William Goodwin, *Learning and Human Abilities: Educational Psychology,* 4th ed. (New York: Harper & Row, 1975), p. 227.
8. A.H. Maslow, "A Theory of Human Motivation," *Psychological Review* 50 (1943):394–95.
9. James Moffett and Betty Wagner, *Student-Centered Language Arts and Reading, K–13: A Handbook for Teachers* (Boston: Houghton Mifflin, 1976).
10. E.L. Thorndike, *Educational Psychology* (New York: Lemcke & Buechner, 1903), p. 80.
11. C. H. Judd, *Psychology of Secondary Education* (Boston: Ginn, 1927), p. 441.
12. Henry A. Ellis, *The Transfer of Learning* (New York: Macmillan, 1965), pp. 72–74.
13. D. O. Lyon, "The Relation of Length of Material to Time Taken for Learning, and the Optimum Distribution of Time," *Journal of Educational Psychology* 5 (1914):155–63, cited in J.B. Stroud, *Psychology in Education* (New York: Longman, Green, 1946), p. 521.
14. Albert J. Harris and E. R. Sipay, *How to Increase Reading Ability,* 6th ed. (New York: David McKay, 1975), pp. 486–87.
15. Benjamin S. Bloom, ed., *Taxonomy of Educational Objectives—Handbook I: Cognitive Domain* (New York: Longman, Green, 1956), pp. 201–7.
16. Sanders, *Classroom Questions,* p. 23.
17. Asahel D. Woodruff, *Basic Concepts of Teaching,* concise ed. (San Francisco, Chandler, 1961), p. 184.
18. Ronald Raven and Richard Salzer, "Piaget and Reading Instruction," *The Reading Teacher* 24 (April 1971): 634.
19. Ibid., p. 635.
20. Hilda Taba, *Teachers' Handbook for Elementary Social Studies* (Palo Alto, Calif.: Addison-Wesley, 1967), pp. 7–10.
21. Ibid., pp. 91–117.
22. Jerome S. Bruner, *Toward a Theory of Instruction* (Cambridge, Mass.: Harvard University Press, 1966), pp. 102–12.
23. Benjamin Bloom, *Human Characteristics and School Learning* (New York: McGraw-Hill, 1976).

24. Ibid., pp. 115–27.
25. B. F. Skinner, "Why We Need Teaching Machines," in *Human Dynamics in Psychology and Education,* ed. Don Hamachek (Boston: Allyn & Bacon, 1968), pp. 224–25.
26. David R. Krathwohl et al., *Taxonomy of Educational Objectives—Handbook II: Affective Domain* (New York: David McKay, 1964), pp. 176–85.
27. Ibid., pp. 49–50.
28. Louis E. Raths et al., *Values and Teaching: Working with Values in the Classroom* (Columbus, Ohio: Charles E. Merrill, 1966), p. 30.
29. Ibid., pp. 4–6.
30. Ibid., pp. 51–62.
31. Ibid., pp. 260–61.
32. Rudyard Kipling, *The Jungle Book* (New York: Doubleday, 1964); Laura Ingalls Wilder, *Little House on the Prairie, On the Banks of Plum Creek, The Long Winter* (New York: Harper & Row, 1932–43); Booker T. Washington, *Up From Slavery* (Boston: Houghton Mifflin, 1917).
33. Elizabeth Yates, *Amos Fortune, Free Man* (New York: E.P. Dutton, 1950).
34. Doris Gates, *Blue Willow* (New York: Viking Press, 1948).
35. E. B. White, *Charlotte's Web* (New York: Harper & Row, 1952).
36. Fred Gipson, *Old Yeller* (New York: Harper and Brothers, 1956).
37. Wilson Rawls, *Where the Red Fern Grows* (Garden City, N.Y.: Doubleday, 1961).
38. Frances Cavanah, *Abe Lincoln Gets His Chance* (Chicago: Rand McNally, 1959), p. 78.
39. Eleanor Estes, *The Hundred Dresses* (New York: Harcourt, Brace & World, 1944); Esther Forbes, *Johnny Tremain* (Boston: Houghton Mifflin, 1943); Marguerite de Angeli, *Yonie Wondernose* (New York: Doubleday, 1944); Joseph Krumgold, *And Now Miguel* (New York: Thomas Y. Crowell, 1953); Jade Snow Wong, *Fifth Chinese Daughter* (New York: Scholastic Book Services, 1963); William H. Armstrong, *Sounder* (New York: Harper & Row, 1969); Jean George, *Julie of The Wolves* (New York: Harper & Row, 1972); Lawrence Yep, *Dragonwings* (New York: Harper & Row, 1975); Jane Wagner, *J.T.* (New York: Dell, 1969); John Gunther, *Death Be Not Proud* (New York: Pyramid Books, 1949); Margaret Craven, *I Heard the Owl Call My Name* (New York: Dell, 1973).
40. Dora V. Smith, *Communication: The Miracle of Shared Living* (New York: Macmillan, 1955), p. 57.

Linguistic Foundations for Reading Instruction

A Cognitive Map: Linguistic Foundations for Reading Instruction

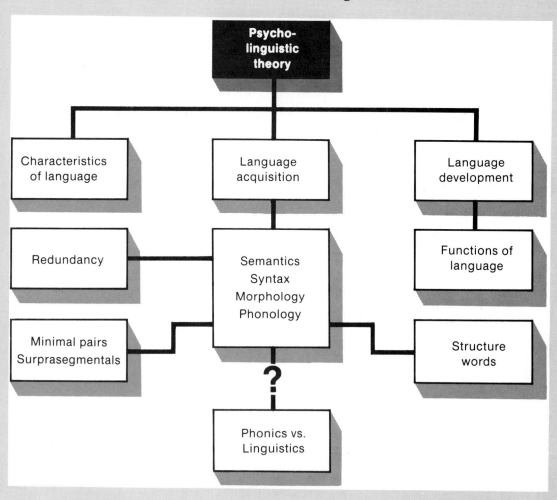

3

Guide Questions

1. What are the general characteristics of language?

2. Define in your own words: syntax, semantics, morphology, phonology.

3. Study table 3.1. Why might syntax be a more primary need than phonology in language learning?

4. Which facets in language structure contribute most to getting meaning from print?

5. How does psycholinguistic theory help in teaching reading?

Terminology

deep structure

grapho-phonics

inflected forms

linguistics

minimal pairs

morphology

psycholinguistics

redundancy

semantics

sociolinguistics

suprasegmentals

syntax

Language is the system of speech sounds by which people communicate with one another in their social group. The study of the nature of language is called *linguistics*. Teachers of reading must know something of the nature and components of language.

The study of language as an expression of human behavior is called *psycholinguistics*. Knowledge of psycholinguistics is as important to the teacher as knowledge of *descriptive linguistics,* the study of the phenomenon of language itself. *Sociolinguistics* is the scientific study of language in the context of the cultural values, practices, attitudes, and ideals that are expressed through language, including also the social context of who says what to whom, how, when, and for what purpose.

Current psycholinguistic theory has significantly changed reading methodology and textbook planning in the past two decades. The emphasis has been on whole language, comprehension, a schematic organization of thinking, language/environment relationships, and child-centered interests, attitudes, and motives. Key principles identified by Goodman and Goodman include:[1]

1. Meaning is constructed during listening and reading. Readers build meanings by using what they have already learned and by interacting with the text content.
2. Reading is a process of prediction, selection, confirmation and self-correction.
3. The three systems—grapho-phonic, syntactic and semantic—interact in the language process and cannot be taught as separate parts of a whole. (These terms are defined in the glossary at the end of this chapter.)
4. Comprehension is the center of every lesson in reading.
5. Learning must be functional, and literacy is an extension of natural language learning.
6. Teachers motivate learning, arrange stimulating learning environments, monitor learning activities, provide relevant materials for learning, and encourage and suggest. But it is always *the learner* who extracts what is meaningful to him or her.
7. Learning to read is *not* learning to recognize words; it is learning to make sense of printed text. Predictability builds vocabulary more than the simple repetition of words being read does.

Characteristics of Language

There are eight general characteristics of language that have especial implications for the classroom teacher.

1. Language is uniquely human. Only people use language as an expression of abstract thought. While bees, dolphins, and a few other animals may use sequences of signs and signals, linguists do not consider these to be language systems of communication. They do not combine sound with specific meanings.

2. Language is speech; it is oral. Writing is only a representation of the oral language. In written language, most of the important phonological features of stress, intonation, and juncture are left out. For example, "Are you going to wear that dress?" could have different kinds of stress and therefore meaning: "*Are* you going to wear that dress?" "Are you going to *wear* that dress?" "Are you going to wear *that* dress?" Each of these three sentences means something different. But just as the spoken language cannot completely express thought, so the written language cannot completely encode speech. Spoken language is the natural expression commonly used by the native speaker, with its contractions, idiomatic expressions, and slang and one-word answers. "How are you?" may be spoken as if it were one word, "Howarya?" And "It is a book" is spoken, "Itza book."

3. Language expresses a people's culture. The following examples illustrate how a people's attitudes and values are inherent in the structure of their language. For example, in English we would say, "I dropped the plate." But the equivalent in Spanish translates, "The plate fell from me." Young illustrates the need for understanding translation difficulties from Navajo to English:

Navajo culture does not have a heritage of coercive religious, political or patriarchal family figures. In the Navajo scheme of things one does not usually impose his will on another animate being to the same extent and in the same ways as one does from the English point of view. "I *made* my wife sing" becomes, in Navajo, simply "even though my wife did not want to do so, she sang when I told her to sing." From the Navajo point of view, one can compel his children to go to school in the sense that he drives them there; or he can *place* them in school, but none of these terms reflect the imposition of one's will independently of physical force—the children do not comply with a mandate.[2]

Kaulfers has illustrated clearly how language is an integral part of people's culture. Language is the means by which thoughts and feelings are expressed; language guides our thinking about social problems and processes. Kaulfers wrote:

How translation can defeat its own ends if words are merely transverbalized without regard for their pleasant or unpleasant associations is illustrated by the difficulties missionaries have sometimes in trying to convert remote populations to Christianity. Most Eskimos, for example, eat no bread. Few like it, because it has no taste or smell. Consequently, early missionaries found it difficult to explain the phrase, "Give us this day our daily bread." To win the natives, they had to substitute walrus, polar bear, and deer. This illustration is but one of many that could be cited to show how an expert command of a second language always requires a thorough understanding of the attitudes, likes, dislikes, customs, and standards of values of the people.[3]

4. Every language has a distinctive structure that is arbitrary and systematic. This structure determines the nature and placement of sounds that make words, and it determines the form of the words that make sentences—subjects, verbs, and objects or modifiers. The letters "blla si rde het" have no meaning. Rearrange the sounds to make English words of them, "ball the red is," and there is still no meaning. But if the words are arranged in the order "the ball is red," there is meaning. Word order is not important in all languages, but in English it is very important. However, arrangement of the sounds that make up words is important in all languages.

   Children internalize the structural features of their language. These structural features include such things as the distinctive sounds of the languages and how they combine, how words are formed from sub-word units called morphemes, and the relationships of one word to another. When they read, "The glings glongled glorgily in the goag," we can be sure that "glings" is the subject of the sentence, "glongled" is a verb, "glorgily" is an adverb, and "goag" is a noun used as the object of the preposition *in*.[4]

5. Language is unconscious, learned behavior. Native speakers are not conscious of each sound or word they say nor of the sequence of the sounds of words. They are primarily conscious of the ideas or thoughts they are trying to convey. The stringing together of sounds in certain positions is an unconscious act. The structure of a child's language is internalized and automatic by the time the child enters first grade. When children learn their first language in a free, relaxed, trial-and-error atmosphere, there is time for error, correction, and repetition without conscious effort. Whenever another language is superimposed as a second language, there is interference between the two sound patterns. Therefore, much guided repetition, self-correction, and motivated drill are indicated.

6. Language is personal. It is the reflection of the speaker's self-image. It is a person's primary means of expressing all that he or she is or aspires to be. Each person has certain expressions that are distinctively his or her own.

7. The language of a given group is neither "good" or "bad" nor "right" or "wrong"; it is communication. Dialects of English other than standard English are referred to as *non*standard rather than *sub*standard. This topic is discussed in detail in chapter 16.

8. A language is always slowly changing its sounds, its lexicon, and its syntax. There is certainly sufficient permanence in the lexicon of any language that the elders use most of the same basic words as the young. However, the lexicon of English has increased enormously in the twentieth century to include in everyday usage such new words as *blitzkrieg, hara-kiri, television.* Some slang expressions become

established and are added to the dictionary. Others disappear with the generation that created them—as, for example, calling something "the bee's knees" or "the cat's pajamas."

Teachers can easily demonstrate to boys and girls that language changes markedly through the centuries. But they must also teach that language is consistent and dependable and that change is always slow and never severe. A teacher could show passages from *Beowulf* or Chaucer or Robert Burns to show how the further away from us in time, the more different is each form of English from our own. For example, following are some lines from *Beowulf,* written about the seventh century A.D.:

Nealles him on heape handgesteallan,
ae elinga bearn, ymbe gestodon
hildecystum, ac hy on holt bugon,
ealdre burgan. (2596–99a)[5]

In modern English, they would be:

In no way did those war-comrades,
those sons of noblemen, take
their stand around him in formation as fighting-men should; no
they fell back into the forest
and took care of their own lives.

Following are some lines from the Prologue to the *Canterbury Tales* by Geoffrey Chaucer, who lived in the fourteenth century:

Whan that Aprill with his shoures soote
The droghte of March hath perced to the roote,
And bathed every veyne in swich licour
Of which vertu engendred is the flour;[6]

In modern English, they would be:

When April comes with its sweet showers
It abruptly ends the March drouth,
And bathes the spring plants in such moisture
So they burst into beautiful flowers.

Or, following are some lines from Robert Burns's poem "To a Louse," written in 1786 after he saw a louse on a lady's bonnet in church. The poem ended with this verse:

O wad some Power the giftie gie us
To see oursels as ithers see us!
It wad frae mony a blunder free us,
An' foolish notion:
What airs in dress an' gait wad lea'e us,
An ev'n devotion![7]

Ways to Describe Language

Linguists have given us words to use to describe language. *Phonology* is the study of the distinctive sounds of a language, called *phonemes*. *Morphology* is the study of the smallest meaningful units of a language, called *morphemes;* they are mainly words and parts of words. *Syntax* is the grammar of the language—the set of rules by which words are combined into sentences.

Table 3.1 contains definitions and descriptions of phonology, morphology, syntax, and semantics. There are forty-four phonemes in the English language, represented graphically by the twenty-six letters of the alphabet. Phonemes (distinctive sounds) need to be distinguished from morphemes (meaningful units); phonemic differences can constitute minimal pairs in the child's language. The suprasegmentals, pitch, stress, and juncture are other distinctive features in the English language. Morphology is important in the understanding of compound words, inflectional endings, prefixes and suffixes, and Greek and Latin combining forms.

Syntax is the grammar of the language and includes word order in sentences, "kernel" sentence patterns, and sentence transformations. Semantics is the study of the meanings communicated through language. Learning to use context clues to search out meanings is a semantic skill, as is the knowledge of figures of speech and idiomatic and slang expressions. Suprasegmentals, listed graphemically as phonology, are also semantic because they communicate meaning changes.

The information in table 3.1 is basic to understanding later chapters in the text that deal with beginning reading, phonic and structural analysis, teaching English as a second language, teaching reading to bilinguals, and teaching reading to speakers of nonstandard English.

Language Acquisition

Learning to talk the language of one's extended family appears to be a very simple task for almost everyone. One could say that speaking the language is virtually self-taught. Well before the age of six months, infants begin trying to reproduce the sounds around them that represent communication, differentiating those sounds from the total range of sounds possible. From that point, children do not try to imitate their elders exactly so much as they experiment with approximations of what the elders say to see if they too can communicate meaningfully. Then, rather than merely repeating what someone else has said, they imitate sentence patterns and spontaneously produce new sentences that are their own. Psycholinguists call the process by which children test out their own abilities to express themselves "hypothesis testing."

The second step in this process is what children do with the response they elicit from others. If they ask for something or tell their mothers something and get no response, they conclude that they are not communicating the way adults around them do. However, if they get a positive response, their efforts are reinforced. Feedback is what everyone needs to encourage them to keep trying, keep learning, keep experimenting. A child may say, "Milk!" and mother asks, "Do

Table 3.1 The structure of language.

Phonology	Morphology	Syntax	Semantics
Phonology is the study of the distinctive sounds of language.	Morphology is the study of the smallest meaningful units of language, called *morphemes*, which are mainly words or parts of words. Morphemes especially important in elementary school teaching are:	Syntax is often thought of as the grammar of a language. More precisely, it is the set of rules governing how morphemes are combined into sentences.	Semantics is the study of the meanings communicated through language.
1. There are 44 distinctive sounds, called *phonemes*, in the English language. (Sources differ: 40, 44, 45, 47.) The alphabet is an imperfect representation of those sounds.	1. Compound words. 2. Inflectional endings *er, est, ed, ing, s, es.* 3. Prefixes and suffixes. 4. The common Greek and Latin combining forms.	1. Word order, an important distinctive feature of English, is an aspect of syntax (a *pocket watch* is not the same as a *watch pocket*).	1. English is a language with a rich vocabulary, or lexicon, which has many words borrowed from other languages.
2. Phonemes combine into distinctive meaningful units, called *morphemes*, which are words or parts of words.		2. Basic ("kernel") sentence patterns:	2. The listener or the reader must rely on context clues; meanings depend upon context.
3. Minimal pairs are two words with only one phonemic difference, which changes meaning (pick-pig, map-mat, big-pig, big-bag).		a. Noun—transitive verb—object b. Noun—linking verb—predicate noun or adjective c. Noun—verb—prepositional phrase	3. The language contains many figures of speech, idiomatic expressions, and slang expressions.
4. Stress and juncture (called *suprasegmentals*) are also distinctive features of English, comparable to phonemes, which change meaning. (*You* bought that. You bought *that.* You bought that. A blue bird is not necessarily a bluebird.)		3. Transformations: a. Negative statements b. *Or* changes c. Expansions d. *There* changes e. Question changes f. Passive changes g. Combined kernel sentences h. *Until, if, because* changes i. Tense changes	4. The vocabulary contains antonyms, heteronyms, homographs, homonyms, synonyms.
5. The phoneme-grapheme relationships are often confusing in English because the same sound may have many variant spellings, and different sounds may have the same spellings.			5. Suprasegmentals, which are phonemic because they change meanings, are also semantic in communicating meaning changes.

you want more milk?" while she gets some more. The child has created communication; the mother understood and responded; and the child is rewarded for having mastered one more step in the effort to learn how to talk.

There is perhaps a third step in this process. The significant adult in the child's environment expands the child's language competence just by talking and thereby providing a model. The parent may even try consciously to expand the child's language by *correcting* it. However, the very young child is apt to pay little attention to the correction, as the following conversation reported by Cazden indicates:

> Child: Nobody don't like me.
> Mother: No, say "Nobody likes me."
> Child: Nobody don't like me.
> (Eight repetitions of this dialogue)
> Mother: No, now listen carefully; say, "Nobody likes me."
> Child: Oh! Nobody don't likes me![8]

Young children rely on exposure to language, from which they can make inferences about the syntax of the language and create their own set of rules regarding that language. Then, in their own speech, children hypothesize correct language usage, test their hypotheses, and eliminate incorrect patterns because they are not rewarded.

Cazden further reported:

> Evidence on the role of correction in the child's learning of syntax is wholly negative. In hundreds of hours of recordings of Adam, Eve, and Sarah talking with their parents, we found corrections of misstatements of fact, but no correction of immature syntactic forms.[9]

The school needs to provide for talking so the student has a body of knowledge for hypothesis-testing. After children adjust to a talking environment, they are anxious to participate openly and naturally in fruitful ways. It seems that children initiate their own learning more than they are taught by those who try so hard to teach!

John cautions us that the learning styles of children with varying cultural backgrounds may make significant differences in their use of language when they enter school. She suggests that Indian children of the Southwest are visual in their approaches to the world and that they absorb their world through sight and touch:

> Language lessons are introduced as the most valued aspect of education, but they are presented in ways that contradict aspects of Navajo children's preschool life. The shape and cold feel of the buildings in which they live and are taught deprive them of sensory impressions they are used to: the look of the sky, the feel of the wind, the smell of smoke. I was struck ... how often the little ones clustered around each other, touching their buddies' hair and arms and holding hands even during lessons. This is one of the ways in which they keep literally in touch with the familiar.[10]

Halliday prefers the term *language development* instead of *language acquisition*. He says:

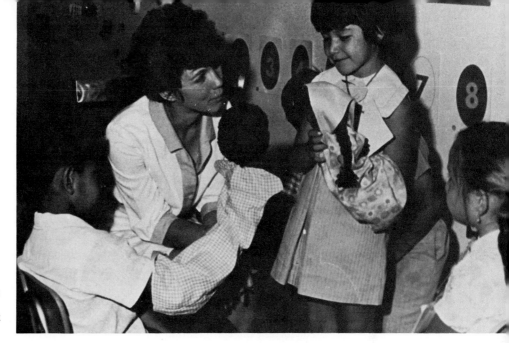

Children grow in their ability to use language in classrooms if they are encouraged to talk openly and naturally.

. . . the term acquisition is a rather misleading metaphor, suggesting that language is some sort of property to be owned—(but language development) needs to be seen as the mastery of linguistic functions . . . learning the uses of language, and the meanings, or rather the meaning potential, associated with them. . . . Learning language is learning how to mean.[11]

The School and Language Development

Much of the difficulty with language in school is caused by the fact that the typical child is required to accept an inflexible, stereotypic use of language ("school language" or "textbook language") that is often quite different from the language he or she has internalized in life outside the school. The reading and writing tasks of first grade, for example, may not parallel the child's previous uses of language.

Halliday delineates several functions of language:[12]

1. The instrumental function, language used for the satisfaction of material needs.
2. The regulatory function, the "do as I tell you" function, language in the control of behavior.
3. The interactional function, language used in getting along with others.
4. The personal function, the expression of identity, of the self, which develops largely through linguistic interaction.
5. The heuristic function, the use of language for learning, to explore reality.
6. The imaginative function, the "let's pretend" where the child can explore his own mind through language.
7. The representational function, that of communication of content.

Thus language is defined for the child by the uses he or she has for it.

From Theory to Practice 3.1
Observation and Evaluation of Child Language

Linguistic performance is very important to a child's learning to read. Teachers need to be able to observe and make some judgments about linguistic competence of boys and girls. With this in mind, your task is to identify various aspects of linguistic competence/performance. (We need to judge competence by performance, since competence cannot be directly observed.)

Assignment: Locate a situation where children interact. Then identify one or two children who are talking (between themselves or with an adult). If there is little *talk,* switch to some other children. Gather conversational speech for a minimum of twenty minutes.

Suggestions: Make yourself as inconspicuous as possible to keep from distorting the conversation. (Hint: If you wish to observe Abner and William, position yourself to appear to be watching Abigail and Freda.)

Make yourself as complete a record of the *real* conversation as possible.

If the language comes fast and there are significant things happening about language, make notes of these particular items instead of concentrating only on a complete recording of conversation.

Be sure to take time when you finish to immediately go back over your notes and make notations in the margins to identify significant language production or to complete some of the notes you might otherwise forget.

Evaluation: Some suggestions for evaluating the corpus of speech are:

1. Length of child's sentences?
2. Fragments? What kinds? One-, two-, or three-word sentences?
3. Articulation errors?
4. Different types of sentences: statements, questions, commands, exclamations?
5. Phrases and clauses?
6. Errors in grammatical usage? Faulty hypotheses?
7. Does the child play with language?
8. Does he use past and future (verb tenses) as well as present?
9. Does he talk about other people, other places, other times?
10. Does the child falsify? Romance? Imagine?
11. What language does the child speak? Use two languages?
12. Is language labored? Does the child struggle for words, sounds, sentences?

13. Is his speech egocentric or is it socialized? Piaget divides child speech into egocentric and socialized speech. When the child talks to himself or when a group of children is talking (but each only to and for himself or herself) that is egocentric speech. Piaget says half of the speech of children up to the age of 7 or 8 is egocentric. On the other hand, information giving, criticism, questions, answers, commands, requests, and threats are examples of socialized speech. Look for examples of egocentric and socialized speech in the children you observe.
14. If an adult is present, how does the adult respond to "errors," questions, need for feedback, silence?
15. Note the child's use of: gerunds, plurals, possessives, negations, tag questions, passive voice, progressive verb forms, noun phrases and verb phrases.
16. Be sure to note or estimate the ages of the speakers for across-age comparisons later.

From the child's point of view, much of the language of the adults may be representational—especially if teachers are viewed as only transmitting content to be learned. This may explain why the communication between adult and child breaks down—there are many other registers of language in which the child has a very real need to function.

The nature of language is explained in terms of its function in the social structure. In order to understand language, we must understand how values in a society are transmitted, how the rules of behavior are defined, the rigidity or the permissiveness in the attention to "duty," and the behavior patterns expected at all levels of the maturing person's life. Language is the principal means by which the culture is transmitted. In this sense, language is socio-semantic; the emphasis in its use is on the functions it performs. Meaning potential is registered not in terms of cognitive structure (the art of knowing), but rather in the life values embedded in one's cultural experience.

Thus, one might conclude that the child's development of language, that is, his enhancement in useful meaning potential, is from the social reference in which he uses language, to the semantic meanings entailed in the language, to the "accepted" grammatical form that makes his use of language readily understood.

The total range of potential meaning realized by the child in her language system is determined by the context of cultural experience she has had. Language develops as it functions in the child's social structure, and her detailed daily behavior is a "reading" of her cultural values, beliefs, and practices. Halliday refers to this as context of *culture* versus context of *situation*.[13]

Britton makes clear that in Infant's Schools (children ages 3 to 7) boys and girls do not spend the day sitting in straight rows of desks. He says:

. . . they are here, there, and everywhere, up and about; going off to ask somebody something or tell him something else; going off to see for themselves; standing at a bench or a table, moving around to get a better grip or take a longer look; working or playing in different parts of the room or the building in accordance with what is to be found to do there.[14]

Britton reminds us that we cannot forget what has gone on in the life of the child before, that he is *not* making a fresh start, and that he has deep roots already in the life he has lived outside of school. The classroom must merge into the world outside it, and *school learning* must merge into the processes of learning that begin the day one is born and continue throughout life.

We learn by talking. The child both learns by talking and learns to talk by talking.[15] Children must continue to use oral language to make sense of their world.

Schools Should Encourage More Talking

Hart, in "The New Brain Concept of Learning" emphasizes that students must talk if they are to learn well because much of the brain is devoted to language activity.[16] Much thought is clarified, extended, corrected, or adjusted by talking out beliefs and opinions, by comparing different ways of thinking about a topic, and by responding to well-framed questions. The school desperately needs to change its traditional strategy of trying to keep boys and girls *quiet* and to promote a very great deal of discussion, explanation, debate, argument, conversation, and questioning. If the teacher takes time to hear what individual children have to say, there will be less need for so many busy work exercises to be completed during study period. There is no way to help children with improvement in the way they use oral language if they are not permitted to talk freely in class.

Extending Oral Language to the Child's First Reading Lessons

With only slight exaggeration, it could be said that teachers have often made learning to read very difficult for many children. They approach the task formally with prescribed lessons to make sure the children understand phonemes, sight words, and then the syntax of language before finally extracting the meaning. These teachers usually organize beginning reading programs in the following order:

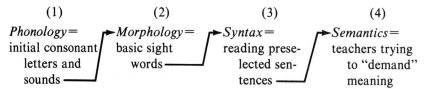

Of course beginning reading doesn't need to happen this way. Burke has shown that *meaning* should be at the core of every reading lesson; that the syntax of the child's personal language guarantees meaning; and that grapheme-phoneme relationships become important only when the child must decode a word to get the meaning.[17] Beginning reading really should begin with ideas or concepts that are personal and important to the child—never only with names and sounds of initial consonants. Burke's concept is diagrammed in figure 1.1.

Therefore, the linguistic schema for learning to read would look like this:

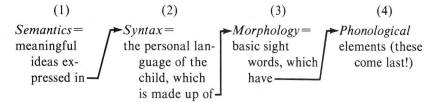

The language-experience approach to reading, which is emphasized throughout this text, is based on this schema.

Holt said that if parents felt as obligated to teach children to talk as first grade teachers do to teach them to read, the results would be disastrous:

> Bill Hull once said to me, "If we taught children to speak, they'd never learn." I thought at first he was joking. By now I realize that it was a very important truth. Suppose we decided that we had to "teach" children to speak. How would we go about it? First, some committee of experts would analyze speech and break it down into a number of separate "speech skills." We would probably say that, since speech is made up of sounds, a child must be taught to make all the sounds of his language before he can be taught to speak the language itself. Doubtless we would list these sounds, easiest and commonest ones first, harder and rarer ones next. Then we would begin to teach infants these sounds, working our way down the list. Perhaps, in order not to "confuse" the child—"confuse" is an evil word to many educators—we would not let the child hear much ordinary speech but would only expose him to the sounds we were trying to teach. . . .
>
> Suppose we tried to do this; what would happen? What would happen, quite simply, is that most children, before they got very far, would become baffled, discouraged, humiliated, and fearful, and would quit trying to do what we asked them. If, outside of our classes, they lived a normal infant's life, many of them would probably ignore our "teaching" and learn to speak on their own. If not, if our control of their lives was complete (the dream of too many educators), they would take refuge in deliberate failure and silence, as so many of them do when the subject is reading.[18]

Cazden has suggested some ways in which learning to read *can* be like learning to talk:

> Consider, as an example, the differences between learning to talk and learning to read. In oral language the child has to learn relationships between meanings and sounds. The raw material for the child's learning processes consists of a rich set of pairings of meanings and sound—for that is what language in the context of ongoing experience is. In reading the child must learn relationships between oral language—which he now knows—and letters of the alphabet. But a rich set of pairings of oral and written language is much less available. It is available when the child is read to while sitting on an adult's lap (not when read to as part of a group in school); it is available when the bouncing ball accompanies TV commercials; it is available whenever the child points to any writing and asks "What's that say?" and it is available

whenever the child himself tries to write. Provision of a rich set of sound-word pairings can be built into deliberately planned environments—in the classroom or on TV. But the necessary pairings don't just happen for written language at school as they do for oral language at home.[19]

Minimal Pairs

Children whose first language is not English must learn to hear all the phonemes used in English that are not used in their native language. For Spanish-speakers learning English, there are several substitutions likely to be made, such as *sumb* for *thumb* or *pass* for *path,* because the phonemes of the Spanish language do not include those consonant distinctions. Vowel sounds vary from one language to the other also. The student must learn to discriminate all these differences. Discriminating minimal pairs and juncture is good practice for sharpening this ability.

Minimal pairs are two words that sound exactly the same except for one phoneme that changes the meaning. Ending consonant sounds are often troublesome. For example, *pick* is spoken as *pig, map* is spoken as *mat.* This auditory discrimination practice, important in second-language teaching, is also important to primary children learning to read.

pic*k*-pi*g*	*t*aste-*t*est	p*ai*n-p*e*n	boa*t*-bo*th*
*b*ig-*p*ig	d*i*p-d*ee*p	shee*p*-shi*p*	b*i*t-b*ea*t
nie*c*e-knee*s*	ma*p*-ma*t*	for*c*e-four*s*	m*a*n-m*e*n
pri*c*e-pri*z*e	dea*th*-dea*f*	la*c*y-la*z*y	*b*ig-*b*ug
*a*ge-*e*dge	bu*s*-buz*z*	tu*ck*-tu*g*	p*o*ke-p*a*ck

Juncture

Juncture is the name given to the "boundary" between consecutive words within a sentence (or between sentences) in speech. Written language usually expresses juncture with a space. The following examples are comparable to minimal pairs and demonstrate that juncture is phonemic because it changes meaning.

Mary was home sick.	Mary was sick at home.
Mary was homesick.	Mary wanted very much to go home.
Was that the green house?	Was it a green color?
Was that the Green house?	Do the Greens live there?
Was that the greenhouse?	Was it a place where plants are nurtured year-round?
I saw a blue bird.	The bird I saw was a blue color.
I saw a bluebird.	It was the variety called "bluebird."
Bob said he saw a horse fly.	The horse had wings.
Bob said he saw a horsefly.	It was a fly that bothers horses.

And in these:

I scream	send them aid	night rate	lighthouse keeping
ice cream	send the maid	nitrate	light housekeeping

Structure Words	Words that have no referent are called structure words. It is estimated that there are no more than 300 such words in the English language, but they comprise nearly half the words in an elementary context. They are termed *markers* for the type of structural element that follows them:

Noun markers: a, the, some, any, three, this, my, few, etc.
Verb markers: am, are, is, was, have, has, had, etc.
Phrase markers: up, down, in, out, above, below, etc.
Clause markers: if, until, because, that, how, when, etc.
Question markers: who, why, how, when, what, where, etc.

Structure words are also called *glue* words or *service* words because in and of themselves they do not convey meaning but are necessary connectors. They should be taught and mastered as early in the reading process as possible. They play a significant part in helping the reader to anticipate meanings of the verbs or nouns that follow in a given sentence structure.

Is It Linguistics? Is It Phonics?

There is no conflict between being skillful at decoding words by phonic analysis and learning whatever one can about *linguistics*.

We are proposing that linguistics encompasses knowledge about how children acquire and extend language through the hierarchy of listening, speaking, reading, and writing. We also propose that the purpose of language is to illuminate meaning. Phonics supports what the teacher does to make "decoding-encoding" of the meaning in reading and writing an efficient operation. *Phonics is never emphasized to the exclusion of meaning.* Table 3.2 should clarify some of these differences.

Table 3.2 contrasts what teachers are apt to *say* in phonics lessons with children with what linguists may be *thinking* about the same concept. There are five vowel *letters* in English, but there are many vowel *sounds*. For the five letters, or graphemes, there are at least twelve distinct sounds, or phonemes. Phonics, as taught with rules in primary reading, may be confusing if the rules have too many exceptions. Clymer concluded that there are few rules worth teaching.[20]

We may say to the child that a consonant has only one sound. Linguists might remind us that letters written on paper do not make sound. We may talk about silent letters, but the linguist would say that letters do not make either sound or silence. Changes in forms of the same root word may change the way it is spoken. Children are not learning to *say* "Mother" when they learn the sight word at age six. Hopefully, they have been saying it for years.

Sustakoski tried to point out for teachers of beginning reading that "letters do not have sound." This misconception is based on the notion that written language is the primary form of language; this notion may be further perpetuated by the misconception that it is the written form that preserves language in its "correct" form. Of course, by necessity, one must prepare much more carefully

Table 3.2   What teachers say compared to how linguists describe language.

In teaching phonics to children, teachers are apt to say:	The linguist would like to remind teachers that:
There are five vowels in the English language.	But this means there are five *graphemes: a, e, i, o,* and *u.* There are more than twice that many vowel *sounds* (phonemes).
Phonics has a set of rules to teach vowel sounds.	Each vowel grapheme represents several different phonemes. One of *several* sounds of ''a'' is/ey/.
Most consonants have only one *sound.*	Letters on paper do not ''have'' *sounds.* The ''written-down'' graphemes are only symbolic representations of a spoken language.
Sound out the word. Sound and connect phonemes into a chain of integrated sounds to make a new word: *s-a-nd-w-i-ch.*	Written letters are only graphic symbols of the sounds (phonemes) that the children have known and produced correctly for a long time.
We have silent letters: *k* is silent in *know; g* is silent in *sign.*	Letters make neither sound nor silence. Changes in English spellings have not kept up historically with changes in English speech (and we still need the *g* in *sign* for the related words *signal and signature*).
Look at the words. (The problem here is with meaning. If we allow children to think that words mean what is ''written down,'' they may believe that words become language by being written.)	Language is speech. Words were oral before they were written with symbols (graphemes).
Children must learn to pronounce a controlled basic sight vocabulary.	This is illogical. Children usually begin reading only words that they have been pronouncing correctly for years.

Adapted from Dorothy Seymour, "The Differences Between Linguistics and Phonics," *The Reading Teacher* 23 (November 1969):99–102, 111.

what is put down on paper. In writing, many of the signals of speech are lacking, including all the intonational features, and this causes the writer to use greater caution in the arrangement of sentences. Thus, Sustakoski wrote:

> The most dangerous aspect of this confusion, as far as the teaching of reading is concerned, is that the teacher attempts to have a child "pronounce" the letters of the word as if the letters had sounds instead of allowing the written configuration to evoke the oral counterpart in the child's mind, which is the *true* nature of the process of reading.[21]

Generalizations Teachers Can Borrow from Linguists

Linguists have helped reading teachers understand the nature and function of language and the part that reading plays in the total communication process. First, they have emphasized the distinction between *grammar* and *usage* of language. Grammar is formalized language structure; usage is the preference or ethical judgment of the user of the language. People do say:

That's where it's at.　　　It's me.　　　　　　No, it ain't.

Second, children do, if they are native speakers, understand the differences between the deep structure and the surface structure of language. The sentences "Time flies like an arrow" and "Fruit flies like a banana" appear very much alike on the surface but the syntax is entirely different.[22] Rutherford illustrates differences between surface structure and deep structure in many pairs of sentences that look on the surface as if they followed the same pattern:[23]

What he wants is *more* of your 　　　What he wants is *none* of your
　　business.　　　　　　　　　　　　business.
It was a moving *train.*　　　　　　It was a moving *experience.*

Third, language is oral. It is speech before it is either reading or writing. Fourth, our writing system is based on an alphabet whose symbols (letters) long ago had a much closer correspondence to the sounds they represented. Spoken language changes over time at a much faster rate than does written language. This fact explains many of what we call the spelling irregularities and peculiarities of English. Nevertheless, our spelling conventions still have a fairly high degree of sound-symbol regularity.

Given these linguistic facts, some facts about reading follow:

1. Efficient reading moves directly to meaning with the least mediation possible in the process. To achieve this efficiency, the reader must learn to make intelligent guesses about what is in the line of print he or she is reading—anticipating meaning before actually seeing the words.
2. Always teach *context.* Letters are only parts of words, words are only parts of sentences or meaningful phrases, and even sentences are only a part of the paragraph, which contains a more complete meaning.
3. We should encourage beginners to get the meaning of the sentence and not to be overconcerned about the preciseness of word-calling. Readers should be able to make mistakes without penalty.
4. Many of the phonics rules we have insisted on in the past were not nearly so important as extracting meaning from the message. Phonics is no help with "read" in the sentences "I will read the book for you" and "I read the book yesterday" since other words in the sentences determine how to pronounce "read."

Some "do's" and "don'ts," then, are:

1. Do not give emphasis to traditional "rules" of reading.
2. Do not depend on phonics rules.
3. Teach letters as parts of words; words as parts of sentences.

4. Accept sensible reproduction of print that conveys meaning.
5. Try to be sure that the context provides feedback to the reader.
6. Focus on the child, not on the method of teaching reading.

Linguists have also shown the following points to be important when teaching reading:

1. A child's dialect is that child's natural language and should be accepted completely by teachers as the place to start teaching. Probably no one *speaks* standard written English. Reading teachers need to study children's dialects in order to help them learn how to move from *their* oral language to *their* written-down language.
2. The language-experience method is undoubtedly the most natural method for learning to read because children read their own language as they "told" it. The child who dictates a story already understands it, so has optimal chances of reading it successfully. The teacher can assist the child by using the rebus technique for some of the nouns in the story.

Daddy shot a 🦃 when he went hunting.

3. The cloze technique reveals the student's ability to sense meaning and anticipate what will happen next in the story. Cloze lessons are easy to prepare and are adaptable. They require filling in missing words in sentences. Cloze is discussed in more detail in chapter 10, "Comprehension Skills."
4. Miscue analysis is the means by which the teacher decides whether the student has adapted the reading to his or her dialect, has substituted a meaningful word that would ordinarily not have been used, or has made some other miscue that is not exactly like the printed line. In the event the reader is using the language correctly, is understanding the message, and is confidently getting the point of the story, *no error* has been made, and the miscue should be accepted without penalty. Graphic miscues, such as confusing *b* and *d* or *th* and *wh,* may cause the student to have to repeat phrases to correct the meaning in the sentence. Semantic miscues are more significant because the student will lose meaning unless the miscue is corrected. If a sentence is written "Away the bird flew and then she came back" and the child reads aloud "The bird flew away and then she came

back," the meaning is clear and the miscue need not be corrected. However, if the sentence "They practiced conservation" is read as "They practiced conversation," the meaning is lost.

5. Semantics is the study of the meanings communicated through language. Helping children develop an ever larger vocabulary, both oral and written, is one way to help them increase their grasp of meaning. Teachers can also begin introducing even first graders to multiple meanings of common words, word opposites, homonyms, idiomatic expressions, similes, and other devices by which language usage conveys meaning.

Redundancy

One of the features about language that we need to analyze in helping children learn to read is its redundancy. In the sense in which the word is used here, it is *not* deprecatory and does not imply that needless or undesirable features are present. On the contrary, redundancy in linguistic structure makes anticipating meaning in the line of print easier for the reader. Osgood's theory of communication suggests that redundancies and transitional probabilities facilitate the transmission and receipt of messages:

Redundancy: For example, "man coming" means the same as the redundant statement "a man is coming this way now." It is suggested that the latter is more like ordinary English; it indicates the singular number of the subject three times (by "a," "man," and "is"), the present tense twice ("is coming" and "now"), and the direction of action twice ("coming" and "this way"). Such repetitions of meaning ... make it possible to replace "is," "this," "way," or "now," should they be deleted.[24]

Information helpful to the reader in completing the meaning while reading may be pictorial, orthographic, syntactic, or semantic.[25] The typical efficient reader, though he may be quite unaware, makes skilled use of redundancy. There are few words that begin with *dw* or *tw;* there are fifteen common prefixes the good reader already knows; or the first three or four letters of a polysyllabic word may be the only clue necessary. Such are the details that allow the reader to hurry on with absorbing the meaning of a paragraph. "This kind of prior knowledge, which reduces the alternative number of possibilities that a letter or word can be, is termed redundancy."[26]

Goodman explained:

Redundancy facilitates language processing. This term, derived from information theory, means the tendency in language for information to be carried by more than one part of the signal. Language is redundant to the extent that each element carries more than a single bit of information.

In the sentence *He was watching Mary, watching* has three cues to its function as a verb: its position in the sentence, the use of *was* with it, and its *ing* ending. Sequential constraint contributes considerably to redundancy. Since *q* must always be followed by *u,* no new information is provided by the *u.* Redundancy makes it possible to sample without losing information. It also provides a possibility of verification, since multiple cues must be consistent.[27]

A Short Glossary of Linguistic Terms

A brief glossary of terms that may be useful to classroom teachers is included here.

affix: A morpheme that occurs as a prefix or suffix. It is called a "bound morpheme" because it cannot stand alone.

alphabet: The letters of a writing system in which there are graphic symbols to represent the phonemes of the language.

cultural determinism: The belief that one's personality and personal values are shaped by one's culture.

deep structure: The "kernel" sentences underlying the grammatical transformations represented by the surface structure of a sentence.

derived forms: Words composed of a root plus a prefix or suffix or both—for example, *unhappiness; politeness.*

diacritical marks: Marks added to graphemes to give them specific pronunciations; marks that augment an alphabet so that each phoneme in the language can be accurately identified.

dialect: The distinctive phonological, morphological, and syntactic patterns of a language in a given part of a country or of a given social group.

digraph: The combination of two letters (graphemes) to represent a single phoneme: vowel digraph—r*ea*d; consonant digraph—*th*ink.

diphthong: The combination of two vowel sounds, the one gliding into the second, as *oi* in *boil.*

embedding: A sentence-combining process in which one clause is inside another. (The girl *that rode the bus* went to the library.)

ethnography: Descriptive anthropology, which can include the study of language in particular cultural and social contexts. (One has to know when to talk, when to be silent, and how much to talk. One has to know how to talk to one's boss, to one's mother, to one's best friend, to one's peer, and to a total stranger.)[28]

grammar: The rules that govern the structure of a language.

grapheme: The *written symbol* used to represent a phoneme.

grapho-phonic: Noting the phonic relationships between the sounds and symbols of a language.

homographs: Words written in exactly the same way but having entirely different meanings.

homophones: Words pronounced alike but having different meanings or spellings.

inflected form: A suffix that changes the form of the word but not its meaning, such as adding *s, ed,* or *ing.*

intonation: Pitch of the voice to change meanings.

jargon: A hybrid language simplified in vocabulary and grammar for communication between peoples of different speech; the technical terminology or characteristic idiom of a special group; for example, *media center* for library or *student stations* for desks.

juncture: The "boundary" between consecutive words in a stream of speech: the juncture of *an + aim* is different from *a + name.*

kernel sentence: A simple declarative sentence that illustrates one possible pattern of English sentences: *John reads.*

language: A system of arbitrary oral symbols by means of which a social group interacts.[29]

language acquisition: The process of learning either a native or a second language.

language development: The continuous growth in the effectiveness with which each child uses language.[30]

lexeme: The dictionary form of a word to which affixes may be added to modify meaning. *Walk* is the lexeme for *walked* and *walking* but not for *walk-on* or *walk-up*.

lexicon: The total vocabulary of a language.

linguistic analysis: The application of linguistic principles to some aspect of language.

linguistics: The scientific study of language.

literacy: The ability to read and write to a degree thought desirable by a society.

metalinguistic awareness: The ability to reflect on and talk about language.

minimal pair: Two linguistic items whose meaning difference is the contrast of one phonemic difference: ma*t* and ma*p*; *p*ig and *b*ig.

morpheme: The smallest meaningful units of a language—mainly words or parts of words. *Albuquerque* is one morpheme, for example; *un-dy-ing* is three morphemes.

morphology: The study of word formation of a language—the origin and functions of inflections and derivations especially.

morphophoneme: A given phoneme within a given morpheme whose pronunciation changes, bridging the gap between morphological levels and phonemic levels. Compare the vowel changes in *verbose—verbosity; divine—divinity.*[31]

morphophonemics: The study of the relationships between the sound structure and the word structure of the language. May be thought of as the bridge between morphology and phonology.

oracy: Fluency in speaking and listening.

phoneme: The smallest significant unit of speech. A phoneme is technically not to be thought of as a syllable or letter. There are 44 phonemes and only 26 letters in English.

phonetics: The analysis of speech sounds with respect to their articulation and acoustic properties.

phonic analysis: Phonic analysis is the application of a knowledge of consonant and vowel sound clues to the pronunciation of a word.

phonics: The teaching of techniques about the sounds of written words so that children acquire letter-sound correlations.

phonology: The study of the patterns and distribution of speech sounds, or phonemes.

pitch: The tonal quality in speech that signals meaning variation; pitch has four discrete sound ranges in spoken English.

pragmatics: A branch of linguistic science that studies the relationship between things (facts) and verbal expressions and the people who use the verbal expressions.

psycholinguistics: A study of the interdependence of linguistic and psychological behaviors of an individual or group.

rebus: A picture or a symbol that suggests a word in a sentence.

rhythm: A recurring emphasis in the flow of oral or written speech; cadence.

schema: (*pl.* schemata) A conceptual plan for understanding something.

semantic cue: Evidence in the general sense of a written or spoken communication that aids in the identification of an unknown word.

semantics: The study of meaning in language.

sociolinguistics: A study of linguistics in its social context: who says what to whom, how, when, and to what purpose.

stress: The degree of prominence a syllable has, usually identified as primary, mid, and weak.

suprasegmentals: The phonological entities of pitch, stress, intonation, and juncture—equivalent to phonemes because they can signify meaning.

surface structure: The words we speak to communicate.

syntax: The rules for combining words to form grammatical sentences.

utterance: A meaningful unit of spoken language; it may or may not be a sentence.
vernacular: Pertaining to the everyday speech of one's native language and dialect.
word: A segment of language recorded as an independent entity in dictionaries.[32]

Summary

Linguistics is the scientific study of language. Language can be studied through its phonology, morphology, syntax, and semantics. Phonology is the study of the distinctive sounds of language (forty-four phonemes in English); morphology is the study of the arrangement of phonemes into meaningful units of language; syntax is the set of rules that determine how morphemes are combined into sentences; and semantics is the study of the meanings communicated through language.

Psycholinguistics and sociolinguistics have provided a great deal of relevant information about language and how it is learned and used. Psycholinguistics is a study of psychology and linguistics that examines language behavior. It incorporates the study of language elements, language acquisition (either as a first or second language), language analysis, and semantic meanings. Sociolinguistics relates language to social behavior. It is the study of speech patterns in the community of speakers, the ways the media use language, and the effect of the economic power structure on the language differences in society. It has been said that sociolinguistics is the study of "*who* says *what* to *whom* and for *what* purpose."

Mastering the language for school success requires that boys and girls utilize semantic and context clues, redundancy in normal language use, basic kernel sentences, and transformations. Children who live in a rich oral language environment should have little difficulty sensing differences in surface and deep structure usage.

For Further Reading

Britton, James. *Language and Learning*. Coral Gables, Fla.: University of Miami Press, 1970.

Carroll, John B. *Language and Thought*. Englewood Cliffs, N.J.: Prentice-Hall, 1964.

Cazden, Courtney, Vera John, and Dell Hymes. *Functions of Language in the Classroom*. New York: Teachers College Press, 1972.

Goodman, Kenneth. "Reading: A Psycholinguistic Guessing Game." In *Theoretical Models and Processes of Reading*. 2d ed. Ed. Harry Singer and Robert Ruddell. Newark, Del.: International Reading Association, 1976. Pp. 497–508.

Goodman, Kenneth, and Yetta Goodman. "A Whole-Language, Comprehension-Centered Reading Program." A position paper, Arizona Center for Research and Development, College of Education, University of Arizona, 1981.

Halliday, M. A. K. *Explorations in the Functions of Language*. New York: Elsevier, 1977.

Hodges, Richard E., and E. Hugh Rudorf. *Language and Learning to Read*. Boston: Houghton Mifflin, 1972.

Malmstrom, Jean. *Understanding Language: A Primer for Language Arts Teachers*. New York: St. Martin's, 1977.

Savage, John F., ed. *Linguistics for Teachers: Selected Readings*. Chicago: Science Research Associates, 1973.

Shuy, Roger, ed. *Linguistic Theory: What Can It Say About Reading?* Newark, Del.: International Reading Association, 1977.

Smith, Frank. *Reading Without Nonsense.* New York: Teachers College Press, 1979.

Notes

1. Kenneth S. Goodman and Yetta M. Goodman, "A Whole-Language, Comprehension-Centered Reading Program" (Position Paper No. 1, Arizona Center for Research and Development, College of Education, University of Arizona, 1981), pp. 2–6.

2. Robert Young, "Culture," in *Language and Cultural Diversity in American Education,* ed. Roger D. Abrahams and Rudolph C. Troike (Englewood Cliffs, N.J.: Prentice-Hall, 1972), p. 41.

3. Walter V. Kaulfers, "Gift of Tongues or Tower of Babel," *Educational Forum* 19 (November 1954):82.

4. John F. Savage, ed., *Linguistics for Teachers: Selected Readings* (Chicago: Science Research Associates, 1973), p. 114.

5. Edward B. Irving, Jr., *A Reading of Beowulf* (New Haven, Conn.: Yale University Press, 1968), p. 7.

6. F. N. Robinson, ed., *The Works of Geoffrey Chaucer* (Boston: Houghton Mifflin, 1961), p. 17.

7. Charles Elliott, ed., *The Harvard Classics* 6 (New York: P.F. Collier & Son, 1909): 199.

8. Courtney B. Cazden, *Child Language and Education* (New York: Holt, Rinehart and Winston, 1972), p. 92.

9. Ibid., p. 114.

10. Vera John, "Styles of Learning–Styles of Teaching: Reflections on the Education of Navajo Children," in *Functions of Language in the Classroom,* ed. Courtney Cazden, Vera John, and Dell Hymes (New York: Teachers College Press, 1972), p. 335.

11. M. A. K. Halliday, *Explorations in the Functions of Language* (New York: Elsevier, 1977), p. 16.

12. Ibid., p. 9.

13. Ibid., pp. 56–57.

14. James Britton, *Language and Learning* (Coral Gables, Fla.: University of Miami Press, 1971), p. 129.

15. Ibid., p. 15.

16. Leslie A. Hart, "The Brain Concept of Learning," *Phi Delta Kappan* 59 (1978): 393–96.

17. Carolyn L. Burke, "The Language Process: Systems or Systematic," in *Language and Learning to Read,* ed. Richard E. Hodges and E. Hugh Rudorf (Boston: Houghton Mifflin, 1972), pp. 24–30.

18. John Holt, *How Children Learn* (New York: Pitman, 1967), pp. 56–57.

19. Cazden, *Child Language and Education,* pp. 140–41.

20. Theodore L. Clymer, "The Utility of Phonic Generalizations in the Primary Grades," *The Reading Teacher* 16 (1963): 252–58.

21. Henry J. Sustakoski, "Some Contributions of Linguistic Science to the Teaching of Reading," in *Oral Language and Reading,* ed. James Walden (508 South Sixth Street, Champaign, Ill. 61820: National Council of Teachers of English, 1969), p. 61.

22. Cazden, *Child Language and Education,* p. 5.
23. William E. Rutherford, "Deep and Surface Structure, and the Language Drill," *TESOL* (Teachers of English to Speakers of Other Languages) *Quarterly* 2 (June 1968): 71–79.
24. Cited in Thomas C. Potter, *A Taxonomy of Cloze Research; Part I: Readability and Reading Comprehension* (11300 La Cienega Blvd., Inglewood, Calif. 90304: Southwest Regional Laboratory for Educational Research and Development, 1968), pp. 2–3.
25. Frank Smith, *Understanding Reading* (New York: Holt, Rinehart and Winston, 1971), p. 20.
26. Ibid., p. 7.
27. Kenneth S. Goodman, "The Reading Process: Theory and Practice," in Hodges and Rudorf, *Language and Learning to Read,* p. 153.
28. From Joel Sherzer, "The Ethnography of Speaking," in *Linguistic Theory: What Can It Say About Reading?* ed. Roger Shuy (Newark, Del.: International Reading Assn., copyright 1977), pp. 144–45.
29. From W. Lehmann, *A Dictionary of Reading and Related Terms,* ed. Theodore Harris and Richard Hodges (Newark, Del.: International Reading Assn., 1981).
30. Dorris M. Lee and Joseph B. Rubin, *Children and Language* (Belmont, Calif.: Wadsworth, 1979), p. 73.
31. From Robert Hall, *Introductory Linguistics* (Philadelphia: Chilton Publishing Co., copyright © 1964), p. 138.
32. Lehmann, cited in Harris and Hodges, *Dictionary of Reading and Related Terms.*

The Informal Reading Inventory

A Cognitive Map: The Informal Reading Inventory

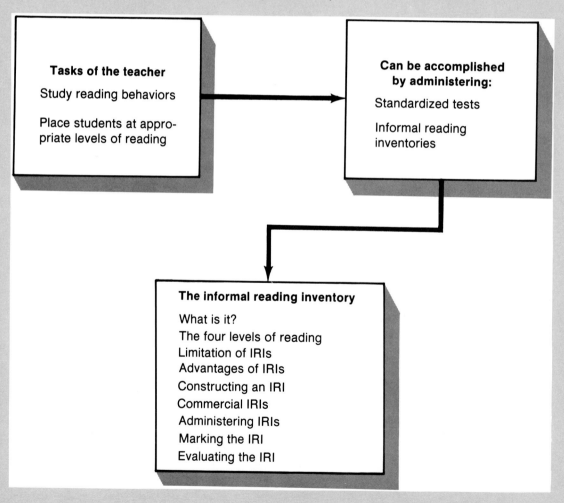

Tasks of the teacher

Study reading behaviors

Place students at appro-
priate levels of reading

**Can be accomplished
by administering:**

Standardized tests

Informal reading
inventories

The informal reading inventory

What is it?
The four levels of reading
Limitation of IRIs
Advantages of IRIs
Constructing an IRI
Commercial IRIs
Administering IRIs
Marking the IRI
Evaluating the IRI

4

Guide Questions

1. What are the components of an informal reading inventory?

2. What are the advantages and disadvantages of the informal reading inventory?

3. How is each of the four reading levels defined?

4. What is the system for administering, marking, scoring, and evaluating an IRI?

5. What is the purpose of giving a word list along with the informal reading inventory?

Terminology

capacity level

frustration level

hesitation

independent level

insertion

instructional level

miscue

mispronunciation

omission

repetition

substitution

trying a book on for size

A primary task of the classroom teacher or the special reading teacher is to become well acquainted with the reading behaviors of the students. In working to accomplish this goal, the teacher also becomes a learner, a student of the reading process. While observing children's reading and puzzling over the kinds of difficulties they experience, the teacher becomes more sensitive to the processes of learning to read (and reading) and relatively less concerned with the quantitative aspects. Such careful observation and thought lead to a primary focus on learners and their strengths, areas for growth, needs, and interests, shifting major concern away from programs, curricula, and skills lists. The teacher's primary concern, then, is focused on children rather than on materials.

A second major task of the teacher is to make sure that children use reading materials that are of a suitable level of difficulty. Appropriate materials are those at the children's *instructional* and *independent* levels.

One of the most serious problems in elementary school classrooms today is the very large percentage of children who are kept reading at their *frustration* level. If a book is too difficult, if too many new concepts appear and are not repeated several times, and if the decoding process of unlocking new words has not been learned, boys and girls spend much time in school trying to gain information that is beyond their grasp. When teachers look at standardized test results and on that basis divide all the children in their rooms into three reading groups, they may be asking some children to stay frustrated all day long. Learning does not progress when children work at the frustration level.

One of the best ways to focus attention on children's reading needs is to administer informal reading inventories to students at the beginning of the school year. Some people say that doing this takes too much time, but when compared with the time that is wasted when children spend a whole year reading materials that are too difficult or in other ways inappropriate, the time needed to administer reading inventories is time well spent.

Standardized reading achievement tests do have a very important place in assessment of the total school reading program. Also, they provide each teacher with a distribution of his or her students from best to poorest performer. However, they do not provide an adequate measure by which the teacher can determine which books are appropriate for which children to read at their respective *instructional* levels. The standardized test, if it is a timed test, is a power test, and may more nearly measure a child's frustration level of reading for a short period of time.

Teachers have found that standardized test scores may yield grade placement equivalents one or even two years higher than children can actually read with understanding.[1] Wheeler and Smith found that the grade placement scores on standardized reading tests in the primary grades often have little relationship to the child's actual instructional reading level.[2]

The teacher cannot meet each child at his or her level of functioning and provide instruction from which the child can profit unless the teacher can somehow determine with a fair degree of accuracy what that functioning level is. An informal reading inventory will provide the classroom teacher with this fundamental information.

What Is the Informal Reading Inventory?

An informal reading inventory (IRI) is an individual test in which the child reads both orally and silently from increasingly difficult material until he or she becomes frustrated because of not knowing the words, not being able to pronounce them, or not understanding the ideas presented. IRIs are informal tests for reader level, sometimes referred to as "trying on a book for size." The informal reading test is diagnostic in that it allows the teacher to study the child's reading behavior. Clearly, the value of the IRI depends entirely upon the competence of the teacher to make judgments as the child reads. An informal reading inventory should provide a selection of oral and silent reading at each level from preprimer through the high school level. Comprehension questions must be provided to measure the child's understanding of what is read.

The child should read from the book while the teacher has a reproduced copy on which to mark errors and make notes and evaluations. At the level at which the child makes too many miscues in word identification or errors on comprehension questions, the teacher begins reading one passage orally at each reading level and then asks prepared questions to measure the child's capacity for understanding ideas when he listens to someone else read the material. This is referred to as the child's *capacity* level, listening level, or hearing comprehension level.

The Four Reading Levels to Be Defined

The IRI will provide the teacher with information about levels of reading appropriate for the child's instructional work in class, the level at which he or she might most enjoy free reading, and a level of understanding ideas in written context even when it is too difficult for the child to read the material. These levels are called: (1) independent; (2) instructional; (3) frustration; and (4) capacity levels.

The *independent level* of reading is the *highest* level at which the child can read fluently and with personal satisfaction but without help. In independent reading, the child encounters practically no mechanical difficulties with the words and no problems with understanding the concepts in the context. The level is generally defined as that level where the child makes no more than one miscue in one hundred words in the mechanics of reading and where he or she has no difficulties in comprehension. Much of the material the child selects for free reading from the library as well as some of the collateral reading he or she does for unit work in social studies and science should be at this level.

The *instructional level* of reading is the teaching level. This is defined as the *highest* level at which the child makes no more than five uncorrected miscues in reading one hundred consecutive words with at least 75 percent comprehension. Such materials are difficult enough to be challenging but sufficiently easy so that the student can do independent seatwork with only the usual readiness help from the teacher when assignments are made. *The most important task of the elementary teacher is to establish each child's instructional level of functioning in reading and provide him or her with work at that level.* Material at the child's instructional level should be read silently before it is read orally. Then there should be no difficulties with phrasing, punctuation, finger pointing, or tension. Studies reported here indicate that many children are never given the opportunity to read at this level in school. The instructional level is reached when the child uses a conversational tone, without noticeable tension, with satisfactory rhythm, and with suitable phrasing. He or she also makes proper use of word recognition clues and techniques.[3]

The *frustration level* is the *lowest* level at which obvious difficulties cause confusion, frustration, and tension in the reading situation. Betts lists inability to anticipate meanings, head movements, finger pointing, tension, slow word-by-word reading, vocalization, and too many substitutions, omissions, repetitions, and insertions as evidences of frustration.[4]

The teacher understands that a clear line of separation does not exist between the instructional and frustration levels. The teacher's purpose is to keep the child on the growing edge of learning without pushing the learner along too fast. The teacher will do well to choose the lower of two possible reader levels when there is a question about which is appropriate for a given individual. It is preferable to let the child have more practice at an easier level and thus strengthen abilities and skills than to assign material that is too difficult and impede progress.

The *capacity level* for reading is the *highest* level at which the child can understand the ideas and concepts in informational material that is read to her. In determining this level, the teacher begins reading to the student at the level of difficulty at which she stops oral or silent reading because of reaching the frustration level. The same questions prepared to ask if the child reads the material are also appropriate to ask her after the teacher reads the material. Comprehension of 75 percent, the same proportion used for establishing instructional level, is the figure used for establishing capacity level. It is important to determine a child's capacity level so it can be compared to the child's instructional level. If the instructional level is only second level of second grade (2^2) and the capacity level for reading is fourth grade, the child's reading retardation is 1.5 years. This is one indication that the child has the innate ability to read much better than he or she is reading.

Limitations of the Informal Reading Inventory

The severest limitation of the informal reading inventory is the competence of the teacher administering it. However, with a minimum amount of practice, any classroom teacher can use the technique confidently and will be convinced that it is a necessity. It is the most accurate test of a child's ability to use textbooks for instructional purposes.

Some classroom teachers who have never administered an IRI expect it to be a technical and complicated instrument. For this reason they avoid it. But being a teacher must involve such responsibility. The reading inventory should be the very core of the teacher's whole reading-work program for the year. A teacher dare not believe that it is too technical and still think that he or she is functioning as a teacher.

Any teacher can learn to prepare that part of a complete reading inventory that meets the immediate need, and with study and practice, learn a great deal about the abilities and disabilities of the boys and girls in his or her classroom with respect to developmental reading.

Since the child is reading only brief passages and the test situation represents only one small sample of the child's total behavior, it is easily possible that there are facets of reading not adequately assessed and that on another day or at another time, the same individual might perform somewhat differently.

Spache feels that the individual texts in any basal reading series are not accurately graded and that a readability formula needs to be applied to determine the level of difficulty. He also suggests that a passage needs to be sufficiently long to represent four minutes of reading time in order to adequately check comprehension of ideas.[5] Further, Spache reports that classroom teachers have been found to be very inaccurate in recording errors in the informal reading inventory.[6]

While these limitations described by Spache are valid criticisms, they in no way change the fact that it is the classroom teacher who, in the final analysis, *must make all the decisions* about the child's reading ability in day-to-day work. The teacher must, *unavoidably,* select reading materials in language arts, social studies, arithmetic, science, and literature. It is to be hoped that shelves of books of many levels of difficulty will be provided for students to choose from, but the scope of the selections is the teacher's responsibility.

Improvement in the accuracy of the interpretation of the IRI develops with practice—if this practice is guided, or based on further reading and study. An excellent way for a beginning teacher to acquire initial skill in administering an informal reading inventory is to record the child's oral reading on a tape recorder so that it can be played back a number of times. Most clinicians are apt to hear some errors the second time that they missed completely the first time. Without a specific plan of what to listen for, the listener is probably not able to make any kind of objective summary of the results of the oral reading.

Advantages of the Informal Reading Inventory

Betts has pointed out the advantages of the informal reading inventory as the teacher's primary tool in teaching developmental reading skills:[7]

1. The teacher uses the materials at hand; there is little cost.
2. With direct and rapid administration, the teacher gets some needed answers quickly.
3. In terms of textbook reading the child will do, it is more valid than other tests.
4. Informal reading inventories can be either group or individual for appropriate purposes.
5. The student can be made aware of how well he reads.
6. The student can be made aware of progress as he achieves it.
7. As achievement is appraised, specific needs are revealed.
8. Interesting materials can be selected to use in the inventory.
9. Readability of materials can be checked in series of texts.
10. The test situation can be a valuable instructional situation also.

Construction of the Informal Reading Inventory

The first step in preparing the inventory is the selection of a series of books, probably a series of readers. Preferably a series of readers not already familiar to the children being tested would be used. While there are many words *not common* to two series of readers, the controlled vocabularies, the picture clues, and the context clues all help the child anticipate meanings, and most of the words are already in the typical English-speaking child's vocabulary.

Some teachers may write stories at increasingly difficult levels for use in preparing their IRIs. Even children's writing samples may be ordered in levels of difficulty and made into IRI passages. Questions will be prepared the same as for passages from readers.

Selections from preprimers, primers, and first and second readers need to contain 60 to 125 words and to be sufficiently informational so that questions can be constructed to measure understanding of the ideas in what is read. For grades three to six, passages need to be somewhat longer, perhaps 100 to 200 words in length.

One selection must be identified to be read orally and one to be read silently. The selection from each book should be taken from near the end of the first third of the book. It should not be from the first stories, which contain mostly review words from previous books in the series, but should fall close enough to the front of the book to include the newly introduced words before the progressively more difficult reading that follows.

When the child reads, even if it is at the beginning of a story, the teacher should first give a synopsis of the story, or otherwise clue the child in to the place where the reading begins. It is wise to select for silent reading the selection immediately following the oral reading selection so the child can continue reading without teacher explanation and, thus, save time.

The comprehension questions should be carefully thought out so that they measure understanding as completely as possible. Different levels of questioning are appropriate: factual or memory items; inferential items requiring reading between the lines; vocabulary items to test concepts; and items to test ability to use context clues.

Authors need to provide meaningful definitions for new or difficult vocabulary items: "Erosion, which is the washing or blowing away of the soil, is therefore a serious problem."[8] The careful reader can now answer the question: "What is erosion?" "The stumpage, or timber in standing trees, is sold to lumbermen, who come in and cut the timber that is marked by the rangers for cutting."[9] The careful reader can answer the question: "What is stumpage?"

When choosing selections for the informal reading inventory, teachers should consider the nature of the context material. Can good comprehension questions be framed concerning the story? Vocabulary, sentence structure, human interest, and the number and complexity of the ideas dealt with influence the comprehension level of the material. Complexity of the ideas may be estimated by the number of prepositional phrases. The teacher should prepare questions that can be answered from the reading material, not from what the child already knows. Also, the questions should require recall, not merely a *yes* or *no*. For example, "What color was the hound?" *not,* "Was the hound in the story red?"

Patty, in the fourth grade, was referred for a reading evaluation because she was unable to do her work in her content subjects. When she was reading the *Gilmore Oral Reading Test,*[10] paragraph 2, she had little difficulty with the words. She read, "The cat is looking at the girl. He wants to play ball, too." But when she was asked, "What does the cat want?" she replied, "Cat food." In paragraph 3, she read, "After father has gone to work, the children will leave for school." To the question, "When will the children leave for school?" she responded, "When they're ready." This child apparently needs much help to improve concentration on what she is reading. If she had been asked *yes-no* questions, her inattention to the content of the story might have been much less evident.

Depending upon the content of the material read, there should be five to seven questions to measure comprehension. If the questions are of different types as suggested, this will provide some measure of the individual's understanding.

The child should read from the book itself. This gives him or her the book format, the appropriate size print, and picture clues. The selections need to be reproduced so that the examiner has a copy for marking reading errors, making notes in the page margins, checking comprehension, and observing the child's behavior in the reading situation. As teachers develop sophistication in asking a child to "try the book on for size," they need to be able to apply their techniques for marking errors and checking comprehension of the available material in the classroom. The word "informal" in informal reading inventory emphasizes that it allows the teacher to check quickly to see if a book is appropriate for a particular child's functioning reading level.

From Theory to Practice 4.2
Selecting and Testing a Passage for the IRI

Select a passage of 75 to 150 words from a basal reader. The number of words may vary depending on the level of the reader. Be sure the passage you select has enough content to allow you to prepare questions.

After you have selected the reading passage, prepare five questions about the material that would be suitable to ask the child. Try to have various kinds of questions: recall, word meaning, inferential, and affective, for example.

Finally, ask a child to read the passage and answer your questions. Was the child able to do the task? Did he or she make any comments about your questions?

While any teacher can construct an informal reading inventory, there are a number published for teachers to use. With practice in administering and interpreting them, teachers will develop their own preferences about such inventories. Some of them are:

Bader, Lois A. *Reading and Language Inventory.* New York: Macmillan, 1983. Levels preprimer (pp) through 12.

Burns, Paul, and Betty Roe. *Informal Reading Assessment.* Chicago: Rand McNally, 1980. Levels pp through 12.

Ekwall, Eldon. *Ekwall Reading Inventory.* Boston: Allyn & Bacon, 1979. Levels pp through 9.

Johns, Jerry. *Advanced Reading Inventory.* Dubuque, Iowa: Wm. C. Brown, 1981. Levels 7 through college.

————. *Basic Reading Inventory.* 2d ed. Dubuque, Iowa: Wm. C. Brown, 1981. Levels pp through 8.

La Pray, Margaret. *On-the-Spot Reading Diagnosis File.* New York: Center for Applied Research in Education, 1978.

Miller, Wilma. "Individual Reading Inventory." In *Reading Diagnosis Kit.* 2d ed. West Nyack, N.Y.: Center for Applied Research in Education, 1978. Levels primer through 12.

Silvaroli, Nicholas J. *Classroom Reading Inventory.* 4th ed. Boston: Allyn & Bacon, 1979. Levels pp through 8.

Spache, George D. *The Diagnostic Reading Scales.* New York: McGraw-Hill, 1972. Levels 1 through 6; poor readers 7 through 12.

Sucher, Floyd, and Ruel Allred. *Sucher–Allred Reading Placement Inventory.* Oklahoma City: The Economy Co., 1973.

Woods, Mary Lynn, and Alden Moe. *Analytical Reading Inventory.* 2d ed. Columbus, Ohio: Charles E. Merrill, 1981.

**Administering
the Informal
Reading
Inventory**

Estimating
Reading Level

Before the teacher can decide what selection to give the child to read, he or she needs some idea of the child's functioning level. There are several ways to acquire information for making this decision.

The *San Diego Quick Assessment* is a very short, easy-to-administer word-recognition test. It is included here. It has been found useful for finding a starting place to begin work with a child. Following are the instructions, the steps in administering, and the test itself.

San Diego Quick Assessment[11]
Margaret La Pray and Ramon Ross

Instructions:

1. Have the student read lists until he misses three words in one list.
2. The list in which a student misses no more than one of the ten words is the level at which he can read independently. Two errors indicate his instructional level. Three or more words identify the level at which reading material will be too difficult.
3. Be sure to analyze the errors.
4. Observe behaviors that accompany the reading.

Administration:

1. Type out each list of ten words on index cards, one list to a card. If available, type the first three or four lists with primary type.
2. Begin with a card that is at least two years below the student's grade level assignment.
3. Do not put the reading level on the cards where the student can read it. Do your coding on the back of the card.
4. Ask the student to read the words aloud to you. If he misreads any on the list, drop to easier lists until he makes no errors. This indicates the base level.
5. Write down all incorrect responses or write them on the copy of the test.
6. Encourage the student to read words he does not know so that you can identify the techniques he uses for word identification.
7. Keep reading lists until he misses three words on any one list or all lists are exhausted.

The Test:

PP	*Primer*	*1*	*2*	*3*
see	you	road	our	city
play	come	live	please	middle
me	not	thank	myself	moment
at	with	when	town	frightened
run	jump	bigger	early	exclaimed
go	help	how	send	several
and	is	always	wide	lonely
look	work	night	believe	drew
can	are	spring	quietly	since
here	this	today	carefully	straight

4	5	6	7	8
decided	scanty	bridge	amber	capacious
served	certainly	commercial	dominion	limitation
amazed	develop	abolish	sundry	pretext
silent	considered	trucker	capillary	intrigue
wrecked	discussed	apparatus	impetuous	delusion
improved	behaved	elementary	blight	immaculate
certainly	splendid	comment	wrest	ascent
entered	acquainted	necessity	enumerate	acrid
realized	escaped	gallery	daunted	binocular
interrupted	grim	relativity	condescend	embankment

9	10	11
conscientious	zany	galore
isolation	jerkin	rotunda
molecule	nausea	capitalism
ritual	gratuitous	prevaricate
momentous	linear	risible
vulnerable	inept	exonerate
kinship	legality	superannuate
conservatism	aspen	luxuriate
jaunty	amnesty	piebald
inventive	barometer	crunch

Other ways to "guesstimate" reading level:

1. In September the teacher can check the cumulative record from the previous year to see what book the child was reading when the school year ended and choose accordingly. If the book selected is too difficult, the teacher will simply move to easier material.

2. The teacher may be able to assemble subgroups of children in reading circles very early in the year and ask them to "read around the circle" sampling a story that the teacher has developed readiness for. For children who have difficulty, only one sentence is sufficient. For those who read well, a much longer passage is fine.[12]

3. If the teacher estimates that a book at second level of first grade is appropriate, a sampling of words can be made from the list in the back of the book to make a word-recognition test of twenty words. The sample will be obtained by dividing the total number of words in the list by twenty and then selecting words from the list at intervals of that quotient. For example, if there are 200 words in the list, $200 \div 20 = 10$; the teacher will thus select every tenth word in the list. A child who knows at least 80 percent of these words at sight will

Figure 4.1
A system of marking
sight recognition of
the first forty words on
the Dolch list.

From E. W. Dolch, *The
Dolch Basic Sight Word
Test* (Champaign, Ill.:
Garrard Press, 1972).

Name _____ Date _____

1. by   at   a   it
2. in   I   be   big *good*/go
3. did   good   do   go
4. all   are   *many*/any   an
5. *has*/had   *had*/have   him   drink
6. its   is   into   if
7. *as*/ask   may   as   are
8. *c*/many   cut   keep   know
9. *do*/does *good*/goes *doing*/going and
10. has   he   his   *for*/far

probably be able to read from the book. The following list of twenty-
five words represents every eighth word in a list of 207 new words in
the back of the book *Fields and Fences, Readiness Second Reader.*[13]

uncle	sister	people	already	brought
easy	nuts	threw	loud	hopped
getting	hide	shark	send	broke
past	Teddy	paw	held	bumpity-bump
it's	both	branch	whole	drum

If the child can pronounce twenty or more of these words at sight,
this would be an appropriate book to sample for the child's
instructional level of reading.

4. The *Slosson Oral Reading Test* can be useful for suggesting the
   child's oral instructional level and entry to the informal reading
   inventory.[14]
5. The Dolch Basic Sight Word List can be administered as a recall
   test. This is done by asking the child to pronounce all the words, line
   by line, on the *Dolch Basic Sight Word Test.*[15] Generally, the teacher
   has one copy of the test and writes comments and marks errors as the
   child works (see figure 4.1). The child needs a three-by-five-inch
   index card to move down the page and hold under each word as it is
   being pronounced. The teacher strikes a line through each word

Table 4.1 Approximate reader levels based on the *Dolch Basic Sight Word Recall Test.*

Dolch Words Known	Equivalent Reader Levels
0–75	Preprimer
76–120	Primer
121–170	First reader
171–210	Second reader or above
Above 210	Third reader or above

From Maude McBroom, Julia Sparrow, and Catherine Eckstein, *Scale for Determining a Child's Reader Level* (Iowa City: Bureau of Publications, Extension Division, University of Iowa, 1944), p. 11. Reprinted by permission.

recognized *at sight.* The McBroom-Sparrow-Eckstein scale of known sight words indicates approximately which book in the reading series the child may be able to read.[16] (See table 4.1.)

Criteria for knowing a Dolch Basic Sight Word are as follows:

1. The child looks at the word and pronounces it correctly.
2. The child does not sound the word letter-by-letter.
3. The child does not need more than a few seconds to say the word.

A child having difficulty and missing half of the sight words should be allowed to stop the test. With older children making many errors, the teacher may decide to do only Part I or Part II of the Basic Sight Word Test Sheet.

Some sample errors made by a child on Part I are shown in figure 4.2. It is possible to make an analysis of these errors by grouping them into the following categories: wrong beginnings, wrong middles, wrong endings, reversals, wrong several parts, and words not pronounced—as in table 4.2. The analysis shows that the child makes all types of errors. However, if *brown* for *down* is caused by reversing *b's* and *d's,* and *now* for *how* is caused by confusing *n's* and *h's,* there were fewer errors in beginnings. This is significant since, at the level at which the child will be able to read context, attention to "How does the word begin?" seems most appropriate. Since the child has pronounced about 55 of the 110 words in Part I of the test at sight, we could project another 55 out of 110 on Part II. For this estimated score of 110, the McBroom, Sparrow, Eckstein scale (see table 4.1) indicates a primer level of reading.

Wrong beginnings is probably the lowest level of error, since first grade teachers work very hard at helping children perceive words from left to right. The teacher will probably want to give the child some help with studying the word all the way through to be sure to get the ending right. The analysis of errors

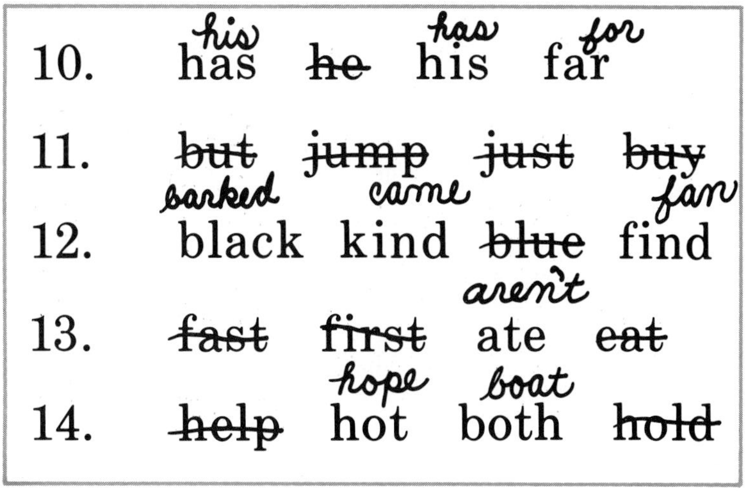

Figure 4.2
A sample of a child's errors on Part I of the *Dolch Basic Sight Word Test.* The teacher crosses out all words pronounced at sight and writes in the substitution errors the child makes.

From E. W. Dolch, *The Dolch Basic Sight Word Test* (Champaign, Ill.: Garrard Press, 1972).

10.	has (*his*)	~~he~~	his (*has*)	far (*for*)
11.	~~but~~ (*barked*)	~~jump~~ (*came*)	~~just~~	~~buy~~ (*fan*)
12.	black	kind	~~blue~~	find
13.	~~fast~~	first (*aren't*)	ate	~~eat~~
14.	~~help~~ (*hope*)	hot (*boat*)	both	~~hold~~

Table 4.2   Analysis of errors made on Part I, *Dolch Basic Sight Word Test.*

Wrong Beginnings	Wrong Middles	Wrong Endings	Reversals	Wrong Several Parts	Failed to Pronounce
it for *at*	*hid* for *had*	*his* for *him*	*me* for *am*	*barked* for *black*	drink
brown for *down*	*here* for *have*	*bringing* for *bring*	*brown* for *down*	*came* for *kind*	ask
now for *how*	*my* for *may*	*boat* for *both*	*now* for *how*	*fan* for *find*	as
gray for *give*	*his* for *has*	*became* for *because*		*aren't* for *ate*	found
gray for *gave*	*has* for *his*	*less* for *let*	(3)	*hope* for *hot*	eight
	for for *far*	*go* for *got*		*get* for *grow*	better
(5)	*a boat* for *about*	*can* for *came*		*a little* for *always*	light
	fall for *full*			*game* for *again*	done
	bean for *been*			*afraid* for *after*	draw
	like for *live*	(7)		*couldn't* for *clean*	get
	din't for *don't*			*four* for *five*	
	came for *come*			*bus* for *best*	(10)
				lake for *laugh*	
	(12)			*hard* for *hurt*	
				could for *carry*	
				could for *call*	
				heard for *here*	
				had for *here*	
				(18)	

From E. W. Dolch, *The Dolch Basic Sight Word Test* (Champaign, IL: Garrard Press, 1972).

makes it clear that vowel sounds are giving the child a great deal of difficulty in the middle of words. As the child's reading level increases to second grade, complete instruction in the vowel skills will be needed.

Specific Difficulties

Word Recognition

Many children finish the third grade without establishing mastery of the 220 Dolch Basic Sight Words. Because this list is composed of the service words that constitute half of all the text words in elementary school textbooks, they must be mastered. No nouns were included in the basic sight word list, since Dolch did not consider naming words to be service words. But he also identified the ninety-five most common nouns in children's reading experience. Any corrective reading program must provide for the teaching of these most used words. Suggestions for such teaching are included in chapter 9, "Word-Recognition Skills."

Sometimes it can be arranged for the rest of the class to work on independent activities so the teacher is free for fifteen or twenty minutes in one corner of the room where the child can complete the inventory. A relatively uninterrupted environment is necessary. Some teachers arrange to test one child each day during a recess.

The easiest way to establish rapport with a child is to explain exactly what you are doing and why determining the child's instructional level of reading is so important. If the child is interested, point out how the size of print changes in more difficult books, therefore increasing the amount of reading on a page, and how the use of pictures decreases. The child must not be made to feel that the test is a "threat" to his or her status, and if the child is the type who continually asks for reassurance (Am I doin' good?), the teacher needs to be completely reassuring.

If the child makes more than five uncorrected errors in reading the first selection attempted, the teacher may select an easier book and have the child continue reading until a satisfactory instructional level is found. Occasionally a child makes more errors on the first passage than on a subsequent more difficult one. The teacher has to be alert to such a possibility and to any psychological factors that may cause it to happen in order to be sure that the child's instructional level is correctly identified.

While the pupil is reading, the teacher should record all word substitutions, hesitations, mispronunciations, repetitions, omissions, and insertions. The method of marking and scoring is discussed in the next section of this chapter. The busy teacher will find it helpful to record the pupil's reading with a tape recorder and replay it when the children are gone so that more concentrated attention can be given to the reading.

Comprehension

Before the child reads, the teacher should explain that comprehension questions will be asked at the end of each oral and silent passage. When the questions are asked, the teacher should make note of the answers given. The teacher may wish to leave the reading material with the child for reference in answering. Removing

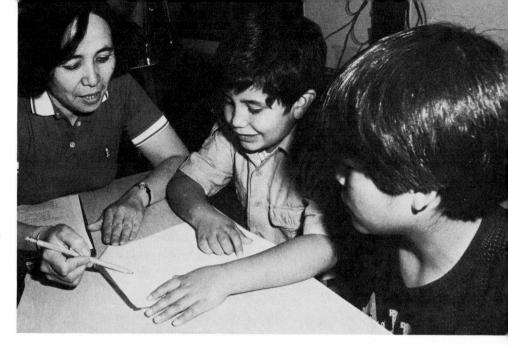

After the teacher administers an IRI to a student, she has an excellent estimate of his instructional reading level. She can then give him material at the appropriate level of difficulty to read.

the materials combines the tasks of comprehending and remembering. Kender and Rubenstein found that children who did not understand the questions and the material on which the questions were based could not answer even with the material available for inspection.[17] Children who did understand but did not remember referred back and answered the questions satisfactorily. The teacher should be aware of the task the reader faces and the implications of the adult's decision, whether the choice is to leave or remove the material.

The child continues to read selections until the teacher is certain the child's frustration level has been reached. Then the teacher reads one selection at each subsequent level so long as the child can answer the comprehension questions.

Marking and Scoring the IRI

The system of marking errors in oral reading described by Gilmore will meet the needs of most teachers for scoring the IRI. The errors to be noted include substitutions, omissions, insertions, hesitations, words pronounced by the examiner, and repetitions. The important point is that the teacher have a definite, well-learned system of marking that will be meaningful. By such a method, a child may read a passage of three hundred words, for example, with twenty errors in the mechanics of reading. Measurable growth is shown if three months later the student can read the same passage with only five errors. However, the system of recording errors must be consistent if the pre-/posttest record is to have value. Durrell[18] and Gates[19] have also provided detailed systems for marking errors. Each teacher must know one system well.

With only a minimum amount of practice, groups of experienced teachers find they mark children's oral reading with a very high percent of agreement. So, even though administering the IRI has subjective elements, and many judgments must be made informally and quickly by the teacher, the results will yield objective data for the competent teacher after some practice.

The following types of oral reading errors represent most of the difficulties children have.[20]

Hesitation. Mark after two seconds of hesitation with a (✓). Proper nouns are given to the child as needed and are not scored as errors unless the proper noun is a word that most children would know, like Brown, Green, or Smith.

Word pronounced for the child. If a pupil hesitates for approximately five seconds on a difficult word, the teacher should pronounce it and make a second check mark (✓ ✓).

Mispronunciation. This results in a nonsense word, which may be produced by: (1) wrongly placed stress, (2) wrong pronunciation of vowels or consonants, or (3) omission, addition, or insertion of one or more letters without creating a real or new word. Example: *crēt'ik* for *critic.* Write the child's pronunciation above phonetically. Notice word attack methods and enunciation. If errors come too rapidly for recording, draw a line through mispronounced words. Do not count foreign accent or regional speech mannerisms. If a proper noun that most children would know is miscalled several times in one passage, the teacher must decide whether to count this as only one error. For example, the child may have read regularly about Tom and Betty and consistently pronounce Fred as Tom in the IRI reading. This should be counted as only one error.

Omissions. Circle the omitted word, syllable, letter sound, or endings that are omitted. Count as only one error the omission of consecutive words.

Punctuation. Put an X on punctuation marks that the child ignores or passes over.

Substitutions. When one sensible or real word is substituted for the printed word, write the substituted word directly above the word presented in print. Notice whether it makes sense or is irrelevant to the context. If the child makes one substitution error and then in the same sentence makes a second error to get proper grammatical structure with verbs or pronouns, count this as only one error. In basic sight word substitutions, the error should be counted each time it occurs. If the reader says "then" for "when" three times, this is three errors.

Insertions. When the child reads words that do not appear in the printed material, place a caret ($\wedge$) and write the added word or words. Count as only one error the insertion of two or more consecutive words.

Repetitions. Repetition of a word, part of a word, or groups of words may indicate that the child is having trouble understanding what he or she reads. Draw a wavy line under the repeated words.

The teacher must record the child's responses to the comprehension questions as they are given. When the child's comprehension falls below 70 to 75 percent, there is no need to have the child continue reading even if few mechanical difficulties are showing up.

Nervous mannerisms such as fidgeting, hair twisting, nose picking, heavy sighing, or undue restlessness indicate discomfort and frustration and should be noted on the child's test. Some other signs that should be noted are losing the place in the story, holding the book close to the face, finger pointing, or head movements.

In silent reading, the child may vocalize everything he or she reads, read very slowly, or need encouragement to keep on reading.

Figures 4.4 and 4.5 contain story passages on which oral reading errors are marked according to the system described for the *Gilmore Oral Reading Test* (figure 4.3). A single exercise does not adequately identify the child's instructional level of reading, however. Before making a firm decision, a classroom teacher should ask the child to read some less difficult selections.

The teacher will be able to summarize the results of the IRI reading in a chart such as the following:

Oral

Level of book	Total words	Total errors	Percent of error	Percent accuracy	Level of difficulty
————	————	————	————	————	————
————	————	————	————	————	————
————	————	————	————	————	————
————	————	————	————	————	————
————	————	————	————	————	————

Silent

Level of book	Total words	Time in seconds	Rate per minute	Percent com-prehension	Level of difficulty
————	————	————	————	————	————
————	————	————	————	————	————
————	————	————	————	————	————
————	————	————	————	————	————
————	————	————	————	————	————

Figure 4.3
Recording errors in oral reading.

Adapted, with permission, from John V. Gilmore and Eunice C. Gilmore, *Gilmore Oral Reading Test. Manual of Directions* (New York: Harcourt, Brace & World, © 1968), pp. 6–7.

Type of Error	Rule for Marking	Examples
Substitutions.	Write in substituted word.	*black* The boy is back of the girl.
Mispronunciations (nonsense words).	Write in the word phonetically or draw a line through word.	*sĭm'-bol-ik* symbolic
Words pronounced by examiner (after hesitation of 5 sec. or more).	Make two checks above the word pronounced.	It is a ✓✓fascinating story.
Disregard of punctuation.	Mark punctuation disregarded with an *X*.	Jack, my brother, ˣis in the navy.
Insertions (including additions).	Write in inserted word or words.	The dog and ˄*the* cat are fighting.
Hesitations (pause of two or more seconds).	Make a check above the word on which hesitation occurs.	It is a ✓fascinating story.
Repetitions (a word, part of a word, or group of words repeated).	Draw a wavy line beneath the word or words repeated.	He thought he saw a whale.
Omissions (one or more words omitted).	Encircle the word or words omitted.	Mother does all (of) her work with great care.
Corrections.	Write a *C* next to a mistake when the child corrects the error.	*going* I am ᶜtoo unhappy about leaving you.

Figure 4.4

An example of oral reading errors made by a student reading without previous preparation. Two substitutions were self-corrected. Number of miscues is expressed as a percentage of number of words.

This passage was taken from the writing of children and prepared by students in the Navajo Teacher Education Project of the University of New Mexico, Albuquerque, N.M., 1982.

Herding Sheep

Last summer my dog and I went to my grandmother's house to stay with her for about a week. It was fun to herd sheep. One day I herded sheep for my grandmother. First, I let the sheep out of the corral in the morning. I herded them to the forest with my dog, and at about 4:00 o'clock in the evening I herded them back to my grandmother's house. When I counted the sheep, there were five sheep missing. I told my dog to go find them. He left, and in a few minutes I heard the dog barking. I ran outside, and there he was chasing the five sheep back into the corral. All the sheep were safe at the end of the day. I really like my dog. I think you can see why.

(handwritten annotations: hard, harded, all, let, hear, thank)

1. What did the writer do while he stayed at his grandmother's house? +

2. Who found the lost sheep? +

3. What kinds of things would you see in a forest? +

4. Why do you think the boy likes his dog? 0

75% comprehension

Level of difficulty: 2nd reader

Number of words: 137

Substitutions	3
Hesitations	1
Words pronounced by examiner	3
Repetitions	3
Omissions	2
Insertions	1
Total uncorrected errors	13
Percentage of miscues	9.5%
Percentage of accuracy	90.5%

Oscar's Airplane Ride

When Mr. Zabriski decided to go to Los Angeles, Oscar wanted to go with him. But Mr. Zabriski only shook his head. "I'm sorry," he said, "but I can't be bothered with a seal on this trip, not even a famous seal. You must stay here in New York. I have secret work to do."

Poor, neglected Oscar! He just couldn't stay in New York all alone! "We always go everywhere together," he said to himself. "I know Mr. Zabriski doesn't mean to be selfish. The first thing tomorrow I'll talk him into taking me along. I need a vacation."

Then Oscar got into his bathtub and slept until morning.

The next morning, when the seal climbed from his bathtub, he found that his trainer was gone. In a few minutes, he saw a letter leaning against a large fish - Oscar's favorite food. The letter said:

Dear Oscar:

I can't bear to say good-by. I am too unhappy about leaving you. Take good care of yourself until I come back.

Your Trainer,

Zabriski

What did Mr. Zabriski tell Oscar? +   Substitutions 9/5

What did Oscar think about this? 0   Hesitations 2

Where did Oscar sleep? +   Words pronounced by examiner 9/7

What is Oscar's favorite food? +

What did the letter tell Oscar? +   Repetitions 2

comprehension adequate.   Omissions 1

Insertions 0

TOTAL UNCORRECTED ERRORS 17

Percentage of error: 11%

Level of difficulty: 3²

Number of words: 160   Percentage of accuracy 89%

From Theory to Practice 4.3
Administering the Informal Reading Inventory

Administer an informal reading inventory. The one chosen to administer will be identified by your instructor. You may be asked to administer the sample IRI in Appendix 2. It was written by children living on the Zuni and Navajo reservations in western New Mexico.

It is important to tape the entire session so that you may study the child's reading behaviors until you are satisfied that you have marked each passage correctly.

It is most helpful if you share the administration, scoring, and evaluation with others carrying out the same task. Talking over the various responses of the reader with others will help to clarify how markings should be recorded and what the implications of the child's performance might be.

Summary

The regular classroom teacher has the inescapable responsibility for accurate assessment of each child's oral and silent reading abilities. The informal reading inventory is a useful tool for this purpose.

The IRI is a technique for measuring what the independent, instructional, and frustration reading levels are for a child by having the child read graded material and what the capacity level is by reading to the child. The difference between the instructional level of reading and the capacity level for understanding represents the extent of the child's reading retardation.

The limitations of the informal reading inventory and how to construct, administer, mark, score, and interpret the results in terms of difficulty levels of books for children have been presented.

For Further Reading

Ekwall, E. E. "Using Informal Reading Inventories, the Cloze Procedure, and the Analysis of Reading Scores." Chapter 11 in *Diagnosis and Remediation of the Disabled Reader,* pp. 260–91. Boston: Allyn & Bacon, 1976.

Harris, Albert, and E. R. Sipay. "Assessing Reading Performance, II." Chapter 9 in *How to Increase Reading Ability,* 7th ed., pp. 209–50. New York: Longman, 1980.

Heilman, Arthur, Timothy Blair, and William Rupley. *Principles and Practices of Teaching Reading,* 5th ed., pp. 328–40. Columbus, Ohio: Charles E. Merrill, 1981.

Jongsma, Kathleen, and Eugene Jongsma. "Test Review: Commercial Informal Reading Inventories." *The Reading Teacher* 34 (March 1981): 697–705.

Marzano, Robert, et al. "The Graded Word List Is Not a Shortcut to an IRI." *The Reading Teacher* 31 (March 1978): 647–51.

Pikulski, John J., and Timothy Shanahan, eds. *Approaches to the Informal Evaluation of Reading.* Newark, Del.: International Reading Assn., 1982.

Rubin, Dorothy. "Diagnostic Reading Tests and Techniques I: Emphasis on the Informal Reading Inventory." Chapter 9 in *Diagnosis and Correction in Reading Instruction,* pp. 108–43. New York: Holt, Rinehart and Winston, 1982.

Zintz, Miles. *Corrective Reading,* 4th ed. Dubuque, Iowa: Wm. C. Brown, 1981.

Notes

1. William D. Sheldon, "Specific Principles Essential to Classroom Diagnosis," *The Reading Teacher* 14 (September 1960): 8.
2. Lester R. Wheeler and Edwin H. Smith, "A Modification of the Informal Reading Inventory," *Elementary English* 34 (April 1967): 224.
3. Miles A. Tinker, *Bases for Effective Reading* (Minneapolis: University of Minnesota Press, 1965), p. 274.
4. Emmett A. Betts, *Foundations of Reading Instruction* (New York: American Book Co., 1946), p. 448.
5. George D. Spache, *Reading in the Elementary School* (Boston: Allyn & Bacon, 1964), p. 245.
6. Ibid., pp. 248–49.
7. Betts, *Foundations of Reading Instruction,* pp. 478–79.
8. Ernest Horn et al., *Reaching Our Goals,* Progress in Reading Series (Boston: Ginn, 1940), p. 138.
9. Ibid., p. 145.
10. John V. Gilmore, *Gilmore Oral Reading Test* (New York: Harcourt, Brace and World, 1952).
11. Margaret La Pray and Ramon Ross, "San Diego Quick Assessment," in *Teaching Children to Become Independent Readers* (New York: Center for Applied Research in Education, 1972), pp. 62–65.
12. E. W. Dolch, "How to Diagnose Children's Reading Difficulties in Informal Classroom Techniques," *The Reading Teacher* 6 (January 1953): 10–14.
13. William D. Sheldon, Mary C. Austin, and Richard E. Drdek, *Fields and Fences, Readiness Second Reader* (Boston: Allyn & Bacon, 1957), pp. 188–91.
14. Richard L. Slosson, *Slosson Oral Reading Test* (East Aurora, N.Y.: Slosson Educational Publications, 1963).
15. E. W. Dolch, *Dolch Basic Sight Word Test* (Champaign, Ill.: Garrard Press, 1942).
16. Maude McBroom, Julia Sparrow, and Catherine Eckstein, *Scale for Determining a Child's Reader Level* (Iowa City: Bureau of Publications, Extension Division, State University of Iowa, 1944).
17. Joseph Kender and Herbert Rubenstein, "Recall Versus Reinspection in IRI Comprehension Tests," *The Reading Teacher* 30 (April 1977): 776–79.
18. D. D. Durrell, *Manual of Directions, Analysis of Reading Difficulty* (Yonkers-on-Hudson: World Book Co., 1955).
19. A. I. Gates, *Manual of Directions: Gates Reading Diagnostic Test* (New York: Teachers College Press, 1953).
20. Dianne Brown, "The Preparation, Use and Analysis of the Results of the Informal Reading Inventory" (Master's thesis, University of New Mexico, 1968).

A Good Beginning

Part 2

A good beginning for boys and girls in the primary grades is based on adequate screening and sorting to determine which children learn best verbally, which children lack adequate motor coordination, and which children enter school emotionally immature. This is how diagnostic teaching begins.

Diagnostic teaching continues with the teacher continually examining and reexamining teaching failure in order to insure that children are taught at levels at which they can succeed. Teaching diagnostically demands that causes of reading failure be carefully analyzed to permit successful teaching.

Lee has very wisely said:

> Diagnostic teaching permits the child to deal with familiar concepts and procedures as he continues his growth in the unfamiliar school setting. When the school year opens with *a* plan of procedures, *a* set of materials, *a* topic on which to focus, many children are placed at a disadvantage; the teacher loses much valuable time and a variety of opportunities for enriching the learning that children already have.
>
> Some instructional programs are now swamping children with a multitude of experiences which their meager backgrounds ill prepare them to perceive or from which they gain little meaning.*

*Dorris M. Lee, *Diagnostic Teaching* (1201 Sixteenth St., N.W., Washington, D.C. 20036; Department of Elementary-Kindergarten-Nursery Education, National Education Association, 1966), p. 9.

Assessment of Prereading Skills

A Cognitive Map: Assessment of Prereading Skills

Factors
- Intelligence
- Language
- Emotional maturity
- Social maturity
- Visual discrimination
- Auditory discrimination
- Attendance in kindergarten
- Handedness
- Reading experiences
- Concepts learned

Which factors count the most

Tests
- Formal Reading readiness tests
- Informal Assessment tools
- Predictive index
- Social maturity scale
- Ready steps
- Early detection of reading difficulties
- Piagetian tasks

5

Guide Questions

1. What is meant by the term "prereading skills"?

2. What factors affect beginning reading performance?

3. What is the relationship between language and concept formation?

4. What are some common ways to assess the student's readiness to begin reading instruction?

Terminology

auditory discrimination

color blindness

concept

concepts about print

minimal pair

planned sequential verbal bombardment

prereading skills

reading readiness

reading readiness test

running record

visual discrimination

Since our society is deeply entrenched in a traditional practice of starting all children in first grade at age six, chronological age has become the only criterion for deciding if children are ready for this new and exciting adventure. Chronological age will be the only characteristic that many of these children have in common even though it is the least important in assessing whether each child has the psychological, intellectual, and neurological maturity to profit from this experience.

Because the school accepts children who are chronologically six, it needs to provide for much better sorting and selecting after the children arrive so that each one can be kept learning and developing *appropriate behaviors at his or her growing edge of learning.* Children who are already reading should be encouraged to continue reading, with proper precaution that reading isn't being emphasized to the exclusion of all the other areas of growth and development. For those children who are ready to read, there is no reason to insist that they complete all the pages in a readiness workbook just because the school has a copy for each child to use. They should read if they are ready to read. However, many children, perhaps a sizable minority, lack language skills, vocabulary concepts, and experiences with the middle-class life pictured and assumed in most of the textbooks children will read. Moreover, for perhaps one child in ten or twelve, English has not been the first language of the home. Because of our extremely mobile population today, every elementary teacher should know something about teaching English as a second language.

There is an optimal time for learning. Skills that build upon currently developing behaviors are most easily learned. Behaviors for learning to read have been developing for most of the child's life. Assessing the child's ability to perform these behaviors will help the teacher to predict and plan for the child's adjustment to the reading situation. If skills or knowledge are missing at any step of the way, they should be developed before the child is confronted with the abstract process of reading.

The more mature the learner, the less adaptation is needed to attain a given level of proficiency in specific skills. This is clearly demonstrated in any large group of six-year-old children. Some few have learned how to read, some are optimally ready for learning to read, and some will not exhibit this developing behavior for some time. Children who are permitted to learn to read *when they are ready* will generally learn easily and read a great deal.

Teaching formal readiness or prereading skills before the child has appropriate neurological, psychological, or intellectual maturation is almost sure to result in failure to achieve the standards set by the school. This too early attempt may prevent the child from developing natural curiosity about reading and may be the beginning of emotional problems that will later become stumbling blocks to learning.

Children who are becoming readers have achieved an adequate level of intellectual development, possess a body of relevant knowledge, and have control of the grammar of the language. They also understand how reading works, know some purposes for reading, and feel that they are capable of becoming good readers. Obviously, these statements are subjective and have only relative value. Children must reach a minimum functioning level in their use of concepts, verbalizing, and general understanding before they become greatly interested in such an abstract process as deciphering the printed word.

Teachers need to be aware of the values placed on reading by children's families. The fact that a child's family and society influence children's reading is an important perspective that can no longer be ignored. Success in learning to read, and in school generally, must be viewed as the shared responsibility of the school and the home.

Two important related areas that the teacher should also consider are the child's emotional stability and maturity and his or her physical and neurological development. A child who has problems in vision and hearing or who lacks the visual-perceptual skills required for reading will not learn to read well.

The jobs of the first grade teacher, then, are to evaluate children's skills when they come to the first grade, to determine their degree of readiness for formal reading instruction, and to make sure that those who give evidence of a lack of readiness in any area have opportunity to develop needed abilities *before* they are given formal reading tasks.

Much of what has traditionally been done in readiness programs has been ineffective because whole groups of children have been asked to work through skills that many of them already knew well and a few understood neither before nor after the teaching.

The present point of view is that teachers must evaluate—with supplemental judgments from the principal, school nurse, school social worker, school psychologist, and reading supervisor—the learning levels of children and keep them growing toward maturity without regard to their place on a learning continuum when they enrolled in school.

The Complexity of "Being Ready": Factors Affecting Performance in Beginning Reading

Some of the factors the teacher will observe in appraising a child's maturity for reading are (1) intelligence, (2) use of language, (3) emotional and social maturity, (4) visual discrimination, (5) auditory discrimination, (6) left-handedness, (7) attendance in kindergarten, and (8) informal reading experiences at home. However, the teacher's informal appraisal of these factors should not be interpreted narrowly. Rather, they should be viewed in relation to the child's total growth and development, participation in all types of activities, and communication through nonverbal signals as well as oral language.

Intelligence

While intelligence is a major factor in learning to read, teachers should be aware that the standard measures of intelligence may not be valid for a large percentage of children who do not communicate using the standard English of the teacher and do not relate to the middle-class experiences emphasized in the school. Cultural biases are at work against the lower socioeconomic class, against those who speak nonstandard English, and against those whose first language is not English. The teacher can observe the child's general reactions in situations all day long:

on the playground, in discussions, when working with mechanical devices, when solving problems not related to language expression, the type of leadership exercised among peers, and how the child's nonverbal behavior changes (facial expression, motivation, emotional response) when activities related to early reading experience are presented. Formal intelligence tests that must be administered in selected cases need to be selected carefully to prevent cultural and linguistic bias as much as possible, and to minimize the effect poor reading ability may have on the results. Scores obtained need equally careful interpretation and application.

Use of Language

Teachers must find time to read a great deal to young children: stories, both fanciful and true, and selected poetry, rhymes, and jingles. Of course, readiness for literature depends on the child's stage of language cognition. All children in a group will not see, hear, and feel the same things when the teacher reads to them. Especially with children who have not had broad experiences, the teacher should try to compensate for the deficit. *Jam* is a poem that can be enjoyed and "tasted" until it is a meaningful experience for all the boys and girls in the class.

Jam

Jam on biscuits, jam on toast,
Jam is the thing I like the most.
Jam is sticky, jam is sweet,
Jam is tasty, jam's a treat—
*Rasp*berry, *straw*berry, *goose*berry, I'm *very*
FOND . . . OF . . . JAM!

Jam in the morning, jam at noon,
Bread and jam by the light of the moon.
Jam . . . is . . . very . . . nice.

—by Russell Hoban[1]

Another poem that children can enjoy because it speaks of experiences common to all is *Choosing Shoes*. There are varied possibilities for children to respond to the ideas expressed by its author.

Choosing Shoes

New shoes, new shoes,
Red and pink and blue shoes.
Tell me, what would *you* choose,
If they'd let us buy?

Buckle shoes, bow shoes,
Pretty pointy-toe shoes,
Strappy, cappy low shoes;
Let's have some to try.

From Theory to Practice 5.1

Sharing Poetry with Children

Your text suggests several sources of poetry to share with children to aid in developing concepts and to extend their appreciation of the rhythm of the language. Search through these or other collections of poetry for children. Then do the following:

1. Select two poems and prepare to read them with children.
2. Read the poems to children of appropriate ages. Afterwards, engage in discussion with the children about the poems.
3. You may wish to design some activity related to the ideas expressed in the poems that the children would enjoy doing.
4. As the children talk, listen carefully to their language, or even record the whole event. Do they give evidence of understanding the concepts? Do you think that some children may have broadened a concept already partially developed?
5. What could be done to help the children develop concepts further?
6. Be prepared to discuss with your classmates your experience with children, either in a small group or as a class.

Bright shoes, white shoes,
Dandy-dance-by-night shoes,
Perhaps-a-little-tight shoes,
Like some? So would I.

But

Flat shoes, fat shoes,
Stump-along-like-that shoes,
Wipe-them-on-the-mat shoes,
That's the sort they'll buy.

—by Frida Wolfe[2]

Sources of good materials for literature in grade one include: May Hill Arbuthnot,[3] Geismer and Suter,[4] and *The Real Mother Goose.*[5]

Facility with language may be one of the most important factors in reading readiness. Language facility will vary tremendously in any random group of six-year-old children, of course. The gamut includes the little girl of three and one-half years, who, after playing with paper boats in nursery school one morning, asked her mother to make her a paper boat to float in the dishpan of water in the afternoon. In a few minutes she brought a crumpled piece of wet paper to her mother in the living room and said, "My boat has *disintegrated* in the water."

The other end of the continuum includes both the child who has very meager language and gives one-word answers or says "Me go," meaning "I want to go," and the child whose native language is not the language of the school.

Language is being developed when parents, other adults, and teachers encourage children in the use of the language; when they answer many of the child's questions; when they model for children so they can understand concepts in a conversation; and when they ask children to correctly repeat sentence patterns, to form verb phrases correctly, or to straighten out pronunciations. These are always done in an informal, encouraging way. Thus the child learns, unlearns, and relearns the language through trial and error.

One reason culturally advantaged children often seem to display more verbal fluency than other children apparently stems from the way adults talk to them, answer their questions, ask them questions, ask them to amplify answers, and so on. If, on the other hand, children are talked to in one-word commands, or given instructions with minimal word usage, they respond in the same way and remain much less articulate than children who are answered, asked to amplify answers, given synonyms for many words they know, and so on.

Speaking and understanding spoken language utilizing concepts; asking questions or presenting problems; using language to formulate concepts; differentiating words that sound similar but mean different things; inferring meanings from context when one word has many meanings; and holding ideas in mind and organizing and classifying them in sequential order—all of these mental operations are evidences of language power and correlate highly with success in developing reading skills and academic learning. Needlessly carrying on an extensive readiness program for children who are already prepared is as foolish as ignoring readiness activities when they are needed. Some five-year-olds are more advanced intellectually, physically, socially, and emotionally than some six-year-olds. It should be just as possible to offer a long continuum of learning experiences in a kindergarten or first grade class as in any other. In that way, some point along the continuum should match each child's optimal readiness for learning.

Environmental experiences are needed—trips and excursions; fact and fancy in stories and poems; skills and habits in visual-auditory/visual-motor discrimination; creative expression through art, music, games, and rhythms.

Telling a story, seeing it written down, hearing it read back, and listening to its contents and knowing that it is what was said before—this sequence helps the child understand what reading is.

Children can learn in many informal experiences to *extend* their vocabulary:

Not, "It's a bird"; rather, "It's a robin."
Not, "It's a tree"; rather, "It's a maple tree."
Not, "It's a dog"; rather, "It's a big collie dog."

Emotional and Social Maturity

Many activities in the first two years of school life contribute to a child's emotional and social growth. A teacher who is sensitive to such traits as timidity, aggression, fear, anxiety, and the need for success and approval can create opportunity to help each child in terms of his or her need. Children learn through planned group work experiences to work cooperatively to achieve group goals, to share with each other, and to exchange ideas through informal conversation. Comfortable emotional and socializing experiences contribute to greater maturity, stability, and confidence when a child is confronted with the formal learning-to-read process. In the informal atmosphere of a kindergarten or first grade classroom, the teacher can promote vocabulary enrichment, correct English usage, fluency in extemporaneous speaking, and the ability to give attention in listening, all of which are skills essential in the learning-to-read process. (See figure 1.3.)

Visual
Discrimination

It is clear that good vision is an asset to becoming a good reader. Reading requires the ability to see clearly at close range for extended periods of time. Some children are sure to come to school with visual problems for which adjustments can be made. The teacher must be alert to observe whether the child appears to have vision problems and must make sure that the proper referrals are made. Reading clinicians, reading clinics in large school systems, and school nurses will be able to administer such tests as the *Snellen Chart,* the *Eames Eye Test,* or the *Keystone Visual Telebinocular Survey Test.*[6] When indicated, medical referrals will then be made.

Because of the great amount of color used in pictures and in all teaching media today, the child who is color-blind has a distinct disadvantage. These children need to be identified and given special help when identification, naming, and use of color are required. Possibly auditory methods can be emphasized more with the color-blind child. About 4 percent of the children enrolled in a school are likely to be color-blind, and almost all will be boys.[7]

Olson screened 275 first grade boys at the end of the school year with the AO H-R-R Pseudo-Isochromatic Plates and identified twelve color-blind boys.[8] She matched these with twelve boys who were not color-blind and compared their achievement on the *California Reading Test,* Lower Primary, Form W, given in May. The differences in achievement were significant at the .01 level of confidence in favor of the boys who had color vision.[9]

Schiffman identified 201 color-blind boys in first grade. The teachers of fifty-one of these boys were told about the color blindness, but no other treatment was given. At the end of the year, the fifty-one whose teachers had been informed performed better than the rest of the color-blind boys, whose teachers were not informed. The difference was statistically significant at the .05 level of confidence.[10]

Children should be screened early in their school careers for color blindness. For those identified, adjustment should be made early in the course of study to prevent failure. Parents and teachers should plan to give support to the child in meeting psychological and societal demands if adjustments are necessary.

In addition to planned activities that may permit the assessment of visual discrimination abilities, teachers may learn much about their pupils' visual discrimination skills through careful observation. Typical planned assessment activities might include picking out one word that is different from three of four

Working with puzzles is one way for a young child to learn to attend to details, to develop new vocabulary, and to exercise motor skills.

others, identifying words in language-experience stories that begin with certain letters, and underlining a given word every time it appears in an experience story. The teacher may observe children matching one letter or word to another, comparing one another's names, commenting that one word begins like another word, copying letters and words carefully from models, and exhibiting curiosity about the different forms letters take in book print and cursive writing. Careful anecdotal records of the observed behaviors may provide a more complete assessment of visual discrimination abilities than will a few isolated, and rather contrived, planned experiences.

Other ideas for assessing visual discrimination abilities may be found in the subsection "Visual Configuration" in chapter 9, "Word-Recognition Skills."

Auditory Discrimination

In order to learn to read, children must have acquired skills in auditory discrimination. Boys and girls need to be able to identify likenesses and differences in beginning and ending sounds of words, and to hear and correctly identify consonant sounds, vowel sounds, consonant clusters, diphthongs, pitch, and intonation. The prereading program must include many nonverbal, expressive kinds of activities to compensate for grammatical or syntactical differences or confusions in verbal activities. Some oral exercises that teachers may use to strengthen auditory discrimination are:

1. List all the words you can think of that have the same beginning sound as the word *dog.*
2. Tell me the sound you hear at the beginning of *Ruth.*
3. Do *man* and *mother; dog* and *boy* begin alike?
4. Which word does not begin like the others?
   mother   money   Nancy   milk
5. Which words do not begin with the same sound as in *mother?*
   money   something   milk   never   said
6. Tell me some words that rhyme with *tall.*
7. Supply the rhyming words at the ends of lines of *Mother Goose.*
8. Name all the things you can see that start with the same sound as the beginning sound of *red.*

Minimal pairs are two words containing all the same sounds except one phoneme, which changes the meaning of the word. Several examples of minimal pairs are given in chapter 3, "Linguistic Foundations for Reading Instruction."

The importance of visual and auditory discrimination is further emphasized in chapter 9, "Word-Recognition Skills."

The Left-Handed Child

About 7 percent of the children in school are left-handed. Since a relationship between changing handedness of young children and stuttering was hypothesized some decades ago, most teachers have accepted the idea that if children enter school using their left hands, they should accept that fact and make no attempt to change.

If young children do not demonstrate a definite handedness preference by the time they are between twenty-four and thirty months of age, mothers might well see if the practice of always handing the child objects from the right side might cause him to decide to be right-handed. If there is no strong preference, a small amount of encouragement might be all that is necessary to have a child decide to be right-handed, and he will find that society is organized for right-handed people. However, if a child enters school at age five or six with a preference for the left hand, she should certainly be encouraged to use it.

In view of the large number of children who do not learn how to write successfully with the left hand, however, it seems necessary to offer a word of advice to teachers. Rather than take a complete "hands off" attitude toward the left-handed child, they should show the child how to hold a pencil comfortably and firmly in the left hand just as they would if the child were right-handed. They can also provide affective support and encouragement. When the child is ready for cursive writing, they can demonstrate how to turn the paper at a forty-five degree angle to the right, just as the opposite arrangement is used for the right-handed child. While many children are able to work at tables where writing is comfortable with either hand, the school administrator should provide chairs with arms on the left side instead of on the right and make any other adjustments needed.

Attendance in Kindergarten	Children who attend kindergarten are exposed to many types of socializing experiences that provide for small group interaction and development of language. They hear stories and listen to records and play rhythm and singing games that develop skills in physical, emotional, social, and intellectual areas. Children who do not attend kindergarten need a longer period of time in first grade to make their adjustment to school and to participate in many of these activities. For many children who do attend kindergarten, there is a genuine need to continue their informal activities at the beginning of first grade to make the second year of school a continuation of the first but leading to more complex types of activities.

While there is some controversy about teaching reading in kindergarten, wise kindergarten teachers do not make any formal attempt for all the children to have any such lessons. All types of beginning reading experiences are available, but each child is allowed to demonstrate his or her own readiness and motivation *before* the teacher begins to place importance on "what words are." When a child points to a word and asks "What's that word?" the child should, of course, be told and commended for wanting to know. When the child draws a picture, the teacher can encourage the child to make up a sentence about it, which can be written below the picture to tell a story. But the child need not remember any of the individual words as part of a sight vocabulary. It is hoped that the child's attention span will grow to the point of wanting to hear stories read by the teacher, but a child should be permitted to leave the group when no longer interested.

Informal Reading in Relation to Home Environment	The teacher will be interested in determining the extent to which the child's parents read, because this helps determine the importance the child will place on reading. The teacher will observe whether there are books in the home and whether the parents place value on learning through reading. If a mother asks for ways she may help her child informally, she can be advised that trips to the supermarket provide opportunity for the child to identify words on signs, cans, and packages where the picture is a guide to the contents. Also, many inexpensive books are available in the supermarket that can be read to the child and that the child can then reread by studying the pictures. Teachers counseling parents might emphasize that a happy child with parents who love him, who spend time with him, and who strengthen his self-concept is likely to adjust well anywhere.

Parents need to understand that the following activities lead to readiness for formal reading:[11]

1. Many, varied opportunities for oral expression.
2. Practice in listening to other people tell about things; for example, "show and tell" time.
3. Discussing experiences or things shared by others.
4. Opportunities to hear stories and poems read by the teacher or presented on records and tapes.
5. Field trips and other excursions, preceded by preparedness directions and followed by discussion and experience charts.

6. Activities such as choral speaking, dramatization, radio or television skits, and practice with a tape recorder, to promote accurate pronunciation and enunciation.

7. Arranging pictures into a story sequence. This is carried out in a variety of situations, including flannel boards and pictures mounted on individual cards.

8. Interpreting a picture by telling a story about it: what the people are doing; where they are going; do they look happy?

9. Practice in recognizing the central ideas in stories read by the teacher.

10. Extensive practice in auditory discrimination and identification of familiar sounds. This may be thinking about things in the kitchen that begin with *p* (*p*an, *p*ot, *p*itcher, *p*late). Or it may be identifying different animal or traffic sounds or sounds like wood on wood, spoons being tapped together, paper being crumpled, or shoes scraping.

11. Making children aware of reading in their daily lives by having them distinguish their own names, looking at and talking about stories, reading or seeing signs, bulletin boards, and messages.

12. Keeping records of interesting or unusual words that have been used in conversation.

In addition, parents may be encouraged to talk with and listen to the child, read and enjoy stories and poems as well as make them up, take the child to the library regularly, play learning games within the family, encourage activities that require coordination such as cutting, jumping, and playing ball, and broaden the child's background of experience.[12]

Language and Concept Development

In order that the teacher may place sufficient emphasis on developing language concepts, provide for thinking in the language, and deliberately work for expanded vocabulary, *planned sequential verbal bombardment* is called for. Such a strategy is important for all children, but it is probably the only way the culturally different child can ever hope to catch up sufficiently to profit from the compulsory subjects in middle-class schools. A well planned verbal environment will keep the children on the growing edge of learning for as much of their short school day as possible.

Since reading success correlates most highly with verbal behavior, it is recommended that teachers place their greatest emphasis on types of oral language lessons that will *develop and extend concepts* in children when they enter school. The development of concepts in young children is heavily dependent on opportunities for direct interaction with the environment. This interaction, accompanied by verbal interpretation and elaboration, is the critical element in conceptual growth in young readers. The primary teacher who wishes to facilitate the growth of concepts, and thereby the growth of language and readiness for formal reading, will make sure that the classroom environment provides many

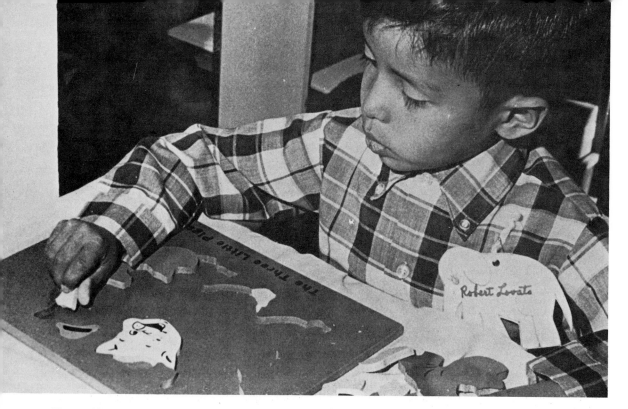

Young children need to work with classroom materials every day if language and concept development are to be encouraged.

occasions to operate with real materials and objects and that there are frequent opportunities for children to talk with each other and with the teacher about the materials.

Teachers may also use themselves as language models, deliberately employing certain oral language forms in interactions with their students. If teachers consistently model the language they hope their students will use, they will usually hear children using the forms after a period of time.

Language- and concept-building exercises such as those that follow should be helpful. Particular types of exercises are presented in isolation to focus attention on the concepts and language forms being employed. When such activities are done with children, they should be embedded in meaningful, natural learning situations. Such situations would occur when children experience genuine reasons for communicating with peers and with adults. Rarely will isolated drills on such concepts and language forms be effective with young learners.

1. Using word "opposites" in meaningful ways:

big–little	winter–summer	clean–dirty
on–off	good–bad	above–below
in–out	before–after	left–right
long–short	open–close	stop–go
up–down	front–back	sick–well
over–under	first–last	push–pull
boy–girl	wide–narrow	noisy–quiet

2. Classifying things:

red, blue, and yellow	colors
two, three, four	numbers
lion, tiger, giraffe	wild animals
cat, dog, goldfish	pets
Tom, Dick, Harry	boys' names
man, woman, boy, worker, nurse	people
sofa, chair, stove, table	furniture
pants, suit, hat, socks, shirt	clothes
houses, barns, stores, restaurants, hotels,	buildings
robin, wren, blackbird, sparrow, warbler	birds

3. Counting concrete objects and recognizing numbers of things to five:

How many baby chickens?

How many cherries?

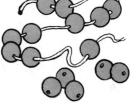

How many beads are
not on the string?

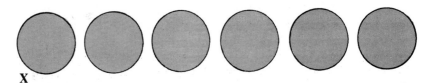

X

Which is the fifth circle from the **X**?

4. Associating words in pairs:

cow–calf	ring–finger	mail–postman
knife–fork	hen–chicken	shirt–tie
cup–saucer	cat–kitten	doll–dress
mother–baby	frog–tadpole	sheep–lamb

ball–bat	milk–milkman	horse–colt
cream–sugar	pen–pencil	dog–pup
salt–pepper	comb–hair	fire–fireman
hammer–nails	dog–bone	pan–lid

5. Using common prepositions: A large chart published by Ginn and Company (see figure 15.1) to illustrate the ten most common prepositions is useful in first grade where the children are all speakers of English. *In, out, on, between, up, down, over, across, into* and *under* are presented. Special attention needs to be given to the presentation of such prepositions when teaching English to speakers of other languages. The list of common prepositions in children's speech is not long and the teacher can provide opportunity to make sure children have control of many of them:

about	before	from	on	until
across	beneath	in	out	up
after	beside	inside	outside	upon
against	by	into	over	with
along	beyond	like	since	without

6. Finding homonyms, to control use of *both* meanings in oral language:

to–too–two	blew–blue	no–know	through–threw
knew–new	deer–dear	ate–eight	cheap–cheep
our–hour	sale–sail	son–sun	waist–waste
week–weak	he'll–heel	tale–tail	by–buy
read–red	fair–fare	rode–road	right–write

7. Using words with several meanings:

We went to the state *fair* yesterday.
The weather will be *fair* today.
Boys should play *fair*.

The leaves *fall* from the trees in October.
We start to school in the *fall*.
Please *fall* in line! (Take your place.)

There is a *fire* in the furnace.
The soldiers will *fire* at the enemy.
His boss will *fire* him.

Most of the girls wear *bangs*.
Bang! went the gun.
The baby was *banging* the pots and pans together.
(If children volunteer "Tom banged the door" or "Mother says not to bang the door," very good.)

He was cutting the *bark* from the tree.
The dog will be sure to *bark*.

We sat on the river *bank*.
John put his money in a savings *bank*.
(If any children know "Bank the fire" or "Don't bank on that," be sure to praise them.)

8. Completing word association exercises:

You sit on a chair; you sleep on a _____ .
A bird flies; a fish _____ .
Soup is hot; ice cream is _____ .
Feathers are light; stones are _____ .
You have fingers on your hand; you have toes on your _____ .
You can cut with scissors; with a pencil, you can _____ .
A rabbit goes fast; a turtle goes _____ .
A mile is long; an inch is _____ .

9. Practicing word inflections:

I have one apple. There are two *apples*.
Here is a box. Now there are two *boxes*.
This one is long. This one is *longer*.
This one is big. This one is *bigger*.
This one is pretty. This one is *prettier*.
Here is a mouse. There are two *mice*.
Here is a child. There are two *children*.
Here is a goose. There are two *geese*.
I do my work every day. Yesterday I *did* it.
I go to work every day. Yesterday I *went* to work.
I throw the ball to Jack. Yesterday I *threw* it.

10. Testing readiness concepts for quantitative thinking; teachers may use the following list as a guide in informal conversations with beginners and identify which children lack the concepts:

Up and *down*	*Round*	*Kilogram*
Big and *little*	*Rectangle*	*Some*
Before and *after*	*Afternoon*	*Next*
Near and *far*	*Straight*	*One-half* of single objects
Fast and *slow*	*Above*	*Less than* and *more than*
Under and *over*	*Cupful*	*More* and *most*
Thick and *thin*	*Jarful*	*Faster* and *slower*
All and *none*	*Liter*	
Night and *day*	*Meter*	

11. Answering some comprehension questions that help teachers evaluate a child's understanding of concepts:

Why do we have books?
Why do we have stoves?
How old are you?
Where do we put the paper that is no good?
What are two things that you wear on your head?
What tells us what time it is?
Does a house have doors?
What color is the flag?
Is a baby cat a puppy? What is it?
What two things can you do with a pencil?
What things fly?
What animals have long ears?
What do we call a baby dog? cat? goat? hen? cow? sheep?
Where does the bird put her eggs?
What do you see in the sky in the daytime?
When do you need an umbrella?
Can you write with scissors? What can you do with them?
How many days do you come to school in a week?
What are all the things that you can do with a ball?
What does a car have to have to make it go?

12. Using interesting pictures to encourage conversation and discussion. Some of the major publishers of children's textbooks have sets of large pictures emphasizing elementary concepts in social studies, science, and health that can be very useful in this respect. One of the learning aids provided by the Field Enterprises Educational Corporation is a 25″ by 38″ picture with city life depicted on one side and country life on the other. Suggestions for the teacher for use of these pictures are also provided.[13]

13. Making up rhymes. After the teacher illustrates with phrases like "A *pig* can *jig*," and "A *boy* has a *toy*," the boys and girls either make up similar phrases or supply rhyming words:

A goat in a _____ .   A fox in a _____ .   A nose smells a _____ .
A hen in a _____ .   A girl has a _____ .   A horse, of _____ .

Testing Readiness for Reading

Upon completing a program of activities with first graders that includes many different elements of linguistic and cognitive knowledge and skills, the teacher may wish to administer a standardized reading readiness test. Such a test will supplement the teacher's judgment and can be used as a criterion for moving the child into more formal reading activities. It is logical to assume that a readiness test would also predict the child's success in learning to read.

Reading readiness tests currently available have rather serious limitations with respect to accurate prediction of future reading success, however. Reading success in first grade may depend less on cognitive learning than on the affective factors that surround the child's life and the extent of the child's enriched oral language competence. Attention span and experiential background may be factors too, but they are not measured on a readiness test in many cases.

Although the commonly administered readiness tests do not have high validity in predicting reading success for first graders, they may have diagnostic usefulness. Analysis of the errors made on the test may help teachers to plan subsequent exercises for the child.

Commonly used reading readiness tests are the following:

1. *Clymer-Barrett Prereading Battery* by Theodore Clymer and Thomas Barrett (Princeton, New Jersey: Personnel Press, 1969). A prereading test that measures letter recognition, shape completion, sentence-copying, discriminating ending sounds, discriminating beginning sounds, and matching words.

2. *The Metropolitan Readiness Test* by Joanne R. Nurss and Mary E. McGauvran (New York: Harcourt Brace Jovanovich, 1976). A school readiness test for end of the kindergarten year or beginning first grade. In addition to the reading readiness activities, there is a number readiness subtest, and space for a child's drawing of a man. The subtests of reading readiness include: (1) word meaning, (2) understanding sentences, (3) using information, and (4) visual discrimination of pictures.

3. *Harrison-Stroud Reading Readiness Tests* by M. Lucille Harrison and J. B. Stroud (Boston: Houghton Mifflin, 1956). A reading readiness test that may be used in the first grade when the teacher believes the child is ready for reading. It measures visual discriminations, use of context clues, auditory discriminations, use of context and auditory clues, and identification of the letters of the alphabet.

4. *Murphy-Durrell Reading Readiness Analysis* by Helen Murphy and D. D. Durrell (New York: Psychological Corporation, 1965). Six scores may be obtained: sound recognition, letter names both capital and lower case, total of letters named, learning rate, and a total score. It requires two sessions to administer.

5. *Gates-MacGinitie Reading Tests: Readiness Tests* by Arthur Gates and Walter MacGinitie (Boston: Houghton Mifflin, 1969). Eight subscores may be obtained: listening comprehension, auditory discrimination, visual discrimination, ability to follow directions, letter recognition, visual-motor coordination, auditory blending, and word recognition.

Informal Assessment Tools

A variety of assessment tools, other than reading readiness tests, is available to teachers and support persons to help them make decisions about the readiness of children to engage in formal reading activities. The assessment tools provide ways of looking at social and emotional status, cognitive levels, knowledge about print and books, and physical and motor development.

Predicting Reading Failure

De Hirsch, Jansky, and Langford selected ten tests that can be administered at the kindergarten level for determining the child's readiness for formal schooling. These ten tests can be administered in about forty-five minutes by a teacher who is familiar with them. The authors have established critical score levels below which they expect a child will have difficulty.[14] Table 5.1, which shows the critical score levels, was developed by comparing the scores of children who failed in beginning reading with the scores of children who did not fail.

De Hirsch and Jansky found that six tests could identify the failing readers, the slow starters, and the high achievers with respect to school success at the end of the second grade.[15] They were the Bender Gestalt, the drawing of a human figure, auditory discrimination, classifying or putting things in categories, presence of reversals, and word recognition. With limited study and instruction, first grade teachers could evaluate beginning first grade boys and girls on all these abilities and rank them, after some experience, with considerable confidence. Such an endeavor could be a much-needed step toward prevention of failure, because it could set the stage for the diagnostic teaching needed to overcome weaknesses.

De Hirsch and Jansky, concerning early identification of school failure in children, stated:

> Since development is by and large a consistent and lawful process, it seemed safe to assume that a kindergarten child's perceptuo-motor and oral language level would forecast his performance on such highly integrated tasks as reading, writing, and spelling. The tests covered several broad aspects of development: behavior and motility patterning; large and fine motor coordination; figure-ground discrimination; visuo-motor organization; auditory and visual perceptual competence; ability to comprehend and use language; and more specifically, reading readiness.[16]

Table 5.1 Critical score levels on ten kindergarten tests included in the predictive index.

Test	Score Range (Best-Poorest)	Critical Score Level
1. Pencil Use	0–2	0 (level expected for age)
2. Bender Visuo-Motor Gestalt (A, 1, 2, 4, 6, 8)	0–6	1 (at least 5 designs copied correctly)
3. Auditory Discrimination (Wepman)	0–11	1 (X-error)
4. Number of words	594–54	226 words
5. Categories	0–3	0 (all series correctly categorized)
6. Reversals (Horst)	0–9	4 (at least 5 rows correctly matched)
7. Word Matching (Gates)	0–12	3 (at least 9 words correctly paired)
8. Word Recognition I (Pack)	0–2	0 (both words identified)
9. Word Recognition II (Table)	0–2	0 (both words identified)
10. Word Reproduction	6–0	3 (no. of letters reproduced correctly)

From *Predicting Reading Failure: A Preliminary Study of Reading, Writing, and Spelling Disabilities in Preschool Children*, by Katrina de Hirsch, Jeanette Jefferson Jansky, and William S. Langford. Copyright © 1966 by Katrina de Hirsch and Jeanette Jefferson Jansky. By permission of Harper & Row, Publishers, Inc.

The Vineland Social Maturity Scale

The *Vineland Social Maturity Scale*[17] is a scale for measuring social development. The information for checking the scale is obtained by a skillful interview with the parent and may be supplemented by direct observation of the child. The items evaluate self-help, locomotion, communication, self-direction, and socialization in relation to expected normal development in children. A social age is determined by the total number of items passed. A social quotient is obtained by dividing the child's social age by the chronological age. For example, children at age two may be expected to ask to go to the toilet; children at age four may be expected to wash their faces unassisted; and children at age six go to bed unassisted.

This test and the two intelligence tests mentioned above require technical preparation of whoever administers them, so are usually administered by the school counselor, psychologist, or diagnostician.

Ready Steps

Ready Steps is a diagnostic and instructional tool designed to identify those children who need additional language experiences before engaging in formal reading instruction.[18] The diagnostic component is planned to assess auditory discrimination, instructional language, ability to follow directions, listening comprehension, sequencing, oral language development, general vocabulary, categorizing skills, use of oral context, and letter form discrimination. After diagnosis, the teacher may use the other component of *Ready Steps* for instruction. The *Ready Steps Resource Kit* provides a variety of games, activities, records, and books for use by the teacher in building language competence.

The Early Detection of Reading Difficulties

Marie Clay has developed a group of assessment procedures that, taken together, provide a comprehensive diagnosis of the child's early success with print.[19] The most well-known portion of her test materials is *Sand*;[20] often it is administered as an isolated test. This practice is most unfortunate, since much more data on the young reader may be obtained by combining the *Sand* test with the rest of Clay's assessment battery. In *The Early Detection of Reading Difficulties,* the following procedures should be carried out:

1. Taking a running record of oral reading. The teacher may gain information about word recognition generally, directional difficulties, error rate, error behavior, self-correction strategies, and attempts to obtain meaning.
2. Letter identification during which the child is tested on knowledge of both lower- and upper-case forms.
3. Concepts about print, using either the *Sand* booklet or the newer *Stones* booklet. This assessment will be discussed in some detail in the following paragraphs.
4. Word list tests.
5. A standardized reading test.
6. Writing samples along with an inventory of words the child can think of and write. The child is also asked to write from dictation.
7. Writing a story, expected of somewhat more able children.
8. Spelling test.

Clay has long been concerned that many of the difficulties children have in reading stem from a lack of knowledge about how print is organized and misunderstandings of the vocabulary associated with reading. In both the *Sand* and *Stones*[21] booklets, while the child is being read a little story, the teacher asks a series of questions that may reveal the confusions and gaps in the child's knowledge. Twenty-four items are tested, ranging from knowledge of the front of a book and understanding that the print and not the picture is read, to recognition of various punctuation marks and understanding of the concepts of letters and words.

Figure 5.1 shows an example of Clay's *Sand* test. On this page the child is asked where to start reading, which direction one will read, and where one will read after completing the first line. Figure 5.2, also from *Sand,* allows the teacher to determine where the child will begin reading when there is print on facing pages. One may also find out if the child is noticing words that are in the wrong order and words in which the letters are ordered incorrectly. Data from pages 12 and 13 of the test provide the teacher with information concerning how carefully the child is attending to the print on the page. A child who does not notice

I dug a little hole
and the waves
splashed in .

I sat the in hole
and I splashed my with feet .

I sat ni eth hole
and I wondered .
Could a boat float heer ?
Could a whale wsim here ?

the incorrect order of words is not prepared to note the incorrect letter sequences. The child who fails to note the incorrectly written short words is not yet ready to distinguish slight differences in much longer words, as well as other small variations in print.

If the teacher wishes to administer the various tests in *The Early Detection of Reading Difficulties,* it is good to know that the information from the standardized reading test, the various writing samples, the story writing, and the spelling test can be obtained by working with groups of children. The only individual tasks are taking a running record of reading, checking on letter knowledge, administering the *Concepts About Print* assessment, and checking the recognition of individual words. Taking a running record of reading can be done as children read orally during the normal school day, while checking letter knowledge and the recognition of isolated words takes only a few minutes per child and can be done easily over a few days during individual conferences. Only the *Concepts About Print* assessment requires more time, typically about ten minutes. Ten minutes can be found at such times as self-selection, recess or after school, during quiet study, or while the other children are doing independent seatwork. The teacher can obtain a large amount of data on each child within the first month of school.

A number of studies by Downing,[22] Reid,[23] Johns,[24] and Clay[25] suggest that lack of understanding of the technicalities of print and confusions about the technical language used in discussing reading and books may be contributing factors in reading problems. Children may be more confused and disturbed by these kinds of questions than by the kinds of skills and information usually taught. Teachers should be sensitive to the possible vocabulary, directional, and print confusions, and should take time to explain, demonstrate, and answer questions children have about these ideas.

Piagetian Tasks

Several writers, among them Duckworth,[26] Kirkland,[27] and Raven and Salzer,[28] reported possible relationships between reading growth and the attainment of the stage of concrete operations as defined by Piaget. It was suggested that children need to have attained that level of intellectual development to deal with the abstractness of print and with the problems inherent in seeing words as groups of letters that can be decomposed to individual letters, yet regrouped into words and sentences again. Raven and Salzer question whether preoperational thinkers can engage in this form of mental gymnastics successfully.[29]

Assessing the children's intellectual development by asking them to engage in various Piagetian tasks could provide useful information to the teacher of beginning readers. Children might work with balls of clay of equal mass; the shapes are changed by rolling one ball of clay into a"snake" or making it into a "pancake." Usually, preoperational children believe that the mass of clay has been changed because the shape has been changed. Still another task requires the child to observe equal amounts of colored water being poured into containers of various diameters and heights. The preoperational child believes the quantity of liquid changes when the height of the liquid in the glass changes. The child has difficulty taking into account the two variables that must be considered—the height and the width of the container.

Carrying out various Piagetian tasks provides useful information to the teacher of beginning readers.

It is also useful to observe the day-to-day behaviors of the children both at work and at play. Careful observation may reveal evidences of preoperational thought as effectively as will asking children to perform tasks such as those just described.

Summary

This chapter has dealt with the concept of being ready to read and the factors that appear to be important in determining a child's readiness for formal reading instruction. The nature and importance of language and concept development, along with suggestions for the kinds of activities that could facilitate them were discussed. Traditional reading readiness tests were listed and described following comments on the general nature of such tests. In addition to formal readiness tests, other assessment strategies were considered. These included *Predicting Reading Failure, the Vineland Social Maturity Scale, Ready Steps, The Early Detection of Reading Difficulties,* and some Piagetian tasks.

The factors that appear to be important in determining a child's readiness for formal reading are: (1) *physical-neurological factors,* including the ability to see and hear well, visual and auditory discriminatory abilities, length of attention span, willingness to attend, and the presence of specific disabilities that may be neurological dysfunctioning; (2) *emotional and social factors,* such as ability to adjust to and cooperate in the group, adequate attention span, and the possible presence of behavioral disorders; and (3) *intellectual factors,* including cognitive development in relevant knowledge, comprehension, quantitative thinking, word association, story sequence, and extensiveness of vocabulary. It is in the intellectual area that the teacher hopes to develop curiosity about reading and a genuine interest in learning how to read.

It is detrimental to growth to "push" a child into reading before he or she has the prerequisite skills. The most important prerequisite is a functional language background that the child can use in reading. Children who exhibit little interest in reading the printed page need lots of opportunity to use language orally. They need to think and express their thoughts, to solve problems, to tell and guess riddles, to become curious about print, to *see purpose* in making use of reading. A delay in efforts to make children learn words and read from early readers will pay big dividends if the children are working on expanding and enriching their oral language repertoire.

Since chronological age has not been demonstrated as a defensible criterion for enrolling all children in first grade, it becomes very important that the kindergarten and first grade years be used for competent assessment of maturity for the reading process. Learning to read makes use of the child's previous learning, attention span, ability to follow instructions, and attainment in language. The first grade teacher must plan the room organization and language interaction with the class so observations about each child can be made. Does the child:

1. Talk easily and use a big vocabulary to relate experiences?
2. Have a sufficiently long attention span to become engrossed in some tasks for long periods?

3. Become engrossed in activities based entirely on language when the occasion fits?
4. Prefer active games or physical movement, and have difficulty sitting still for very long periods of time?
5. Think and spontaneously answer the teacher's questions with ease?
6. Follow directions and finish the jobs started?
7. Recognize whether sounds are alike or different?
8. Observe well and note salient features?
9. Have motor control in writing his or her name; in following the line?
10. Recognize the left-to-right progression of printed words?
11. Handle books with care?
12. Exhibit a desire to read?

For Further Reading

Clay, Marie. "Exploring with a Pencil." *Theory Into Practice* 16 (December 1977): 334–41.

Dallman, Martha, et al. *The Teaching of Reading,* 6th ed. Chaps. 5A, 5B, pp. 61–106. New York: Holt, Rinehart and Winston, 1982.

Dunn, Lloyd, et al. *Peabody Language Development Kits.* Circle Pines, Minn. 55014: American Guidance Services, 1976.

Durrell, Donald, and Helen Murphy. "A Prereading Phonics Inventory." *The Reading Teacher* 31 (January 1978): 385–90.

Gambrell, Linda, and Robert Wilson. *28 Ways to Help Your Child Be a Better Reader.* Silver Springs, Md.: Reading Education, 1977.

Heilman, Arthur, et al. *Principles and Practices in Teaching Reading,* 5th ed. Chap. 4, pp. 78–112. Columbus, Ohio: Charles E. Merrill, 1981.

Hohmann, Mary, et al. *Young Children in Action.* Chapter 6, pp.147–69. Ypsilanti, Mich.: High Scope Educational Research Foundation, 1977.

Lindfors, Judith. *Children's Language and Learning.* Chapter 8, pp. 201–27. Englewood Cliffs, N.J.: Prentice-Hall, 1980.

Teale, William. "Positive Environments for Learning to Read: What Studies of Early Readers Tell Us." *Language Arts* 55 (November/December 1978): 922–32.

Notes

1. Excerpts from "Jam" from *Bread and Jam for Frances* by Russell Hoban. Text copyright © 1964 by Russell C. Hoban. By permission of Harper & Row, Publishers, Inc.
2. "Choosing Shoes" by Frida Wolfe. Published by Sidgwick & Jackson Ltd. London, England. Reprinted by permission.
3. May Hill Arbuthnot, ed., *The Arbuthnot Anthology of Children's Literature* (Chicago: Scott, Foresman, 1952).
4. Barbara Geismer and Antoinette Suter, *Very Young Verses* (Boston: Houghton Mifflin, 1945).
5. *The Real Mother Goose* (Chicago: Rand McNally, 1944).
6. *The Snellen Chart,* American Optical Company, Southbridge, Mass. *The Eames Eye Test,* Harcourt, Brace, and World; *Keystone Visual Telebinocular Survey Test,* Keystone View Division, Mast Development Company, 2210 East 12th St., Davenport, Iowa 52803.

7. A. Chapanis, "Color Blindness," *Scientific American* 184 (1951): 48–53; F. E. Kratter, "Color Blindness in Relation to Normal and Defective Intelligence," *American Journal of Mental Deficiency* 62 (1957): 436–41.

8. L.H. Hardy and others, *AO H-R-R Pseudo-Isochromatic Plates—A Manual* (Buffalo: American Optical Company, 1957). AO H-R-R Pseudo-Isochromatic plates are available from American Optical Co., Vision Park, Southbridge, Mass. 01550.

9. Arleen L. Olson, "An Experimental Study of the Relationship Between Color Blindness and Reading Achievement in the First Grade" (Master's thesis, The Graduate School, University of New Mexico, 1963).

10. G.B. Shiffman, *The Effects of Color Blindness upon Achievement of Elementary School Males,* Experimental Research Series Report No. 106 (Towson, Md.: Board of Education, 1963).

11. From Warren G. Cutts, *Modern Reading Instruction* (Washington, D.C.: Center for Applied Research in Education, 1964), p. 18. See also Roma Gans, "This Business of Reading," *Progressive Education* 21:70, 72, 93, 94; and Lucille M. Harrison, "Getting Them Ready to Read," *NEA Journal* 40:106–8.

12. Doreen Croft, *Parents and Teachers: A Resource Book for Home, School, and Community Relations* (Belmont, Calif.: Wadsworth, 1979), pp. 31–32.

13. *Farm Life* (1963) and *City Life* (1965) (Chicago: Field Enterprises Educational Corporation).

14. Katrina de Hirsch, Jeanette J. Jansky, and William S. Langford, *Predicting Reading Failure* (New York: Harper & Row, 1966).

15. Katrina de Hirsch and Jeanette J. Jansky, "Early Prediction of Reading, Writing, and Spelling Ability," in *Corrective Reading in the Elementary Classroom,* ed. Marjorie Seddon Johnson and Roy A. Kress, Perspectives in Reading No. 7 (Newark, Del.: International Reading Assn., 1967), p. 50.

16. Ibid., p. 47.

17. E.A. Doll, *Vineland Social Maturity Scale* (Minneapolis: American Guidance Service, 1965).

18. Robert Aukerman, *The Basal Reader Approach to Reading* (New York: Wiley, 1981), pp. 160–62.

19. Marie Clay, *The Early Detection of Reading Difficulties: A Diagnostic Survey with Recovery Procedures* (Auckland, New Zealand: Heinemann, 1979).

20. Marie Clay, *Sand* (Auckland, New Zealand: Heinemann, 1972).

21. Marie Clay, *Stones* (Auckland, New Zealand: Heinemann, 1979).

22. John Downing, "Children's Developing Concepts of Spoken and Written Language," *Journal of Reading Behavior* 4 (1972): 1–19.

23. J. F. Reid, "Learning to Think About Reading," *Educational Research* 9 (1966): 56–62.

24. Jerry Johns, "First Graders' Concepts About Print," *Reading Research Quarterly* 15 (No. 4, 1980): 529–49.

25. Marie Clay, *Reading: The Patterning of Complex Behaviour,* 2d ed. (Auckland, New Zealand: Heinemann, 1979).

26. Eleanor Duckworth, "Language and Thought," in *Piaget in the Classroom,* ed. Milton Schwebel and Jane Raph (New York: Basic Books, 1973), pp. 132–54.

27. Eleanor Kirkland, "A Piagetian Interpretation of Beginning Reading Instruction," *The Reading Teacher* 31 (February 1978): 497–503.

28. Ronald Raven and Richard Salzer, "Piaget and Reading Instruction," *The Reading Teacher* 24 (April 1971): 630–39.

29. Ibid., p. 634.

Teaching Beginning Reading

A Cognitive Map: Teaching Beginning Reading

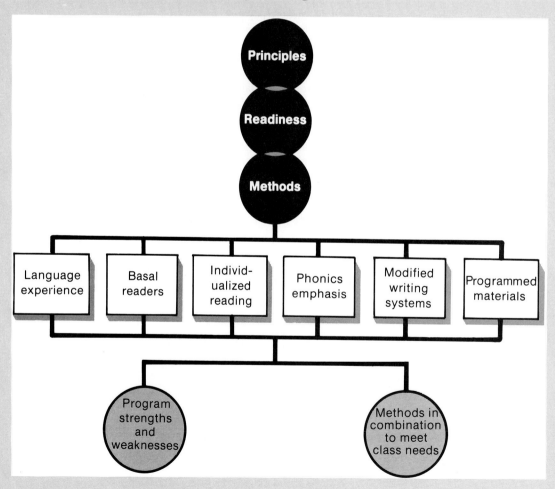

6

Guide Questions

1. What are the important principles that undergird the emergent stage of reading (literacy)?

2. What are the characteristics of the major approaches to the teaching of beginning reading?

3. What are the strengths and weaknesses of each of these approaches?

4. Where does phonics fit into the reading program?

5. What are the values of some of the modified writing systems?

6. How does the computer contribute to reading instruction?

Terminology

basal reader approach

computer instruction

directed reading lesson

emergent stage of reading

experience charts

individualized reading

i/t/a

language-experience approach

phonics-oriented approach

rebus

Without meaning, there is no reading. The process of reading is first and foremost a thinking process, from the very first reading lesson. Of course, the visual perception of words and the ability to call up meanings they represent make word recognition a prerequisite. Word recognition is supported if the child is aware of the predictive nature of the reading process and the system of cues that exists in meaningful text.

How Reading Begins

As explained in the definition of the reading process in chapter 1, the very first lessons in how to read must teach children that *ideas* are contained in the printed symbols. Children need to watch ideas being written down on paper, preserved, and then restated in exactly the way they were stated the first time. To demonstrate this process from the very first lesson, the teacher should work from the children's own experiences. Children utilizing their own grammar to express ideas personal and important to them can then see their stories recorded. All this must happen before they become concerned with the sound-symbol relationships of letters in the words authors have used to provide stories for them to read. They learn *first* how the reading process works.

It must be reemphasized that children of six or seven years bring to school a well-developed language and that they possess all the skills to think and reason orally using that language. A primary responsibility of the teacher is to understand what kind of language a child has. Is it standard English, as used in school textbooks? Is it any one of many nonstandard dialects of English? Is it English spoken with interference from a second language? Or is it a language other than English? If a child's *primary* language can be categorized in any of these areas, the child should be introduced to reading through a language-experience approach using that "kind of language."

The first language-experience reading of a child whose primary language is Spanish should be in the Spanish language. The first language-experience reading of the child who speaks Black English should be in that dialect of English. Similarly, a child who speaks standard English should learn reading *first* in that dialect. (See the diagram suggested by Burke in figure 1.1.)

With every reading lesson, the child needs to relate first to meanings and, next, to the language used to express the meanings. Only then should the child be concerned about analysis of phonic or structural elements. When the teacher's effort is centered on meanings, the child's opportunity to see the task as a whole is enhanced. In all teaching of reading, a primary consideration must be the development of concepts—the translation of concrete experiences into abstractions. In order to be a good reader, one must be able to do abstract and critical thinking.

The concepts required to read successfully must be created by the learners themselves. The more concepts children have, the more interconnections they can make. Schools, then, should be places where children can develop concepts and make connections between them. In reading, children need two levels of concepts: (1) those about the reading process itself that will facilitate reading and (2) those about the content of the material being read. If teachers keep the child at the

Figure 6.1
Model for child-centered, experience-based learning.

From Ethel Buchanan, ed., *For the Love of Reading* (Winnipeg, Manitoba: The C.E.L. Group, Inc., 1980), p. 1.

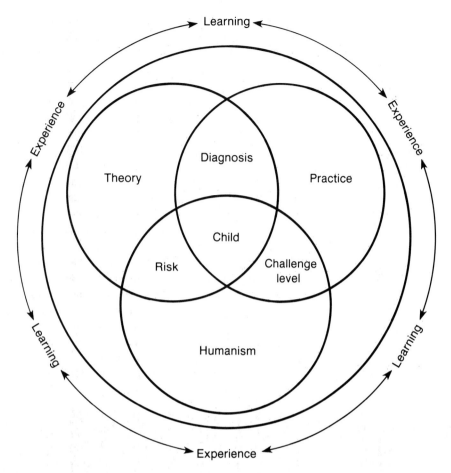

center of planned experiences and the hoped-for learning, and such elements of teaching as theory, diagnosis, practice, challenge, risk, and humanism serve to link the two (see figure 6.1),[1] then they can reasonably believe that they are providing the best opportunities for children to experience genuine learning.

Heath suggests that for all readers there are seven uses of literacy: (1) instrumental—information about practical problems of daily life; (2) social-interactional—information pertinent to social relationships; (3) news-related—information about third parties or distant events; (4) memory-supportive—such written messages as address books or innoculation records; (5) substitutes for oral messages—such messages as notes from parents to explain to their child when they'll be back; (6) provision of permanent record—for example, necessary legal records; and (7) confirmation—support for attitudes or ideas already held.[2]

Heath reports the working philosophy of one first grade teacher:

Reading and writing are things you do all the time—at home, on the bus, riding your bike, at the barber shop. You can read, and you do everyday before you ever come to school. You can also play baseball. Reading and writing are like baseball and football. You play baseball and football at home, at the park, wherever you want to, but when you come to school or go to a summer program at the Neighborhood Center, you get help on techniques, the gloves to buy, the way to throw, and the way to slide. School does that for reading and writing. We all read and write a lot of the time, lots of places. School isn't much different except that here we work on techniques, and we practice a lot—under a coach. I'm the coach.[3]

Harris warns us that children are apt to fail to learn the meaningful nature of reading if teachers spend undue time teaching phonic elements in isolation. If, from the child's first conscious exposure to written language, that language does not communicate, then the chances are high that the beginning reader will get a false idea of the purpose of the reading lesson. Even recently published materials often may present the alphabet or phonic skills or sight words in isolation as immediate goals of learning. It is therefore possible that children will *not* start by demanding meaning in reading, and reading groups may show evidences of boredom and low levels of motivation.[4]

The concept of developing skills sequentially has been adhered to closely in all traditional teaching materials. When children understand the reading process as an extension of their total use of language in communication, beginning with the language-experience approach, rigid sequencing loses its importance from the *child's* standpoint. If we accept two premises—(1) that the child's thinking skills are developed in oral language to a mature degree, and (2) that the language-experience approach to reading is each child's avenue to reading something that is interesting and personal—then we cannot feel bound to teach phonic and structural analysis skills in any rigid sequence. However, it is important to emphasize that the teacher must know the sequence of skills that helps a particular child move from the known to the unknown, from the simple to the complex, from the old to the new. The teacher can thus help the child develop the skill needed *when* it is needed.

Some of the characteristics of a primary reading program are:

1. It extends the communication arts from listening and speaking to reading and writing.
2. It emphasizes the principle that reading is recorded talk, that writing preserves talk.
3. It emphasizes that reading is primarily a thinking process.
4. Its primary objective is that children accumulate a vocabulary of sight words they can use automatically.
5. It teaches appreciation so that children begin early to like to read and to anticipate enjoyment in good books.
6. It does not rely on only one method or technique for learning; a good teacher's methodology is eclectic.
7. It requires interesting, exciting, changing things in the room to read—bulletin boards, displays, labels, questions, current events.
8. It emphasizes that phoneme-grapheme relationships translate symbols into worthwhile ideas.

9. It teaches a variety of approaches to new words so the independent reader can discover new words: configuration, similarity to known words, context clues, picture clues, sounding out, analyzing the word structure.

Children who are mastering a sight vocabulary of some fifty words are already profiting from directed lessons in auditory discrimination of initial consonant sounds. From pictures, they are becoming aware of the beginning sound of "goat," "girl," "goose," and "gun" and labeling it as the *g* sound. They will learn to recognize the visual symbol as soon as they have learned to read a few *g* words in print. As soon as they associate the phoneme (sound as spoken) with the grapheme (letter as written), children can make systematic use of phonics. Most reading series will present a sequenced program in phonic analysis through the sixth grade, with the heaviest dosage in grades two and three. Structural analysis will be taught all the way through public school, but by the end of grade three, children will already have much familiarity with compound words, root words, prefixes, suffixes, and syllables.

Beginning formal reading, then, is the transition from expanding language development, through the acquisition of an acuity in auditory discrimination of English phonemes, to some understanding of the relationships between oral language and print. This understanding should result in knowledge of a basic sight vocabulary of from fifty to one hundred words and some fluency in reading meaningfully. This period in the child's life is sometimes referred to as the emergent stage of literacy.[5] Holdaway writes:

> The vital learnings of this emergent stage of literacy development centre around the tasks of creating a healthy 'literacy set'. . . . Most children enter school with a poorly developed literacy set—they have not mastered the tasks of the emergent reading stage. To pass them through a pre-reading programme which is not oriented towards literacy, and then move them on into early reading before they have developed a strong literacy set, seems very unwise. . . .[6]

Holdaway defines "literacy set" as being composed of motivational factors (high expectations of print), linguistic factors (familiarity with the oral form of the written material), operational factors (strategies for working with print), and orthographic factors (knowledge of the conventions of print).[7]

Readiness

One of the most important things for a teacher of young children to bear in mind always is that six-year-olds show great variability in what they are ready to learn in school. This is true because of the great range in what they already know, in what they can already do, in the length of their attention span, and in what they value as worthwhile.

Classroom practices that are predicated on the assumption that all children of any *given age* are ready to read is false and unfair to *all* children. All teachers have probably observed such sharp differences among children as the following:

The shy, timid, self-absorbed child versus the more aggressive, brave, gregarious child.

The child with no interest in books, print, or learning to write versus the child who pores over pictures and illustrated books, "reading" and creating stories.

The quiet daydreamer versus the loud, obnoxious mixer.

The socialized, demure child versus the eternally curious child.

The undernourished child or the one with little resistance to disease versus the "healthy" child who seems to stay well.

The child who has enjoyed few toys of his or her own versus the child of affluence who has "too many things."

The child whose parent is busy and does not know the responsibilities of parenting versus the one whose parent is patient, takes time, is concerned and helpful and motivating and encouraging.

These individual differences undoubtedly have more bearing on how the great majority of children will respond to future reading experiences than will the results of currently used intelligence and achievement tests.

One wonders why educators have not widely accepted the logical notion that some few children learn to read at three; more learn when they are four; some when they are five; the great majority when they are six; and some few need more time and will learn if permitted to do so when they are seven, or eight, or nine. Learning centers such as described in chapter 7 could make it possible for young children of all stages of readiness to have profitable days at school indefinitely. Those interested in reading may do so, and those who have other needs to be met first are permitted to delay formal reading until a later time.

Methods

Teachers today usually have the option of using six methods of teaching reading, with emphasis distributed as they wish: (1) a language-experience approach; (2) a basal reader approach; (3) an individualized reading approach; (4) an approach based on a modified or special writing system; (5) an approach strongly oriented to phonics, often exemplified by programmed materials or systems approaches; and (6) utilization of microcomputer technology and materials. The strengths and weaknesses of some of these approaches are summarized in tables later in this chapter.

At the same time young teachers are learning methods of teaching reading, they may be introduced to certain dogmatisms. Jastak and Jastak have some pertinent advice to teachers about two particular dogmatisms.

The literature on reading instruction contains various prescriptions as to what children should not be encouraged to do in learning to read. Sometimes such prescriptions are in the form of indirect allusions that children are slowed down when they use certain ways of learning. Among the Taboos are pointing with the finger, moving lips, oral reading, reading without comprehension, spelling aloud before reading, reading without inflection, phonic reading, breaking words up into syllables, etc. These interdictions are taught with complete confidence in their validity without evidence that they are bad habits except that they "slow children down." Furthermore, they are applied as absolute rules to persons of any age and at any point of the learning stage. We have heard of supervisors and reading specialists visiting classrooms for the sole purpose of checking whether any of the children move their lips or point with their fingers while reading. Teachers whose children move their lips are condemned as inferior and are given poor professional ratings. This strange behavior on the part of supervisors and reading experts causes more retardation in reading than any moving of the lips or pointing with the fingers has ever done. It can be demonstrated that some children who point with their fingers read faster and more accurately than when they do not. The fallacy of "being slowed down" stems from the observations that good readers do not point with their fingers but poor readers do. It is known however to students of statistics that correlation is not causation. The poor reader, finding that he loses his way or that his performance is not what it should be, hits upon the device of using his finger to help himself. Pointing with the finger becomes an important temporary aid in overcoming the coordination difficulties that exist in poor readers. Pointing with the finger is not a cause but an effect of reading disability. It is helpful in the early stages of learning to read and is spontaneously abandoned as the skill of reading gains in efficiency.[8]

Language-Experience Approach

In the language-experience approach, the children dictate stories based upon their activities during or after school hours. Experience stories may be individual, small group, or planned and dictated by the class as a whole.

Early in the first grade year a kitten may be brought to school for sharing time. If the group shows enthusiasm, the teacher may catch some of their sentences and make a story on the chalkboard.

A Kitten
Tim has a kitten.
It is all black.
It came to school.
Tim likes his cat.

Or one child may tell the teacher:

My Toys
I have a ball.
I have a wagon.
I have a tractor.
I have a car.
I like to play with them.

The language-experience approach is the most promising method of meeting the reading objectives to help the child relate the written form of language to the spoken form. Experience stories written in the language of the child will demonstrate that reading is useful for remembering things; they will make reading rewarding because they preserve the child's ideas; and they will provide good practice for all the skills required later for more formal reading.

Twenty elements that constitute the language-experience approach to reading are:[9]

Converting experiences to words:
1. Sharing experiences
2. Discussing experiences
3. Listening to stories read
4. Telling stories
5. Dictating
6. Summarizing
7. Making and reading books
8. Writing independently

Studying the words themselves:
9. Developing word recognition skills
10. Developing basic sight vocabulary
11. Expanding English vocabulary concepts
12. Studying words

Recognizing words and relating them to experience:
13. Improving style and form
14. Using a variety of resources
15. Reading a variety of symbols: facial expressions, pictures, calendar, clock, map, road signs
16. Reading whole books
17. Improving comprehension
18. Outlining
19. Integrating and assimilating ideas
20. Reading critically

Writing down the language contributions of a young child is one of the most natural ways of extending the child's learning in the communication arts. The teacher stops at a child's desk and admires a picture the child is making. When the teacher asks about the picture, the child says, "Ducks can swim by pushing their feet." The teacher can say, "Texie, would you like me to write that under your picture?" Of course she would, because the teacher is preserving something personal and valuable to her. The result is presented in figure 6.2.

The kindergarten class goes to the baby animal zoo for a field trip. When they return to the classroom and talk about their trip, the teacher encourages a great deal of discussion—verbalization about whatever topics of conversation are of most interest to the children. By encouraging the children's responses, the teacher may spur each child to express one idea and illustrate it with crayon. As these pictures evolve, the teacher can write a sentence for each child's picture about what it tells. The teacher could then bind all the pictures into a big book for the reading table, which the children may peruse in their free time. Children are apt to remember their own sentences and, although they do not know individual words at this time, they will be able to "read" to the class what their own pictures "say." Children build vocabulary while gaining new ideas, discussing

Texie

Ducks can swim by pushing their feet.

with others, asking questions about things they see, and listening as the teacher talks with the group. Children should be able to acquire a sight vocabulary of approximately one hundred words with this approach. They then have sufficient reading power to read several books with controlled vocabularies.

The heightened effect produced by the teacher arranging to meet individually with each child, albeit for only very short periods, to write down what the child would like to record, develops a sensitivity to oral and written language and encourages the child to be more observant of his or her environment and the language he or she hears, and more impressed with the recording of oral language as a means of preserving ideas.

The language-experience method of operating with small groups or individuals in the classroom has been clearly described in recent publications.[10]

Experience Charts and other Displayed Reading Materials

Experience charts provide the teacher several avenues to language development that are practical and useful in daily activities in the classroom. They can contain: (1) short written accounts of children's experiences that can be read and reread for review; (2) announcements, directions, reminders, or lists of duties; (3) summaries of subject matter discussed; (4) samples of children's creative writing; or (5) plans for the day or for special work periods.[11]

It is important that much of the reading material displayed be needed in order for the child to function in the classroom. This is an important way to create "an environment that demands reading."[12] Some teachers have made a practice of posting important information (changed *each* day) in an obvious place, perhaps the classroom door. The child *must* read the sign in order to know about some event of the day. He or she soon learns the necessity of being able to read in order to function in the environment. The concept that print carries a meaningful message is also stressed. Typical door signs are shown in figures 6.3 and 6.4.

Figure 6.3
Door sign containing important news for children as they arrive at school.

From Halene Weaver, Albuquerque Public Schools, Albuquerque, N.M., 1979.

Tomorrow is our first bus trip. Come and find the sign that tells where we will go.

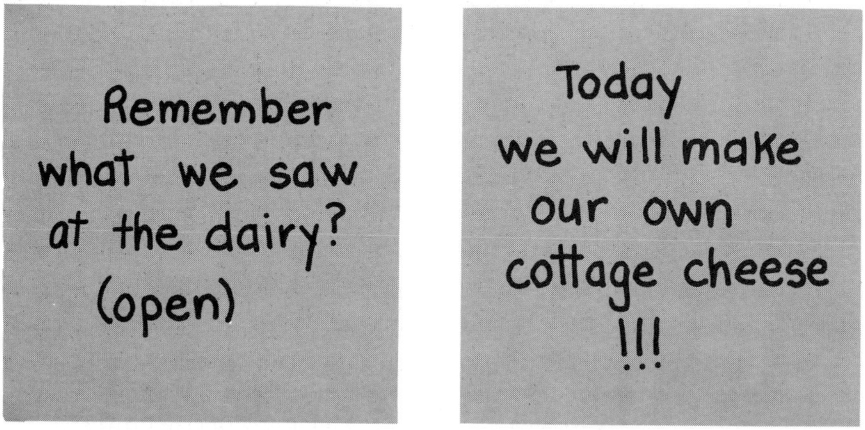

Figure 6.4
A door sign announcing something exciting for the school day. The sign on the right was under the first sign, requiring the child to get involved in order to acquire the whole message.

From Halene Weaver, Albuquerque Public Schools, Albuquerque, N.M., 1979.

Remember what we saw at the dairy? (open)

Today we will make our own cottage cheese !!!

The following outline details the steps for making experience charts.

I. Getting ready to make an experience chart:
   A. The teacher needs to select an experience that has been common to all the children. Many charts can be based on usual happenings in daily school routine. A common experience of the group, such as an excursion, provides a basis for several stories. (See the story "The Ice Plant" dictated by the kindergarten class in figure 6.5.)
   B. After the experience has been selected, it is necessary to develop, through group discussion, the important concepts and to state them in complete sentences.

150

Figure 6.5
Experience stories
dictated by groups of
children.

The Duck Pond

We walked over to the
duck pond.
We found a duck that was
half brown and half white.
Two ducks ran around us.
One was a mallard.
It started biting the
other duck.
We chased him away.

The Ice Plant

We went to the ice plant.
It was awfully cold.
The ice was in big chunks.
We touched it.
We stuck our tongues on it.
We got warm on the bus.

Figure 6.6
Zaner-Bloser
alphabet.

Used by permission of the
Zaner-Bloser Company,
Columbus, Ohio 43215.

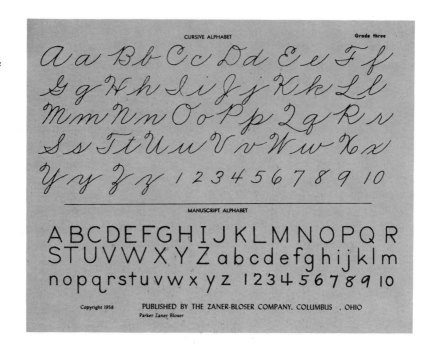

C. The concepts need to be analyzed and organized so that different members of the group will present the concepts in proper chronology.

D. The teacher writes the sentences in the story as they are dictated by the children. Other children in the group may edit sentences or extend the discussion to clarify concepts.

II. The chart should contain:

A. Sentences dictated by individual children.

B. Complete sentences.

C. All sentences "one-line" length in early charts.

D. Ideas clearly and accurately stated.

III. Making the experience chart:

A. Use large size chart paper, 22 by 30 inches or larger. The lines should be spaced three-fourths of an inch apart. Such lined paper is available commercially for primary teachers.

B. Center the title three spaces from top of page.

C. Capitalize only the first letters of words in the title.

D. Leave a two-inch margin on the left and a neat margin on the right.

E. Begin the first line three spaces below the title.

F. Use three spaces for each line of manuscript writing. A middle space is the base line for writing, a space above is for the tall letters and a space below for the letters with stems below. (See *Zaner-Bloser* alphabet, figure 6.6.)

    G. Leave a fourth space for separation of lines of manuscript writing.

    H. Make lines fairly uniform in length, if possible.

    I. When a sentence is too long for one line, be sure to break it between phrases without regard to length of written line. (See story "The Duck Pond".)

After children have read a number of experience stories, the teacher can identify the basic sight words that have been used several times and prepare *reading charts* using the names of the children in the room. This provides some interesting practice for overlearning the most used words in primary reading.

Teachers should practice appropriate editorial skills so that charts will be finished with both good form and good content. They can be displayed in the room bound into books and reused at later times. Some of the editorial skills include organization on the page, line arrangement, spacing, the use of pictures, editing, and expanding to include additional information when indicated. An excellent handbook outlining the range of uses for, the preparation of, and the rationale for experience charts is *Using Experience Charts with Children* by Herrick and Nerbovig.[13]

Lamoreaux and Lee wrote:

In general, . . . certain principles can be drawn which distinguish good charts. First, each chart must serve the purpose it is intended to serve, and, over a period of time, charts should serve a variety of purposes. They should be simple and unified. They should be suited to the ability of the children for whom they are intended. There should be adequate word control. The mechanics should be good, the print clear and large enough, and the lines well spaced. The sentences should be correctly phrased in thought units and indented in regular paragraph form.[14]

| Rebus Reading | Rebuses are symbols, usually pictures, that represent words. Pictorial rebuses make possible the reading of simple stories before children learn to pronounce all the words that would be used. Hopefully, the author can prepare a more interesting story if he or she is not so severely limited with words in the reader's sight vocabulary. |

If the child can rely on the rebus, he or she can: (1) give more attention to meaning; (2) avoid frustration with abstract symbols he or she may not know; and (3) get absorbed in the story a little more quickly. Rebuses are used occasionally in children's magazines to "entertain" young readers. They are used in preprimers for young children to accommodate the use of words not yet mastered as sight vocabulary. See figure 6.7.

Research and Writing

The research and writing method is useful for later grades, as the language-experience method is useful for beginning readers.

Good writing skills strengthen reading power. Of course, all of the four skills of communication—listening, speaking, reading, and writing—are interrelated. Optimal communication skill requires that they all function well. But the research and writing way to reading, when well motivated, has especially great value. It is the most useful means of expanding horizons—and, indeed, is used throughout a child's school career.

Especially when used in elementary school, the research and writing method requires that the teacher be sophisticated in what word-recognition and comprehension skills the children need and how best to teach them. An experienced teacher who feels confident about the skills and work habits children need can encourage development of these skills and work habits through work produced by the children themselves. Of course, such a program is supplemented with a great deal of reading, including basal readers. But the primary objective is for the children themselves to produce stories, articles, and small illustrated books

Mary went on the bus.
Mary saw the 🦒 .
Billy went to the zoo.
Billy saw the 🐘 .

John went to the zoo.
John saw the 🦁 .
Jean went to the zoo.
Jean saw the 🐫 .

Figure 6.7
Example of a story
dictated after a zoo
trip, using rebuses to
replace animal names.

worth reading. Such a program is also dependent upon a teacher who has a broad knowledge of children's literature so that children will be encouraged to pursue their own individualized reading programs.

The Basal Reader Approach

Some basal readers have been heavily criticized as shallow, repetitive, and uninteresting. In the recent past, basal readers did not present life realistically for children not from a middle-class culture. Even now they may not motivate those children who bring to school divergent cultural experiences, especially if the stories portray the comfortable life of children from the middle-class neighborhood. However, the recent editions of basal readers seem to present an improved representation of minorities, other cultures, and divergent life styles.

Basal reader materials generally are a series of books and auxiliary materials designed to stimulate systematic development of reading abilities. Basal reading series provide (1) carefully sequenced presentation of skills, (2) continuity of all skills through the grades, and (3) integration of materials and skills to facilitate independent learning. Series are usually organized to provide gradual progression to more difficult steps and gradual broadening of children's conceptions of social organization, vocabulary, word analysis skills, and evaluative abilities.

If a child cannot recognize a word, probably the child will have difficulty gathering meaning from a sentence containing it. For very young children beginning the reading process, it is safe to assume that if they cannot pronounce a word, they will not be able to get the full meaning of a sentence in which it appears. Therefore, reading programs generally try to teach children to recognize a small stock of sight words so they can extract meaning from the very first books of a reading series. Some first preprimers will have no more than twenty different words. The significant point is that a child will, with this limited stock of words, read meaningful sentences and little stories for which the teacher will ask guide questions and build story plots. And from the beginning, the teacher will request children to "read with their eyes and not with their lips" so that they will form the habit of recognizing all the words in a sentence and then practice saying them as they might speak instead of reading word-by-word slowly and with observable difficulty.

Stone has identified the one hundred words used most in early reading in first-grade basal reading programs. (They are listed in chapter 9.) These words must be learned as sight words. They do provide a core of service words to be used in a great deal of easy reading practice.

Dolch made a list of *service* words most needed by children in all textbook reading in the elementary school. The list of 220 words contains no nouns and constitutes about *two-thirds* of all the words read by children in first and second grade books and *half* of all the words read by boys and girls in fourth, fifth, and sixth grade books. Since they appear over and over in all elementary reading, knowing them as sight words is crucial for all readers. The first 300 words of the Fry "instant words" list include the service words that appear most often in children's reading. This list, found in chapter 9, contains almost all of the Dolch words.

Salisbury has pointed out that stories that focus on American middle-class children and their interests may not be applicable in many areas of our country, in binational schools outside the United States, and in other outlying areas.[15] This condition makes it even more difficult to write interestingly with a drastically limited vocabulary.

Nevertheless, for the *beginning* teacher who must meet the demands of all the children in the classroom each day, basal readers provide gradual introduction of skills, necessary repetition, ready-made seatwork, and tests. In other words, basal texts make it possible for inexperienced teachers to offer a well-worked-out reading program to a class.

Usually there are readiness materials—often in the form of a workbook for the child, three preprimers introducing the first sight vocabulary, a primer or two, and a first reader for the first grade reading program. In second and third grades, there are usually two books for each grade—for example, *second grade, semester one* and *second grade, semester two*. For all of these books, publishers provide workbooks of exercises and teachers' editions of the readers or separate manuals. More recently, in an attempt to eliminate grade level distinctions, publishers have renumbered the books in basal reader series. The first six books might constitute the grade one program; then numbers seven through ten would be for the grade two program; eleven and twelve, the grade three program; and thirteen, fourteen, and fifteen, for grades four, five, and six, respectively.

Under the impetus of the Elementary Secondary Education Act (ESEA), Title I, which made federal money available for purchase of materials, publishers have provided text films, filmstrips, recordings, word and phrase cards, and many supplementary reading materials.

Many publishers of reading series also provide supplementary aids for teachers: placement tests for each level of achievement; mastery tests for each level of achievement; sets of overhead transparencies for skill development; reading time books; tape cassettes; spirit duplicating masters; and teacher materials for additional learning aids.

Estimates of school systems using reading series as basal readers run as high as 90 percent with many schools recommending a second and third series as co-basal and tri-basal. Basal readers also provide much material for supplementary reading.

After young teachers have taught basal reading programs and learned the skills sequences, they need to organize their own resources and venture more broadly into language-experience approaches and/or individualized reading programs. Needless to say, the confidence of teachers in their ability to carry out a competent program is the first requisite. Until they feel confident that they understand the many word-recognition and comprehension skills that children need for reading in today's world, they must adhere to an organized program that will insure success for the children they teach. Their goal must be to see children as individuals, and their approach to teaching must be diagnostic with respect to the learning needs of each one.

Many major publishers now provide reading series for use all through the elementary grades and the middle school or junior high school:

Allyn & Bacon: *Pathfinder,* K–6, 1978. Robert B. Ruddell, senior author.

American Book Company: *The American Readers,* K–8, 1980. No one senior author.

Economy Company: *Keys to Reading,* K–8, 1980. Louise Matteoni, Wilson Lane, Floyd Sucher, and Versie Burns, authors.

Ginn and Company: *Rainbow Edition, Reading 720 Series,* K–8, 1980. Theodore Clymer, senior author.

Harcourt Brace Jovanovich: *The Bookmark Reading Program,* K–8, 1979–80. Margaret Early, senior author.

Harper & Row: *Reading Basics Plus,* K–8, 1980. No one senior author.

Holt, Rinehart and Winston: *Holt Basic Reading,* K–8, 1980. Bernard Weiss, senior author.

Houghton Mifflin: *Houghton Mifflin Reading Program,* K–8, 1981. William Durr, senior author.

Laidlaw Brothers: *Laidlaw Reading Program,* K–8, 1980. William Eller and Kathleen Hester, senior authors.

Lippincott: *Basic Reading,* K–8, 1981. Charles Walcutt and Glenn McCracken, senior authors.

Macmillan: *Series r: Macmillan Reading,* K–8, 1980. Carl Smith and Ronald Wardhaugh, senior authors.

Charles E. Merrill: *Merrill Linguistic Reading Program,* K–6, 1980. Rosemary G. Wilson and Mildred K. Rudolph, major authors.

Open Court Publishing Co.: *The Headway Program,* K–6, 1979. Different authors at each level.

Riverside Publishing Co.: *Rand McNally Reading Program: Young America Basic Series,* K–8, 1981. Leo Fay, senior author.

Scott, Foresman: *Scott, Foresman Reading,* K–8, 1980. Ira Aaron, senior author.

The Basal Reader Program: The Directed Reading Lesson

A directed reading lesson requires more time than many new teachers realize. Such a lesson may be introduced and the guided silent reading completed during one period. It can be recalled and finished in a second session. Some stories need more time than others, and some lessons may be guided during one period with the teacher and then finished independently. The teacher's manual will include for each lesson one or two specific skills to be stressed—phonic analysis, structural analysis, comprehension, or interpretation. Manuals also afford many opportunities for teachers to evaluate children's development in the affective as well as the cognitive areas.

A guided reading lesson usually follows five sequential steps.[16] These are:

1. Motivating an interest in the lesson by:
   a. Studying the pictures that illustrate the story;
   b. Talking about new or unusual words in the story;
   c. Relating the ideas in the story to the background of experience of the class.
   d. Setting up a purpose for reading, i.e., reading to find out something.

2. Teaching new vocabulary and reviewing words "that cause trouble" by:
   a. Presenting new words in meaningful ways;
   b. Practicing flash card drills;
   c. Playing games that teach or give practice matching, comparing, arranging, etc., the basic vocabulary.
3. Guiding the silent reading of the lesson by:
   a. Asking guide questions so that pupils read to find specific information;
   b. Completing the story section by section with attention to understanding the plot of the story;
   c. Checking pupils' understanding as indicated throughout the story.
4. Interpreting the story by:
   a. Reading orally conversation parts;
   b. Reading orally favorite parts;
   c. Retelling the ideas in the story in proper sequence;
   d. Reading sentences or paragraphs to answer specific questions or to evaluate pupil's opinions;
   e. Evaluating the happenings in the story with such questions as:
      (1) Would you have done what Bob did? or
      (2) Is this true or only imaginary?
5. Providing related activities (follow-up) by:
   a. Using seatwork exercises to give:
      (1) Further practice on vocabulary;
      (2) Attention to phonic and structural skills;
      (3) Comprehension checks.
   b. Extending the lesson through:
      (1) Free reading at the book table;
      (2) Searching encyclopedias for additional information;
      (3) Art work, writing, dramatization as related to the lesson;
      (4) Shared oral reading in small groups.

Most reading lesson plans follow similar outlines. The teacher will attempt to motivate an interest in reading the story; teach the new vocabulary and review difficult words; guide the silent reading of the story and discuss the content; interpret the story through questioning or rereading parts; and provide related activities as a follow-through for the lesson.

Motivating an Interest

Thumbing through the pages may show that the story is accompanied by colored illustrations that reveal incidents in the story that can be discussed. The teacher may have related pictures from the materials center, or may talk about new or unusual words in the story, or perhaps raise questions to guide children's thinking. The incident around which the story is built needs to be related to the experience of the class so the children can decide whether it is fact or fiction, real or imaginary. Finally, the teacher must establish a purpose for reading. The child starts reading to "find out something."

Making Sure of Vocabulary	New words should be presented in context and discussed so that they are meaningful to the boys and girls. The words can then be reviewed with flash card drills or games that give practice in matching, comparing, or using them in sentences. Children should be led to discover new words for themselves if they have sufficient word analysis skills to do so. If they use their skills to unlock new words, there will be fewer and fewer strange words to present as they gain in reading independence.
Guiding the Silent Reading	In the first books, very young children need to be guided sentence by sentence or section by section to make sure they are learning that the words on the page are telling them something, just as a conversation using these words would. Guide questions should be specific enough to cause children to look carefully for specific information. As children gain in reading power, they can read longer and longer parts of stories without detailed teacher guidance. In the intermediate grades, students reading at grade level should be able to read the entire story after adequate preparation and after the purpose is established.
Interpreting the Story	It is important for the teacher to ask questions to make sure the reader understood the story, but that is only a minor part in evaluation. Understanding the sequence of events and what the author said is prerequisite to using the story information for evaluation of ideas requiring judgment, reasoning, and analysis of values.

Most teachers' questions have tended to fall in the memory and translation (paraphrase) levels, according to Bloom's taxonomy (see chapter 2).

While memory and translation questions are necessary to establish common understandings and sequence of story events, it is at the higher, integrative, levels of thinking that interpretation, reflection, application, and evaluation can be developed. As teachers require application, analysis, and evaluation of ideas read, they more closely approach the affective life of the child and require him to reflect on his acceptance of, preference for, and commitment to *values*. There is opportunity for the teacher to use the story as a basis for interpreting other happenings in the light of the children's values. The teacher could analyze at the children's level why the author ended the story as he or she did. Or the teacher could help the children see analogies between the story and actual happenings in their lives or community. Original thinking can be evoked with such questions as "What would you have done if you had been in Bob's shoes?" or "What would have been a more realistic ending for this story?"

Providing Related Activities	Related cognitive activities include comprehension exercises, further work on vocabulary, or practice of phonic or structural analysis skills. Related affective activities require children to connect story incidents to their own experiences and feelings. Children learn that ideas are not *all* right or *all* wrong, *all* good or *all* bad, or *all* true or *all* false; that they have shades of meaning that relate to personal attitudes and position in time and space.

The lesson may be extended through the search for additional information in general references, free reading at the book table, or shared oral reading.

When teachers use basal readers, children who have similar reading abilities are frequently grouped together for instruction.

Individualized Reading

The recognition that reading is an active, thinking process—a complex developmental process—an individual, personal experience—has led to changing concepts of teaching reading in the schools. One response that has evolved from this change is commonly called *individualized reading*. Individualized reading programs show an effort, at least, to let children proceed at their own rates of learning and select the material they want to read. Individualized reading is a broad approach, not entirely new to many competent teachers, and not limiting or restricting insofar as other reading activities are concerned.

Recreational reading is not individualized reading. Recreational reading is easy reading practice to develop greater fluency, to learn that reading is fun, and that there are lots and lots of interesting books.

Individualized reading promotes the principles of self-motivation, self-selection, self-pacing, and self-evaluation. Teachers achieve their objectives in such a program if the children are learning independence in purposeful reading and building lasting reading interests.

In order to initiate a system of self-motivation, self-selection, and self-pacing of reading for each member of the class, it is necessary that the following criteria be met:

1. The classroom provides a variety of all types of reading to meet the needs, interests, and abilities of all the members of the group. Administering and evaluating informal reading inventories for each individual is the best way to obtain this information.
2. Types of reading materials include (a) trade books (library books) of adventure, animals, family life, humor, mystery, history, travel, science, folktales, myths and legends, biography, and poetry; (b) basal and supplementary readers; (c) standard reference books; and (d) newspapers and magazines.

In an individualized reading program, children select their own reading materials.

3. The teacher either takes sufficient time with the group to work out purposes, methods of operating, and ways of reporting or arranges for part of the group to continue with traditional ways of working while one subgroup at a time is introduced to the process of self-selection and independent study.

4. A system of assigning or checking out books needs to be devised so that it is monitored entirely by selected members of the group. This process must continue while the teacher works with other aspects of the program.

5. The reading program should be planned with a week as the basic unit of time. For example, perhaps each child is assured of at least one individual conference each week with Monday, Tuesday, and

Figure 6.8
A sample weekly
schedule for individual
reading conferences.

Group	Monday	Tuesday	Wednesday	Thursday	Friday
I	Conferences 45 min.	Silent reading	Skills exercises	Silent reading and reporting	Weekly Reader 30 min. and reporting 30 min.
II	Silent reading	Conferences 45 min.	Silent reading and reporting	Skills exercises	Weekly Reader 30 min. and reporting 30 min.
III	Skills exercises	Silent reading and reporting	Conferences 45 min.	Silent reading	Weekly Reader 30 min. and reporting 30 min.
IV	Silent reading and reporting	Skills exercises	Silent reading	Conferences 45 min.	Weekly Reader 30 min. and reporting 30 min.

Wednesday being the individual conference days. If there are thirty children in one room, an average of ten conferences must be held each day. If the conferences average from three to ten minutes each, it may be possible for the teacher to hold ten conferences in one reading hour. Some teachers would prefer to have only six conferences on each of the five days and utilize some time each day for a group discussion or special reports given to the whole class.

Scheduling must be sufficiently flexible that any child with a special problem can have a conference the day it is needed. Teachers will be able to note certain skills that more than one child needs to improve; the teacher can form them into a group then and teach these skills.

Some attention must be given to specific work on skills, and the teacher may wish to draw upon programmed materials other than basal reading workbooks for this work. How the teacher plans to keep large numbers of children busy while giving attention to one at a time will be discussed in chapter 7.

While some teachers plan one specific day in the week for skills enrichment, others plan for students to work on skills on two or three days during the week, although the teacher may discuss them with the group on only one day. (See figure 6.8.)

Figure 6.9
A diary record for
individualized reading.

	Std. Tst.		
Name: _____	Score: _____	Date: _____	Grade: ____

September
25:

Is reading *Little House in the Big Woods*. Visited the Laura Ingalls Wilder home in Missouri in the summer. Thoroughly enjoys the story. Will plan a report on Friday recommending it to others. Is beginning SRA: RFU with card No. 26 (Gr. Pl. 5.7).

October 2:

Is working with Betty on a special display and report about the Wilder books and the Wilder Home Museum.

October 9:

Figure 6.9 suggests one method of record-keeping. The teacher keeps a five-by-eight-inch card for each child on which to make notes in brief diary form. The teacher will try to record such observations as: "misses many basic sight words in reading," "cannot divide words into syllables," "had a book that was a bit too difficult this morning," "gets implied meanings well."

Individualized reading implies that children are not in a reading circle in front of the teacher, but are at their desks or at tables with books they have selected. They receive help from the teacher or a helper only when they ask for it. There will be a time to share with the others what they have read, but some skills the children need in order to grow in reading independence will be taught to subgroups as occasions arise.

The social interaction in a class with subgroups can teach children that one group is *average,* one group is *inferior,* and one group is *superior.* It is argued that this problem does not exist with individualized reading. This is only partially valid. It would *not* be a serious problem in regularly assigned groups *if* children understood why they were reading far below grade level, *knew* that they were making good growth at that level, and *felt* they would be rehabilitated.

Knowing that the range of ability within any group of thirty children may have a spread of five to seven grade levels, the teacher uses interest and specified routine to allow children to conduct their own free reading practice. Children read what they *want* to read. They learn how to choose books, how to handle the books, how to come and go in the room, how to get help when it is needed; that is, they learn to function independently. The individualized conferences provide opportunity for the teacher to keep a check on sight vocabulary in the primary grades. If the book is at a child's instructional level, the child will not meet too many *hard* words. The teacher will pronounce the words the child doesn't know and provide opportunities for the child to read these words in many situations. If children are selected to be helping teachers, they will tell words to those who need more assistance.

To help children become acquainted with a wide variety of books, the teacher might encourage the class to share them with and advertise them to one another in interesting ways. The children thus, incidentally, have opportunities to show their ingenuity and creative ability in art, writing, dramatic arts, and other fields while stimulating each other to read more books of good quality.

A *Practical Guide to Individualized Reading* is an excellent source book for teachers.[17] Carlton and Moore raise a list of pertinent questions for the classroom teacher to consider:[18]

1. What is individualized reading?
2. What is the teacher's responsibility?
3. What is the best time to begin an individualized program?
4. Are there any special materials needed for an individualized reading program?
5. How does a teacher acquire enough materials for an individualized reading program?
6. How does a teacher know which books to give a pupil?
7. How can a teacher be sure a child is reading at the level where he should be?
8. Can children be expected to select their own reading material wisely?
9. How do pupils develop a basic vocabulary in an individualized reading program?
10. How are word recognition skills incorporated into individualized reading programs?
11. What is the advantage of using individualized reading instead of the basal reader approach?
12. How does the teacher evaluate pupil progress in an individualized reading program?
13. Why do some studies show little difference in results between individualized reading programs and the more traditional approach of using basal reading with the groups?
14. What are some of the advantages of the individualized reading approach?

Experienced teachers will probably plan a reading program in such a way that more emphasis is given to individualized reading and language-experience reading than to using a basal reader. However, at times they need to rely on the stories in basal readers for group reading practice—for instance, when library books are returned and not reissued on time, or when language-experience writing is not serving a purpose. Teachers need many techniques to maximally develop all children requiring individual programs.

The language-experience, basal, and individualized approaches to reading each have different underlying theoretical bases and distinguishing characteristics. In figures 6.10, 6.11, and 6.12, each approach or program is described in terms of these characteristics.

Figure 6.10
A reading program emphasizing students writing text material.

Corrective Reading

Corrective reading is the remedial work done by the regular class teacher to help children develop sequentially their reading skills—filling in what has been missed and relearning what has been forgotten.

Programmed Texts

Sequenced skill development is well worked out in: *Programmed Reading* and *Programmed Remedial Reading* (McGraw-Hill): SRA *Reading for Understanding* and SRA Elementary Labs; EDL *Study Skills; Standard Test Lessons in Reading* and *Practice Exercises in Reading* (Teachers College Press.)

The Research and Writing Way to Reading

Through a series of planned lessons in keeping written records of their work—for example, of the fifth grade year—the primary reading job could be the production of stories and well illustrated books related to the fifth grade course of study for the school year.

For beginning readers, this is a language-experience approach to reading: talking about interesting or common experiences and then writing about them; building sequences of such stories into interesting little booklets; also reading carefully written reading charts that repeat vocabulary learned.

Individualized Reading

Self-motivation, self-selection, and self-pacing are the key words in helping children develop individual reading habits. Each child reads what he or she enjoys, wants to learn about, and finds useful.

Lots of trade books and some kind of reading record are important.

Basal Readers

The teacher organizes small groups and uses basal readers to teach skills. This is especially necessary for students in any grade whose instructional level of reading is third grade or below.

Interesting stories in readers should be shared as oral reading practice.

Figure 6.11
A reading program based primarily on the use of basal readers and teachers' guides.

Corrective Reading

Corrective reading is the remedial work done by the regular class teacher to help children develop sequentially their reading skills—filling in what has been missed and relearning what has been forgotten.

Language-Experience Reading

Utilizing learning experiences in reading helps the beginner understand that reading is talk written down, and that written down, it is preserved and can be read back.

Older boys and girls can utilize and extend writing skills by well illustrated booklets about the units of work they are doing in school.

Basal Readers

A basal reader approach with reading groups provides the new teacher with direction, well planned lessons, and source materials.

This well planned framework will give teachers security; as they learn through experience what constitutes an adequate program, they will gain self-confidence.

Through the year, as varying levels of ability and different kinds of reading problems become apparent, the teacher will move toward more individualizing of children's work.

Individualized Reading

Self-motivation, self-selection, and self-pacing are the key words in helping children develop individual reading habits. Each child reads what he or she enjoys, wants to learn about, and finds useful.

Lots of trade books and some kind of reading record are important.

Special Reading Activities

Dramatizing parts of stories.

Collecting information about books; making book week displays; studying favorite authors.

Using reading games and puzzles.

Using standard references.

167

Figure 6.12
A reading program based primarily on the individualized reading approach.

Individualized Reading

Requires resources of a well stocked school library. Minimum of 100 selected books in the classroom at one time—to be changed each month—range of difficulty to fit the entire class.

Most books will be trade books, but good stories in readers are fine too. Minimum of one individual conference weekly; both child and teacher keep records. Must provide opportunity for class reporting, discussing, and evaluating.

Basal Readers

The teacher organizes small groups and uses basal readers to teach skills. This is especially necessary for students in any grade whose instructional level of reading is third grade or below.

Interesting stories in readers should be shared as oral reading practice.

Corrective Reading

Corrective reading is the remedial work done by the regular class teacher to help children develop sequentially their reading skills—filling in what has been missed and relearning what has been forgotten.

Programmed Texts

Sequenced skill development is well worked out in *Programmed Reading* and *Programmed Remedial Reading* (McGraw-Hill); SRA *Reading for Understanding* and SRA Elementary Labs; EDL *Study Skills*; *Standard Test Lessons in Reading* and *Practice Exercises in Reading* (Teachers College Press.)

Language-Experience Reading

Writing original stories; writing illustrated content lessons; reporting.

Figure 6.13
Phonics, as traditionally presented, will be helpful only at the word-perception level in demanding meaning in the reading process.

Reading is a process of thinking, evaluating, judging, imagining, reasoning, and problem-solving.

1
Word Perception (ability to pronounce the words)

Approaches That Are Strongly Phonics-Oriented

Many phonics systems have been published through the years to provide children with methods of decoding printed words for reading. Fifty years ago the Beacon Charts were widely used to teach children many isolated sounds and then to provide practice in integrating these sounds into family endings and sight words.[19]

Usually the pages in the primers contained sentences unrelated to each other. They were prepared for the specific purpose of giving the child a number of repetitions in pronouncing the phonic element being taught.

Today phonics is not considered a *method* of teaching reading. Phonics is a very necessary skill in word analysis and word identification. As emphasized throughout this text, this is not *reading*. With respect to Gray's four-step definition—"Reading is perception, comprehension, reaction, and integration"— phonics can possibly be of help only with the first step. Of course it is necessary to perceive words before reading can take place, but perceiving what words are is not reading. This is illustrated in figure 6.13, which repeats the circle presented in figure 1.2, but with only one quadrant identified to show that word perception helps the child only with the first quarter of the circle.

Any child who has low word-recognition abilities after being taught developmental reading might profit from some instruction specifically in phonic skills. Such workbooks as those provided by Rand McNally, *Phonics We Use,* and by McCormick Mathers, *Building Reading Skills,* are useful.

Some phonic systems intended for classroom use are:

Programmed Reading, McGraw-Hill.

The Phonovisual Method, Phonovisual Products, Inc., 4708 Wisconsin Avenue, N.W., Washington, D.C.

The SRA Basic Reading Series, Workbooks Level A, B, C, D, E, Science Research Associates, Chicago, Illinois.

Modified Writing Systems

The Initial Teaching Alphabet

The Initial Teaching Alphabet has forty-four symbols instead of the conventional twenty-six. Each of the forty-four symbols represents only one sound. The i/t/a is basically phonemic rather than phonetic. Capital letters in i/t/a are only larger duplicates of the small letter. Thus, instead of small letters in manuscript and capital letters in manuscript, then small letters in cursive and large letters in cursive, the beginning reader has to learn only forty-four symbols that always stay the *same.*

While the vowel sound in the word *pie* is called a long *i,* that same sound can be spelled many different ways in other words in traditional orthography. Not in i/t/a. This sound is spelled the same in *buy, sigh, aisle, island, kite,* etc.

Most children are ready to make the transition from i/t/a to traditional orthography by the end of the first grade. The traditional basal readers rewritten into i/t/a would serve no purpose since i/t/a vocabulary is not as severely controlled. The traditional reading program is apt to introduce the child to only 350 words the first year but i/t/a may introduce that many words in a few weeks. Once children learn the sounds and realize they remain constant, they can read much more widely much more quickly.[20] The alphabet in i/t/a and a few sentences written with the i/t/a alphabet are shown in figures 6.14 and 6.15.

Use of the Rebus in Beginning Reading

The Peabody Rebus Reading Program, American Guidance Services, Inc., Circle Pines, Minnesota 55014, is a method of using pictographs so a child can read a sentence without all the English words being presented in their printed form. With the rebus technique, pupils first learn to read pictures of objects that stand for words (rebuses). They can thus direct their first learning efforts to how the reading process works. After learning to read the rebuses and understanding the way the reading process works, the pupils proceed through a controlled transition process in which spelled words are substituted for the pictures.

Either rebus or structured phonics materials may be especially appropriate for emotionally disturbed or neurologically impaired children who need to work in tightly structured situations, sheltered from the confusion of many other children working near them (see figure 6.16).

These systems are not intended to take the place of a regular reading program that expands sight vocabulary, develops meaning vocabulary, and provides a great deal of easy reading practice. They should be used as parallel teaching materials.

Figure 6.14
Pitman's Initial
Teaching Alphabet,
with its 44 symbols
and words illustrating
the sounds these
symbols represent.

Reproduced by permission
of Initial Teaching
Alphabet Publications, Inc.,
New York, N.Y.

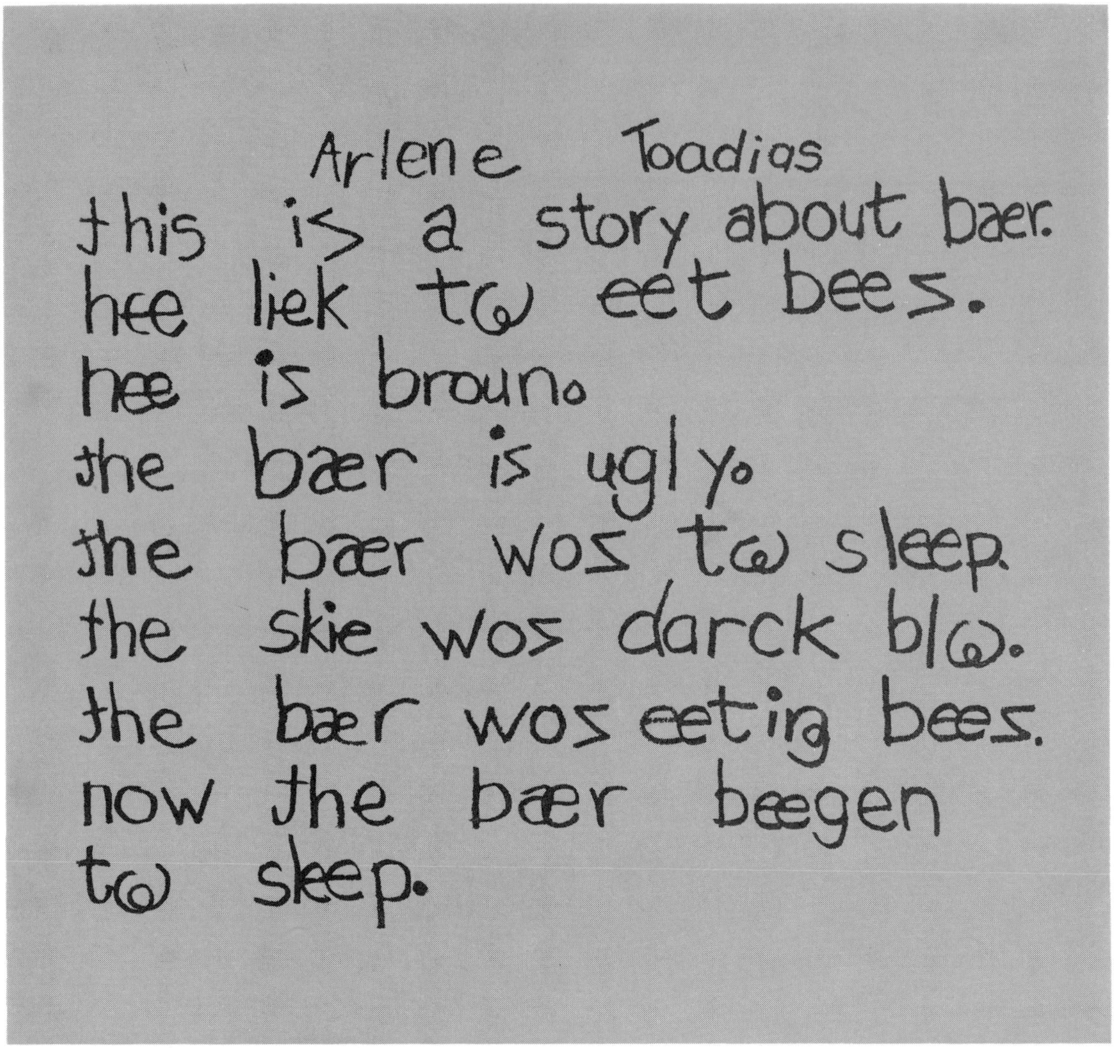

Arlene Toadias

this is a story about bær.
hee liek tω eet bees.
hee is brouno
the bær is uglyo
the bær wos tω sleep.
the skie wos darck blω.
the bær wos eeting bees.
now the bær beegen
tω sleep.

Figure 6.15
This first grader wrote
a story about a bear in
i/t/a.

Programmed Reading Materials

Teachers should have available many exercises that teach developmental reading and study skills. The SRA Reading Laboratories,[21] the EDL Laboratories,[22] *New Practice Readers,*[23] and *McCall-Crabb Test Lessons in Reading*[24] are some of these. Kits such as these make it possible for sophisticated teachers to assemble individualized developmental reading programs as diversified as they are capable of directing. Under the impetus of the Elementary Secondary Education Act, Title I, with large amounts of money available to help purchase materials, publishers have provided text films, filmstrips, recordings, word and phrase cards, and many other supplementary reading materials.

However, teachers are cautioned that very phonemically oriented materials that require extensive and continued phonics practice as programmed exercises or independent seatwork are profitable only under the close supervision of skilled teachers. Schools are ill-advised to spend large sums of money on systems primarily based on teaching the decoding process.

Micro-Computer Instruction

An addition to the available approaches and materials for reading instruction is the microcomputer. To date, most of the materials prepared for use with the microcomputer have been lessons on decoding and lower-level comprehension skills. However, with a creative approach to the potential of microcomputers, it is likely that lessons may move into areas more representative of the total reading process. Schools can use microcomputers as storage sites for children's stories and other creative products. These can then be retrieved by the authors or by other children for reading enjoyment. Microcomputers could be used to illustrate

The microcomputer adds an important new dimension to literacy in the classroom.

multiple meanings of words, to serve as libraries of all kinds, and to provide opportunities for sentence construction.[25] One has only to pass a group of children engrossed in one of the video games or to note the growing acceptance of home microcomputers to become aware of the need of schools and teachers to explore the educational opportunities that are available or waiting to be developed.

Evaluation of First Grade Reading Methods

By observing in elementary schools, one can see that the differences among classrooms are greater than the differences among the methods being used to teach reading. The most important factors are the teachers themselves and their individual abilities to relate to the children being taught.

Nevertheless, some evaluation of different methods for teaching reading is in order. The strengths and weaknesses of various methodologies are summarized in tables 6.1, 6.2, 6.3, and 6.4.[26]

Table 6.1 Summary of strengths and weaknesses of the language-experience approach to teaching reading.

Strengths	Weaknesses
1. Shows children that reading is just talk written down.	1. Vocabulary may be too uncontrolled.
2. Encourages communication—free and easy talk.	2. May not provide continuity in teaching phonics skills.
3. Makes reading a personal and meaningful experience.	3. May not learn thinking, problem-solving skills in comprehension.
4. It is flexible.	4. Important gains in child progress may not be measured on standardized test at end of school.
5. Encourages greater creative experience in writing original stories.	5. Classroom may seem disorganized during reading class.
6. Children provide their own source of materials.	6. Charts used must seem to the children to have specific purposes.
7. Gives opportunity for the teacher to emphasize the left-to-right direction in beginning sentence reading.	7. Requires extra preparation by the teacher: chart-making, planning firsthand experiences.
8. Children learn to share their own ideas—but, more importantly, they learn to listen to the ideas of others.	
9. Children learn use of punctuation marks.	
10. Pitch, intonation, and stress can be more meaningful using child's natural spoken language in his sentences.	

Adapted from James F. Kerfoot, ed., *First Grade Reading Programs,* Perspectives in Reading, No. 5.

Table 6.2 Summary of strengths and weaknesses of the basal reader approach to teaching reading.

Strengths	Weaknesses*
1. Eclectic in nature with practices integrated from all systems.	1. Too much vocabulary control—dull, repetitious.
2. *Sequential* order in presentation of skills.	2. Limited content in preprimers: shallow, unrealistic, lack of literary style.
3. *Continuity* of all skills through the grades.	3. Lack of visibility in the way skills are developed.
4. *Integration*—coordination of materials and skills.	4. Stories often not related to children's interests.
5. Gradual introduction of vocabulary and word analysis skills.	5. Sentence patterns appear haphazardly without repetition or mastery.
6. Organization is horizontal (coordination of materials) and vertical (social organization, vocabulary, word analysis skills, comprehension).	6. Race and ethnic groups are stereotyped and stylized.
	7. Tell only easy and comfortable life.
	8. Attitudes: society not realistic.
	9. Not enough done to stimulate curiosity.
	10. Need to make important things *interesting.*

On the basis of revisions in children's readers since Kerfoot's work was published, some of these criticisms do not apply as generally as they did in 1965.

Adapted from James F. Kerfoot, ed., *First Grade Reading Programs,* Perspectives in Reading, No. 5.

Table 6.3 Summary of strengths and weaknesses of a strong phonics approach to teaching beginning reading.

Strengths	Weaknesses
1. Aids in auditory perception.	1. Inhibits other skills if overemphasized in the beginning.
2. Aids in visual-auditory discrimination.	2. Over-reliance narrows flexibility in reading.
3. Aid to word recognition.	3. Memorizing phonics rules *does not* assure ability to use them.
4. Aid to unlocking new, strange words.	4. Meaning is really much more important than sounding.
5. Systematic system of learning letter sounds.	5. Too many sounds are spelled alike.
6. Builds confidence in word recognition.	6. Too many rules—and most of them have exceptions.
7. Useful in spelling and composition.	7. No good for children with hearing defects.
	8. Intensive drill can kill interest in reading.

Adapted from James F. Kerfoot, ed., *First Grade Reading Programs,* Perspectives in Reading, No. 5.

Table 6.4 Summary of strengths and weaknesses of the individualized reading approach to teaching reading.

Strengths	Weaknesses
1. Self-selected books are more likely to satisfy reading interests.	1. Inadequate library materials in the schools.
2. Greater opportunity for interaction among students in bringing together ideas gained from independent reading.	2. Danger of insufficient skill development.
3. Children progress at their own rate.	3. Puts heavy clerical burden on the teacher.
4. Individual teacher-pupil conferences develop rapport.	4. Difficult to find time for enough individual conferences.
5. Diminishes competition and comparison; avoids stigma of being in lowest group.	5. Young children need much guidance in material selection.
6. Each child experiences greater self-worth; takes more initiative.	6. Hard to judge difficulty of books.
7. Flexible—no ceiling on the learning.	7. Is only one of possible ways to accommodate for differences in children.
8. Some children can be introduced to a much greater variety of reading materials.	8. Teacher needs to have read many books in children's literature.
9. Small groups are formed as needed for specific purposes.	9. Teacher needs to be able to teach skills as needed.
10. Through time, teachers should develop greater skill and flexibility in teaching.	10. Inefficient to teach a skill to an individual that half a dozen need at that time.
11. Some children can be guided in more oral and written expression and in critical thinking.	11. May encourage carelessness in reading and lack of thoroughness.
12. Combines well with other methods.	12. Difficult to administer written seatwork.
	13. Control (discipline) of room may be more difficult for teacher.
	14. Teacher must do a good job of interpreting program to the parents.

Adapted from James F. Kerfoot, ed., *First Grade Reading Programs*, Perspectives in Reading, No. 5.

Summary

Beginning reading instruction should include all the methodological skills that the teacher can incorporate. Teaching reading should begin with the language-experience approach to written language. This places the emphasis on *meaning* as the core of the reading process. Children's personal language is used for whatever message they wish to convey. They need to learn phoneme-grapheme relationships only after trying to interpret their own messages in written form. Language-experience gives children the opportunity to select the vocabulary they wish to read *first* instead of having to read a controlled vocabulary selected by others.

To go beyond reading their own experiences, children need to develop a sight vocabulary of the most commonly used words; to learn a set of skills for phonic and structural analysis of strange words (any words decoded become a child's own sight words); to develop skills of selection, comprehension, and evaluation; and to practice reading in many rewarding situations.

The problems of teaching developmental reading stem much more from the complexity of children and their learning processes than from the deficiencies of any particular teaching method.

This chapter emphasizes introduction of reading by the use of language-experience stories, then discusses basal reader approaches, individualized reading, phonic approaches, modified writing systems, and computer instruction.

For Further Reading

Aukerman, Robert C. *The Basal Reader Approach to Reading.* New York: Wiley, 1981.

Clay, Marie M. *Reading: The Patterning of Complex Behaviour.* 2d ed. Auckland, New Zealand: Heinemann, 1979.

Clinard, Linda M. *The Reading Triangle.* P.O. Box 2862, Farmington Hills, Michigan 48018: Focus, 1981.

Hall, Mary Anne. *Teaching Reading As a Language Experience.* 3d ed. Columbus, Ohio: Charles E. Merrill, 1981.

Lee, Dorris M., and Joseph Rubin. *Children and Language.* Belmont, Calif.: Wadsworth, 1979.

McCracken, Robert A., and Marlene McCracken. *Reading, Writing, and Language: A Practical Guide for the Primary Teacher.* Winnipeg, Manitoba: Peguis, 1979.

Smith, Frank. *Understanding Reading.* 3d ed. New York: Holt, Rinehart and Winston, 1982.

Temple, Charles A., Ruth G. Nathan, and Nancy A. Burris. *The Beginnings of Writing.* Boston: Allyn & Bacon, 1982.

Weaver, Constance. *Psycholinguistics and Reading: From Process to Practice.* Cambridge, Mass.: Winthrop, 1980.

Notes

1. Ethel Buchanan, ed., *For the Love of Reading* (Winnipeg, Manitoba: The C.E.L. Group, 1980), p.1.
2. Shirley Brice Heath, "The Functions and Uses of Literacy," *Journal of Communication* 30 (Winter 1980): 128–29.
3. Ibid., pp. 130–31.
4. Stephen G. Harris, "Reading Methodology: What's Radical, What's Traditional," *The Reading Teacher* 27 (November 1973):135.
5. Don Holdaway, *The Foundations of Literacy* (Sydney, Australia: Ashton Scholastic, 1979), pp. 56–57.
6. Ibid., p. 57.
7. Ibid., p. 62.
8. Careth Ellingson, *The Shadow Children* (Five North Wabash Avenue, Chicago, Ill., 60602: Topaz Books, 1967), pp. 92–93, quoted from J. F. Jastak and S. R. Jastak, *Wide Range Achievement Tests—Manual of Instructions* (Wilmington, Del.: Guidance Associates).
9. Wilhelmina Nielsen, "Twenty Language Experiences Which Form the Framework of the Experience Approach to the Language Arts," *Claremont Reading Conference: On Becoming a Reader* (Claremont, Calif.: Claremont Graduate School, 1965), pp. 168–74.

10. See Russell Stauffer, *The Language Experience Approach to the Teaching of Reading* (New York: Harper & Row, 1970); Robert A. McCracken and Marlene J. McCracken, *Reading Is Only the Tiger's Tail* (San Rafael, Calif.: Leswing Press, 1972); Jeannette Veatch et al., *Key Words to Reading: The Language Experience Approach Begins,* 2d ed. (Columbus, Ohio: Charles E. Merrill, 1979); Mary Ann Hall, *The Language-Experience Approach to Teaching Reading: A Research Perspective,* 2d ed. (Newark, Del.: International Reading Assn., 1978).

11. Virgil E. Herrick and Marcella Nerbovig, *Using Language Experience Charts with Children* (Columbus, Ohio: Charles E. Merrill, 1964), pp. iii–iv.

12. Marie Hughes (Workshop presentation in Albuquerque Public Schools, Albuquerque, N.M., February 1973).

13. Herrick and Nerbovig, *Using Language Experience Charts with Children,* pp. iii–iv.

14. Lillian A. Lamoreaux and Dorris M. Lee, *Learning to Read Through Experience* (New York: Appleton-Century-Crofts, 1943), p. 180.

15. Lee H. Salisbury, "Teaching English to Alaska Natives," *Journal of American Indian Education* 6 (January 1967):4–5.

16. Miles Zintz, *Corrective Reading* (Dubuque, Iowa: Wm. C. Brown, 1966), pp. 336–37.

17. Board of Education of City of New York, *A Practical Guide to Individualized Reading* (Board of Education, Bureau of Educational Research, 110 Livingston St., Room 732, Brooklyn, N.Y., 1960).

18. Lessie Carlton and Robert H. Moore, "Individualized Reading," *NEA Journal* 63 (November 1964): 11–12.

19. James H. Fassett, *The Beacon Primer* (Boston: Ginn and Company, 1912).

20. Albert J. Mazurkiewicz, *New Perspectives in Reading Instruction,* "The Initial Teaching Alphabet (Augmented Roman) for Teaching Reading" (New York: Pitman, 1964) pp. 539–44.

21. Chicago: Science Research Associates, various dates.

22. Huntington, N.Y.: Educational Development Laboratories, various dates.

23. New York: Webster Division, McGraw-Hill, various dates.

24. New York: Teachers College Press, various dates.

25. George E. Mason and Jay S. Blanchard, *Computer Applications in Reading* (Newark, Del.: International Reading Assn., 1979), p. 24.

26. James F. Kerfoot, ed., "First Grade Reading Programs," *Perspectives in Reading* No. 5 (Newark, Del.: International Reading Assn., 1965).

Facilitating Instruction in the Classroom

Part 3

Teachers may have a great amount of knowledge about the reading process and how children acquire the ability and desire to read. However, they may still experience difficulty in teaching unless they have developed classroom organization and management skills and the ability to work with parents as they carry out their instructional programs.

Managing time and space advantages and restrictions wisely, as well as viewing positively the uniqueness of the children in the classroom, will contribute to effective and satisfying management strategies. The teacher will want to know various strategies for reading instruction, as well as ways of preventing behavior problems or handling them when they arise. Establishing clear, honest, and open communication between teacher and child will help in maintaining an environment for learning. All of these ideas are addressed in chapter 7, "Organizing the Classroom Reading Program."

Children's learning is facilitated by home-school cooperation. It is imperative that the teacher promote this relationship in a variety of ways, from parent-teacher conferences to encouraging parents to spend time working in their children's classrooms. The end result is greater parent understanding of their children and how they grow and learn. The teacher gains a better understanding of the children, their homes, and their cultures. Chapter 8, "Parent-Teacher Cooperation," is designed to provide information for teachers as they work with their students' parents.

Organizing the Classroom Reading Program

A Cognitive Map: Organizing the Classroom Reading Program

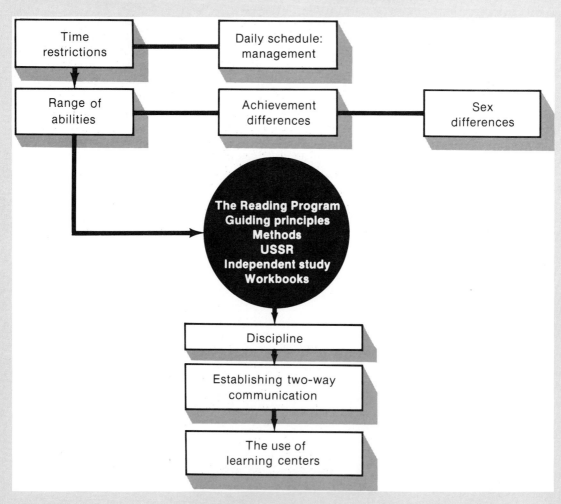

7

Guide Questions

1. How can a daily schedule for reading instruction be developed that takes into account differences and abilities in the pupils and includes the varied aspects of a comprehensive reading program?

2. What strategies can a teacher employ to make management and discipline positive aspects of the classroom program?

3. How might a classroom be organized around learning centers?

Terminology

achievement differences

children's independent work

direct interaction pattern

indirect interaction pattern

influence techniques

learning center

reading period

sex differences

three-group plan

uninterrupted sustained silent reading (USSR)

workbooks

The primary goal for the teacher is to organize the classroom to permit each child to learn. The teacher needs both methodology and materials to help each child progress in the acquisition of sequenced, developmental reading skills.

The teacher needs to complete an informal reading inventory for each child in order to assign the child to an appropriate working group. Finding an oral instructional reading level, a silent reading level with adequate comprehension, and an estimated capacity for understanding for each child is a comprehensive task for the teacher. By the end of the first month of school, the teacher will have determined at least the oral instructional reading level for each student and completed as much additional informal testing as time permits.

The teacher must often use less than exact group methods for finding out approximate reading abilities of boys and girls. During the first week of school the teacher can ask groups of children to read a selected story orally. The teacher should give a synopsis of the story and then ask the members of the group to read around the circle, taking turns and passing the book along to each succeeding person to read. Children who read well can read a long passage. Children who have difficulty can read a short one. If the level is obviously frustrating for a child, only one sentence need be read. Any child who does not wish to read or can't *should not be required to do so* but should be given priority for a personal conference. The child can try the informal reading inventory then, by which method the teacher can establish temporarily the level of difficulty appropriate for that child, and for most members of the class. The few children who cannot read can be given worksheet types of assignments until further testing is completed.

Cumulative records, standardized test results, and conversations with children's previous teachers and principals are also sources of evidence, both cognitive and affective, for grouping children at the beginning of the year. These supplement, but do not substitute for, the teacher's listening to children read individually or in small groups.

The teacher can expect to find in the classroom a wide range of differences in reading performance. Since differences in mental, physical, emotional, and social development are completely normal in children, the teacher *must accept* as normal the great variability in school achievement. With good teaching the *differences get greater, not less,* as the year progresses.

Time Restrictions

Improving instruction by meeting the needs of a classroom of boys and girls depends on the skills the teacher can develop to fulfill the responsibilities of the job. A new teacher may be able to plan carefully how to teach reading lessons for assigned reading groups in the classroom but may have considerable difficulty with the rest of the class because its time has not been sufficiently planned. As every teacher knows, idle hands do often get into mischief. Knowing how to plan specifically for each child's work period without direct supervision may be more crucial than careful study of the teacher's manual for teaching one sub-group.

Teachers find that the demands and restrictions on their time fall into three general categories during reading instruction: (1) time for instruction of small groups or individuals; (2) time for giving directions and instructions to the entire group, small groups, and individuals; and (3) time for monitoring the independent work of groups and individuals. Finding time to respond to all of these needs during a single period requires careful planning by the teacher. The next section of the chapter will discuss this task, including some of the problems the teacher must overcome and suggestions for dealing with these problems.

Figure 7.1 suggests one way in which an hour of reading instruction may be divided to provide time for small group instruction, directions and instructions, and independent work. Each instructional segment is prefaced by a few minutes in which the teacher plans with the children for the best use of their time when they are working independently. These times minimize or eliminate the need for children to interrupt the teacher during instructional periods. In such a plan the teacher has time to instruct each of three groups of children. The children have time for independent work, which is important if they are to become increasingly responsible for their own learning.

Reading in the Teacher's Daily Schedule

Most state courses of study recommend the minimum amount of time that teachers should spend teaching developmental reading in the elementary classroom. The amount is usually longer for the primary grades than for the intermediate grades. Many teachers in the primary grades spend more than the minimum recommended time teaching reading and may, in fact, spend more than half their teaching day in the teaching of reading. Upper grade teachers are apt to feel pressured to teach a great deal of content material in various subjects. Often, to the detriment of the children, they concentrate more on the subject than upon the student. The individual teacher needs to adapt the quantity of work to be done to the amount of time available. And unless the teacher adapts the teaching of content to the particular children being taught, confusion rather than learning results.

This discussion now focuses on management of the classroom for efficient teaching, since it is not possible to teach small groups in the room effectively if the teacher has not provided for relatively quiet, constructive work for all those not responding directly to the teacher.

Probably the most difficult task for new teachers to master is keeping two-thirds or more of the group actively working and motivated while they teach or lead a worthwhile discussion with a small group in the class. If the teacher plans to spend one hour teaching reading to the class, this hour must be broken down into plans for the activities of each group of children. The lesson plan will be sufficient to keep the teacher busy teaching, checking other groups, and managing the room. The problem is very different from each child's point of view. If the teacher works directly with one group for fifteen minutes, what will that group do the rest of the hour? They will not be busy very long doing the two or three pages provided in the workbook if they know how to do it when they begin. If they do not know how to do it when they begin, they will either need to interrupt the teacher to ask questions, talk to their neighbors, or do the work incorrectly.

	Group 1	Group 2	Group 3
5 minutes	The teacher answers questions and reminds individuals and groups about work to be done in independent work periods. The students ask questions and get ready to complete independent seatwork.		
Period I 15 minutes	Directed teaching of a reading lesson—probably for the least able readers first, because they will be least able to plan independently. The teacher may plan to develop only some of the steps in a directed reading lesson.	Interest centers, exercises to practice skills; free reading; committee work; preparing reports; games to teach skills.	
3 minutes	Teacher gives attention to progress of individual and group work; answers questions.		
Period II 15 minutes	Interest centers, etc.	Directed teaching of a reading lesson. Less attention should be given to formal teaching in how to read the lesson than to free discussion of ideas in the story and making value judgments about it.	Interest centers, etc.
3 minutes	Teacher gives attention to progress of individual and group work; answers questions.		
Period III 15 minutes	Interest centers, etc.		If this group is the highest achieving group, greater attention can be given to vocabulary development, evaluating, and making critical judgments.

Figure 7.1
Planning work for the reading period. What independent seatwork will each child do?

While his teacher conducts a directed reading lesson with one group, a child may use a cassette recorder to practice a needed reading skill.

How do teachers develop independence in children so they keep working when there are, of necessity, long periods when the teacher cannot directly supervise their work?

First of all, they should not be given *busywork* that only keeps their hands occupied. Coloring, cutting, and pasting are not instructive after the child knows how to do them. Constructive seatwork that has a purpose must be planned. Children must understand what they are doing and see sense in the assignment. Such routine directions as "Draw a picture about some part of the story that you liked" soon get tiresome for even young children. And as the children see less value in such a task, they will require less and less time to complete it.

From Theory to Practice 7.1

Interviewing Teachers Who Teach Reading

Each teacher has his or her own approach to the reading instruction period. No one would expect all teachers to approach it the same. It is good for prospective teachers or those wishing to look at a number of alternatives to study various plans for managing time during reading instruction.

After studying the plan for reading instruction shown in figure 7.1, interview three teachers about the structure of their reading periods. You will surely hear about variations on the basic plan—variations that meet the needs of individual teachers and their students.

Prepare diagrams of the three instructional plans, using figure 7.1 as a model. Plan to share these with your instructor and other class members.

It is apparent that the teacher can be very busy teaching during the hour allotted to teaching reading, but *unless careful planning is done with the entire class, many boys and girls may not use much of this time profitably*. Some of the cautions that might be stated then, in summary, are:

1. With respect to improving reading ability, the teacher must be concerned with what *each child needs* and that the child is provided with exercises that help to meet these needs.
2. The teacher's biggest job is to *manage* the total reading program by selecting appropriate methods of teaching. Keeping the individuals in the group busy and interested is the best assurance that discipline does not become a problem.
3. No child is going to profit from trying to handle material at the frustration level; children cannot work quietly at their seats without asking questions if they neither understand the instructions nor are able to read the material required for completion of a given task.
4. If children understand their assignment, they are able to use their time wisely and can continue with the job the next day if they need to.

Individual Differences

One of the realities of teaching reading is the range of differences to be found in any group of children. The successful teacher of reading takes the differences into account in planning instruction. Some of the differences have to do with the range of ability among the students, achievement differences, and sex differences.

Range of Abilities   Teachers recognize that their pupils will vary in general ability to do schoolwork. The wise teacher plans a daily program that accommodates this range of abilities and finds ways to allow children to utilize whatever skills and abilities they have. Both teachers and children value these differences and see them as strengths rather than as problems. (See "Capacity" in chapter 2.)

Teachers will find that their pupils vary in ability in many ways. Some are talented in art; others are chess champions. Still others are gifted musicians, while their friends are often the peacemakers in disputes. The wise teachers organize their classrooms and design their programs in ways that accentuate these talents and promote the discovery of abilities in each and every pupil.

Achievement Differences   In this section on individual differences, achievement differences should be noted again. This type of difference was discussed in chapter 2. The two most useful concepts to remember are that at any grade level there will be a significant range of achievement within a class of children, and that the range of achievement will widen with good teaching and as children progress through the grades.

Sex Differences in First Grade   Until recently, children were expected to behave in accordance with stereotyped sex roles. The Mother Goose rhyme was only a mild exaggeration:

> What are little girls made of?
> Sugar and spice and all that's nice
> That's what little girls are made of.
> What are little boys made of?
> Snaps and snails and puppy dog tails
> That's what little boys are made of.

These sex roles were often evident in the ways parents, especially fathers, expected their sons to be little men when the boys really felt like crying! Boys were supposed to learn to defend themselves, never to act like sissies, and to display some masculine aggression. Little girls were expected to wear dresses, sit quietly like little ladies, and be agreeable. A mother whose little girl turned out to be a tomboy sometimes expressed disappointment.

Whatever may be the causes, girls are likely to speak in sentences, use longer sentences and more of them, and achieve clear enunciation of all the phonemes of the language at an earlier age than are boys.

These differences mean that girls may enter first grade with two distinct advantages over boys: (1) greater ability to sit still and do seatwork, and (2) greater facility with language. Add to this the probability of a child having a woman teacher, who may emphasize traditional female values, and it is apparent that girls *do* have an advantage. Perhaps these facts explain why girls are apt to have a more favorable attitude toward school all the way through. Boys are more apt to rebel, become belligerent, or fail to see reasons why school should be largely unrelated to life.

There is some evidence that women have greater difficulty giving birth to male babies. It has been theorized that the male baby may be larger and the head therefore subject to greater danger of injury during the birth process, with resulting minimal brain dysfunction, neurological impairment, or brain lesions. Statistically, about 53 births in 100 are male, which may be nature's way of compensating for the "weaker" sex in order to insure equal numbers of males and females in the population.

While, on the average, girls have more school success than boys (whatever the causes), individual differences within each sex are just as great as between the sexes. In other words, boys fall along the whole continuum of readiness for reading in school, as do girls. Therefore, it is clear that *some* boys at age six are much more ready for formal school than *some* girls of the same chronological age. The suggestion, occasionally voiced, that girls might enter school a year younger than boys cannot be generalized to *all* six-year-olds.

> The average girl of six is more advanced than the average boy of that age in general development, including skeletal structure, and she maintains this superiority throughout the usual span of ages of the primary grades. In both height and weight, as well as in other aspects of size, the average boy surpasses the average girl.[1]

Deutsch found important sex differences among black children in severely culturally deprived areas.[2] Black girls could aspire to jobs as clerks, clerk typists, and secretaries with some likelihood of achieving them. Black boys were apt to see that black men were usually thwarted in job opportunities if whites were available to fill them. Also, black children more often saw the mother as the family authority figure. The man, more often less able to contribute to the family's needs, and with no economic value to the family, had little ego strength and was a negative psychological force rather than a positive one. We recognize today that both sex differences and ethnic or racial differences are the result of social forces. Such attribution was beyond the scope of Deutsch's work, however.

Stanchfield reported a study designed to determine whether boys might experience greater success in reading if taught in classes of boys only.

> Using 550 children in the first grades of the Los Angeles City Schools, reading was taught in sex-segregated groups. Care was taken to provide a wide range of socioeconomic levels. Two reading periods were offered, one in the morning and one in the afternoon. The outcome of this study was that, after statistical analyses of reading achievement and reading growth, boys taught in the absence of girls did not show more significant gains in achievement or in growth than boys taught in mixed groupings. Again, the girls as a group achieved more significantly than boys and showed greater reading growth.[3]

Following are comments of teachers who taught "boys only" groups in Stanchfield's study.

> "Boys are so overwhelmingly active, so frighteningly energetic, so terribly vigorous, so utterly strenuous." "It's so hard for a six-year-old boy to keep himself occupied with reading a book." "Boys tend to wiggle, twist, push, turn, shove, and, in general, bother each other instead of reading."
> "Girls are so quiet and controlled—they can sit quietly and read a book." "Girls are easier to teach—so ladylike and easy to handle."

Generally, boys were less anxious to please the teacher, less motivated to develop good work habits, lacked desire to assume responsibility and were less self-motivated in learning to read. Gates . . . suggested that boys in the culture have had less goal-direction for the act of reading than the girls, while they have more motivation for physical involvement and activity.[4]

Betts made these observations about sex differences and beginning reading:

First, there is some evidence to the effect that girls are promoted on lower standards of achievement than boys are. Second, girls use reading activities for recreation more often than boys do. Third, there is a need for more reading materials to challenge the interests of boys.[5]

Yet, at the same time, Betts cautioned:

Sex differences in readiness for reading may be over-emphasized. After all, there is considerable overlap between sexes. Girls as well as boys may be characterized by speech defects and delayed language development.[6]

Statistics have been reported for some time showing that boys referred to reading clinics or for special reading instruction outnumber girls by large ratios. Koppitz reported, for example, that the ratio of boys to girls in special classes for learning-disabled was six to one.[7]

Another study questioned whether all the *girls* who would profit from remediation get reported in the literature. Naiden examined the results of the Metropolitan Reading Tests for all fourth, sixth, and eighth graders in the Seattle public schools. She found that there were only three boys to every two girls among the disabled readers. Then she found that boys outnumbered girls four to one in remedial classes. These findings suggest that boys without skills get referred more often than do girls without skills. Naiden suggested:

1. Boys in general tend to display more overt undesirable behaviors. Teachers do not readily refer underachieving children if they are not discipline problems.
2. Teacher expectation for boys and girls may differ. Do teachers feel that boys need to learn to read more than girls in order to be successful in later years?[8]

Principles for Planning a Reading Program

The teacher will surely allow for flexibility in planning the reading program in order to incorporate a variety of activities to best develop the range of abilities within a class. The teacher will probably rely on basal readers but will also utilize an individualized reading program, a language-experience approach, and a writing way to reading while at the same time providing activities to keep each child profitably working. The following principles should be kept in mind:

1. The basal reader program is not sufficient to provide for all the children in a given classroom.
2. The same amount of time need not be spent with each child. Equal time is not to be equated with providing equal opportunity.

3. The notion that for any given grade there is a *basic book* that all children must finish is absurd and must be discarded.
4. Having children read in a group and then answer memory questions about the story is a superficial activity that must be changed so that reading can be followed by higher levels of questioning that evaluate the story read and reveal the child's understanding of the story as a whole.
5. A whole set of study skills must be developed for the process to constitute developmental reading.
6. At least as much attention needs to be given to attitudes toward and interest in reading as is given to instruction in the reading process itself, if lifelong reading habits are to be nurtured.

Some suggestions for adapting basal readers made by Dallmann and her colleagues are appropriate here:

> . . . reliance should not be placed on a single basal reader for the whole class; indeed, it should not be placed on an entire single series. It is fortunate that, increasingly, newer reading textbook series have, as their basic plan of organization, levels of reading which cut across grade designations. If a series is organized by grade levels, with arrangements for variations in needs of boys and girls, the reader should not be labeled according to grade level of difficulty, although the publisher's estimate of difficulty level may be indicated by some code device. All basal readers should be amply supplemented with general reading materials on many subjects and representing many levels of reading difficulty.[9]

Methods for the Reading Class Period

Teachers often share their experiences about procedures in teaching reading. One may emphasize learning how to handle reading groups. This procedure gets things compartmentalized well, and once the organization is taken care of, the operation runs smoothly. These teachers usually manage three groups. Others talk about having four or five groups, and occasionally a teacher refers to a classroom as a "regular three-ring circus." Many listeners to such a conversation might wonder what a teacher does to adequately *manage* a room with many things going on.

More and more teachers are talking about individualized reading in their rooms. Different problems are sure to arise if the teacher organizes the room for individual teacher-pupil conferences.

Then there are those teachers who are committed to the language-experience approach to reading. How do they operate?

Knowing that children are all different from each other, and that the longer the children attend school the greater the range of difference becomes in all types of skills, abilities, interests, and ambitions, teachers cannot rely on teaching any *one* thing to all members of a given class. Consequently, any teacher who *accepts the facts* about the way children grow, develop, learn, and satisfy their curiosities must be searching for ways to manage the classroom so that each child does have opportunity to stretch outward *on the growing edge of learning*.

Some tangible supports to which to anchor lesson plans will help the novice teacher learn and develop security. It may well be that dividing a class into three reading groups using the previous teacher's recommendations and the informal reading inventory is the most practical way to get a good year underway. Teacher's manuals contain storehouses of worthwhile information that many beginning teachers do not know. There can be nothing wrong in first acquiring that information.

There is no three-group plan that could provide for all the individual differences that exist in a class. Nevertheless, each teacher must decide what his or her limits are in organizing the classroom for productive learning. The beginning teacher will probably plan the reading program around the use of a basal reading series as a starting point. However, the teacher sensitive to needs will soon begin to borrow from other reading approaches, and the plan will become more flexible.

The teacher's first job is to develop techniques that work well. Having gained some confidence and security in teaching developmental reading skills, the teacher can then explore ways to direct the enthusiasm, interests, and aptitudes of all the boys and girls in his or her charge. Some of these ways are sure to involve individualized work, language-experience assignments, and small groups organized for specific teaching purposes during the year.

The most efficient interaction between teacher and groups of children takes place when the teacher meets children in groups of no more than five or six. This is the maximum number with which there can be personal exchange, eye contact, and opportunity for full exchange of ideas. Therefore, teachers must continually search out management techniques that work with large groups. Peer teaching is one. Having teachers' aides direct small group work is another. The teacher can set up varieties of learning centers in the room, being sure to change the content or the objectives of the centers often. Cross-age grouping can be used. And programmed materials that provide for needed practice in skill development for all levels of difficulty and all types of skill exercises are useful.

Beyond these challenges lie more complicated tasks: (1) planning a program in corrective reading for the child who has missed many needed skills; (2) planning an adjusted reading program for the educable mentally retarded child who is mainstreamed; (3) providing an environment in which the emotionally disturbed child can spend at least a part of the day in the regular classroom; and (4) providing for the child of normal intelligence who has some physical handicap such as a learning disability, limited vision, or defective hearing.

The teacher is also responsible for all the special activities that are related to the reading lessons themselves. These may include (1) preparing a TV program in which parts of stories are dramatized; (2) promoting reading of interesting books through oral book reports or panel discussions of books read; (3) compiling reports by committees about authors of favorite children's books and about books awarded the Newbery Medal or the Caldecott Medal; and (4) tape recording each child's voice reading a passage at the child's instructional level of reading.[10]

The primary consideration is that teachers decide what they *can* do and how they can best function within their limitations. Teachers have individual differences, just as do the children they teach. They vary considerably in the amount of noise they can tolerate in the classroom and in the amount of freedom they can allow to the committees or small groups talking among themselves across the room. Such statements as "Nothing *shakes* him" and "She's *so* conscientious" suggest different levels of tolerance.

Some methodologies that require good management skills, discipline as a constant classroom concern, and teacher-child interaction strategies will be discussed in the remainder of this chapter.

Uninterrupted Sustained Silent Reading

Uninterrupted sustained silent reading (USSR) is an activity assigned at a specific time each day when *everyone* reads silently for a predetermined amount of time. It may seem strange, but it is undisputably true, that such a designated period is necessary in order to provide the opportunity for *all* students to read *something* of their choosing and to persist at it for a given amount of time. One might think, since school success depends to a high degree on reading ability, that everybody has the opportunity to read. Because there are problems in all schools with unmotivated students, with reluctant readers, and with disabled readers, teachers must be continually seeking out ways to cause students to read because they want to, not because they must.

Teachers and other adults in the schools must be models to establish the sincerity of the objectives of USSR. Students may expect not only teachers to read during this time, but also other adults, such as the nurse, custodian, principal, and counselor, to join them. When all of these adults become engrossed in their own books and magazines, an essential feature of this activity is being carried out.

There must be guidelines. Everybody needs to be involved in the reading activity. Everybody must keep the same book or other type of reading material through the period so as not to disturb others. A timer or alarm clock can be used to mark the end of the reading so no one needs to watch the clock. In some schools, when everyone reads at the same time, the school bell may be used to indicate the beginning and end of the reading time. No book reports or detailed records of any kind are required. Voluntary sharing may be encouraged, with the teacher leading the way.

Sustained silent reading should have many positive values. Students select what they wish to read. They should develop some permanent reading habits if they find value in what they have read. And they learn that "free reading" is a pleasurable, fulfilling activity.

Kindergarteners and first graders not yet reading freely from books may engage in sustained silent reading. They are not expected to read the words but over time may begin to attend to an increasing amount of the print. The reading time each day will be brief, perhaps no more than five minutes, but children can still learn that books bring pleasure and that one can become involved with a book.

Initiating such a daily activity requires trust on the part of the adults that children will respond positively as a group. The period can be short the first day and lengthened as the abilities of the group merit. However, USSR can be only one of several vital parts of a total reading program.

<table>
<tr><td>

Promoting
Independent
Study

</td><td>

One of the teacher's goals should be to encourage the ability of students to work independently. The teacher must consider the physical arrangement of the classroom so that places for independent work are provided. Necessary materials must be available, and children must have access to them. Children will need any required directions clearly defined; task cards may be used to guide some independent work.

</td></tr>
</table>

Children carrying on activities worthwhile to them need to have freedom to move about, and they will need to talk quietly to one another occasionally, so there *will be* noise in the classroom. If it is work noise, and the teacher's tolerance level is sufficiently high, this is no problem. Teachers must establish the kind of room climate in which they can function efficiently.

The following activities are suitable for the period of independent study. Some are more suitable for one grade level than another.

1. After appropriate preparation while in the reading group, children may complete the exercises in the reading workbook.
2. If the group wishes to prepare a series of pictures to tell a story, children may each draw a designated scene from the story in the day's lesson.
3. Some children like to be encouraged to write their own stories. They may or may not relate to the day's lesson. All need to be urged to do some writing of original paragraphs. In writing original paragraphs, the primary consideration should be having ideas to write about. However, it provides a teacher an excellent diagnostic instrument to determine which children lack sentence sense, which omit all mechanics of writing, which cannot spell common words, and which have special difficulties with the order of letters in words. At any grade level, a teacher will occasionally have a student who has an extremely poor sense of phoneme-grapheme relationship and needs training in auditory discrimination.
4. The reading table should contain appealing books so that any child who finishes work can read, browse, or study pictures, charts, graphs, and maps. Also, each child can always have a library book checked out and kept in his or her desk.
5. There are many word games that can be kept in one corner where small groups of children can utilize them. Such games as *Go-Fish,* first and second series; *Vowel Dominoes,* from Remedial Education Center, Washington, D.C.; *Take,* from Garrard Publishing Co., Champaign, Ill.; and *Old Itch, Bingobang, Full House,* and *Syllable Count,* from Rand McNally, Chicago, are excellent for this purpose. (See chapter 9.)

After children have been instructed in reading by their teacher, an aide or parent in the classroom can extend their experiences with books during their independent study time.

6. Each child may choose a partner to study with, for example, by writing regular spelling words or mastering the multiplication facts or division facts.

7. If some unit construction work, murals, models, or dioramas are in progress in the room, it may be desirable for children with individual assignments there to work on them in their free time.

8. A child may read a story that he or she has practiced onto a tape as part of a continuing record of reading growth.

9. Younger children may enjoy playing quietly with manipulative toys or puzzles. They may also practice and expand language in a housekeeping area or in caring for classroom pets.

10. Children may view filmstrips alone or in small groups, using and caring for the projector as they have been taught. A listening center may also be enjoyed by some students.

Materials for Independent Seatwork

Anderson, Donald G. *New Practice Readers.* 2d ed. New York: Webster Division, McGraw-Hill, 1978. Grades 1–6.

Bamman, Henry A. et al. *Breakaway: The EMC Basic Comprehension Series.* St. Paul, Minn.: EMC Corp., 1980.

Barbe, Walter B., Virginia Lucas, and Judith Streb. *Lessons in Reading Comprehension.* Grades 1–3. Columbus, Ohio: Zaner-Bloser, 1981.

Barnell Loft Specific Skills Series: Midway Overview. Baldwin, N.Y.: Barnell Loft, Ltd., 1980. Workbook format. *Detecting the Sequence, Using the Context, Working with Sounds, Following Directions, Locating the Answer, Getting the Facts, Drawing Conclusions,* and *Getting the Main Idea.* All books grades 1–6 and advanced.

Boning, Richard A. *Supportive Reading Skills.* Baldwin, N.Y.: Barnell Loft, Dexter and Westbrook, 1980. Grades 1–6 and advanced. *Primary Overview, Intermediate Overview, Advanced.*

Cohen, Lawrence H. *Neighborhood Stories: A Comprehensive Program for the Middle Grades.* Providence, R.I.: Jamestown Publishers, 1982. Levels 3–6.

Gates, A. I., et al. *Gates-Peardon-LaClair Reading Exercises.* East Aurora, N.Y.: Slosson Educational Publications, 1982. A, B, and C Levels (Gr. 1–6) on following skills: *Read and Remember, Read Beyond the Lines, Follow Directions—Step by Step.*

Herr, Selma E. *Learning Activities for Reading.* 4th ed. Dubuque, Iowa: Wm. C. Brown, 1982.

Liddle, William. *Reading for Concepts.* New York: Webster Division, McGraw-Hill, 1977. Levels A through H teach a variety of comprehension skills. The child reads a short story and answers a set of questions. Reading levels grades 2–6.

McCall, William A., and Lelah Mae Crabbs. *Standard Test Lessons in Reading.* New York: Teachers College Press, 1979. A series of six levels, from grade 3 through high school.

Williston, Glenn R. *Comprehension Skills Series,* Middle Level. Providence, R.I.: Jamestown Publishers, 1982. Levels 4–8.

Wolfe, Josephine B. *Merrill Phonics Skilltext Series: The Sound and Structure of Words.* Columbus: Charles E. Merrill, 1979. Grades 1–6, Books A–F.

Use of Workbooks

In order to find time to individualize instruction in the classroom, the teacher will need to have seatwork exercises that can be done by children independently while the teacher is busy with subgroups in the room. Workbooks that accompany basic reading series provide some of the necessary practice children need in order to acquire the word analysis and comprehension skills of reading. Wisely used, they have a definite place in the reading program. The quality of exercises they contain, and the quality printing and format provided by publishers are both undoubtedly superior to the majority of teacher-made exercises quickly prepared and reproduced.

Criteria for the Selection of Workbooks or Other Seatwork

1. The workbook exercises the child does are usually related to the reading lesson of the day. In primary reading, this gives the child needed repetition in a new context of vocabulary being taught. With emphasis on context reading situations, this further practice helps to fix vocabulary for the child.

2. The workbooks for a class must be geared to the reading levels to be found in that class. Thirty identical workbooks for thirty third-grade children who have a reading range of at least five years is completely unjustifiable. Workbooks have no value unless they vary in relation to the reading abilities of the boys and girls using them.

3. Workbook exercises should be used for groups that need them, can profit from them, and can complete them successfully. Exercises that are not needed and do not teach needed skills should not be used. The workbook itself does not take care of individual differences in the class, but judicious use of the exercises in selected workbooks may make it possible for the teacher to accommodate differences.

4. Workbooks must not be given an undue amount of time in a child's working day. They tend to be mechanical and stereotyped and are apt to crowd out more active and enriching experiences the child should have. Workbooks leave little opportunity for a child to express initiative and to be creative in communication skills. If the teacher recognizes such limitations of workbooks and is providing these other experiences for the child, the role of the workbook falls into proper perspective.

5. In general, workbooks provide good practice with developmental reading skills. The gradual introduction of skills in a specifically planned sequence makes it possible for the child to learn to read by reading. Study skills, selecting titles for paragraphs, judging whether an anecdote is fact or fancy, and giving definitions for new words are all skills introduced early.

6. It is necessary that children be able to accomplish work assigned in the workbook. They must *feel* that they can do it. If a child has had unfortunate failures, or just marks answers without reading the exercises, the work may be too difficult for the child's reading power. Children cannot work independently for any length of time until they have sufficient reading power to keep them motivated.

A workbook that accompanies a basic reader can have many advantages for the student if it is well taught. Presented in good format, with clearly stated instructions, the exercises are likely to be superior to those prepared by the classroom teacher. Boys and girls can learn work habits and personal responsibility with attention to duty for extended periods of time while the teacher is busy with other individuals or subgroups in the class.

Workbooks can teach such study skills as following directions and using general reference materials. They can help children improve their organizational ability and develop and expand their vocabulary.

In the primary grades, workbooks have an added value of reteaching and giving the child practice on the sight vocabulary being taught in the stories in the child's reader.

Teachers are misusing them, however, if they are "using workbooks indiscriminately with all children; failing to check workbook activities; failing to develop workbook pages with children who are not able to work independently with them without preceding explanations."[11]

Smith suggests *desirable* uses of workbooks:

> Use workbooks as they are needed as a whole or in parts, the latter being more desirable. With slower children develop new workbook activities before leaving children to work by themselves. By all means *check* the workbook results carefully after each use. Study these results to ascertain skills needed. Follow up with additional help for children whose workbook activities reveal special needs.[12]

The cost of buying workbooks for every child in a class could be greatly reduced. Individual worksheets classified by skill to be developed and sequenced in order of difficulty of exercise could be used much more flexibly than workbooks by any teacher who knows the study skills and level of difficulty needed. Such worksheets need to be so programmed that the child can check his own work as soon as he finishes it. Individual teachers have built such files of materials by removing pages from many workbooks, mounting them, sequencing them into a skills program, and placing each one in a plastic envelope so that the child writes on the plastic with a grease pencil.

Teachers may consider the following statements in judging the value of workbooks:

1. Workbooks give more practice on the vocabulary in the readers.
2. Workbooks teach word-attack skills in sequence to give the child greater independence in reading.
3. The systematic approach to reading skills is more expertly done than a classroom teacher will likely be able to do.
4. The teacher must rely on seatwork to keep many children working independently while attention is given to subgroups in the room.
5. Workbooks provide *some* exercises to teach skills and concepts; children may need much more practice with some types of skills than workbooks provide.
6. The teacher needs a greater *variety* of approaches to learning than daily use of workbook exercises alone will provide.
7. If an exercise is not appropriate, or if for any reason it serves no purpose for a given child, it need not be used.

Relationships Between Discipline and Classroom Organization and Management

An *effective teacher* needs to be aware of the interpersonal relations among the members of a class. The teacher is therefore continually assessing the emotional and social climate in the room.

Many young teachers working in a departmentalized program with older children have experienced frustration with groups of sixth or seventh graders who are noisy, somewhat tense, and brusk when they storm into the classroom to start a new class period.

Mr. Jones noted such behavior early in the year when his seventh grade groups came to reading-language class. He responded by listening long enough to pick up some thread of the conversation. Then, instead of moving directly to the day's lessons, he chaired a discussion with the boys and girls about their behavior. After perhaps ten minutes, several gripes had been aired and the class settled down to work.

In a casual conversation with Miss Quiet, a colleague who taught these groups the previous period and who had taught in the school system more than twenty years, Mr. Jones related the episode about the very restless behavior.

Miss Quiet assured him they were *not* restless in her room, that they worked very quietly, and that she tolerated no impudence from youngsters who tried to talk back.

Mr. Jones soon learned from colleagues of the pin-drop silence in Miss Quiet's room and the rules about "no pencil-sharpening," "no whispering," and the introduction of *no* topic except the day's lesson.

It was not difficult to understand that after a twenty-minute home room study period and a fifty-five minute recitation and study period with Miss Quiet just prior to reading-language with Mr. Jones, many of the twelve-year-olds had been "still and quiet" about as long as was physically possible.

Mr. Jones accepted the problem of a sudden transition from a highly authoritarian teacher for one long, quiet period to a period which he hoped would be a free, interacting, group-planning, group-conversation atmosphere. With this in mind, he closed his classroom door when the bell rang for classes to begin and planned for a controlled conversation period that could last ten minutes if necessary, in order to reduce tensions and let the held-in exuberance escape. Only then did he get the group back to the assignments of the hour.

It is hoped that most new teachers will not face such extreme teacher-behavior environments. However, just as teachers are admonished to accept children *as they are,* so faculties must accept teachers as *they* are. Teachers naturally range from extremely authoritarian to extremely democratic. Some, confused about the two ends of the continuum, invite chaos because they fail to teach such discriminations as the difference between freedom and license, privilege and irresponsibility, decision making based on logical reasoning or fact and decision making based on personal whim.

Yet the primary purpose of education as a socializing institution is to foster intelligent decision making. Therefore, finding ways to become sensitive to people's feelings, attitudes, and needs is basic to providing for social and intellectual needs in all human interaction.

Teachers probably tend to feel that they have a great deal of information (facts) that they must convey to a group of students in a short period of time. For this reason, they are inclined to use oral language as their means of *telling* boys and girls what they *need* to know. They overlook the need for students to communicate with each other and with the teacher. Learners must have the chance to think through a problem, exchange ideas, and talk to their peers in order to crystallize their thoughts and correct some of their fallacious thinking. Teachers sometimes forget that communication has to be a two-way process if it is to be effective.

Discipline and Techniques That Can Influence Student Behavior

The word *discipline* suggests that there has to be a response to negative behavior. All teachers know, of course, that when thirty or more youngsters are working, living, and playing together in one room for a school year, negative behavior is sure to appear occasionally. The danger is, though, that teachers have in mind a specific standard of behavior that is acceptable to them and they wish to "demand" this standard of behavior from everyone. Mature, confident teachers who feel secure in their work do not *fear* the impatience of an *anxious child* or the aggressive, impulsive response of an *angry one*. Rather, they accept these behaviors as normal and maintain a room climate in which these behaviors can be tolerated by the group.

Mental hygienists have taught us the dangers of impulsive, punitive behavior on the part of the adult. Far too many adults judge the ability to discipline a class by just what they see on the surface.

"He used a naughty word so I washed his mouth out with soap. That worked!"

"He was impudent and sassed me so I slapped him. That worked!"

These responses to overt behavior treat *symptoms,* not *causes.* They force the pain, the hurt, the anger (the cause of this behavior) to be more deeply repressed by the offender, thereby practically guaranteeing recurrence in some form eventually.

In helping children to grow in positive directions, in giving positive emphasis to expected behavior, teachers must look for the kinds of *influence techniques* that will help children to help themselves in exercising self-control.[13]

Teachers need a repertoire of techniques so they can anticipate difficulty and perhaps avoid it while at the same time giving children assistance or support when they are apt to get into trouble or are in a crisis. They need to know how to work through a situation without threatening, nagging, or becoming demanding. Some influence techniques are described below.

1. Get the child's attention if he or she is about to commit an antisocial act. If the teacher catches the child's eye and can convey a message by frowning, shaking the head, raising a finger, or clearing the throat, this may be a *warning* that helps the child to exercise self-control. Many children forget, and trouble is avoided by merely helping them remember to conform.
2. Place yourself in close proximity to the child. If the teacher remains cautiously in a position to be tripped by a pair of legs extended across the aisle, the legs are likely to be retracted and placed under the seat. A pat on the shoulder or a friendly reminder spoken in an undertone would not be used to make the child fearful, but rather would help the child find the strength of self-control.

3. Make sure the assignment the child is attempting to do is one the child has the ability to do. Much classroom disorder results from children not being able to cope with the problem in front of them at the moment. Children who can't read need to be taught how, not punished for squirming, making noise, or leaving their seats too much.
4. Encourage children to talk about their feelings. Then accept the feelings and evaluate them. Such frankness from a confident teacher can reduce tension.
5. Humor is a good way to change a tense situation into a face-saving reduced-tension atmosphere. Boys and girls consider humor evidence of poise and self-confidence based on security.
6. A certain amount of routine so that children have some idea of *how* the day is going to be spent is a steadying influence. The younger the class, the more important is knowing "what are we going to do next?" Everyone needs a certain amount of routine in his life.
7. Isolating a child is occasionally a necessity, for many reasons. It is important that teachers not evince anger, hostility, or rejection in doing the isolating. A hyperactive child often needs to be encouraged to work in a quiet, sheltered corner—not as a punishment but because he or she will be able to concentrate better, will be able to attend to the learning task, and will be able to regain self-control.

    Occasional temper tantrums, kicking, name-calling, or just "uncontrollable giggles" are all reasons for isolating a child. The important thing is the teacher's behavior in doing the isolation. It should not be punishing but rather should be seen as allowing the child opportunity to regain self-control. If occasionally an industrious child wishes to get a task finished when considerable activity is going on and the teacher can *permit* one child to leave the group, this is not only a good reason for isolation, it also demonstrates that isolation is not punishment but a constructive way to help. Frequent isolation of one child from a class to sit in the corridor for long periods of time is a crass misuse of this technique. Isolation without constructive help for such a child is only avoiding the real problem and encouraging more negative attitudes.
8. The teacher should try to help class members anticipate, as much as possible, changes in their routine. New situations create some anxiety and tensions. The first time a group goes to the auditorium to practice, to the dark room to see a movie, or on a field trip, getting set in advance will pay dividends.
9. Changing activity when everyone is beginning to get tired is a good way to avoid trouble ahead. With younger children, if the job needs to be done that day, it may be well to say something like this: "Let's leave everything just where it is and line up by the door." Or, "Let's move the papers over to the library table so we are free to march up

and down the aisles here." Five minutes of brisk walking, singing favorite tunes, formal arm and leg exercises, and time for drinks and toilet may revive almost everyone so that finishing the job doesn't look so forbidding. With older students, it may be necessary only to say, "We have this much more to get done before lunch. If you need to stand up and stretch or get a drink, do it quietly and let's give it a hard try." If most of the group want to finish (are allied with the teacher), this may be all the encouragement they need.

10. Having a fairly well understood way of operating without getting bogged down with too many rules to quibble about will help children define their own limits. Because the teacher has to be at different times a judge, a referee, a detective, a helper, an ego-supporter, or a leader of a group, children need a mature adult whose reactions to behavior situations are reasonably consistent, fair, supportive, and not punitive. Adults who basically do not like children have no business in the classroom.

Specific Suggestions to Help New Teachers with Discipline

When teachers talk about behavior of boys and girls in their classes, they reveal a great deal about their philosophy of classroom discipline. In this respect, teachers place themselves on a long continuum from strictly enforced discipline to constructively guided discipline. The authors are deeply committed to the philosophy of constructively guided discipline. Children are encouraged to express their attitudes, feelings, and ideas and are then guided in directing them in socially acceptable ways according to the standards of conduct understood by their local environment. Industry, cooperation, and acceptance of a plurality of ideas are desirable ends. The desirable goals may be contrasted with such undesirable ones as *passive* children in very quiet, orderly rooms dominated by an authoritarian teacher.

The discipline recommended here is more difficult to maintain since it is based on a friendly, cooperative spirit prevailing and on a consensus about such matters as behavior, values, and the importance of knowledge. In such an atmosphere, good, effective teaching generates good discipline in most boys and girls. Well-planned lessons, careful attention to individual differences in both achievement and behavior, and a constructive, optimistic, worklike atmosphere will eliminate emphasis on behavior *per se* most of the time.

The new teacher may profit from a careful perusal of the following suggestions in preparation for the very complex job of guiding the learning of a roomful of boys and girls for the first time.

1. Learn as quickly as possible to call the boys and girls by their names. Study their names on the class roll before they arrive and connect name to child as quickly as you can.

2. Take charge of the room by talking in a strong, confident voice; present definite plans of work for each hour the first day; conduct business in an impartial, confident way; and provide a variety of tasks and keep everybody busy *all the time* the first day.

3. Accept the standard of conduct for the group that fits the neighborhood in which you teach. While you *must not permit* children to continually tell you "Miss Smith let us do that last year," or "We never did it that way last year," so too, you *must not admonish* your group to behave the way you did when you were a child—or the way children do out in a city suburb.

4. Use every opportunity to make friendly comments throughout the day. These interchanges will cause the boys and girls to feel that you have a personal interest in them. Tell Mary she has a pretty ribbon in her hair, tell John that you appreciate the way he came in very quietly for a change, or write a one-sentence note to Jack's mother and tell her the first time Jack gets all his spelling words right.

5. Begin every class promptly and enthusiastically. Being businesslike, however, does not change the fact that a good sense of humor and a friendly smile are two of your greatest assets. Knowing the lesson well will win respect for you as the teacher. A courteous use of enthusiasm, businesslike behavior, knowledge of the subject matter, and a good sense of humor are sure to win the confidence of the group in the long run.

6. Don't talk too much. Many a sixth grade boy has explained to his mother about his teacher who talks much too much. "We just turn off our hearing aids!" The lecture method has *no* place in the elementary school. This arbitrary point of view is intended to mitigate the far too prevalent situation in which teachers spend long periods of time telling students what is important and on what content they will be examined. The less response teachers stimulate or accept from the group, the more they are apt to carry on an interminable monologue.

7. Sometimes teachers use words and sentence patterns that the children do not even understand. One third grade teacher teaching children for whom English was a second language in the Southwest asked the boys and girls to be quiet while she talked to a visitor. They were soon talking with each other instead of working. The teacher turned to them and said in a firm voice, "It seems that I cannot relax my vigilance for one minute!" They became quiet for a second, so she turned back to talk to the visitor. Then they continued their conversations in an undertone.

8. When a situation arises that must be handled by the teacher, be sure to keep calm, dignified, and select something that you can carry through to resolve the problem. The child may be asked to take a chair and sit outside the room *once* until the child and the teacher can have a private conference. *But* no child gets an education sitting out in the hall every day.

9. From the first hour of the day, your eyes must be skilled at catching each child's variant behavior no matter where you are standing in the classroom. The first few days, *do not* plan to turn your back on the

class for such activities as writing extensively on the blackboard. If material needs to be written on the board, it can be done before the group comes in. Later in the year you may be able to select a mature student to put things on the board for you. Little elementary school teaching is done in a sitting position. The first week you probably shouldn't sit down at all.

10. When you are having a large group discussion, or when you are teaching subgroups, develop the practice of asking the daydreamer or the mischievous one a question, speak the child's name, or make a casual comment about whether or not "X" is going to get the work done today. When a child's attention is beginning to waver, a reminder may be all that is needed.

11. When a fracas has taken place, either between two students or between a student and teacher, don't insist on apologies. An insincere apology teaches hypocrisy.

12. Do not punish the whole class for a mistake committed by one or a few.

13. As a class proceeds, the teacher should note the number of *indifferent* pupils. In a class of twenty-nine fifth graders studying topic sentences for paragraphs, only five girls near the front were paying attention. This teacher needed to reevaluate her goals.

14. Do *not* end the lesson on a sarcastic note: "Nobody had the lesson well prepared today." "Most of you didn't get it—but then I didn't think you would!" Under such conditions, each succeeding lesson will probably get *worse*.

Student-Teacher Interaction

One kind of teacher promotes integrative social forces in the classroom through stimulating, clarifying, encouraging, and reflecting feelings and attitudes expressed by students either verbally or behaviorally. Another kind of teacher exercises those skills that control or manage the class much more in a superior-subordinate kind of relationship. The two patterns are characterized as follows:[14]

The indirect, integrative, pattern:
  a. Accepts, clarifies, and supports the ideas and feelings of pupils.
  b. Praises and encourages.
  c. Asks questions to stimulate pupil participation in decision making.
  d. Asks questions to orient pupils to schoolwork.

The direct, dominative, pattern:
  a. Expresses or lectures about own ideas or knowledge.
  b. Gives directions or orders.
  c. Criticizes or deprecates pupil behavior without intent to change it.
  d. Justifies own position or authority.

When the curriculum is based more upon process and less upon content, the teacher operates as a group-centered person. This situation may be contrasted with a classroom climate that is teacher-dominated. The first teacher may be thought of as a leader, who relies mainly on indirect influence; the second teacher relies on direct influence.

Direct influence—through lecturing, giving directions, criticizing, and justifying one's own use of authority—restricts freedom of action by focusing attention on the problem or on the teacher's authority.

Indirect influence—asking questions, accepting and clarifying ideas and feelings, and encouraging student response—consists of the verbal statements of the teacher that expand a student's freedom of action by encouraging verbal participation and initiative. Higher classroom behavior standards can be achieved by asking questions and then using student ideas, perceptions, and reactions to build toward greater student self-direction, responsibility, and understanding.[15]

One might hypothesize that indirect teacher influence increases pupil learning when the student's perception of the objective is clear and acceptable.

Figure 7.2
Various types of
communicative
relationships between
teachers and
students, in order of
their effectiveness.

From Henry C. Lindgren.
*Educational Psychology in
the Classroom* (New York:
John Wiley and Sons, ©
1956), p. 266. Reprinted by
permission.

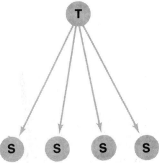

1. *Least effective.* The teacher
attempts to maintain one-way
communication with individual
students.

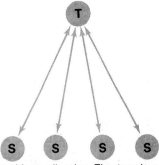

2. *More effective.* The teacher
tries to develop two-way
communication with individual
students.

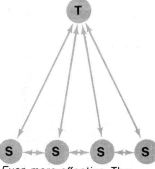

3. *Even more effective.* The
teacher maintains two-way
communication with individual
students and also permits
some communication among
students on a rather formal
basis.

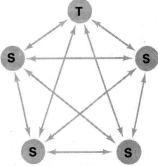

4. *Most effective.* The teacher
becomes a member of the
group and permits two-way
communication among all
members of the group.

Lindgren has illustrated four types of teacher-student language interaction in figure 7.2.[16] Type 4 allows free and open discussion, which provides each member of the group the opportunity to participate, to answer any other member of the group, and to continue the discussion indefinitely without domination by the teacher.

The kind of language communication within the group should be determined by the objectives to be met during a specific period of time. Certainly there are a few periods of time when the teacher should be imparting needed information to the class, with every member of the group giving the teacher undivided attention. However, the statement sometimes made by junior high school teachers that they lecture to their classes for a forty-minute class period suggests that these teachers do not recognize that boys and girls of that age can neither concentrate on an abstract academic lecture that long nor take adequate notes to have a record of the material covered. For the great majority of elementary and junior high students, lecturing by the teacher is a sheer waste of effort. Many elementary teachers, as well as students, talk too much.

Classroom verbal interaction is a complex process and determines many important aspects of teacher-pupil interaction. Observers can categorize behaviors as arising in the cognitive domain or in the affective domain.

The cognitive system deals with the thinking process. Different kinds of teacher information, teacher questions, and pupil responses are distinguished.

The four dimensions of affective behavior are:

1. Teacher reactions to pupils' ideas or cognitive output.
2. Teacher reactions to pupils' feelings or emotional output.
3. Teacher reactions to pupils' attempts to manage classroom procedure and set standards.
4. Teacher reactions to pupils' nonverbal behaviors.

Affective behavior can be rated on a continuum from *accepting-praising, encouraging, neutrally accepting, ignoring,* to *rejecting.*

Learning Centers and the Learning Laboratory Concept

The desired teaching-learning environment is one in which both teacher and children are motivated and actively learning. The less experienced teacher is sure to need a less complex environment and enough sense of "control" to have some security. Experienced teachers should be able to allow the group itself to evolve the structure it *needs* in order to permit each of its members to be active, creative learners. A great deal of wisely used freedom is necessary if the teacher is to encourage different behaviors, keep natural curiosity alive and working, and provide the educational resources children need to keep on learning, questioning, problem-solving.

In spite of how different the learning tasks of first and sixth graders are, we traditionally expect them to operate in very similar settings: uniform physical spaces; similar teacher behavior; formal school tasks to be achieved. To accommodate the extreme differences in children—and this includes all types of difference: aptitude, motivation, intelligence, etc.—all teachers need classroom arrangements that allow maximum flexibility so individuals can work undisturbed and at tasks where they have reasonable assurance of success.

Loughlin says:

The arranged environment consists of extensive learning materials and furnishings, their physical organization for access by the learner, and the spaces created by the organization. The arranged environment is organized to respond appropriately to the specific learning needs of the individuals who work in it. As growth and learning occur, changes in the resources, the equipment, and the space patterns meet the increasing maturity and the changing activity needs of the learners. The arranged environment is in a continuing state of adaptation. . . . The teacher works with the arranged environment by arranging places to work, choosing materials, and organizing them to support purposes of teacher and learner.[17]

Such a teacher is prepared from day to day to give necessary directions, ask appropriate questions, help the child who is confused about the work, and encourage students when they are moving in promising directions.

Van Dongen states the need for a reading environment:

> If children are to construct a personal view of reading which tells them that reading is a meaningful, functional activity, involvement and interaction with an environment which sustains needs for reading must be carefully planned. Opportunities for children to behave as readers at any level of competency which they have provide criteria for creating and evaluating a rich reading environment.[18]

Learning centers, if designed with the promotion of reading in mind, can provide many opportunities for expanding the desired literate environment in the classroom. Each learning center may contain carefully written step-by-step directions, signs and labels, and finished written work of children who have used the center previously. A classroom organized around learning centers requires record keeping on the part of the children as well as the teacher. The writing and reviewing of such records provide for more functional reading.

It is important to have a variety of learning centers in an active environment. We must remember that the purpose of any arrangement of classroom space is to facilitate movement within the room and to allow grouping so children can work together and interact in accordance with principles we have known for a long time: that we learn to do by doing; that learning is an active process, not passive.

"Children do not arithmetic, science, or phonic."[19] Rather, they experiment, they argue, they interact, they build, they measure, they chart courses of activities, they write, they read, and they calculate.

If there is no classroom library for children to browse in, the environment is inadequate. If the classroom bookshelves are in a corner behind the teacher's desk and accessible for only brief moments at dismissal time, the environment is still inadequate.

When the teacher arranges learning centers, they should be easy to supervise, easy for small groups of children to use, and materials and equipment should be accessible. Care should be taken not to have long, straight aisles that can become runways, or large empty spaces that can facilitate "horseplay."

When the learning environment is arranged to accommodate a wide selection of ongoing activities (see figure 7.3), it is no longer necessary for every student to have a "permanent station," a personal desk. Each student can follow a daily schedule of planned work, moving about the room as the day progresses. However, all students need places for their own things, which can be supplied by a chest providing small drawers or by a series of cardboard boxes that can be easily stacked along one wall of the classroom.

The learning laboratory is the conceptual counterpart to the learning center kind of physical arrangement. If teachers are going to take seriously the principle that great differences in intellectual, social, emotional, and physical maturity exist in every group, then the classroom in the elementary school must become

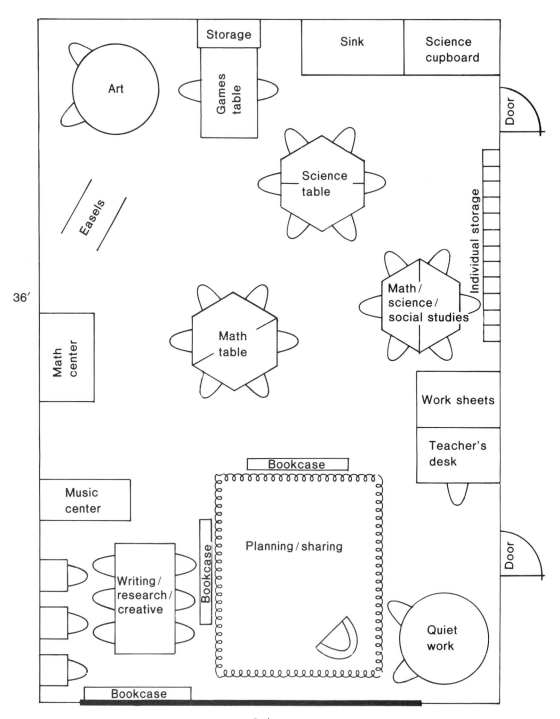

Figure 7.3
A learning center arrangement for the classroom.

a learning laboratory where children can carry on a wide variety of learning activities simultaneously. In a challenging learning laboratory, children can experiment with a wide variety of avenues to learning. A variety of equipment and materials and a well-stocked library must be provided if the classroom is to be a learning laboratory.

In a learning laboratory, there are jobs to do for which children see real purpose; jobs that will satisfy those who need immediate goals and those who can work toward long-range goals; jobs that are easy and jobs that are difficult; jobs that can be performed by individuals and jobs that will be performed by groups. Planning time is crucial, for the teacher must feel sure that each child has definite goals in mind for the work period. Planning time should be a structured period when questions are asked freely and arrangements are made to help those who will need either student or teacher help in finishing tasks.

The learning laboratory has another basic criterion: there are no minimum or maximum levels of performance set as standards for any class group for any given year. Learning is an active, participating process. Problem solving, creative thinking, memory work, and drill are all engaged in—at all levels of difficulty, from readiness (if indicated) to mature levels of reading, evaluating, reporting, and discussing.

Operating this kind of classroom requires maximal group interaction yet leaves the teacher free to work with small groups within the class during the greater part of the school day. In this kind of a classroom, a clear understanding of interaction analysis and how it works is very important.

Summary

Effective organization and management skills are required if the teacher is to have a successful reading program. The daily schedule should allow time to meet with groups and individuals as needed. The range of abilities and needs among the students must be acknowledged in the daily schedule, as well as in the materials and activities that are presented. Besides having a carefully developed reading program using a variety of teaching strategies, the teacher must plan ways for children to work independently. Teachers are advised to pay more attention to strengthening their repertoire of influence techniques that cultivate positive behavior than to disciplining students. Several influence techniques were presented in this chapter. Two-way communication is stressed; effective communication will surely contribute to appropriate behavior in the classroom. Finally, the use of learning centers as an instructional strategy is discussed, especially as they relate to reading instruction.

For Further Reading

Charles, C. M. *Individualizing Instruction.* 2d ed. St. Louis: C.V. Mosby, 1980.

Hong, Laraine K. "Modifying SSR for Beginning Readers." *The Reading Teacher* 34 (May 1981): 888–91.

Jones, Elizabeth. *Dimensions of Teaching-Learning Environments.* 714 West California Blvd., Pasadena, Calif.: Pacific Oaks, n.d.

Kitagawa, Mary M. "Improving Discussions or How to Get the Students to Ask the Questions." *The Reading Teacher* 36 (October 1982): 42–45.

Kritchevsky, Sybil, and Elizabeth Prescott. *Planning Environments for Young Children: Physical Space.* Washington, D.C.: National Association for the Education of Young Children, 1969.

Loughlin, Catherine, and Joseph Suina. *The Learning Environment: An Instructional Strategy.* New York: Teachers College Press, 1982.

Martin, Mavis. "A Talk with Marie Hughes." *Insights Into Open Education* 11 (March 1979): 2–8.

Martin, Mavis. "A Talk with Marie Hughes, Continued." *Insights Into Open Education* 11 (April 1979): 2–11.

Petreshene, Susan. *The Complete Guide to Learning Centers.* Palo Alto, Calif.: Pendragon House, 1978.

Purkey, William W. *Inviting School Success.* Belmont, Calif.: Wadsworth, 1978.

Reed, Marilyn. "Reading in the Open Classroom." *Theory Into Practice* 16 (December 1977): 392–400.

Taylor, Anne, and George Vlastos. *School Zone: Learning Environments for Children.* New York: Van Nostrand Reinhold, 1975.

Notes

1. Martha Dallman, *Teaching the Language Arts in the Elementary School,* 2d ed. (Dubuque, Iowa: Wm. C. Brown, 1971), p. 16.
2. Martin Deutsch, *Minority Group and Class Status as Related to Social and Personality Factors in Scholastic Achievement,* Society for Applied Anthropology, Monograph No. 2 (Ithaca, N.Y.: Cornell University, 1960), pp. 8–13.
3. Jo M. Stanchfield, "Do Girls Learn to Read Better Than Boys in the Primary Grades?" in *New Directions in Reading,* ed. Ralph Staiger and David Sohn (New York: Bantam Books, 1967), p. 60; see also Jo M. Stanchfield, "Boys' Achievement

in Reading," in *Reading and Inquiry,* ed. J. Allen Figurel, International Reading Association Conference Proceedings 10 (1965): 290–93.

4. Stanchfield, "Do Girls Learn" pp. 60–61; see also Arthur I. Gates, "Sex Differences in Reading Ability," *Elementary School Journal* 61 (May 1961): 431–34.

5. Emmett Albert Betts, *Foundations of Reading Instruction* (New York: American Book Company, 1950), p. 137.

6. Ibid.

7. Elizabeth M. Koppitz, "Special Class Pupils with Learning Disabilities: A Five-Year Follow-up Study," *Academic Therapy* 8 (1972–1973): 133–39.

8. Norma Naiden, "Ratio of Boys to Girls among Disabled Readers," *The Reading Teacher* 29 (February 1976): 439–42.

9. Martha Dallman, Roger L. Rouch, Lynette Y.C. Char, and John DeBoer, *The Teaching of Reading,* 6th ed. (New York: Holt, Rinehart and Winston, 1982), pp. 412–13.

10. The tape recorder will be mentioned many times throughout the text. It is an excellent self-teaching device. Upper elementary children can operate it themselves and practice oral reading in any quiet corner or empty closet space.

11. Nila Banton Smith, *Reading Instruction for Today's Children* (Englewood Cliffs, N.J.: Prentice-Hall, 1963), p. 100.

12. Ibid., p. 102.

13. Fritz Redl and W.W. Wattenberg, "Influence Techniques," chapter 12 in *Mental Hygiene in Teaching* (New York: Harcourt, Brace, 1951).

14. Ned Flanders, "Teacher Influences, Pupil Attitudes, and Achievement," in *Studying Teaching,* 2d ed., ed. James Raths, John R. Pancella, and James S. Van Ness (Englewood Cliffs, N.J.: Prentice-Hall, 1971), p. 47.

15. Ibid., pp. 64–66.

16. Henry Clay Lindgren, *Educational Psychology in the Classroom* (New York: Wiley, 1956), p. 266.

17. Catherine Loughlin, "Understanding the Learning Environment," *Elementary School Journal* 78 (November 1977): 127, 128.

18. Richard Van Dongen, "Young Children Move into Reading Supported by a Classroom Reading Environment," *Insights Into Open Education* 12 (November 1979): 4–5.

19. Loughlin, "Understanding the Learning Environment," p. 128.

Parent-Teacher Cooperation

A Cognitive Map: Parent-Teacher Cooperation

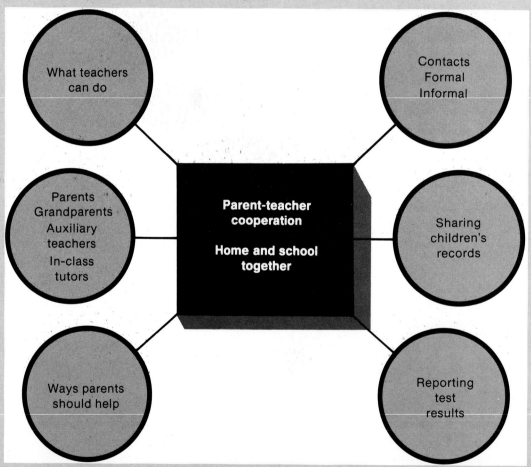

8

Guide Questions

1. How can teachers promote home-school cooperation for the benefit of children?

2. How should a parent-teacher conference be conducted?

3. How can parents be encouraged to cooperate with the school?

Terminology

grandparent program

parent-teacher conference

parent tutors

The title of this chapter is meant to emphasize that teaching children is a cooperative venture between parents and teachers. Teachers should recognize that parents are not just people to work *with* or counsel; parents have both information and concerns that can be most helpful in careful planning for a child. Indeed, educators are becoming increasingly aware of the profound influence parents and the children's community have on their progress in reading.[1]

As the school has come to take a more and more important place in the education of children, the parents' roles have become, perhaps, less well defined. Sometimes parents are criticized by teachers, and at times teachers are criticized by parents. Stereotyped and prejudiced attitudes can develop on both sides. Sometimes parents are indifferent to school; sometimes they misunderstand the policies of the school.

Teachers must exercise caution in carrying out their responsibility when having parent conferences about the academic progress of their children. A teacher once said to half a dozen parents in her classroom prior to the regular PTA meeting, in response to a question about the school testing program: "Oh, our testing program. We've been giving some IQ tests." Then after a slightly embarrassed laugh, she continued, "But none of you folks have anything to worry about."

The teacher might more constructively have said something like: "The tests are being given to obtain more information about the children's general abilities and to help us in future planning both *for* and *with* the children."

An educator once mimicked the jargon a teacher is said to have used during a conference with a boy's parents: "He's adjusting well to his peer group and achieving to expectancy in skill subjects. But I'm afraid his growth in content subjects is blocked by reluctance to get on with his developmental tasks." Parent-teacher conferences need to adhere to language clearly understood by both teachers and parents.

It has been suggested that there is an important fourth *R* to be added to *Readin', 'Ritin',* and *'Rithmetic*. It is *Relationships,* focusing on a clearer relationship between teacher and child, teacher and parent, and the child's school life.

The conflicts pointed out by Redl and Wattenberg are very real conflicts.[2] Parents who fear trouble for their children in school are apt to be the parents who feared trouble for themselves when they were children in school. And teachers who hope to maintain a safe distance between themselves and parents may remember unpleasant experiences from their past in dealing with adults. Many teachers and principals have, in the past, been predisposed to think that parents who come to the school are in trouble, apt to expose trouble, or predisposed to make trouble.

Merrill has suggested:

Some of the negative undercurrents in parent-teacher relationships come from feelings most of us have about authority. We normally respond to those in authority in various ways, mixing hostility and submissiveness, the anxiety to please, awe, respect, and perhaps fear. . . . Parents and teachers tend to see each other as authority figures. . . . Many teachers and parents feel ambivalent about being cast in an authority role. They enjoy the prestige but do not wish to cope with negative feelings directed toward those in authority.[3]

Insights into these ways of feeling may be helpful in accepting and dealing with them.

While these comments may seem negative to the beginning teacher, they reflect situations as they exist in some schools. However, increasingly, parents are finding their way into the classrooms and offering their services in constructive ways to further the educational experiences of their children. They want cooperative sharing and planning in order to best structure the total environment of their children.

School-Home Cooperation

Schools need to join forces with parents, first, in order to help parents understand more about the growth and development of their own children and children in general. Some parents need to learn that children are not miniature adults. They need to learn that a continuous growth process starts at birth and goes on during all the waking hours of a child, wherever the child is. Actually, it began long before birth, but perhaps for the teacher's purposes this will be an adequate place to start. Being ready for school requires that from infancy a child be taught the meaning of things in the environment, taught what the environment is, and taught how to use it. Language—not just words, but cognitive growth of concepts—is of first importance in the preschool years.

Schools also need to extend parents' knowledge of the availability of services of many community agencies that serve families, adults, or children. This includes making parents aware of their own need for services that they may have felt were only needed by others. It may also include acquainting parents with the importance of encouraging children to have library cards in their community library, taking their children to the city museum, or subscribing to, and reading, the PTA magazine.

Further, schools should try to cement mutual understanding and acceptance between teachers and parents. When teachers and parents meet and talk, the face-to-face acquaintance permits building the kind of partnership that works for positive results. Written reports and report cards are, at best, limited in helping parents understand their child's progress in school. Parents should have an opportunity to talk directly with the teacher about their child's academic progress.

Negative reactions and feelings are more apt to be engendered when teachers say, "I sent a note asking the mother to come in but she never did," or when mothers say, "I couldn't write her a note; I couldn't spell the words." It is much better to establish friendly relations on a face-to-face basis early in the year so that parent and teacher feel they know each other *before* there is any need to meet to thresh out a difficult problem that neither adult understands and that each might like to blame the other for.

A further by-product of school-home cooperation is that often teachers can make use of many parents of the children in their rooms. Some fathers could help the third grade boys make bird houses more easily than the teacher could. Some mothers could teach sixth grade girls how to knit. Many mothers would be glad to drive a carload of children to the airport, to the museum, or to the public library. At the same time, when parents have opportunities to meet and talk with other parents, they often find that they have many common interests and aspirations for their children.

Parent-Teacher Contacts

In the course of a school year, teachers will have contacts with many of the parents of their students. These will occur in many contexts—a chance meeting in the market with Billy's mother; a formal conference with the parents and other school personnel to consider a special placement for Rhonda; several occasions when Ted's mother, the room mother, comes to help with parties; and regularly scheduled conferences with each parent when progress reports are sent home.

Teachers may find it difficult to arrange meetings with some parents for a variety of reasons. Parents may have problems with lack of transportation or child care for younger children, feelings of extreme discomfort with being in the school, and work schedules that include school hours. Occasionally, parents seem not to be interested in their children's progress, but the teacher must not jump to the conclusion that this is the case without examining the circumstances.

In this section of the chapter, the discussion will center around two forms of parent-teacher contact—the parent-teacher conference and informal contacts.

Parent-Teacher Conferences

There are a few important points for the teacher to have in mind when meeting with one or both of the child's parents. The conference will be most satisfying for everyone if careful pre-planning is done. The conference itself should begin and end on a pleasant and constructive note. Both teacher and parents should

A child profits greatly from a well-planned and carefully conducted conference with her parents and teacher about her progress in reading.

feel at ease in the conversation, and the teacher must be a good listener. After the conference, the teacher must make some record of what was said and done, and must follow up on any recommendations that were made.

As soon as the conference is scheduled, the teacher should begin preparing. The child's records should be studied and made ready to share with the parents. Samples of the child's work should be gathered and organized. A tape recording of the student's reading may be made ready to share and analyze with the parents. The teacher may wish to discuss the conference with the child, getting his or her ideas about topics to be discussed. Perhaps the teacher will invite the child to attend part of the conference and share some of the school work and the tape. A comfortable, private place for the conference will be obtained. Perhaps notes or an outline will be developed as a guide for the discussion; the guide may not be followed, but it is there if needed.

The teacher should initiate the conference with some pleasant aspect of the child's school experience. The content of the conference will probably focus on the child's work, formal and informal assessments, evidences of progress, and plans for the future. Time needs to be allowed for the parent to ask questions and to make comments. The teacher must be alert to comments that may have hidden meanings—meanings other than the specific references in an anecdote the parents may relate. The teacher must be able to ask appropriate questions, make tactful answers, extend the parent's conversation, or just listen. The teacher should be constructive if the parent asks direct questions, but should be careful to convey to the parent that in the area of serious learning problems, there may be a need for help from specialists. As the conference draws to a close, the teacher will probably wish to indicate that the time is nearly gone, then summarize the important points of the conference.

During the conference the teacher will want to avoid discussing the work or progress of other children. It is important not to become involved in criticism of other teachers or parents or to make promises about how much the child is going to learn. One cannot promise the learning of another person, even a student you know well.

After the conference, the teacher should write a succinct report of the conference for the child's file. Notes may have been taken during the conference, and these can form the basis of the report. If promises were made to do specific things for the child, such as having hearing checked or obtaining a workbook for use at home, these things should be done immediately. Finally, those aspects of the conference that the child should know about and the instructional plans that were made should be put into effect. The child can then almost immediately appreciate the value of the conference.

Informal Parent-Teacher Contacts

The following general suggestions may be helpful in planning initial contacts with parents or in working out informal ways of keeping them involved in the school program of their child.

1. Plan an opportunity to meet the parents of the children in your room as early in the school year as is convenient. Explain in general terms to the parents in a total group about the work for the year. Emphasize the extent of individual differences and how the range of achievement increases within a class as boys and girls progress through the school.
2. Invite parents to bring individual questions to private conferences. If individual kinds of questions are raised in group discussions, the teacher should make a constructive statement but arrange for a private conference later to discuss the specific problem.
3. To keep channels of communication open, send short informal notes home with the child whenever there is an occasion—to report a good performance some day, to offer encouragement, or to suggest a way for mother to help with a special assignment.
4. Occasional telephone calls to parents to report something positive about the child's work or behavior is an important teacher responsibility. Too many parents never get telephone calls unless something unpleasant must be reported.
5. Encourage parents to visit the classroom to observe the children at work. Do not permit parents to carry on a conversation with you about children in front of them. But, do plan to meet a parent in a suitable conference environment and allow sufficient time for questions and discussion.

6. Discuss freely with the parents the meaningful records that the school has in the child's cumulative folder. If the child is performing below grade level in reading, for example, make sure that parents understand that the class average, or median, represents that level below which half of the class achieves. A sample performance on the informal reading inventory would provide a concrete illustration of how well the child reads context and what kinds of errors are made. When parents ask about intelligence tests, teachers must explain their limitations. Group intelligence tests are dependent upon reading ability and sample a child's performance for only a short period of time in a special situation. At best, such a test can only predict whether a child is a rapid learner, above average, average, below average, or a possible slow learner. Neither the teacher nor the parent should accept a group test result as a diagnosis of the limit of intellectual ability of a child. An individual intelligence test provides a much more reliable estimate of general learning ability. Parents are entitled to the best information the school can provide if they are to plan realistically for the future education of their children.

7. Encourage parents to give their children enriching learning experiences that are available to them. Studying the TV guides to seek out worthwhile educational programs will improve the quality of the viewing of many school children. Traveling with parents and learning about places firsthand will make reading about them later more meaningful. A library card at the local public library can be an enriching opportunity for any child.

8. When children's work is sent home, the teacher may duplicate notes of explanation and fasten them with the completed papers. Often parents cannot tell why a particular task was done or what the teacher's expectations may have been. Such an explanation can answer many questions.

Sharing Children's Records

In the last decade, records of pupil achievement have come to be viewed in a new light. Records are open to the student involved and to the student's parents. At the same time, records of students' progress and test scores are protected by the student's right to privacy and must be handled as privileged information.[4]

In keeping and consulting a child's record, several ideas should be kept in mind. Material entered into the records needs to be carefully and accurately prepared. Records of behavior and performance are desirable, but the teacher's interpretation of such information is of questionable value. Data in the records need to be kept current, but should include only those items that relate directly to the child's school performance.

In using records, keep in mind they may be shared only with the child and his or her parents. One should view with suspicion two pieces of contradictory information. In addition, one should never make recommendations based on the scores of a single test. Several test scores that seem to produce a pattern are far more reliable than a single score. Finally, information in files that is not dated and signed has little credibility and should not be seriously considered.

Reporting Testing

Often, teachers must interpret test results to parents. It is important to be able to explain such testing terms as grade score, percentile, and stanine. They are not discussed here, but are explained in chapter 19.

Many teachers find that reporting standardized test results in stanines is most useful, since a range of scores is represented by each stanine. Teachers know that the differences between individual scores usually mean little. They find explaining these small differences difficult and detracting from the more important discussion of the implications of the child's test performance for individualization of instruction.

When the teacher discusses the results of an informal reading inventory with parents, much of the conversation will be qualitative. The teacher will want to describe the reading behaviors that were observed, share what was learned about the child's comprehension, and perhaps contrast the oral and silent reading performances. Without being unduly technical, the teacher may find it useful to explain the child's different reading levels. Helping the parents to understand the meaning of the independent level may give them insight about what books to choose on visits to the library or when buying books as gifts. The parent may understand why the child is reading somewhat more difficult material under the teacher's supervision than when reading independently. Finally, the parent will be aware that the child can better understand and enjoy more difficult material when it is read aloud by someone else.

When several test scores are reported at once, there is likely to be a discrepancy among them. The teacher must be able to explain this discrepancy. Different skills may have been tested; different test formats may have been used; different modalities or modality integrations may have been employed; or, the child may simply have been better able to perform at one time than at another. There are many other reasons for discrepancies. Whatever the reasons may be, the teacher should have thought this matter through well before meeting with the parents.

Ways Parents Should Help

Economic changes in family life have transferred much of the traditional work of the home to outside agencies. Industrial technology has not only eased the burden of running the household and providing the food for the family, but has also permitted millions of mothers to work outside the home. In this kind of home, children have become an economic burden where once they were an economic asset. Child labor laws, compulsory education, and social and humanitarian motives of society have freed the child from work responsibilities—but may also have created some anxieties for children about loss of independence, concern about personal security in the family, and many other problems.

Because the family has undergone changes resulting in different child-parent relationships, parents may need help from the school in defining their roles and identifying ways they can help their children be successful in school. A few specific suggestions that teachers may make to parents are:

1. Be sure your child is in the best physical health and gets adequate sleep and rest. Pay attention to hearing, vision, and neurological problems or symptoms.
2. Be sure the child feels secure and confident both in the home and in school.
3. Provide the child a reading environment and a positive attitude toward reading at home. This means a place to study and evidence that adults in his home also read. Parents should read aloud to their children; and children should be encouraged to read aloud to their

parents. Children will likely favor this if they are successful. Encourage parents to always tell children unknown words when they are reading. If the child misses too many, the material is too difficult and he should seek out easier stories to read.

4. Encourage the child to purchase paperbacks and join book clubs for exchanging them with others to provide wider reading.

There are also ways in which parents should *not* help. The emotional involvement of being the parent of a child who has problems in learning how to read often causes the parent to be anxious or frustrated. In such a situation, the parent may overtly express the idea that the child is stupid or convey it in nonverbal ways. Parents should heed the following admonitions:

1. Do not compare the child with siblings who are more successful in school.
2. Do not punish the child for making poor marks in school.
3. Do try to avoid losing patience, raising voices, or otherwise causing the child anxiety.
4. Do not try to teach phonic elements, new words, or other reading skills without fairly clear instructions from the teacher as to suitable methods.
5. Do not try to work with the child when he or she is upset, anxious, or feeling pressured about school.

A Seminar for Parents

How the Developmental Reading Process Works

Parents often have vague notions about how the reading process is being taught but inadequate understanding of many of the things they have "heard." Is phonics being taught? Why can't my boy spell? "Look-say" is inadequate. Is the controlled vocabulary necessary?

Six-week, eight-week, and ten-week seminars have been planned for parents in which the methods of teaching reading in a given school are explained with opportunity for questions.[5]

Similarly, a series of tapes for studying *The Ways of Teaching Children to Read* has been made available.[6] Tapes that could serve as bases for discussion include: (1) "Major Methods of Teaching Children to Read"; (2) "What Parents Need to Know about Child Development and Reading"; (3) "Helping Your Child with Reading."

Parents as Auxiliary Teachers

Wilson and Pfau have suggested that since there are so many more children with reading problems than there are clinicians to help them, perhaps teachers should take another look at the ways parents might be able to help.

1. There are types of instruction in remedial reading that are reinforcing practice, and these might be done by parents if they were helped to distinguish these from other types of instruction to be done

When a parent helps the teacher in the classroom, there is more time to attend to the needs of individual children.

only by teachers. Such things as mother helping seven-year-old Billy list all the things in the kitchen that start with *P* or *C,* or playing *Go-Fish* or *Vowel Domino* are examples.

2. The teacher must teach the parent how to do correctly the activity he is to enjoy with the child. If the parent is going to listen to the child read, he must be a good listener, give his undivided attention, and be interested in discussing the story after it is read. He should tell the child the word he doesn't know, not make him "sound it out."

3. Parents should have a chance to try the activity; if a game, to play it with the clinician and child; if an exercise in the workbook, to ask the clinician any question they may have.

4. Let the parent decide whether she can establish a good working relationship with her own child. If frustration mounts or the parent is too emotionally involved—still too concerned about possible mental retardation—still burdened with some guilt about the child's failure—then she should understand that it is better to discontinue parent help.[7]

Parents can be a valuable resource, collectively, for all the teachers in a building. One elementary school made a brief survey of the special skills, abilities, travel experiences, hobbies, and other interests that the parents in the district possessed. A surprising number of parents had traveled to Europe and returned with boxes of excellent colored slides, which they were happy to show and talk about to a class; others had traveled to many other interesting places and returned with artifacts, costumes, furniture, books, pictures, and musical instruments of endless variety. One man was a glassblower. One could demonstrate and teach elementary judo. Several women could knit, crochet, tat, weave, braid, do textile painting, and one had learned flower-arranging skills in Japan.

> In helping children to succeed in school, parents and teachers play similar roles. Both need to offer the child a warm, supportive climate; opportunities for success; a variety of experiences; and above all, a chance to become actively involved in his own learning.[8]

When parents ask how they can best help their child, some of the following suggestions may be appropriate:[9]

1. Demonstrate an appreciation of books: (a) set up a library shelf; (b) plan regular trips to the library; (c) ask the librarian for lists of recommended books; (d) use books as gifts; and (e) let your children see *their* parents use reading as *their* enjoyable activity.
2. Read to your children often. Make it an enjoyable experience.
3. Accept each child as he or she is, understanding the child's strengths and weaknesses. Avoid comparing siblings. Praise when it is earned.
4. Include your children in shopping excursions. Initiate conversation and keep the dialogue going.
5. Plan little excursions to points of interest where you live. Use them for extending vocabulary.
6. Include your children in decision-making processes where they can participate. If you give them alternatives from which to choose, then abide by their choices.

Parents As In-Class Tutors

Many teachers and parents have worked out arrangements that allow the parents to work in the classroom in a variety of ways. Parents may repair or make materials or do certain types of clerical tasks. Perhaps the most rewarding experiences, though, are the opportunities to work with children. Parents may find it most satisfying to work with children other than their own. However, some parents and their children find that they can work well together.

Tasks that parents may be able to do include listening to children read, taking down stories as children dictate them, typing dictated stories, reading or telling stories to children, helping small groups with tasks the teacher has explained thoroughly, and helping children with questions and problems while the teacher works with reading groups. When the teacher and parents have planned together well, both will find working together in the classroom satisfying and stimulating.

One innovative program involves the use of a valuable human resource, senior citizens, in the classroom. They have much to share with the young, many of whom have never had close experiences with people older than their parents. These "grandparents" can provide links with the past in ways ranging from sharing the folklore of an earlier era to helping children learn nearly-forgotten crafts. Of course, they can also do the same kinds of tasks with children in the classroom as were suggested for parents.

Linking children's lives with the past can be an important function of older persons in the classroom.

A child can get individualized and caring help with reading from a ''grandmother'' in the classroom.

What Teachers Can Do

Working with parents is one of the teacher's most important jobs, and he or she should make it a high priority. Some of the most important things teachers can do in working with parents are:

1. Be sure the relationship with parents is a cooperative, rather than an adversary, one.
2. Work to help parents understand the classroom program—its intent, methods, and materials.
3. Help the parents to understand and appreciate their children, knowing that every person has areas of strength and areas for growth. Parents and teacher together can become students of childhood.
4. Encourage each parent to get involved in some way in the instructional program. Make parents welcome in the classroom.
5. Interpret correctly the meanings of various test scores, and help parents put test information in perspective compared to general performance in the classroom.

Reports from Teachers of Home-School Cooperation

The more parents there are who come to the school so that they actually see the school program in operation and participate in some activity, the more the community is apt to think the school does the best it can under the circumstances.

In a community with a wide range of cultural systems, a somewhat transient population, disparity in family incomes, and widespread lack of interest in school, a group of teachers wanted to identify basic behavior problems. They found that inconsistencies within the school staff as well as inconsistencies between home and school with respect to rules and expectations created many of the problems.

The student council in the school, a committee of parents chosen to represent all socioeconomic areas of the district, and a teacher committee laid the foundation for working on the problem:

1. Teachers and children should work together to establish realistic goals and standards.
2. Conflict areas should be analyzed for causes and reasons.
3. Role-playing procedures should be used to analyze discipline and behavior problems.
4. School behavior units should be developed at each grade level.
5. Pupil interests and special abilities should be utilized.
6. Children, teachers, and parents need to understand all discipline regulations.
7. A conference and home visitation program should be developed.
8. Existing teaching methods and the curriculum should be evaluated.

When report cards were distributed through parent-teacher conferences, 96 percent of the parents responded to the invitation for such a conference. Observable changes in attitude and behavior were evident not only in the boys and girls, but also among teachers and parents![10]

To provide for personal communication with parents of her fifth grade class, one teacher gave each child a folder in which to file day-to-day exercises, homework exercises, study sheets, tests, and quizzes. At the end of each month the children wrote their parents letters describing interesting happenings at school, the program in physical education, music, art, and other special subjects, as well as explaining the papers in the folders. The teacher also included in the folder a note to the parents. This effort is time-consuming but pays big dividends in promoting the desirable team effort of parent-child-teacher in encouraging the child's growth in academic skills. Typical parent comments reinforced the teacher's evaluation:

> About all we can say for the spelling is that it's original. At least 'Duey Desmal Sistom' surpasses them all!
>
> I was disappointed that he hadn't shown much improvement over last month.
>
> For the first time since my son started school, I finally know what is going on.[11]

Just before report cards were due, one primary teacher invited parents to come to school to observe their children for a complete day. She gave those who came a list of things to look for:[12]

> How well does he seem to know what to do?
> Does he work steadily at a given task?
> What distracts him?
> What response does he make to his teachers?
> What troubles does he have and how does he solve them?
> Who does he play with?
> Does he seem to have special friends?
> Does he play alone or with other children?
> Is his work the best he's capable of?
> Are you satisfied with his progress?

Such visitations were sufficiently encouraging to cause the teacher to plan for other all-day visits before succeeding report card days.

One school has a parents' waiting room with comfortable arm chairs, tables, exhibits of children's work, announcements, and magazines for parents. A nursery school encourages mothers to bring a child for visits, both staying only a short time at first. In some schools, parents are encouraged to visit often in their child's classroom. They see their own child in contact with and in comparison with other children. The teacher helps them enlarge their perceptions of their child.[13]

In some schools, parents are often called on to give minor assistance, helping to make or repair something, assisting with school excursions, teaching skills the teacher lacks. One school arranged parent-teacher conferences during the school day and asked mothers to come to school to monitor classroom activities while the teacher conferred with other parents.

The child should not be lost sight of in parent-teacher conferences. Three-way conferences of child-parent-teacher are sometimes needed, too. Teachers are occasionally able to enjoy such a conference with both parents and their child when they are invited into the home either for a meal or just to visit in the living room when the child feels free to participate in the conversation. Many conferences in the intermediate grades might be more profitable if the student, parents, and teacher all met together.

Summary

Teachers and parents must cooperate in a relationship of mutual respect and dependence. Parents do have a great deal of information about their children. They need an opportunity to talk with someone who can help them evaluate this information and plan how to use it to effect behavior change. The following suggestions summarize how parents can best prepare their children for success in school; how teachers may counsel with parents about their child's behavior; and how to conduct successful parent-teacher conferences. Parents are doing their part when they make sure that their children:

Are in an optimal state of physical health.
Feel secure and confident in the family circle.
Live in a reading environment.
Have a rich background of firsthand experiences.
Get undivided attention when reading aloud to either parent.

Parents must be counseled by teachers to modify their behavior toward their children if they:

Take a punitive attitude toward a child who fails.
Think a child is lazy or unwilling to try.
Force a child to study when it is playtime.
Nag, scold, or punish because a child fails.
Compare a child with siblings.
Feel guilty and defensive about a child's lack of success.

In conducting a parent-teacher conference, the teacher should:

Try to meet parents early in the school year to get acquainted.
Put parents at ease during the conference.
Assure parents of concern for their child.
Open the conference by giving a parent the opportunity to talk first.
Give an honest evaluation of the child's reading status: Does the child know basic sight words? Does the child know phonics and structural analysis? Does the child know how to write and spell (in manuscript or cursive) and at what level?
Discuss anecdotal records with parents.
Assure parents that it takes a long time to learn how to read.
If other services are indicated, either in the school or elsewhere (psychological, medical, speech and hearing, remedial reading, or other), discuss these candidly with the parent.

For Further Reading

Butler, Dorothy, and Marie Clay. *Reading Begins at Home*. Exeter, N.H.: Heinemann Educational Books, 1982.

Clinard, Linda M. *The Reading Triangle*. Farmington Hills, Mich.: Focus Publishing, 1981.

Criscuolo, Nicholas. "Effective Ways to Communicate with Parents About Reading." *The Reading Teacher* 34 (November 1980): 164–66.

Croft, Doreen. *Parents and Teachers: A Resource Book for Home, School, and Community Relations*. Belmont, Calif.: Wadsworth, 1979.

Harper, Robert J. II, and Gary Kilarr, eds. *Reading and the Law*. Newark, Del.: International Reading Assn., 1978.

Kroth, Roger. *Communicating with Parents of Exceptional Children*. Denver: Love Publishing, 1975.

Kroth, Roger, and Richard Simpson. *Parent Conferences as a Teaching Strategy*. Denver: Love Publishing, 1977.

Larrick, Nancy. *A Parent's Guide to Children's Reading*. 4th ed. New York: Bantam, 1975.

Monson, Dianne L., and DayAnn K. McClenathan, eds. *Developing Active Readers: Ideas for Parents, Teachers, and Librarians*. Newark, Del.: International Reading Assn., 1979.

Swick, Kevin J., and R. Eleanor Duff. *The Parent-Teacher Bond*. Dubuque, Iowa: Kendall/Hunt, 1978.

Notes

1. Shirley Brice Heath, "The Functions and Uses of Literacy," *Journal of Communication* 30 (Winter 1980): 130.
2. Fritz Redl and William W. Wattenberg, "Working with Parents," in *Mental Hygiene in Teaching*, 2d ed. pp. 452–76 (New York: Harcourt, Brace and World, 1959).
3. Barbara Merrill, "Under the Surface of Parent-Teacher Relationships," *The Instructor* 75 (November 1965): 35.
4. Rita M. Bean and Robert M. Wilson, *Effecting Change in School Reading Programs: The Resource Role* (Newark, Del.: International Reading Assn., 1981), p. 54.
5. Alma Harrington, "Teaching Parents to Help at Home," in *Parents and Reading*, ed. Carl B. Smith (Newark, Del.: International Reading Assn., 1971), pp. 49–56.
6. The Jab Press, Box 213, Fair Lawn, N.J. 07410, 1976.
7. Robert M. Wilson and Donald W. Pfau, "Parents Can Help," *The Reading Teacher* 21 (May 1968):759–60.
8. Glennys G. Unruh, "Parents Can Help Their Children Succeed in School," *NEA Journal* 55 (December 1966):14–16.
9. Pat Koppman, San Diego, Calif., City Schools (Lecture, Sixth Annual New Mexico International Reading Association Convention, 15 January 1977).
10. Jack L. Roach, "We Found Better Ways to Improve Pupil Behavior," *The Instructor* 76 (February 1967): 29.
11. Martha J. Hamblet, "Keeping in Touch with Parents," *The Instructor* 77 (January 1968): 34.
12. Magdalen Eichert, "Parents Come to School," *The Instructor* 75 (October 1965): 50.
13. H. H. Stern, *Parent Education, An International Survey* (173 Cottingham Road, Hull, England: Institute for Education, University of Hull, 1960), p. 41.

The Skills of Reading

Part 4

Part 4 contains the chapters that discuss the various developmental skills necessary for boys and girls to become independent readers. It begins with teaching word-recognition skills in chapter 9, teaching comprehension skills in chapter 10, and developing study skills in chapter 11. Guidelines are given for developing (1) a stock of sight words, (2) phonic and structural analysis skills, and (3) comprehension of the ideas contained in the material read.

At the same time, helping children learn to exercise critical judgment, to develop oral reading skills, and to establish permanent reading habits are other essential aspects of a good developmental reading program. Chapter 12, "Reading in the Content Fields," shows the distinction between reading the expository writing of content textbooks and the narrative writing of the basal readers.

Helping students become critical readers may well be the most important task of the teacher. Critical reading requires thinking, reasoning, problem-solving, evaluating, and synthesizing. The skills needed to achieve the ability to read critically are discussed here.

Word-Recognition Skills

A Cognitive Map: Word-Recognition Skills

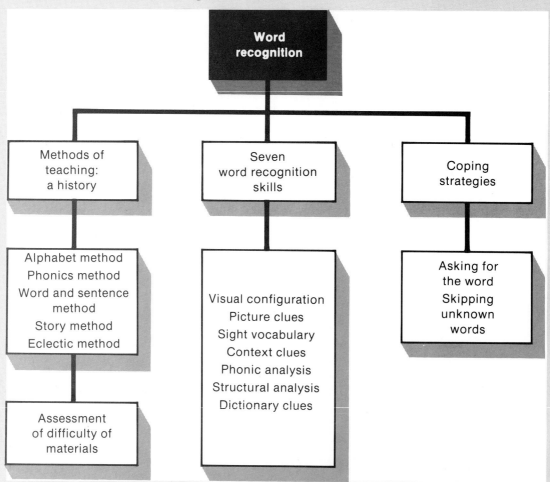

9

Guide Questions

1. Why should teachers know something about the history of reading instruction and reading methods?

2. Identify each of the seven word-recognition skill areas. How would you utilize each in reading instruction?

3. What importance do the coping strategies have for reading instruction?

Terminology

alphabet method

basal readers

context clues

coping strategies

dictionary

Fry graph

minimal pairs

phonic analysis

phonics method

picture clues

readability

sight words

story method

structural analysis

visual configuration

word-and-sentence method

Growth in the ability to recognize words in print is the most *basic* skill in learning how to read. None of the other necessary abilities can develop until the child has an accessible stock of words in a reading vocabulary.

In beginning reading the child needs to know the meaning of a word when pronouncing it in order to grasp the principle of demanding meaning from what is read. This presupposes an adequate listening and speaking vocabulary so that all of the concepts the child tries to read will be understood.

The typical middle-class, first grade child comes to school with a relatively large vocabulary. Actually the child has not one but several vocabularies. Of these, at age six, the *listening* vocabulary is likely to be the largest. That means that the child understands many words spoken in context that he or she would not use in his or her own *speaking* vocabulary. Typically, the *reading* vocabulary will be limited to a very few words, if it exists at all. And many six-year-olds do not have a *writing* vocabulary. It has been estimated that a typical middle-class six-year-old child may have as many as 8,000 to 10,000 words in a listening vocabulary; 5,000 to 7,000 in a speaking vocabulary; and, at the beginning of school, no reading or writing vocabulary of significance. As the child progresses through elementary school, these vocabularies change greatly. The sizes of reading vocabularies vary greatly with children after they have learned word-attack skills for discovering new words for themselves. By grade five or soon thereafter, the reading vocabulary will become larger than the speaking vocabulary for the able reader. Eventually, too, the reading vocabulary will become greater than the listening vocabulary, and the child must develop the dictionary habit in order to find quickly the meanings of new words or meanings of old words in new contexts.

Methods of Teaching Word Recognition: A History

Historically, teachers have used several different methods in trying to help children learn word-recognition skills. When Bible reading was the main purpose for learning to read and the Bible was the source used, learners probably resorted mostly to configuration clues and repetition to remember words. They could then learn to recognize syllables and sound out words by syllables. Undoubtedly, many children learned by this method, but there are few statistics to show how many boys and girls *did not learn* to read by it.

Synthetic methods may be defined as building larger elements (the word) from simpler elements (the letters), or "going from the parts to the whole." The alphabet-spelling and phonics methods are synthetic methods, both based on putting letters together to make words.

The Alphabet Method

In the alphabet method, the letters in the word are named in sequence and then the word pronounced. One difficulty of using this method in English is that the names and the sounds of the letters have little similarity. *Bat* would be spelled as *bee aye tea* and then pronounced *bat*. In languages where the letter names are essentially the same as their sounds, this is much more effective, as, for example, in Spanish.

The Phonics Method

The phonics method introduces many of the sounds of letters and letter combinations so the child can put them together to make words. The 1912 *Beacon Primer* introduced the child to some 150 phonetic elements on large charts, which the child could practice sounding. After mastering the charts, the child was ready to begin reading context. For example, having learned the sounds *ra, ha, ma, ta,* and *sa,* the child could use the consonant *t* and pronounce *ra-t, ha-t, ma-t, ta-t,* and *sa-t,* which, by pronouncing more rapidly, then became the words *rat, hat, mat, tat,* and *sat* (see figure 9.1).

Figure 9.1
The Beacon system used the initial blends *ra, ha, la, ma, ta* as the basis for sounding out words. This may be contrasted with the final blends used similarly in the *Gordon Primer.*

Beacon Primer, page 1, copyright © 1912 by Ginn and Company. Reprinted by permission.

BEACON PRIMER

PHONETIC TABLES

This book is planned to be used in connection with the Phonetic Chart. The following tables and exercises should not be taught until the Phonetic Chart is completed.[1]

After finishing the tables found in the chart, the child should come to this work with considerable phonetic power. The following words should be recognized silently and given as wholes at the rate of thirty to forty per minute.

had	map	rag	cat	had
ham	mat	ran	fan	lap
hat	pad	rat	fat	man
lad	pan	tag	bad	sat
lag	sad	tan	bag	rap
lap	sap	tap	nag	bag
man	sat	can	nap	fan

[1] If it is impossible to use the Phonetic Chart, teach the sounds of the following letters: *s, f, h, t, b, r, n, m, c, k, g, d, l, p,* and the short sound of *a;* also *ba, ha, la, ma, na, pa, sa, ra, ta, ca, ga, fa.* When the child has mastered these, build groups upon the blackboard as follows:

ra-n	ha-d	la-d	ma-d	ta-g
ra-p	ha-m	la-g	ma-n	ta-n
ra-t	ha-t	la-p	ma-t	ta-p

1

"I will make a picture of what each word says after you sound it."

Children sound : Teacher draws with simple outlines :

First method				*Second method*	
1	2	3		1	2
m-at	mat			at	mat
r -at	rat			at	rat
h -at	hat			at	hat
c -at	cat			at	cat
s -at	sat			at	sat

Require each child to sound one of these illustrated words before passing to his seat. Those who have gained perception of the blend will do this with little difficulty, as the picture helps in getting the word.

LESSON 26. — BLENDING OF INITIAL CONSONANT

Write family names upon the blackboard : *an, at, ash, op, eet, ilk.* By means of the letter squares, present a succession of initials to be used with them as in the previous exercises, or prefix the same initial to each family name ; as,

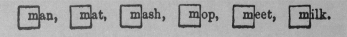

man,   mat,   mash,   mop,   meet,   milk.

In the *Gordon Primer* one learned initial consonant sounds and joined them to a "family" to make long lists of words (see figure 9.2). For the *at* family, for example, the child combined it with the sound of *m* and pronounced *mat.* Then, with *r*, the child could build *rat,* and with *h, hat.*

Some controversy continues about which of the two approaches to sounding is better. Should one read ra-t or r-at as the word rat? Does it make a great deal of difference so long as children know what they are doing? There is one problem in sounding consonants separately at word beginnings. The child is probably sounding *b* as if it were *bŭ* as in *but* and saying *bŭ-at* for *bat.*

Emphasis on *sounding,* or phonics, as a method of introducing reading to young children has appeared, disappeared, and reappeared through the years. There are undoubtedly several reasons. The most significant reason is that most primary teachers have not been aware of the contribution that some understanding of linguistics could make to reading instruction. Chapter 3 is devoted to that topic. But even if reading teachers have some linguistic background, the question of what children should learn first—how to decode words, or that reading is an intellectual thought process—has still not been satisfactorily resolved. How can both of these jobs be accomplished to the greatest advantage for the child? The authors believe that heavy emphasis on phonics early in the typical child's school life will be much less meaningful or intrinsically interesting than putting reading sentences to work to manipulate ideas. There is the possibility that some children, not highly motivated with abstract phonics drills, may become word-callers and exhibit labored attempts at reading. Finally, believing that phonics *is* reading, a child may develop negative attitudes toward the whole reading process.

The Word-and-Sentence Method

The word-and-sentence method may be illustrated from a page taken from the *Aldine Primer* (figure 9.3). When children read such sentences as "Rain, rain, go away/Boys and girls want to play," they learned the few new words they needed as sight words. Then the sentences on the remainder of the page gave some practice with the same vocabulary. One shortcoming with this attempt to put words in context was that it provided insufficient practice on the new sight vocabulary. Also, the pages provided isolated practice on a few words and did not tell a story so that reading did not have a meaningful purpose.

The word method was based on the point of view that the word was the smallest thought unit that the child needed to read for meaning. Proponents of the word method believed that a beginning reader need not already know the letters of the alphabet in order to read the whole word. The reader could learn to recognize the word *look* as easily as he or she can learn the letter *k,* for example. With the severely controlled vocabularies in present-day preprimers, a child learns enough words in a relatively short time to read an entire book. The child's memory of visual configurations is sufficient for this beginning.

As early as 1838, Horace Mann recognized the advantage of the whole-word method over the phonics or the spelling approaches to teaching reading. He wrote:

Figure 9.3
The *Aldine Primer*
taught a "word-and-sentence" method
that flourished for
several years.

Catherine I. Bryce and
Frank E. Spalding, *Aldine
Primer*, p. 23, copyright ©
1907, 1915, 1916. (New
York: Newsom & Co.)
Reprinted by permission.

Rain, go away.
Boys and girls want to play.
Boys want to jump.
Girls want to run.

The girls want to come with me.
The boys want to go away.

The girls want to play with me.
The boys want to run away.

Go away, boys.
Run away to the tree.

Come with me, girls.
Come and play with me.

Presenting the children with the alphabet is giving them what they never saw, heard, or thought before.... But the printed names of known things (dog, cat, doll) are the signs of sounds which their ears have been accustomed to hear, and their organs of speech to utter. Therefore, a child can learn to name 26 familiar *words* sooner than the unknown, unheard of and unthought of letters of the alphabet.[1]

The Story Method

The story method of teaching beginning reading was based on the belief that, from the beginning, children should be exposed to good literature. The authors of these series believed that such material could be written within the vocabulary reach of beginning readers. Free and Treadwell rewrote nine old folk tales, including "The Little Red Hen," "The Gingerbread Boy," and "The Old Woman and Her Pig," so they became the beginning reading lessons.[2]

The teacher would read a complete story from the reader while the children followed along or listened. They learned the story sequence as it was reread so they were able to retell it in detail. Also, as the teacher read, the children joined her in chorus on the many repetitions in such a story. The story was then dissected into episodes, sentences, phrases, and finally words. After a few weeks, the child was expected to be able to read the story and recognize the individual words.

If the study of one story continues for many days, it is questionable whether many children continue to find it interesting.

Such folktales as "The Little Red Hen," "The Billy Goats Gruff," or "The Gingerbread Boy" do provide much repetition of sight words as the sequences in the stories unfold. They are stories that provide conversation parts for dramatization or dialogue reading, and children can illustrate sequence of ideas in pictures.

The story of the gingerbread boy is a classic example of vocabulary practice provided in repetitive episodes as the gingerbread boy runs away. Examine the section of the story as the gingerbread boy came to the fox:

> The gingerbread boy
> came to a fox.
> The gingerbread boy said,
> "Good morning, Fox.
> I am a gingerbread boy,
> I am, I am, I am.
> I ran away
> from the little old woman.
>
> I ran away
> from the little old man.
> I ran away from the hen.
> I ran away from the duck.
> I ran away from the goat.
> I ran away from the dog.
> I can run away from you.
> Here I go."[3]

Basal Readers

Basal readers use what might be called an *eclectic* approach to reading. Such a method utilizes desirable attributes of all other methods. The child masters a sight vocabulary *first* in order to be able to read stories written with a severely limited number of words. Second, he or she begins learning about auditory discrimination of sound, which is the beginning of word-attack skills. The effective teacher achieves an appropriate emphasis in each of these jobs. To keep interest in reading at a high level so that children find it exciting to move on to new stories requires that they acquire enough phonic and structural analysis skills so that they can increase their independence in attacking new words and reading harder material. Unless there is attention to getting meaning, reading may degenerate into a word-calling process. However, without word-attack skills, reading can be a word-guessing game.

Figure 9.4
Fry's Readability
Graph extended
through preprimer
level.

From George Maginnis,
"The Readability Graph
and Informal Reading
Inventories," *The Reading
Teacher* 22 (March 1969):
518.

FRY'S READABILITY GRAPH

EXTENDED THRU PREPRIMER LEVEL

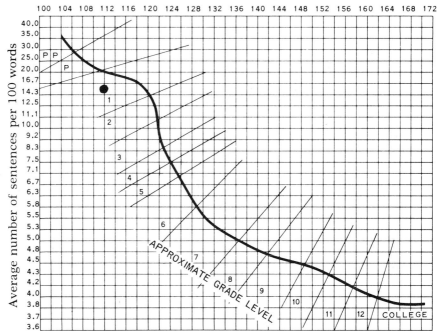

Assessment of Difficulty of Materials

As children read beyond the basal readers, teachers may feel more comfortable if they have a way to estimate the difficulty of the materials. The Fry Readability Graph as adapted by Maginnis (see figure 9.4) can be a useful tool for making these estimates. It is based on the notion that the difficulty of reading passages is based on the length of words and the length of sentences. The longer the word, the more difficult it is assumed to be; the longer the sentence, the greater its difficulty. The Fry graph does not take into account the child's motivation, knowledge of the subject to be read about, or knowledge of the language in which the material is written. However, even with these limitations, it offers some support in the making of decisions about books and other reading materials.

The steps in using the Fry graph are:

1. Count out three 100-word passages in the book or story. Each passage should start at the beginning of a sentence.
2. Find the average number of sentences in the three passages.
3. Find the average number of syllables in the three passages.

4. Find the point of the X axis that represents the average number of sentences in the passages. Find the point on the Y axis for the average number of syllables in the passages.
5. Locate the point in the grade level areas where the two lines meet. That is the estimated difficulty of the three passages. If the lines meet in the upper right-hand corner or the lower left-hand corner, the estimate is likely to be invalid. A new sample should be taken.

Seven Word-Recognition Skills

The child learning a basic sight vocabulary of about fifty words is also beginning phonics training by hearing words that begin the same, hearing rhyming words, and finding pictures of things that begin with the same sound. Whenever words the child is learning have characteristics in common, the teacher points them out. Even in kindergarten, the teacher will help children to see that Mary, Mike, and Michele all have names that begin alike. When three or four words that begin with *d—dog, down, doll, duck—*have been learned, the child is ready to see that they have the same beginning letter and to hear the same sound at the beginning of each.

In summary, the eclectic method attempts to:

1. Emphasize the meaningful nature of reading as the most important factor in reading.
2. Teach an initial vocabulary of sight words learned (memorized) as visual configurations. This is achieved through chart reading, experience stories, labels in the room, blackboard work, workbook lessons, and direct teaching of the words commonly used by young children in their stories or of the words in the first preprimer.
3. Begin systematic teaching of phonic and structural analysis skills simultaneously with the first reading lessons.
4. Include in the child's reading basal preprimers, experience stories, chart reading, reading labels, following directions, and trade books.
5. Encourage children to "write books" of their own that can be bound by the teacher and kept on the reading table.
6. Emphasize the developmental, functional, and recreational nature of a balanced reading program.

Word-recognition skills are all those skills and abilities the student must acquire in order to be able to "unlock" words independently and rapidly while reading. Memorizing a small stock of sight words may work very well for many children to be able to read the first preprimers in a reading series, but extending independent reading requires additional skills. Picture clues are also useful in the beginning and may be effectively used if the reading materials are well illustrated. However, the reader must be prepared to continue reading when there are no illustrations to convey the story theme. There are some other skills, then, that the teacher must develop with boys and girls to give them the independence in word recognition that is imperative for reading success.

Techniques for mastering a sight vocabulary may or may not include extensive study of word patterns or word structure as emphasized by a linguistic approach to reading. Similarly, a linguistic approach emphasizes patterns of speech, systems of phoneme-grapheme relationships, and word order in sentences. These points are mentioned under different subheadings that follow.

The following discussion covers seven word-recognition skills. While the first two are of considerable initial value, they have not been determined to contribute significantly to the later successful practice of reading.

1. Remembering visual cues in a small number of words.
2. Using picture clues for story meaning and word recognition.
3. Building a large stock of common words recognized at sight.
4. Identifying new words by using context clues in the rest of the sentence.
5. Using a sequence of phonic analysis skills.
6. Using structural analysis skills.
7. Learning to use the dictionary for help in both pronunciation and word meaning.

Visual Configuration

Young children are more motivated to read a story in the process of learning to read than they are in learning all the language, word analysis, and word identification that are involved in independent reading. If the teacher can help boys and girls to read a story containing twenty words, and they can then successfully read that story to their parents, they have reached one of their primary objectives in reading. The first preprimer in most basal reading series is prepared with a severely controlled vocabulary so that no more than fifteen to thirty words are used in the entire little book. By combining the picture clues that convey the story element and the noun words, visual configuration makes the early reading of such a book easier. The child will rely on the look-and-say method for recognizing these few words at this time.

As indicated in the preceding section, it is as easy for the child to learn *look* as a sight word as to remember the letter *k* as the last letter in the word. For a young child, learning the whole word is probably easier since the word is a concept while the letter *k* is not. From a typical first preprimer, as in figure 9.5, one can see that the child can learn these words by their differing configurations without too much confusion. When printed in lowercase characters, the letters provide some cues from ascenders (stems above the line) and descenders (stems below the line). Children can see that *come* and *ride* or *come* and *can* have different configurations. More important for beginners may be the more gross differentiations. *Tomorrow* or *grandmother* may be much easier to remember because of the length of the words compared to *come* or *can*. Also, long words with many ascenders and descenders may be easy to differentiate visually.

Ability to notice the different shapes of words may be of some value to readers if it teaches the habit of observing visual characteristics of new words that need unlocking. It must be pointed out, however, that visual configuration is not helpful to young children with pairs of words like *house* and *horse, these* and *those, tired* and *tried.*

Figure 9.5
Printing in lowercase
letters provides
children some clues
because words have
different shapes.

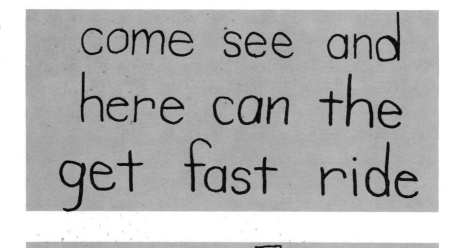

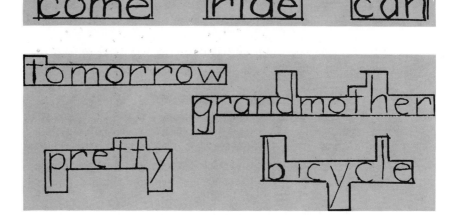

Some research has been done to identify the role of configuration clues in effective reading. Huey[4] notes that words can be read at a distance before the letters can be seen. McClelland[5] reports several of his own studies suggesting that adults utilize configuration information in reading. Haber and Haber[6] review the earlier studies, some of which had indicated that configuration plays little or no role in reading. However, they conclude that such clues are utilized by readers of all ages, that older, better readers use them even more than younger, poorer readers, and that configuration clues are most effective in conjunction with semantic and syntactic information.

Picture Clues

Picture context can be as helpful to the beginning reader as sentence context is helpful later on. A picture portraying action can help the reader identify verbs in sentence structure. Teachers should utilize pictures more than they do now. In the intermediate grades, for example, social studies material will be better

245

The fox galloped along beside the fence. He crashed under a clump of blackened brush and leaped to the top rail of the fence.

The dog went racing past.

The fox went on along the fence. The charred wood crumbled between his toes. He jumped down and raced lightly through the vineyard.

Now, far in the distance, he could hear the unhappy yelps of the dog.

Then there was silence.

Back in the barnyard, the dog trotted up, panting loudly, and the chickens scolded softly and settled down again to sleep.

The fox did not return.

understood if teachers discuss the pictures contained in the reading as a readiness activity. Questions that the teacher can raise about pictures may help to motivate students to study. The picture in figure 9.6 from the book *Fox and the Fire* by Miska Miles will help a child anticipate meaning if the teacher asks the appropriate questions before the child reads.

Picture dictionaries can be useful in helping children recognize words through the use of picture clues. Young children can learn more from a picture dictionary than to associate a printed word with a picture representing it. They learn that they can find information for themselves by going to the dictionary. Some picture dictionaries available are:

Jenkins, William A., and Andrew Schiller. *My First Picture Dictionary*. Glenview, Ill.: Scott, Foresman, 1975. Presents 800 words. Arranged by categories, but entries within a category are alphabetized. Accompanied by a student exercise book.

Jenkins, William A., and Andrew Schiller. *My Second Picture Dictionary*. Glenview, Ill.: Scott, Foresman, 1975. Alphabetically arranged.

Monroe, Marian, W. Cabel Greet, and Andrew Schiller. *My Pictionary*. Glenview, Ill.: Scott, Foresman, 1975. Arranged and color-coded by subjects. Contains 524 entries.

My First Dictionary: An American Heritage Dictionary. Boston: Houghton Mifflin, 1980. Contains 1,700 main entries. Includes 500 words basic to most reading programs.

Ogle, Lucille, and Tina Thorn. *The Golden Picture Dictionary:* A Beginning Dictionary of More than 2500 Words. New York: Western Publishing Co., 1976. Presents 2,500 words.

Reid, Hale C., and Helen W. Crane. *My Picture Dictionary*. Lexington, Mass.: Ginn, 1977.

Scarry, Huck (illus.). *My First Picture Dictionary*. New York: Random House, 1978.

Siculan, Dan (illus.). *Picture Book Dictionary*. Chicago: Rand McNally, 1970.

Young readers can use realia and picture dictionaries to learn many words and to expand their knowledge of the world around them.

A trend in first dictionaries appears to be to identify a fictional character popular with children and to organize an entire volume around that person. Examples of these picture dictionaries are:

Geisel, T. S., and Philip Eastman. *The Cat in the Hat Beginner Book Dictionary*. New York: Random House, 1964. Written by the Cat himself, this was a premier dictionary in the use of a single fictional character as an organizer. Presents vocabulary of 1,350 words.

Heyward, Linda. *The Sesame Street Dictionary*. New York: Random House, 1980. Based on the various characters of "Sesame Street." Presents 1,300 main entries.

Holmes, Mary Z. (editorial director). *The Super Dictionary*. New York: Holt, Rinehart & Winston, 1978. Features Superman and his associates.

Walt Disney's Winnie the Pooh Dictionary. New York: Golden Press, 1981. Typical of several paperback dictionaries available in supermarkets and discount houses as well as bookstores; current cost 95¢.

Developing Sight Vocabulary

The first problem in learning to read is that the learner must *know some words*. As the definition of reading in figure 1.2 shows, word perception is the first element of the four-step process of reading.

Early in the school year in first grade, children generally become word-conscious as a result of various techniques used by the teacher. One of these techniques is labeling many things in the classroom. Each child's name written in manuscript and taped to his or her desk is useful in classroom management, but it is also a way to help children fix the idea that everything has a name that can be written on a label. The labels *door, window, desk, toy box, teacher,* and *reading table* confirm the idea that printed or written words correspond to real objects.

These children are learning a large number of sight words as the result of lots of meaningful reading practice.

The best way for children to learn a small stock of sight words is by using them to read for meaningful purposes. As soon as they have a small stock of words, there are many interesting little stories and books that they can enjoy. *Using* reading is basic to developing the habit of reading.

By using the most common service words in group and individual experience stories, by labeling objects in the classroom, and by using the vocabularies in the first books to be read, the teacher helps children build a small stock of words they will encounter frequently in their reading.

One of the teacher's most difficult tasks is fitting this phase of beginning to learn a sight vocabulary to the wide range of differences in the reactions of first graders learning the vocabulary. Children who do not have well-developed spontaneous oral language abilities should certainly have an extended oral language program before attempting to read. Children who lack the visual motor coordination skills required in writing and in following consecutive lines of print may profit from special readiness teaching to promote these abilities. Children with poor auditory discrimination need to develop these skills. Even among children who possess all these readiness skills, there will be some who have little interest in learning to read just because the teacher considers it important. Other children will have problems in the affective domain that will influence their adjustment to school. Many children are fearful, others are anxious, some are hostile. These children need understanding and attention to their emotional adjustment before they will successfully retain what the teacher teaches.

Among the children who are not handicapped by the limitations just mentioned, the teacher will find fast learners, adequate learners, and slow learners in the different kinds of tasks in the school curriculum. A few first graders may already possess a sizable sight vocabulary. The teacher must identify these students and encourage their continued growth in reading skills.

The High-Frequency Service Words of Reading

Stone[7] compiled a list of one hundred high-frequency words in children's beginning reading. It is useful for teachers to be able to identify which of the words used in children's stories are the ones the children most need to master. This list is as follows:

a	dog	I	not	the
after	doll	in	now	then
am	down	into	oh	they
and	father	is	on	this
are	find	it	one	three
at	for	jump	out	to
away	fun	kitten	play	too
baby	funny	laughed	rabbit	two
ball	get	like	ran	up
big	girl	little	red	want
blue	go	look	ride	was
bow-wow	good	make	run	we
boy	good-by	may	said	went
came	had	me	saw	what
can	have	milk	school	where
car	he	morning	see	who
cat	help	mother	she	will
color	here	my	some	with
come	home	new	something	yes
did	house	no	stop	you

The teacher may record the children's dictation as follows:

Tom said, "May I go with you?"
George said, "Where are we going?"
Tom said, "Let's go to the park.
We can play ball in the park."
"OK," said George, "I'd like to go."

It is apparent that several words in the story are high-frequency service words. The following sixteen are on Stone's list:

said	with	are	the	ball
may	you	we	can	in
I	where	to	play	like
go				

Following is another story that might be dictated by first grade boys and girls:

Kee is a Navajo boy.
He lives in a hogan in the canyon.
He lives with his mother and father.
Kee has a pony.
It is a red pony.
He likes to ride his pony.
His pony can run fast.

The following seventeen words are on Stone's list.

is	in	and	red	ride
a	the	father	like	can
boy	with	it	to	run
he	mother			

All of the high-frequency words from the Stone list except nouns are also among the 220 words in the Dolch Basic Sight Vocabulary.[8] This is another list of service words every child must know as sight words in order to read well. The words are those common to three lists containing words used or understood by primary grade children.[9] No nouns are included since nouns change with subject matter and can be illustrated. Dolch also selected ninety-five common nouns as a useful list for teachers.

Following is a child's story about dinosaurs.

This is a dinosaur.
It is an animal *of long, long* ago.
Dinosaurs grew *very* large.
Dinosaurs laid eggs.
Dinosaurs *ate and ate.*
Some dinosaurs *ate only* plants.
Some dinosaurs *ate only* animals.
Maybe *little* animals *ate the* dinosaur eggs.
Maybe *the* land dried *up.*
Maybe *there was not* enough food.
Maybe *the* climate changed *to very cold* winters.
All the dinosaurs died.

Table 9.1 Percentage of words in school textbooks that are basic sight vocabulary.

Textbook	No. of Series Used	Grade I	II	III	IV	V	VI
Reading	4	70	66	65	61	59	59
Arithmetic	2			62	63	57	57
Geography	2				60	59	54
History	2				57	53	52

From E. W. Dolch, *Teaching Primary Reading* (Champaign, IL: Garrard, Copyright © 1941), p. 208. Reprinted by permission.

There are sixty-three words in this story; thirty-three, or 52 percent, are words from the Dolch Basic Sight Word List. They are italicized.

Preprimers and their accompanying teacher's manuals provide teachers with a sequenced introduction of vocabulary to be learned by the children preparatory to reading a first book with twenty or fewer different words.

Based on 1,000-word samplings from elementary school texts, Dolch found that 70 percent of the words in grade one readers were on the Dolch list; 66 percent in the second grade readers; 65 percent in the third grade readers; 61 percent in the fourth; 59 percent in the fifth and sixth (see table 9.1).

McNally and Murray worked from a basic word list of twenty thousand words.[10] They report that only *twelve words* constitute, on the average, 25 percent of the running words in printed material. These twelve words are:

a	I	it
the	and	in
of	to	he
is	that	was

All but "of" and "that" are on the Stone list of one hundred words; all twelve appear on the Dolch list. McNally and Murray believe that with eighty-eight additional words—one hundred in all—one has a list that, on the average, constitutes *half of the different words* used in most reading material. Adding another 150, making a total of 250, makes the list account for about 60 percent of the running words in reading and writing. This compares favorably with the Basic Sight Word List prepared by Dolch. The lists given by McNally and Murray are very significant for elementary teachers. (See figure 9.7.)

Fry's Instant Words   Fry selected a list of most frequently used words that could be mastered in remedial reading situations to give the child maximum flexibility in reading.[11] By arbitrarily combining and selecting from several word lists, Fry compiled a list of 600 words, which he divided into twenty-four groups of twenty-five words each.

Figure 9.7
McNally and Murray show the significance of the highest frequency words with their proportional representation of the most used words in English as applied to the vocabulary of an average adult.

J. McNally and W. Murray, *Key Words to Literacy* (London: Schoolmaster Publishing Co., Ltd., 1968), p. 1. Used with permission.

a and he

I in is

it of that

the to was

12

all as at be but are for had have him his not on one said so they we with you

20

about an back been before big by call came can come could did do down first from get go has her here if into just like little look made make me more much must my no new now off only or our other out over right see she some their them then there this two when up want well went were what where which who will your old.

68

After Again Always Am Ask Another Any Away Bad Because Best Bird Black Blue Boy Bring Day Dog Don't Eat Every Fast Father Fell Find Five Fly Four Found Gave Girl Give Going Good Got Green Hand Head Help Home House How Jump Keep Know Last Left Let Live Long Man Many May Men Mother Mr. Never Next Once Open Own Play Put Ran Read Red Room Round Run Sat Saw Say School Should Sing Sit Soon Stop Take Tell Than These Thing Think Three Time Too Tree Under Us Very Walk White Why Wish Work Woman Would Yes Year Bus Apple Baby Bag Ball Bed Book Box Car Cat Children Cow Cup Dinner Doll Door Egg End Farm Fish Fun Hat Hill Horse Jam Letter Milk Money Morning Mrs. Name Night Nothing Picture Pig Place Rabbit Road Sea Shop Sister Street Sun Table Tea Today Top Toy Train Water

150

This area represents 19,750 further words. Space does not permit the printing of these words.

He tried to arrange them in graduated difficulty from easiest to hardest to learn. The lists from which Fry selected included the Lorge-Thorndike, Rinsland, and the Dolch service words. His first 300 words will be very useful to all classroom teachers.

The first 100 words of the Fry list include 95 of the Dolch service words; the second 100 include 55 of the Dolch words; and the third 100 include 56. Thus, 206 of the total 220 Dolch service words are among the first 300 Fry instant words. These 300 can serve the same purposes as the comparable list prepared by Dolch.

The following lists are Fry's first hundred instant words, second hundred, and third hundred, each group being arranged in alphabetical order:

First Hundred

a	did	if	on	this
about	do	in	one	three
after	down	is	or	to
again	eat	it	other	two
all	for	just	our	up
an	from	know	out	us
and	get	like	put	very
any	give	little	said	was
are	go	long	see	we
as	good	make	she	were
at	had	man	so	what
be	has	many	some	when
been	have	me	take	which
before	he	much	that	who
boy	her	my	the	will
but	here	new	their	with
by	him	no	them	work
can	his	not	then	would
come	how	of	there	you
day	I	old	they	your

Second Hundred

also	each	left	own	sure
am	ear	let	people	tell
another	end	live	play	than
away	far	look	please	these
back	find	made	present	thing
ball	first	may	pretty	think
because	five	men	ran	too
best	found	more	read	tree
better	four	morning	red	under
big	friend	most	right	until
black	girl	mother	run	upon
book	got	must	saw	use
both	hand	name	say	want
box	high	near	school	way
bring	home	never	seem	where
call	house	next	shall	while
came	into	night	should	white
color	kind	only	soon	wish
could	last	open	stand	why
dear	leave	over	such	year

Third Hundred

along	don't	grow	off	stop
always	door	hat	once	ten
anything	dress	happy	order	thank
around	early	hard	pair	third
ask	eight	head	part	those
ate	every	hear	ride	though
bed	eyes	help	round	today
brown	face	hold	same	took
buy	fall	hope	sat	town
car	fast	hot	second	try
carry	fat	jump	set	turn
clean	fine	keep	seven	walk
close	fire	letter	show	warm
clothes	fly	longer	sing	wash
coat	food	love	sister	water
cold	full	might	sit	woman
cut	funny	money	six	write
didn't	gave	myself	sleep	yellow
does	goes	now	small	yes
dog	green	o'clock	start	yesterday

Techniques for Teaching Sight Words

Most reading series provide children the opportunity to discover new words for themselves if they have already learned the necessary skills to do so. For example, using sight words already known, the child can be shown how to make the following new words. If the series does not do so, the teacher should provide opportunities for these newly identified words to be added to the child's growing collection of words recognized at sight.

From the *T* in *Tom* and the *oy* in *boy*, make the new word *toy*.

From the *fl* in *fly* and the *ing* in *sing*, make *fling*.

From the *sh* in *show* and the *ore* in *tore*, make *shore*.

From the *tr* in *tree* and the *end* in *send*, make *trend*.

From the *ch* in *children* and the *ance* in *dance*, make *chance*.

The teacher can use language like the following to give children practice.

Take *b* away from *boy*, put in *t* and you have *toy*.

Take *s* away from *sing*, put in *fl* and you have *fling*.

Take *t* away from *tore*, put in *sh* and you have *shore*.

The Reading for Meaning Series[12] of basal readers provides the teacher with a number of models for reference in planning word recognition exercises:

1. Recognizing capital and small letters: Are *print* and *Print* the same?
2. Recognizing long vowel sounds: Does *idea* begin with the same sound as *island* and *idle*?

3. Discriminating between beginning sounds: Do *ice, iris, make,* and *isle* all begin with the same sound?
4. Hearing consonant clusters at the beginnings of words: Put *br* and the word *bridge* on the board; say a list of words—*brown, brook, could, letter, brave*—and ask the class to identify the *br* words.
5. Discovering new words: From the word *say* take away *s,* put in *pr* and make *pray.*
6. Substituting final sounds: Take *d* away from *bud,* put in *t* and make *but;* put in *n* and make *bun;* put in *s* and make *bus.*

The best technique for giving practice with sight words is undoubtedly to offer lots of opportunities to read material that is easy and meaningful for the child. The teacher should make every effort *to fill the room* with a variety of materials to read so that all students can find something to read that is comfortably easy and purposeful, from the children's point of view.

However, teachers may want to make or buy games that are intended to give practice with sight words. The teacher can easily invent bingo, checkers, and domino-type games that will give practice on sight words. Those games that are designed to put the sight words in sentences or phrases instead of in isolation are probably the best learning tools.

Some Problems That May Be Encountered

Some boys and girls have much difficulty with the abstract service words or often confuse certain pairs of words.

Since many structure words in sentence building are abstract and very difficult to illustrate visually, it is imperative that children learn them early in reading. Such words as *of, the, on, since,* and *because* were presented as "markers" in chapter 3. They are necessary sight words for early meaningful reading.

Children often confuse words like *then* and *when, where* and *there, what* and *that.* The question words *which, what, where, when,* and *why* also cause some children difficulty. These words appear over and over in reading at the second grade level, so teachers should use whatever devices they have found successful to help children distinguish them.

Exercises can be prepared by the teacher to give the child practice reading a troublesome word in context in sentences, when the child has been told that the word will be used; practice reading sentences in which the correct word must be supplied; and, later, practice reading sentences in which the word appears randomly along with words with which it is often confused.

A child who has much difficulty confusing *then* and *when* might first complete exercises that use only one of these words; then complete exercises that use only the other one; and finally complete exercises in which a choice between the two words must be made. Teachers can prepare sentence exercises like those shown in figure 9.8.

1. Write *then* in the blank and read the sentence.
   a. Put the book on the table, _____ bring me your paper.
   b. What will you do _____ ?
   c. _____ the teacher told us a story.

2. Write *when* in the blank and read the sentence.
   a. _____ is Bill coming home?
   b. _____ will it be time to go?
   c. Tell me _____ you are ready to go.

3. Read the sentence. Decide whether *when* or *then* belongs in the blank. Write in the correct word:
   a. I don't know _____ he is coming.
   b. He did his work; _____ he went home.
   c. The flowers will be blooming _____ .
   d. Apples are ripe _____ they are red.

Figure 9.8
Practice for overcoming "when-then" confusion.

From Theory to Practice 9.1
Developing Sight Word Vocabulary

Sometimes it is hard to trust that children will get enough practice with sight words when they are encouraged to do most of their reading from stories they have written or dictated. An analysis of several children's stories will make one feel more secure that the children are getting sufficient practice on sight words.

Collect at least five children's stories—stories that they have either written or dictated. Analyze each story for its sight words. A good word list to use in this analysis would be the Stone list or the first hundred words of the Fry list. Make a list of the sight words present in each of the stories. Determine how many sight words are used in the five stories. Bring your stories and your analysis to share with your classmates and your instructor.

Minimal Pairs

Hearing differences in words that sound almost alike is another difficulty with which teachers must help some boys and girls. Failing to discriminate the proper vowel sound within a word or consonant sound at the end of a word may cause a child to misunderstand or be misunderstood. Discriminating minimal pairs is discussed in chapter 3. Minimal pairs are word pairs that sound exactly alike except for one phoneme that differs. For example, *look* and *book* constitute a minimal pair because they differ only in initial consonant sound. However, the minimal pairs that present difficulty are likely to involve vowel or final consonant or consonant cluster differences.

While these difficulties in perceiving differences in sound are very common with children learning English as a second language, they are by no means limited to them. Common errors are final *g* and *k* confusion, as in *pig* and *pick; th* and *f* as in *death* and *deaf; s* and *z* as in *rice* and *rise; f* and *v* as in *leaf* and *leave*. Vowels such as *ee* and *i* as in *sheep* and *ship;* and *a* and *e* as in *age* and *edge* also cause difficulty.

A short list of minimal pairs follows:

pi*g*—pi*ck*	du*g*—du*ck*	wrea*th*—ree*f*
be*t*—be*d*	*c*old—*g*old	bu*zz*—bu*s*
*p*each—*b*each	ro*p*e—ro*b*e	play*s*—pla*ce*
cu*p*—cu*b*	p*oo*l—p*u*ll	ri*se*—ri*ce*
ca*p*—ca*b*	li*f*e—li*v*e	boa*t*—bo*th*
lea*f*—lea*v*e	*sh*eep—*sh*ip	*th*ick—*t*ick
toe*s*—toa*st*	b*i*t—b*ea*t	p*ai*n—p*e*n
a*g*e—e*dge*	dea*th*—dea*f*	

In teaching phonic analysis skills, teachers will provide practice in the auditory discrimination of such word pairs.

Context Clues

Word perception and pronunciation is the first step in the reading process. If the process stops with word calling, then reading as defined in chapter 1 does not take place. For hard-of-hearing and deaf children, modes of learning must maximize other avenues than auditory.

The next step is to use meaning or conceptual skills to relate what is being read to what is already known. This may be thought of as comprehension of the idea. It is depicted in figure 1.2 as the second step in the four-step process of reading.

The reader constructs a concept or a meaning when the last word in a sentence is perceived:

bank

John played the drums in the band

bang

bond

The reader first perceives that the four-letter word *is* ban*d* and not ban*k* or ban*g* or b*ond*. Step one requires the proper *pronunciation* to match the graphic form of *band*.

At the *comprehension* level, the reader must, in this case, know what a *band* is. However, this word has more than one meaning. Before moving to step three in the reading process, to *react* to the sentence as a unit, the reader must understand the use of the word *band* in the sentence and the use of all the words in the sentence as they relate to the meaning stored in the concept *band*.

This comprehension of words in any context necessitates a great storehouse of word meanings readily available to the reader. Children must be taught many ways of arriving at adequate meanings. Techniques for doing so will be explored in greater depth in later chapters, but at the elementary level they include teaching multiple meanings of common words, synonyms, homonyms, antonyms, perceiving word relationships in the sentence, and choosing the best dictionary definition. At the same time, the importance of word order in an English sentence is a further context clue.

Multiple Meanings of Common Words   The printed form of the word *run* represents many different words in our language. Horn illustrated:[13]

The disease has *run* its course.
The fence *runs* east and west.
To *run* to seed.
To *run* a garage.
To *run* a splinter in a finger.
To *run* out of money.
To *run* to ruin.

To *run* a risk.
To *run* up a bill.
To *run* across a friend.
To knock a home *run*.
A *run* on a bank.
The common *run* of persons.

Note the elementary uses of *down:*

I will walk *down* the stairs.
Jack likes to sleep under a *down* comforter.
The boy went *down* town.
The struggling swimmer went *down* for the third time.
The boxer was *down* for the count.
Jack fell *down*.
Elevators go up and *down*.

Teachers' guides and preparatory books provide many exercises to help children understand the variant meanings of common words by asking them to match meanings, as in the following exercise:

Directions: Read the sentences in group 1. Then find the sentence in group 2 that uses the word in italics in a similar way. Put the appropriate matching letter on the line in front of the sentence.

Group 1
a. Did you pay the gas *bill?*
b. Uncle *Bill* came to see us today.
c. Did you *bill* them for the medicine?
d. The bird's *bill* was broken.

Group 2

_____ The boy paid the grocery *bill* today.

_____ The chicken pulled the worm out with his *bill*.

_____ Will *Bill* go to school tomorrow?

_____ He *billed* us for the things we bought today.

Comparing and Contrasting Word Meanings

The teacher can provide exercises to develop children's abilities in giving synonyms, antonyms, or deciding whether words presented in pairs are alike or opposite in meaning.

1. Exercises giving synonyms:

   We followed a winding _____ . (path, trail, road)
   We brought water in a _____ . (bucket, pail, container)
   Snow sometimes _____the trail. (hid, covered, concealed)

2. Exercises identifying antonyms:

   John went *up* the hill. I wanted to go _____ .
   That rose was *rare* around here. It is getting more _____
   The light was *red;* it changed to _____ .
   He was *tired* last night but this morning he seemed _____ .

3. Exercises deciding whether words are synonyms or antonyms. For the child the instructions will read: "Write *s* on the line if the two words mean the same; write *o* if the meanings are opposite."

large	small	o
huge	gigantic	s
conceal	hide	s
common	rare	o
try	attempt	s

4. Worksheet exercises could ask the child to choose the correct spelling from among groups of homophones to fit a particular context.

scent	to	their	pear	sew
cent	two	there	pair	sow
sent	too	they're	pare	so
sight	right	rowed	vane	rain
site	rite	road	vein	reign
cite	write	rode	vain	rein

5. Perceiving relationships between or among words. Use the words in each group in *one* sentence.

   harvest, sale, cotton
   teacher, student, principal
   seed, irrigation ditches, planting

6. Choosing the best meaning in a given context. The child is asked to read the definitions and match the appropriate one with each example:

Scale: 1. Instrument for weighing
      2. Covering of the fish
      3. Size represented on a map

———— a. The *scale* used was 1 mile equals 1 inch.
———— b. They removed the *scales* with sharp knives.
———— c. They weighed the fish on the *scale.*

Phonic Analysis

Many phonic generalizations have been taught in an effort to help boys and girls anticipate pronunciation in new situations. However, some word-count studies have indicated less than complete effectiveness in selected generalizations taught. Those considered most useful are presented. However, if one hopes that phonics will be the child's answer to word recognition, the poem "Our Queer Language" shows some of the difficulties and inconsistencies in grapheme-phoneme relationships in the vocabulary to be mastered.

Our Queer Language

When the English Tongue we speak
Why is "break" not rhymed with "freak"?
Will you tell me why it's true
We say "sew" and likewise "few"?
And the maker of the verse
Cannot cap his "horse" with "worse"
"Beard" sounds not the same as "heard"
"Cord" is different from "word"
Cow is "cow" but low is "low"
"Shoe" is never rhymed with "foe"
Think of "hose" and "dose" and "lose"
And think of "goose" and not of "choose"
"Doll" and "roll," "home" and "some"
And since "pay" is rhymed with "say"
Why not "paid" with "said" I pray?
"Mould" is not pronounced like "could"
Wherefore "done" but "gone" and "lone"
Is there any reason known?
And in short it seems to me
Sounds and letters disagree.

                          Source unknown.

Smith describes how phonics instruction has been emphasized and deemphasized in cycles through the past two centuries.[14] The misplaced heavy emphasis on phonics in learning to read has already been discussed.

With the new emphasis on reading for meaning in the mid-thirties and concomitant attention to silent reading exercises to emphasize understanding, the teaching of phonics was deemphasized to the point of neglect. Of course, the

Figure 9.9
Many teachers help boys and girls learn letters by collecting pictures of things whose names begin with the same letter. These pictures were used for the "B" page in a first grade book of sounds.

pendulum has swung back now so that *phonics is being taught today*. The great majority of teachers are teaching phonic and structural analysis skills. Today teachers encourage children to use phonic skills along with several other strategies such as context clues, analyzing word structure, checking for meaning, and using the dictionary for recognizing words.

Phonic skills are now taught to children with a different emphasis. They are taught sequentially throughout the reading program and with spaced reviews. The sequence is designed to develop all the necessary abilities to unlock new words. Phonic skills are introduced gradually in reading series as an integral part of the complete set of techniques in the eclectic approach. This approach was identified and developed by Gates as the intrinsic approach to teaching phonics. Teaching phonics functionally in relation to the reading children are doing and as a way of attacking difficulties as they arise is a defensible practice.

Beginning in the kindergarten, children have a great deal of informal practice in auditory discrimination. (1) They hear how each other's first names begin, as in Carl, Carolyn, Kate, and Karen. (2) They hear Mother Goose rhymes, as in "Jack and *Jill* went up the *hill*." (3) They hear the teacher call attention to words used in their own conversations, as when one child says, *"home, house, and hospital,"* and the teacher points out that all begin with *h*, or that a string of words rhyme, as in *at, bat, cat, dat, gat, lat*. (See figure 9.9.)

The phonic elements to be taught include:

1. The sounds of the single consonant letters. (*Q, X, Y,* and *Z* will not be needed early in the program.)
2. The consonant cluster sounds in both initial and final positions in words:

Initial position: *sm*art, *sk*ill, *st*ick, *tr*ain, *sw*eep, *str*ing.
Final position: cha*sm*, whi*sk*, ta*sk*, mou*nds*, fore*sts*, mea*sles*.

3. The consonant digraphs: *ch, sh, th, wh* in initial and final positions in words:

Initial position: *ch*eck, *sh*all, *th*ink, *wh*en.
Final position: bu*nch*, wa*sh*, ba*th*.

4. The short and the long sounds of the vowels:

Short vowel words: b*a*g, b*e*g, b*i*g, b*o*g, b*u*g.
Long vowel words: m*a*te, m*e*te, m*i*te, b*o*ne, m*u*te.

5. The consonant-vowel-consonant (CVC) generalization:

The vowel in a closed syllable usually has its short sound, as in f*i*n ish, c*a*n dor, l*o*t tery, b*u*t ter, g*e*t ting.

6. The vowel digraphs: *ay, ai, au, ee, ea, ei, eu, ew, ie, oa, oo, ow.*
7. The vowel diphthongs: *oi, oy, ou, ow.*
8. In a syllable ending in a vowel, the vowel is usually long, *he, she.* (This is the consonant-vowel [CV] generalization.)
9. In a short word with a middle vowel and ending with *e*, usually the *e* is silent and the middle vowel is long. (This is the CVCV generalization.)
10. The schwa sound: (ə), as in *a*bout, penc*i*l. It occurs only in unstressed syllables. The following list of words containing the schwa are taken from Cordts:[15]

_ə_ bout	fath_ə_ r	Sat_ə_ rn	cupb_ə_ rd
at_ə_ m	doct_ə_ r	tap_ə_ r	surg_ə_ n
circ_ə_ s	doll_ə_ r	fash_ə_ n	tort_ə_ s

11. The clues to silent letters in words. Silent consonants designate those letters in syllables that are not sounded when the syllable is spoken. Cordts gave the following generalizations:[16]

The letter *b* is silent after *m* and before *t:* debt, doubt, climb, comb.
The letter *g* is silent before *m* and *n:* gnat, gnu, sign, diaphragm.
The letter *h* may be silent before any vowel or when preceded by *r:* rhyme, rhinoceros, honest, herb.
The letters *gh* are silent after *a, i,* or *o:* high, eight, bought, caught.
The letter *k* is silent before *n:* knock, know, knife, knee.
The letter *l* is silent before *k, d,* or *m:* talk, would, calm, salmon.
The letter *p* is silent before *s, t,* or *n:* psalm, pneumonia, ptomaine.
The letter *t* following *s* or *f:* listen, often, thistle, soften.
The letter *w* before *r:* wrist, write, wren, wrong.

12. Several consonant sounds have more than one sound:

The hard sound of *g*, when *g* is followed by *a, o,* or *u.*
The soft sound of *g*, when *g* is followed by *e, i,* or *y.*
The hard sound of *c*, when *c* is followed by *a, o,* or *u.*

The soft sound of *c*, when *c* is followed by *e*, *i*, or *y*.

The *s* sound as *z* in *fuse;* *sh* in *sugar;* and *zh* in *treasure.*

The *x* sound as *ks* in box; *gz* in *exact;* and *z* in *xylophone, Xerxes.*

13. Syllabic consonants. There are many words in which there is no vowel in the unaccented syllable. The consonants *l*, *n*, and *m* sometimes function as syllables by themselves. In the word *little*, *lit* forms one sounded syllable and the letter *l* forms the other. In the word *garden*, *gard* forms one sounded syllable and the letter *n* forms the other. In the word *rhythm*, *rhyth* forms the first sounded syllable and the letter *m* forms the other. Because *l*, *m*, and *n* are capable of forming a syllable by themselves, they are known as syllabic consonants.

There are many examples in English words where phoneme-grapheme relationships are irregular or inconsistent. However, when there are few examples in children's work, it seems best not to teach an element, or its exceptions, until needed. Examples include *ph* as *f;* *qu* always sounds like *kw;* the *s* is silent in *isle, aisle,* and *island.*

The pronunciation of suffixes beginning with *t*, as in *tion, tious, tial*, must also be taught as a special sound of *sh* for the letter *t*.

By second grade the child has met at least six spellings for long *a* (ā)—p*a*per, *a*te, pl*a*y, pr*ai*se, f*ai*l, gr*ea*t—and eight different sounds spelled by *ea*—gr*ea*t, br*ea*d, w*ea*r, *ea*t, h*ea*rt, s*ea*rch, b*ea*uty, bur*ea*u.

Cordts found forty-seven different sound-letter associations for the letter *a* in words actually occurring in first, second, and third readers.[17]

Fifty years ago Horn raised the question whether English spelling is so unphonetic as to make teaching phonic generalizations in the primary grades impractical.[18]

English spellings often seem irregular—even irrational—and are therefore difficult to teach. The seeming lack of correspondence between the sounds and the spellings of the English language is a product of the history of the language. The spelling of *knight* is an example. It fully corresponded to speech at the time the *k* was pronounced and the *gh* represented a phoneme of English that has since gone out of the language.

Most phonic generalizations that have been developed take into account only surface details, not underlying historical facts about the language. They have limited scope, therefore.

The value of teaching rules for phonic and structural analysis is open to serious question if some of the first words the child reads and tries to apply the rule to happen to be exceptions. For example, the child may learn that "when two vowels go walking" the first one has its long sound—but then must learn to cope with *bread* and *break* about as soon as with *team* and *cream.*

Oaks[19] in 1952 found that vowel situations requiring explanation appear as early as the primer in basal readers. Clymer[20] in 1963 found that many generalizations being taught had limited value and that teachers must teach many exceptions to most generalizations being taught. Of forty-five generalizations that he found in primary grade teachers' manuals for basal readers, when checked against all the words in a composite word list, the percent of utility was too low to justify teaching many of them. Using 75 percent as an arbitrary criterion value of usefulness, he found only eighteen generalizations worth teaching.

Burrows and Lourie[21] found that teachers might look for other ways to pronounce double vowels than to try to use the "when two vowels go walking" generalization.

Emans[22] studied the applicability of Clymer's generalizations in grades four and above and found that a few of Clymer's generalizations had less applicability above fourth grade and that there were a few not included by Clymer that had more applicability.

Bailey[23] evaluated the utility of Clymer's forty-five generalizations and found some of them clearly stated and especially useful. She found some less useful, and others difficult to interpret.

Burmeister[24] sifted results from the studies of Oaks, Clymer, Fry,[25] Bailey, Emans, and Winkley, combined them with her own data, and developed a list of especially useful generalizations. The following are selected from that list:

The behavior of consonants:
When *c* and *h* are next to each other, they make only one sound.
Ch is usually pronounced as it is in mu*ch, ch*eck; not like *sh*.
When *c* or *g* is followed by *e, i,* or *y,* the soft sound is likely to be heard;
    otherwise they will have a hard sound.
When *ght* is seen in a word, *gh* is silent.
When a word begins with *kn,* the *k* is silent.
When a word begins with *wr,* the *w* is silent.
When two of the same consonants are side by side, only one is heard.
When a word ends in *ck,* it has the same last sound as in *look*.

The behavior of vowels:
If the only vowel is at the end of a one-syllable word, the letter usually
    has its long sound.
The *r* gives the preceding vowel a sound that is neither long nor short.
When the letters *oa* are together in a word, *o* gives its long sound and *a* is
    silent.
Words having double *e* usually have the long *e* sound.
When *y* is the final letter in a word, it usually has a vowel sound.
When *a* is followed by *r* and final *e,* we expect to hear the sound heard in
    care.

Rationale for Vowel Spellings

It is not possible to offer a helpful and simple set of generalizations for the spelling-sound correspondences of the five English vowel graphemes. Generally, the spelling-sound relationships of the vowel letters show little regularity. Nevertheless, there are some patterns that teachers of reading, especially in the early elementary grades, will find helpful.

1. The one-syllable word ending in a consonant—the closed syllable, CVC—will contain a vowel that usually uses its short sound; for example: c*a*n, m*e*n, f*i*n, c*o*t, b*u*t, c*a*ndle, m*e*ntion, f*i*nishing, c*o*ttage, b*u*tterfly.

   The many three-letter words fitting the following pattern suggest that this is a very important generalization for boys and girls to learn early in the reading program:

bad	bed	bid		bud
bag	beg	big	bog	bug
bat	bet	bit		but
		dig	dog	dug
Dan	den	din	don	dun
fan	fen	fin		fun
ham	hem	him		hum
hat		hit	hot	hut
lad	led	lid		
mad		mid		mud
mat	met	mit		
	net	nit	not	nut
pan	pen	pin		pun
pat	pet	pit	pot	put
	red	rid	rod	
sat	set	sit		
tan	ten	tin		
tap		tip	top	

2. The vowel followed by a consonant followed by final *e* (V + C + e) usually has its long sound, c*a*ne, m*e*te, f*i*ne, r*o*te, m*u*te.

   The teacher may teach many short sounds of the vowels first. However, children do learn from contrasting, too. It may be helpful for some children to contrast *not* and *note, hat* and *hate,* etc., by listening to the separate sounds of the vowels as they look at both words together. A short list of common pairs in this pattern follows:

tap	tape	plan	plane	mop	mope	rid	ride
can	cane	bad	bade			dim	dime
pan	pane	fat	fate	pin	pine	fin	fine
man	mane			slid	slide	rip	ripe
hat	hate	not	note	win	wine	kit	kite
mad	made	hop	hope	bit	bite	hid	hide

3. The vowel may retain its long sound if the vowel is followed by a consonant followed by another vowel within the word:

   c*a*nine   l*a*dle   p*i*lot   m*e*ter   p*o*tent   m*u*sic

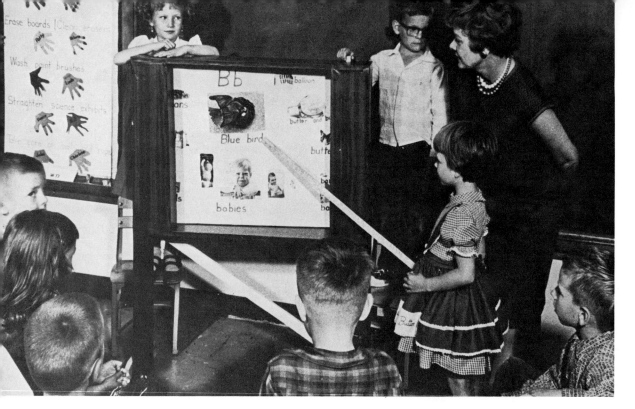

These children are reviewing phonics knowledge using a "television program" of words that begin with certain sounds and letters.

The vowel sound is short if the vowel is followed by a consonant cluster (*dg, x*) or by geminate consonants (*dd, gg, nn*). Geminate means occurring in pairs—as twin consonants, ca*bb*age, ru*bb*ed, and se*tt*ing.

badge   saddle   *exit*   antenna   taxi   cognate

4. The long vowel sound in V + C + e changes to a short sound in words that add syllables like *ic* or *ity* or when geminate consonants (twin consonants) appear:

sane	sanity	later	latter
mete	netting	caning	canning
cone	conic	hoping	hopping
rose	roster	motel	mottle
site	sitting	super	supper
induce	induction	biting	bitter
		tubing	tubbing

5. The V + C + e pattern may also produce long vowel sounds in polysyllabic words:

file	domicile	late	matriculate	size	nationalize
fume	resume	gene	gangrene	robe	microbe

6. Boys and girls need direct teaching of specific application for much of their beginning work with double vowels in one-syllable words. Double *e* producing long *e* and *oa* producing long *o* will be consistent in the words in the elementary school.[26] But *ea* may be long *e* in *lean* and *beat,* short *e* in *bread,* and long *a* in *break.* The double vowel *oo* uses one of its sounds in *book* and the other in *moon. Ou* and *aw* sound alike in a few words but have variant sounds in others.

Structural Analysis

Structural analysis is the means by which the parts of a word that form meaning units or pronunciation units within the word are identified. Structural analysis includes recognizing the root word as a meaning unit, identification of compound words, prefixes and suffixes, and generalizations about syllabication. Very important in this task is appreciating the influence of stress on syllables as spoken.

Dictionaries usually try to retain the base word or the root as nearly as possible in its original form when showing how words can be divided at the end of a line of print. In other words, dictionaries show primarily how the written, not the spoken, word is divided. Cordts says:

> The syllabication of the spoken word may or may not coincide with the way the word is divided when the word is written. The simple word *selfish* offers an example. When writing the word, it is correctly divided as *self ish,* but the spoken word is *sel'fish.*[27]

Inflectional Variants

1. Possessive forms: John's, the man's.
2. Plural nouns with *s* or *es:* apples, cups, boxes, bananas.
3. Verbs changed by:

   s or *es:* walks, finishes, takes, jumps
   d or *ed:* walked, finished, hoped, filed
   ing: walking, finishing, hoping, filing
   n or *en:* taken, given, loosen, tighten

4. Comparison using *er* and *est:*

   faster, fastest, taller, tallest.

5. Dropping final *e:*

hope	hoping	tape	taping
bare	baring	mope	moping
cane	caning	stare	staring
mate	mating	pine	pining

6. Doubling final consonant:

hop	hopping	tap	tapping
bar	barring	mop	mopping
can	canning	star	starring
mat	matting	pin	pinning

7. Changing *y* to *i*:

happy happiest	crazy craziest	pretty prettiest

8. Changing *f* to *v*:

half halving	shelf shelving	calf calving

Independent Parts of Compound Words

The parts of compound words are, by definition, complete words by themselves:

something	became	broadcloth
grandmother	lifelike	newcomers
airplane	outlaw	wanderlust

Roots, Prefixes, and Suffixes

Each italicized root has both a prefix and a suffix:

en *camp* ment	dis *approv* ing	in *adequate* ly

Fifteen common prefixes constitute the majority of prefixes used in writing for elementary school children.[28] It is important that they be taught meaningfully to boys and girls in the fifth and sixth grades. Boys and girls need to learn that these letters' appearance at the beginning of a word is not a definite indication that they represent a prefix. Learning the meanings and selecting examples is a suitable exercise for sixth graders who perform at grade level. In the lists below, the most common meaning of the prefix or suffix is given along with one or two examples:

Prefix	Meaning	Examples
ab	from	abnormal
ad	to	admit, adhere
be	by	bedecked
com	with, together	compact, commiserate
de	reversal	deduct, depose
dis	reversal	disappear, disengage
en	in	enjoy
ex	out	exhale, export
in	inside	inhabit, inhibit
in	not	incorrect, inadequate
pre	before	preview, prediction
pro	for, forward	propel, pronoun
re	again	renovate, reconsider
sub	under	submarine, subjugate
un	not	unhappy, uncommon

Suffix	Meaning	Examples
able	having the potential	suitable
al	having the property of	magical, national
ance	act, process, or fact of being, quality, state of	disappearance

ant	promoting an action	assistant, observant
ary	belonging to, or connected with	legendary, momentary
en	consisting of, or cause to be	wooden, sweeten
ful	full of or characterized by	sorrowful, healthful
hood	a state or condition of	manhood, falsehood
ion	result of an act or process	expression, perfection
less	without	needless, regardless
ly	in the manner of	gladly

Children should be asked to complete exercises like the following:

Choose *less, like, ful, ness,* or *ly* as a suffix to make the word being defined.

In a cruel manner _____ (*cruelly*)
Without hope _____ (*hopeless*)
Full of being good _____ (*goodness*)
Like a bird _____ (*birdlike*)
Full of peace _____ (*peaceful*)

Greek and Latin Combining Forms

Making charts like the following is helpful to boys and girls:

Combining Forms			Literal Meanings		
bio	+	logy	life	+	science of
geo	+	graphy	earth	+	to write about
thermo	+	meter	heat	+	to measure
tele	+	scope	far away	+	to view

Exercises to Develop Understanding of Structural Analysis

Exercises like the following are useful:

Copy the word that is italicized. Write down what it means.

Everyone needs a *friend.*
I lost my *friend's* address.
He is a *friendly* person.
Jim acts *friendlier* than Ted.
Ed is sometimes *unfriendly.*
I hope I never am *friendless.*
I admire his *friendliness.*
I need your *friendship.*
The Red Cross will *befriend* the flood-stricken people.[29]

The teacher or the students can make charts like the following:

Building inflected and derived forms with root words

	come				come	ly
	come	s		in	come	
	com	ing		wel	come	
be	come				come	back
be	com	ing		over	come	

	cross			cross	country
a	cross		double	cross	
	cross	es	hot	cross	buns
	cross	ed		cross	wise
	cross	ing		cross	eye
un	cross			cross	roads
	cross	section	criss	cross	

Syllables are classified as open or closed and as accented or unaccented. Open syllables are those that end with a vowel sound; closed syllables are those that end with a consonant sound.

Open Syllables	Closed Syllables
se′ cret	sun′ set
po′ nies	mon′ key
ti′ ger	but′ ter
sto′ ries	rain′ bow
pota′ to	dif′ ferent
fa′ mous	cir′ cle

Rules for Syllabication

Students must understand that the rules of syllabication that indicate how a written or printed word may be broken are not applicable to spoken words. The following rules are followed by most publishers.

1. When there are two consonants between two vowels in a polysyllabic word, the syllables will divide between the two consonants unless the first vowel has its long sound. VCCV indicates letter order: vowel-consonant-consonant-vowel in words.

VCCV Words	VCCV Words with the First Vowel Sound Long
mon·key	se·cret
ob·li·gate	mi·crobe
cir·cum·fer·ence	
per·fect	
mis·take	

2. When there are twin consonants between the separated vowel sounds, the word is divided between the consonants:

but·ter	lad·der	skim·ming
cab·bage	cop·per	com·mon
sum·mer	cot·tage	bal·loon

3. When a word is composed of two complete words—that is, a compound word—it is first divided between the two words that make up the compound word:

any·one	grand·mother	bird·house
some·where	sun·set	school·yard
any·thing	pop·overs	air·plane
who·ever	cow·boy	tooth·brush

4. Syllables usually do not break between consonant cluster letters or special two-letter combinations:

chil·*dr*en   an·*gr*y   lea*th*·er   bro*th*·er

5. When there is one consonant between two vowels, the consonant usually goes with the next syllable if the preceding vowel has its long sound, and with the preceding syllable if the vowel has its short sound or some other sound (VCV indicates letter order—vowel-consonant-vowel in words):

VCV Words, Consonant Begins Second Syllable		VCV Words, Consonant Remains with Preceding Syllable		
fa·tal	to·tal	shiv·er	tax·i	per·il
pa·per	a·muse	nov·el	ex·ert	rock·ets
de·lay	a·corn	trav·el	mim·ic	mon·ey
o·ver	po·lite	sol·id	ban·ish	fath·er
be·gin	ti·ger	rap·id	rob·in	sec·ond
sa·ble	gro·cer		cour·age	com·et
pro·vide	be·tween			

In most of these examples, if the first syllable retains the long vowel sound, the consonant begins the second syllable. Also, if the consonant between the two vowels is either *x* or *v*, this letter often remains with the preceding vowel to form a syllable.

6. When two adjacent vowels in a word form separate syllables, the word is divided between the two vowels. For example, *ru·in, gi·ant, fu·el, Su·ez, cre·ate, li·on, po·etry.*

It is not expected that boys and girls will attempt to learn rules of syllabication until they have derived the generalization based on seeing a large number of words syllabicated in each of the various ways provided by these rules.

Little words in big ones.   Children cannot generalize about finding little words in big words:

At is not *at* in attack, dated, eat, fatal, fathom, material, patriot, path, patrol, station, water, watch.[30]
Up is not *up* in pupil, puppet, rupee, supervisor, superman, cupid, cupola, duplicate, duplex.

Teachers need to give some consideration to stress in pronunciation. Some general statements are possible about the use of stress even though there are few widely applicable rules that can be taught.

In a two-syllable word, one syllable is usually stressed more than the other. In many polysyllabic words, one syllable gets a primary emphasis or stress and another gets a secondary stress. Boys and girls will best learn about stress by generalizing from the examples in which they apply stress to make the intonation and rhythm of their spoken language communicate properly. A vowel grapheme usually has a distinctive sound only when in an accented syllable. It usually has the schwa sound (ə) when in an unaccented syllable.

In a two-syllable word in which the first syllable is *not a prefix,* the stress usually falls on the first syllable. For example, *res'cue, stu'pid, fun'ny.*

In a polysyllabic word with a root and prefixes and suffixes, the root of the word is often stressed: *en camp' ment, im prove' ment, sur round' ing.*

In a polysyllabic word ending in *tion, cion, sion, tious, cious,* stress usually falls on the next to the last syllable: pre ven' tion, grav i ta' tion, pre ten' tious, un con' scious.

Cordts recommends three generalizations about placing stress in polysyllabic words but emphasizes that all such generalizations will have exceptions:[31]

1. Two-syllable words that are used as both nouns and verbs will likely be stressed on the first syllable as nouns and on the last syllable as verbs: *per'fume* is a noun; *per fume'* is a verb.

Nouns	Verbs
rec' ord	re·cord'
prog' ress	pro·gress'
pro' test	pro·test'
sur' vey	sur·vey'
per' mit	per·mit'
in'sult	in·sult'
con' flict	con·flict'

2. Words having three or more syllables are apt to have both a primary stress (') and a secondary stress ("), as in *con" sti tu' tion, mul" ti pli ca' tion.*

3. In counting, the first syllable of a number name is stressed, but in saying the numbers, both syllables are accented. One counts *fif' teen, six' teen, sev' en·teen, eigh' teen;* but one says *fif' teen', six' teen', sev' en·teen'.*

There are many words that have an accented syllable in which the vowel sound changes to an unaccented sound—that is, the schwa—when another form of the word is used:

Vowel Sound	Schwa Sound
at′ om	ə·tom′ ic
cor′ al	kər·ral′
up′ per	əp·on′
par′ ti·cle	pər·tik′ yə·lər

Winkley tried to find out whether stress generalizations should be taught.[32] Using the eighteen stress generalizations listed by Gray,[33] Winkley prepared a test requiring students in the intermediate grades to underline the stressed syllables, select the correct vowel sound for the stressed syllable, and choose the correct meaning of the word. As a result of her testing, she concluded that the following generalizations should be taught in grades four to six:

1. When there is no other clue in a two-syllable word, the stress is usually on the first syllable. Examples: *ba′sic, pro′gram.*
2. In inflected or derived forms of words, the primary stress usually falls on or within the root word. Examples: *box′es, untie′.*
3. If *de-, re-, be-, ex-, in-,* or *a-* is the first syllable of a word, it is usually unstressed. Examples: *delay′, explore′.*
4. Two vowel letters together in the last syllable of a word may be a clue to a stressed final syllable. Examples: *com·plain′, con·ceal′.*
5. When there are two like consonant letters within a word, the syllable before the double consonants is usually stressed. Examples: *be·gin′ner, let′ter.*
6. The primary stress usually occurs on the syllable before the suffixes *-ion, -ity, -ic, -ian, -ial,* or *-ious,* and on the second syllable before the suffix *-ate.* Examples: *af·fec·ta′tion, dif·fer·en′ti·ate.*
7. In words of three or more syllables, one of the first two syllables is usually stressed. Examples: *ac′ci·dent, de·ter′mine.*

Use of the Dictionary

To find words needed, determine proper pronunciation of words, and establish meanings appropriate to the context in which the word is being used, every child must become proficient in the use of the dictionary. Third grade boys and girls who read at or above grade level should be developing some of the dictionary skills outlined in this section. Much time will be devoted to teaching dictionary skills in both fourth and fifth grades because all children will not acquire the skills when they are taught, and the teacher must provide for much reteaching and review.

The skills needed for dictionary usage have been classified into location, pronunciation, and meaning skills (see table 9.2).

In order to find words quickly in the dictionary, children need to know how entries are made and how different forms of a word are handled in the dictionary. If a child is looking for *reporting* and there is no entry for this word, the child must know that *reporting* is derived from *report* and that the word must be looked for under the *report* entry.

Table 9.2 Location, pronunciation, and meaning skills needed by boys and girls in the elementary school in the use of the dictionary.

Location Skills	Pronunciation Skills	Meaning Skills
1. Ability to arrange words in alphabetical order from the initial letter to the fourth letter.	1. Ability to use the pronunciation key at the bottom of each page.	1. Learning meanings of new words by reading simple definitions.
2. Ability to find words quickly in an alphabetical list.	2. Ability to use the full pronunciation key in the front of the dictionary.	2. Using pictures and definitions in the dictionary to arrive at meanings.
3. Ability to open the dictionary quickly to the section in which the desired word is to be found—to the proper fourth of the book.	3. Ability to use and interpret stress marks, both primary and secondary.	3. Using an illustrative sentence to arrive at meanings.
4. Ability to use the two guide words at the top of the page.	4. Ability to select the correct pronunciation for a homograph; for example, *rec'ord* or *re·cord'*, *ob'ject* or *ob·ject'*.	4. Using two different meanings for the same word.
5. Ability to think of the names of letters immediately preceding and immediately following the letter being located.	5. Ability to identify silent letters in words pronounced.	5. Ability to approximate real life sizes by using dictionary pictures and explanatory clues.
6. Ability to use special pronunciation-meaning sections of the dictionary; for example, medical terms, slang expressions, musical terms, and foreign words and phrases.	6. Ability to recognize differences between spellings and pronunciations (lack of phoneme-grapheme relationship).	6. Ability to select the specific meaning for a given context.
	7. Ability to use phonic spelling for pronunciation.	7. Understanding special meanings: idioms, slang expressions, and other figures of speech.
	8. Ability to discriminate vowel sounds.	8. Use of the concept of *root word*.
	9. Ability to use diacritical marks as an aid in pronunciation.	9. Interpreting multiple meanings of words.
	10. Understanding how syllables are marked in dictionaries.	10. Ability to know when meaning has been satisfied through dictionary usage.
	11. Ability to identify unstressed syllables in words.	
	12. Arriving at pronunciation and recognizing it as correct.	

From Theory to Practice 9.2
Use of the Dictionary

Make arrangements to work with three to five boys and girls at a grade level between third and sixth. Your task will be to have some experiences with the dictionary. Each child will need a dictionary.

Listed here are three suggested activities. Select one and carry it out with the children.

1. One initial problem children have is just being able to turn quickly to the part of the dictionary where the entry is located. Play a two- or three-minute game with the children in which they try to open the dictionary to the letter named. For example, you might say "S." The children will try to open their dictionaries to the "S" section on the first try. Name other letters that have long lists of entries. If the children can do this task well, you may wish to try some of the letters with few entries—j, q, x, or i. This is a game to be played quickly and for a short period of time.

2. Prepare a list of sentences such as those that follow for the children to read. Have them look up the underlined words and find the definitions that match the meanings in the sentences. Many children find it difficult to locate the correct meaning from among the various meanings presented.

   Joe made a <u>run</u> in the ball game.
   The cowboy found the <u>shoe</u> his horse had lost.
   The carpenter bought a new <u>saw</u> for her work.
   The club members voted to <u>table</u> the motion.
   The detective found the <u>key</u> to the mystery.
   The class put on a <u>play</u> for the parents.
   Sam's mother will <u>order</u> clothes from the catalog.

3. Children may not always realize the relationship between root words and words that are related to them. For example, they may not associate the following root and its related words: *prove*—proved, proving, provable, prover, proven.

   Have the children look up *some* of the following words and find all of their related words. Talk about how each of the forms might be used. The number of the words chosen will depend on the ages and reading levels of the children. Few children will remain interested if more than three or four of the words are used.

boot	coat	neighbor
expect	depend	yellow
rain	thin	detect

Prepare a record of what happened during the experience. The record may be taped or written. Bring it to class to share as your instructor desires.

A number of dictionaries are designed for elementary school children. Classrooms should have sufficient copies of a good one so that they are easily accessible to each child. This is necessary in order to develop the dictionary habit.

A few of the elementary school dictionaries of recent copyright are:

Beginning Dictionary. William D. Halsey, editorial director. New York: Macmillan, 1977. Accompanied by *School Dictionary Practice Book.*

Children's Dictionary: An American Heritage Dictionary. *Fernando de Mello Vianna,* editorial director. Boston: Houghton Mifflin, 1979. Over 30,000 entries.

Ginn Intermediate Dictionary. Lexington, Mass.: Ginn, 1977. Grades three through six; 34,000 entries.

The HBJ School Dictionary. Harrison G. Platt, ed. New York: Harcourt Brace Jovanovich, 1977. Grades four through eight; 46,000 entries.

Scott, Foresman Beginning Dictionary. E. L. Thorndike, Clarence L. Barnhart. Glenview, Ill.: Scott, Foresman, 1979. Contains 25,000 main entries.

Scott, Foresman Intermediate Dictionary. Clarence L. Barnhart, ed. Glenview, Ill.: Scott, Foresman, 1978.

Webster's Beginning Dictionary. Springfield, Mass.: Merriam, 1980. Grades three through six; 32,000 entries.

Webster's New World Dictionary for Young Readers. David B. Guralnik. Cleveland: Collins, 1979. Grades four through eight; 46,000 entries.

Another reference tool, the thesaurus, can provide children with help in word recognition and word meanings. Two examples are:

In Other Words: A Beginning Thesaurus. Andrew Schiller and William A. Jenkins. Glenview, Ill.: Scott, Foresman, 1977. Suited for upper elementary students. Has accompanying exercise book.

In Other Words: A Junior Thesaurus. Andrew Schiller and William A. Jenkins. Glenview, Ill.: Scott, Foresman, 1977. Suited for late primary students. Has accompanying exercise book.

The Microcomputer As an Instructional Tool

For decades the conventional tools for reading instruction and additional practice have been basal readers, workbooks, duplicated worksheets, and chalkboard exercises. Now the time of the microcomputer has arrived. School systems across the country are in the process of spending millions of dollars for hardware and the accompanying software(the instructional packets). Increasingly, parents are buying microcomputers for their children's use at home. It is necessary that teachers move quickly to become literate in using the microcomputer.

A related component of the microcomputer is the word processor. Its use allows students to create, revise, edit, store and retrieve their ideas in print. It has great potential for the language-experience approach to reading and for creative writing.

A representative sample of the software packets for word-attack skills is given below. These materials come from different companies and are prepared for various microcomputers.

Alphabet Keyboard by Betamax (New York: Random House).

Word Blaster (cloze activities) with Bill Martin as consultant (New York: Random House).

Intermediate Reading Skills, including programs for "Compound Words" and
"Prefixes and Suffixes" for grades 3 and 4 (Wilmington, Del.: BLS, Inc.).
Consonant-Vowel-Consonant, a program for short vowels for grades 2 to 4. Pet
(Englewood Cliffs, New Jersey: Scholastic, Inc.).

Games and Devices

Games and devices, if they are carefully chosen, can provide some of the necessary drill in reading skills. If they offer the child an opportunity to win, they may even provide motivation. Winning the game will be its own reward. At the same time, the child will experience success in learning a reading-related skill.

The mechanics of the game should *not* be such that little time is spent on the learning of the skills needed in reading. The fun part should center around a reading skill rather than a physical skill not related to the reading act.

Available commercial games, a few selected games that teachers can devise, and a brief list of sources of good games and devices are given below.

Commercial Games

1. The *Group-Sounding Game* gives the child practice in self-help sounding at different levels (Champaign, Ill.: Garrard).
2. *Go-Fish* is a card game for practicing and reinforcing auditory discrimination of initial consonant sounds (first series) and consonant blend sounds (second series) (Kingsbury Center, 2138 Bancroft Place, N.W., Washington, D.C. 20008: The Remedial Education Press).
3. *Vowel Dominoes* is a card game played like dominoes that practices and reinforces the short vowel sounds (Kingsbury Center, 2138 Bancroft Place, N.W., Washington, D.C. 20008: The Remedial Education Press).
4. *Take* is a card game designed to practice hearing the sounds at the beginning, in the middle, or at the end of the word (Champaign, Ill.: Garrard).
5. *Quizmo* is a bingo game designed to practice hearing initial consonant, consonant blend, and initial short vowel sounds. The box contains directions, a list of words for the teacher to call, and thirty-eight bingo cards (Springfield, Mass.: Milton Bradley).
6. *The Syllable Game* is a card game in which words from the intermediate grade vocabulary are divided into syllables. Designed to help the student recognize and remember the commonest syllables in words. Like syllables become matched pairs. It may be played as a form of *solitaire* or as a group game (Champaign, Ill.: Garrard).
7. *Word Wheels.* A word wheel is usually two circles of different diameters fastened together at the center. They rotate in such a way that initial consonants and consonant blends on the smaller circle can be matched to family words on the larger circle. Also, prefixes or suffixes can be matched to root words. *Phono Word Wheels* are available from the Steck Company, Box 16, Austin, Texas. *Webster Word Wheels* are available from the Webster Division, McGraw-Hill, New York.

8. *Phonic Rummy* is a game played by matching vowel sounds. There are four sets of cards with sixty cards in each set. One set is for grades 1 and 2; one set is for grades 2 and 3; one set is for grades 2, 3, and 4; and one for grades 3, 4, and 5 (Buffalo, N.Y.: Kenworthy Educational Service).

9. *Phonics We Use Learning Games Kit.* Games for two or more players reinforce primary phonics skills: *Old Itch*—for initial consonant sounds; *Spin-a-Sound*—initial consonant sounds, symbols; *Blends Race*—initial consonant blends, symbols; *Digraph Whirl*—initial consonant digraphs, symbols; *Digraph Hopscotch*—initial and final consonant digraphs, symbols; *Vowel Dominoes*—long and short vowels, symbols; *Spin hard, Spin soft*—hard and soft *c* and *g* sounds; *Full House*—vowels, vowel digraphs, diphthongs; *Syllable Count*—syllabication and stress (Chicago: Rand McNally, 1967).

10. *Opposites* and *Beginning Sounds* are simple games for young readers (Springfield, Mass.: Milton Bradley).

11. *Shortcut,* an all purpose game board suitable for use with any vocabulary the teacher wishes to write in. *Functional Signs* are environmental signs suitable for young readers or older remedial readers. Can be used in a variety of game situations (Niles, Ill.: DLM).

Microcomputer Games

A new game format is here! Schools have moved into the computer age. Teachers, parents, and children together are discovering the potential of the microcomputer as an instructional tool. Software, the actual instructional packet, is available in great variety. Some materials are far more challenging and appropriate to the medium than others. The following games are typical of those available for practice on word recognition and attack:

Hangman has three levels: Beginning, Intermediate, and Expert for ages 8 to adult. For Atari (Chatsworth, Calif.: Opportunities for Learning, Inc.).

Word Master is a logic game guessing computer-generated three-letter words. Part of *Story Builder/Word Master* designed for different microcomputers. Elementary level (Chatsworth, Calif.: Opportunities for Learning, Inc.).

Minicrossword contains crossword puzzles generated by microcomputer. For all ages (Greenwich, Conn.: Program Design, Inc.).

Code Breaker is for ages 10 and up (Greenwich, Conn.: Program Design, Inc.).

Fishing for Homonyms is an Atari game for grades 3 to 6 (Garden City, Mich.: T.H.E.S.I.S.).

Hidden Words is a word search game for Atari, grades 1–8. (Garden City, Mich.: T.H.E.S.I.S.).

Blastoff 100 is a game for word recognition, grades 1–6 for Pet (Englewood Cliffs, N.J.: Scholastic, Inc.).

Word Scrambler is a game for word identification for grades 1–8, Pet (Englewood Cliffs, N.J.: Scholastic, Inc.).

Games for the Teacher to Make

1. *This to That.* Starting with one word, one of the letters in the word is changed each time, making a series such as: *his, him, ham, ram, ran, run.* The game can also be played by changing one- or two-letter combinations, as: *sheep, sheet, shoot, shook, spook, spoke, broke.*
2. *Fishing.* One word, a phrase, or a short sentence is printed on each of a number of small cardboard cutouts in the shape of fish, to which paper clips are attached. The child picks up a fish by means of a tiny horseshoe magnet on a string (his fishing pole). He may keep his card if he can read it correctly. The one with the most fish wins the game. Similar games can be devised doing such things as pulling leaves off trees, etc.
3. *I'm thinking of a word that begins like … :* (a) Use sight words learned and put them in the chart holder. One child says, "I'm thinking of a word that begins like *run."* The second child says, "Is it *ride?"* The child who guesses the right word gives the next clue.
   (b) This game also can provide practice in auditory discrimination. The child says, "I'm thinking of a word that begins like *dog."* This child then whispers his choice to a scorekeeper. Children then may respond with any word that begins with *d.*

Books of Good Suggestions

Coody, Betty, and David Nelson. *Successful Activities for Enriching the Language Arts.* Belmont, Calif.: Wadsworth, 1982.

Dolch, Marguerite P., and Lillian Ostrofsky. *My Puzzle Book.* Book I and Book II. Champaign, Ill.: Garrard, 1964.

Ekwall, Eldon. *Locating and Correcting Reading Difficulties.* 3d ed. Columbus, Ohio: Charles E. Merrill, 1981.

Heilman, Arthur. *Phonics in Proper Perspective.* 4th ed. Columbus, Ohio: Charles E. Merrill, 1981.

Herr, Selma. *Learning Activities for Reading.* 4th ed. Dubuque, Iowa: Wm. C. Brown, 1982.

Higley, Joan. *Activities Desk Book for Reading Skills.* West Nyack, N.Y.: Parker, 1977.

Hollinger, Ray, and Curt Shreiner. *Games Teachers Make.* Willow Street, Penn.: Instructional Design Association, 1979.

Platts, Mary E. *Anchor.* Stevensville, Mich.: Educational Service, 1970.

Platts, Mary E. *Spice. Suggested Activities to Motivate the Teaching of the Language Arts in the Elementary School.* Benton Harbor, Mich.: Educational Service, 1960.

Russell, David H., and Elizabeth F. Russell. *Listening Aids Through the Grades.* 2d ed. New York: Teachers College Press, 1979. Revised and enlarged by Dorothy G. Hennings.

Russell, David, Etta Karp, and Anne Marie Mueser. *Reading Aids Through the Grades.* New York: Teachers College Press, 1975.

Schubert, Delwyn, and Theodore Torgerson. *Improving the Reading Program.* 4th ed. Dubuque, Iowa: Wm. C. Brown, 1976.

Smith, Carl B., and Peggy G. Elliott. *Reading Activities for Middle and Secondary Schools.* New York: Holt, Rinehart and Winston, 1979.

Figure 9.10
A worksheet for identifying word-recognition skills which are involved in basal reader lessons as planned in teacher's manuals.

| Your name _____ | Title of reading text _____ | |
| Date _____ | Grade level of reading text _____ | |

Type of Skill	Example	Example
(For example: "Using context clues"; "Strengthening memory of word forms"; "Applying phonetic understandings"; etc.)	(Give example and page no. in teacher's manual where found.)	

Keeping Records of Word-Recognition Skills

Since so many skills are introduced in the teacher's manuals of basal readers that teachers use in the course of a year, it may be advisable to prepare a chart to help keep track of them. The teacher may simply list the skills to be taught along with book titles, page numbers, and brief notations about the activities. A chart such as the one in figure 9.10 may be a way of organizing these references.

Coping Strategies

Sometimes none of the techniques described in this chapter seem to work separately or in combination to provide the information needed to attack a word successfully. Two possible resources are left—asking for help with the word or skipping it, at least for the moment. Children seem to know intuitively that these are useful coping strategies with difficult words. Teachers should encourage children to recognize that these strategies exist and should help them to use them wisely. Children may need support in deciding how many words can be omitted and still acquire the needed level of understanding. They need to learn to be sensitive to the loss of meaning that occurs when too many words are omitted or when certain critical words are not identified.

Children also need to know that it may be useful to ask for help with a word. They may also learn that there are other ways to find out the name of the word besides asking directly. They may hear someone else reading the word and identify the context in which that word is likely to occur. They may also hear the

From Theory to Practice 9.3
Making Word-Recognition Games

Every teacher needs a collection of homemade reading games. Building that collection is a time-consuming process that should begin early in one's professional career and be continued at every opportunity. Ideas for games may come from the teacher's own creativity, from idea books such as the ones listed in this chapter, from professional journals, from children's ideas, or from other teachers.

Prepare a game for helping children with some phase of word recognition. (Note that games and other papers should be laminated if you wish to keep them very long.) Prepare clear directions for playing it. Bring it to class on a day your instructor sets aside for playing each other's games. After several people play your game, you will get feedback concerning how easily it may be played, how clear the directions are, and how interesting it is. You will also get a chance to see and make notes on several other games.

word used in discussion and identify its printed form because of similar contexts. The child may be shown that meaning is lost when too many words have to be asked of someone; the frequent interruptions can cause loss of meaning.

Summary

This chapter has contained a discussion of word-recognition skills. The techniques discussed were teaching a basic sight vocabulary, recognizing that meaning is essential to develop reading as a thinking process, using phonic and structural analysis clues, and learning to use the dictionary. Studies that review the usefulness of phonic generalizations presented in teachers' manuals that accompany basal readers were summarized. Games and devices for strengthening word-recognition abilities were discussed, and a brief list of resources for teachers was presented.

For Further Reading

Bradley, Virginia N. "Improving Students' Writing with Microcomputers." *Language Arts* 59 (October 1982): 732–43.

Charles, C.M. "Individualizing Instruction." In *Individualizing Instruction*. 2d ed. St. Louis: C.V. Mosby, 1980.

Clay, Marie. *Reading, The Patterning of Complex Behaviour*. 2d ed. Auckland, New Zealand: Heinemann Educational Books, 1979.

Cunningham, Patricia. "Teaching Were, With, What, and Other 'Four-letter' Words." *The Reading Teacher* 34 (November 1980): 160–63.

Dallman, Martha, Roger L. Rouch, Lynette Y. C. Char, and John J. DeBoer. "Word Recognition" and "Developing Skills in Word Recognition." In *The Teaching of Reading*. 6th ed. New York: Holt, Rinehart and Winston, 1982.

Dickerson, Dolores P. "A Study of Use of Games to Reinforce Sight Vocabulary." *The Reading Teacher* 36 (October 1982): 46–49.

Ehri, Linnea C., Roderick W. Barron, and Jeffrey M. Feldman. *The Recognition of Words*. Newark, Del.: International Reading Assn., 1978.

Gray, William S. *On Their Own in Reading*. Rev. ed. Glenview, Ill.: Scott, Foresman, 1960.

Harris, Albert, and Edward R. Sipay. "Developing Word-recognition Skills" and "Remedial Procedures for Overcoming Word-recognition Problems." In *How to Increase Reading Ability*. 7th ed. New York: Longman, 1980.

Hull, Marion A. *Phonics for the Teacher of Reading*. 3d ed. Columbus, Ohio: Charles E. Merrill, 1981.

Mason, George E., and Jay S. Blanchard. *Computer Applications in Reading*. Newark, Del.: International Reading Assn., 1979.

Rinsky, Lee Ann, and Barbara Griffith. *Teaching Word Attack Skills*. Dubuque, Iowa: Gorsuch Scarsbruck, 1978.

Rosso, Barbara, and Robert Emans. "Children's Use of Phonic Generalizations." *The Reading Teacher* 34 (March 1981): 653–57.

Smith, Nila B., and H. Alan Robinson. "Developing Word Approximation and Identification Strategies." In *Reading Instruction for Today's Children*. 2d ed. Englewood Cliffs, N.J.: Prentice-Hall, 1980.

Williams, Johanna, Ellen L. Blumberg, and David Williams. "Cues Used in Visual Word Recognition." *Journal of Educational Psychology* 61 (1970): 310–15.

Notes

1. Lillian Gray, citing Horace Mann's *Report to the Board of Education in Massachusetts in 1838,* in *Teaching Children to Read,* 3d ed., p. 47 (New York: Ronald Press, 1963).

2. Harriette Taylor Treadwell and Margaret Free, *Reading-Literature: The Primer* (Evanston, Ill.: Row-Peterson, 1910).

3. Miriam Blanton Huber, Frank Seely Salisbury, and Mabel O'Donnell, *I Know a Story* (New York: Harper & Row, 1962), pp. 20–21.

4. Edmund Huey, *The Psychology and Pedagogy of Reading* (Cambridge, Mass. The MIT Press, 1908), pp. 73–74.

5. James L. McClelland, "Letter and Configuration Information in Word Identification," *Journal of Verbal Learning and Verbal Behavior* 16:137–50.

6. Ralph N. Haber and Lyn Haber, "The Shape of a Word Can Specify Its Meaning," *Reading Research Quarterly* 16 (1981): 334–45.

7. Clarence R. Stone, *Progress in Primary Reading* (New York: McGraw-Hill, copyright © 1950). Reprinted by permission.

8. E.W. Dolch, *The Dolch Basic Sight Word Test* (Champaign, Ill.: Garrard, 1942).

9. A.I. Gates, *A Reading Vocabulary for the Primary Grades* (New York: Teachers College Press, 1926); The Child Study Committee of the International Kindergarten Union, *A Study of the Vocabulary of Children Before Entering First Grade* (1201 Sixteenth Street, N.W., Washington, D.C.: International Kindergarten Union, 1928); and H. E. Wheeler and Emma A. Howell, "A First Grade Vocabulary Study," *Elementary School Journal* 31 (September 1930): 52–60.

10. J. McNally and W. Murray, *Key Words to Literacy* (London: Schoolmaster Pub. Co., 1968).

11. Edward Fry, "Developing a Word List for Remedial Reading," *Elementary English,* November 1957, pp. 456–58. Reprinted by permission.

12. Paul McKee, M. Lucille Harrison, Annie McCowen, and Elizabeth Lehr, Teacher's Edition for *Come Along,* rev. ed. (Boston: Houghton Mifflin, 1957), pp. 478–83.

13. Ernest Horn, "Language and Meaning," *NSSE Yearbook. The Psychology of Learning* (Chicago: University of Chicago Press, copyright © 1942), pp. 398–99. Reprinted by permission.

14. Nila B. Smith, *American Reading Instruction* (Newark, Del.: International Reading Assn., 1965). Also, Nila B. Smith, *Reading Instruction for Today's Children* (Englewood Cliffs, N.J.: Prentice-Hall, 1963), pp. 187–95.

15. Anna D. Cordts, *Phonics for the Reading Teacher,* copyright © 1965, pp. 134–35, 162, 164. CBS Publishing, New York. Reprinted by permission.

16. Ibid., pp. 134–35.

17. Ibid., p. 164.

18. Ernest Horn, "The Child's Early Experience with the Letter A," *Journal of Educational Psychology* 20 (March 1929): 161–68.

19. Ruth E. Oaks, "A Study of the Vowel Situations in a Primary Vocabulary," *Education* 71 (1952): 604–17.

20. Theodore L. Clymer, "The Utility of Phonics Generalizations in the Primary Grades," *The Reading Teacher* 16 (1963): 252–58.

21. A.T. Burrows and Z. Lourie, "When 'Two Vowels Go Walking,'" *The Reading Teacher* 17 (November 1963): 79–82.

22. Robert Emans, "The Usefulness of Phonic Generalizations Above the Primary Grades," *The Reading Teacher* 20 (February 1967): 419–25; "When Two Vowels Go Walking and Other Such Things," *The Reading Teacher* 21 (December 1967): 262–69.

23. Mildred Hart Bailey, "The Utility of Phonic Generalizations in Grades One Through Six," *The Reading Teacher* 20 (February 1967): 413–18.

24. Lou Burmeister, "Usefulness of Phonic Generalizations," *The Reading Teacher* 21 (January 1968): 349–56; "Vowel Pairs," *The Reading Teacher* 21 (February 1968): 445–52.

25. E.A. Fry, "A Frequency Approach to Phonics," *Elementary English* 41 (1964): 759–65ff.

26. A few exceptions to this valid *oa* generalization are *boa,* as in boa constrictors; *goa,* the gazelle of Tibet; or *Goa,* a small land area in India.

27. Cordts, *Phonics,* p. 172.

28. Russell C. Stauffer, "A Study of Prefixes in the Thorndike List to Establish a List of Prefixes that Should Be Taught in the Elementary School," *Journal of Educational Research* 35 (1942): 453–58.

29. *100 Good Ways to Strengthen Reading Skills* (Chicago: Scott, Foresman, copyright © 1956), p. 16. Reprinted by permission.

30. William S. Gray, *On Their Own in Reading* (Chicago: Scott, Foresman, 1948), p. 80.

31. Cordts, *Phonics,* p. 178.

32. Carol K. Winkley, "Which Accent Generalizations Are Worth Teaching?" *The Reading Teacher* 20 (December 1966): 219–24.

33. William S. Gray, *On Their Own in Reading* (Chicago: Scott, Foresman, 1960), pp. 66–199.

Comprehension Skills

A Cognitive Map: Comprehension Skills

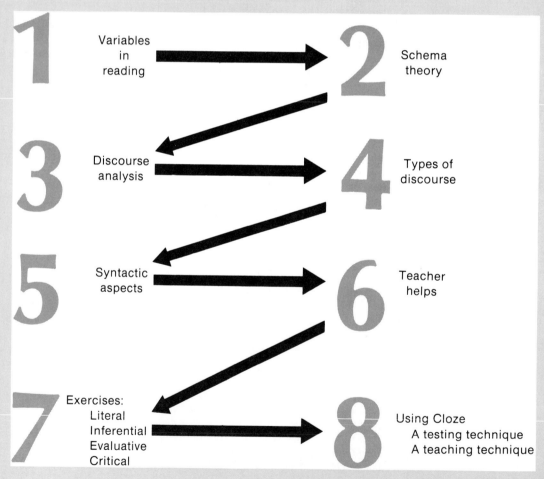

1. Variables in reading

2. Schema theory

3. Discourse analysis

4. Types of discourse

5. Syntactic aspects

6. Teacher helps

7. Exercises:
   Literal
   Inferential
   Evaluative
   Critical

8. Using Cloze
   A testing technique
   A teaching technique

Guide Questions

1. What are the variables in reading? In addition to the *person* who reads and the *text* the person reads, there is also the *context* in which the reading is to be understood. What does *context* in this frame of reference mean to you?

2. What is meant by discourse analysis? How does the reader analyze discourse to search out meaning?

3. How can teachers help students discover meaning in reading?

4. What methods and materials are available for teaching comprehension?

5. What is an adequate balance among the following levels of questioning: literal, inferential, evaluative, and creative? How will you insure this balance in your classes?

6. Why is cloze a good way to test for meaning in reading? How might cloze be effectively used to teach comprehension in reading?

Terminology

anaphora

cloze technique

context

convergent/divergent thinking

creative questioning

critical comprehension

discourse

discourse analysis

inference

interpretive (inferential) questions

literal comprehension

metaphor

outlining

pragmatics

schemata

schema theory

syntax

text

Variables in the Reading Act

Comprehension in reading is the process by which people who read derive meaning from text. This process might be viewed as a three-pronged affair: (1) the reader, or the person who reads, (2) the text an author has written, and (3) a context, which is all the environmental cues present. The experiences, background knowledge, skills, and abilities that the reader brings to the reading situation determine the level of comprehension that will ensue.[1]

The act of comprehending is the construction of ideas out of preexisting concepts. Adams and Bruce state that "comprehension is the use of prior knowledge to create new knowledge."[2]

Thorndike, in 1917, defined reading as a process of *reasoning*.[3] Understanding a paragraph is like solving a math problem. It consists of selecting the right elements of the situation and putting them together in the right relations and with the right amount of weight or influence or force for each. The mind is assailed, as it were, by every word in the paragraph. It must select, repress, soften, emphasize, correlate, and organize, all under the influence of the right mental set or purpose or demand.

Being a good student requires that one be aware of what one does and does not understand. One problem for teachers is to give their students greater awareness of what they do understand well and can easily paraphrase and of what they do not clearly understand. An old Arabian proverb might be useful to many of our students:

Men are Four
He who knows, and knows that he knows,
He is wise—follow him.
He who knows, and knows not he knows,
He is asleep—awake him.
He who knows not, and knows not that he knows not,
He is a fool—shun him.
He who knows not, and knows he knows not,
He is a child—teach him.

A major part of the teaching of comprehension is the developing of those skills that enable students to "learn how to learn." While students need to learn how to solve the problems that confront them today, the ultimate value of the learning is to be able to solve the problems that have not yet been formulated, those that will arise later in their lives. Brown outlines four major variables that enable students to learn how to learn: (1) the nature of the material to be learned; (2) the critical tasks, or the "need" or "motive" for which the learner will use the material; (3) learning activities engaged in; and (4) characteristics of learners, such as prior experience, background knowledge, abilities, and interests.[4]

Students need to gain some insights into the learning situation, they need to understand their own learning abilities, they need to know what study strategies work best for them, and they need to select appropriate study skills and know how to apply them. In doing these things, they learn how to learn from reading.

Teachers need to be aware that textbook passages may make it difficult for the child to carry out these suggestions. Sometimes the text contains so many unfamiliar concepts in a few sentences that the readers are unable to apply productive learning strategies. An example is this passage from a fifth grade science text:

> Jet engines work on the principle of jet propulsion. The scientist has a special name for the jet-propulsion engine. He calls it a *reaction engine*.
>
> An English scientist, Sir Isaac Newton, first set forth the scientific principle that explains why a jet engine works.
>
> Newton's principle is the *third law of motion*. This law states that *for every action, there is an equal and opposite reaction.*
>
> The *third law of motion* has been on record for a long time. Newton lived from 1642 to 1727. The law is as true today as it was in the time of Newton.[5]

If teachers are aware of the concept load of textbooks, they can help children prepare for such reading assignments so that they contribute to the children's growing knowledge of the world. Singer writes:

> . . . we conceive of the entire curriculum, including all the direct and vicarious experiences that students gain in and out of school, as contributing to the range, depth, and altitude of an individual's schema hierarchy and knowledge of the world. The schemata, stored in the reader's mental encyclopedia, enable readers to explicate passages, make inferences, and assimilate information. They are a major contributor to the individual's reading comprehension.[6]

Schema Theory

A schema is a data structure for representing the generic concepts stored in memory. A schema contains a network of interrelations that is believed to hold normally among the constituents of the concept in question. Schemata are *active* processes.

Schemata are complex, interacting structures of knowledge. Their function is to help the individual decide how accurate or precise his judgments are in this active, decision-making process. These schemata, then, are the building blocks of cognition.[7]

Rumelhart suggests three reasons for misunderstanding the passage read:[8]

1. The reader may not have the appropriate schemata.
2. The reader may have the appropriate schemata, but the clues provided by the author may be insufficient to suggest them.
3. The reader may find a consistent interpretation of the text but may not find the one intended by the author.

Many readers will find the following paragraph difficult. In this case the author has failed to give enough information to suggest the clues needed to read with understanding:

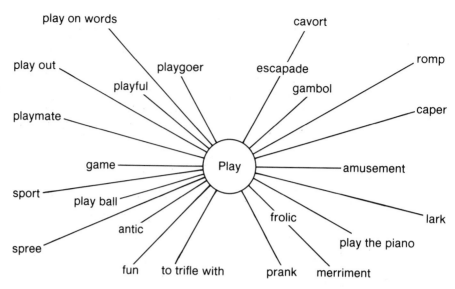

Figure 10.1
The word *play* can conjure up in your mind as many of the meanings identified here as you have already experienced in your life.

The procedure is actually quite simple. First you arrange things into different groups. Of course, one pile may be sufficient depending on how much there is to do. If you have to go somewhere else due to lack of facilities, that is the next step, otherwise you are pretty well set. It is important not to overdo things. That is, it is better to do too few things at once than too many. In the short run this may not seem important but complications can easily arise. A mistake can be expensive as well. At first the whole procedure will seem complicated. Soon, however, it will become just another facet of life. It is difficult to foresee any end to the necessity for this task in the immediate future, but then one can never tell. After the procedure is completed, one arranges the materials into different groups again. Then they can be put into their appropriate places. Eventually they will be used once more and the whole cycle will then have to be repeated. However, that is part of life.[9]

Schema theory may be the new gestalt that will help us to understand how to teach reading comprehension. A schema is a conceptual system for understanding something. Hart in *How the Brain Works* explains that young children with good guidance from the adults around them develop innumerable schemata in their brains so that they have myriad program structures that enable them to carry on an extensive amount of program structuring simultaneously.[10] He says that much of the brain structuring is unconscious—no conscious thought is needed to put on one's shirt and socks, for example. As long as the brain functions, new program structures—schemata—are being acquired. These schemata represent a kind of encyclopedic knowledge of the world with both denotative (direct or cognitive) and connotative (non-literal or affective) meanings. (See figures 10.1 and 10.2.)

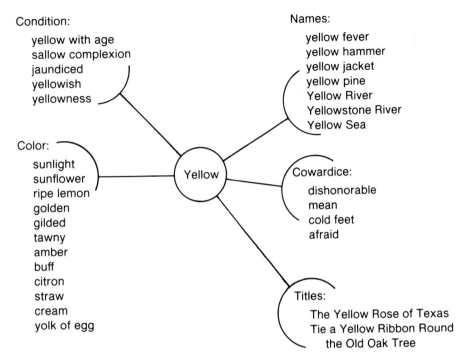

Figure 10.2
What the word *yellow* means to you depends on your previous experience with it. (Meanings under *cowardice* are connotative; others are denotative.)

Condition:

yellow with age
sallow complexion
jaundiced
yellowish
yellowness

Names:

yellow fever
yellow hammer
yellow jacket
yellow pine
Yellow River
Yellowstone River
Yellow Sea

Color:

sunlight
sunflower
ripe lemon
golden
gilded
tawny
amber
buff
citron
straw
cream
yolk of egg

Yellow

Cowardice:

dishonorable
mean
cold feet
afraid

Titles:

The Yellow Rose of Texas
Tie a Yellow Ribbon Round
the Old Oak Tree

A schematic-theoretical view of reading is based on the interaction between the reader and the text; it specifies how the reader's knowledge shapes the information on the page and defines how that knowledge must be organized to support the interaction. This restructuring of one's cognitive base is analogous to the terms *assimilation* and *accommodation* used by Piaget to explain the acquisition of new learning.

Building Schemata
to Increase
Understanding

Schemata are mental structures that provide the ability to interpret linguistic, contextual, or situational forms. The schema is essential for comprehension, storage, and retrieval of information being learned. It is the schemata in the reader's mind that enable him or her to use reading the way it is defined in the psycholinguistic frame of reference. Reading is a sampling, selecting, predicting, comparing, and confirming activity in which the reader selects a sample of useful graphic cues based on what he or she sees and expects to see.[11]

Perhaps more simply, *schema* refers to all the little pictures or associations you create in your mind when you hear or read a word or a sentence. You have a schema for the word *tree*, for instance. Your concept of tree includes trunk, branches, leaves, roots; it includes fruits, nuts, cones, lumber, shade, nesting places for birds, even furniture for houses. (See figure 10.3 on developing a concept.) If you have an organized schema for *tree* in your head, it puts things about trees in categories: parts of trees, names of trees, products of trees.

Trees provide:

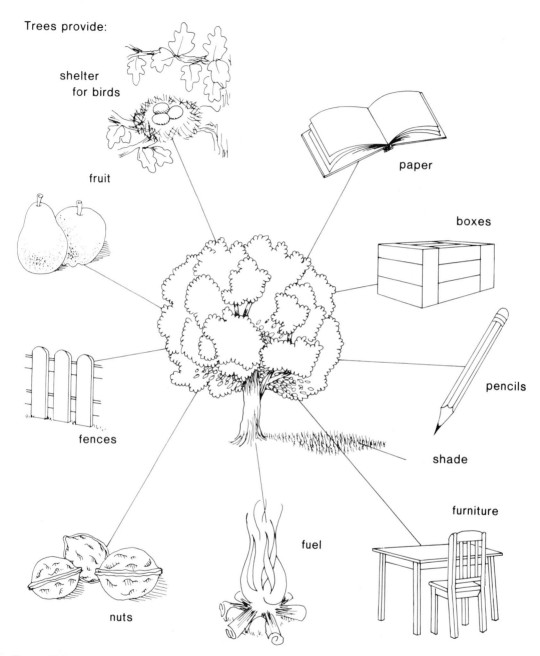

shelter for birds

fruit

paper

boxes

pencils

fences

shade

furniture

nuts

fuel

Figure 10.3
Concept: trees are useful to people.

These schemata have a great deal to do with reading for understanding. Reading comprehension requires not only making decisions about what parts of the text are important to remember, but also making decisions about information that does not appear in the text that must be added or inferred. To illustrate, a few paragraphs from one of Laura Ingalls Wilder's books follow. In *On the Banks of Plum Creek*, Laura Ingalls Wilder describes the setting up of the new cook-stove in the wonderful new house Pa had just finished. How different the story-and-a-half frame house with glass windows seemed compared to the dugout in which they had lived.

> He lifted the marvelous stove and set it in the living-room, and put up the stovepipe. Piece by piece, the stovepipe went up through the ceiling and the attic and through the hole he sawed in the roof. Then Pa climbed onto the roof and he set a larger tin pipe over the stovepipe. The tin pipe had a spread-out, flat bottom that covered the hole in the roof. Not a drop of rain could run down the stovepipe into the new house.
>
> That was a prairie chimney.
>
> "Well, it's done," Pa said, "Even to a prairie chimney."
>
> There was nothing more that a house could possibly have. The glass windows made the inside of that house so light that you would hardly know you were in a house. It smelled clean and piny, from yellow-new board walls and floor. The cook-stove stood lordly in the corner by the lean-to door. A touch on the white-china door knob swung the boughten door on its boughten hinges, and the door knob's little iron tongue clicked and held the door shut.
>
> "We'll move in, tomorrow morning," Pa said. "This is the last night we'll sleep in a dugout."
>
> Laura and Mary took his hands and they went down the knoll. The wheat-field was a silky, shimmery green rippling over a curve of the prairie. Its sides were straight and its corners square, and all around it the wild prairie grasses looked coarser and darker green. Laura looked back at the wonderful house. In the sunshine on the knoll, its sawed-lumber walls and roof were as golden as a strawstack.[12]

What will the boys and girls in your room this year *know* about *dugouts* where people lived on the prairie; or about *stovepipes,* or the tin pieces that spread out to make the roof rainproof?

What will children today think when they read "There was *nothing* more the house could possibly have?" Will they think it had a bathroom, hot and cold running water, central heat, a refrigerator that is half cooler and half freezer, a vacuum cleaner that picks up most "messy things" off the rugs, and a television-video recorder and playback unit so no program need be missed? What will they think about a store-bought door, store-bought hinges, and store-bought white-china door knobs? And if the boards that smell "piny" were the wonderful golden color of a strawstack, what's a strawstack?

Of course, for many of us, the artifacts that Laura Ingalls Wilder wrote about were real and a part of our first-hand experience; but for boys and girls today, we may need to find good educational motion pictures and well-organized local museums, or make an excursion to Mansfield, Missouri, if we want to get the fullest meaning out of the Wilder books. If boys and girls share many of the pictures or photographs they will find in standard reference books, they can clarify many of these concepts.

Many children are unaware of the fact that they *do* possess relevant schemata. They become so involved with decoding all the words that they do not comprehend many ideas. They need help in making sure their prior knowledge is organized and available.

Some children may read rapidly and only expect to get the gist of what the story is about. They will often miss the subtleties of language, the polysemous words, the details in technical information, and the melody of poetry. Reading is an interactive process in which students approach a passage with preconceived ideas but are constantly restructuring their present knowledge to incorporate the ideas they encounter in their reading.

In a schematic approach to reading, we are talking about the interface between the reader and the text—allowing the reader to use his or her previous knowledge to construct or reconstruct meaning from the material being read. Pearson and Spiro provide an excellent explanation of schema theory for classroom teachers in the May 1982 *Instructor*.[13] Part of their explanation is reprinted later in the chapter.

Discourse Analysis

Discourse analysis is the study of the structure and function of language units longer than a single sentence. The meanings to be assigned to words in extended discourse depend on the context in which they are used. Instead of a fixed abstract meaning, a word can be conceived to have a "family" of potential meanings. For example:[14]

1. *Chicago* has a new mayor. (A political entity)
2. A blizzard has engulfed *Chicago*. (A geographical entity)
3. There were serious riots in *Chicago* last night. (A social entity)

Word meanings are context sensitive. If one reads the two sentences—

4. The fish attacked the swimmer.
5. The fish avoided the swimmer.

—one might conclude in the first sentence that the fish is a shark; in the second, the fish is not a shark.

Discourse analysis goes beyond the consideration of word recognition and "understanding the sentence." It is necessary to look at characteristics of paragraphs and appreciate the relationships between the sentences. The basic premise of discourse analysis is that readers must approach the context of what they are reading from the point of view of the author's writing pattern or "form of discourse." The ability to comprehend must be taught according to specific forms of discourse, which means that the writer must recognize the common patterns of writing that will be used. The usual patterns of discourse are narration, explanation, classification, description, and argument.

Types of Discourse

Types of discourse, or different writing patterns, are illustrated here. The reader is also referred to the subsection on writing patterns in chapter 12, "Teaching Reading in the Content Fields."

Explanation

Pearson and Spiro explain the meaning of schema:

What *is* a schema? It's the little pictures or associations you conjure up in your mind when you hear or read a word or sentence. You can have a schema for an object (chair, boat, fan), an abstract idea or feeling (love, hate, hope), an action (dancing, swimming, buying), or an event (election, garage sale, concert). It's like a concept but broader. For example, you see the word *tree* and you conjure up the concept of a tree—trunk, branches, leaves, and so on. Your schema for a tree includes all this, plus anything else you associate with trees—walks down country lanes, Christmas trees, birds' nests, and so on. A schema includes behavioral sequences, too. For example, your schema for the word *party* could include not only food, friends, and music, but also what you will wear, how you will get there, how long you plan to stay, and so on. And, of course, your schema for *party* is based on your experiences at parties, which may differ substantially from someone else's. A schema is an abstraction of experience that you are constantly fine-tuning and restructuring according to new information you receive. In other words, the more parties you attend, the more schema adjustments you'll make.[15]

Classification

Blough and Schwartz present teachers with the standard classification system for cloud types:

Three basic forms of clouds are recognized: cirrus, cumulus, and stratus. Cirrus, meaning "curl," are the most delicate of all clouds. These clouds, sometimes called "mare's tails," are white, feathery, and filmy. They do not obscure the sun very much. Cirrus clouds are the highest of all clouds, averaging six miles in altitude. They are composed of ice crystals. Cumulus, meaning "heap," are dense clouds that build up huge heaps. They have flat bases, are white and billowy above, and cast shadows on the earth. Cumulus clouds are formed in rising currents of air and are the characteristic clouds seen on fair days. Stratus, meaning "layer," refers to clouds that cover the whole sky, obscuring the sun. They give us smooth gray skies. Stratus clouds are composed of water droplets in summer and ice crystals in winter. A fog is a stratus cloud on the ground.[16]

Description/ Narration

Townsend, in *The Intruder,* describes a rainy evening in this way:

The rain wasn't continuous. It came in gusts, carried on the wind, almost horizontal. Gray clouds ran, ragged and rapid, across the sky. Down on Peter's right, the sea was indigo, flecked with white horses. As he rounded the headland the wind came at him more fiercely, caught his cape like a sail, changed his course, twice nearly blew him off. It would be safer to walk, but Peter didn't feel like walking. In the wild, swooping ride round Skirl Bay was a desolation that matched his mood. Words wheeled in his mind like sea gulls in the air. ". . . Could be anywhere in the world, or out of it for that matter . . . Nothing to do with me, nothing . . ."[17]

Argument

Justice Thomas R. Berger visited the native peoples of the far north and interviewed them concerning their feelings about the building of the oil pipeline through the MacKenzie River Valley in northern Canada. One Indian chief responded with this argument:

Our Dene Nation is like this great river. It has been flowing before any of us can remember. We take our strength, our wisdom and our ways from the flow and direction which has been established for us by ancestors we never knew, ancestors of a thousand years ago. Their wisdom flows through us to our children and our grandchildren, to generations we will never know. We will live out our lives as we must, and we will die in peace because we will know that our people and this river will flow on after us.

We know that our grandchildren will speak a language that is their heritage, that has been passed on from before time. We know they will share their wealth and not hoard it, or keep it to themselves. We know they will look after their old people and respect them for their wisdom. We know they will look after this land and protect it, and that 500 years from now, someone with skin my color, and moccasins on his feet will climb up the Ramparts and rest, and look over the river, and feel that he, too, has a place in the universe, and he will thank the same spirits that I thank, that his ancestors have looked over his land well, and he will be proud to be a Dene.[18]

Semantic/ Syntactic Aspects

Syntactic aspects of reading comprehension become significant when students are unable to determine easily the deep structure meanings when reading "surface structure" sentences. In these sentences—

1. The customer is ready to eat.
2. The omelette is ready to eat.

—the surface structure is the same, but, of course, the meaning embedded in the deep structure is entirely different.
Sentence 3 reads innocently enough:

3. The missionary is ready to eat.

But when it is edited to sentence 4, it carries quite a different meaning:

4. "The missionary is ready to eat," said the cannibal.[19]

There are several causes of comprehension failure in boys and girls:[20]

1. The semantic complexity being communicated may be too difficult for the child. Integrating or interrelating ideas may be difficult.
2. The syntactic form in which content is encoded may be beyond the child's competence. If the aim is to enrich content, then the syntax must be understood by the reader.

Pragmatics

Pragmatics is the study of meanings in social or cultural contexts or a study of language in its everyday use. Pragmatics is the study of all aspects of language use not covered by the specific, literal meanings. It is a relationship between the nonverbal signs or linguistic expressions and their users. It is based on experience rather than on ideas or principles.

Inference

Inference is the "missing connection" between the surface structure of the text and the reader's knowledge of the world.[21] To infer is to be able to conclude or to find out by reasoning.

1. The people inferred that so able a governor would make a good president.
2. When they saw the pile of paper on the teacher's desk, the class made the inference that they would receive written work.

The meaning derived from the following paragraph will depend upon the ability to draw inferences intended by the writer.

> He plunked down $5.00 at the window. She tried to give him $2.50, but he refused to take it. So when they got inside, she bought him a large bag of popcorn.[22]

The paragraph on page 288 explaining how laundry is done is another example of the importance of inference. It will be understood only with adequate inferencing.

Lessons to develop inferential thinking might include the following:

1. Children usually enjoy riddles. Reading or listening to riddles requires children to utilize clues to infer "what am I?"
2. After children have read passages or stories that are not accompanied by pictures, they may be asked to draw pictures of what was read. Inferential thinking is required.
3. Mystery stories that stop short of their conclusions are useful for developing the ability to infer. Children must provide satisfactory conclusions based on inferences from the information provided.

Metaphor

Metaphors are unique and powerful ways of expressing the new in terms of the old. Using and understanding metaphor may be related to acquiring insight. Use of metaphor can be a way of knowing and a way of coming to a new understanding. The ability to see similarities and differences, as in metaphors, is innate and can perhaps be utilized to extend insight.[23]

The vividness of metaphor can make learning more intense or more lasting once the metaphor is understood.

1. The ship plows the sea.
2. He had a heart of stone.
3. We watched the copper late-evening sky.

A metaphor is a word or phrase denoting literally one kind of object or idea in place of another to suggest a likeness or an analogy.

4. Time flies.
5. The iron horse crossed the nation with incredible speed.

A *dead metaphor* is a comparison of two things that has become so commonly used that it is no longer considered a metaphor, such as, "the eye of the needle," "the mouth of the river," or "the leg of the table." In the sentence, "The smoke from the forest fire was pea soup," the *topic* (subject) is "smoke"; the *vehicle* (term being used metaphorically) is "pea soup"; and the *ground* (that which topic and vehicle have in common) is the concept of density or thickness.[24]

When Baldwin, Luce, and Readence asked thirty-nine fifth graders to write the meanings of fourteen stimulus sentences (seven metaphors and seven similes), only 57 percent of the students wrote correct interpretations. Thus, 43 percent of the fifth grade students failed to interpret the meanings in the figures of speech.[25] A few of their examples are:

The smoke from the forest fire was pea soup.
The man's feet were like blocks of ice.
When he is with other people, he is a turtle.
The television is like a cyclops.

Baldwin, Luce, and Readence point out that the metaphor in "The television is a cyclops" requires two matching attributes: one-eyedness and monster. Not one of their fifth graders gave them *both* of these attributes. Perhaps the difficulty of the metaphor is determined by the number of attributes that must be compared.[26]

Lessons to help boys and girls learn about metaphors might include:

1. Provide children with many magazines containing a variety of advertisements. Ask them to clip examples of metaphors that may be used to form a class collage.
2. Make a dictionary of metaphors suitable to the reading needs of the children. Let the children draw pictures to illustrate the denotative and connotative meanings of the words involved. A sentence should accompany each metaphor listed.

Anaphora

Anaphora is one of several devices that transfers meaning from one sentence to the next. Choosing appropriate antecedents requires some special skill on the part of the reader.

A. Antecedents or referents
   1. George shared his lunch with me.
   2. I thanked him very much for *it*.

   "It" refers, not just to any lunch, but to the specific one George shared.

   3. Jack met his two sisters at the hotel.
   4. They took a taxi home.

   The inference is that all three people went home in a taxi.

   5. Jack did not find his sisters at the hotel.
   6. They took a taxi home.

   Here, the inference is that the two sisters went home in a taxi.

B. The role of inference
   1. Jack can watch the traffic and play ball in the street.
   2. John can, *too*.

C. Deletions of key words
  1. Adjectives
    a. Andrew is a dependable guy.
    b. Henry is *not*.
    c. An elephant is large.
    d. A brown bear is, *too*.
  2. Clauses
    a. Mother didn't buy a cake for my party. She baked *one*.
    b. Jack plays ball very well. *So* does John.
D. Demonstrative pronouns or adverbs
  1. My new assignment is in Nome, Alaska.
  2. It will be very cold *there*.
  3. The plane touched down safely.
  4. *Now,* we could relax.
E. Synonyms
  1. The neighbor's dog bit me yesterday.
  2. The *vicious beast* should be on a leash.
  3. John brought his wife to the convention.
  4. But *spouses* had not been invited.
F. Quantitative terms
  1. Melody and Mike came in. The *former* is tall, but the *latter* is short.
  2. Mary, Ginger, and Miles went to the movies. They *all* enjoyed the show. They *all* ate popcorn.
G. General substitutions
  1. The two boys went up into the tree house.
  2. But *that old thing* isn't very safe.
  3. Violence in the streets is on the increase.
  4. The police must take care of *this problem*.

Directed lessons for teaching anaphora:

1. To develop the idea that one word can take the place of another word preceding it, students can write the meaning:

   Andy is a good friend. *He* lives at my house.

   The student writes: " 'He' means Andy."
   The student can also exhibit knowledge of meaning by drawing an arrow from the noun to its antecedent:

   Andy is a good friend. He lives at my house.

   Another example might be:

   The dog next door barks a lot. That animal is driving me up the wall.

   The student writes: " 'That animal' means the dog."

2. Younger children can mark or color pictures to demonstrate understanding of anaphora. Under a suitable picture one might write:

   "Father came home from work. *He* looked very tired."

   The child would mark or color the picture that shows who "he" is.

Levels of Questioning

Students need the help of good *questioning techniques* from their teacher to better understand their textbooks. The right "levels" of questions need to be asked by the teacher, and, in turn, encouraged to evolve from students in their discussions. Teachers can stimulate the learning environment of their students by the types of questions they ask. They should try to become adept at deciding which students to ask specific questions. They also need to create accepting environments for divergent thinking and differences of opinions. Levels of comprehension questions based on the taxonomies of Bloom,[27] Sanders,[28] and Barrett,[29] are:

Literal questions—listing, defining, recalling, naming, locating, labeling.
Interpretive (inferential) questions—reading between the lines, selecting and relating relevant information, generalizing, or concluding.
Critical (evaluative) questions—making a judgment about the truth, accuracy, or validity of a statement with acceptable criteria.
Creative questions—thinking beyond the information presented, extending divergent approaches to a problem.

Using the story "A Special Day" in *Macmillan Reading,* Series R (1980), Smith and Wardhaugh illustrate these questioning levels.[30]

The comprehension questions that follow focus on a discussion of the story as a whole. The questions should be used selectively after the general discussion. You may wish to have the children read orally in response to specific questions or for general enjoyment:

From Theory to Practice 10.2
Asking Questions at Different Levels

Every teacher needs to practice preparing (and asking) questions at different levels. It is very difficult to ask a variety of levels of questions without conscious effort and practice.

Select a story from a basal reader. After reading the story, prepare a set of questions you might ask children after they had read the story. Prepare at least two questions in each of the four categories of questions just discussed.

Bring your story and the questions to class to share with classmates. You will want to encourage them to make suggestions that could make your questions even better.

Literal Comprehension

1. *What special day was it?* (Mexican Independence Day)
2. *What part of the show did Mama and Papa especially want to see?* (the dancers from Mexico City)
3. *What did the Queen of Independence Day give Rosa?* (a prize for the most beautiful costume in the parade)

Interpretive Thinking

1. *Why were Rosa and Anita able to celebrate three Independence Days?* (They lived in Texas, in the United States; and their family had come from Mexico. All three places celebrate their own Independence Days.)
2. *Why was the Queen so happy that Rosa's family took such good care of the costume?* (It helped them to remember the country from which their families came.)

Critical Thinking

1. *Do you think that it is important to celebrate Independence Days? Why or why not?* (Help the children realize the importance of being free from the domination of another country.)
2. *Why is it important to preserve the things that have been in a family for generations?* (It helps to keep alive our cultural heritage; it reminds us that America is made up of people from many different backgrounds.)

299

Creative Thinking

1. *What kind of costume do you think would be appropriate at a celebration of the United States' independence? Why?* (Answers may vary.)
2. *Do you think people should be encouraged to attend celebrations of the national holidays of different ethnic groups?* (Answers may vary. Point out that attending such a celebration helps us understand other people.)

Teacher Helps

Built into print are several cues that help readers make sense out of print. Teachers need to be extremely sensitive to these cues, and they need to make their students equally sensitive to them. Enough time should be spent on these "helps" so that their utilization becomes routine with children.

Getting Meaning from Text

Writers for children need to make use of techniques that will help children learn meanings of new words within the context of what they are reading. Such techniques have been prescribed by Artley and McCullough.[31] They include:

1. A brief explanation of the word can be given in parentheses or in a footnote:

    The *cacique* ordered an inquisition of the intruders who came into the village.
    (The *cacique* is the chief, or person of the highest authority in the village.)

2. A phrase that explains the meaning of the word can be inserted in the sentence:

    At certain times during the year in the northern skies one can see the *aurora borealis,* a colorful display of flickering, shifting lights.
    Moss, grass, and flowers grow in the *tundra,* the treeless plains found in arctic regions.

3. A synonym or substitute phrase is used to indicate the meaning:

    shrimp, a small shellfish
    the *lobby,* a small waiting room
    the *cacique,* the chief of the tribe

4. A new word is *emphasized* by using italics, quotation marks, or boldface type to call attention to it:

    The farmer uses a machine called a *combine* to harvest the wheat.
    Pioneer farmers used a "cradle," a scythe with a wooden frame attached, to harvest the grain.
    Farmers who shared their crops with the landowner were called **sharecroppers.**

5. A direct explanation of the word can be presented in a full sentence:

In the hot desert, the man makes his garden in an oasis. An oasis is a green spot where there is a water supply.

The nomads of the desert are coming to the trading center. Nomads are people who constantly move about and who have no settled home.

The farmer could guide his oxen by shouting "Gee!" or "Haw!" The oxen had learned that *Gee* meant to turn to the right and *Haw* meant to turn to the left.

The preceding examples will help children develop the ability to anticipate meanings in the following ways:

1. Sometimes a new word is set off by boldface type, italics, or quotation marks to call attention to it.
2. Sometimes the new word is followed by a parenthetical expression explaining its meaning.
3. Sometimes the new word is followed by a less technical or more generally known synonym or substitute phrase.
4. Sometimes the new word will be defined in the sentence following.
5. Sometimes the new word is one with several meanings, but in its current context it can have only one intended meaning.
6. A pictorial illustration may help clarify a new concept.

Boys and girls will profit from directed practice in arriving at meanings through such techniques as the following:

1. Study the context to look for clues to the meanings.
2. Relate the word to previous content in the subject.
3. Study the word structure. If it has a prefix, root, or suffix that is already known, combine context and word structure to arrive at specific meaning.
4. Read the dictionary meanings; find the one that fits.
5. Once the word is understood, think of synonyms or antonyms.
6. Once the word is understood, use it purposefully in several situations.

Punctuation

Punctuation marks in written material give meaning to connected written discourse. Reading the punctuation accurately, quickly, and meaningfully enhances comprehension significantly.

Failure to give proper attention to punctuation is certain to weaken meaningful understanding of sentences and longer reading units. Underachievers in reading often fail to read smoothly and fluently and need help in establishing the practice of watching for and using punctuation. Children need to learn precise uses of periods, question marks, commas, colons, semicolons, and exclamation marks.

Children themselves sense the need for punctuation in print. Graves reported the conversation of two first graders discussing punctuation in writing and reading:

"If you want your story to make sense, you can't write without punctuation," Alan says now. "Punctuation tells people things—like if the sentence is asking, or if someone is talking, or if you should yell it out."

Chip agrees. Readers need punctuation. "It lets you know where the sentence ends, so otherwise one minute you'd be sledding down the hill and the next minute you're inside the house, without even stopping."[32]

Working with the cloze procedure often highlights the importance of punctuation. The following sentence is from *Charlotte's Web*.

When the children grew tired *of* swinging, they went down *toward* the pasture and picked *wild* raspberries and ate them.[33]

When the underlined words are deleted, readers often have trouble with the comma, declaring it should be a period. They come to this conclusion because they try to insert "then" or "finally" in the first blank, slightly altering the meaning. It is only when they see the comma that they realize their word choice is incorrect. Since the sentence has been typed, they often are sure that the typing is at fault.

Children often enjoy reading a sentence with different punctuation marks at the end. They find it fun to use their voices to convey the intended meanings.

You ate all your cereal. (statement)
You ate all your cereal! (expressing amazement, approval)
You ate all your cereal? (expressing doubt)

Young readers also enjoy sentences in which commas inserted or omitted make a difference.

The boy said the principal is coming.
The boy, said the principal, is coming.

Convergent and Divergent Thinking

Convergent thinking is directed toward finding a correct answer to any question or problem. It has been overused in elementary school to the extent that children often think there has to be a right answer to whatever question the teacher may ask. As suggested by Guszak's report on levels of teachers' questioning, the students are apt to become habituated to unproductive, closed, *convergent* types of thinking, reasoning, and responding.[34]

Divergent thinking, on the other hand, encourages children to respond to different types of questions and problems with open, creative, and imaginative answers. Such a question as, "How many different uses can you think of for a brick used by a brick mason?" may produce a dozen valid uses other than just the construction of sturdy homes. Naturally, people do both convergent and divergent thinking in life outside the school. However, it behooves the school system to encourage the openness and the creativity of divergent and speculative thinking.

Again, levels of questioning and questioning strategies assume primary importance, as pointed out by Taba:

> The role of questions becomes crucial and the way of asking is by far the most influential single teaching act. A focus set by the teacher's questions circumscribes the mental operations which students can perform, determines what points they explore, which modes of thought they learn. A question such as "What are the important cities in the Balkans?" provides poor focus in several respects. Because no criterion of importance is available, such questions develop an unproductive mode of thinking, in addition to training in arbitrary judgment. Such questions (1) suggest that one can judge the importance of cities without a criterion. For example, does one look for large cities, capitols, ancient ones or what? Most students faced with such questions have only two alternatives: guessing what the teacher wants, or trying to recollect what the book said, both cognitive not productive. Asking "right" answer questions also (2) builds a "convergent" mind—one that looks for simple right answers, and which assumes that "right" answers depend on authority rather than on rational judgment.[35]

Our concern that divergent thinking will be sacrificed to emphasis on convergent thinking is illustrated clearly by Iverson:

> In the classes I have observed, assignments have rarely been open-ended. Instead, students were told to "work" on assignments that had *single* right answers. Such assignments develop linear and logical thinking at the expense of more expansive and intuitive thinking. I found only one exception. In a sixth grade English class, the students read a brief mystery story up to, but not including, its resolution. Then the teacher asked the students to tell what they would do in a similar situation. Students debated the best solution, discussed all aspects of the story, and brought personal knowledge into their arguments. After 34 minutes of discussion, the teacher had them read the end of the story. During that lesson there was no right answer, nor were there boundaries to the knowledge students might bring to bear on the problem. The students were combining ideas in new forms rather than hunting for the "right" answer.[36]

Iverson concludes her article in this way:

> Schooling today needs to address the rapid obsolescence of facts and promote the adaptive strategies needed to deal productively with change. If one of the long-term purposes of education is to prepare children to take their places in our fast-changing society, they will need open, flexible minds and the ability to combine information in new ways.[37]

Exercises

Reading with good comprehension requires the flexible use of a variety of intellectual abilities: developing vocabulary, comparing and contrasting, putting things in categories, ordering events into the proper sequence, recognizing antecedents (understanding anaphora), being able to remember, and asking and responding to questions. Downing has recently asked the question, "Is the learning of separate subskills necessary for learning how to read?"[38] Or, do children learn to read by reading when they use reading to solve problems, to answer their own questions, or to entertain themselves?

Following are a variety of types of exercises to help children comprehend at the literal, inferential, creative, and evaluative levels. They stand as useful learning experiences. However, it will often be possible to build such types of exercises into the children's personal needs for reading, providing increased opportunities for meaningful learning.

Literal
Comprehension

Example 1. Using the rest of the sentence to determine the meaning.[39]

Mrs. James was *puzzled* by Joyce's idea and even more *bewildered* by her actions.

Mrs. Collins *praised* her daughter, *saying that her idea was very good.*

Mr. Warren kept a plow, a hayrake and other *implements* in the barn.

George *looked over* the cleaning job, and when he had completed his *survey,* he said, "I think this basement looks fine."

"See how *sleek* Danny looks after he's curried," said Art as he eyed the pony's *smooth, glossy* coat.

*Expanding
Vocabulary
Concepts*

Example 2. Matching word meanings.

What does each worker do? Read carefully through the list of workers:

minister	shoemaker	surveyor	student	author
farmer	swimmer	sculptor	general	actress
fireman	magician	doctor	artist	grocer
teacher	miner	clown	king	conductor

In the following list, find the matching word for each word in the preceding list. On your paper, write the words that go together, for example, "1. minister preaches."

digs	preaches	sells	commands	paints
dives	reigns	juggles	studies	cultivates
measures	collects	acts	rescues	heals
writes	carves	jokes	mends	instructs

Example 3. Putting words in categories.

All of the following words can be classified as four types: flowers, foods, animals, and ways of describing behavior. Rule your paper as shown, and put each of the words in its proper category.

Flowers	Foods	Animals	Describing behavior

The words are: primrose, kangaroo, prunes, happy, beets, peony, healthy, butter, helpful, tulip, tortoise, buffalo, kind, pansy, donkey, dahlia, zebra, salad, giraffe, cocoa, busy, mule, polite, cheese, chimpanzee, generous, cheerful, brave, thrifty, lilac, interesting, careful, soup, punctual, dandelion, industrious, cauliflower, sandwiches.

Example 4. Choosing synonyms.

Read the following list of words:

finally	entrust	gradually	comment
declared	resented	despair	surveyed
grumbled	difficult	ridicule	compliment

Now read the following list of words or expressions and find one that means the same or nearly the same as each of the words in the preceding list. On your paper, match the word with its synonym:

complained	was angry at	at last	hopelessness
remark	give	said	hard
make fun of	term of praise	looked at	little by little

Example 5. Recognizing the sequence of ideas within a sentence.[40]

Each group of words here is a part of a sentence—a beginning, a middle, or a last part. When you put them in the right order, they make a sentence. In each box you are to put *1* in front of the first part, *2* in front of the middle part, and *3* in front of the last part of the sentence.

_____ Friday was the day
_____ on her vacation
_____ that Miss Spruce started

_____ clear the table
_____ Patty helped
_____ and wash the dishes

_____ and disappeared
_____ the starving beast
_____ leaped from the cage

_____ these new books in the right order
_____ on the bookshelf"
_____ Ruth said, "I'm going to put

_____ so that the bee would fly out
_____ the window of the bus
_____ Mr. Hunger was going to raise

Example 6. Deciding whether the sentence explains when, where, why, how, or who.

Read the sentence on the left and then write in the blank space on the right whether it tells *when, where, why, how,* or *who.*

The man sat *in the shade of the house.* _____

Mary cried *because she could not go.* _____

Tell me *when you have finished.* _____

They lived *happily* ever after. _____

The boys won the ball game *easily.* _____

Do you always work so *rapidly?* _____

McKee introduced the following type of exercise at the second grade level.[41]

In each sentence the part that is italicized tells where or when or how. Read each sentence. After the sentence you will see three words. Draw a line under the one word that shows what the italicized part of the sentence tells:

A golden coach came *down the street.*	When Where How
Our cat likes to stay out *at night.*	When Where How
I went to the store *in a hurry.*	When Where How
Bob ran *as fast as he could go.*	When Where How
Last summer I drank some goat's milk.	When Where How
Would a goat ride *in a golden coach?*	When Where How

Getting Meaning from the Context

Example 7. Reading to find answers.

The following exercise lends itself to factual questioning that reconstructs the story content.

"Dingdong Bell"[42]

Dingdong, dingdong! Sunday morning bells ring out, calling people to church. These bells are heard in both city and country.

Fire engines still carry a bell. Firemen pull a rope to ring the bell when they go racing off to a fire. They also sound their sirens.

On board ship, bells ring every hour and half-hour to tell sailors the time.

In the old days children came into their schoolroom when the teacher rang a bell. Sometimes this was a big handbell. Sometimes the bell was on the roof of the school house.

The most musical bells were the old sleigh bells. You heard them when the horse trotted over the snow, pulling the sleigh. Their merry tinkling, jingling sound in the frosty air is almost forgotten now.

Depending upon the maturity of the student who reads the story, there are many questions possible. For example: "What is the story about?" The story tells about five kinds of bells. The question "What kinds of bells are told about?" could lead to making a simple outline:

Different kinds of bells
1. Church bells
2. Fire engine bells
3. Ship bells
4. School bells
5. Sleigh bells

Or,

1. The church bell calls _____ .
2. The fire bell tells _____ .
3. The bell on the ship tells _____ .
4. The school bell told the children _____ .
5. Sleigh bells made music when _____ .

Inferential
Comprehension

Example 1. Understanding antecedents or pronoun referents in the sentence.

Directions: In each sentence here two pronouns are *italicized*. These pronouns refer to a person or thing in the sentence. Read each sentence. Write in the blank the name of the person or thing to which the pronoun refers.[43]

Anaphora

A stranger asked the policeman, "Can *you* tell *me* where Pennsylvania Street is from here?"

you _____
me _____

George saw at a glance that *his* boat had broken away from the dock and that *it* was stuck on a sand bar.

his _____
it _____

Jane carefully put *her* scrapbook on the highest bookshelf so that *it* would not be lost.

her _____
it _____

Paragraph Titles

Example 2. Selecting the best title for a paragraph.

After boys and girls read a paragraph or story, they can (1) select the best title from a number of suggested titles, (2) decide whether or not the title given tells what the paragraph or story is about, or (3) think of a good title. This will help to develop understanding of paragraph meaning and organization. The following exercise is an example of providing the student practice in selecting the best title after reading a paragraph:[44]

Fresh vegetables for a salad should be washed and dried carefully. Then they should be placed in a refrigerator for a time. Just before the salad is to be served, the greens should be broken into pieces and put into a salad bowl. Then strips of carrot, rings of onions, or other vegetables may be added. Next, a small amount of French dressing should be poured over the contents of the bowl. The salad should be tossed lightly until each part of it has become coated with dressing.

Put a check (✓) before the title that tells the main idea of the paragraph.
_____ 1. Preparing a Salad
_____ 2. How to Toss a Salad

Topic Sentences

Example 3. Identifying the topic sentence of a paragraph.

Boys and girls should learn that a good paragraph deals with only one topic, and the paragraph contains a topic sentence that tells what the paragraph is about. All the details of a good paragraph develop the topic sentence. Being able to identify the topic sentence will help a reader understand and organize the ideas being read.

However, children must also learn that not all writers are careful in their writing, and many paragraphs in the textbooks they read will not have a topic sentence. Further, they will have to accept paragraphs that contain details (extra sentences) that do not amplify the topic sentence for the paragraph.

Generally, in the elementary school, children will find that paragraphs contain a topic sentence, which may be the first sentence in the paragraph. Sometimes the topic sentence is a kind of summarizing sentence placed at the end of the paragraph. Boys and girls need practice identifying topic sentences found at either the beginning or the end of the paragraph.

In the following paragraph, the first sentence tells what the whole paragraph is about. Since it states the topic of the paragraph, it is called the topic sentence.

The separate bones are held together by joints in ways that help make movement of the body possible. The joints in the neck make it possible for a person to move his head up or down as well as from side to side. The joint at the shoulder makes it possible for him to move his arm in a round-the-circle manner. It is because of joints that we are able to bend the back, pick up articles with our fingers, and perform other actions.[45]

In the following example, the topic sentence is at the end of the paragraph.

Each person was in his proper place. Flags were flying. The band had begun to play a lively march. Suddenly there was a burst of applause as the marching began. The Fourth of July celebration was starting off with a big parade.[46]

In the following paragraph all the sentences relate to the general topic of roasting corn. The whole paragraph tells two ways to roast corn. The first sentence is the topic sentence because it indicates that the paragraph will tell about two ways to roast corn over an open fire.

I know two different ways to roast corn on an open fire. One way is to dip the ears, husks and all, in water. Then you put the ears on a grill over the fire to steam. These are good, but I like the second way even better. You take off the husks and put butter and salt on the ears. Then you wrap them in aluminum foil and roast them in the coals.[47]

Boys and girls in the intermediate grades should be able to underline the topic sentences in material like the following paragraphs.

When Marco Polo was seventeen years old, he went to China with his father and uncle. While there, he traveled through many little-known parts of the country in the service of the ruler. Many places he visited were very wild, and Marco had some exciting times. Then, three years after he returned to his homeland, he was called on to serve in a war. He was captured and was imprisoned for nearly a year. Marco Polo had many interesting adventures during his life—both in foreign lands and in his homeland.

By following a few simple directions, anyone should be able to raise lettuce. Light, well-fertilized soil should be used. The lettuce seeds should not be dropped too close together. If they are dropped close together, some of the young plants should be thinned out. There should be frequent stirring of the soil to encourage growth of the plants. Large amounts of water are not necessary for growing lettuce.

One of the oldest and most common of the human qualities is that of wanting animals as pets. Children at an early age learn to love pets. A small child will hug his toy dog and love it, but he will gladly exchange it for a live pet. Although we think of children as the persons who most desire and need pets, most older persons also love pets. Those who lose a pet are often very sad, until they get another, or until they become accustomed to being without a pet.[48]

Learning to Anticipate Meanings: Predicting What Will Happen Next

Example 4.[49]

Read the paragraph and two sentences in each column below. Then draw a line under the sentence that answers the question correctly.

The red fox was clever and full of tricks, and never had trouble finding something to eat. In summer he caught small animals and birds. In winter he caught fish through a hole in the ice.

How will the red fox get along without the white fox?

He will go hungry. He will have all that he needs.

The white fox did very little. He sunned himself in front of the den in summer. He slept in his warm bed during the cold, dark winter. Every day he waited for the red fox to come home.

How will the white fox get along without the red fox?

He will go hungry. He will have all that he needs.

1. What the white fox did _____ .
2. What the red fox did _____ .

Example 5.[50]

Read each of the next two paragraphs and the statements that accompany them.
Underline the statement that best predicts the outcome for each paragraph.

> One winter day a country boy was driving a team of horses. It began to snow, and
> the wind blew the snow in his face. All around him the falling snow was like a thick
> curtain. He drove the horses where he thought the road was. Soon he knew he was
> lost. Then he remembered that horses always know the way home, even in a bad
> storm.
>
> > The horses ate the grass by the road.
> > He let the horses find the way home.
> > He made the horses stand still.
> > He took his sister in out of the storm.
>
> A boy who had never seen snow was taken to a place where snow fell every winter.
> He could hardly wait to see the snow for he had heard how fluffy and white it was.
> He had been told that it made fences, roads, and even trash heaps beautiful. One
> morning when he opened his eyes he saw a strange white world through the window.
> It had snowed.
>
> > He turned over and went back to sleep.
> > He pulled down the window shade at once.
> > He ran to the window and looked out.
> > He waited until the winter came.

Role of Conceptual Thought in Inference

Elementary concepts have a three-part structure: differentiation, ordering, and abstraction. This is illustrated in figure 10.4. (See also chapter 12, "Teaching Reading in the Content Fields.")

Work by curriculum experts in elementary education has emphasized the job of the classroom teacher in developing understandings, concepts, and generalizations. Taba states that the content of learning for the child consists of various levels of thinking:

> One level is that of specific facts, descriptive ideas at a low level of abstraction, and specific processes and skills. . . .
>
> Basic ideas and principles represent another level of knowledge. The ideas about causal relationships between human culture and natural environment are of this sort. So are scientific laws and mathematics principles, the ideas stating relationships between nutrition and metabolism of the human body, or ideas about how such factors as climate, soil, and natural resources produce unique constellations of a geographic environment. . . .
>
> A third level of content is composed of what one might call concepts, such as the concept of democracy, of interdependence, of social change, or of the "set" in mathematics.[51]

Taba's levels of thinking are basic theoretical material for the reading teacher who is going to help boys and girls develop reading skills that embody the full definition of reading: comprehending, reacting, and integrating. Levels of questioning as prescribed in Bloom's taxonomy (see chapter 2) and the refining of conceptual thinking for critical reading ability are positively related.

Figure 10.4
Elementary concepts have a three-part structure: differentiation, abstraction, and ordering. Differentiating involves distinguishing one element from another. Abstracting from such elements a concept that some are food and some are not food would be another mental operation. Ordering things that are conceptualized into different categories is yet another mental operation. Whether these three operations follow a fixed sequence is not clear, although they are often diagrammed in a hierarchy as here.

From Margaret Greer, "The Effect of Studying the Structure of Concepts and Cognitive-Emphasis Social Studies Units on Selected Cognitive Processes of Fifth-Grade Children," Unpublished doctoral dissertation, Graduate School, University of New Mexico, Albuquerque, New Mexico, 1969, p. 70.

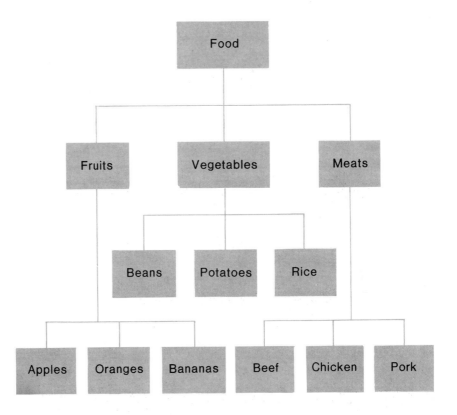

Outlining. As an initial step in helping children learn to outline, the teacher needs to guide the discussion about the content of the paragraph and to list, perhaps on the chalkboard, the main points, the subordinate points, and the details that the paragraph contains.

Growing and Exporting Bananas

Growing and exporting bananas is the most important industry in Ecuador. Bananas require both a tropical climate and hard work. The plants grow in the lowlands near the Pacific coast, where the temperature is always hot and there is abundant rainfall. The farmers must care for the plants many months before the fruit is mature. Then they select the largest bunches to sell. The bunches are cut from the stalk, and the stalk is then cut off near the ground. Trucks drive to the edge of the fields, and men load the heavy stalks of bananas by hand. If the bananas must be carried any distance to the truck, men carry them on their backs or tie them on the backs of burros. Exporting, or the marketing process, requires hauling the crop to the seaport and loading it on ships. The trucks carry the bananas to the docks in Guayaquil. At the docks, the bananas may be carried by hand and put into large nets that will be lifted by crane and lowered into the holds of ships. These vessels carry great quantities of green bananas to many parts of the world. Some weeks later, the fruit, now ripened and yellow, is ready to be sold in fruit markets and supermarkets in your hometown. Many people never think about the thousands of miles the delicious banana on their breakfast table had to travel to get there.

Growing and Exporting the Banana

Growing Conditions	Farmers	Transporting	Exporting
climate	planting	hauling to trucks	throughout the
tropical	cultivating	to docks in	world
lowlands	harvesting	Guayaquil	food markets
rainfall	selling	filling large nets	eating
		loading into holds	
		of ships	

This list can be rearranged into a topical outline:

Growing and Exporting the Banana in Ecuador

I. Growing bananas
   A. Climate
      1. Tropical
      2. Lowlands
      3. Rainfall
   B. Farmers at work
      1. Planting
      2. Cultivating
      3. Harvesting
      4. Selling
II. Exporting bananas
   A. Transporting
      1. With trucks from farm to docks
      2. Loading on ships
   B. Marketing
      1. Distributing throughout the world
      2. Food markets
      3. Eating the banana

Drawing Inferences   **Based on factual information.**   In order to draw inferences based on factual information, it is necessary for the reader to retain, select, and evaluate the information read and then follow the directions to draw conclusions based on the evidence.

Ideas implied but not stated.   A student able to evaluate while reading—that is, able to read critically—will be able to draw inferences and arrive at conclusions. Such an ability is achieved by practice. This skill is necessary in evaluating the characters in a story, with just descriptions of their behavior given. In the story presented in figure 10.5, sixth graders are asked to infer appropriate meanings or to draw conclusions based on the reading.

Figure 10.5
Critical reading
requires the student to
extend the given
information to
formulate proper
conclusions.

From Guy L. Bond, Marie
C. Cuddy, and Leo C. Fay,
Fun to Do Book to
accompany *Stories to
Remember* (Chicago, Ill.:
Lyons and Carnahan,
1962), p. 60.

Read and Think

Read the story and be ready to answer some questions about it.

Part I

Obed Swain was an old sailor, or, as he would have put it, "an old sea dog." He had once been captain of the good ship *Catawba* and had sailed the seven seas. Now that he was old, he had settled down to life in a village. The only difficulty which he had not been able to surmount was that of monotony. The captain had been accustomed to monotony at sea, but had always found diversion in regaling his shipmates with tales of his adventures. People in the village, which Obed Swain called a "landlocked town," did not seem to understand his seafaring language. At first they found it a diversion just to listen to the old captain talk, but soon they lost interest in his tales.

Mark your answer with a check (✓).

What is an "old sea dog"?

_____ 1. A dog that goes to sea

_____ 2. A worn-out ship

_____ 3. An old sailor

What do you think Obed Swain meant by a "landlocked town"?

_____ 1. A town with no land to sell

_____ 2. An inland town away from the sea

_____ 3. A town far away from other towns

Part II

Shortly after the captain settled down in his new home, a railroad was built through the village. Almost everyone was excited about it, but Obed Swain had paid no attention to the event until the day the first train came in. The sight had an electrifying effect on the captain.

"What kind of contrivance is that?" he asked. Then, seeing the smoke pour from the smokestack, he exclaimed, "See that black smoke! That contrivance must burn sperm oil!"

When the train stopped, the captain went over to look at the locomotive. As he approached it, a jet of vapor issued from the side of the engine.

"Thar she blows!" shouted the captain. "Thar she blows on the larboard side!"

When the vapor had disappeared, Captain Swain talked to the engineer.

"Ho, there! Are you the captain of this craft?" inquired Obed. "Where's your ratlines? I want to come aboard."

The engineer did not know what ratlines were, but he helped the old gentleman get up into the locomotive. Obed Swain asked questions about different devices he saw. He understood engines, so he and the engineer had an enjoyable time.

From that day on, the captain looked forward to train time.

Mark your answer with a check (✓).

Which of the following show that the story probably did not take place in recent times?

_____ 1. A railroad was just being built into the town.

_____ 2. The old man did not know a locomotive when he saw it.

_____ 3. Black smoke was coming out of the smokestack.

60

Drawing Generalizations	One lesson in generalizing is being able to read material such as a fable and decide what it illustrates.[52]

1. One sunny day two ducks went out for a walk. "Child," said the mother duck, "you're not walking very prettily. You should try to walk straight without waddling so."

   "Dear Mother," said the young duck, "if you'll walk the way you want me to walk, I'll follow you."

2. A lamb on a rooftop saw a wolf pass by on the ground below. The lamb shouted, "Get away from here, you terrible creature! How dare you show your face here!"

   "You talk very boldly," replied the wolf. "Would you be as bold if you were down on the ground?"

3. After fishing for a whole day, a fisherman caught only a single small fish. "Please let me go," begged the fish. "I'm too small to eat now. If you put me back into the pond, I'll grow. Then you can make a meal of me."

   "Oh, no!" said the fisherman. "I have you now. I may not catch you again."

4. One warm day a hungry fox spied a delicious-looking bunch of fruit. It was hanging on a vine that was tied to a high fence. The fox jumped and jumped, trying to reach the fruit. But each time he just missed it. When he was too tired to jump again, he gave up.

   "I'm sure that fruit is spoiled," grumbled the fox as he went away.

   A bird in the hand is worth two in the bush.
   It is easy to dislike what you cannot get.
   Setting a good model is the best way to teach.
   It is easy to be brave from a safe distance.

Creative Comprehension	It has been stated that we learn to appreciate our base ten number system by working with other bases. Because our system is so familiar to us, we fail to attend to its organization and structure until we are faced with a different system.

Children often fail to appreciate the organization and structure of their language(s) because they have known nothing else. Older boys and girls may be challenged by trying to create a new language. They will be confronted with the significant aspects of language—its sounds, its structure, and its meanings. These, of course, are the major aspects of language that facilitate comprehension. Even if the children never finish their task, they will have come face to face with the primary components of language and some of the means by which understanding is conveyed.

Other possible ways to work with creative comprehension are:

1. After a story or book is completed, children may be encouraged to write or dictate a further chapter or several more paragraphs. It must be consistent with the story that has been read.

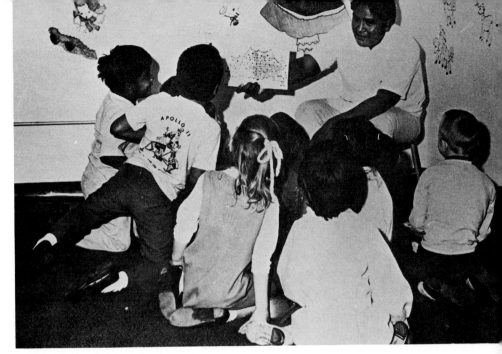

After children have heard an interesting story, they may wish to engage in creative comprehension by turning the story into a play.

2. Children may be asked to turn a story into a play. Completing this task requires that children invent scenes, dialogue, settings, and perhaps costumes. The children will need to make many inferences, and in addition they will have to exhibit creative thought.
3. Children may be asked to develop several different possible endings for a story.
4. The reading and writing of poetry are certainly creative experiences and require creative comprehension. Hennings writes, "It is in poetry that writers create the most striking pictures from words; and it is, therefore, through poetry that teachers help students appreciate the beauty of word pictures and create vivid images of their own."[53]

Evaluative Comprehension

Helping children become evaluative and critical readers is an important part of the teacher's job. Following are some possible strategies to help children develop and refine this aspect of comprehension.

1. Have children compare the entries on specific topics in encyclopedias. Try to obtain an encyclopedia at least twenty years old, another from about a decade ago, and a current one. Topics such as "moon," "space flight," and "airplanes" are good ones. Children can evaluate the effects of date of publication on the validity of information.
2. Help the children to make a chart on which *they* list the characteristics of a good story. As stories in the basal readers or in trade books are read, evaluate each using the predetermined list of characteristics of good stories.

3. After reading a given selection, discuss why the children think the author wrote the story or article. If possible, help the children to cite evidence in the selection to support their beliefs.
4. Involve the class in sending for some item that is advertised on a cereal carton or the container of some other product. When it arrives, compare it carefully with the way it was described and the way individuals thought it would look.
5. Help children to identify stories as "real" or fanciful. Also, lead them to identify statements of fact and opinion.

Learning to Anticipate Meanings: The Cloze Procedure

Cloze is a procedure in which the reader tries to anticipate meaning from context and supply words deleted in a message. Taylor defines the cloze procedure as "a method of intercepting a message from a 'transmitter' (writer or speaker), mutilating its language patterns by deleting parts, and so administering it to 'receivers' (readers and listeners) that their attempts to make the patterns whole again potentially yield a considerable number of cloze units."[54]

Using Cloze as a Testing Techniuqe

The cloze procedure does not require special expertise in test construction. It merely presents the reader with a series of contextually interrelated blanks in a passage. A cloze test is constructed by selecting a passage of a minimum of 250 words and mutilating it by (1) omitting every *nth* word throughout and leaving in their places blanks of some standard length, or (2) omitting every *nth* noun or every *nth* verb. Students read the passage and write in the missing words. It follows that the better the passage is understood, the more likely the reader can anticipate what words are missing. Schneyer found that cloze tests have adequate validity for evaluating reading comprehension for most general uses.[55] The first type of omission correlates more highly with vocabulary and reading comprehension; the second with story comprehension.[56]

The generally acceptable criteria for developing cloze exercises include the following:[57]

1. Every "nth" word is deleted. (N may equal any number between 5 and 12.)
2. The minimum passage length must be 250 words.
3. At least fifty deletions are used to insure adequate sampling of content.
4. For scoring for determining instructional level, the exact word deleted must be used by the reader in order for the scoring criteria to be valid.
5. Other scoring systems (synonyms, form classes) provide less interscorer reliability and require substantially more time.
6. The separate scoring of form classes or content and function words may provide specific information for specialized purposes.

While the cloze has been evaluated as a testing device, little has been said about its use as a teaching device. Sentences with blank spaces in which children write the word that best completes the thought, or sentences in which the children think of synonyms for the underlined word are types of exercises that develop skill in the use of this technique.

An individual's performance on a cloze test is a measure of ability to understand the meaning of the material being read. Meaning is based upon general language facility, vocabulary relevant to the material, native learning ability, and motivation.[58]

In evaluating the cloze test results, the percentage of correctly completed cloze units is used to assign levels of reading comprehension. For example, a percentage of correct answers of forty or below is equated with the frustration level of reading comprehension; a percentage of correct answers between forty and fifty is equated with the instructional level of reading comprehension; a percentage of correct answers above fifty is equated with the independent level of reading comprehension.

Practice exercise 1.

Directions: In this exercise you will use context clues to think accurately and to supply the missing word to give the meaning. Read the selection all the way through before filling in the blanks. You will need only *one* word for each blank.

Life in the Desert[59]

In the northern part of Africa is a great amount of hot, dry (1) _____ called desert. This desert is larger than our (2) _____ . The driest parts of the desert have hills and (3) _____ of sand. No one tries to live there. In some other parts, most of them where the (4) _____ is higher, there is enough rain for some plants to grow.

In these desert (5) _____ , there are hundreds of places where water (6) _____ from springs or wells throughout the year. Such a place (7) _____ called an oasis. At an oasis we find palm trees and (8) _____ . Sometimes several hundred or even several thousand people live near a place with water.

Many of the (9) _____ of the desert lands move about from one place to another. They do so to (10) _____ more water and grass for their animals. These traveling people (11) _____ called nomads.

Most of the land in desert country (12) _____ not owned by anyone.

Cloze Scoring Key.* (Grade level = 4.5)
1. *land,* country, area, region, sand
2. *United States,* country, land, nation, deserts, state
3. *drifts,* dunes, abundance
4. *land,* altitude
5. *lands,* wastelands, areas, regions, parts, places

6. *comes,* spurts, collects, splashes, flows, pours
7. *is*
8. *gardens,* plants, shade, water, spring
9. *people,* nomads, occupants, natives, tribes
10. *find,* supply, get, gather, have, locate, provide, fetch
11. *are*
12. *is*

*The word used by the author is in italics.

Practice exercise 2.

Directions: This is an elementary story about a woodsman who lost his ax. Read the story all the way through quickly and then fill in the blanks. Use only one word for each blank.

The Octopus and the Ax[60]

Once upon a time there was a poor man who lived near the sea. In summer, he fished for a (1) _____ . In winter he cut wood to (2) _____ .

One day, as he was working, (3) _____ ax fell into the water.

"Help!" (4) _____ the man. "I have lost my (5) _____ ." To his surprise, an octopus came (6) _____ . He was waving a gold ax (7) _____ one of his long, black arms.

(8) "_____ this the ax you lost?" asked (9) _____ octopus.

"No," said the man. "My (10) _____ is made of wood."

The octopus (11) _____ down again. This time he brought (12) _____ a silver ax.

"Is this the (13) _____ you lost?" asked the octopus.

"No," (14) _____ the man again. "My ax is (15) _____ wood."

Again the octopus went down. (16) _____ time he came up holding an (17) _____ of wood.

"Is this the ax (18) _____ lost?" asked the octopus.

"Yes! That (19) _____ it!" cried the man. "How can (20) _____ ever thank you?"

"Your honesty is (21) _____ the thanks I need," said the (22) _____ . He gave the man the lost (23) _____ , and the gold and silver ones, too.

Then, with a wave of his (24) _____ black arms, he went back to (25) _____ bottom of the sea.

Key:

1. living	6. up	11. went	16. This	21. all
2. sell	7. in	12. up	17. ax	22. octopus
3. his	8. Is	13. ax	18. you	23. ax
4. cried	9. the	14. said	19. is	24. long
5. ax	10. ax	15. only	20. I	25. the

A cloze test.

Directions: In the following story, every seventh word has been left out. Read through the whole story quickly to see what the general idea is. Then anticipate the meaning the author had in mind by using all of the context clues you can find. Write the appropriate word on each blank. Remember you will need only one word for each blank.

Outwitting Brindle[61]

Uncle Hyatt Frame bought a cow named Brindle. He was pleased with his buy (1) _____ he milked her for the first (2) _____ . It took only two minutes for (3) _____ to discover that she was (4) _____ "switcher." Now, it is bad enough (5) _____ have a cow that keeps her (6) _____ going in fly time, but in (7) _____ there is not a bit of (8) _____ excuse for it. A blow in (9) _____ face from a long, stringy tail (10) _____ sure to cause a strong feeling (11) _____ to anger.

At the first switch (12) _____ Brindle's tail, Uncle Hyatt shouted, "Hey!" At (13) _____ second, he hit the cow in (14) _____ . At the third, he got off (15) _____ milking stool, found a piece of (16) _____ , and tied the tail to a (17) _____ .

Warm weather came. Uncle Hyatt moved his (18) _____ outside. At the first switch, he (19) _____ the tail and tied it to (20) _____ boot strap. When he finished the (21) _____ , he got up and picked up (22) _____ pail of milk. Then he gave (23) _____ a slap. Brindle moved away, taking (24) _____ left leg with her. His right (25) _____ followed.

Looking from the kitchen window, Aunt Emily (26) _____ amazed. She saw Uncle Hyatt hopping quickly (27) _____ the yard after the cow. Milk (28) _____ from the pail. Aunt Emily had no (29) _____ what the trouble was. The only (30) _____ she could see was that a (31) _____ milking was rapidly going to waste. (32) _____ called loudly from the open window, (33) " _____ out for the milk!" Then she (34) _____ to the door.

By this time, (35) _____ and Brindle had reached the farther (36) _____ of the yard. They had even (37) _____ on the return trip. Brindle had (38) _____ air of someone who knew where (39) _____ was going. Uncle Hyatt hopped after her, (40) _____ holding the milk pail, which grew (41) _____ and lighter.

"Stop her!" cried Uncle Hyatt.

(42) _____ was between them, so Aunt Emily did (43) _____ know the reason for Uncle Hyatt's strange (44) _____ . She ran through the gate, waving (45) _____ apron and calling, "Whoa, Brindle."

The (46) _____ cow began to run. The milk (47) _____ flew off to one side. Uncle Hyatt (48) _____ and moved quickly along at Brindle's (49) _____ , grabbing at anything in sight.

Finally (50) _____ boot strap broke. Brindle ran to (51) _____ farthest corner of the yard. Aunt Emily (52) _____ Uncle Hyatt to his feet, took him (53) _____ the kitchen, and worked over him (54) _____ liniment. "Tell me something, Hyatt," she (55) _____ . "If you had to tie the (56) _____ to a leg, why didn't you (57) _____ it to Brindle's?"

Key:

1. until	16. rope	30. thing	44. behavior
2. time	17. rafter	31. whole	45. her
3. him	18. milking	32. She	46. frightened
4. a	19. grabbed	33. Look	47. pail
5. to	20. his	34. hurried	48. fell
6. tail	21. milking	35. Uncle Hyatt	49. heels
7. winter	22. the	36. end	50. his
8. an	23. Brindle	37. started	51. the
9. the	24. Uncle Hyatt's	38. the	52. helped
10. is	25. leg	39. she	53. into
11. leading	26. was	40. still	54. with
12. of	27. about	41. lighter	55. said
13. the	28. splashed	42. Brindle	56. tail
14. anger	29. idea	43. not	57. tie
15. the			

From Theory to Practice 10.3
Administering and Scoring a Cloze Test

Learning how to construct and use the cloze procedure is an important part of learning how to teach reading.

Select a story, probably from a third to sixth reader level. Prepare it as a cloze test. It will need to be typed with every *nth* word deleted. It is suggested that you delete every fifth word. Make each blank the same size. Duplicate the sheet for use by two or more students.

Administer the cloze test to two or more children, after explaining to them carefully what they are to do. When each child has completed the sheet, ask him or her to explain to you why at least some of the blanks were filled as they were.

After the children have gone, score the sheets for the author's words. Determine the percentage of correct answers. Was this cloze test at each child's instructional level? Frustration level? Independent level?

Plan to share your cloze test and the results with other class members and your instructor.

Using Cloze As a Teaching Technique

The cloze procedure is usually associated with testing techniques. However, teachers should also think of it as an instructional tool.

Cloze activities may be used to help children improve their reading comprehension abilities. The activities may be done orally with both familiar and unfamiliar materials, in committees or other groups, or individually. Teachers may have children choose appropriate words or try to identify the author's words. In doing these activities, children are encouraged to use syntactic and semantic clues, punctuation clues, and their own knowledge, all elements of successful comprehension.

Teachers may make cloze activities from a variety of materials. Any textbook in use can be the source of material for a cloze lesson. Newspaper articles, magazine selections, library books, and even children's writing are other sources.

When teachers are participating in textbook selection, they may wish to make cloze lessons from proposed texts. If children cannot score at least forty percent on such worksheets, the proposed text is probably too difficult for use.

Materials for Teaching Comprehension

Many kits, workbooks, sets of worksheets, and games are available commercially to help teach comprehension skills. A sampling of these includes:

Boning, Richard A. *Cloze Connections.* Baldwin, N.Y.: Barnell Loft, 1980. Levels 3 to 9.

Lapp, Diane, and James Flood. *Clues for Better Reading.* North Billerica, Mass.: Curriculum Associates, 1982. Kit I for grades 2 and 3; Kit II for grades 4 to 6; Kit III for grades 7 to 9. Activities focus on such skills as Main Idea, Cause and Effect, Inferring, and Propaganda.

Barnell Loft Specific Skill Series. Primary, Elementary, and Midway Levels. Baldwin, N.Y.: Barnell Loft, 1980. Workbook format.

Cohen, Lawrence H. *Neighborhood Stories.* Providence, R.I.: Jamestown Publishers, 1982. For 4th, 5th, and 6th grades. Focus on vocabulary, details, inference and conclusion, and subject matter and main idea.

Gaining fluency in writing simple programs for the microcomputer contributes both to word recognition and to comprehension.

Some microcomputer software is available for practice on comprehension. Examples of available materials include:

Fry, Edward, and Lawrence Carrillo. *Reading Comprehension Tutorprogram.* Wilmington, Del.: BLS. For Apple II. Reading levels 3 and 4, contents levels 3 to 6. Additional program for reading level 5 and 6, content level 4 to 7.

Reading Comprehension: What's Different? Greenwich, Conn.: Program Design. For ages 8 and up. Five programs in which student picks word that does not belong.

Reading Comprehension. Chatsworth, Calif.: Opportunities for Learning. Set of ten programs elementary level and up. For four different microcomputers.

Summary

Comprehension has been defined as being dependent on the interactions between reader, text, and context. Discussions of schema theory and discourse analysis have been provided to extend and clarify the meaning of comprehension. Literal, inferential, creative, and evaluative comprehension have been discussed, along with suggested activities for each. Literal comprehension was defined as understanding vocabulary concepts, integrated ideas in sentences, paragraph organization, and getting ideas from context. Inferential comprehension includes understanding anaphora, working with paragraphs, anticipating meanings, developing concepts, outlining, and developing generalizations. Creative comprehension includes aspects of going beyond the information on the page and thinking in divergent ways. Finally, critical comprehension focuses on assessing the truth or validity of information, on the importance of authorship and the motives of authors, on the date of publication, and on the differences between real and fanciful, fact and opinion. The cloze procedure has been discussed as an effective comprehension teaching and testing technique.

For Further Reading

Crowell, Doris C., and Kathryn Hu-pei Au. "A Scale of Questions to Guide Comprehension Instruction." *The Reading Teacher* 34 (January 1981): 389–93.

Dallman, Martha, et al. "Comprehension" and "Developing Comprehension." In *The Teaching of Reading,* 6th ed. pp. 158–208. New York: Holt, Rinehart and Winston, 1982.

Davidson, Jane L. "The Group Mapping Activity for Instruction in Reading and Thinking." *Journal of Reading* 26 (October 1982): 52–56.

Downing, John. "Reading—Skill or Skills?" *The Reading Teacher* 35 (February 1982): 534–37.

Guthrie, John T., ed. *Comprehension and Teaching: Research Reviews.* Newark, Del.: International Reading Assn., 1981.

Hansen, Jane. "The Effects of Inference Training and Practice on Young Children's Reading Comprehension." *Reading Research Quarterly* 16, no. 3 (1981): 391–417.

———. "An Inferential Comprehension Strategy for Use with Primary Grade Children." *The Reading Teacher* 34 (March 1981): 665–69.

Pearson, P. David, and Dale D. Johnson. *Teaching Reading Comprehension.* New York: Holt, Rinehart and Winston, 1978.

Santa, Carol M., and Bernard L. Hayes. *Children's Prose Comprehension.* Newark, Del.: International Reading Assn., 1981.

Smith, Nila B., and H. Alan Robinson. "Nurturing Reading Comprehension." In *Reading Instruction for Today's Children,* 2d ed., pp. 203–37. Englewood Cliffs, N.J.: Prentice-Hall, 1980.

Taylor, Wilson L. "Cloze Procedure: A New Tool for Measuring Readability." *Journalism Quarterly* 30 (Fall 1953): 415–33.

Wilson, Cathy, and Carol Hammill. "Inferencing and Comprehension in Ninth Graders Reading Geography Textbooks." *Journal of Reading* 25 (February 1982):424–28.

Notes

1. Judith A. Langer and M. Trika Smith-Burke, eds., *Reader Meets Author/Bridging the Gap* (Newark, Del.: International Reading Assn., 1982), p. vii.
2. Marilyn Adams and Bertram Bruce, "Background Knowledge and Reading Comprehension," in Smith-Burke, *Reader Meets Author,* pp. 22–23.
3. E. L. Thorndike, "Reading as Reasoning: A Study of Mistakes in Paragraph Reading," *Journal of Educational Psychology* 8 (1917): 323–32.
4. Ann L. Brown, "Learning How to Learn from Reading," in Langer and Smith-Burke, *Reader Meets Author,* pp. 42–43.
5. John G. Navarra and Joseph Zafforoni, *Today's Basic Science* (New York: Harper & Row, 1967), p. 77.
6. Harry Singer, "Hypotheses on Reading Comprehension in Search of Classroom Validation," reprinted from *Directions in Reading: Research and Instruction,* ed. Michael Kamil (Thirtieth yearbook of the National Reading Conference. Washington D.C.: The National Reading Conference, 1981), p. 12.
7. David E. Rumelhart, "Schemata: The Building Blocks of Cognition," chapter 2 in *Theoretical Issues in Reading Comprehension,* ed. Rand J. Spiro, Bertram C. Bruce, and William F. Brewer (Hillsdale, N.J.: Lawrence Erlbaum Associates, 1980).
8. Ibid., p. 48.
9. J. D. Bransford and M. K. Johnson, "Contextual Prerequisites for Understanding Some Investigations of Comprehension and Recall," *Journal of Verbal Learning and Verbal Behavior* 11 (1972): 717–26.
10. Leslie Hart, *How the Brain Works* (New York: Basic Books, 1975).
11. Kenneth Goodman, "Schema," in *A Dictionary of Reading and Related Terms,* ed. Theodore L. Harris and Richard E. Hodges (Newark, Del.: International Reading Assn., 1981), p. 286.
12. Laura Ingalls Wilder, *On the Banks of Plum Creek* (New York: Harper & Row, 1937, 1953, 1971), pp. 116–17.
13. P. David Pearson and Rand Spiro, "The New Buzz Word in Reading Is Schema," *Instructor* 91 (May 1982): 46–48.
14. Richard C. Anderson and Zohara Shifrin, "The Meaning of Words in Context," in Spiro, et al., *Theoretical Issues in Reading Comprehension,* p. 332.
15. Pearson and Spiro, "The New Buzz Word in Reading Is Schema," pp. 46–47.
16. Glenn O. Blough and Julius Schwartz, *Elementary School Science and How to Teach It,* Fourth Edition (New York: Holt, Rinehart and Winston, 1969), pp. 217–19.
17. John Rowe Townsend, *The Intruder* (New York: Dell, 1969), p. 149.
18. Thomas R. Berger, *Northern Frontier, Northern Homeland, The Report of the Mackenzie Valley Pipeline Inquiry* (Toronto, Ontario: James Lorimer and Company, 1977), p. 100.

19. A. W. F. Huggins and Marilyn J. Adams, "Syntactic Aspects of Reading Comprehension," in Spiro, et al., *Theoretical Issues in Reading Comprehension,* p. 103.

20. Ibid., p. 109.

21. Allan Collins, John Seely Brown, and Kathy M. Larkin, "Inference in Text Understanding," in Spiro, et al., *Theoretical Issues in Reading Comprehension,* p. 386.

22. Ibid., p. 387.

23. Andrew Ortony, "Metaphor," in Spiro, et al., *Theoretical Issues in Reading Comprehension,* pp. 349–65.

24. R. Scott Baldwin, Terrence S. Luce, and John E. Readence, "The Impact of Subschemata on Metaphorical Processing," *Reading Research Quarterly* 17, no. 4 (1982): 529.

25. Ibid., pp. 534, 536.

26. Ibid., p. 542.

27. Benjamin Bloom, ed., *Taxonomy of Educational Objectives, Handbook I: Cognitive Domain* (New York: Longman, Green, 1956).

28. Norris Sanders, *Classroom Questions: What Kinds?* (New York: Harper & Row, 1966).

29. Thomas Barrett, "Taxonomy of Cognitive and Affective Dimensions of Reading Comprehension," in Theodore Clymer, "What Is Reading?: Some Current Concepts," in *Innovation and Change in Reading Instruction,* ed. Helen M. Robinson, 67th Yearbook, National Society for the Study of Education, Part II (Chicago: University of Chicago Press, 1968), pp. 19–23.

30. Carl B. Smith and Ronald Wardhaugh, "A Special Day," in *Macmillan Reading,* Series R, is cited by Robert Aukerman, *The Basal Approach to Reading* (New York: Wiley, 1981), p. 220.

31. A. S. Artley, "Teaching Word Meaning Through Context," *Elementary English Review* 20 (1943): 68–74; Constance M. McCullough, "The Recognition of Context Clues in Reading," *Elementary English Review* 22 (1945): 1–5.

32. Donald H. Graves, "When Children Want to Punctuate: Basic Skills Belong in Context—Lucy McCormick Calkins," *Language Arts* 57 (May 1980): 569.

33. E. B. White, *Charlotte's Web* (New York: Harper & Row, 1952), p. 70.

34. Frank J. Guszak, "Teachers' Questions and Levels in Reading Comprehension," in *Perspectives in Reading: The Evaluation of Children's Reading Achievement,* ed. James F. Kerfoot (Newark, Del.: International Reading Assn., 1967), pp. 97–109.

35. Hilda Taba, S. Levine, and F. F. Elzey, *Thinking in Elementary School Children* (San Francisco: San Francisco State College, U.S. Office of Education, Cooperative Research Project No. 1574, 1964), pp. 53–54.

36. Barbara K. Iverson, "Play, Creativity, and Schools Today," *Phi Delta Kappan* 63 (June 1982): 694.

37. Ibid.

38. John Downing, "Reading—Skill or Skills?" *The Reading Teacher* 35 (February 1982): 534.

39. William S. Gray and Gwen Horseman, *Basic Reading Skills for Junior High School Use* (Chicago: Scott, Foresman, 1957), p. 13.

40. William S. Gray, Marian Monroe, and Steryl Artley, *Think-and-Do Book* to accompany *Just Imagine!* Teacher's Edition (Chicago: Scott, Foresman, 1953), p. 24; and Guidebook to accompany *Basic Reading Skills for Junior High School Use,* Teacher's Edition (Chicago: Scott, Foresman, 1957), p. 19.

41. Paul McKee, et al., *Workbook for On We Go* (Boston: Houghton Mifflin, 1963), p. 25.

42. Arthur I. Gates and Celeste C. Peardon, *Reading Exercises, Preparatory,* Level A (New York: Bureau of Publications, Teachers College Press, 1963), story no. 5.

43. Gray and Horseman, *Basic Reading Skills,* p. 21.

44. Guy L. Bond, Marie C. Cuddy, and Leo C. Fay, *Fun to Do Book* to accompany *Stories to Remember* (Chicago: Lyons and Carnahan, 1962), p. 22.

45. Ibid., p. 34.

46. Ibid.

47. Harold Shane, et al., *Using Good English, Book Five* (River Forest, Ill.: Laidlaw Bros., 1961), p. 84.

48. Harold Shane, et al., *Using Good English, Book Six* (River Forest, Ill.: Laidlaw Bros., 1961), p. 81.

49. William Burton, et al., *Flying High,* Developmental Reading Text Workbook, Grade Five (Indianapolis: Bobbs-Merrill, 1964), p. 98.

50. Arthur I. Gates, *Gates Silent Reading Test, Type B: Reading to Predict the Outcome of Given Events,* Form 1, Grades 3–8 (New York: Bureau of Publications, Teachers College Press, 1926).

51. Hilda Taba, *Curriculum Development: Theory and Practice* (New York: Harcourt, Brace and World, 1962), pp. 175, 176, 178.

52. From *Just Imagine Think-and-Do Book* by W.S. Gray et al. Copyright © 1962 Scott, Foresman and Company. Reprinted by permission.

53. Dorothy Grant Hennings, *Communication in Action* (Chicago: Rand McNally, 1978), p. 245.

54. Wilson L. Taylor, "Cloze Procedure: A New Tool for Measuring Readability," *Journalism Quarterly* 30 (Fall 1953): 416.

55. Wesley J. Schneyer, "Use of the Cloze Procedure for Improving Reading Comprehension," *The Reading Teacher* 19 (December 1965): 174.

56. W. W. Weaver and A. J. Kingston, "A Factor Analysis of the Cloze Procedure and Other Measures of Reading and Language Ability," *Journal of Communications* 13 (1963): 253.

57. Thomas C. Potter, *A Taxonomy of Cloze Research, Part I, Readability and Reading Comprehension* (11300 La Cienega Blvd., Inglewood, Calif. 90304: Southwest Regional Laboratory for Educational Research and Development, 1968), pp. 39–40.

58. Taylor, "Cloze Procedure," p. 416.

59. Marian Tonjes, "Evaluation of Comprehension and Vocabulary Gains of Tenth Grade Students Enrolled in a Developmental Reading Program" (M.A. thesis, University of New Mexico, 1969) pp. 66–67.

60. Clarence R. Stone and Ardis Edwards Gurton, *New Practice Readers,* Book A (New York: Webster Division, McGraw-Hill, 1960), pp. 90–91. Reprinted by permission.

61. Clarence R. Stone and Charles C. Grover, *New Practice Readers,* Book D (New York: McGraw-Hill, 1962), pp. 82–83. Reprinted by permission.

Study Skills

A Cognitive Map: Study Skills

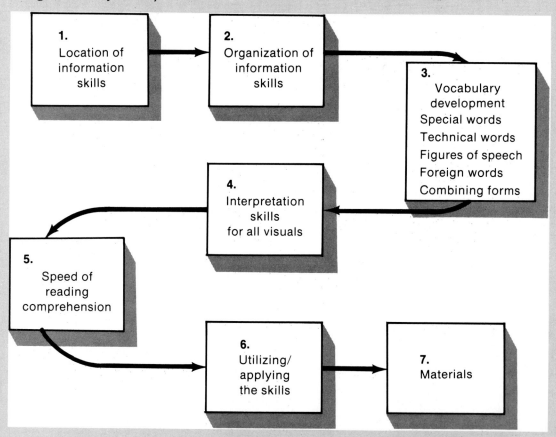

11

Guide Questions

1. What aspects of the study skill *location of information* does a teacher need to know?

2. What are the critical ideas for a teacher about skills for organizing information?

3. What are the important aspects of vocabulary development in connection with the study skills?

4. What does a teacher need to know to teach children about the interpretation of information?

5. How does the teacher plan to have children apply the study skills in meaningful ways?

Terminology

applying study skills

combining forms

Dewey Decimal System

figures of speech

foreign words

functional skills of reading

interpretation skills

locational study skills

mining a book

outlining

rate of reading

skills for organizing information

specialized vocabulary

study guide

summary (précis)

teaching unit

technical vocabulary

Study skills, sometimes identified as the *functional skills of reading,* deserve greater emphasis in the developmental reading program than is often given to them. The level of mastery of these skills will determine how efficiently a student will be able to learn in all the content areas of the curriculum.

Some elementary teachers have failed to accept responsibility for the planned, sequential development of specific abilities such as making outlines, locating information, or learning to read maps, graphs, and charts efficiently. A detailed outline list of such specific skills is presented at appropriate points throughout the chapter.

Teachers must be mindful not only of the need to teach study skills, but also of the importance of spaced review and reinforcement later in the school program to insure that the skills are practiced and retained.

Reading in Subject-Matter Areas

The reading in subject-matter areas is generally more difficult than the reading in organized reading classes. Such reading requires special vocabulary; comprehension of concepts; ability to locate and read maps, graphs, and charts and apply their content in further reading in the text; and organization and evalution of the reading.

Fay identified the following difficulties with reading in the content areas.[1]

1. There is an unduly heavy load of facts and concepts.
2. Variations in typographical arrangement from one area to another may confuse the pupil.
3. All too frequently the materials are uninteresting to the pupils.
4. Materials are often less readable than are basic readers.
5. Many writers tend to assume the children have more background than is the case.

Fay concluded that materials to be read for subject matter should be carefully fitted to children and instruction in reading such materials carefully organized.

Locational Study Skills

The study skills can be divided into four large subcategories: locational skills, skills of organizing information, skills in interpreting information, and skills in utilizing and applying that information. Obviously, skills in locating information are fundamental to the other three areas.

Location of information skills include those having to do with making effective use of the parts of a book. Using reference books and indexes constitutes another large area of locational skills; using such materials requires the abilities to alphabetize, to utilize pronunciation keys and definitions, to select volumes from information on book spines, to utilize guide words, and to choose from given information that which is appropriate for one's needs. Other locational skills have to do with the use of the library—the card catalog and the arrangement of materials on shelves and in files, the utilization of references such as maps, charts, graphs, and pictures, the use of audiovisual materials, and the employment of various automated retrieval systems. Finally, students need to learn to obtain information directly from people and from what Moffett calls "lower-order documents": eyewitness accounts, journals and diaries, correspondence, autobiography, municipal files, archives, the *Congressional Record,* photos, newspapers, census reports, historical societies and other clubs and organizations, and museums.[2]

Using the Parts of a Book

One of the first groups of skills children can begin to acquire has to do with using the parts of a book. Children can gain a sense of "mining a book," using every part of the book to find what one needs to know.[3]

Young readers can be made aware of the title page, and shortly afterwards can begin to understand the meaning of author and date of publication. Learning about the concept of author can be facilitated if children are allowed to experience authorship themselves. It may help children to think that a given book was published the year they were born or the year they were in kindergarten. Older readers can begin to appreciate the importance of authorship and the impact of copyright on the validity of information.

As children become more proficient readers, they will need guided lessons in the use of the index, glossary, footnotes, bibliography, and appendix. They must become aware of what kinds of information can be found in each of these book parts. Teachers must not assume that children will discover this information for themselves, but must plan to include initial instruction and review on the uses of each of these parts of a book. Social studies and science texts are excellent tools to use in context to teach children about the index and how it differs from the table of contents. Glossaries are often found in the backs of basal readers; using them for their intended purposes demonstrates their usefulness to students.

Using Reference Books

The dictionary may be the first reference book many children use. Suggestions for helping children learn to use the dictionary were given in chapter 9.

Children need many experiences with encyclopedias. Before they are ready to use them alone, the teacher may model the use of the encyclopedia by talking about where the entry will be found. The teacher might say:

> Now, we want to look up *engine.* So we'll look in the *E* volume. The second letter in *engine* is *n,* so it's probably over halfway through the book. Here's *emu,* so we're getting close. Oh, here's the guide word *energy* (pointing), and here's *engine* on the next page.

If this technique is used often with children, they will soon have a verbal model of how to find an entry.

After the children have learned to find entries by themselves, they need help in reading the article for desired information. They should have specific purposes for finding articles, and these purposes should suggest what information is to be obtained from the reading. Children will often read or copy whole articles unless purposeful, specific reading is taught.

Children need to be made aware of indexes that are available. Since these indexes vary in how they locate information, children should have planned experiences with the materials. The *Reader's Guide to Periodical Literature,* the *World Almanac,* and the thesaurus are examples of this type of reference. Teachers may give children references in connection with social studies and science units that will require them to work with these and similar materials.

Using the Library

The children's earliest experiences with the library may be with a collection of books marked "Easy." Children are rarely aware of or interested in the arrangement of these books, which is often alphabetical. By late second or third grade, children usually begin to evidence some interest in the card catalog, and at that time the teacher and librarian may begin to help them understand some of its "mysteries." The use of enlarged author-title-subject cards is helpful so that all of the children can see clearly the parts of the cards while they are being explained. It is important for the teacher and librarian to spend time with individual children as they learn how to find desired cards. In the late elementary years, children are able to understand the categories of the Dewey Decimal System or perhaps the Library of Congress system. Many librarians have attractively illustrated cards for each of the ten Dewey Decimal System categories as references for children. Games may be played in which the children order themselves according to a Dewey number each is holding. However, the best way for the child to learn the library classification and shelving systems is to have extensive experience in using the card catalog and locating the desired books.

The library contains many other kinds of materials. Special storage is usually provided for such references as maps, pictures, charts, and models. The curriculum should be designed to provide ample, genuine needs for locating these kinds of materials, as well as using them to obtain information. Too often the teacher finds it easier and quicker to find such material for the children; the children are denied experiences they need.

Children can be taught quite early how to operate simple audiovisual equipment so that information can be derived independently from filmstrips, records, tapes, and slides. Adults may find it desirable to operate more complicated and expensive equipment until children are in the middle grades. Sometimes children view time spent with audiovisual materials as entertainment. Preliminary discussion of what is to be learned, or preparation of study guides for older children, will help students view such experiences as occasions for learning.

Children will find in the next few years that libraries, and even their classrooms, are going to have instant access to amazing amounts of information through the computer.

> . . . online computer research will allow people to reach vast sums of information quickly—information that those who live far from our great, well-stocked libraries may have great trouble reaching today . . . those who have no access to the computer, or who do not know how to use it, or who cannot afford the charges, may be frozen out.[4]

Students need careful supervision by the teacher or librarian until they can use the card catalog easily.

It is incumbent on teachers and librarians to learn to take advantage of information retrieval systems so that children will have access to the stored knowledge that is rapidly becoming available. Attending classes or workshops may be quick ways for adults to obtain the needed information. The rush to information retrieval systems has been described as the "third revolution."[5] It becomes a responsibility of the school to prepare children to live and function in such a world.

Other Sources for Locating Information

Frequently, the message is given to children that all knowledge is to be found in print. It is important for them to realize that there are other sources, often more informative and satisfying than print. Children usually learn more by talking with a "real" rodeo rider or chemist than when reading about what these people do. They also profit greatly from working with objects and materials. Every teacher should keep an ever-growing file of such resources; in this file, for example, can be names and telephone numbers of people with interesting collections and hobbies, tour guides for zoos and museums, and directors of museums with suitcase displays. In addition, teachers should be collectors of all kinds of potential learning materials for classroom use.

Children should be given opportunities to learn from Moffett's "lower-order documents."[6] While participating in unit experiences, children can gather information from newspapers, government documents, bulletins, letters, and other similar materials. Even in the lower grades, teachers should bring such materials into the classroom when appropriate for sharing and discussion.

An Outline of Basic Study Skills

Van Dongen surveyed several graded series of readers to find out which study skills are commonly taught.[7] The following outline is a synthesis of his research.

I. Ability to locate information
  A. Ability to locate information by using the aid of book parts
    1. Cover, title page, title, author, publisher, location of publisher, editor's name, name of series, and edition
    2. Copyright page and date of publication
    3. Preface, introduction, foreword
    4. Table of contents and locating topics by pages
    5. Table of contents to locate topical organization of book or determine importance of topic by number of pages devoted to it
    6. Footnotes and references at end of chapters
    7. Glossary
    8. Indexes, select and use key word, cross-references
    9. Locate and use the appendix
    10. Locate and use the bibliography
  B. Ability to locate information by using knowledge of alphabetizing
    1. Ability to locate any given letter quickly
    2. Knowing sections: beginning, middle, end
    3. Ability to alphabetize
  C. Ability to locate information by using references
    1. Locate information by using the dictionary
      a. Finding words quickly
      b. Locate the pronunciation key
      c. Ability to use the dictionary as an aid in pronunciation
      d. Use of dictionary to determine meanings
        (1) Select meaning from context
        (2) Pictorial or verbal illustrations
        (3) Determine what part of speech a word is

      e. Use of dictionary as an aid in checking spelling

      f. Locate base word as an entry

      g. Derivations of the base word

  2. Locating information in the encyclopedia

      a. Locating volume from information on the spine of the book

      b. Using initial letters and guide words

  3. Ability to use and locate other references

      a. Selecting appropriate references for locating information

      b. Locate and use various guides and sources:

         (1) Almanac

         (2) Atlas

         (3) City directory

         (4) Government publications

         (5) Junior book of authors

         (6) Newspapers and periodicals

         (7) Posters

         (8) Radio or television schedules

         (9) Telephone directory

         (10) Time schedules

         (11) Yearbooks

  4. Ability to use textbooks and trade books for locating information

D. Ability to use the library and its aids for locating information

  1. Card catalog

      a. Desired topic, author, or title

      b. Alphabetical arrangement in card catalog

  2. Organization of the library for locating material

      a. Shelf plans, labels, and floor plans

      b. Dewey Decimal System, Library of Congress, or other methods

      c. Locate reference books

      d. Locate and use the magazine file

      e. Locate and use appropriate indexes

         (1) *Readers' Guide to Periodical Literature*

         (2) *Who's Who*

         (3) Biographical dictionaries

         (4) Thesaurus

         (5) Unabridged dictionary

         (6) *Subject Index to Poetry for Children and Young People, 1957–1975*

E. Locate information by using maps, graphs, charts, pictorial material

Skills for Organization of Information

After information has been located, the child's next step is to organize it for use. If there is a genuine need for the information, its organization will indicate whether enough information has been found or whether there are gaps and more must be located.

Outlining is probably the organizational form that first comes to mind. However, children should have experiences with summaries, both as synthesizing experiences and as outlines converted to expository form. Children should also experience note-taking as a means of organizing their thinking about a body of information, as a means of supporting memory, and as a source of accurate quotation of the writing of others.

Outlining

Outlining is often introduced in the middle grades. Frequently, children view outlining as a difficult task, as indeed it is. The need to comprehend the content, to organize the ideas into a hierarchy, and to establish the descending order of concepts or generalizations at each step is a complicated task. In addition, the child must master a new form of writing with Roman numerals, capital letters, Arabic numerals, and other elements.

Kindergarteners and primary children can begin to master the tasks basic to outlining, and through a series of steps over several years can arrive at formal outlining with much less trauma. Suppose young children are going to visit the zoo. Small note pads with sturdy cardboard backs and pencils attached with strings can be made for each child. At the zoo, children make quick drawings of the animals or other events seen or experienced. Back at school, the teacher helps the children build a "story" of the trip by writing captions such as "Big Cats," "Kinds of Bears," "Water Animals," etc., on large paper. Children paste their appropriate pictures, perhaps in a row, under the labels. Somewhat later, the experience of building a model can be dictated to the teacher, who writes the steps of the process in phrases in a simple outline form:

Getting the materials
    Buy plastic
    Find scrap lumber
    Ask parents for leftover paint
    Getting nails, hammer, and saw from custodian
Making model
    Make pattern
    Draw pattern pieces on plastic and wood
    Cut out pieces
    Nail and glue pieces together
    Paint model
Displaying model
    Ask librarian to display in library
    Make sign explaining model
    Set up in library

After such organization of personal experiences, children may be led to organize in a similar way stories or other information that they have read. It is a short step from this task in third or fourth grade to formal outlines, since all that is missing is the Roman numeral-capital-Arabic numeral, etc., sequence. Frequent experiences such as these during the elementary school years can lead children fairly easily into outlining, since the steps in the process have been broken down and initially made personal.

Following are sample lessons in outlining that might be completed by elementary children.

Sample Lesson   Read the following essay.[8]

How to Become a Good Oral Reader

Good readers select very carefully what they are to read. They try to choose an interesting story or a worthwhile article, one that their listeners will surely enjoy. If they are reading to prove a point, they read only the sentences that are necessary. If they are reading an interesting story or part of a story, they select one that is not too long to be interesting. Here is the first rule: If you want people to like to hear you read, select your story or article carefully.

Good readers know well the story or article that they are to read. In the first place, they know the exact meaning of what they are to read. It would be hard to give the meaning to other people if the readers themselves did not know the meaning. In the second place, they know the words in the selection so that they do not pronounce them incorrectly and spoil the meaning for the listeners. This all takes time and study, but it is necessary if people are to read aloud well. The second rule is: Know well the selection you are to read aloud.

Good readers keep their audience interested in what they are reading. They read loudly enough to be heard easily. They read clearly, so that the listeners do not have to guess what they are saying. They make the important points in the selection stand out plainly, and they read with expression so that the characters talk like real people. Good readers work and practice to do all these things well, in order to keep their audience interested. And so the last rule is: Keep your listeners interested to the very last of what you read.

Directions to the student:

In this article, you have read three rules for reading aloud well to others. Perhaps you noticed that the topic sentence at the beginning is the same as the rule stated at the end of each paragraph. The skeleton outline that follows tells you to find three details in paragraph one, two details in paragraph two, and four details in paragraph three. Complete the skeleton outline.

How to Become a Good Oral Reader

I.
  A.
  B.
  C.
II.
  A.
  B.
III.
  A.
  B.
  C.
  D.

Other forms of outlining include time lines and the construction of charts and tables. Each requires the child to organize events or ideas in some type of sequence.

A Time Line

A time line is a graphic presentation of a chronological outline showing important facts in outline form. By the fourth grade the child should have had the concept of time introduced to him in terms of his own experience, such as the passing of a day as the earth rotates once, weeks, months, seasons, and his own birthdays. He will thus be ready for historical time lines in fifth and sixth grade. The time line in figure 11.1 shows many of the "events" presented in a fifth grade social studies program.

Greer suggests that the child at the sixth grade level can see the analogy between the chronology of mankind's history and the chronology of the child's personal history.[9]

Before you were born, your parents were children and lived with their parents; later your parents had a home of their own; then you were born; you learned to walk, to talk, and started to school. In your lifetime there have been special events you remember most vividly.

Mankind's history is divided into two parts: B.C. and A.D. In history, man lived in caves. He learned to make tools and use them in hunting. He began to live in groups called tribes. After Christ was born many events occurred in man's history. America was discovered; people came to live here; cars and planes were invented.

| 5 | 4 | 3 | 2 | 1 | 0 | 1 | 2 | 3 | 4 | 5 |

your birth
Christ's birth

Charts and Graphs

Charts and graphs are unique forms of outlines, in that two or more variables must be considered in their construction and interpretation. In a simple graph of the birthdays of children in the class, both the months of the year (probably

| 1000 | 1100 | | 1200 | 1300 | | 1400 | 1500 | | 1600 | 1700 | | 1800 | 1900 |

(1000) Leif Ericson discovers America

(1260) Marco Polo's journey to China

(1492) Columbus discovers America

(1519) Magellan circumnavigates globe

(1609) Hudson discovers River and Bay

Make a time line (A.D. 1000–1875) like the one above and add the following events:

1420 Prince Henry establishes a school for sailors	1534 Cartier explored Gulf of St. Lawrence	1636 Williams founded Rhode Island
1486 Dias sailed to Cape of Good Hope	1541 DeSoto discovered Mississippi	1647 First public school in America
1497 Cabot explored North America	1577 Drake began world voyage	1664 New Netherland seized by English
1498 Columbus made third voyage	1608 Champlain founded Quebec	1682 Pennsylvania settled by Penn
1500 Cabral claimed Brazil	1620 Mayflower Compact signed	1814 First Power Loom built
1513 Balboa discovered the Pacific	1623 New Netherland settled	1825 Erie Canal opened
1513 Ponce de Leon explored Florida	1630 Massachusetts Bay Colony settled	1831 Steam locomotive pulled train
		1859 First oil well drilled in U.S.

Figure 11.1
This time line presents many of the significant events usually taught in the fifth grade social studies program.

Prudence Cutright, A. Y. King, Ida Dennis, and F. Potter, *Living Together in the Americas* (New York: Macmillan, copyright © 1960), Teachers Guide, pp. 59, 61; text, p. 63. Reprinted by permission.

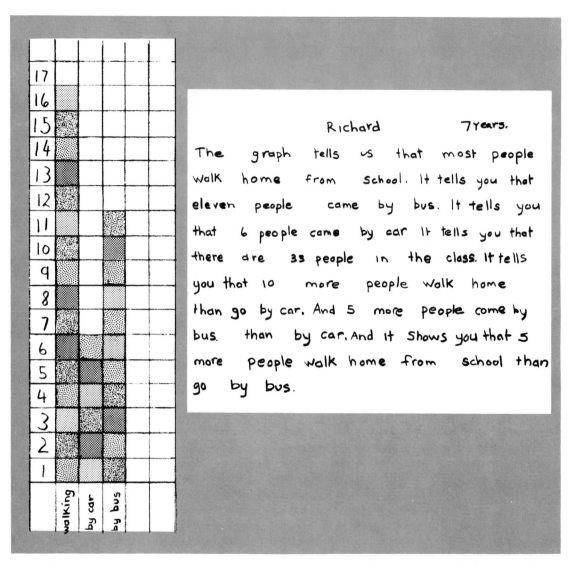

The graph tells us that most people walk home from school. It tells you that eleven people came by bus. It tells you that 6 people came by car It tells you that there are 33 people in the class. It tells you that 10 more people walk home than go by car. And 5 more people come by bus. than by car. And it shows you that 5 more people walk home from school than go by bus.

Richard   7 years.

Figure 11.2
Richard's bar graph and his paragraph in which he explains what the graph contains.

Reproduced from: Nuffield Foundation (1967), Nuffield Mathematics Project Pictorial Representation. Chambers/ Murray/Wiley.

in correct order) and the number of persons with birthdays in each month must be kept in mind. In a chart of production of wheat by nations over a ten-year period, three variables must be considered—countries, total wheat production by countries (in some unit such as tons), and each year in the ten-year period. Children will be able to interpret such presentations of information if they have made graphs and charts routinely since their earliest school years.

Figure 11.2 is an example of graphing done by a young child. Graphing is an excellent means of combining study skills, mathematics, and writing in an integrated experience for the child.

Using Climatic Charts As an Organizer in the Study of Geography

The climatic chart is an example of an aid to guide intermediate grade students in generalizing about a geographic location. They need to study first the climatic chart representative of the area where they live so they can use it as a reference point in later work. They learn to notice the length of the frost-free, or growing, season; the amount of cold, cool, warm, and hot weather throughout the year, and during which months; and the amount of rainfall and its distribution throughout the year. The students can then learn to generalize. The example in figure 11.3 of a climatic chart for Chicago, Illinois illustrates how the basic elements of climate appear when graphed.

Conceal the station information at the top of the chart and see if you can answer the following questions by studying only the rainfall, temperature, and growing season.

1. Is the growing season long enough to grow different cereal crops?
2. Is there sufficient annual rainfall to grow different cereal crops?
3. Is there sufficient hot weather at one time to ripen crops?
4. Would you expect to find four distinct seasons in this place?
5. Is this place north or south of the equator?
6. Will tropical fruits grow in this place?
7. What kind of vegetation would you expect to find here? Desert, mountain, tropical, or temperate zone?
8. Might there be snow here to add to the annual precipitation?
9. Since there is sufficient moisture, could two crops be produced annually on the same soil?

Writing Summaries

The first steps in summarizing are oral steps. Children may be asked to tell *briefly* about what they did at the Saturday picnic or what the story just read was about. The emphasis is on brevity and relating the most important aspects of the event. The teacher may then write down these brief statements, which may be compared with longer stories that provide much more detail. Repeated experiences with recorded summaries will help children understand the crucial differences between them and complete stories or records. Finally, children may be asked to write their own summaries.

Taking Notes

In the section on outlining, it was suggested that very young children, even children not yet reading, can learn to take notes by drawing simple pictures. These notes can help children organize bodies of information and prompt their memories. When children are able to write, written notes can serve the same purposes. It should be stressed that notes are for personal use and are functional if they serve the purposes of organizing ideas and triggering memory. Writing mechanics are of no concern, as long as the individual can read the notes. Children should be encouraged to have personal note pads in which notes on a variety of topics may be recorded. They should be guided to refer to these notes frequently in the course of a school day.

Figure 11.3
Climatic chart for
Chicago, Illinois.
Average monthly
rainfall is represented
by the bar graph;
average monthly
temperatures are
represented by the
line graph; and the
length of the growing
season is represented
by the rectangle at the
top (end of April to
early October).

From H. L. Nelson,
*Climatic Data for
Representative Stations of
the World* (Lincoln:
University of Nebraska
Press, 1968), p. 69.
Reprinted by permission.

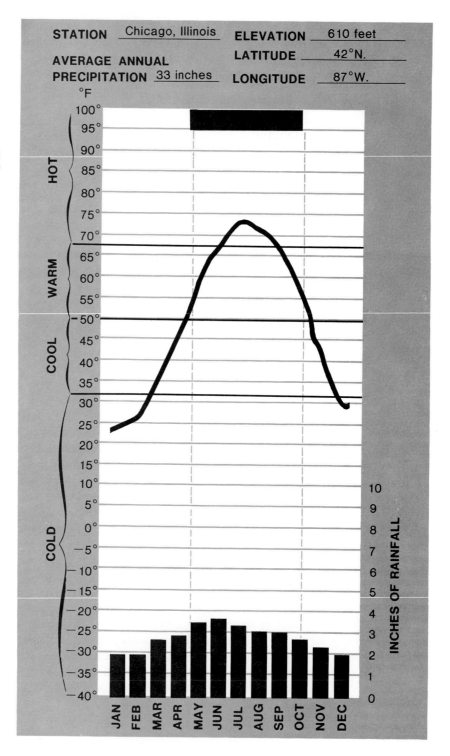

When notes are taken for the purpose of citing authors in an essay or paper, children need to learn the need for accuracy in recording quotations and their sources. At that point, students need to be able to record accurately full bibliographic information.

Outline of
Organizational
Skills

Van Dongen, in his research on study skills, found the following ones presented in basal reading series.[10] This is a continuation of his outline presented earlier in this chapter.

II. Ability to organize information
   A. Use knowledge of alphabetizing or organizing information
   B. Construct an outline
      1. Ability to put material in sequence
         a. Arrange steps of a process in order
         b. Construct a time line
      2. Classify information on two-way charts, tables
      3. Construct an outline
         a. Find main headings
         b. Give main and subordinate topics
         c. Provide subordinates when given main heading or provide main heading when given subordinates
         d. Outline single paragraphs
         e. Outline short selections
         f. Outline more complex selections
         g. Put ideas together from various sources in outline form
         h. Outline what has been read and use outline in a presentation—either written or oral
   C. Ability to summarize material
      1. Summary statement for a paragraph
      2. Write summary statements for a short selection
      3. Write summary statements for more complex selections
      4. Use a summary as data for oral or written reports
      5. Bring together information from several sources
      6. Write a summary using an outline
      7. Construct maps, graphs, charts, or pictorial material as a summary of information
   D. Ability to take notes
      1. Take notes in brief—they may be grammatically incorrect and abbreviated
      2. In outline form—formal or informal
      3. In précis writing (spaced intervals of listening or reading)
      4. Take notes in fact-inference charts
      5. Note origin of information for footnotes and bibliography

From Theory to Practice 11.2

Teaching Organizational Skills

In order to have an experience helping children learn about organizational skills, make arrangements to work with a small group of youngsters. Be sure the group is no larger than five. The children may be of any grade level; you will have to adjust what you do to their grade level.

Suggested here are three activities. Select the one you would prefer to do and carry it out with your group. Taping your experience will help you go back and analyze what happened. You may want to share your tape with fellow students and with your instructor.

1. Plan an outlining experience appropriate for the grade level you have chosen. You will need to provide an experience that can be developed in outline form for younger children or an appropriate reading passage if you work with older children.
2. Help individuals in your group develop a time line. Your time lines may be of the children's lives, of events in the school year, or even of a day at school. After sharing the time lines with students in your class, you will want to return them to the children.
3. Plan a graphing experience with your group. Very simple, but interesting, data may be graphed. Birthdays, pets owned by the children, favorite foods, cars owned by families, and heights of children are possibilities. You can think of other interesting topics.

Vocabulary Development

Beyond the simplest kinds of information location and organization, reading vocabulary becomes a critical factor. Of first concern is the child's ability to recognize the sight words and other basic vocabulary words. If the child can read the typical vocabulary at the appropriate grade level, then the teacher's concern must be directed toward helping the child master a specialized vocabulary peculiar to the text being read. This specialized vocabulary falls into several categories: special words, technical words, figures of speech, foreign words, and combining forms (words made using prefixes and suffixes).

The Specialized Vocabulary

Each student has several different vocabularies: his oral vocabulary, which he uses in conversation; his listening vocabulary, which enables him to understand what others say; his reading vocabulary, which he, generally speaking, *begins* when he learns how to read at school; and his writing vocabulary, which enables him to communicate on paper with others and to record his own thoughts. Generally for young children the listening vocabulary is the largest, and, if the youngster has lived with adults who use a diversified vocabulary, she may enter school with a very large listening vocabulary. The reading vocabulary for the successful reader will, by fifth or sixth grade, begin to equal and surpass the listening and speaking (oral) vocabularies.

The student's reading vocabulary must assimilate many types of words. Structure words, or transition words, predetermine the facility of the reader to assimilate the ideas expressed in writing. Such structure words include: *however; in the first place; finally; moreover; nevertheless; therefore; as well as; because; when; but; as . . . as; if . . . then; not only . . . but also.*

Each subject has its own specialized vocabulary. Attention must be directed to the science vocabulary, the mathematics vocabulary, or the history vocabulary.

In addition, there are some problems to be dealt with in the multiple meanings conveyed by many commonly used words in children's vocabularies. These are the *common* words that have very different meanings when used in different subject matters. For example, children soon learn from both home and school that they must pick up the *litter* they normally leave about. They evolve a meaning for *litter* that says: "Litter is the disorder created when little things are left lying around or in a state of disorder." However, children will soon add another meaning when they learn that Sally's dog has a new *litter*. A third meaning of *litter* may be "straw or hay used as bedding for animals." Then, eventually, the student will add the additional meaning "a stretcher used for carrying a sick person."

Such concepts need to be developed through guided instruction just as understandings for *centigrade* or *Celsius, theocracy,* or *kinetic energy* need to be developed.

A comb is an instrument for arranging the hair or for holding the hair in place. But it can also mean "to search through" as in, "We *combed* the whole library to find the lost book." Or it can be the red, fleshy piece on a rooster's head, or the cellular structure in which bees store honey.

Young children understand: "I got it right"; "I'm all right, mother"; "He did the right thing." Then meanings expand to: "He has his rights"; "I have the right to vote"; "She always does the right thing"; "Tommy looked all right; I didn't know he'd been sick"; "It's on your right side"; "Is this the right side of the cloth?"; "He writes with his right hand"; "Turn right"; "They set it upright"; "Your book is right where you left it"; "Look me right in the eye!"

The word *foot* has several common meanings:

He has frozen his left *foot*. (a part of the body)
The army moved on *foot*. (a means of travel)
The *foot* of the hill. The *foot* of the page. (the base or bottom of something)
Who will *foot* the bill? (to have to pay)
Twelve inches make a *foot*. (a measure of length)
The lines of poetry were each four *feet*. (a unit of poetry)

In addition, *foot* combines with other words to determine meanings of new words: *foot*ball, *foot*board, *foot*hill, *foot*hold, *foot*ing, *foot*man, *foot*note, *foot*pad, *foot*path, *foot*print, *foot*rest, *foot* soldier, *foot*step, *foot*stool, *foot*work.

*Technical
Vocabulary*
Technical vocabulary needs to be presented in context and practiced to allow students to gain familiarity with it. Perhaps it might be well to have a quiz or play a game using some of the new terminology even before it appears in silent reading.

Pictures from science texts may offer suggestions for projects youngsters might work on in groups of three or four to prepare, demonstrate, and explain such things as the following:

> A child's balloon and a piece of aluminum foil can show how jet propulsion works. How?
>
> Centrifugal force can be demonstrated with a ball and a string. How?

In science, Greek and Latin combining forms include:

bio (life) and *logy* (study of)	biology
geo (earth) and *graph* (write)	geography
pan (all-everything) and *chrom* (colors)	panchromatic
micro (small) and *meter* (measure)	micrometer
tele (far) and *phon* (sound)	telephonic

In mathematics:

octo (eight) and *gon* (angle)	octagon
dia (through) and *gon* (angle)	diagonal
peri (around) and *meter* (measure)	perimeter
quadri (four) and *lateral* (side)	quadrilateral
bi (two) and *sect* (separate)	bisect

In social studies:

demo (people) and *crat* (government)	democratic
mono (one) and *theist* (belief in God)	monotheism
epi (over) and *dem* (people)	epidemic
sub (under) and *terra* (earth)	subterranean
trans (across) and *globe* (world)	transglobal

In general use:

bio (life) and *graph* (write)	biography
gen (beginnings) and *logy* (study of)	genealogy
crypt (secret) and *ic* (being)	cryptic
em (put into) and *path* (state [disease]) and *ic* (being)	empathic
psych (mind) and *social* (relating to)	psychosocial

Figure 11.4
A morpheme tree bulletin board display or mobile would be a useful addition to a classroom. The trunk of the tree labeled with two or more morphemes in a subject being taught. Students can be asked to contribute words based on the morphemes as labels for the tree's branches or as leaves or ornaments for the tree.

Adapted from Lou E. Burmeister, "Vocabulary Development in Context Areas Through the Use of Morphemes," *Journal of Reading* 19 (March 1976) pp. 484–85. Reprinted with permission of the International Reading Association and Lou E. Burmeister.

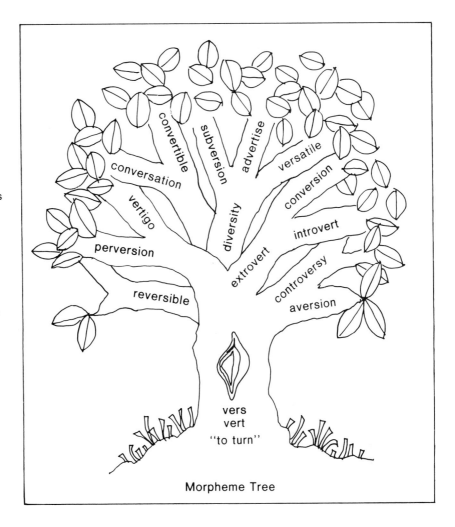

Morpheme Tree

Teachers will find Burmeister's article "Vocabulary Development in Content Areas Through the Use of Morphemes" useful.[11] Figure 11.4 illustrates her use of a morpheme tree or mobile for teaching specialized vocabulary.

In an article in *The Journal of Reading* Vacca suggested an interesting way to use the magic square to reinforce specialized vocabulary.[12] Students should enjoy doing such exercises in small groups.

The following sources offer word lists related to specific subjects:

Aukerman, Robert C. *Reading in the Secondary School Classroom.* New York: McGraw-Hill, 1972.

Burmeister, Lou E. *Reading Strategies for Middle and Secondary School Teaching.* 2d ed. Reading, Mass.: Addison-Wesley, 1978.

Thelen, Judith. *Improving Reading in Science.* Newark, Del.: International Reading Assn., 1975.

Willmon, Betty. "Reading in the Content Area: A 'New Math' Terminology List for the Pr. Grades." *Elementary English* 48 (May 1971): 463–71. Reprinted in Earle, Richard A., *Teaching Reading and Mathematics,* Appendix B. Newark, Del.: International Reading Assn., 1976. Contains 473 words appearing most frequently in primary mathematics texts, compiled from eight basal arithmetic series, grades 1–3.

Figures of Speech

Figures of speech, foreign words in English language context, and prefixes, suffixes, and combining forms all require precise understanding on the part of the critical reader.

Expressions and words used for other than their ordinary or literal meaning add beauty and force to our language. Yet, many adults use such expressions without knowing their origin. "Mad as a hatter," "my man Friday," "sour grapes," or "a Pandora's box" would all be more meaningful if we were familiar with the source of the expression.

Many such figurative expressions are derived from the Bible, and teachers should remind themselves that many boys and girls grow up without hearing references to the Old or the New Testament. Some biblical expressions commonly used as figures of speech are:

> as old as Methuselah
> as patient as Job
> whither thou goest I will go
> there entered into the garden a snake
> the golden rule
> doubting Thomas
> the land of milk and honey
> it was a David and Jonathan friendship
> a voice crying in the wilderness
> the wailing wall
> they crucified her
> vanity, vanity, all is vanity, saith the preacher
> it's a whited sepulchre
> like the seven plagues
> though your sins be as scarlet
> the wisdom of Solomon
> and the walls came tumbling down

Seven Types of Figures

Simile. A simile expresses a likeness between two things that in most respects are totally unlike:

> After one day on his new job, Jack said the next morning, "I'm *stiff as a board* today."
> In making his choices, he was *as sly as a fox.*

Metaphor. A metaphor is an implied comparison that omits the words *like* or *as:*

He has a *heart of stone.*
Tom stood *rooted* to the spot.

Irony. Irony is a method of expression in which the ordinary meaning of the words is the opposite of the thought in the speaker's mind (subtle sarcasm):

Thanks for forgetting to show up to help with all this work!
You are setting a *fine* example for the rest of the class!

Hyperbole. Hyperbole is a figure of speech that uses exaggeration for effect:

Waves *mountain high* broke over the reef.
The horses sped *like the wind* over the prairie.

Personification. Personification is endowing animals, plants, and inanimate objects with personal traits and human attributes:

Death won in the traffic race.
Duty calls us.

Synecdoche. The figure of speech that puts a part for a whole *or* a whole for a part is called synecdoche:

She had lived in the house fifty springs.
Two heads are better than one.
Or:
The world is too much with us.
Modern medicine has virtually conquered the scourge of malaria.

Metonymy. Using the name of one thing for another, of which it is an attribute or with which it is associated, is a further kind of figure of speech, called metonymy:

Handsome is as handsome does.
The White House announced a new energy policy.

Foreign Words in English Context

Many expressions in common use are borrowed directly from other languages. The selected list below contains some that are sure to appear occasionally in the reading done by critical readers:

Expression	Language	English dictionary meaning
à la mode	French	in the fashion
a posteriori	Latin	inductive argument from observed facts
a priori	Latin	deductive argument from self-evident propositions

ad infinitum	Latin	to infinity
ad valorem	Latin	according to the value
alma mater	Latin	a school, college, or university one has attended
coup d'état	French	violent overthrow of government
e pluribus unum	Latin	one composed of many
esprit de corps	French	the shared spirit and enthusiasm of a group
ex cathedra	Latin	by virtue of high authority
ex officio	Latin	by virtue of one's office
ex post facto	Latin	after the fact; retroactively
in loco parentis	Latin	in the place of a parent
in memoriam	Latin	in memory of
ipso facto	Latin	by the nature of the case
laissez-faire	French	philosophy of noninterference
modus operandi	Latin	method of procedure
noblesse oblige	French	the obligation of a person of high rank to behave generously
nom de plume	French	pseudonym
non sequitur	Latin	a statement that does not follow from preceding statements; unwarranted conclusion
papier-mâché	French	a light, strong molding material made of paper
par excellence	French	being the best of a kind
per diem	Latin	by the day
poco a poco	Spanish	little by little
pro rata	Latin	in proportion
sine qua non	Latin	an indispensable condition
status quo	Latin	the existing state of affairs
sub rosa	Latin	secret or confidential
tabula rasa	Latin	the hypothetical blank mind before receiving outside impressions
tempus fugit	Latin	time flies
terra firma	Latin	solid earth; a safe footing
vice versa	Latin	the terms being exchanged
vis-à-vis	French	face to face with; in relation to

Following is a glossary of Spanish words used often in the western United States. For many children, these are not foreign words, but are parts of their first language.

acequia irrigation ditch

adobe unburnt brick dried in sun used for building

angoras chaps made of goat hide with hair retained

broncho-busting horse-breaking

bronco; broncho unbroken Mexican or California horse

buckaroo; buccarro cowboy (Northwest)

caballada band of horses

caballero Spanish knight or horseman; happy cowboy; expert horseman

caballo horse

cabestro rope; horsehair rope halter

calabozo Spanish name for jail

caracole to make a half turn to the right or left on horseback

cataloes cross-breed of cattle and buffaloes

cholla type of large cactus with sharp spines

compadre boon companion; pal

conchas silver disks worn for decoration on chaps, hats, etc.

corral pen for livestock

dinero money

frijole, frijol type of bean much cultivated in Mexico for food

hacienda in Spanish America, a large plantation on which the owner is resident; an establishment for raising stock

jacal small hut or cabin

javalina a wild boar

junta the junction; sometimes refers to business meeting

latigo leather strap attached to girth and used to fasten saddle on horse's back

lobo wolf

loco crazy; foolish

maguey a century plant from which the fibers are used in making rope

mañana tomorrow; late

mantas type of blanket or wrap

mesa elevated tableland

mestizo half-breed

peso Mexican dollar; hence, any dollar

pinto piebald; small calico horse of the Western plains

pueblo group of buildings constructed by Indians of the Southwest

ranchero rancher; especially Mexican rancher

reata leather rope; lariat

remuda band of saddle horses; extra mounts

romal whip fashioned from leather thongs and attached to bridle or saddle

serape blanket worn as cloak by Mexicans

sudaderos leather lining or underside of saddle

vaquero cowpuncher; cowboy

vara Spanish measure of length equal to about a yard

Prefixes, Suffixes, and Combining Forms

Linguists use the term *morpheme* to refer to parts of words that carry meaning in their own right. Prefixes, suffixes, and what are called here "combining forms" are such parts.[13]

Common Prefixes

Prefix	Meaning of prefix	Example	Literal meaning of example
in	in	inhabit	to live in
com con col	together with	collaborate	to labor together
dis	not	disapprove	not approve
pre	before	prejudice	to judge before
sub	under	submarine	under the water

Common Suffixes

Suffix	Meaning of suffix	Example	Literal meaning of example
ive	relating to	decorative	relating to decoration
ful	full of	helpful	full of help
less	without	needless	without need
ship	state of being	friendship	having friends
tion	act, state of being	conjunction	act of joining with

Combining Forms

Word parts	Meaning	Example	Literal meaning of example
bio logy	life study of	biology	study of living things
geo graph	earth write	geography	write about the earth
therm meter	heat measure	thermometer	measure the heat
poly gon	many angle	polygon	having many sides
tele phone	far sound	telephone	sound from far away

Use of study skills and relevant vocabulary in lessons before a field trip contributes to a successful experience for a class.

Interpretation Skills

Locating and organizing information will be of little use to the learners unless they can take the next step, using interpretive skills. Interpretation of text has been discussed thoroughly in chapter 10; in this chapter the focus will be on interpretation of the information contained in maps, graphs, charts, tables, diagrams, and pictures, and on globes.

Interpreting Maps and Globes

Maps are very common in the everyday experiences of boys and girls in the elementary school, beginning with the road map that helps the family plan the vacation trip. Maps on television newscasts show where major events are happening. Newspapers, magazines, and advertising material present outline maps that pinpoint events and commercial products. Even restaurants are apt to have placemats that are printed with an outline map that locates the place where you are now eating and the one where you should eat next!

Yet many boys and girls learn to pay little attention to these maps because they do not understand the legend or the vocabulary and they do not understand the map form of representation. If adults do not take the necessary few minutes to orient children, then the children are missing a very useful lesson that could make maps and diagrams meaningful to them. The nine-, ten-, and eleven-year-olds in the intermediate grades are apt to be very interested in the symbols, signs, and codes in the legends that make maps meaningful if they are guided in their understanding.

Children need to understand projections so that the difference between a Mercator and a polar projection is clear to them. It has been suggested that cutting an orange peel in sections so it can be flattened will show the polar projection when the world is produced on a flat map. A hollow rubber ball could also be used and could be preserved indefinitely.

Teachers will find useful the *Maps and Globes Kit* marketed by Science Research Associates. It provides skills practice for effective use of maps and globes for grades 4–8. The kit contains exercise cards, resource cards, and skills starter cards.

A careful look at the maps in figures 11.5 and 11.6 can suggest to boys and girls questions about which they can do their own research.

1. Where is corn the principal crop?
2. Is coal mined in your state?

Interpreting Graphs, Charts, Tables, Diagrams, and Pictures

Graphs, charts, and tables are given special attention by Welton and Mallan. They write that such devices are frequently avoided by children, and they suggest why this might be so.

> Two aspects of quantitative or statistical data deserve special attention. First, quantitative data is, by nature, raw and uninterpreted information . . . individuals must interpret (or process) the data in order to draw their own conclusions. It takes a certain amount of mental effort to do this . . . which may account in part for the "bad breath" feeling sometimes associated with quantitative data. . . . A second aspect of dealing with quantitative data is the fact that charts, graphs, and tables are extremely efficient forms of presenting information . . . so efficient that it doesn't take long before many students begin to suffer from information overload.[14]

Probably the best way to avoid the pitfalls described by Welton and Mallan is to initiate work with tables, charts, and graphs using information that is personally meaningful to children. Care should be taken to use only those devices that present a limited amount of data. And teachers should spend whatever time is needed to help children understand the meanings involved. It is also important to begin such studies early in the children's school careers and to work with them throughout the grades. One of the most serious problems is waiting to present tables, charts, and graphs until the upper grades, when not only is the information complex, but so are the techniques by which it is presented.

Interpreting Diagrams and Pictures

Picture study should begin at the start of a child's school experience; it is a normal part of reading primary textbooks. As children move to more difficult materials with more complex pictures, care must be taken to see that legends under the pictures are read and the details are noticed and understood. Teachers need to study the pictures before teaching the lessons so that they have noted important aspects to call to the children's attention, have developed fitting questions, and have developed the appropriate vocabulary to make full use of the illustrations.

Diagrams may present specific problems, since they are usually schematic representations without the reality of pictures. Often a diagram identifies parts of a whole or attempts to develop or extend a concept. Teachers need to discuss diagrams until they are sure the children have understood what the intent of the author was. (For some examples, the reader is referred to tables and figures throughout the text.)

Figure 11.5
Distribution of corn production in the United States.

From Prudence Cutright, Allen Y. King, Ida Dennis, and Florence Potter, *Living Together in the Americas* (New York: Macmillan, copyright © 1958), pp. 199, 251. Reprinted by permission.

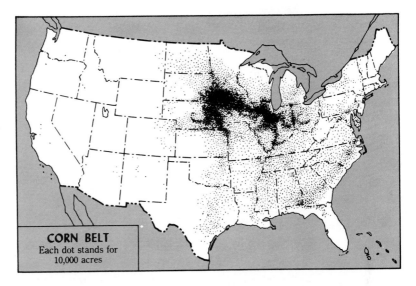

CORN BELT
Each dot stands for 10,000 acres

Figure 11.6
Distribution of coal deposits in the United States.

From Prudence Cutright, Allen Y. King, Ida Dennis, and Florence Potter, *Living Together in the Americas* (New York: Macmillan, copyright © 1958), pp. 199, 251. Reprinted by permission.

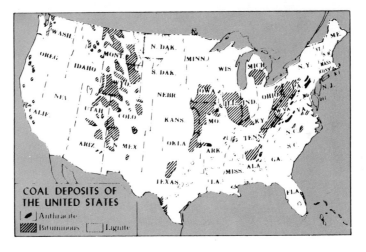

COAL DEPOSITS OF THE UNITED STATES
Anthracite
Bituminous Lignite

Students need
repeated, first-hand
experiences with
globes and maps if
they are to become
skilled in their use.

Table 11.1   Average rates of reading with comprehension in grades 1–6.

Grade	McCracken* Words per Minute		Harris and Sipay**
	Oral	Silent	Silent
1	60	60	—
2	70	70	86
3	90	120	116
4	120	150	155
5	120	170	177
6	150	245	206

*Robert A. McCracken, "The Informal Reading Inventory as a Means of Improving Instruction," *Perspectives in Reading: The Evaluation of Children's Reading Achievement* 8 (1967): 85.
**Albert J. Harris and Edward R. Sipay, *How to Increase Reading Ability,* 6th ed. (New York: Longman Co., 1975). Reprinted by permission.

Summary of
Interpretive Skills

In his outline of basic study skills, parts of which have already been presented in this chapter, Van Dongen presented the following summary of the interpretive skills in basal reader series:[15]

III. Ability to use and interpret maps, graphs, charts, and other pictorial material
    A. Use and interpret maps and globes
        1. Ability to locate desired information
           a. Interpret key and map symbols
           b. Use map scales
           c. Interpret directions
        2. Ability to demonstrate understanding of map distortions or type of projection
    B. Use and interpret graphs, tables, diagrams, and other pictorial material
        1. Interpret graphs
           a. Bar graphs
           b. Circle graphs
           c. Line graphs
        2. Interpret tables
        3. Interpret diagrams
        4. Interpret time lines
        5. Interpret other pictorial material
    C. Read and use charts

Rate of Reading: Speed of Comprehension

While rate of reading is unimportant unless the student comprehends the material, it is certain that most people could read much more efficiently than they do and obtain just as much from their reading. It is safe to generalize that fast readers get more from their reading.

In the elementary school, however, it is necessary to establish mastery over the mechanics of reading before giving attention to the rate of reading. Until children have mastered the words to use in reading, they cannot hurry up the process of assimilating the ideas expressed in those words.

Many adults, unsophisticated in the complexities of the reading process, think about reading speed when they talk about reading problems. If a child is already tense in the reading situation because he does not know how to break words into syllables, or because parts of words reverse themselves in the line of print (quiet—quite; form—from; angel—angle), or if he occasionally reads a word from the line above and then one from the line below the one he is really reading, to challenge him at that point with "Now, read faster!" the teacher is creating emotional problems that may be difficult to overcome.

Average rates of reading at each grade level in the elementary school have been provided by Harris and McCracken. These are given in table 11.1.

By November, Tom was well into his senior year of high school. He was being pressured to get ready to go to the university the next year in spite of serious reading difficulties. His parents were college graduates and expected Tom and his brother to complete college also. In his first interview, Tom discussed his difficulties with reading, writing, and spelling. In his second session in a reading clinic, he read material of approximately sixth grade level of difficulty at a speed of 111 words per minute with 65 percent comprehension.

During the six months that followed, Tom worked on the following elements.

1. Word forms. He faced problems of reversals of word parts by comparing, pronouncing, writing, and spelling many paired words commonly confused.
2. Word meanings. He learned about roots, prefixes, suffixes, and Greek and Latin combining forms.
3. Writing original paragraphs. He selected philosophical or esoteric topics according to his ephemeral interests and wrote short paragraphs that he and the tutor analyzed and corrected.
4. Rate of reading. He kept graphs of his speed and comprehension in reading Simpson's *Reading Exercises,* Books I and II.[16] From a speed of 111 words on the first story, he improved to a rate of 328 words per minute on one exercise. By graduation time, he was maintaining a speed of about 290 words per minute, which is adequate for college success if other study conditions are satisfactory. The graphs of his speed and comprehension are shown in figures 11.7 and 11.8.

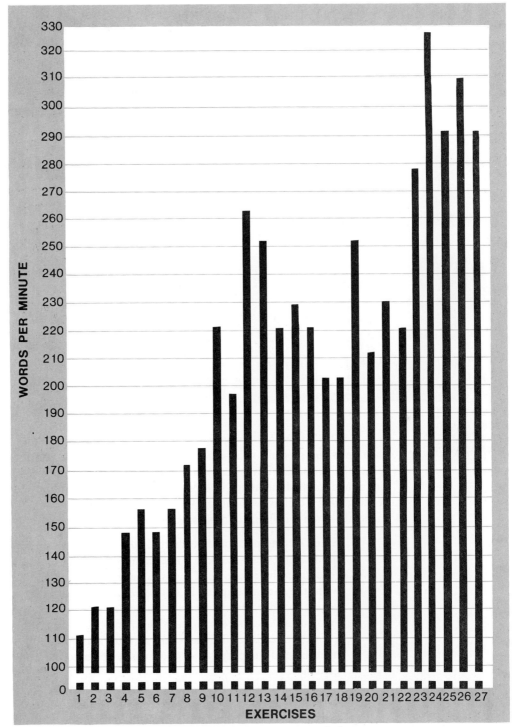

Figure 11.7
A graph of Tom's
reading speed on the
twenty-seven
exercises.

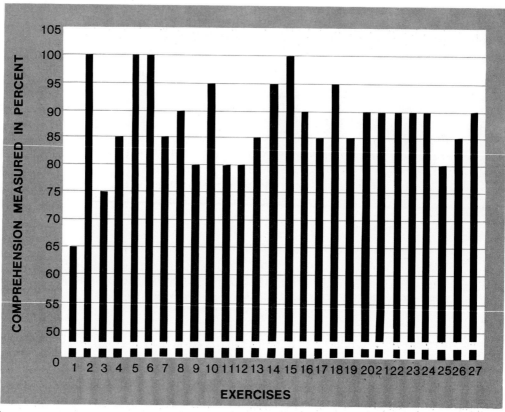

Figure 11.8
A graph of Tom's comprehension on tests over twenty-seven reading exercises.

Ideally, Tom's rate of reading will approximate his rate of thinking, since the rate of comprehension is basically being considered. Because of the wide individual differences within peer groups in ability to read silently and identify both literal and implied meanings in a passage, there is no *standard* or *best* rate of reading for all children. However, there are some generalizations that may be made about the individual and his silent reading:

1. Speed of reading should be partially determined by the purpose one has in mind when reading. Children need to adjust their speed in reading to their purpose. They will learn to "shift to a lower gear" when they are attempting to solve a verbal problem in arithmetic or general science. But they can "resume full speed" when they are enjoying an exciting story and wish to know the outcome.

2. Growth in reading efficiency—i.e., at rates appropriate to the material and the purpose—is most easily achieved by good teacher guidance.

3. Clear-cut purposes that are understood beforehand enable the reader to decide whether she can skim rapidly to acquire the general idea or whether she must read slowly for details that must not be missed.

Utilizing/ Applying Skills

Teachers at all grade levels need to find many ways for children to practice the study skills. These opportunities may range from the first grade visit to the potato chip factory with its follow-up mural and roleplaying, to the sixth grade term paper assignment in which students go through the steps of locating, organizing, and interpreting a body of information.

Unit teaching is an instructional strategy that provides many opportunities for teachers to have children practice study skills. When this work is done during a unit in which children are interested, the study skills practice is done in context, making it more meaningful than when it is taught from isolated drill sheets.

In unit teaching, there is a need in the beginning to arouse interest based on what everybody already knows and what everybody would like to learn. This requires free discussion. Then there is need for organized, fairly formal planning so that everyone can go to work efficiently to find information. Next, the unit plan requires sharing in committees, writing about information gained, discussing in small groups, and talking together quietly to crystallize thinking. Then, the entire group is ready to share, question, agree or disagree, and summarize. Finally they need some method to demonstrate that the original objectives for the unit of study have been met. These five steps in the development of a unit of work are presented in table 11.2 with types of interaction between teacher and students.

Simon and Sarkotich have suggested nine skills that need to be strengthened if teachers are to be sensitive to individual students' verbal needs and aware of positive group interaction in the class.[17]

1. Growing accustomed to being nonjudgmental with one another's ideas.
2. Allowing the other person to have attitudes and feelings different from one's own.
3. Growing in the skill of asking and answering questions—without being defensive.
4. Learning to listen for clues in responses.
5. Using neutral questions to expand the responses or to turn attention in new directions.
6. Learning how to report, diagnose, and evaluate classroom problems in group interaction.
7. Using open-ended questions: "How do you feel about this?" "Is there something else important?"
8. Learning that observation, participation, and feedback have real meaning in problem-solving situations.
9. Learning to use "acceptance" and "silence" when useful in getting both participation and interaction.

How to Teach a Unit of Work

The teacher may think of the unit as having five distinct steps, as shown in the following outline.

I. *Orientation*
   A. Create interest on the part of the class.
   B. Give the class some notion of the scope of the problem involved.
   C. Discuss with the group the purpose and possibilities of the unit so they can see the kind of problem the unit will help them solve.
   D. An orientation period may require varying lengths of time, from a day to a week.

II. *Teacher-pupil planning*
   A. Set down in writing the questions or problems to be answered by completing the unit of work.
   B. Many of the questions will be raised by the members of the class.
   C. The teacher is also a participating member and should raise questions not raised by the class.
   D. A teacher-pupil planning period may evolve a number of experiments to be performed, a list of questions to be answered through reading, or a study guide to provide direction to the *gathering information* phase of the unit.

III. *Gathering information*

In the lower grades, children will work for short periods with frequent questioning and evaluation. In the higher elementary grades, a class may work for several class periods gathering information from a variety of sources in a variety of ways.

IV. *Sharing information*

A sharing period would make it possible for the students to share information they have obtained from different sources, so that all members of the class need not read the same thing. The sharing period is especially important, too, for correcting any erroneous ideas children may have gotten in their reading.

V. *Culminating activity*

There needs to be some way to summarize what the group has learned with the completion of each unit of work. This may be done in any one of several ways.
   A. Prepare a program of reports for another group of children, for the class, or for the parents.
   B. Make notebooks that compile summary statements about work done in the unit.
   C. Take a unit test covering the information that has been taught in the class.
   D. Discuss, plan, and draw a mural that tells the story of the unit. The discussion of what the class has learned is very important, since they need to handle the concepts of the unit through oral discussion.

Table 11.2 Formal steps in development of a unit of work suggesting significant teacher-pupil interaction at each step.

Orientation to the Unit of Work	Teacher-Pupil Planning of Assignments	Information Gathering Time	Information Sharing Time	Culmination
Problem identification.	Problem selection.	Planning and organizing.	Synthesis of ideas.	Evaluation.
Problem exploration.	Goal setting.	Coordinating and communicating.	End product.	Demonstration that objectives have been met.
Informal class interaction.	Teacher-directed discussion.	Committees, small groups, and some individuals doing research and writing activities.	Informal class interaction: sharing information; correcting erroneous ideas; summarizing; selecting important ideas to remember.	Student performance: making and explaining a mural; preparing and performing a play; giving a panel discussion; performing a unit test.

The teacher-pupil planning period can be the most important both in setting up the objectives to be met, and in guiding the students in planning what they think is important—how they can carry out the activities of the unit, and which of them can exercise leadership in working with the teacher.

This method of teaching affords the teacher excellent opportunities to have students work together in small groups or committees and help each other. Organizing committees in the intermediate grades can be frustrating for a teacher if the boys and girls have never worked in this manner before. Yet, once they have learned to study together efficiently, many very important social interaction skills and social values are learned that are just as important as the subject matter being studied. If group work is new to the children, the teacher must guide the process skillfully. For example, groups can be set up for just one short period with no indication of their continuing after this first meeting. Then if the groups have a clear purpose for meeting and the teacher has planned ahead with the chairmen of the groups, the teacher can move from group to group and lend assistance where needed. The boys and girls themselves must evaluate the technique afterward as a group and reveal their own weaknesses and decide how to move ahead.

The Study Guide
The study guide is another tool whose purpose is to encourage children to learn important study skills. Graded study guides can help give children specific direction for doing silent-study exercises. They are among the best ways for children to study their content subjects such as science, history, geography, or hygiene. The tasks to be outlined in the study guide will be determined by the planning done by the group with the teacher.

A study guide should be just what the name implies, a *guide* to help children understand, organize, and remember what they are reading. It should concentrate primarily upon thought processes, understanding, relating reading to children's experiences, seeing relationships, and paraphrasing ideas to insure retention.

The detailed suggestions given here about making and using study guides as an aid in studying the material are presented as general suggestions or ideas. They are intended to be useful to a teacher who must plan many types of job-sheets, study sheets, or test-exercises to help boys and girls better understand what they are studying.

Five points to keep in mind are:

1. If a child cannot pronounce the words, he or she needs word-recognition exercises over the material before trying to read it silently.
2. If a child does not know the meanings of words, he or she needs vocabulary-building exercises before reading silently to try to understand.
3. In most textbooks, the hard new words are introduced too fast and not repeated often enough for children to learn them. Study guides should require close reading of small amounts of material and also rereading for different purposes.

4. Textbook sentences may sometimes have unusual or difficult syntax. Study guide exercises should require some restating or paraphrasing of ideas in the text.

5. Often children have not had enough experience with the ideas in the reading material. For example, children may have difficulty with the sentence "Joe's father is working on the ditches that carry the water to irrigate the vegetable fields." If they have not had experience with ditches, irrigation, or vegetables raised in large areas, they need experience, either firsthand or vicarious, to remove this difficulty. Pictures in film, filmstrip, or a flat-picture collection; going to see the thing described; or reading easy material that describes it in terms the child already knows are ways of removing the difficulty.

The study guide should help the child think about and use the material read. Some of the reasons why a child cannot, or does not, think about and use material after reading it are these:

1. The child may have had no clear-cut purpose in reading the material other than to get through the lesson.

2. A child may be so engrossed with the details of every sentence, such as pronouncing hard words, that he or she does not see the larger purposes of the material being read.

3. The child may consider all the sentences of equal value and therefore will need to be taught that some ideas have more importance while others are subordinate. Study sheets are needed, which require a child to identify the main ideas and minor ideas and to outline, summarize, and evaluate a selection.

Durrell, in his book *Improving Reading Instruction,*[18] suggests that the teacher needs to plan *levels* and *types* of study tasks in social science and science. The following suggestions will help in such planning.

1. A series of short tasks is easier than a single long task.

2. Multiple-choice answers or short oral answers are easier than unaided summaries.

3. Questions posed prior to reading provide more help than questions asked after reading.

4. Evaluation of the material immediately after the reading is more beneficial than evaluation at a later time.

A study guide for a unit of work needs to be prepared at two or three levels. It can be used in several ways, depending upon the group and its needs. The easiest level may be presented in the form of a list of questions for which children can find specific answers in a text; or they read the text and then select the right choice in multiple-choice questions. This task is easier when the answers are given orally than when they are written. At a more difficult level of functioning, the children are asked to write a summary paragraph about a lesson they have read and discussed.

Following are illustrative questions for a study guide for American history from 1860 to 1865 in fifth grade. The level I questions represent literal comprehension; level II, interpretive comprehension; and level III, evaluation.[19]

Three-Level Study Guide, Fifth Grade

Level I. Check the statements that are accurate and appeared in the reading selection.

1. Hamilton believed that small farmers and merchants should be protected by the government.
2. The majority rules in our democratic form of government.
3. Jefferson formed a new political party to represent his ideas about government.
4. The Southern states controlled the House of Representatives in the fight over slavery.
5. The tariff benefited the North and hurt the South; so the Southern states threatened to ignore the tariff.
6. The cotton gin was an example of Northern industrialism.
7. The cotton gin increased the South's need for slavery.
8. With the expansion of the U.S. territory, states were being forced to enter the Union as either free or slave states.

Level II. Check the statements that are correct *interpretations* of the reading selection.

1. Southerners felt slaveholders should have more rights than free men.
2. A political party holds a common set of beliefs and goals.
3. In a democracy, people in the minority on an issue may not feel their needs are being met.
4. The tariff actually benefited the South.
5. The power of the federal government vs. the state government became a large issue in the Civil War.
6. The cotton gin probably was a factor in causing the Civil War.
7. The Missouri Compromise was a permanent solution to the free vs. slave state issue.
8. Popular sovereignty (the right of a state to decide) agrees with the Constitution, so the Missouri Compromise must be unconstitutional.

Level III. Which of the following statements best expresses or summarizes the meaning of the reading selection?

1. Compromise cannot work unless it deals with the real problems, not just symptoms.
2. Our federal Union should be like a happy marriage.

3. States' rights vs. federal control was one of the real issues of the Civil War.
4. When emotional discussions overrule rational thought and discussion, a break becomes inevitable.

Since study guides require time to prepare, they should be saved for future use as a reference to assist the teacher in updating and improving future lessons. Until study guides are provided with textbooks, teachers—individually or in groups—will have to prepare them. A few have been prepared and are provided commercially, but there is the problem of fitting the guide to the specific activities you wish to complete in your classroom.

Materials

Many materials to help children learn study skills have been mentioned throughout the chapter. Included would be such materials as atlases, encyclopedias, card catalogs, and dictionaries. It is important to note here other types of materials.

Using the Newspaper to Teach Skills

Newspapers offer a continuous source of material for teaching skills as well as content. Piercey has pointed out several specific ways newspapers can be useful to teachers.[20] They can help students strengthen comprehension skills, critical reading, study skills, vocabulary, and creative writing. News stories are tailor-made to help students extract main ideas because they give the important facts in the first one or two paragraphs. In the opening of a news story, called the lead, are answers to who? what? where? why? and when?

Newspapers can help students find supporting details. After a couple of paragraphs covering the main facts, details are usually unfolded in an organized way. Also, byline columns on and opposite the editorial page offer good debate material for critical readers.

Throw-Away Materials

Creative teachers have found uses for several kinds of materials normally tossed in the waste can. Included might be some junk mail, restaurant place mats, paper bags, chamber of commerce and state tourist bureau materials, brochures obtained from foreign embassies, retail catalogs, and even matchbook covers. If teachers build files of such materials and also encourage children to collect them, they will have an amazing amount of information to apply to a variety of units and projects. Some of the information will come from the print; some will be pictured.

Commercial Materials

One may buy workbooks, ditto books, or even microcomputer software for teaching study skills. Almost all workbooks accompanying basal readers have some pages devoted to this skill area. Such materials should be studied carefully to determine their usefulness for specific groups and individuals. Undoubtedly, the best way for children to learn important study skills is in context during unit study or as a by-product of individual research or class projects. While such learning experiences are being developed, the teacher can plan experiences that will require the use of the appropriate study skills.

Summary

The abilities needed to put reading to work identifying and solving problems are called the study skills. Study skills utilize all the abilities of the student in vocabulary and concept development; they are based upon the student's mastery of reading comprehension skills. The primary study skill is the ability to locate appropriate information, followed by the organization of that information. Before one can interpret the data obtained, a vocabulary of special, technical, and foreign words may be needed, along with a knowledge of figures of speech and combined word forms. Finally, interpretation skills are needed, facilitated by necessary reading speed. Teachers should provide many opportunities for students to apply study skills. Units and projects provide in-context situations that are generally better for developing study skills than are isolated drills.

For Further Reading

Allen, Roach V. "Organizing Ideas and Information" and "Searching and Researching Multiple Sources." In *Language Experiences in Communication,* pp. 380–92, 413–29. Boston: Houghton Mifflin, 1976.

Coody, Betty, and David Nelson. "Making the Most of Media: Books and Nonbook Materials in Partnership." In *Teaching Elementary Language Arts: A Literature Approach,* pp. 278–302. Belmont, Calif.: Wadsworth, 1982.

Dupuis, Mary, and Eunice N. Askov. "The Unit as the Central Organizer" and "Teaching Study Skills." In *Content Area Reading, An Individualized Approach,* pp. 107–14, 215–30. Englewood Cliffs, N.J.: Prentice-Hall, 1982.

Hartner, Stephen P., and Kenneth F. Kister. "Online Encyclopedias: The Potential." *Library Journal* 106 (September 1981): 1600–1602.

Hater, Mary A., Robert B. Kane, and Mary A. Byrne. "Building Reading Skills in the Mathematics Class." *The Arithmetic Teacher* 21 (December 1974): 662–68.

Heilman, Arthur W., Timothy R. Blair, and William H. Rupley. "Study Skills." In *Principles and Practices of Teaching Reading,* 5th ed., pp. 268–308. Columbus, Ohio: Charles E. Merrill, 1981.

Smith, Carl B. "Study Skills: The Key to Independent Learning." In *Teaching Reading in Secondary School Content Subjects: A Book Thinking Process,* pp. 251–81. New York: Holt, Rinehart and Winston, 1978.

Smith, Nila B., and H. Alan Robinson. "Developing Study Strategies in the Content Areas." In *Reading Instruction for Today's Children,* 2d ed., pp. 263–303. Englewood Cliffs, N.J.: Prentice-Hall, 1980.

Tonjes, Marian J., and Miles V. Zintz. "Improving Study Skills." Chap. 8 in *Teaching Reading/Thinking/Study Skills in Content Classrooms.* Dubuque, Iowa: Wm. C. Brown, 1981.

Wright, Jone P., and Nann L. Andreasen. "Practice in Using Location Skills in A Content Area." *The Reading Teacher* 34 (November 1980): 184–86.

Yonan, Barbara. "Encyclopedia Reports Don't Have to Be Dull." *The Reading Teacher* 36 (November 1982): 212–14.

Notes

1. L. C. Fay, "What Research Has to Say About Reading in the Content Areas," *The Reading Teacher* 8 (1954): 68–72.

2. James Moffett and Betty Wagner, *Student-Centered Language Arts and Reading: K–13* (Boston: Houghton Mifflin, 1976), p. 369.

3. Arthur Heilman, Timothy Blair, and William H. Rupley, *Principles and Practices of Teaching Reading* (Columbus, Ohio: Charles E. Merrill, 1981), p. 277.

4. Richard M. Neustadt, "The Third Revolution in Information: A Challenge to Libraries," *Library Journal* 106 (July 1981): 1376.

5. Ibid.

6. Moffett and Wagner, *Language Arts and Reading,* p. 369.

7. Richard D. Van Dongen, "An Analysis of Study Skills Taught by Intermediate-Grade Basal Readers" (M.A. thesis, University of New Mexico, August 1967), pp. 47–54.

8. Ernest Horn, Bess Goodykoontz, and Mabel I. Snedaker, *Progress in Reading Series: Reaching Our Goals,* Grade Six (Boston: Ginn, 1940), pp. 271–73.

9. Margaret Smith Greer, "The Efficiency of the Use of Analogy in Teaching Selected Concepts at the Sixth Grade Level" (M.A. thesis, University of New Mexico, 1966), p. 40.

10. Van Dongen, "Study Skills," pp. 47–54.

11. Lou Burmeister, "Vocabulary Development in Content Areas Through the Use of Morphemes," *Journal of Reading* 19 (March 1976): 481–87.

12. Richard T. Vacca, "Readiness to Read Content Area Assignments," *The Journal of Reading* 18 (May 1975): 587–90.

13. For more extensive lists of prefixes and suffixes, see Dale D. Johnson and P. David Pearson, *Teaching Reading Vocabulary* (New York: Holt, Rinehart & Winston, 1978), pp. 84–87; and Dolores Durkin, *Strategies for Identifying Words* (Boston: Allyn & Bacon, 1976), pp. 48–49.

14. David A. Welton and John T. Mallan, *Children and Their World,* 2d. ed. (Chicago: Rand McNally, 1981), p. 273.

15. Van Dongen, "Study Skills," pp. 47–54.

16. Elizabeth Simpson, *SRA Better Reading Books I and II* (Chicago: Science Research Associates, 1951).

17. Dan Simon and Diane Sarkotich, "Sensitivity Training in the Classroom," *NEA Journal* 56 (January 1967): 12–13.

18. D. D. Durrell, *Improving Reading Instruction* (New York: Harcourt, Brace, and World, 1956), pp. 285–308.

19. We are indebted to Mrs. Anne M. Anderson, Reading Consultant, State Department of Education, Santa Fe, New Mexico, for the list of questions presented in three levels. They are based on the text *The Social Sciences: Concepts and Values,* Grade 5 (New York: Harcourt Brace Jovanovich, 1970), pp. 248–50.

20. Dorothy Piercey, "Teachers Use Newspapers as Aid to Reading," *The Arizona Republic,* 6 March 1966.

Teaching Reading in the Content Fields

A Cognitive Map: Teaching Reading in the Content Fields

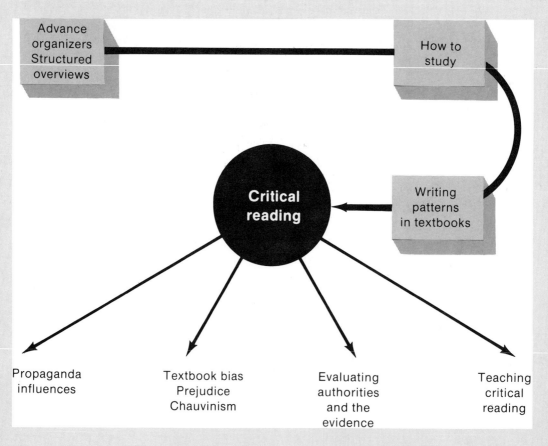

12

Guide Questions

1. A structured overview is a form of advance organizer. What do you see as the purposes of structured overviews? How might you use them with children?

2. What would you teach elementary schoolchildren about how to study?

3. After reading about different writing patterns, study some of your own textbooks. Try to find examples of the different writing patterns. Do some cause more trouble than others? Why?

4. What are the types of critical reading abilities children need to learn? Why is not learning them so dangerous?

Terminology

advance organizer

author bias

bandwagon

cardstacking

cause-and-effect

enumeration

generalizations

glittering generalities

name-calling

plain folks

prejudice

reference points

sequence

SQ3R

stereotypes

structured overview

testimonials

transfer

Susan is now in the sixth grade and is having some difficulty with the study assignments in science class. Susan has always perceived herself as a "good" student who follows the teacher's precise directions and works diligently to complete her written assignments. She has never had any difficulty with reading *in reading class*. But this year the science units have demanded considerable vocabulary, and they presupposed some previous knowledge of concepts and generalizations. Susan can remember that she memorized quite a few things last year before unit tests in science, but the teacher hadn't sounded so "scientific" as this year.

Susan's new unit is about rockets and space travel. Tomorrow she needs to know how to explain things like: "For every action, there is an opposite and equal reaction," and words like "gravity," "centrifugal force," "inertia," and "escape velocity."[1] The words have definitions in the glossary of her textbook, and she knows she could memorize them, but the teacher wants everyone to give examples and ask questions.

Susan is not the only child having such problems in the sixth grade world. But because she is conscientious and habitually tries to please the adults in her world, she may *feel* very much alone. Actually she is studying very abstract subject matter. The teacher may need to provide much more time for some of the students to assimilate elementary concepts than is necessary for the "real scientists" in the class. Also, the teacher should have quite different expectations for different students at the end of the unit.

Susan needs to be reassured that she *can* read many of the things she needs to read. She needs her confidence restored so she can approach science work positively. And she needs to get a "picture" of what is expected of her in the science class.

The teacher may build background—through reading to the class, asking those who have had more experience with Newton's Laws to do experiments for the others, or presenting an educational motion picture that shows how a rocket works. New vocabulary presented first orally in meaningful context, then in written context, will help some of the class to assimilate it.

What Susan is experiencing is the difference between reading expository material and reading narrative. Her successes have been primarily with narrative in her basal readers; now, in a serious confrontation with subject matter texts, the demands on the reader are different. Susan doesn't realize what is happening or why, and possibly her teacher does not, either.

It may help if the teacher were to present an overview in diagrammatic form for the whole unit and then keep the overview handy for reference as the unit progresses. Such an overview might be structured like the one in figure 12.1.

Then perhaps Susan could begin by reviewing what she was previously taught about gravity. Or she could read elementary biographies of scientists who were interested in conquering space. Or she could participate in some experiments to demonstrate how jet propulsion works.

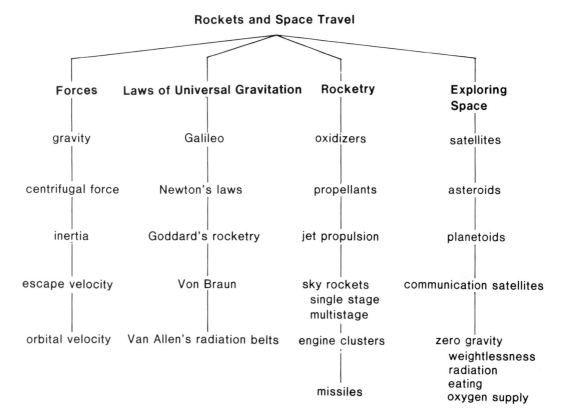

Rockets and Space Travel

Forces	Laws of Universal Gravitation	Rocketry	Exploring Space
gravity	Galileo	oxidizers	satellites
centrifugal force	Newton's laws	propellants	asteroids
inertia	Goddard's rocketry	jet propulsion	planetoids
escape velocity	Von Braun	sky rockets single stage multistage	communication satellites
orbital velocity	Van Allen's radiation belts	engine clusters	zero gravity weightlessness radiation eating oxygen supply
		missiles	

Figure 12.1
A structured overview of concept relationships in rocketry and space travel.

From John G. Navarra and Joseph Zafforoni, *The Young Scientist: His Predictions and Tests,* published by Harper & Row, New York, copyright © 1971. Reprinted by permission.

Reading is a very elaborate procedure, involving a weighing of each of many elements in a sentence, their organization in the proper relations one to another, the selection of certain of their connotations and the rejection of others, and the cooperation of many forces to determine final response. In fact we shall find that the act of answering simple questions about a simple paragraph . . . includes all the features characteristic of typical reasoning.[2]

Teachers must not consider the reading of a textbook or related assignment as a passive, undiscriminating task. Reading a textbook assignment requires the exercise of critical skills, judgment, and organization and association of ideas. It is no small task for the student to really learn what the book is saying. The teacher's primary problem is to be inventive or stimulating enough to cause students to become sufficiently *interested* and *motivated* that they will want to make the necessary effort.

Reading skills include: (1) word recognition, context clues, word structure, and dictionary techniques; (2) understanding meanings, which involves literal comprehension, interpretation, critical judgment, and knowing specific word meanings; and (3) flexibility of rate so that it can be accommodated to the reason for reading the material and the nature of the subject matter.

Study skills include location skills, organization skills, interpretation skills, special vocabulary skills, adjusting speed to fit the content, and using skills to solve problems. Teachers must know which students can already apply all of these reading and study skills, which students need additional instruction, and which students do not have any of these skills.

Reading in the content fields requires the use of all of the comprehension skills that have already been presented and illustrated in the chapters on comprehension and study skills. Application of these skills is basic to meaningful study in the content fields. In addition, the expansion of vocabulary, the ability to identify purposes, and concept building will be used daily by teachers and students as they study the content subjects.

This chapter will include the following sections:

1. Structured overview.
2. How to study an assignment.
3. Writing patterns in textbooks.
4. Critical reading, including propaganda influences, textbook bias (prejudice and chauvinism), evaluating authorities and the evidence, and teaching critical reading.

Structured Overviews

A structured overview, an advance organizer, is a diagram that attempts to give students a *visual* approach to the structure of a unit. It is probably most valuable when it can be developed *with* students. It presents the important vocabulary to be taught and suggests ways that technical terms may be related to each other. Preparing such an overview also helps the teacher to define the reasons for conducting the lesson.[3] Examples of structured overviews may be found at the beginning of the chapters in this book.

Such an overview should help students understand the objectives of a particular lesson. It can also provide the stimulus for discussion of relationships between terms. And it can help students see the interrelationships among separate parts of reading assignments. While any overview may appear to be oversimplified, its usefulness in the classroom depends upon its being used as a stimulus for the teacher and students to *question* sufficiently to clarify concepts and add supporting details to the outline. The teacher needs to be a good questioner, to be able to elicit information from the group, and to be able to supply explanations.[4]

Two structured overviews are presented here. Figure 12.2 is designed to help eleven-year-olds understand an abstract term such as *democracy* as it is exemplified by the government of the United States of America.

Figure 12.3 presents a structured overview that could be the basis for a discussion prior to reading about the problem of hunger throughout the world.

Figure 12.2
A structured overview
for the concept of
democracy.

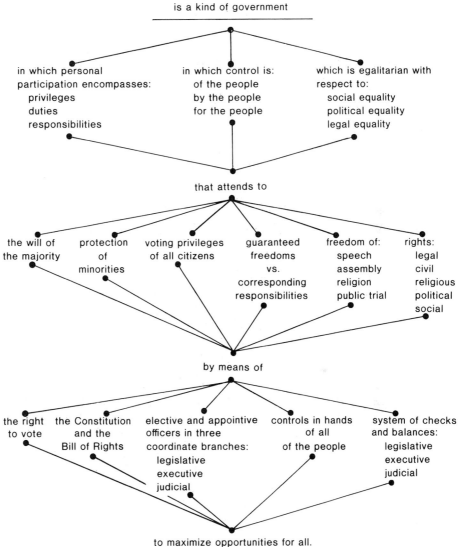

A democracy,

as represented by the United States of America,

is a kind of government

in which personal
participation encompasses:
   privileges
   duties
   responsibilities

in which control is:
   of the people
   by the people
   for the people

which is egalitarian with
respect to:
   social equality
   political equality
   legal equality

that attends to

the will of
the majority

protection
of
minorities

voting privileges
of all citizens

guaranteed
freedoms
vs.
corresponding
responsibilities

freedom of:
   speech
   assembly
   religion
   public trial

rights:
   legal
   civil
   religious
   political
   social

by means of

the right
to vote

the Constitution
and the
Bill of Rights

elective and appointive
officers in three
coordinate branches:
   legislative
   executive
   judicial

controls in hands
of all
of the people

system of checks
and balances:
   legislative
   executive
   judicial

to maximize opportunities for all.

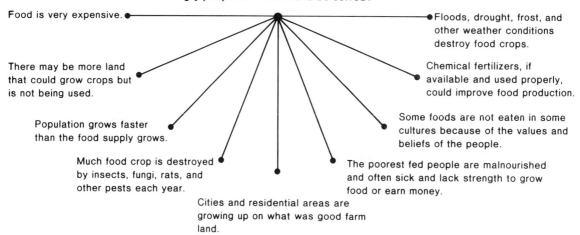

How will the problem of so many hungry people in a rich world be solved?

Food is very expensive.

Floods, drought, frost, and other weather conditions destroy food crops.

There may be more land that could grow crops but is not being used.

Chemical fertilizers, if available and used properly, could improve food production.

Population grows faster than the food supply grows.

Some foods are not eaten in some cultures because of the values and beliefs of the people.

Much food crop is destroyed by insects, fungi, rats, and other pests each year.

The poorest fed people are malnourished and often sick and lack strength to grow food or earn money.

Cities and residential areas are growing up on what was good farm land.

Figure 12.3
A structured overview relating to the problem of hunger throughout the world.

Adapted from the Starting Points Learning Activity Poster, "Hungry People in a Rich World." Special permission of *Learning, the Magazine for Creative Teaching,* December 1976. Copyright © 1976 by Education Today Company, Inc.

From Theory to Practice 12.1
Preparing Structured Overviews

Learning to prepare useful structured overviews is a skill that requires much effort to do well. As suggested in the chapter, many teachers actually build them *with* their students. However, for you to get practice in carrying out this aspect of teaching, it may be useful to begin by making overviews by yourself.

Select a fourth or fifth grade social studies or science text that is organized in unit format. Identify a single unit and study it carefully. You may also want to study the accompanying teacher's manual. Then create a structured overview for that unit that would promote your teaching and the students' learning.

Bring your structured overview and the textbook from which it was drawn to class to share with other students and your instructor.

How to Study a Lesson

Students need guidance in their preparation for study, they need suggestions from teachers in ways to read more efficiently, and they need to be taught new techniques that work in different subject areas.

Readiness usually incorporates establishing purposes, building some background for understanding, and teaching unfamiliar vocabulary.

Most students will profit from being given an oral summary of key points contained in text material before they begin reading. Especially if the text contains two or three major issues to be evaluated, students will grasp them more quickly if the teacher presents them briefly beforehand and permits time for discussion. This background information presented to make reading the lesson easier for students to understand is called an *advance organizer*. Or students will profit from *directed prereading activities* such as seeing a film or filmstrip or listening to a tape or developing a *structured overview* of the major or minor topic. Also, a few guide questions can make the purposes for reading much more specific.

The extent of previous learning that a student brings to the reading determines how well the reading will be understood. Big differences in quality of reading done by students in a given class relate to a large extent to differences in the readers' background information.

It may be necessary to develop concepts and ideas in some detail to insure that the lesson is understood. Enlarging the context of the topic is the responsibility of the teacher *before* the reading is done. Such preliminary activities as locating places on maps or a globe, comparing new places with familiar *reference points,* seeing an educational motion picture, and studying pictures, travel posters, and illustrations in magazines may all help students.

Establishing Reference Points	In order to compare new places with familiar reference points, students need to understand physiographic concepts such as altitude, longitude, latitude, equator, rainy season, growing season, frost-free season, weather, and climate. Once they understand each of these terms with reference to where they are, they can then compare or contrast their own region with another region.

When one basic text has been provided for the entire class, the teacher should identify which students cannot read it with understanding and should provide other reading materials for them. This may be done by (1) finding alternative books at lower readability levels, (2) selecting additional texts with lower reading levels, (3) making different assignments for different children, (4) rewriting textbook materials at easier reading levels, or (5) preparing tapes of the text for children to hear. Each teacher should be continuously selecting and adding to the classroom library books that relate to any subject matter being taught. These materials should be available to all students and should span a wide range of levels of difficulty and interests. Hansell makes some excellent suggestions for teachers who wish to help students improve their reading skill when reading in content areas.[5]

Once students have been introduced to a unit of work, have been motivated to find information, and have specific objectives for reading, they should be allowed time for independent study. They need opportunity to work alone or in small groups, opportunity to talk informally about what they are finding, and opportunity to question or to verify facts. Then the teacher needs to provide for sharing information, interpretations, analyses, syntheses, and evaluation of concepts and generalizations presented. Reviewing and summarizing are final

Table 12.1 A plan for helping students study the content material in subject fields.

Step 1	Step 2	Step 3
An overview.	Development of vocabulary.	Sample content to motivate study.
What is the present unit going to be about?	Discussion should come first, followed by several kinds of matching exercises.	*Discussion* needs to be emphasized here.
Study pictures, illustrations, maps, or see an educational motion picture.	Some work on roots, prefixes, suffixes, as needed.	All students need *not* read the same text.
Listen to a recording or anecdotes read to the class by the teacher.	The class, under teacher guidance, formulates a list of questions based on the overview and vocabulary study.	Some may *listen* to tapes of the text read aloud.
		Some may read *more elementary material* that does not answer all of the questions.

Step 4	Step 5	Step 6
Read, study and share.	Do further research.	Summarize and review.
By now the class may be able to set up a list of questions that require *interpretation* and *application* on what is read and to use maps, charts, globes, diagrams, or tables to help *explain* the narrative.	*Individual research* or reading or study, fiction or nonfiction, in the library. Some means for keeping a record of *extensive related* reading.	May be *generalizing* kinds of questions.
Discussion in which students *share* with each other is very important.		May be *diagrammatic* or schematic *presentations*.
A shelf of books at *many levels of difficulty*—fiction and nonfiction—related to the subject may be available. Biography is important here.		May be *reports* on special books or articles read and interpreted.

steps. Table 12.1 shows six steps by which a teacher can guide students through a unit of work: (1) overview; (2) development of vocabulary; (3) sample content to motivate study; (4) read, study, and share; (5) do further research; and (6) summarize and review. When children have little background for a lesson, these steps cannot be covered hurriedly.

The common reading skills that students should be using need to be consciously reinforced over and over by the teacher. These include separating main ideas and details; drawing inferences; recognizing the author's purpose; using a table of contents, index, appendices, and standard references to locate information.

Specific lessons need to be provided for *subgroups* in the class to allow practice in (1) reading to grasp the general significance of the argument; (2) selecting generalized statements and then searching for objective proof; (3) identifying problems and then finding solutions or summarizing evidence for decision making; and (4) identifying an effect as given in the reading and then looking for causes that lead to this effect.

Teachers should also teach the *specific study skills* needed in a unit of study. Will sequencing in a chronological timetable be useful? Will comparison and contrast be a primary focus? Will categorizing, enumerating, or solving problems be important?

Teachers can give suggestions and can demonstrate to boys and girls how to study a reading assignment. Following are some steps that most students should follow as they study a lesson. Teacher guidance will be necessary in order for students to establish the habits.

1. Look through all the pages of the assignment. Chapter headings, chapter subheadings, guide questions, and captions for pictures, maps, and tables should be read because they begin to circumscribe the topic under study. They will provide some information that should later fit into an organized unit plan.
2. Read the introductory paragraphs at the beginning of the chapter and at the beginning of each subsection of the assignment. Find the last paragraph in each subsection and read this summary. A good summary will present important points that have been made.
3. If there are questions at the end of the assignment, or if the teacher has given a list of questions to be answered, the student should read them carefully now, *before reading the assignment,* because they will pinpoint what the author or the teacher thinks is important.
4. If words have been identified that are not in the students' vocabulary, a dictionary or glossary definition should be consulted before reading the assignment.
5. If main ideas are explained by presentation of details, notes in outline form should be made after each subsection is read. Writing down information helps one to remember it.
6. When an assignment has been read, the student needs to take a few minutes to *reflect* on the reading, to decide whether preliminary questions posed were answered, and to think through the major points covered.
7. Notes taken during reading need to be compared with the teacher's explanation later, and if they are to be remembered, they need to be reviewed.

Many successful science projects begin with the student's knowledge of appropriate study and research skills.

SQ3R

Are there specific steps that might help anyone get more out of reading? Robinson has suggested an easy-to-remember formula that has proved very useful.[6] He calls it the SQ3R method of study—*Survey, Question, Read, Recite,* and *Review*. It can be summarized as follows:

> *Survey:* Glance over the headings in the chapter to see the main points that will be developed. Also read the final summary paragraph if the chapter has one. This survey should not take more than a minute and will show the three to six core ideas around which the discussion will center. This orientation will help to organize the ideas as you read them later.

> *Question:* Now begin to work. Turn the first heading into a question. This will arouse your curiosity and so increase your comprehension. It will bring to mind information already known, thus helping you to understand that section more quickly. And the question you have raised in your mind will make important points stand out while

explanatory detail is recognized as such. Turning a heading into a question as it is read is not difficult, but keeping the question in mind as one reads to find the answer requires a conscious effort.

Read: Read to answer that question, at least to the end of the section. This is not a passive plodding along each line, but an active search for an answer.

Recite: Having read the section, look away from the book and try to recite briefly the answer to your question. Use your own words and include an example. If you can do this, you know what you have read; if you can't, glance over it again. An excellent way to do this reciting from memory is to jot down cue phrases in outline form on a sheet of paper.

Review: When the lesson has been completely read, look over your notes to get a bird's eye view of the points and their relationship and check your memory as to the content by reciting the major subpoints under each heading.

SQ4R is an adaptation of Francis Robinson's SQ3R formula, to which the word *Reflect* has been added.[7] Fay has recommended the specific study skill SQRQCQ to increase the student's problem-solving ability.[8] It is an adapted form of SQ4R and involves the following steps:

Survey: The material is read quickly to determine its nature.

Question: What is the problem presented in the reading?

Read: Reread for details and interrelationships.

Question: What process will I use?

Compute: Carry out the computation.

Question: Is the answer correct?

Writing Patterns in Textbooks

Even though children have succeeded in reading the basal readers, they may run into serious difficulties in fourth or fifth grade when they are expected to read the content of science, social studies, and mathematics. That is sufficient reason for teaching specialized skills for those content subjects.

One of the student's problems is that the expository writing in the textbook is more difficult to read than the basal reader. It has greater frequency of unknown technical words and a more academic approach to topic presentation. Another problem is that more complex skills are required of students to enable them to keep their purposes in mind while they cope with the written material.

The subject matter teacher who can select what is cognitively important in the subject is the logical person to provide some appropriate reading and study strategies to insure efficient learning. Burmeister has outlined specific techniques for helping students understand some material through sequencing.[9] She has suggested, helpfully, that sequencing may be chronological, spatial, or expository and can be expressed accordingly as follows:

                    Sequencing
                        Chronological order
                            Flow chart
                            Outline
                            Time line
                            Tree chart
                        Spatial order
                            Sketch
                            Map
                            Floor plan
                        Expository order
                            Outline
                            Chart
                            Graphs
                                Map
                                Pie
                                Bar
                                Line
                                Pictograph

Enumeration

Another technique involves recognition of major patterns commonly used in content writing. *Enumeration* is a pattern that presents descriptions or attributes to help the reader understand and remember subtopics. For example, the following quotation about clouds defines three main cloud types by describing their characteristics. (See "Classification" as a type of discourse, chapter 10.)

Clouds

Clouds come in many different shapes, sizes, and colors and are found at different heights. By knowing what to look for, you can tell what kind of weather each kind of cloud may bring.

There are three main cloud shapes:

1. *Cirrus* means feathery. How does their name describe their shape? These clouds are found very high up . . . up to 40,000 feet high. They are made of ice crystals. Why do you think ice crystals form instead of water drops? Cirrus clouds are formed in fair weather, but often mark a change in the weather.

2. *Stratus* means layer. Why is this a good name for this type of cloud? Stratus clouds form an overcast-looking sky which often turns to rain or drizzle.

3. *Cumulus* means heap. These white, billowy clouds are seen in fair weather.[10]

Sequence

Sequence is a pattern that presents the steps of a process. The following quotation, "How coal was formed," is an illustration. The reader should be able to identify the several steps.

How coal was formed

If you like to collect ancient things, you should have a lump of hard coal in your collection. Most hard coal is over two hundred million years old!

Scientists believe that coal was made long ago, in the Paleozoic era. This was a time very long ago when the climate was hot and steamy, like a tropical rain climate. There were many large swamps in many parts of the earth. Treelike plants and huge ferns grew and died and sank into the water. Others grew on top of these dead plants, died, and sank into the water, too. The dead plants were covered with water.

For many centuries the layers of dead plants piled up, thicker and thicker. In places the land sank. The swamps became lakes or seas. Through many centuries destructional forces washed sediments over the dead plants.

Pressure and the heat of the sediments changed the plant material.

What happens when plant material is heated without air? You can find out.[11]

Generalizing

Generalizations may be based on supporting or clarifying information. The example quoted below, "Chemical energy in living things," first states the importance of green plants to all living things. Then the process of photosynthesis is explained. Finally the generalization is made: "Photosynthesis is the most important energy transfer in the world."

Chemical energy in living things

A fuel is a high-energy substance. You take in a fuel called food. In your body the fuel combines with oxygen. The fuel is oxidized. During the oxidation there is an output of heat energy. This is what keeps your body warm. There is also an output of mechanical energy. This is what makes your muscles move.

Of course, this is just a very bare outline of how chemical energy is used by your body. You know that your body needs food for other purposes besides releasing energy. You will find out in a later chapter about the chemical changes that prepare food and change it into body materials.

Living things get their energy by feeding on high-energy substances. The cat feeds on a mouse that ate the cheese that was made from the milk that came from the cow that ate the grass. Mouse, cheese, milk, grass—these are all high-energy foods.

No matter what food chain you follow, you come to green plants.

Green plants make food for all other living things. They make it out of substances that animals cannot use as food.

Plants take molecules of water from the soil and molecules of carbon dioxide from the air. These are low-energy substances. With the energy of sunlight, the plants separate these molecules into their atoms and then combine them into new molecules with high energy—molecules of sugar and oxygen.

This process is called **photosynthesis.** *Photo* means "light"; *synthesis* means "put together."

Photosynthesis is the most important energy transfer in the world. Can you tell why?[12]

Cause-Effect

In *cause-and-effect* the reader is typically presented with an effect, such as in the following passage.

Lincoln was a minority president—not the first and not the last. But far worse, in the eyes of Southerners, he was also a sectional President. Not a single southern or border state had voted for him. Southern leaders had long been prepared to leave the Union rather than be ruled by the North. Now they did it. Less than eight weeks after Lincoln's election, the people of South Carolina voted to secede from the Union. Georgia, Florida, Alabama, Mississippi, Louisiana, and Texas quickly followed.

From Theory to Practice 12.2
Identifying Writing Patterns

Teachers need to be able to recognize different writing patterns almost at a glance, if they are going to be consistently ready to help their students read content area materials effectively.

Search through a number of different textbooks for different grades and subjects. Identify at least one example of each writing pattern discussed in chapter 12.

Bring the textbooks with the patterns marked. These could be shared with other students in several ways, one of which would be to read selections and ask others to identify the patterns. Other groups might want to make collections of examples of different patterns.

In February 1861, delegates from these states met and formed their own government. They called it the Confederate States of America. Its Constitution was much like that of the United States. But it stressed the right of each state to decide most of its own laws. It also protected slavery wherever it existed. Jefferson Davis of Mississippi was elected president of the new Confederacy.[13]

These two paragraphs give several causes for an effect. The teacher could ask the student to list the causes under the effect in their order of importance, as in the following example.

Effect: Seven Southern states seceded from the Union.
Causes: 1. _____ [sectionalism; not be ruled by a Northerner]
             2. _____ [supremacy of states' rights]
             3. _____ [maintain slavery]

Other Patterns

Some other writing patterns are *classification, comparison and contrast,* and *problem-solving.*

Critical Reading Ability

We do not believe everything we read. If we tried to, we would become hopelessly confused. We relate new ideas that we hear, see, or read with our previous knowledge, or prejudice, and then accept or reject the new idea.

Politicians try to say what they think people want to hear. Many compromises are made with the whole truth, and many promises made can be only partially fulfilled.

Reread some of the lines from the "Ballad of Davy Crockett."

Born on a mountaintop in Tennessee
Greenest state in the land of the free
Killed him a b'ar when he was only three.

Raised in the woods so he knew every tree.
Fought single-handed through the Injun war
'Till the Creeks was whipped and peace was in store.

He went off to Congress and served a spell
Fixing up the government and laws as well
Took over Washington so we heard tell
'N patched up the crack in the liberty bell.[14]

Was he born on a mountaintop? Is Tennessee the greenest state? Can anyone kill a bear when he is only three years old? Does one know the names of all the trees in a forest just because he lives there and sees them? Could anyone fight a war single-handed? Does any *one* person do much to stabilize or improve the government of the country? And the crack in the Liberty Bell is not patched!

The ballad is intended to honor the legendary hero, of course, without being taken literally. Teachers might explain that the author was not trying to relate facts, but rather portray a heroic, gallant spirit to whom all good citizens can respond emotionally, with warmth and affection. Education should help us distinguish between what is intended as figurative and what factual and should teach us that different kinds of evaluation are called for.

The Socratic method taught people to demand accurate definition, clear thinking, and exact analysis.[15]

> Socrates collected opinions, asked questions, clarified terms and ideas, and indicated commitments. That is all he did. All that was required of those who took part with him was that they should try to think and to understand one another. They did not have to agree among themselves. If they came to conviction, they did so by their own free will. The only constraint upon them was the law of contradiction. They could not answer "Yes" and "No" to the same question at the same time.[16]

Today educational literature stresses that the primary aims of education are to teach problem-solving approaches, the decision-making process, weighing and evaluating, and making logical use of knowledge.

> . . . while a good education can be a great good, a bad education can be a very great evil; it can be infinitely worse than no education at all. With a good education a child learns to think clearly and to draw sound conclusions from evidence; with a bad education he will learn to accept plausible falsehoods, to confuse propaganda with truth. With a good education he will come to cherish what is most worthwhile; with a bad education he will learn to value the trivial. With a good education he will learn to make ethical judgments even when they are unpopular; with a bad education he will learn to follow the crowd wherever it may lead him and to be convinced that he is right in so doing.[17]

To achieve such educational aims, we must insure the success of the Socratic method. We must, above all, help boys and girls develop critical reading abilities.

"Critical reading," as the term is used here, encompasses both of the following broad definitions:

. . . merely getting the facts is not critical reading. The reader must first determine whether he is reading facts or merely opinions and/or assumptions. Sensing the relationships among the facts, comparing the facts with experience, knowing when the facts are relevant, evaluating these facts against other facts to arrive at some conclusion, and going beyond the facts to get the inferred, but not explicitly stated, meaning are aspects of critical reading.[18]

To really think while reading, to evaluate, to judge what is important and unimportant, what is relevant or irrelevant, what is in harmony with an idea read in another book or acquired through experience, constitutes critical reading.[19]

Teachers must themselves possess those virtues of attention, curiosity, courage to be themselves, and adherence to high standards that they try to nourish in their students. They must know how to accept and evaluate opposing points of view or dissenting opinions. Teachers must have knowledge. They can guide discussion properly only if their own information and skill in thinking are adequate.

The student who is not taught the habit of critical attention is apt to arrive at adulthood with superficial knowledge and, in turn, base poor judgment on inadequate knowledge.

Critical reading cannot be done without *knowledge*. Through knowledge, the reader is able to make comparisons and judge relevance. If judgments are not based on knowledge, the judgments will not be valid.

Detecting and Resisting Propaganda Influences

Are most people able to make critical evaluations? The testimony that many are not can be found in the full-page advertisements in color in all of the popular magazines and the frequency of advertising spots on radio and TV. Their high cost is readily paid for by the gullibility of the audiences.

By helping children develop critical reading ability, we also help them achieve critical judgment about appeals through all media, including TV and radio.

How do people learn to *see through* the propaganda techniques in constant use all about us? We may doubt that millions of people will respond to such phrases as "Be the first on your block to own a Volkswagen!" or "And nothing but nylon makes you feel so female!" or "Remember how great cigarettes *used* to taste? Luckies still do!" But the advertisers who pay for them must find them profitable!

Attitudes, beliefs, and biases interfere more with critical reading than they do with literal comprehension. The cognitive process is colored by the affective process.[20]

Henry writes of the psychology of advertising.[21] Through television, advertisers whet children's appetites for certain toys. Children then let their parents know that nothing else will do for Christmas, and desperate parents comb stores, for they *do want to* buy what their children want! "Deprive business of its capacity to appeal to children *over the heads of their parents,* and what would happen to most cereals, some of the drugs, and many toys?"[22]

Most boys and girls, by the time they pass to the sixth grade, have had the personal experience of being a victim of rumor in the course of their school life. "The teacher said . . ." "The coach is going to . . ." "Anybody who can't work these problems in arithmetic . . ." These and many similar expressions implying threat or instilling anxiety or fear are often passed around. The one who has little to fear from the threat may be the one who most enjoys spreading it among the less fortunate, for whom it was probably an agonizing experience for a short time.

Propaganda is defined as "any plan or method for spreading opinions or beliefs." The definition makes it apparent that advertisements and rumors have much in common with propaganda.

Frequently propaganda is sincere, or at least harmless; sometimes, however, it deliberately skirts or conceals the truth. One needs to be alert to the devices and able to evaluate them. Propaganda devices that can mislead have been described by the Institute for Propaganda Analysis, New York City.

1. *Name-calling* consists of using labels instead of discussing the facts. This technique usually involves attaching a negative symbol to someone—for example, calling a politician a crook, or labeling a person whose ideas are unpopular a fascist. By branding a person with these negative symbols it is often possible to avoid citing facts. The names, not facts, are used to get the desired reaction.

2. *Glittering generalities* implies use of vague phrases that promise much. They usually try to associate positive symbols, slogans, and unsupported generalizations with an idea or person—as for example, saying in a political campaign that "this act will benefit all Americans and will enhance our position abroad." Only a careful weighing of the facts will determine whether such a glittering generality has any substance.

3. *Transfer* means applying a set of symbols to a purpose for which they are not intended. This method of convincing people consists primarily of transferring the attraction of strong positive symbols or the repulsion of strong negative symbols to some person, group, or idea. For example, a subversive group might display the American flag and pictures of Washington and Lincoln at their meetings. These positive symbols help gain public support. Only careful thinking on the listener's part can determine whether these symbols are compatible with the situation.

4. *Testimonials* involve getting some prominent person to endorse an idea or product in order to induce others to react favorably to it. Motion picture stars and outstanding athletes are often used for this purpose.

5. *Plain folks* device requires pretending to be "one of the folks." People are sometimes persuaded to vote for a candidate for office because he takes a "folksy" approach to problems. In other words, he uses simple language and repeats old proverbs. Sometimes the plain

folks approach includes kissing babies, wearing Indian feathers, or posing with a fishing rod in hand. Although very common in American politics, it proves little, if anything, about the qualifications of a candidate for office.

6. *Bandwagon* means claiming that "everyone is doing it." The bandwagon method of persuading people is effective because many people don't make up their own minds and instead follow the lead of the majority. The bandwagon approach consists of giving the impression that everyone is doing it, or voting a certain way, or buying some product, and so one should get on the bandwagon if one wants to keep up with the crowd. It is an appeal to the desire to conform. To resist this approach, one must stand firmly on one's right to make up one's own mind. Appealing to the desire to "keep up with the Joneses" is one of the most common methods used to persuade people to do certain things, and is one of the *most difficult to withstand*. Boys and girls in the intermediate grades have already learned to use the "getting on the bandwagon" technique. How many mothers have allowed themselves to be coaxed and wheedled to say "yes" to something when, if they had telephoned other mothers, they would have found more than enough agreement to have said "no" with no ill effects. Boys and girls will acknowledge to a teacher whom they trust and in whom they have confidence that it is very necessary to know how to "play the game." They can cite examples of specific situations where they and their friends achieved their goal by convincing their separate parents that everyone else highly approved of something. Occasionally a child has felt *pressure* on the one hand to do what the rest of the group wants to do, but felt considerable anxiety on the other hand because he or she didn't really want to be a participant at that time.

7. *Cardstacking* is presenting only facts that favor one side. Examples are using quotations out of context, omitting key words from a quotation, or using favorable statistics while suppressing unfavorable ones. The important thing to keep in mind is that a series of half-truths usually add up to a complete lie. And, since cardstacking usually involves citing some reliable facts, one must be astute to see the flaws and falseness of this approach. In other words, cardstacking is one of the most effective propaganda devices; effort and intelligence are required to see through it.

Reading is becoming increasingly important in our society, and its ultimate end is to make the reader ably critical. Any thinking, participating citizen in our free society must read critically and make value judgments all the time. Resisting propaganda, discarding irrelevant information, choosing between two opinions when both are strongly supported, and being able to change one's thinking patterns when new evidence proves an old idea wrong or obsolete are all benefits of well-developed critical reading ability.

Awareness of
Author Bias or
Prejudice in
Textbooks

Cultural pluralism has been accepted theoretically as the objective of American education. The melting pot theory has proved unworkable and, instead, the tremendously rich ethnic diversity in America is now being recognized. But present-day education lags behind, partly because it relies to a great extent upon the written word. Therefore, cultural pluralism must get so deeply imbedded in all the reading materials of boys and girls that its values, attitudes, beliefs, cognition, and affect are learned right from the beginning and throughout their school years.

Much of the reading material now available to students still represents only the dominant culture. It needs to be completely rewritten to delete subtle biases and judgmental descriptive words that attribute such values as right and wrong, good and bad, or civilized and uncivilized to one or another set of cultural traditions.

Evaluating textbooks for such biases is a very time-consuming task. Many of the objectionable words, phrases, and illustrations are not readily detected by all teachers. We need to make this transition and achieve a more acceptable library of reading materials as quickly as possible and with maximum fairness and good judgment.[23]

Recent analyses of social studies books used in schools indicate that the great majority are still presenting a view of the world, both historically and currently, that is largely white, Anglo-Saxon, and Protestant. Since textbooks are, and will continue to be in the foreseeable future, the most universally used teaching tool, it is imperative that they be carefully evaluated not only for *what they contain,* but also for *what they imply subtly* and *what they omit.* A monograph by Marcus sets forth seven evaluative criteria:[24]

1. *Inclusion.* (Students need to read the truth about the Nazi persecution before and during World War II.)
2. *Validity.* (Statements need to present accurate, pertinent information.)
3. *Balance.* (Both sides of an issue should be presented fairly.)
4. *Comprehensiveness.* (Encourage diversity; eliminate stereotyping.)
5. *Concreteness.* (The material should be factual and objective.)
6. *Unity.* (Information about a topic should be unified, coherent, and concentrated in one place.)
7. *Realism.* (Social evils must be presented frankly and openly with students encouraged to think individualistically about better ways to solve them.)

A fifth grade social studies book asks the question: "Can you see one reason why North American Indians never had cities?"[25] It is not true, according to modern archaeology, that North American Indians never had cities. In the twelfth century a community of 30,000 people lived at Cahokia, Illinois (near present-day St. Louis).[26] The same book states a few pages later: "The man who discovered America was an Italian sailor, Christopher Columbus." Josephy[27] has suggested that perhaps nearly a million Indians were living in what is now the United

States when Columbus came to America. Another fifteen million may have lived in Mexico and Central and South America. Didn't *they* discover America?

The subtle implications of such statements are unacceptable. It behooves teachers to become critical, discerning readers. And they must help students to develop their own critical, evaluative skills so they can recognize such writing.

The Council on Interracial Books for Children has suggested some ways to analyze books for racism and sexism that may be helpful:[28]

1. Check the illustrations for stereotypes, tokenism, life styles.
2. Check the story line—relationships, measure of success, viewpoint.
3. Check the author's perspective.
4. Check the author's competency to write about this minority.
5. Check for the effect on self-image, self-esteem.
6. Check the copyright date. The minority experience is recent—late '60s and early '70s.
7. Watch for loaded words.

Similarly, Rudman raises the following pertinent questions: "How aware are we of the connotations and innuendos in the books that our children read? . . . What of the popular fantasies and novels and even works of so-called nonfiction that are rife with racist ideas? . . . How can we recognize our acts of omission?"[29]

Stereotypes   Cata analyzed children's fictional literature in which one main character was an Indian. She identified 89 verbal stereotypes used to describe North American Indian characters in 401 fictional stories for children. Eight negative stereotypes that appeared thirty or more times were: superstitious, stolid, revengeful, savage, warlike, cruel, physically dirty, and hostile.[30]

According to Klineberg, "the existence of ethnic stereotypes may play an important part in preventing the improvement of race relations on the basis of increased contact between two conflicting groups. It may result in a literal inability to see those things which do not fit into the stereotype."[31]

The following paragraph by Rogers and Muessig was characteristic of findings two decades ago:

> Too many texts are filled with slanted "facts," stereotypes, provincial and ethnocentric attitudes, and superficial, utopian discussions which skim over conditions as they actually exist today. Texts which have sections devoted to life in our United States, for example, too often portray "Americans" as white, Anglo-Protestant, white-collar, and middle class. Perusing a number of books, one gets the impression that all Americans live on wide, shady streets in clean suburban areas, occupy white Cape Cod houses, drive new automobiles, have two children (a boy and a girl, of course), and own a dog. Characters in texts have first names like Bill, Tom, and John, rather than Sid, Tony and Juan and last names like Adams, Hill, and Cook, rather than Schmidt, Podosky, and Chen.[32]

McDiarmid and Pratt, in a monograph entitled *Teaching Prejudice,* ask the serious question whether *teaching children to be prejudiced* may not be exactly what we are doing.[33] They identified six categories of people: Christians, Jews,

Moslems, blacks, Indians, and immigrants. They then asked students to select from a list of descriptive words the ones that most frequently applied to each group. The result was that Christians are devoted, Jews are a great people, Moslems are infidels, blacks are primitive, Indians are savage, and immigrants are hard working. In a study of pictorial stereotypes of Africans, Asians, and Indians, the Native Americans emerged as the least favored and were portrayed as primitive, unskilled, aggressive, and hostile.[34]

In 1973 the Manitoba Indian brotherhood evaluated a number of social studies textbooks used in sixth grade classes across Canada. They titled their monograph *The Shocking Truth About Indians in Textbooks.*[35] They quoted from a text that told sixth graders about the use of tobacco:

> Raleigh was also responsible for making tobacco fashionable in England. Tobacco is a New World plant that was not known in Europe until after the discovery of America. Sir Walter Raleigh introduced the custom of smoking to his friends, and it was not long before elegant Englishmen were puffing away as contentedly as the naked savages of North America. [p. 21]

And from another text:

> Perhaps the sailors made friends with the Indians as you would make friends with a puppy—by offering them something to eat. [p. 93]
>
> Champlain grew fond of the Indian people as one grows fond of children, and he made plans to help them. [p. 96]

Such statements demean the dignity of Indians as people. They demonstrate one of the most objectionable attitudes: that Indians are childlike, and therefore others *must decide* what is best for them and do things *for* them.

Yet another text contained these statements:

> The Pueblo Indians had even learned how to dig ditches to bring water to their fields from the nearby streams and rivers, to keep crops growing when there was no rain. It is interesting to think that this art, which is called irrigation, was already known in North America when the white man came. [p. 13]

Use of the word "even" conveys no historical information, but it certainly emphasizes a patronizing attitude toward the Indians. The whole paragraph seems to express great surprise that another group of people could possibly know about such technology before the white man arrived. Contrast the above paragraph with the following in the book by Josephy:

> The Pueblo people depended primarily on intensive agriculture with corn as the principal crop. In the west, where matrilineal clans were important social units, the women owned the crops, as well as the houses and furnishings. . . .
>
> Along the Rio Grande, in the east, Pueblos planted their crops in the river bottoms near their towns and irrigated their fields. The people also raised squash, beans, cotton, tobacco, and gourds, using wooden sticks and hoes with which to cultivate their plots. Farm work was difficult in a country with an average of only 13 inches of rain a year and the men did all the labor in the fields.[36]

It is no wonder that Mary Gloyne Byler, a member of the eastern band of Cherokees of North Carolina, after analyzing hundreds of children's books about Indians written by non-Indians, wrote the following:

There are too many books featuring painted, whooping, befeathered Indians closing in on too many forts, maliciously attacking "peaceful" settlers or simply leering menacingly from the background; too many books in which white benevolence is the only thing that saves the day for the incompetent, childlike Indian; too many stories setting forth what is "best" for the American Indian.

It is time for American publishers, schools, and libraries to take another look at the books they are offering children and seriously set out to offset some of the damage they have done. Only American Indians can tell non-Indians what it is to be Indian. There is no longer any need for non-Indian writers to "interpret" American Indians for the American Public.[37]

It is apparent that there is need for criteria by which to judge writing for American schoolchildren. The criteria might include such questions as these:

1. Is there any way the gist of what is written could deprive *anyone* of his or her human rights?
2. Does the author develop the role of American minority groups in a scholarly, factual, and effective manner?
3. Is the context a balanced treatment?
4. Is there any chance that the context can create or increase race or class hostility, national rivalries, prejudice, or religious bias?
5. Does the text adequately emphasize the pluralistic nature of our multiracial, multiethnic, and multireligious society?
6. Are all groups of people represented in varied and diverse settings?
7. When individuals are recognized, are there only white middle-class *men* or are all minority groups and women properly represented?

Evaluating Authorities and Evidence

Blough raises the question of what to do when the community disagrees with the principle the elementary teacher wishes to teach. Teachers should remember that young children are not, generally, ready to be asked to choose between "what father says" and a scientific principle in the textbook. Blough suggests that teachers may point out that scientists *search for answers*. Scientists themselves do not claim to know all the answers. Many statements in textbooks are tempered with, "It is generally believed that . . . ," "Evidence seems to show . . . ," "Some scientists think . . . ," or "Probably. . . ." Teachers can keep the conversation open with comments such as, "Everyone has a right to his or her own belief. As time goes on, most of us keep on thinking and learning, and we often change our thinking about some things."[38]

The ultimate goal of the school is to help the student find his or her own defensible position between the conformist on the one hand and the nonconformist on the other. Students will conform to the standards they accept based on careful evaluation of the situation in terms of what they have learned.

Conformity to the group without *basis in reason* implies lack of creative thinking and is the result of too much dependence on the teacher as a voice of authority or the textbook as the source of fact.

Critical reading requires all the steps in problem-solving: (1) knowing where to go to find information; (2) knowing how to select the specific information needed from various sources; and (3) knowing how to evaluate the adequacy, validity, and relevance of information. It also requires separating fact from opinion even when opinion is subtly disguised as fact, determining the author's legitimate authority and his biases, and recognizing propaganda.

Criticism, to be valid and consistent, must be based on specified criteria. Teachers and children should set up their criteria for evaluating oral reporting, storytelling, units of work, and many other activities throughout the year.

Developing critical reading abilities means (1) establishing standards of judgment; (2) developing the ability to make comparisons; (3) judging the authority and background of the source; (4) recognizing relevance and irrelevance, fact and opinion; and (5) making inferences and drawing conclusions.

Elementary schoolchildren must be provided opportunities for making judgments. They can be asked to rate each other on some performance, such as giving an oral report. Probably children should be asked to evaluate each other's work periodically. If work has been done by committees so that groups rather than individuals are being evaluated, it may be easier to keep the discussion on relative merits of the project itself rather than personalities.

Social studies projects lend themselves to such evaluation. Children may be severely critical of each other at first, and always forget to mention desirable qualities of work, but this is the method by which they eventually learn to evaluate on more objective bases. When the peer group evaluates, benefits accrue to both the judges and the judged.

Teachers are apt to feel that quiet time with each student performing individually in writing is more profitable learning time than an unstructured guided discussion. But time is well spent in class discussion of such problems as one student monopolizing class time, decisions being based on personal feelings about individuals, and arguments being proposed without supporting facts. Many adults exhibit similar behavior; possibly they might have developed better ways of solving problems if time had been given to these types of discussion in their schoolrooms.

Teaching Critical Reading

Piekarz reports asking teachers in graduate classes in reading to read a passage and construct five questions that they might ask pupils. The result: about 97 percent of all questions are of a literal nature, 2.7 percent are of an interpretive nature, and .3 percent are of an evaluative nature. She concludes:

> Students who spend 97 percent of the time answering literal questions during the twelve years of elementary and high school should expect to experience difficulty with critical reading and thinking when they reach college. Expecting otherwise is unrealistic.[39]

Teaching critical reading can begin very early and should continue throughout the child's school career.

> In intellectual development, the child is increasingly able to understand cause-effect relationships, to form generalizations, and to think logically. He makes amazingly clear distinctions between fact and fancy. When problems are within his experience, his thinking appears to be like that of an adult.[40]

Providing an environment that enhances learning is one of the teacher's primary goals. As has already been stated, the attitude of the teacher in the class sets the climate for the thinking of boys and girls.

> The teacher introduces the children to the world of thought through the kinds of rules and rituals with which she surrounds the thinking process; the kinds of content she introduces, accepts, and rejects from the children; the kinds of approaches to problem solution she encourages and sustains; the amount of freedom she allows for independent and explanatory thinking; the speed with which she closes down inquiry; the respect she shows for their fumbling, their confusion—all create for them an image of that world and a set of expectations about their own potency as learners and thinkers.[41]

Although critical reading is the most difficult of all reading skills to teach, a checklist of elements can be made. Boys and girls in the elementary school can learn to read carefully for the following:

1. Unwarranted generalizations
2. Making everything a dichotomous—either/or—situation
3. Half-truths
4. Quoting words or sentences out of context
5. Emotionally charged words
6. Sensing biases in writer's accounts

Other critical reading skills that can be taught in the developmental reading program are:

7. Investigating sources
8. Comparing and contrasting different reports
9. Searching for the author's purpose
10. Separating fact from opinion
11. Forming judgments
12. Detecting propaganda

Among the most difficult skills needed for critical reading are:

13. Determining the relevance of the material
14. Evaluating the reliability of authors
15. Examining assumptions
16. Checking data
17. Detecting inconsistencies

18. Drawing conclusions, based upon gathering of adequate information; testing possible conclusions in the light of the data; or reaching tentative conclusions subject to revision if new information is discovered.[42]

Much too much time is spent in traditional schools making children's minds act like sponges that will accept authority of parents, teachers, and textbooks without question.

The mythical "cherry tree story" can be put in proper perspective by a more mature evaluation of the character and leadership qualities of the first president.

Is the story of Lincoln's undying love for Ann Rutledge another myth? Was the story started by Lincoln's law partner, William Herndon, because he had such an active hatred for Mary Todd Lincoln and wanted to discredit her? Do the historians agree?[43]

The period of the Civil War can be used to sample and evaluate differing viewpoints. Students might find any one of the following statements in their reading. They should decide which of the contradictory statements in each of the following pairs has the most supporting evidence.

One opinion	A differing opinion
John Brown was insane.	John Brown was a great abolitionist.
The South had superior leadership.	The South was led by unrealistic cavaliers.
The North did not know what it was fighting for—therefore there were many desertions and much lack of interest.	The North was fighting a moral battle to free the U.S. from slavery.
The *Merrimac* was victorious!	The *Monitor* was victorious in the famous sea battle of the ironclads.
The South did not lose, she simply stopped fighting.	The North won the Civil War.

In summary, all of the following kinds of evaluation are important in critical reading.[44]

1. Identifying and selecting material directly relevant to a given topic.
2. Selecting material appropriate for a particular assignment, audience, or occasion.
3. Distinguishing fact from opinion; sense from nonsense.
4. Comparing the ideas in different sources of information; finding contradictions to a given point of view.
5. Considering, and accepting or rejecting, new ideas or information in light of previous knowledge.
6. Sensing biases in an author's point of view.
7. Identifying and rejecting gross overstatements and dogmatic statements with unfounded claims.

From Theory to Practice 12.3
Recognizing Bias, Prejudice, Racism, and Sexism

On this task, you are asked to work with a partner.

Select three textbooks for elementary school students. Social studies and science books might be appropriate; grade level is not significant. It is suggested that the books be intended for use with different ages or grades.

Go through the books carefully together, looking for examples of bias, prejudice, racism, and sexism. Examine pictures as well as text. Make a chart of the examples you find. The organization of your visual presentation will depend on the information you find to present.

Bring it to your class to share with others. Add to your experience by examining their findings also.

Summary

Reading with competence in the content fields demands that the reader acquire study skills so that he or she can complete assignments without undue frustration. To achieve these ends, the reader must:

1. Grasp an overview of the material presented.
2. Know how to study.
3. Recognize how specific strategies or writing patterns can be used in studying different kinds of materials.
4. Practice critical reading skills, including the recognition of author bias or prejudice and propaganda.

For Further Reading

Adams, Abby, Douglas Carnine, and Russell Gersten. "Instructional Strategies for Studying Content Area Texts in the Intermediate Grades." *Reading Research Quarterly* 18 (No. 1, 1982): 27–55.

Burmeister, Lou E. *Reading Strategies for Middle and Secondary School Teaching,* 2d ed. Reading, Mass.: Addison-Wesley, 1978.

Cleary, Donna McKee. *Thinking Thursdays.* Newark, Del.: International Reading Assn., 1978.

Earle, Richard A. *Teaching Reading and Mathematics.* Newark, Del.: International Reading Assn., 1976.

Gentile, Lance M. *Using Sports and Physical Education to Strengthen Reading Skills.* Newark, Del.: International Reading Assn., 1980.

Lehr, Fran. "Content Area Reading Instruction in the Elementary School." *The Reading Teacher* 33 (April 1980): 888–91.

Lundstrum, John, and Bob L. Taylor. *Teaching Reading in the Social Studies.* Newark, Del.: International Reading Assn., and Boulder, Colo.: ERIC Clearinghouse for the Social Studies, 1978.

McDiarmid, Garnet, and David Pratt. *Teaching Prejudice.* Toronto: Ontario Institute for Studies in Education, 1972.

Manitoba Indian Brotherhood. *The Shocking Truth About Indians in Textbooks.* Winnipeg: Manitoba Indian Brotherhood, 1974.

Marcus, Lloyd. *The Treatment of Minorities in Secondary School Textbooks.* New York: Anti-Defamation League of B'nai B'rith, 1963.

Norton, Donna. "A Web of Interest." *Language Arts* 54 (November/December 1977): 928–32.

O'Mara, Deborah. "The Process of Reading Mathematics." *Journal of Reading* 25 (October 1981): 22–30.

Thelen, Judith. *Improving Reading in Science.* Newark, Del.: International Reading Assn., 1976.

Thomas, Keith. "The Directed Inquiry Activity: An Instructional Procedure for Content Reading." *Reading Improvement* 15 (Summer 1978): 134–40.

Tonjes, Marian J., and Miles V. Zintz. *Teaching Reading/Thinking/Study Skills in Content Classrooms.* Dubuque, Iowa: Wm. C. Brown, 1981.

Notes

1. John G. Navarra and Joseph Zafforoni, "Travel Beyond the Earth," in *The Young Scientist: His Predictions and Tests* pp. 338–72 (New York: Harper & Row, 1971).
2. Edward L. Thorndike, "Reading as Reasoning: A Study of Mistakes in Paragraph Reading," *Journal of Educational Psychology* 8 (June 1917): 323.
3. Richard T. Vacca, "Readiness to Read Content Area Assignments," *The Journal of Reading* 20 (February 1977): 387–92.
4. Richard A. Earle, *Teaching Reading and Mathematics* (Newark, Del.: International Reading Assn., 1976), p. 34.
5. T. Stevenson Hansell, "Increasing Understanding in Content Reading," *Journal of Reading* 19 (January 1976): 307–11.
6. Francis P. Robinson, *Effective Reading* (New York: Harper and Bros., 1962), p. 31.
7. Robinson, *Effective Reading,* p. 31; Ellen Lamar Thomas and H. Alan Robinson, *Improving Reading in Every Class* (Boston: Allyn & Bacon, 1972), p. 70.
8. Leo Fay, "Reading Study Skills: Math and Science," in *Reading and Inquiry,* ed. J. A. Figurel (Newark, Del.: International Reading Assn., 1965), pp. 92–94.
9. Lou E. Burmeister, *Reading Strategies for Secondary School Teachers* (Reading, Mass.: Addison-Wesley, 1974), pp. 163–79.
10. Herman and Nina Schneider, *Science in Our World,* 4th ed. (Lexington, Mass.: D. C. Heath, 1973), p. 20.
11. Ibid., p. 332.
12. Ibid., p. 135.
13. *Social Studies Concepts and Values,* Grade 5 (New York: Harcourt Brace Jovanovich), p. 241.
14. Words by Tom Blackburn. Copyright 1954 by Walt Disney Music Company, Glendale, Calif. Used by permission.
15. Will Durant, *The Story of Philosophy* (New York: Pocket Books, 1953), p. 6.
16. Robert M. Hutchins, *The Conflict in Education* (New York: Harper and Bros., 1953), p. 96.

17. Paul Woodring, *A Fourth of a Nation* (New York: McGraw-Hill, 1957), p. 4.
18. Ruth K. Flamond, "Critical Reading," in *New Perspectives in Reading Instruction,* ed. Albert J. Mazurkiewicz (New York: Pitman, 1964), p. 256.
19. Walter T. Petty, "Critical Reading in the Primary Grades," *Education Digest* 22 (October 1956): 42–43.
20. Anne S. McKillop, *The Relationship Between the Reader's Attitude and Certain Types of Reading Responses* (New York: Teachers College Press, 1952).
21. Jules Henry, *Culture Against Man,* chapter 3 (New York: Random House, 1963).
22. Ibid., pp. 75–76.
23. Paula Grinnell (chairperson, Textbook Committee, Dallas Chapter, The American Jewish Committee, Southwest Office, 1809 Tower Bldg., Dallas, Texas 75201), "A Study of Racial Bias in Social Studies Textbooks," n.d.
24. Lloyd Marcus, *The Treatment of Minorities in Secondary School Textbooks* (New York: Anti-Defamation League of B'nai B'rith, 1963), p. 9.
25. Gussie M. Robinson, *Man and Society* (Morristown, N.J.: Silver Burdett, 1972), pp. 37, 48.
26. George E. Stuart, "Who Were the Moundbuilders?" *National Geographic* 142 (December 1972): 789.
27. Alvin M. Josephy, Jr., *The Indian Heritage of America* (New York: Bantam Books, 1968), pp. 50–51.
28. Council on Interracial Books for Children (1841 Broadway, New York, N.Y. 10023), "Ten Quick Ways to Analyze Books for Racism and Sexism," *The Bulletin* 5 (March 1974): 1, 6.
29. Masha K. Rudman, *Children's Literature: An Issues Approach* (Lexington, Mass.: D.C. Heath, 1976), pp. 173–74.
30. Juanita O. Cata, "The Portrait of American Indians in Children's Fictional Literature" (Doctoral dissertation, University of New Mexico, 1977), p. 67.
31. Otto Klineberg, *Social Psychology* (New York: Henry Holt, 1954), p. 489.
32. Vincent R. Rogers and Raymond H. Muessig, "Needed: A Revolution in the Textbook Industry," *The Social Studies* 54 (October 1963): 169.
33. Garnet McDiarmid and David Pratt, *Teaching Prejudice* (Toronto: Ontario Institute for Studies in Education, 1972).
34. Cited in Verna J. Kirkness, "Prejudice About Indians in Textbooks," *The Journal of Reading* 20 (April 1977): 597.
35. The Manitoba Indian Brotherhood, comp., *The Shocking Truth About Indians in Textbooks* (Winnipeg: The Manitoba Indian Brotherhood, 1974).
36. Alvin M. Josephy, Jr., *The Indian Heritage of America* (New York: Knopf, 1971), pp. 163–64.
37. Mary Gloyne Byler, *American Indian Authors for Young Readers, A Selected Bibliography* (432 Park Ave., New York, N.Y. 10016: Association on American Indian Affairs, 1973), pp. 5, 11.
38. Glenn O. Blough, Julius Schwartz, and Albert J. Huggett, *Elementary School Science and How to Teach It,* rev. ed. (New York: Holt, Rinehart and Winston, 1958), pp. 77–78.
39. Josephine Piekarz Ives, "The Improvement of Critical Reading Skills," in *Problem Areas in Reading—Some Observations and Recommendations,* ed. Coleman Morrison (Providence, R.I.: Oxford Press, 1966), p. 56.

40. Nelson B. Henry, ed. *Development In and Through Reading,* 60th Yearbook, National Society for the Study of Education, Part I (Chicago: University of Chicago Press, 1961), p. 288.

41. Edna Shapiro, "Study of Children Through Observation of Classroom Behavior," in *Theory and Research in Teaching,* ed. Arno A. Bellack (New York: Bureau of Publications, Teachers College, 1963), p. 101.

42. Dorothy Fraser and Edith West, *Social Studies in Secondary Schools* (New York: Ronald Press, 1961), pp. 222–27.

43. William Herndon, *Life of Lincoln* (Fine Editions Press, 1949), p. 106; Ruth P. Randall, *Lincoln's Sons* (Boston: Little, Brown, 1955), p. 242; Benjamin P. Thomas, *Abraham Lincoln* (New York: Knopf, 1952), p. 51.

44. The reader may also wish to read: Donald D. Durrell, *Improving Reading Instruction* (New York: Harcourt, Brace and World, 1956), pp. 305ff; Albert J. Harris, *How to Increase Reading Ability,* 5th ed. (New York: Longman, Green, 1970), p. 431ff.

Oral Reading

A Cognitive Map: Oral Reading

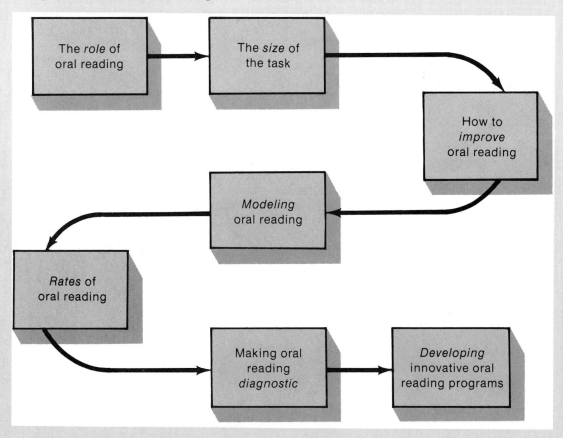

13

Guide Questions

1. Oral and silent reading are like two sides of a coin. What is the relationship between these two types of reading?

2. What factors contribute to a good oral reading experience?

3. What values are there in teachers reading to children?

4. What can one learn about children's reading by listening to them read individually?

Terminology

context reader

modeling oral reading

oral reading situation

predictable books

rate of reading

reader's theater

word-by-word reader

Prior to 1930 the emphasis in teaching children to read was largely on "good oral reading." Correct enunciation and pronunciation and proper inflection, emphasis, and feeling tone were primary goals. McCutchen stressed oral reading skill in the preface of his fourth reader, published in 1883, as follows:

> A critic of the day has observed that "in the great Republic of North America reading aloud is justly considered to be one of the most important elements of a child's education."
>
> Reading aloud, if properly directed, serves a double purpose: it tends to correct errors in articulation and pronunciation, and to break up certain careless habits of speech; and it also enables the teacher to see whether the pupil *comprehends* what he is reading.
>
> It is the business of the teacher to insure exactness in articulation and pronunciation purely by the force of example; the class thus become mere imitators of a good model. . . . It is only when the meaning is too abstruse for the pupil, or when it is desirable to give examples of modulation or style for those pupils who rarely hear good reading, that the teacher may read for the class and let them imitate his emphasis, his pauses, his inflections, as well as his articulation and pronunciation.[1]

In 1911 Baldwin and Bender were emphasizing oral reading skill as follows:

> The design of this series of School Readers is to help children to acquire the art and the habit of reading so well as to give pleasure not only to themselves, but also to those who listen to them. The selections have been chosen and arranged with strict reference to the capabilities and tastes of the pupils who are to read them, thus making every exercise in oral reading both easy and enjoyable as well as instructive.
>
> The notes under the head of "Expression," which follow many of the lessons, are intended to assist in securing correctness of pronunciation and enunciation, a clear understanding of what is being read, and the intelligible and pleasing oral rendering of the printed page. These notes should be carefully studied by both teacher and pupils.[2]

By 1930 emphasis was changing. Silent reading, comprehension, and study skills were being emphasized.

At the present time some teachers devote too much class time to oral reading under poor conditions.[3] Also, many teachers could do more effective *teaching* of oral reading. Ability to read aloud well is, after all, often necessary in adult life. It is still important to be able to read aloud—for such purposes as reading the minutes of a meeting, reading stories to one's children, or participating in group reading in church or social gatherings.

It is regrettable but true that oral reading can be one of the most abused aspects of the reading program. Some teachers ask children to read by turns just so everyone in the group reads one page. When such reading serves no other purpose, the result is fruitless for everyone. Children should have an opportunity to read silently any material they are expected to later read orally, but a group should not be asked to sit and listen quietly while one child reads something they have all already read and discussed. With new material, taking turns around the group is sure to frustrate the fast readers, who are "sneaking" ahead, and to embarrass the slow readers, who cannot read fluently or pronounce all the words. An authoritarian teacher who demands that all the class listen quietly while one person struggles through a paragraph is teaching many negative values and few, if any, positive ones.

The Role of Oral Reading

There seems to have been for the past few years, and continues to be today, considerable controversy about the place of oral reading in the reading program. This controversy is due in part to some people's belief that if children are put in an oral reading situation in which they do not do well, the result will be very damaging to their personalities. And, of course, if they are expected to read at their frustration level all the time, it will do such damage. Another argument in the controversy goes as follows: People do no oral reading outside the school setting—that is, all their outside reading will be silent reading; therefore, they should do only silent reading in school. These two arguments have some validity.

Valid criticisms can be leveled against oral reading in situations that are *not oral reading situations.* (1) If children do not have a purpose for reading or do not understand the purpose; if they are given too little help on technical difficulties prior to oral reading; if a selection is not suitable for audience reading because of either type of material or level of difficulty for the reader, then the oral reading will be neither helpful to the reader nor interesting to the listeners. (2) Situations in which all the people in the audience have copies of the material that the child is reading are *not* audience situations. (3) Many teachers now evidence little interest in oral reading. Teachers themselves may be deficient in oral reading ability. Oral reading that the child does under such adverse conditions as those described here will not constitute a worthwhile experience for him or her.

These criticisms can be overcome by teachers who acknowledge a legitimate place for oral reading in the total reading program for all children. Oral reading has a place for any student who is reading at a *primary reading level,* no matter what the grade placement may be. First of all, oral reading is more like talking, something the child does all day long in and out of school. When children begin a formal reading program in first grade, they may feel that it is less strange if it continues to be a talking kind of language. In first grade, the teacher can expect to commit about 50 percent of the time to oral reading and 50 percent to silent reading. From the beginning of formal reading through the first grade, the teacher will have reading groups first read silently whatever story they are learning how to read. They will reread most of these stories orally during the first year. While the teacher will set up new purposes for the child for the second reading, one of *the teacher's purposes* is to provide the child reading practice on the basic sight vocabulary.

Oral reading, when it is effective, gives students opportunity to entertain others. The child's self-confidence is strengthened too when he or she reads well to an appreciative audience. For the alert teacher, the child's oral reading gives an opportunity to evaluate the quality of the reading performance.

In second grade, children reading at second grade reader level should have more time for silent reading and less time for oral. Perhaps those children now able to do independent reading should spend two-thirds of their reading time on silent reading and one-third on oral. This provides time for all children to have an opportunity to read aloud. After children establish an independent third grade reader level, the amount of time spent on oral reading is sure to decrease. Probably not more than 20 percent of the time in developmental reading classes above third grade level will be given to oral reading. This should include the teacher's evaluation of reading in all subjects, not just in the reading class itself.

Children should have an opportunity to entertain others by their reading. But when are others entertained? Not when the reading is the wrong kind of material or the reader cannot read it well. When do children get satisfaction and security in oral expression? Only when they express themselves reasonably well. Children can get satisfaction through group participation only when giving something that the group anticipates or understands. Children get effective speech practice only when they have poise, self-confidence, and the feeling that they are doing a good job.

The following poems can serve these objectives for many children, but probably not *all* the children in a group.

Mice

I think mice
Are rather nice.

Their tails are long,
Their faces small,
They haven't any
Chins at all.
Their ears are pink,
Their teeth are white,
They run about
The house at night.

They nibble things
They shouldn't touch
And no one seems
To like them much.

But *I* think mice
Are nice.

     Rose Fyleman[4]

Galoshes

Susie's galoshes
Make splishes and sploshes
And slooshes and sloshes,
As Susie steps slowly
Along in the slush.
They stamp and they tramp
On the ice and concrete,

They get stuck in the muck in the mud;
But Susie likes much best to hear

The slippery slush
As it slooshes and sloshes,
And splishes and sploshes,
All round her galoshes.

Rhoda Bacmeister[5]

Eletelephony

Once there was an elephant,
Who tried to use the telephant—
No, No, I mean an elephone
Who tried to use the telephone—
(Dear me, I am not certain quite,
That even now I've got it right.)

Howe'er it was, he got his trunk
Entangled in the telephunk;
The more he tried to get it free,
The louder buzzed the telephee—
(I fear I'd better drop the song
Of elephop and telefong!)

Laura Elizabeth Richards[6]

Arbuthnot[7] suggests that the poem "Where's Mary?" be called a study in irritability. The woman searching for Mary gets angrier with each succeeding line.

Where's Mary?

Is Mary in the dairy?
Is Mary on the stair?
What? Mary's in the garden?
What is she doing there?
Has she made the butter yet?
Has she made the beds?
Has she topped the gooseberries
And taken off their heads?
Has she the potatoes peeled?
Has she done the grate?
Are the new green peas all shelled?
It is getting late!
What! She hasn't done a thing?
Here's a nice to-do!
Mary has a dozen jobs
And hasn't finished two.
Well, here IS a nice to-do!
Well, upon my word!
She's sitting on the garden bench
Listening to a bird!

Ivy O. Eastwick[8]

From Theory to Practice 13.1
Reading Orally with Children

Meet with three to five children individually to select a story or poem each would like to read to other girls and boys. Arrange for each child to practice his or her choice of reading material until it is ready to be shared. Suggest that if a story is chosen, it should be rather short, since several stories will be read.

At a convenient time, gather the children together to share their stories. Conduct the activity as an enjoyable time of reading and discussing whatever is read. You may want to either begin or end the session with a story or poem of your own.

During the oral reading session, you will want to be an active observer as well as participant. Among behaviors and events to observe might be:

1. How does the reader use eye contact, gestures, voice, or expression to convey meaning?
2. What does the reader do if a miscue causes loss of meaning? How do the listeners react to loss of meaning?
3. How do children alternate listener/reader roles?
4. How do the children include you in the experience?
5. How does the reader handle the book being read from?
6. How do the children respond in follow-up discussion—with questions, comments, evaluation, no response?

Immediately after the children leave, record as many details and impressions of the experience as possible. Share these with your class and instructor.

Arbuthnot has done as much as any other teacher of children's literature to emphasize the effective use of oral reading to encourage boys and girls to read freely from the great storehouse of well-written children's books available to them today.

Certainly reading aloud is the way to introduce children to exceptional books that they might not choose for themselves or might not enjoy without this added lift of family enjoyment and the reader's enthusiasm. *The Wind in the Willows, The Children of Greene Knowe, The Gammage Cup, Rifles for Watie, Smoky* . . . just a sampling of the choice books. . . . To hear *Penn* or *Johnny Tremain* beautifully read is a literary treat; and to read *Winnie-the-Pooh* silently, in solitude, isn't half the fun as to read it aloud or to listen to it read aloud.[9]

In summary, the role of oral reading in the reading program can easily be justified. Teachers recognize that oral reading is more difficult than silent reading. In order to be effective, it not only presupposes the ability to understand and appreciate the selections that one reads, but also involves the attitudes and abilities for portraying these ideas to other people.

The Size of the Oral Reading Task

Children need the opportunity to do a great deal of oral reading until they have established an independent reading level of second grade or above. Of course, this category would include children in the first grade, most of the children in the second grade, many children in the third grade, and also some in the fourth, fifth and sixth grades.

The "real-life" purpose of reading aloud to others is to convey information to them, to entertain them, or to share a good story that they do not have. Under such circumstances, then, the audience being read to will not have copies of the material in their hands. Similarly, oral reading is best used in the classroom, not for its own sake, but, rather, for achieving other purposes. Some of these might be as follows:

1. Giving a report, either individual or committee.
2. Giving specific directions to be followed, sharing announcements of interest to the group, or sharing special items of interest.
3. Trying to prove a point, settle an argument, or give evidence of a different point of view.
4. Sharing the many aspects of recreational reading.

For good oral reading the reader must be prepared beforehand. This means that the reader has help with technical difficulties in the reading, understands the content of the passage very well, and can pronounce all the words. A child may practice reading orally before his or her own reading group.

The selection to be read should lend itself to the oral reading situation. If it will not generate interest, if it will not easily appeal to the listeners, the teacher may suggest other content to be read.

Children enjoy sharing their reading when they have confidence in their ability to read well and they find the story interesting. This sharing an enjoyable experience has much affective value for boys and girls. Oral reading also makes it possible for the teacher to enjoy with the reading group the most interesting parts of stories they have read.

For several reasons, it is important that the teacher hear each child read orally on occasion during the school year. By evaluating the kinds of errors a child makes in reading—word recognition errors, punctuation errors, omissions and insertions, failure to use context clues, or inability to attack unfamiliar words—the teacher can arrange teaching emphasis to help the child. For the child in trouble, the teacher can interject questions, stop the reading to discuss or clarify a point, take turns reading pages or paragraphs, and generally lend encouragement. The teacher can promote the child's optimal growth by helping the child build confidence.

Ongoing evaluation also has diagnostic value in helping the teacher appraise pupil growth throughout the year. Until children have established at least a fluent second grade level of reading, the teacher needs a careful check on how accurately they read. Some kind of checklist that could be easily kept up to date would be helpful for recording evaluative impressions of each child's oral reading. The teacher can develop with the children criteria for improvement in abilities to read well for others. The two conditions under which the child reads orally should be distinguished: (1) reading *at sight* (without first reading silently), as in the informal reading inventory; and (2) reading something aloud that the child has had an opportunity to read silently first.

Improving Oral Reading

Reading aloud to an audience requires, first, a purpose that is meaningful to the listeners and to the child who is doing the reading. Ideally, the reader shares information that the members of the audience want and do not already have, and they do not have a copy of whatever is being read to them.

Second, the selection read should be appropriate as well as interesting for an audience. It should be on the level of difficulty that the child can handle as his independent or instructional level of reading.

Third, adequate preparation is important. That usually involves preliminary silent reading with some attention to vocabulary difficulties, followed by oral reading practice, before the selection is read to the entire class.

If these conditions are present, the reading can then be analyzed for the following qualities:

1. Adequate phrasing.
2. Voice modulated to comfortable speech.
3. Opening the mouth so enunciation is clear.

4. Recognizing punctuation marks.
5. Eliminating distracting mannerisms.
6. Flexible use of stress, intonation, and pitch appropriate to the content of the story being read.
7. Developing a comfortable stance or sitting position.
8. Developing the ability to enjoy the story with the audience.

Children need guidance in these details to become satisfactory oral readers. Tape recorders can be very useful tools.

Greer recommends the following procedure:

> Ask the student to read a few paragraphs from the *Gilmore Oral Reading Test* and then analyze the tape with him. Together, compile a list of items which he should check in his oral reading. Paste this check list in the front of his notebook (so it will not be lost) and he can use the list to check subsequent recordings of oral reading.
>
> Save the original tape and let him listen when he likes. After a while he forgets about this tape but continues oral practice. Then near the end of the semester the teacher can bring out the first tape for comparison with his present reading.
>
> In sixth grade, I've had some really excellent results in oral reading improvement with this technique. An advantage is that the child can take care of much of the practice on his own because he knows how to operate the tape recorder.[10]

Use of tape recorders in classrooms makes it possible for children to record their oral reading, to practice a passage under strong motivation, and to prepare tapes of their best reading for the teacher to save. When holding parent-teacher conferences, the teacher can let the parent listen to a sample of the child's oral reading.

The contribution oral reading can make to personality development will reveal itself in clear speech, self-confidence, poise, and an in-group feeling that results from contributing to the pleasure of a group.

Modeling Oral Reading

Teachers are urged to read aloud to the boys and girls in their classes. If they need to improve their oral reading ability, they should practice first. If they read well, they should read something every day to the children. There are many good reasons. There is a direct relationship between reading aloud to children and the children's own reading performance, their language development, and growth of their reading interests.[11] Reading to young children both acquaints them with the syntactic patterns encountered in book language and exposes them to a wide vocabulary, thereby increasing their own repertoire of words.[12]

Listening to good oral reading is not only a pleasant experience, it provides opportunity for the listeners to enlarge their acquaintance with literature and it motivates individuals to read for themselves. Too many parents neglect the opportunity to make reading to their children an intellectually stimulating activity that they can enjoy together.

Lamme developed a "Reading-Aloud-to-Children Scale" to analyze video-tapes of teachers reading aloud to children. These are some of the elements she identified as important.[13]

1. Involving the child in the reading (the most influential item).
2. Amount of eye contact between reader and audience.
3. Reading with good expression.
4. Reader's voice showing pleasing variety in pitch and volume.
5. Reader pointing to pictures and words in the books.
6. Familiarity with a story that increases the reader's ability to make it interesting to others.
7. Selection of appropriate books, with size and quality of illustrations two important criteria.
8. Grouping the children so all can see the pictures and hear the story.
9. Highlighting rhyming elements, unusual words, or repetitive refrains.

Larson has suggested a "reader's theater" as an innovative technique for improving oral reading in the classroom. She defines a reader's theater as a medium in which two or more oral interpreters cause an audience to experience literature. Of course, the passages read need to be primarily dialogue. The basic characteristics of such a theater are: (1) few props; (2) projecting the mood by voice, restrained gestures, and facial expressions; (3) a narrator who speaks to the audience and unites characters and audience; (4) each reader has a copy of the script; and (5) developing a close relationship between the performers and the audience.[14]

Rate of Oral Reading

The average oral reader who enunciates clearly is probably reading at a rate of between 150 and 170 words per minute. This is about as fast as oral reading will be done. By third or fourth grade, the child should begin to perform more rapidly in silent reading than oral. By the end of the sixth grade, the child should have developed a silent reading rate about double his or her oral reading rate.

Price and Stroud reviewed investigations of children's oral reading and concluded that there was little, if any, evidence to show that oral reading has much effect on silent reading rate.[15] Teachers have two distinct problems: the teaching of silent reading skills on the one hand, and the teaching of oral reading skills on the other. The way to develop good oral reading is to practice reading orally; the way to improve silent reading is to practice reading silently and to work on the necessary skills.

However, effective oral reading habits take time to develop. That time should not be allowed to conflict with the time necessary for developing competent silent reading abilities.

Using Oral Reading As a Diagnostic Tool

Oral reading practice is very important in helping the poor reader establish a level of fluency in reading. Children whose reading ability is limited may never have enjoyed silent reading as a means of acquiring new ideas. Such children must be convinced that reading can be fun and can be a revealing, informative way to learn. It will be helpful for poor readers to have some lessons read to them. Also, interesting books with a low-level vocabulary load are useful to help such children strengthen their reading power because they motivate them to read more. The teacher helps make the reading pleasurable and rewarding by enjoying with the child the point of an interesting, easy story that he does read.

If the child has difficulty giving his attention to the job of reading, the teacher can interject questions or stop to discuss points in the story or lend ego support with encouraging remarks. As the reader's skill in the mechanics of reading improves, less support is needed from the teacher. Poor readers may have developed poor speech habits because they cannot read. If so, they need help in general speech improvement as they gain confidence and begin making reading progress. They may need help with several components of reading: accurate phrasing; modulating the voice to a comfortable level; opening the mouth sufficiently for clear enunciation; putting zest and confidence into the reading; recognizing punctuation marks; eliminating distracting mannerisms developed in the period of frustration about reading; and getting inflection into character parts.

The Word-by-Word Reader	Oral reading allows the teacher to follow the child's reading word by word, syllable by syllable, to find out exactly what kinds of errors are being made. Two common problems in oral reading are word-by-word reading and "guessing-in-context" reading. In word-by-word reading, word-callers plod along slowly, tending to make a noticeable pause after each word. When they do attempt to phrase the reading, the wrong words may be grouped together or punctuation marks may be disregarded or misinterpreted. Keeping the place with a finger is a common practice of word-by-word readers. Children who are word-by-word readers can be helped by being given easier material so they will have to think less about how they read and more about what they read. Thus they will improve memory of the details in what they are reading, and understanding should be somewhat better.

The Context Reader	Context readers, in contrast to word-callers, may sound fluent but be inaccurate in what they are trying to read. They may skip over words, add words, or substitute one word for another. They may be unable to attack any words not already in their sight vocabulary except as they guess at them from context.

Some examples will show the typical kind of reading the context reader does. A sentence may read, *The little rabbit went down the road.* The context reader, studying the picture at the top of the page and then looking at the words in the sentence, may say, *The little bunny hopped down the lane.* The idea is correct, but three basic words in the sentence have been changed. Or a sentence may read, *Behind the band came a man on a big elephant.* But the context reader reads, *After the bandwagon went, a man came by on an elephant.*

Children who are context readers probably need easy material to read for practice. Then their attention should be directed to word-attack skills and to phonic and structural analysis. They should also be encouraged to read with complete accuracy for part of the lesson. The teacher could say, for example, "Now, on the next page I'm going to watch to see if you pronounce every word exactly as it is in the story." Such a case was a sixth grade boy who was reading an easy second grade reader and making several errors. At the end of a page, the teacher said to him, "You are getting the idea across to me, and that is the important thing. But since we are reading an easy book this morning, let's just reread these two pages and be sure we read completely accurately." Without much difficulty, this boy was able to concentrate both on the story, which was elementary, and on the mechanics of how he was reading. He was able to pay more attention to how he was reading and soon stopped reconstructing the sentence the way he thought it ought to be or the way he thought it probably was according to the picture.

A good reader knows how to use context and visual clues, as well as word-attack skills and phonic and structural analysis. A poor reader is apt to have only the visual method of attack, and may often use it incorrectly.

The classroom teacher should keep records such as are suggested in chapter 4 for the informal reading inventory in order to help children analyze specific faults so they can be addressed directly.

Teachers should also become skilled in using a marking technique such as is suggested for administering the informal reading inventory. Then any oral reading the student does—not just in the reading class but in all subjects of the school curriculum—can be quickly marked and scored to determine how it relates to the student's instructional and frustration reading levels.

Developing Innovative Oral Reading Programs

Teachers of young children must be alert to different types of materials being made available to them each year. While only two are mentioned here, several publishers are producing programs that emphasize interesting ways to learn language and to understand the relationships between its oral and written forms. *The Sounds of Language*[16] by Bill Martin, Jr., for instance, is a set of little books that uses colorful illustrations and graphic design to show word, phrase, and sentence patterns as meaningful equivalents of oral language. The child can either hear the teacher read the story first or listen to a phonograph record of the story that includes signals telling him when to turn the pages. Then he may relisten and help tell the story. Finally, he can read the story for himself. Such materials are excellent supplements for a classroom interest center designed to build positive attitudes toward reading. *The World of Language*[17] by Muriel Crosby stimulates oral language for young children through poems, stories, and plays with such concepts as rhyme, imagery, mood, and human interaction. Interwoven is considerable emphasis on self-concept and positive attitudes toward self and others. Such oral language stimulation provides for one of children's very important needs. Some techniques are included in this volume in chapter 5, "Assessment of Prereading Skills" (see the section on "Language and Concept Development").

Some teachers or schools will elect to create oral reading opportunities in ways that do not require commercial materials. Older children may be recruited to read to younger children; older boys and girls may make tapes of younger children's favorite books to build a listening library. Indeed, younger children may participate in the library building activity. Some schools encourage children to read stories and poems (often their own) over the intercom system at selected times. Children, instead of adults, may read the daily announcements to all classrooms. From time to time, oral read-a-thons may be organized.

Within classrooms, teachers may set aside time each day for one or more children to read to the class. Reading to inform or entertain others is stressed.

Teachers of young children may find that "predictable books" are useful materials for encouraging oral reading.[18] These books are simply library books that are written in such a way that students can predict quite accurately what the author is saying. These books allow children to make an easy and early start in reading and lend themselves well to oral reading, since the strain of word identification is eased greatly. A collection of these books in the primary classroom is highly recommended.

Summary

The major purposes of oral reading are (1) to entertain; (2) to give personal enjoyment and satisfaction; (3) to encourage effective group participation; (4) to provide effective practice for speech improvement; and (5) to provide for the teacher a diagnostic measure of the strengths and weaknesses in children's oral reading abilities.

Other important ideas discussed in the chapter included (1) criteria of what constitutes an oral reading (audience) situation; (2) the need for teachers to be able to read well orally; (3) the use of oral reading practice to improve word-recognition skills of poor readers; (4) the use of the tape recorder to allow children to practice oral reading independently; (5) the importance of the teacher understanding the *child's purpose* in oral reading as well as the teacher's purpose; and (6) the use of oral reading to open the doors to the great exciting world of children's literature for all boys and girls.

For Further Reading

Aulls, Mark W. *Developmental and Remedial Reading in the Middle Grades,* pp. 234–52. Boston: Allyn & Bacon, 1978.

Cramer, Ronald L. "Reading to Children: Why and How." *The Reading Teacher* 29 (February 1975): 460–63.

Dallmann, Martha, et al. "Oral Reading" and "Developing Skill in Oral Reading." In *The Teaching of Reading,* 6th ed. pp. 209–20, 221–43. New York: Holt, Rinehart and Winston, 1982.

Harris, Albert J., and Edward R. Sipay. "How to Interpret Oral Reading" and "Increasing the Rate of Reading." In *How to Increase Reading Ability,* 7th ed., pp. 246–50, 551–81. New York: Longman, 1980.

Janney, Kay Print. "Introducing Oral Interpretation in Elementary School." *The Reading Teacher* 33 (February 1980): 544–47.

O'Brien, David. "Monitoring Oral Reading." *The Reading Teacher* 34 (April 1981): 775–79.

Rhodes, Lynn K. "I Can Read! Predictable Books As Resources for Reading and Writing Instruction." *The Reading Teacher* 34 (February 1981): 511–18.

Smith, Nila Banton, and H. Alan Robinson. "Developing Fluency and Flexibility." In *Reading Instruction for Today's Children,* 2d ed., pp. 239–61. Englewood Cliffs, N.J.: Prentice-Hall, 1980.

Taylor, Nancy E., and Ulla Connor. "Silent vs. Oral Reading: The Rational Instructional Use of Both Processes." *The Reading Teacher* 35 (January 1982): 440–43.

Notes

1. Samuel McCutchen, ed., *The Fourth Reader* (Philadelphia: E. H. Butler, 1883), pp. 7, 8, 10.
2. James Baldwin and Ida C. Bender, *Reading with Expression: Second Reader* (New York: American Book Company, 1911), pp. 5, 6.
3. Sarah W. Wildebush, "Oral Reading Today," *The Reading Teacher* 18 (November 1964): 139. Wildebush states that many precious hours are being "consumed in the round robin of continuous oral reading."
4. "Mice" copyright © 1931, 1932 by Doubleday & Company, Inc., from *Fifty-One New Nursery Rhymes* by Rose Fyleman. Reprinted by permission of the publisher.

5. From *Stories to Begin On* by Rhoda W. Bacmeister. Copyright © 1940 by E. P. Dutton. Copyright renewal 1968 by Rhoda W. Bacmeister. Reprinted by permission of the publisher, E. P. Dutton, Inc.

6. From Laura E. Richards, *Tirra Lirra* (Boston: Little, Brown, 1935). Reprinted by permission of the publisher.

7. May Hill Arbuthnot, *The Anthology of Children's Literature: Book I, Time for Poetry* (Chicago: Scott, Foresman, 1952), p. 8.

8. From *Fairies and Suchlike* by Ivy O. Eastwick. Copyright © 1946 by E.P. Dutton. Copyright renewal 1974 by Ivy Olive Eastwick. Reprinted by permission of the publisher, E.P. Dutton, Inc.

9. May Hill Arbuthnot, *Children and Books,* 3d ed. (Chicago: Scott, Foresman, 1964), pp. 647–48.

10. Contribution in a university class, cited by Margaret Greer, Assoc. Prof. of Education, University of Alaska, Anchorage.

11. Sandra McCormick, "Should You Read Aloud to Your Children?" *Language Arts* 54 (1977): 143.

12. Sandra McCormick, "Choosing Books to Read to Preschool Children," *Language Arts* 54 (1977): 545. *See also* Bernard A. Faller Jr., "The Basic Basic: Getting Kids to Read," *Learning* 6 (1978): 100–101.

13. Linda Leonard Lamme, "Reading Aloud to Young Children," *Language Arts* 53 (1976): 886–87.

14. Martha L. Larson, "Reader's Theatre: New Vitality for Oral Reading," *The Reading Teacher* 29 (1976): 359–60.

15. Helen Price and James B. Stroud, "Note on Oral Reading," *Quarterly Journal of Speech* 31 (1945): 340–43.

16. Bill Martin, Jr., *The Sounds of Language* (New York: Holt, Rinehart and Winston, 1967).

17. Muriel Crosby, *The World of Language* (Chicago: Follett, 1970).

18. Lynn K. Rhodes, "I Can Read! Predictable Books As Resources for Reading and Writing Instruction," *The Reading Teacher* 34 (February 1981): 511–18. Provides extensive bibliography of predictable books.

Developing Permanent Reading Habits

A Cognitive Map: Developing Permanent Reading Habits

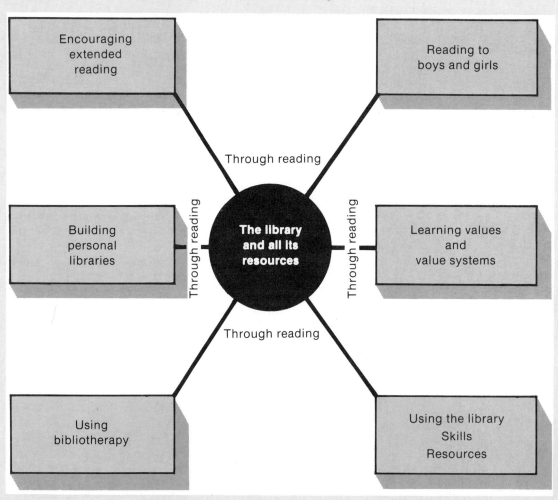

14

Guide Questions

1. The teacher needs to be continually matching children with books that are interesting to them. How will you do this for the boys and girls in your room?

2. Select the grade level you would like to teach. Can you make a list of books you would like to read aloud to these students?

3. What are the skills that girls and boys in the elementary school should have in order to use the school library efficiently?

4. How could *you* apply the principles of bibliotherapy given in the chapter?

5. Select a unit of work in social studies for your grade level. Using the library resources available to you, can you make a bibliography of about twenty-five books to use as collateral reading that expands the subject matter of this unit?

Terminology

bibliotherapy

catharsis

empathy

insight

interest inventory

Library of Congress numbers

multi-level materials

Newbery awards

All teachers want children to develop permanent interests in reading. Attractive bulletin boards showing new book acquisitions, a free reading table, children's book reviews—all are ways teachers try to help children establish a permanent interest in reading. To make reading a permanent habit is, actually, the overall goal of the school's reading program for boys and girls.

Generally, the attitude should be that to read is pleasant. Schools must provide for reading opportunities for all children; children must be guided in making wise choices about which reading materials best serve their purposes; and adequate provision must be made by each teacher to move children toward permanent interests and habits in reading. Reading opportunities for *all* children *require* that:

1. Materials have high interest appeal and be of appropriate difficulty so that children can read with relative ease.
2. Wide ranges of choices be provided: both fact and fiction; travel, history, myth, science, legend, biography, poetry, and plays.
3. They live the incident meaningfully. They must learn to empathize, internalize the feelings, see the sights, smell the smells, hear the sounds.
4. Each child's individual interests be given consideration. Materials can be recommended and made available, but each child will have individual interests, so the teacher should not expect that all children will find particular books, stories, or poems equally appealing just because the teacher feels they have special merit.

Encouraging Extended Reading

The teacher's ability to motivate children to want to read will depend both upon personality interaction with the students and on the teacher's awareness of what conditions work most effectively. The reader is encouraged to reread the comments on motivation found in chapter 2. Some basics include:

1. Knowledge about the child's home life, intelligence, general maturity, and independent reading power.
2. As wide acquaintance as possible with the children's literature available to the child.
3. Knowledge of standard references in juvenile libraries that will help the teacher find, or find out about, the wealth of interesting reading material now available for boys and girls.
4. An inviting reading corner that will entice children to browse when they have the liberty to do so.
5. A provision in every school day that makes it possible for each student to have some time in a pleasant, independent reading environment.
6. Opportunities for children to share what they have read, whether it be through discussion, roleplaying, or shared reading.

Children have few more enjoyable moments in school than sitting with their teacher savoring a good book.

7. Awareness of the many audiovisual aids that can awaken in reluctant readers a desire to read. For example, all the Newbery award books are now available on long-playing records. Teachers need to be alert for radio and television programs and films and filmstrips that will help promote reading interests.

Activities to promote growth in reading interests:

1. Individual card files: annotations about books read
2. A structured plan for record keeping
3. Group discussion once a week or once every two weeks
4. Oral reporting
5. Recommending books to others
6. Oral reading by the teacher
7. Oral reading by individual children

The Interest Inventory

Teachers should learn as much as possible about the personal interests of the boys and girls in their classrooms. This can be accomplished by taking a few minutes to talk privately with each student and make notes when the time is appropriate. Also, children may write autobiographies that reveal interests or attitudes toward themselves and others. Responding to incomplete sentences (I wish. . . . When I was little. . . . I do my best when. . . . What annoys me. . . . When I grow up. . . .) may reveal directions in which the teacher can interact with a student.

A more systematic inventory of a child's interests and background can be obtained by asking boys and girls to complete short interest inventories. What does the student do after school, on Saturdays, or during the winter evenings? What is the student's relationship with siblings and parents? Does the student have special hobbies or collections or take private lessons of any kind? Learning whether the child has taken interesting trips by train, plane, bus, or car and the kinds of places the child's family visits when they travel is important.

A teacher can prepare an inventory of no more than one page that can provide such information. Current events newspapers like the *Weekly Reader* occasionally have interest inventories for boys and girls to use. All information may be useful to the teacher. It may reveal the adequacy of sleep, rest, diet, play, and work in the student's living habits. The more the teacher knows about the interests, activities, and abilities of the student, the more he or she is able to understand the student's behavior. And all such information will provide the teacher useful background information for planning ways to extend the student's reading environment.

When children have a principal who understands and supports reading education, they have extra encouragement to grow in reading ability and to develop positive attitudes about reading.

The Elementary School Library

The basic purpose of the school library is to expose children to much good literature and to develop permanent interest in reading—and in reading a wide variety of materials. It is hoped that good school library experiences will also help develop a child's taste for literature worth reading.

If teachers are to find suitable materials to accommodate the wide ranges of ability in any class, they must rely on the centralized library in the school. Adams urged this function for the school library as follows:

If each child is to reach his highest potential in every subject area at the elementary school level he must have access to vastly different materials and instruction than were offered to that grade level in previous years. A multi-level approach is required and multi-level materials must follow this thinking. Although the multi-level materials are maintained in part within the classroom, it has become evident that many supplementary materials must be utilized, and budgetary consideration makes it advantageous to place them in some type of central repository. The obvious choice for this centralization is the elementary school library.[1]

Arbuthnot reminds us:

One tremendous service a library can render both homes and schools is to supply quantities of those books which bridge the gap between reading ability and reading skill. That lag can, by third or fourth grade, assume discouraging proportions for some children. For instance, a child may be reading at first or second grade level but be capable of comprehending and enjoying books which he can't possibly read for himself at fifth, sixth, or even seventh grade level. Then the experts, among other recommendations, advise that the child be given a lot of practice reading and that he be provided with easy-to-read books in order to acquire the confidence that comes from a sense of comfortable fluency.[2]

And Adams explains:

In the child's mind the library is no longer merely a place where he goes once a week to change a book (or get a book for a book report he must write). It is still a place where a child may on any day take out and return books, but it is also a center of information, a place for leisure time activities, for story hours, for discussion of books and a place to listen to music or view filmstrips.

The teachers, the librarians, and the reading consultant see the library as the center of multi-level materials, the research center and training center for the advancing skills of the students.[3]

The library provides a *comfortable* learning situation where children can "learn how to learn." If children are responsive to this learning environment, they will move easily to junior high, high school, and public libraries as life situations keep encouraging them to read.

The library is planned to meet the individual differences in the reading abilities of large groups of children. The fourth grade boy with third grade reading power can read on his level pursuing his interests; the fourth grade girl reading independently at the sixth grade level can pursue learning much higher on the scale of developmental skills.

Table 14.1   Analysis of book collections.

Subject	Percent of Total
Reference Books	1.2
Religion and Mythology	1.2
Social Sciences and Folklore	9.1
Language	0.3
Science	23.0
Fine Arts	5.0
Literature	3.2
History and Biography	22.5
Fiction	21.5
Picture and Easy-to-read Books	13.0
	100.0%

From American Library Association, *A Basic Book Collection for Elementary Grades* (Chicago, Ill.: American Library Association, 1960), p. 10.

A good central library contains no less than six thousand volumes, made available to all the students and teachers during the entire school day. A balance is maintained between nonfiction books and books for recreational reading and in the various subject fields and fields of children's interests. Intelligent and effective use of available book selection aids will insure the necessary variety of books to extend the experiences of every child. Table 14.1 shows a breakdown of a basic juvenile library book collection suggested by the American Library Association.

If the weeding-out process is properly done, about 10 percent of the books will be discarded annually. The most-used books and those with poor quality bindings will have to be replaced or renovated often.

The issue today is not whether to have either good classroom libraries or a good, well-stocked central library in the elementary school. It is absolutely necessary to have a good central library to be sure a given classroom in the school has interesting, changing library shelves.

Librarians and teachers together select a shelf of books needed for each new social studies unit and make them readily available to the room teacher. The shelf of books that is no longer needed from the previous unit is returned.

Library Skills to Be Learned

Girls and boys can begin early learning to use the card catalog, to locate a book on the shelf, and to recognize quickly the ascending and descending Dewey Decimal or Library of Congress numbers in the area where the book they seek is shelved. Special designations can be learned if pointed out to the children. Certain behaviors will enhance the children's confidence in using and finding the time to use the library. They need to be able to locate easily the books and magazines they like and want. They should be able to withdraw and return on time all the books they can make effective use of. They need to know how to take care of books and to practice good "library behavior."

Greer has suggested seven specific information skills to be taught to elementary school boys and girls.[4]

1. How to locate books by author, title, and subject headings.
2. How to find information in alphabetical order to third or fourth letter.
3. Kind of information on a card in the file: full name of author or authors, complete title, publisher, copyright date, whether or not illustrations are included, and a call number, either Dewey Decimal or Library of Congress.
4. Books are filed by call numbers.
5. Every library book has an accession number, which indicates how many volumes have already been cataloged. If the accession number is 50,000, then the library had already cataloged 49,999 before it arrived.
6. The library has a reference legend explaining which subject headings are assigned to which call numbers on the shelves.
7. Special designations need to be learned: "B" is biography; "F" is fiction; "R" is reference; and "Zi" or "Cla" represents first letters of author's last name.

Sources for the Teacher

There are many general references available that will help teachers to select books to meet the needs and interests of boys and girls and to supplement the units they are teaching. The following general reference books are only a few examples of the many that will be useful:

Arbuthnot, May Hill, et al., eds. *Children's Books Too Good to Miss.* 7th ed. New York: University Press Books, 1980.

Bernstein, Joanne. *Books to Help Children Cope with Separation and Loss.* New York: Bowker, 1977.

Children's Catalog. 14th ed. New York: H. W. Wilson, 1981, with annual supplements.

Cianciolo, Patricia J., ed. *Adventuring with Books: 2400 Titles for Pre-Kindergarten through Grade Eight.* New York: Scholastic Book Services, 1977.

Council on Interracial Books for Children. *Human (and Anti-Human) Values in Children's Books.* New York: Racism and Sexism Resource Center for Educators, A Division of the Council on Interracial Books for Children, 1976.

Field, Elinor W., ed. *Horn Book Reflections on Children's Books and Reading.* Boston: Horn Book, 1969.

Gillis, Ruth J. *Children's Books for Times of Stress: An Annotated Bibliography.* Bloomington: Indiana University Press, 1978.

Horn Book. Magazine published by Horn Book, Inc., Park Sq. Bldg., 31st St. and James Ave., Boston, Mass. 02116. Includes discriminating reviews of children's books and an annual list of outstanding books.

Junior High School Library Catalog. 4th ed. New York: H. W. Wilson, 1980, with annual supplements.

Larrick, Nancy. *Parent's Guide to Children's Reading.* 4th ed. New York: Doubleday, 1975.

Rudman, Masha K. *Children's Literature: An Issues Approach.* Lexington, Mass.: D. C. Heath, 1976.

Spache, George. *Good Reading for the Disadvantaged Reader: Multi-Ethnic Resources.* Rev. ed. Champaign, Ill.: Garrard Press, 1975.

Sunderlin, Sylvia, and Abigail McNamee, eds. *Children and Stress.* Washington, D.C.: Association for Childhood Education International, 1982.

Tway, Eileen, ed. *Reading Ladders to Human Relations.* 6th ed. Washington, D.C.: American Council on Education, 1980.

Values of the People Studied

Social studies textbooks designed to provide the overview of a full year of work for any given grade level must, of necessity, be digests of much factual material. If teachers rely heavily on basic text material, boys and girls will be attempting to absorb many facts for which they may not always see relevance. Typical kinds of abbreviated facts for almost any geographical area include: the important crops, the major cities, the chief industries, the latitude and longitude, the mountain ranges, and the navigable rivers.

To illuminate the cultural, social, and economic values of the people about whom the social studies text is written, teachers need to seek out those fiction and nonfiction accounts that will teach something of the affective life of the people. What was daily living like for the pioneers? What was fun? What games did they play? What were the causes of happiness or unhappiness? What about the fears and anxieties of boys and girls? For historical fiction or biography, the questions need to be in the past tense. Of course, for stories about boys and girls today, the questions should be asked in the present tense.

A special bibliography of such books for children in which Indians are main characters is appended to this volume. The selections were made by Dr. Juanita Cata, Chief, Division of Education, Albuquerque Area Office, Bureau of Indian Affairs.

Cavanah has written a book about Abraham Lincoln's boyhood that many boys and girls enjoy.

> Abe Lincoln was hired to work as a clerk in Denton Offut's general store. Customers could buy all kinds of things there—tools and nails, needles and thread, mittens and calico, and tallow for making candles. One day a woman bought several yards of calico. After she left, Abe discovered that he had charged her six cents too much. That evening he walked six miles to give her the money. He was always doing things like that, and people began to call him "Honest Abe."[5]

Laura Ingalls Wilder has made pioneer days in the Middle West live for many boys and girls in the intermediate grades with her *Little House in the Big Woods, On The Banks of Plum Creek, The Long Winter, Farmer Boy, Little House on the Prairie, By the Shores of Silver Lake, Little Town on the Prairie,* and *These Happy Golden Years.*[6]

The book *Fifth Chinese Daughter* has many episodes that reveal the strong conflict between the parents and the children growing up as first-generation immigrants in San Francisco.

Jade Snow was seventeen and had just arranged her first date without her mother's or father's permission. Her very traditional father chastised her in this way:

"Where and when did you learn to be so daring as to leave this house without permission of your parents? You did not learn it under my roof."

When Jade Snow tried to explain her behavior to her parents, her father became very angry and continued:

"Do I have to justify my judgment to you? I do not want a daughter of mine to be known as one who walks the streets at night. Have you no thought of our reputations if not for your own? If you start going out with boys, no good man will want to ask you to be his wife. You just do not know as well as we do what is good for you."[7]

Louise Stinetorf has written delightfully of the experiences of Abed, a Sudanese boy who lived in the Nubian Desert in North Africa. He took his donkey loaded with his parents' ceramic pots to the marketplace in Fadwa and found a little empty space and began calling out his wares.

Presently a woman stopped in front of the pots and began looking them over. As she moved, Abed heard a little tinkling sound, and although her dress was so long he could not see her feet, he knew she was wearing iron anklets. He knew also, that this meant that God had given her many children, but that God had also taken them away from her.

There was no choice among Abed's wares. Every pot was exactly the same size and shape and color. In Africa, a potter makes exactly one size and kind of pot. If the customer wants something different, he goes to another potter. Abed knew his pots were good ones. His father and mother were careful workmen. They chopped the straw they used until it was almost as fine as flour, and they used enough of it to make their wares good and strong. Their clay, too, was not half sand, but a good red product carried half way across the Sahara Desert on the backs of strong camels.

In spite of all this, the woman lifted up one pot, then another, and examined them all carefully. One pot was too heavy and too shallow, and another made from the same mold was too thin and too deep. At last she chose a pot and offered a price.

Abed took the pot away from the woman, dusted it off carefully, and put it back on the pile. To offer such a tiny price for so excellent a pot was an insult to his ancestors, he told her. The woman seized the pot and pointed out all the rough spots. Abed patted it lovingly as though it were a kitten. The woman thumped the pot with the flat of her hand. See, she cried, it sounded as though there were weak spots in it. It would probably crack wide open the first time she put it over the fire. But she was a charitable woman, and she would offer a little more money for it.

Abed plinked the pot with his thumb nail and cocked his head on one side. It had the ring of strength and purity, he answered. It was sweet toned like a metal camel bell. It had been in the glazing kiln over a fire of hot sheep's dung for two days. It would give hard service for years. Possibly this woman's children would cook in the same pot long after she was dust! But he, too, was charitable and he would take a little less money for the pot although, he assured his customer, it was a very jewel of a pot.

Abed and his customer haggled for some time. She found every possible fault with the pot—and finally every possible fault with Abed and his family, shrieking at him that he was a thief and the child of a family of thieves. But little by little she raised her price.

And the more fault the woman found with the pot, the more Abed praised it. Finally he, too, began to berate her, telling her she was surely blind to find fault with such an excellent pot and saying that if he sold his wares at her price his father and mother would without any doubt starve to death. But little by little he lowered his price.

Then, just when the woman was calling terrible curses down upon Abed's donkey's eyebrow, and it seemed as though they would come to blows, they agreed upon a price. The woman paid Abed, and just as softly as they had sounded loud and angry before, they asked God's blessing on each other and parted good friends. No one seemed disturbed at the shouting nor surprised at the sudden calm and friendship—that is just the way marketing is done in Fadwa![8]

Two recent books about Navaho children provide some insights into the thinking of young Navaho in relatively recent times.

Grandmother decided that Sad-Girl must go away to the off-reservation boarding school to learn the white man's reading and writing. She arranged with the trader at the trading post to have her registered for school, then arranged for her to ride to the trading post at the appointed time with the neighbors, the Yuccas. Enroute to the trading post, the Yucca children explained that the Navaho name was not sufficient in the white man's school and, after due deliberation, named her Rose Smith.

At the boarding school she was awakened one night by the crying of her roommate in the lower bunk. She had been a bit frightened by the strange, muffled sound of the crying. Her first thought was that it might be the ghost of an earth person, because she knew that ghosts appear only after dark and only on moonless nights. Rose must help her friend Isobel.

> If Isobel had contracted sickness or disease it was because she had violated a taboo or had been attacked by a ghost or a witch. If the latter was the case and the spectral attack was very recent, it could be averted or lessened by certain precautions.
>
> She fumbled her way through the darkness to the dresser. Her fingers slipped down, counting, until they arrived at her own drawer. Inside, carefully laid away with her change of underwear and her sweater, was a tiny sack of gall medicine. Grandmother had made it for her just before she left home, so it was fresh and potent. It was composed of dried and pulverized galls of many animals and was a sure cure for anyone who had unknowingly absorbed a witch's poison.[9]

In a book titled *Owl in the Cedar Tree,* Mrs. Momaday presents a conflict between the culture of the Indian and the culture of the white man. Haske, a little boy who rides the bus each day to school from his mother's hogan, makes a painting at school that wins him a prize and allows him to buy the horse that he had wanted for a long time. But woven into the story is the cultural conflict between Old Grandfather and Haske's father. Old Grandfather tells Haske he should become a medicine man when he grows up and that he should start now by going into the hills for four days to fast and pray. His father, however, is determined that Haske must go to school every day and learn the white man's language and culture. One day Haske asks his father to tell the bus driver that he will not be there that day, or the next three days. The father is indignant and tells him that he most certainly will go to school as usual. He also says that the Old One has not given Haske good advice. When Haske returns from school, only his mother and sister are there. He knows that his father has gone to sing for a sick friend and will not return. But he also knows that since Old Grandfather is not there, his father has spoken to him and he has gone away feeling unwanted.

Then Mrs. Momaday explains how the mother resolves the situation:

At supper Riding Woman saw that Haske was not eating his food. By the light of the center fire she saw that her son was troubled, and she understood how he felt.

Finally she said, "Your father told me all about it, my son. This morning he spoke to the Old One and tried to explain that school is good. But Old Grandfather could not understand. He was hurt and offended. He left without saying goodbye."

Haske did not try to hide his tears. He kept his eyes on his mother's face. For the first time in his life he saw the strength and courage in her face. Until now he had seen only the beauty and tenderness. Suddenly he was ashamed of his tears. He stopped crying and smiled at his mother.

Riding Woman said, "Now you feel better and must eat your supper." She put hot food on his plate and warmed his coffee. While Haske ate hungrily, his mother explained all the things he needed to know.

She said, "My son, you have made an anthill look like a mountain. You have worried about which trail to follow. There is only one trail. You have come to believe that some things are all good and some things are all bad. This is not true. The Indian and the white man are not so different as you might think. Both have the same needs, and each must try to understand the other. This is why school is important. At school you learn the white man's language. You cannot understand another person until you can talk with him. By speaking with others you learn what they are thinking and how they feel. This brings understanding between people."

Riding Woman saw that Desbah had gone to sleep by the fire. She picked up the little girl and wrapped a blanket about her. Then she tucked Desbah into her sheepskin bed and sat down again beside Haske.

"So you see, my son, there is only one trail," she continued. "Follow it and keep the best of the old ways while learning the best of the new ways."

Haske felt very happy. His mother had made him understand, and he no longer felt that he was being pulled in two directions. She had set his feet upon the trail as surely as the Navaho gods could have done. And he would make it a trail of beauty.[10]

Reading Good Books to Children

Especially good books may well be read in their entirety to children. Good books that supply background information for units of work but that are too difficult for children to read alone should be read, in whole or in part, to the class.

Books of story type that present such a vivid picture of life in other times and places that the reader is able to recreate them in imagination lend reality to social studies and help children to realize their drama and romance. The voyages of Columbus . . . told by Armstrong Sperry in *The Voyages of Columbus* . . . become a thrilling adventure.[11]

One fifth grade teacher reported reading the following books to her class during the school year. All had a high interest level for the group.

Esther Forbes, *Johnny Tremain* (New York: Houghton Mifflin, 1943).
Sterling North, *Rascal* (New York: E. P. Dutton, 1963).
James Daugherty, *Daniel Boone* (New York: Viking, 1939).
Carol Brink, *Caddie Woodlawn* (New York: Macmillan, 1935).
Joseph Krumgold, *And Now Miguel* (New York: Crowell, 1953).
Elizabeth G. Speare, *The Bronze Bow* (New York: Houghton Mifflin, 1961).

The same fifth grade teacher reported that the first two or three chapters of the following books were read and considerable interest generated. Then the book was given to an individual student who wanted to finish it.[12]

Laura Ingalls Wilder, *On the Banks of Plum Creek* (New York: Harper, 1953).
Laura Ingalls Wilder, *The Little House in the Big Woods* (New York: Harper, 1951).
May McNeer, *Armed with Courage* (Nashville: Abingdon, 1957).
Anna Sewell, *Black Beauty* (New York: Macmillan, 1877).
Scott O'Dell, *Island of the Blue Dolphins* (New York: Houghton Mifflin, 1960).
Joseph Krumgold, *Onion John* (New York: Crowell, 1959).
Lois Lenski, *Strawberry Girl* (New York: Crowell, 1945).
Alice I. Hazeltine, *Hero Tales from Many Lands* (Nashville: Abingdon, 1961).

Julie is explaining about her life at school with her teacher-aunt Cordelia, with whom she also lived. Julie makes clear that Aunt Cordelia was *only* the teacher at school and pretended to know her no better than the other children.

. . . She read aloud to us on Friday afternoons, and she read beautifully; I came very close to loving Aunt Cordelia during those long afternoons when I rested my arms upon the desk in front of me and became acquainted with Jim Hawkins and Huck Finn, with little David and Goliath, with Robinson Crusoe on his island, and with the foolish gods and their kinfolk somewhere above the clouds on Mount Olympus.[13]

The Wind in the Willows is one of the children's classics that should be read aloud to, and enjoyed with, children. Mole, Water Rat, Badger, and Toad are *gentlemen* of the woods and river. Children do enjoy the subtle humor in the behavior of the characters. Peter Green wrote:

The book for me is notable for its intimate sympathy with Nature and for its delicate expression of emotions. When all is said, the boastful, unstable Toad, the hospitable Water Rat, the shy, wise, childlike Badger, and the Mole with his pleasant habit of brave boyish impulse, are neither animals nor men, but are types of that deeper humanity which sways us all. . . . And if I may venture to describe as an allegory a work which critics, who ought to have known better, have dismissed as a fairy-story, it is certain that *The Wind in the Willows* is a wise book.[14]

Fisher evaluated the book for children in this way:

> *The Wind in the Willows* is a wise book; it is a complicated book; yet it has given more pleasure to children than almost any other. Firm and strong it certainly is in its implications. Grahame's story will not push philosophy or satire at a child. It will arouse in him, at different times, pity and anger, enjoyment and laughter; it will satisfy the desire for these things as it satisfied Grahame when he wrote it; and it will leave the animal world where it was, untouched by human sentiment or speculation. The animals return to the river and the wood unchanged; but the reader, young or old, can never again feel blank or indifferent towards them.[15]

Newbery Medal Books

Since 1922, a Newbery Medal Book has been selected annually by a committee of competent librarians as "the most distinguished juvenile book written by a citizen or a resident of the United States and published during the preceding year." The award is made at the annual meeting of the American Library Association.[16]

John Newbery (1713–1767) has come to be known as the father of children's literature. As a London bookseller, he worked diligently to promote the idea that children needed their own shelves of books written especially for them. He printed in all about two hundred little books selling for about six pence each.[17]

The books that have won the Newbery award are, for the most part, excellent books of classic and enduring qualities. Teachers will do well to know these books and use each opportunity to recommend the appropriate book to individuals in their classes. Following is the list of Newbery Medal Books.

1922 *The Story of Mankind*, by Hendrick Van Loon (Liveright).
1923 *The Voyages of Dr. Dolittle*, by Hugh Lofting (J. B. Lippincott).
1924 *The Dark Frigate*, by Charles B. Hawes (Little, Brown).
1925 *Tales from Silver Lands*, by Charles J. Finger (Doubleday).
1926 *Shen of the Sea*, by Arthur B. Chrisman (E. P. Dutton).
1927 *Smoky, the Cowhorse*, by Will James (Charles Scribner's Sons).
1928 *Gayneck: The Story of a Pigeon*, by Dhan Gopal Mukerji (E. P. Dutton).
1929 *The Trumpeter of Krakow*, by Eric P. Kelly (Macmillan).
1930 *Hitty: Her First Hundred Years*, by Rachel Field (Macmillan).
1931 *The Cat Who Went to Heaven*, by Elizabeth Coatsworth (Macmillan).
1932 *Waterless Mountain*, by Laura Adams Armer (David McKay).
1933 *Young Fu of the Upper Yangtze*, by Elizabeth F. Lewis (Holt, Rinehart & Winston).
1934 *The Story of the Author of Little Women: Invincible Louisa*, by Cornelia Meigs (Little, Brown).
1935 *Dobry*, by Monica Shannon (Viking Press).
1936 *Caddie Woodlawn*, by Carol Ryrie Brink (Macmillan).
1937 *Roller Skates*, by Ruth Sawyer (Viking Press).
1938 *The White Stag*, by Kate Seredy (Viking Press).
1939 *Thimble Summer*, by Elizabeth Enright (Holt, Rinehart & Winston).
1940 *Daniel Boone*, by James Daugherty (Viking Press).
1941 *Call It Courage*, by Armstrong Sperry (Macmillan).
1942 *The Matchlock Gun*, by Walter D. Edmonds (Dodd, Mead).
1943 *Adam of the Road*, by Elizabeth Janet Gray (Viking Press).

1944 *Johnny Tremain*, by Esther Forbes (Houghton Mifflin).

1945 *Rabbit Hill*, by Robert Lawson (Viking Press).

1946 *Strawberry Girl*, by Lois Lenski (J. B. Lippincott).

1947 *Miss Hickory*, by Carolyn Sherwin Bailey (Viking Press).

1948 *Twenty-one Balloons*, by William Pene DuBois (Viking Press).

1949 *King of the Wind*, by Marguerite Henry (Rand McNally).

1950 *Door in the Wall*, by Marguerite de Angeli (Doubleday).

1951 *Amos Fortune, Free Man*, by Elizabeth Yates (Aladdin).

1952 *Ginger Pye*, by Eleanor Estes (Harcourt Brace & World).

1953 *Secret of the Andes*, by Ann Nolan Clark (Viking Press).

1954 *And Now Miguel*, by Joseph Krumgold (Thomas Y. Crowell).

1955 *The Wheel on the School*, by Meindert de Jong (Harper & Row).

1956 *Carry On, Mr. Bowditch*, by Jean Lee Latham (Houghton Mifflin).

1957 *Miracles on Maple Hill*, by Virginia Sorenson, illustrated by Beth and Joe Kruch (Harcourt Brace & World).

1958 *Rifles for Watie*, by Harold Keith (Thomas Y. Crowell).

1959 *The Witch of Blackbird Pond*, by Elizabeth George Speare (Houghton Mifflin).

1960 *Onion John*, by Joseph Krumgold (Thomas Y. Crowell).

1961 *Island of the Blue Dolphins*, by Scott O'Dell (Houghton Mifflin).

1962 *The Bronze Bow*, by Elizabeth George Speare (Houghton Mifflin).

1963 *A Wrinkle in Time*, by Madeleine L'Engle (Farrar, Strauss).

1964 *It's Like This Cat*, by Emily Neville (Harper & Row).

1965 *Shadow of a Bull*, by Maia Wojciechowska (Atheneum).

1966 *I, Juan de Pareja*, by Elizabeth B. deTrevino (Farrar, Strauss, & Giroux).

1967 *Up a Road Slowly*, by Irene Hunt (Follett).

1968 *From the Mixed-up Files of Mrs. Basil E. Frankweiler*, by E. L. Koenigsburg (Atheneum).

1969 *The High King*, by Lloyd Alexander (Holt, Rinehart & Winston; also, Dell paperback).

1970 *Sounder*, by William H. Armstrong (Harper & Row).

1971 *Summer of the Swans*, by Betsy Byars (Viking Press).

1972 *Mrs. Frisby and the Rats of NIMH*, by Robert C. O'Brien (Atheneum).

1973 *Julie of the Wolves*, by Jean C. George (Harper & Row).

1974 *The Slave Dancer*, by Paula Fox (Bradbury Press).

1975 *M. C. Higgins, The Great*, by Virginia Hamilton (Macmillan).

1976 *The Grey King*, by Susan Cooper (Atheneum).

1977 *Roll of Thunder: Hear My Cry*, by Mildred Taylor (Dial).

1978 *Bridge to Terabithia*, by Katherine Paterson (Crowell).

1979 *The Westing Game*, by Ellen Raskin (Dutton), grades 5–9.

1980 *A Gathering of Days: A New England Girl's Journal, 1830–1832*, by Joan Blos (Scribner), grades 6–8.

1981 *Jacob Have I Loved*, by Katherine Paterson (Harper & Row), upper grades.

1982 *A Visit to William Blake's Inn*, by Nancy Willard (Harcourt Brace Jovanovich), upper grades.

From Theory to Practice 14.1
Evaluating the Caldecott Medal Books

The Caldecott Medal is an annual award given to an artist for the most distinguished picture book for children. It is named for the English illustrator Randolph Caldecott and has been awarded since 1938.

A few of the Caldecott Medal Award Books are:

Sam, Bangs and Moonshine, written and illustrated by Evaline Ness. New York: Holt, Rinehart and Winston, 1967.
Where the Wild Things Are, written and illustrated by Maurice Sendak. New York: Harper & Row, 1964.
The Snowy Day, written and illustrated by Ezra Jack Keats. New York: Viking Press, 1963.
Once a Mouse, written and illustrated by Marcia Brown. New York: Charles Scribner's Sons, 1962.
Time of Wonder, written and illustrated by Robert McCloskey. New York: Viking Press, 1958.
Song of the Swallows, written and illustrated by Leo Politi. New York: Charles Scribner's Sons, 1950.

Select a few of the Caldecott Medal winners, read them carefully, and plan how and with whom you would like to use these books. Discuss your plans with your classmates.

From Theory to Practice 14.2
Motivating with Newbery Medal Books

From the complete list of Newbery winners in your text, select three that you can hear on long-playing records. Listen to them and be ready to discuss how you could use the records to motivate students in your class to read.

Bibliotherapy and Personal Values

When a person who has a problem follows a planned course of reading about characters in stories who have similar problems in order to gain insights for better self-understanding, the process is termed bibliotherapy. The term literally means therapy through books.

Russell and Shrodes have described bibliotherapy in this way:

> [Bibliotherapy is] . . . a process of dynamic interaction between the personality of the reader and literature . . . interaction which may be utilized for personal assessment, adjustment and growth. This definition suggests that bibliotherapy is not a strange esoteric activity but one that lies within the province of every teacher of literature in working with every child in a group. It does not assume that the teacher must be a skilled therapist, nor the child a seriously maladjusted individual needing clinical treatment. Rather, it conveys the idea that all teachers must be aware of the effects of reading upon children and must realize that, through literature, most children can be helped to solve the developmental problems or adjustment which they face.[18]

Personal values can be cultivated through reading, since children strongly identify with story characters they like and strongly reject those they dislike. Empathy, understanding life experiences of others very different from ourselves, and acceptance of other people's values, attitudes, and beliefs are all character traits desired in the whole generation of elementary school children. Reading can help them develop these traits, especially with respect to handicapped people of all kinds—physically handicapped, economically handicapped by poverty, socially handicapped by loneliness. Such reading may help the nonhandicapped *more* than it does the handicapped.

Nancy Larrick expresses clearly and concisely how teachers help children grapple with the "personal touch" in their affective lives:

> Personal problems are not solved by applying a lotion advertised over television. And a lifetime set of values is not established in a day. Countless factors exert influence. Probably the most effective are the personal ones.
>
> The way a word is spoken may decide the way it is heeded. And the way a book is introduced may make or break its influence on a child. This is particularly true of the books which might have special meaning for a child with problems. Certainly it will not help to say, "Here's a book about a boy who is shy, too." That simply hits where it hurts, and wounds are not healed that way.
>
> But if you read *Crow Boy* in class and show your children those extraordinary pictures, the shy one will hear. The others, not so shy, may realize that their own Chibi yearns for friendship. No word need be said about a lesson in the story unless the children bring it up. If they do, let their discussion flow naturally. As they talk, they may be forming conclusions important to them.[19]

Malkiewicz used Jerold Beim's *Mister Boss* and *Shoeshine Boy* (both Morrow, 1954), Pearl Buck's *The Big Wave* (Day, 1948), and Byrd Baylor Schweitzer's *Amigo* (Macmillan, 1963) with fifth graders. The books helped them identify and discuss social and emotional issues raised in the stories and learn that sometimes problems that seem to be unique are, instead, universal.[20]

Reading about any of the vicissitudes of life can be helpful in identifying and analyzing one's own problems, releasing angry feelings (or pent-up, unidentified feelings), and gaining an insight that enables one to think rationally and normally again. Bernstein suggests that:[21]

1. Reading can help children cope with loss.
2. Reading offers opportunities to identify with "needed others."
3. Reading helps children realize that they are not alone.
4. Reading can extend horizons.
5. Reading can aid the catharsis process that makes insight possible.
6. Reading can facilitate the sharing of problems.

The person who guides bibliotherapy needs to be a good judge of timing and able to listen with empathy. Bernstein makes a distinction between *sympathy* and *empathy* by citing Norman Paul:

> In sympathy . . . the subject is principally absorbed in his own feelings as projected onto the object's special, separate experience. In sympathy, the subject is likely to use his own feelings as standards against which to measure the object's feelings and behavior. Sympathy, then, bypasses real understanding of the other person. . . . The empathic relationship is generous; the empathizer does not use the object as a means for gratifying his own sense of importance, but is himself principally concerned with encouraging the other person to sustain and express his feelings and fantasies.[22]

The dynamics necessary in successful bibliotherapy are:[23]

1. The author's communication with the reader.
2. The reader's ability to understand and respond to what he or she reads.
3. The therapist's ability to perceive alterations in attitude and to bring these changes to the reader's attention.

Cornett and Cornett have outlined the skills of the bibliotherapist to include the following:[24]

1. Ability to determine the needs and interests of the individual.
2. Ability to provide books at the appropriate interest and difficulty levels.
3. Ability to evaluate books for the purpose they will serve in bibliotherapy.
4. Ability to ask a variety of appropriate questions to encourage the individual to verbalize.
5. Ability to use "seconds of silence" and patience to wait for responses after questions have been raised.
6. Ability to be a good listener and to communicate effectively.
7. Ability to weigh carefully the balance between interaction strategies and additional materials to help individuals reach the *insight* stage.
8. Ability to find additional sources of help when appropriate.

Many of the books in this list are cited in the following sources:

Bernstein, Joanne E. *Books to Help Children Cope with Separation and Loss.* New York: R. R. Bowker, 1977.

Dreyer, Sharon S. *The Bookfinder, A Guide to Children's Literature About the Needs and Problems of Youth Aged 2–15.* 2 vols. Circle Pines, Minn.: American Guidance Service, vol. 1, 1977; vol. 2, 1981.

Gillespie, John T., and Christine B. Gilbert, eds. *Best Books for Children: Preschool Through the Middle Grades.* 2d ed. New York: R.R. Bowker, 1981.

White, Mary Lou, ed. *Adventuring with Books: Booklist for Pre-K–Grade 6.* New Ed. Urbana, Ill.: National Council of Teachers of English, 1981.

The books are listed in alphabetical order by author. The level of difficulty is given as primary (kindergarten through grade three), intermediate (grades four through six), and upper (grades seven and above). The primary condition as the subject for therapy is given in parentheses.

Alexander, Martha. *Nobody Asked Me If I Wanted a Baby Sister.* New York: Dial, 1971. Primary. (New sibling) The little boy tries to sell, and then give away, his baby sister. Then when he finds he alone can comfort her, he decides to keep her. Well done.

Armstrong, Wm. H. *Sounder.* New York: Harper, 1969. Upper. (Death) Harsh social customs and poverty make life cruelly difficult for this black boy and his dog, Sounder. Newbery Medal winner.

Blume, Judy. *Deenie.* Scarsdale, N.Y.: Bradbury, 1973. Upper. (Physical handicaps) Deenie, thirteen, is very pretty and her mother hopes Deenie becomes a model. Scoliosis causes poor posture. The cure requires years in a body brace.

Blume, Judy. *It's Not the End of the World.* Scarsdale, N.Y.: Bradbury Press, 1972. Upper. (Divorce) Twelve-year-old Karen's world seems to end when her parents are divorced and her older brother runs away.

Brown, Margaret Wise. *The Dead Bird.* Reading, Mass: Addison-Wesley, 1958. Primary. (Death) Children find a dead bird in the park, give it a funeral, and return daily for a while to pay respects. Highly recommended.

Buck, Pearl S. *The Big Wave.* New York: Day, 1948. Intermediate. (Death) The tidal wave washes Jiya's family away and he lives with his friend's family. He marries and returns to the same beach to live.

Bunin, Catherine, and Sherry Bunin. *Is That Your Sister?* New York: Pantheon, 1976. Primary. (Interracial adoption) Six-year-old Catherine and her sister Carla, both black, are adopted into a white family with two boys.

Burch, Robert. *Queenie Peavy.* New York: Viking, 1966. Intermediate. (Divorce) A defiant thirteen-year-old saves herself from reform school in a Georgia town of the 1930s.

Byars, Betsy. *Go and Hush the Baby.* New York: Viking Press, 1971. Primary. (New siblings) When Willie baby-sits his new baby sister, he is very creative in finding ways to entertain her.

Byars, Betsy. *The Summer of the Swans.* New York: Viking Press, 1970. Upper. (Mental retardation) Charlie is ten years old, retarded and nonverbal; a gentle, shadowy child, accepted with warmth and naturalness by his atypical family. The story centers on Sara's (Charlie's sister's) growth into adolescence, but Charlie is an appealing, if somewhat ill-defined, figure. Recommended.

Carrick, Carol. *The Accident*. New York: Seabury, 1976. Primary. (Death) When the child's dog is killed, his parents allow Christopher to vent all his angry feelings—before tears come and anger disappears.

Cleaver, Vera, and Bill Cleaver. *Me Too*. Philadelphia: Lippincott, 1973. Intermediate/ Upper. (Mental retardation) Lornie and Lydia are twelve-year-old twins. Lornie is retarded and spends her school year in a special school. Lydia is in charge of Lornie's daily supervision when she comes home for the summer. Their lives in this small southern town provide for an entertaining summer.

Cleaver, Vera, and Bill Cleaver. *Where the Lilies Bloom*. Philadelphia: Lippincott, 1969. Upper. (Responsibility) Mary Call Luther, fourteen, follows her father's suggestions to bury him secretly, keep the family together, never take charity, and never allow the landlord to marry her older, "cloudy-headed" sister.

Davidson, Margaret. *Helen Keller*. New York: Hastings, 1969. Intermediate. (Deaf-blindness) The story tells of the early childhood of Helen Keller. Her illness at nineteen months destroys her sight and hearing. The story is mostly concerned with her early years with Annie Sullivan.

DeAngeli, Marguerite. *Yonie Wondernose*. New York: Doubleday, 1944. Primary. (Curiosity) The story of a Pennsylvania Dutch boy whose curiosity was never satisfied.

Estes, Eleanor. *The Hundred Dresses*. New York: Harcourt Brace Jovanovich, 1944. Intermediate. (Acceptance by others) Wanda, a little Polish girl, always wears the same faded blue dress—and is ridiculed by the other children.

Fassler, Joan. *My Grandpa Died Today*. New York: Human Science Press, 1971. Primary. (Death) David's grandfather tries to prepare the boy for the grandfather's death. David does grieve but remembers his grandfather's wish for him to be happy.

Forbes, Esther. *Johnny Tremain*. Boston: Houghton Mifflin, 1943. Upper. (Physical handicap) The moving story of an apprentice silversmith of Paul Revere's day, whose maimed hand causes deep bitterness. Excellent detail about the colonists' fight for their independence. Newbery Medal winner in 1944.

Fox, Paula. *The Slave Dancer*. Scarsdale, N.Y.: Bradbury, 1973. Upper. (Prejudice) Fourteen-year-old Jessie is kidnapped and press-ganged aboard an American slave ship bound for Africa. Newbery Medal winner.

Garfield, James B. *Follow My Leader*. New York: Viking, 1957. Intermediate. (Blindness) Eleven-year-old Jimmy is blinded by a firecracker. He goes to a guide-dog school and gets Leader. This story will be helpful in giving sighted students understanding of the world of the blind.

Gates, Doris. *Blue Willow*. New York: Viking Press, 1948. Intermediate. (Migrant children) Janey moves from one crop to another, always hoping there will be work and shelter. The blue willow plate that she carries as her one treasure is all she has to remind her of better days.

Gilham, Elizabeth Enright. *Kintu*. New York: Holt, Rinehart and Winston, 1935. Kintu, who lives in the African Congo, overcomes his fear of the jungle by making himself venture into the jungle and finds that he knows what to do to keep himself alive.

Glazzard, Margaret H. *Meet Danny, He's a Special Person*. Lawrence, Kans.: H & H Enterprises, 1978. Primary. (Multiple handicaps) Danny's multiple handicaps are explained in simple, authoritative language. Large, clear type with a full-page photograph for each page of text.

Go Ask Alice. Englewood Cliffs, N.J.: Prentice-Hall, 1971. Upper. (Death and drugs) Alice, at fifteen, slips into the drug scene, drawn gradually into the whole spectrum of drugs. She dies of an overdose—but her diary is laced with her love for her middle-class family and their love for her.

Goff, Beth. *Where Is Daddy? The Story of a Divorce.* Boston: Beacon Press, 1969. Primary. (Divorce) Both anger and guilt feelings in a young child. Good to read to young children who feel grief, confusion, and loneliness following divorce. Won an award from the Child Study Association of America.

Gold, Phyllis. *Please Don't Say Hello.* New York: Human Sciences Press, 1974. Primary/Intermediate. (Multiple handicaps) The mother of an autistic child details the experiences of Eddie's family when they move into a new neighborhood. Eddie wins the affection of those around him as he struggles to emerge from the bondage of his autistic shell.

Green, Hannah [pseud.]. *I Never Promised You a Rose Garden.* New York: Holt, Rinehart and Winston, 1964. Upper. (Mental illness) Deborah, sixteen, tries suicide and is hospitalized. She eventually takes an apartment and finishes a GED (high school graduation equivalency). The full spectrum of mental illness is dealt with.

Hunt, Irene. *Across Five Aprils.* Chicago: Follett, 1965. Intermediate/Upper. (War) A young boy from the backwoods of southern Illinois joins the Union forces to fight in the Civil War. His brother joins the Confederacy.

Keats, Ezra Jack. *Peter's Chair.* New York: Harper, 1967. Primary. (New siblings) Peter's crib and high chair have been repainted for a baby sister. Peter must play quietly. His jealousy subsides as his mother and dad make him feel important helping with the baby.

Klein, Norma. *Confessions of an Only Child.* New York: Pantheon, 1974. Intermediate. (New siblings) When Antonia is nine, a new baby brother is born, but lives only one day. The mother then becomes pregnant and a healthy baby is born. Antonia has ambivalent feelings about wanting to be the only one and wanting a baby brother.

Lapsley, Susan. *I Am Adopted.* Scarsdale, N.Y.: Bradbury Press, 1975. Primary. (Adoption) "Adoption means belonging" is the theme. A simple story beautifully told.

Levine, Edna S. *Lisa and her Soundless World.* New York: Human Sciences Press, 1974. Primary. (Deafness) Lisa is born deaf. This story explains signing and finger spelling; lip reading and speech training; and the importance of gesture for the child who does not learn speech normally. This well-told story is an exemplary effort to explain the problem of being deaf in a hearing world.

Levy, Elizabeth. *Lizzie Lies a Lot.* New York: Delacorte, 1976. Intermediate. (Lying) Nine-year-old Lizzie lies about lots of things until her best friend confronts her with lying, and her parents reason that telling the truth might be easier.

Mann, Peggy. *My Dad Lives in a Downtown Hotel.* New York: Doubleday, 1973. Intermediate. (Divorce) Joey, eleven, has heard his parents argue for so long he is shocked when Dad moves out. Presents the bewilderment, anger and guilt felt by the child during such a separation.

Miles, Miska. *Annie and the Old One.* Boston: Little, Brown, 1971. Primary. (Death) Grandmother tells Annie that when the new rug on the loom is finished, it will be time for her to die. Annie cannot imagine her world without her grandmother, who helps her tend the sheep and laughs and plays with her. She slipped out at night and undid the weaving of the day so the rug could not get done. When Grandmother explained that they could not make time stand still, Annie understood and they finished the weaving.

Moore, Lillian, and Leone Adelson. *Old Rosie, the Horse Nobody Understood*. New York: Random House, 1952. Primary. (Understanding) Old Rosie is turned out to sleep, eat, and rest. She becomes very lonesome and misses doing all the things she used to do. She makes a great nuisance of herself until the day she happens to come in at just the right time to frighten away burglars.

Peterson, Jeanne Whitehouse. *I Have a Sister, My Sister is Deaf*. New York: Harper & Row, 1977. Primary. (Deafness) A young girl talks in a gentle, reflective way about her little sister who is deaf. She tells what her sister can and cannot do. Her voice is kind and gentle without sentimentality. Recommended.

Robinson, Veronica. *David in Silence*. Philadelphia: Lippincott, 1966. Intermediate. (Deafness) The story of David, a thirteen-year-old, making his adjustments in a new school with hearing students. Written with knowledge and understanding. Contains valuable information about the social and emotional aspects of deafness.

Smith, Doris B. *A Taste of Blackberries*. New York: Crowell, 1973. Intermediate. (Death) Jamie's best friend dies of an allergic reaction to a bee sting. Jamie's shock, denial, and anger are detailed. Death is presented realistically as a fact of life.

Speare, Elizabeth. *The Witch of Blackbird Pond*. New York: Dell, 1958. Upper. (Courage) Historical romance set in Puritan Connecticut with the theme of witchcraft. A Newbery Medal winner.

Taylor, Mildred D. *Roll of Thunder, Hear My Cry*. New York: Dial Press, 1976. Upper. (Prejudice) Rural Mississippi during the Depression. Cassie Logan's family fights to keep its land. A Newbery Medal winner.

Viorst, Judith. *The Tenth Good Thing About Barney*. New York: Atheneum, 1971. Primary. (Death) Barney is a cat that dies and his master must talk about him at the funeral. He philosophizes that helping the flowers to grow will be the tenth good thing about Barney.

White, E.B. *Charlotte's Web*. New York: Harper and Bros. 1952. Intermediate. (Death, friendship) Charlotte, a spider with a rare personality, spins messages in her web that save the life of Wilbur the pig and endear her to readers of all ages. Charlotte's death near the end of the story and the birth of her spider children explain the cycle of life.

Wojciechowska, Maia. *Tuned Out*. New York: Harper & Row, 1968. Upper. (Drugs) Sixteen-year-old Jim, through his diary, tells of his summer of disbelief and anguish when he learns that his older brother smokes marijuana and uses LSD. Jimmy has his brother hospitalized when he freaks out at home and then waits all summer for the doctor to release him from the hospital.

Yashima, Taro. *Crow Boy*. New York: Viking, 1955. Primary. (Shyness) Picture story of a shy Japanese boy who withdraws to a world of daydreams until his teacher makes him feel at home. Good illustrations.

Young, Miriam. *Miss Suzy's Birthday*. New York: Parents' Magazine, 1974. Primary. (Adoption) Miss Suzy adopts four baby squirrels. At their birthday party, they receive many identical gifts—acorns.

Personal Ownership of Books

The child who grows up in a reading environment, seeing adults read, is apt to develop an early interest in reading. The importance that parents attach to books will be learned very early by children.

Children imitate the adults around them whom they love and respect. If mother or father often has something interesting, funny, or unusual to read aloud to the rest of the family, it is likely that sooner or later the child will appear with something to share, too. Becoming confident in one's ability to read makes it possible for children to use reading as a pleasant way of filling periods of free time.

Some of the books children read will be more appealing, seem more worthwhile, than others. The home has an important responsibility in encouraging not only reading as a permanent habit, but reading books of lasting value. Ideally, the home library will contain a set of encyclopedias and a few other reference books that children may use in pursuing their school assignments and personal interests. Parents who help children begin to accumulate good books as personal possessions are wise. Many youngsters have proudly collected the "Little House" books and read and reread them throughout their childhood years.[25] Inexpensive paperback books make it possible for children to build their own libraries at no greater cost than can be a part of their regular weekly allowance. Scholastic Book Service has made many excellent book choices available to boys and girls—Tab Books for the junior high school level and Arrow Books for the elementary school level. Group orders in classrooms encourage children to obtain books that they would probably not get otherwise. Preparation of the group order is a good school exercise, and the boys and girls enjoy the anticipation of receiving the order. Reading the books in order to evaluate them for the group and recommend them to others is a motivating experience.

The child who has a shelf of books of his own is more apt to have and use a public library card. Caring for one's own books makes one more apt to exercise proper care of borrowed books.

Summary

This chapter has emphasized all the facets of the child's experience that would build permanent interest in reading by the time the child leaves elementary school. Aside from parents, the key person will be the classroom teacher for most children. The teacher must be sufficiently acquainted with children's literature to be able to recommend "the right book for the right child." This ability requires more than a casual, "Why don't you read this one; it looks interesting." The teacher should be able to tell the child why the book is interesting by describing a few episodes or giving a brief synopsis of the whole story.

In order to build broad, permanent reading interests, the school must have a well-stocked central library staffed by a competent librarian; standard references for teachers to use in seeking out the particular materials that fit their courses of study; and adequate reading materials so that teachers can draw from shelves of books related to social studies units being taught.

Teachers and parents who read well to children will encourage them to be curious about the great, wide, wonderful world of books.

For Further Reading

Arbuthnot, May Hill. *The Arbuthnot Anthology of Children's Literature.* 4th ed., rev. by Zena Sutherland. Glenview, Ill.: Scott, Foresman, 1976.

Bernstein, Joanne. *Books to Help Children Cope with Separation and Loss.* New York: R.R. Bowker, 1977.

Cianciolo, Patricia. *Illustrations in Children's Books.* Dubuque, Iowa: Wm. C. Brown, 1970.

Cornett, Claudia, and Charles F. Cornett. *Bibliotherapy: The Right Book at the Right Time.* Bloomington, Ind.: Phi Delta Kappa Educational Foundation, 1980.

Dallmann, Martha, et. al. "Children's Interests in Reading." In *The Teaching of Reading.* 6th ed. New York: Holt, Rinehart and Winston, 1982.

Harris, Albert J., and E. R. Sipay. "Fostering Interests and Tastes." In *How to Increase Reading Ability.* 7th. ed. New York: David McKay, 1980.

Hennings, Dorothy Grant. "Reading Picture Storybooks in the Social Studies." *The Reading Teacher* 36 (December 1982): 284–89.

Larrick, Nancy. *Parents' Guide to Children's Reading.* 4th ed. New York: Doubleday, 1975.

Painter, Helen W., ed. *Reaching Children and Young People Through Literature.* Newark, Del.: International Reading Assn., 1971.

Smardo, Frances A. "Using Children's Literature to Clarify Science Concepts in Early Childhood Programs." *The Reading Teacher* 36 (December 1982): 267–73.

Notes

1. Hazel Adams, "The Changing Role of the Elementary School Library," *The Reading Teacher* 18 (April 1965): 563
2. May Hill Arbuthnot, *Children and Books,* 3d ed. (Chicago: Scott, Foresman, 1964), p. 654.
3. Adams, "Elementary School Library."
4. Margaret Greer, "The Efficiency of the Use of Analogy in Teaching Selected Concepts at the Sixth Grade Level," pp. 44–50 (Masters thesis, University of New Mexico, 1966).

5. Frances Cavanah, *Abe Lincoln Gets His Chance* (Chicago: Rand McNally, 1959), p. 78.
6. Harper & Row, 1953.
7. Jade Snow Wong, *Fifth Chinese Daughter* (New York: Scholastic Book Services, 1963), pp. 163–65.
8. Louise A. Stinetorf, *Children of North Africa* (Philadelphia: J.B. Lippincott, 1943), pp. 53–55.
9. Evelyn Lampman, *Navaho Sister* (New York: Doubleday, 1956), p. 93.
10. Natachee Scott Momaday, *Owl in the Cedar Tree* (Flagstaff, Ariz.: Northland Press, 1975), pp. 82–84.
11. Mabel I. Snedaker, "The Social Studies Curriculum in the Elementary School," *Report of the 36th Annual Conference on Administration and Supervision* (State University of Iowa: Epsilon Chapter of Phi Delta Kappa, College of Education, 1952), p. 6.
12. Mildred Hillyer, "A Report of a Supervised Recreational Reading Program" (Masters thesis, Graduate School, The University of New Mexico, 1968), p. 39.
13. Irene Hunt, *Up a Road Slowly* (Chicago: Follett, 1966), p. 20.
14. Peter Green, *Kenneth Grahame* (Cleveland: World Publ. Co., 1959), p. 259.
15. Margery Fisher, *Intent upon Reading, A Critical Appraisal of Modern Fiction for Children* (New York: Franklin Watts, 1962), p. 64.
16. Lillian Hollowell, ed., *A Book of Children's Literature* (New York: Rinehart, 1959), p. 649.
17. Ibid., p. 8.
18. David Russell and Caroline Shrodes, "Contributions of Research in Bibliotherapy to the Language Arts Program, I," *The School Review* 58 (September 1950): 335.
19. Nancy Larrick, *A Teacher's Guide to Children's Books* (Columbus, Ohio: Charles E. Merrill, 1969), p. 104.
20. J. E. Malkiewicz, "Stories Can Be Springboards," *Instructor* 79 (April 1970): 133–34.
21. Bernstein, Joanne, *Books to Help Children Cope with Separation and Loss* (New York: R.R. Bowker, 1977), pp. 25–29.
22. Ibid., p. 33.
23. Ibid.
24. Cornett, Claudia E., and Charles F. Cornett, *Bibliotherapy: The Right Book at the Right Time* (Bloomington, Ind.: Phi Delta Kappa Educational Foundation, 1980), pp. 36–37.
25. Laura Ingalls Wilder, *Little House in the Big Woods; On the Banks of Plum Creek; Little House on the Prairie; The Long Winter* (New York: Harper & Row, 1951, 1953, 1953, 1953).

Provision for All the Children

Many adults have arrived at their station as classroom teachers without having acquired much understanding of the *one* language that is their only vehicle of communication. The structure of every language conforms to *definite* principles that the teacher should understand. These principles are broken down into the categories of phonology, morphology, syntax, and semantics. In second language learning, contrastive analysis of language differences can be a very useful tool when described within these categories. Contrastive analysis of phonemic differences especially is helpful.

At present, most schools are wrestling with teaching *all* children *in only the English language medium.* Good techniques in teaching English to speakers of other languages will facilitate this process. However, in the relatively near future, it is hoped that bilingual schools will have a place in the public school system. Only in this way can the school help children develop and extend their fluency in two or more languages.

Diagnostic teaching has been tragically neglected in work with children for whom English is a second language. The accepted communication skill hierarchy of listening-speaking-reading-writing has often been violated.

Chapter 3, "Linguistic Foundations for Reading Instruction," has prepared the reader for the next two chapters. Chapter 15 is concerned with teaching reading to the bilingual child and chapter 16 with teaching reading to the child who speaks nonstandard English. Chapter 17 deals with the exceptional child.

Many of the children not functioning as well as they could in the reading process would profit greatly from the teacher's use of corrective techniques in the classroom. Special programs must be provided for the intellectually gifted, the mentally retarded, and the few who have special learning disabilities rooted in neurological impairment or emotional disturbance. Children with learning disabilities are, more often than not, receiving no special help today. They desperately need special methodologies. When a school system makes no provision for their diagnosis and teaching in special clinics, classroom teachers must arrange special reading programs for them. Many professionals can and should help teachers better understand and work with the handicapped child.

Through continuous diagnosis and identification of children's abilities, disabilities, and possibilities, the teacher will be able to create measurable behavioral objectives so that tangible results will reveal whether learning is taking place or whether there is need for further study.

Bond and Tinker* estimate that 75 percent of the children who become remedial reading cases could be helped successfully by the classroom teacher before they reach that stage. The necessary conditions are as follows:

1. All *pressure* from the teacher for every child to complete the same work in the same amount of time with the same amount of practice be *eliminated;*
2. Each child be accepted as an *individual* and permitted to work at his or her *instructional* level of reading, moving only as fast as the child is able to learn;
3. The teacher's effort be bent toward providing many learning activities at many levels of difficulty so that each child would be challenged at his or her growing edge of learning;
4. The philosophy of the school be that other personnel are also concerned about each child's learning so that no teacher need operate alone.

*Guy L. Bond and Miles A. Tinker, *Reading Difficulties: Their Diagnosis and Correction* (New York: Appleton-Century-Crofts, 1967), p. 245.

Teaching Reading to the Bilingual Child

A Cognitive Map: Teaching Reading to the Bilingual Child

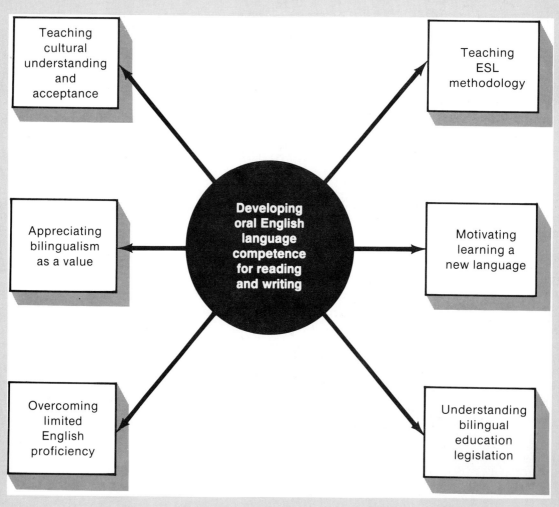

Teaching cultural understanding and acceptance

Teaching ESL methodology

Appreciating bilingualism as a value

Developing oral English language competence for reading and writing

Motivating learning a new language

Overcoming limited English proficiency

Understanding bilingual education legislation

15

Guide Questions

1. What special methods will you need to learn in order to teach students with limited English proficiency?

2. What would a mimic-memorization method of teaching be?

3. What can you do to change the inflexible expectations of the school?

4. How could you use peer tutors to teach English to those for whom English is a second (foreign) language?

5. What is ESL?

6. What will your responsibility be when the child learns to read in his vernacular and you cannot speak it?

7. What are the advantages of a bilingual school?

Terminology

alienation

audio-lingual method

Bilingual Education Act

bilingualism

contrastive analysis

cultural values

dominant culture

ESL

expansion sentences

limited English proficiency

oral language competence

passive voice

tag-ons

transformations

Cultural Differences and English Language Learning

At recess time one cold day in December, a teacher told her class of boys and girls that no one should leave the room until they had put on their *wraps*. Everyone got in line except five little Spanish-speaking children. She questioned why they were not in line, and they said, "But Mrs. Williams, we don't have any wraps." As soon as she said that she really meant to get their *caps* and *coats,* they *wrapped* up and got in line.

Many children who must learn English as a second language after they enroll in school develop negative attitudes and fail to achieve academically. These problems are rooted in the differences of culture, language, and experience.

In a publication entitled *Educating the Children of the Poor,*[1] it is pointed out that adequate theory requires integration of the wisdom of sociologists and psychologists so that environmental factors and personality variables will each receive proper attention. If applied anthropology is left out, a very important portion of the total appraisal of the child has been omitted.

One's cultural heritage shapes all the values, ideals, aspirations, anxieties, taboos, and mores that are represented by a person's behavior. Behavior is the internalized response one makes to the demands placed upon one by the culture.

While this cultural heritage is expressed in many ways, language is probably the most apparent and significant medium of expression. The interdependence of language and culture is discussed throughout this chapter.

Teaching Cultural Understanding and Acceptance

It is important that teachers understand, accept, and appreciate the behaviors and languages of different ethnic and cultural groups. Some excerpts from anthropological literature will help point these out.

Salisbury describes the Alaskan Indian child's problem understanding and relating to the middle-class Anglo-oriented course of study:

> By the time the native child reaches the age of seven, his cultural and language patterns have been set and his parents are required by law to send him to school. Until this time he is likely to speak only his own local dialect of Indian, Aleut, or Eskimo, or if his parents have had some formal schooling he may speak a kind of halting English.
>
> He now enters a completely foreign setting—the western classroom situation. His teacher is likely to be a Caucasian who knows little or nothing about his cultural background. He is taught to read the Dick and Jane series. Many things confuse him: Dick and Jane are two gussuk[2] children who play together. Yet he knows that boys and girls do not play together and do not share toys. They have a dog named Spot who comes indoors and does not work. They have a father who leaves for some mysterious place called "office" each day and never brings any food home with him. He drives a machine called an automobile on a hard covered road called a street which has a policeman on each corner. These policemen always smile, wear funny clothing and spend their time helping children to cross the street. Why do these children need this help? Dick and Jane's mother spends a lot of time in the kitchen cooking a strange food called "cookies" on a stove which has no flame in it.
>
> But the most bewildering part is yet to come. One day they drive out to the country which is a place where Dick and Jane's grandparents are kept. They do not live with the family and they are so glad to see Dick and Jane that one is certain

that they have been ostracized from the rest of the family for some terrible reason. The old people live on something called a "farm," which is a place where many strange animals are kept—a peculiar beast called a "cow," some odd looking birds called "chickens" and a "horse" which looks like a deformed moose.

And so on. For the next twelve years the process goes on. The native child continues to learn this new language which is of no earthly use to him at home and which seems completely unrelated to the world of sky, birds, snow, ice, and tundra which he sees around him.[3]

Evvard and Mitchell analyzed concepts in the stories in the Scott, Foresman basic readers.[4] They contrasted the beliefs and values the books contained with traditional Navajo beliefs and values and found many that conflicted with the young Navajo child's concepts of himself, his family, and his community.

Middle-class, urban values	Navaho values
Pets have humanlike personalities.	Pets are distinct from human personality.
Life is pictured as child-centered.	Life is adult-centered.
Adults participate in children's activities.	Children participate in adult activities.
Germ-theory is implicitly expressed.	Good health results from harmony with nature.
Children and parents are masters of their environment.	Children accept their environment and live with it.
Children are energetic, out-going, obviously happy.	Children are passive and unexpressive.
Many toys and much clothing is an accepted value.	Children can only hope for much clothing and toys.
Life is easy, safe, and bland.	Life is hard and dangerous.

Too many teachers are inadequately prepared to understand or accept cultural values that are different from their own. They come from homes where the drive for success and achievement is internalized early, where "work for work's sake" is rewarded, and where time and energy are spent building for the future. Many children come to the classroom with a set of values and a background of experience radically different from the American middle-class standard. To teach these children successfully, teachers must be cognizant of these differences and must, above all else, seek to understand and not disparage ideas, values, and practices different from their own.

The following paragraph has for *too* long accurately expressed the viewpoint of too many Anglo-American teachers toward Mexican-American students and their parents:

They are good people. Their only handicap is the bag full of superstitions and silly notions they inherited from Mexico. When they get rid of these superstitions, they will be good Americans. The schools help more than anything else. In time, the Latins will think and act like Americans. A lot depends on whether or not we can get them to switch from Spanish to English. When they speak Spanish they think Mexican. When the day comes that they speak English at home like the rest of us, they will be part of the American way of life. I just don't understand why they are so insistent about using Spanish. They should realize that it's not the American tongue.[5]

The attitude of the teacher toward language and other cultural differences is crucially important. Unless the teacher is patient and understanding, the student who must learn English as a second language "develops insecurity instead of security, worry instead of certainty, fear instead of competence, and the teacher makes enemies instead of friends for the English language."[6]

Teachers must be continually alert to the differences in languages, values, customs—the whole cultural heritage. They must seek to understand the students they teach as people whose feelings, attitudes, and emotional responses make them behave the way they do. Most important, they must realize that one way of life is not better, not superior, and not "more right" than another.

Dora V. Smith tells a story of a little Japanese girl who was spending a year in the United States attending an elementary school:

At Christmas time her American classmates sent a package to her school in Tokyo. They decided to write a letter to accompany it. When Reiko was asked whether she wished to add a line, this is what she wrote: "The boys and girls in America sound funny when they talk. We have to read in English, too. But they laugh and cry and play in Japanese."[7]

All teachers should learn what Reiko expressed—that laughing, crying, and playing are a universal language. Time to laugh together and play together allows a kind of communication that helps to counteract the tensions that result from language differences.

Cultural Expectations of the School

Children whose cultural heritage is different from that of the value system perpetuated by the school they attend are in need of special educational services. They need help to master the cultural and language demands of the school *before* they can profit from the typical course of study with which they are apt to be confronted.

Each child coming to the school is expected to become oriented to certain values emphasized in the dominant culture. Some of these values are:[8]

1. Everyone must climb the ladder of success and must place a high value on competitive achievement.
2. Everyone must relate to time by being precise to the hour and minute and must also learn to place a high value on looking to the future.
3. The teachers' reiteration that there is a scientific explanation for all natural phenomena must be accepted.
4. Everyone must become accustomed to change and must anticipate change. (The dominant culture teaches that "change" in and of itself is good and desirable!)

5. Shy, quiet, reserved, and anonymous behavior must be traded for the aggressive, competitive behavior that is socially approved.
6. Everyone must believe that, with some independence, one can shape one's own destiny rather than follow the tradition of remaining an anonymous member of society.

Appreciating Bilingualism as a Value

Bilingualism is a common attribute among most of the people of the world. It is important to view bilingualism as an asset which can be used by teachers to "enhance rather than detract from teaching and learning in the pluralistic society."[9]

The word *bilingual* is used very loosely because it is applied wherever children in school must use a second language as the language of instruction whether or not they know anything about the language. The word is applied as readily to children who know only a nonstandard dialect of English as to those who come to the English-speaking school without ever having used English as a means of communication. Although the real meaning of *bilingual* is "being able to speak in two languages," the term is applied to anyone who is in a two-language environment, even if the person can say only "hello," "thank you," and "good-by" in the second language.

Bilingualism in the Southwest

In the Southwest, children are spoken of as bilinguals if they speak an Indian tongue or Spanish until they enroll in a school where English is the medium of instruction. Naturally, these children are not *bi*lingual by any stretch of the imagination. In the past they were *not* given systematic instruction in the second language so they had little opportunity to become bilingual.

Were the school to take advantage of the child's native language to help him become proficient in the language of the school, the child would then be truly bilingual. With the needs around the world as great as they are today for people to be able to communicate across language barriers, it seems extremely foolish that in the United States the child who brings a language other than English to school has been asked to forget it. If current trends toward bilingual/bicultural programs continue, such children can finish the sixth grade with competent literacy skills in two languages.

The basic problem in the Southwest is *biculturalism,* not bilingualism. Language expresses the values of a culture; culture, by determining behavioral practices and goals, limits the connotations and denotations of the language. The limitations of bilingualism are illustrated in the use of the word *father* in Anglo-American culture and in Zuni Indian culture. For Zuni children, the word *father* represents their mother's husband—a man who enjoys his children as companions. He takes no part in disciplining his children, nor does he have any concern for their economic security. In this matrilineal society, the mother owns the property and her brothers assist in the rearing and disciplining of children. Further, it is said that she may divorce her husband by leaving his shoes and ceremonial garb outside the door while he is away and that this act will be his cue to gather up his belongings and return to his mother's house. The extended family organization does not decree that the marriage relationship is more important than the consanguinal mother-son or sister-brother relationship.

Father for the Anglo middle-class child represents the legal head of a household who is held responsible for the rearing and disciplining of his children. The father's marriage to the child's mother is based, at least theoretically, on a love relationship, and even if dissolved in a court of law, the father may still be held accountable for the full support of the mother and children. It is thus apparent that the term *father* has quite different meanings for the Anglo and for the Zuni child.[10]

The interdependence of language and culture for the young child has been well stated by Davies:

> To change a child's medium of instruction is surely to change his culture; is not culture bound up with language? And if the language should disappear, can the culture remain? Everyone must have his own orientation to life, and language provides the most natural means of reacting to life. In the deepest things of the heart, a man or woman turns naturally to the mother tongue; and in a child's formative stages, his confidence in that tongue must never be impaired.[11]

We believe that teachers plan for far too little use of oral language as an avenue to learning. Too little is done with the language storehouse within the child. Many socio-psychological factors are bound to the values that the child brings to school. If his or her language is not the language of the school, this creates a barrier to be overcome. Home-school alienation, school-child alienation, and then perhaps home-child conflicts over values add to the dilemma.

We must make children feel good about the language they bring to school, and we must accept it as an adequate means of communication. We can demonstrate by the acceptance of that language the acceptance of the child's mother or grandmother and of his entire extended family that speaks that language.

If the teacher reacts negatively to a child's first language, the child will further conclude that only people who speak English are adequate in the teacher's eyes. Both of these things were done to children in the Southwest for many years. They were denied the use of their own language and subtly taught that their language and their people were inferior. One example of this very bad kind of teaching can be cited. A counselor in a border town dormitory for Indian students is reported to have met a bus load of boys and girls at his school in the fall of the year and to have asked them to group themselves around him so that he might say a word to them. He then made the following announcement: "The first thing I want you to do here is to forget that you are an Indian, and the second thing I want to tell you is that we speak only English around here."

Bilingual schools taught in Spanish and English would be natural, workable solutions in many schools in the Southwest. Since Spanish is a major language of the world, books, newspapers, and periodicals are readily available in that language. There are some 200,000,000 speakers of the language in the many nations in the Americas, with libraries, government, business, and schools functioning in Spanish.

The question of young Navajo children receiving instruction in school in the Navajo language is an entirely different matter, though no less important. Although there are no libraries and there is no indicated future literary use, the psychological values are just as valid for Navajo as for Spanish children. At ages five and six, the school should provide for the Navajo language to be used two-thirds or more of the day and planned, sequenced English taught as a spoken means of communication. Learning concepts and reading readiness in Navajo would save children some time later on. At age eight or nine, they would begin learning to read in English, and English would be used as the medium of reading and writing instruction. Thus, the behavior of the adults at school during the first three years would show the children that the school valued their language and cultural heritage, and they might well participate in a Navajo conversation class throughout their school life.

What Is a Bilingual School?

Few truly bilingual programs operate in the public schools of the United States. A bilingual school is one that offers instruction during the school day in more than one language. This means that content subjects are taught in both languages. A child might study mathematics in English and history in Spanish in a Spanish-English bilingual school. In contrast, having children study Spanish for one period of the day as a foreign language, with little attention given to that language except in the class period, does not constitute bilingual education. Furthermore, bilingual education must begin before high school. Few students who begin to study a foreign language in high school are able to master the sound system of that language so they can understand native speakers of that language.

Davies has described a second language learning situation in Wales:

A pleasing feature of parallel-medium or "two-stream" schools in Wales is their complete lack of separatism. The Primary School, Aberystwyth, reorganized in 1948, has 340 pupils, of whom 225 are English- and 115 Welsh-speaking. The staff is bilingual, and the spirit of the school on the whole is Welsh, with Welsh the language of the staff and staff meetings. English is used as the medium of instruction for the English-speaking section throughout, with Welsh introduced as a subject in the second year and taught in every subsequent year. For the Welsh-speaking section, English is introduced during the second half of the first year, the time devoted to it being increased during the second and subsequent years; by the third year, the medium of instruction has become 50% Welsh, 50% English, and by the fourth, equal facility in the use of both languages is aimed at.[12]

Peal and Lambert demonstrated that bilingual children are superior on both verbal and nonverbal intelligence tests when compared with monolinguals. They compared monolingual and bilingual groups of ten-year-old children who were students in six French schools in Montreal, Canada. The groups were matched on age, sex, and socioeconomic status. They concluded that the bilingual subjects had greater mental flexibility than did the monolingual children and, in addition, demonstrated superiority in concept formation.[13]

Richardson reported that bilingual classes in Dade County, Florida achieved as well, on the average, as the monolingual English-speaking classes and had as a bonus their acquired fluency in the Spanish language.[14]

Modiano did a comparative study of two approaches to the teaching of reading in the national languages.[15] She studied reading achievement of native Indians in the Chiapas highlands in southern Mexico, where some of the Indian children are taught to read first in their native Indian languages while others are immediately taught in Spanish. In each of three tribal areas studied, the researcher found significantly better reading ability among children who were first taught to read in their native language.

Modiano's findings are applicable to all schools, and to test this hypothesis she urges experimental programs in schools in the United States having large linguistic minorities. She found no school system in the nation employing the native-language-first approach when she was ready to conduct her study in 1965.

Rock Point Bilingual Program

Rock Point Boarding School is located on the Navajo Reservation near Chinle, Arizona. Several years ago this school passed from the Chinle Agency of the Bureau of Indian Affairs (BIA) to the local community and became a community-controlled "contract" school. The school began developing a bilingual program in 1967 when Title I funds became available for that purpose. However, from 1967 until 1971 the local school board exercised little control and those years were spent developing oral Navajo and oral English, reading readiness in

Navajo, and doing a great deal of thinking about initial literacy. Little material was available in Navajo then, so just planning the curriculum one year at a time was a monumental task. However, the results of the bilingual program at Rock Point are very significant. In a 1978 report, by the end of grade six, Navajo children in the bilingual program were testing at the national sixth grade norms in English reading.[16]

Milingimbi Bilingual Education Program

Milingimbi is an Aboriginal community in the Northern Territory of Australia. Its bilingual program was begun in 1973. Classes for primary children have been conducted since that time in both the Aboriginal language and English. Much testing has been done to identify the effectiveness of the bilingual program.[17]

> Since the introduction of bilingual education at Milingimbi, the children are not only learning to read and write in their own language and furthering their knowledge and respect for their own culture, but they are also achieving better academic results in oral English, reading, English composition, and mathematics than they were under the former English monolingual education system. Milingimbi School is reasonably typical of the larger bilingual schools in the Northern Territory, and thus these results lend support to the whole movement of bilingual education among Aboriginal children.[18]

Overcoming Limited English Proficiency

With the mobility of our general population and the influx of immigrants from all over the world into our country, *every teacher* must now be able to deal with the children who have only limited proficiency in the use of the English language. Even though many schools do have special teachers and special programs, it is really the classroom teacher who must accept the responsibility for the level of literacy in the schools. And mainstreaming, if carefully planned, is a good idea if the classroom teacher can deal with the limited English proficient (LEP) child in a holistic language framework.

The audio-lingual method or the mimic-memorization method of learning a new language that worked well for young adults will work just as well for young children if the teacher takes into account the nature of childhood and the motivations young children have for learning and growing. There are a number of commonly used language patterns that must be practiced over and over, but the practice must be spirited, motivated, and relevant. An LEP student paired with a buddy who is a fluent speaker can practice lots of routines in ways that will be fun for them.

Pictures can be used to teach labels for concepts and to generate sentences. Captions can be written for pictures; pictures can be put in categories; language experience paragraphs can be written.

Wordless picture books can be used with a peer or with an interested listening adult to generate language; trade books with ten, twenty, or thirty different words can be read to the LEP student once or many times, and he can then read them back to his buddy, to the teacher's aid, or to the teacher.

Singing verses of the traditional songs like "Here We Go Round the Mulberry Bush," "Clementine," or "The Wheels of the Bus Go Round and Round," helps LEP students to internalize the rhythm and inflection in English. In this regard, teachers might make use of *Jazz Chants for Children* (Graham, 1979).[19]

Copying familiar dialogues will familiarize the child with the language and help her to read it better. Having the child take dictation in the new language, if not extended for too long a period, is highly recommended.

Language processes—listening, speaking, reading, writing—support and clarify each other, but the teacher must be able to work within the limits established by the children's motivations and endurance. In meaningful contexts, the regular classroom teacher can guide the child with limited English proficiency successfully into the mainstream of learning.

Teaching ESL Methodology

To be a good teacher of bilingual children requires more than a set of classroom techniques. Above all, the teacher should have tact, common sense, and sympathetic understanding of problems the children may have. It has already been stressed that the teacher should also know something of the language of the child's parents and should know something about the cultural practices and contributions of that culture. It is a good idea for the teacher to visit the child's home, not once, but many times. Such visits make it possible for the teacher to explain the basic purposes of the school and clarify erroneous concepts the child may have brought home. It is important for the teacher to feel and to show genuine appreciation for the values of the culture of the parents. Good teaching techniques will produce the best possible results when grounded on such a firm emotional base.

How shall primary teachers develop the language arts in bilingual boys and girls during the primary grades? The first task is to teach the child learning English as a second language the necessary oral language skills so that he can function more nearly the way the native speaker functions.

Finocchiaro has described the second-language teaching-learning process as follows:[20]

1. Learning a language means forming new habits through intensive practice in hearing and speaking.
2. It is deemed advisable that the teacher use and repeat a limited number of sentence patterns and give the children intensive practice in those patterns only. The teacher should learn to pronounce these patterns as perfectly as possible. He should learn when to use them and with which other combinations they are normally used. He should learn how to develop and how to judge accurate pronunciation

in his pupils. Too, he should learn how to give varied, interesting practice in the limited patterns being taught. Improvisation by teacher and pupils at this level is not recommended.

3. *Habitual use of the most frequently used patterns* and items of language should take precedence over the mere accumulation of words. The acquisition of vocabulary should be a secondary goal at the beginning stage. Vocabulary will increase rapidly when reading is begun. To reiterate the same principle—because it is of utmost importance—*learning a foreign language is not primarily acquiring vocabulary,* as necessary as that is. It is much more important for the student to engage in practice which will most quickly form habits of articulation, stress, intonation, word order, and word formation. The sooner these patterns become habit and not choice, the sooner mastery of the language will be achieved.

4. Vocabulary should be taught and practiced only in the context of real situations so that meaning will be clarified and reinforced.

5. Classroom activities should center about authentic speech situations—dialogues, interchanges (I'm six. How old are you?), descriptions, rejoinders ("Are you ready?" "Of course.")—where two or more children are involved.

6. Speech should not be slowed down nor the rhythm distorted because of the mistaken idea that it will increase understanding.

7. New patterns of language should be introduced and practiced with vocabulary that students already know. For example, if one were teaching the interrogative form, "Do you have _____ ?" the point of departure would be a sentence the children already know, e.g., "I have a dog at home."

Children cannot *read* a language they cannot use orally. They must be able to express themselves well in oral English before they can read it with any satisfaction. Even many concepts describing everyday activities will be meaningless if met the first time in textbooks. The teacher's effort will be totally nonproductive if reading and writing are taught before listening and speaking. The *pressure* to move children into formal reading groups before they have learned listening and speaking habits in the language is one of the gravest errors teachers continue to make with young non-English-speaking children.

The aural-oral method of learning a language is a method of instruction that emphasizes *hearing and speaking* the new language, especially in the beginning rather than learning grammatical structure, translation, reading, or writing. When this method is correctly followed, learners say only what they have heard (and understood); read what they have said; and write what they have heard, said, and read.

Teachers can devise many lessons using improvised audio and visual aids to motivate language learning.

Elementary stories and poems can be used to establish meanings. For example, the poem "What Is Black?" could reinforce many meanings for the word *black* if the teacher gathers some pictures from the vertical picture file and some three-dimensional toys from ten-cent stores, drug stores, and department stores.

What Is Black?[21]

Black is good earth where little seeds grow;
Black is the bird that we call a crow.
Black is a berry which grows on a vine;
Black is the night, unless moon and stars shine.
Black are the shoes that you wear on your feet;
Black is the pepper on food that you eat.
Black is sweet licorice—yum, yum, yum!
Black is the spot of ink on your thumb.
Black is the skunk with stripe down his back;
Black is the engine that runs on a track.
Black is a fierce old Halloween cat;
Black is a witch's steeple hat.
Black is the marker with which you write;
Black is the opposite of white!

Louise Binder Scott

Find pictures of natural pairs of objects in magazines and catalogs and mount them on 3-by-5 or 4-by-6-inch cards. Some possible pairs would be:

cup—saucer	fork—knife	doll—doll carriage
pen—pencil	boy—girl	light bulb—lamp
ball—bat	chair—desk	comb—hair
broom—dust pan	shirt—tie	hammer—nail
pan—lid	ring—finger	football player—football
mare—foal	baker—cake	fire fighter—fire truck
cat—dog	nose—face	letter carrier—letter
leaf—tree	paint—brush	dog—bone

Pictures that associate opposite concepts can be collected and mounted. Reading readiness books and picture dictionaries are among sources that should be looked at. Some possible pairs would be:

empty—full	above—below	large—small
in—out	cold—hot	on—off
inside—outside	left—right	tall—short

Pictures that represent seasons of the year can be compiled and classified into spring, summer, fall, winter. Similarly, pictures can be found to represent action verbs: swinging, sitting, reading, pasting, cutting, playing, falling down, getting off of, reaching, falling, kneeling, running, standing, painting, leaning over, setting, jumping, flying, sliding down.

Pictures of clothing we wear can be put in categories of things for mother, father, brother, sister. Catalogs of the big mail order companies are excellent sources for pictures of tools.

Dogs, toys, furniture, time pieces, different kinds of chairs, different kinds of lamps, ways we travel, domestic animals, dishes, money, sharp objects, musical instruments—all such things are categories of pictures that might be compiled in packets for different kinds of games or drills that might be planned with or without direct teacher supervision.

Children are not *functioning* in a language until they can generate sentences of their own. One technique that may be helpful is the use of pictures without background detail. Question words such as *who, what, why,* and *where* can then be used to elicit the necessary parts for constructing complete sentences.

The suggestions given here all emphasize the oral language and language-experience approach. That means teaching language patterns and providing the children much opportunity to talk about their experiences, with the teacher doing the little writing that needs to be done.

Six-year-olds can learn orally why irrigation is necessary in much of the Rio Grande Valley for growing garden vegetables. One kindergarten class became interested in a new house that was being built near the school so were taken to visit the house several times. They discussed how water would be piped into it, how the electricity would work, and all the kinds of skilled workmen who helped to build a house. Because one child was especially interested in the water pipes, a trip was arranged to the city water works department to see a large wall map that showed how the water lines were laid throughout the city.

Through meaningful experiences like these, a teacher can develop a language-experience approach to reading with children learning English as a second language in the same way as she does with children whose native language is English. The children soon learn that:

1. Reading is nothing more than talk written down.
2. Once written down, it can be read back exactly as it was said.
3. The printed word and a picture can mean the same thing.
4. Punctuation can change meaning in written language.

The picture illustrating "helpful little words," figure 15.1, can make common prepositions meaningful and can be useful for review. The teacher must be careful to present such abstract words *one at a time* and to fix their meanings in a way that will not confuse the child. These words will be used naturally in language-experience stories, adding both natural purpose to learning them and much-needed repetition.

Some Methodology in TESOL

The basic methodology of TESOL (Teaching English as a Second Language) includes oral drills in sentence patterns that involve substitutions, expansions, and transformations, among other things. Following are some examples.

Figure 15.1
The common prepositions must be taught one at a time in meaningful situations and with sufficient review provided so that the child uses them confidently.

From Hale C. Reid and Helen W. Crane, *My Picture Dictionary* (Boston, Mass.: Ginn, copyright © 1965), p. 37.

Substitutions

The teacher models a sentence, such as "The school is just around the corner." The whole class repeats it, then, small groups, and then individuals. Then the teacher says only the word *store,* and in sequence, the class, small groups, and then individuals respond, "The store is just around the corner." The teacher says "restaurant," and the class, etc., respond, "The restaurant is just around the corner," etc.

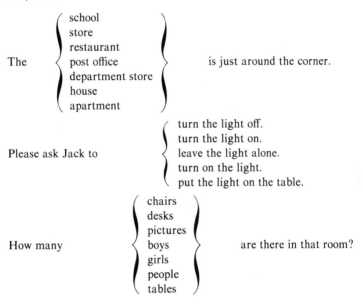

The
$\begin{cases} \text{school} \\ \text{store} \\ \text{restaurant} \\ \text{post office} \\ \text{department store} \\ \text{house} \\ \text{apartment} \end{cases}$
is just around the corner.

Please ask Jack to
$\begin{cases} \text{turn the light off.} \\ \text{turn the light on.} \\ \text{leave the light alone.} \\ \text{turn on the light.} \\ \text{put the light on the table.} \end{cases}$

How many
$\begin{cases} \text{chairs} \\ \text{desks} \\ \text{pictures} \\ \text{boys} \\ \text{girls} \\ \text{people} \\ \text{tables} \end{cases}$
are there in that room?

Expansions

Basic sentence patterns are, of course, made to serve their purposes more clearly for speakers by being expanded. Boys and girls who are native speakers of the language get much practice in this in English lessons. Speakers of nonstandard English will need a great deal of help with these exercises.

	Dogs bark.
	Dogs bark loudly.
The people's	dogs bark loudly.
The people's	dogs bark loudly every night.
We could hear the people's	dogs bark loudly every night.
We could hear the people's	dogs bark loudly every night when we were at grandmother's house.
The roses	are beautiful.
The red roses	are beautiful.
The red roses near my window	are beautiful.
I gave the red roses near my window	to the elderly couple next door.
I can play.	
I can play	this afternoon.
I can play	this afternoon for a while.
I can play	until five o'clock this afternoon.
I can play in the park	until five o'clock this afternoon.

457

Basic sentence structure

The book was lost.
The book was *The Wind in the Willows.*

The man in the library reads almost every evening.
He knows a great deal about Mexico.

Some pupils know the story already.
They should not tell the ending.

I came home early.
The library was closed.

The farmer didn't plant potatoes.
The ground was too wet.

Mother complained.
I didn't help get dinner.

I didn't finish.
The bell rang.

I can't go with you.
My homework isn't finished.

I have to wait.
I get paid on Friday.

I can't buy the groceries.
She didn't give me the list.

I'll stay here.
The library stays open.

José will work every day.
His brother can work too.

It is the end of summer.
School will begin soon.

Girls work.
Boys play.

The teacher was fair.
The teacher was helpful.
The teacher was completely honest.

Subordination

The book that was lost was *The Wind in the Willows.*

The man who reads in the library almost every evening knows a great deal about Mexico.

Pupils who know the story already should not tell the ending.

Subordination using *because, until, when,* etc.

I came home early because the library was closed.

The farmer didn't plant potatoes because the ground was too wet.

Mother complained because I didn't help get dinner.

I didn't finish because the bell rang.

I can't go with you until my homework is finished.

I have to wait until I get paid on Friday.

I can't buy the groceries until she gives me the list.

I'll stay here if the library stays open.

José will work every day if his brother can work too.

It is the end of summer and school will begin soon.

Girls work and boys play.

Compounding with deletions

The teacher was fair, helpful, and completely honest.

Transformations	All English sentences are derived, by transformation and combination, from a few basic sentence types. So the sentence "Four chairs are in the room" can be transformed into a question by changing the positions of the subject and verb: "Are four chairs in the room?"

Lenneberg defined *transformation* in this way.

> We have illustrated a universal principle of grammatical knowledge or understanding: there must be lawful ways in which certain types of structure may be related to other types of structure. The grammatical laws that control these relations have come to be called *transformations*.
>
> Transformations are statements of grammatical as well as semantic and phonological connections.[22]

Observe the many transformations of the sentence "The girl knits her sweater."

The girl knitted her sweater.
The girl did knit her sweater.
The girl was knitting her sweater.
The girl didn't knit her sweater.
The girl wasn't knitting her sweater.
Wasn't the girl knitting her sweater?
Did the girl knit her sweater?
Didn't the girl knit her sweater?
The sweater was knitted by the girl.
Was the sweater knitted by the girl?

More basic sentences and transformations are presented below.

Passive Voice

Basic sentence structure	**Passive transformation**
They built a house.	A house was built by them.
John shot a deer.	A deer was shot by John.
Our country fought a civil war.	A civil war was fought by our country.
The third grade worked that problem.	That problem was worked by the third grade.
The old man planted the garden.	The garden was planted by the old man.

Verb to Noun

	Verb-to-noun transformation
John works.	John is a worker.
Julio gardens.	Julio is a gardener.
Mary teaches.	Mary is a teacher.
Ramon farms.	Ramon is a farmer.
Enrique drives a truck.	Enrique is a truck driver.

Mrs. Jones practices law.	Mrs. Jones is a lawyer.
Marianna cooks.	Marianna is a cook.
Mrs. Chacon makes dresses.	Mrs. Chacon is a dressmaker.
Mr. Acosta plays chess.	Mr. Acosta is a chess player.
Linda studies at the university.	Linda is a student at the university.

*Past
Transformations*

Basic sentence structure

Past transformation

I go to work.	I went to work.
I need help.	I needed help.
I walk to class.	I walked to class.
I bring my books.	I brought my books.
I eat lunch at school.	I ate lunch at school.
I work.	I worked.
He works.	He worked.
She works.	She worked.
You work.	You worked.
We work.	We worked.
They work.	They worked.
I go.	I went.
He goes.	He went.

Question Words

Question-word transformation

John works here.	*Who* works here?
Robert lives in *Arizona*.	*Where* does Robert live?
The books should have cost *ten dollars*.	*How much* should the books have cost?
Bill is in his *office*.	*Where* is Bill?
He studies *geography*.	*What* does he study?
He *works* in an office.	*What* does he do?
He studies in the *afternoon*.	*When* does he study?
He writes letters *at night*.	*When* does he write letters?

**"There," "it," or "does"
transformation/
Question transformation**

A man is at the door.	There is a man at the door./ Is there a man at the door?
Four chairs are at the table.	There are four chairs at the table./ Are there four chairs at the table?
Three boys are in the principal's office.	There are three boys in the principal's office./ Are there three boys in the principal's office?
The day is warm.	It is a warm day./ Is it a warm day?
The job is tough.	It is a tough job./ Is it a tough job?
He reads fast.	He does read fast./ Does he read fast?

Tag-ons

Basic sentence structure

**Tag question, negative tag/
Tag question, positive tag**

You can go.	You can go, can't you?/ You can't go, can you?
He has the book.	He has the book, hasn't he?/ He doesn't have the book, does he?
He is working today.	He is working today, isn't he?/ He isn't working today, is he?
He was in your office.	He was in your office, wasn't he?/ He wasn't in your office, was he?
He will come back soon.	He will come back soon, won't he?/ He won't come back soon, will he?

A year—or longer—much longer if necessary—may be required to teach the most common sentence patterns with dialogue practice, substitution drills, and questions and answers. Such lessons are now commercially available to all teachers. Of course, each teacher will adapt any text to fit the needs and specific experiences of the students being taught.

Contrastive Analysis of English and Spanish

Most teachers of native Spanish-speakers in classrooms where English is the medium of instruction have heard sentences like the following: "We went through the rooms bigs"; "Mary is wear a dress red"; "He no go to school"; "Yesterday your brother I saw"; "I am ready for to read"; "I see you later"; "Is Tuesday";

and "This apple is more big than that one." Usually such sentences represent Spanish structure combined with English vocabulary. It is useful to analyze such sentences in those terms for the students in order to demonstrate *why* Spanish-speakers tend to produce certain kinds of mistakes in English.

The following examples of contrast in structure are adapted from *Teaching English as a New Language to Adults:*[23]

Native English-Speaker	**Spanish-Speaker Learning English**
Not is negative used with verb forms: "Mary is not here."	Spanish negation of verb is *no;* hence, "Mary is no here."
Verb is inflected with *s* in English third person simple present: "The boy eats."	Spanish verbs are fully inflected; hence, in learning our comparatively uninflected English, the student tends to drop even the inflections that persist, to say: "The boy eat."
Negatives are formed with *do, does, did:* "He *did* not go to school."	Spanish has no auxiliaries; hence, "He no go/went to school."
English adjectives usually precede the noun: "The red dress."	Spanish adjectives usually follow the noun; hence, "The dress red."
Going to to express future time: "I am going to sing."	Comparable Spanish construction uses the simple present; hence, "I go to sing."
The auxiliary *will* in English future: "I will see you later."	Tendency is to omit auxiliary and to say: "I see you later."
Use of *it* to start a sentence: "It is Tuesday."	Spanish does not have the "It . . ." construction; hence, "Is Tuesday."
Use of *to be* to express age: "I'm twenty years old."	Spanish uses *to have;* hence, "I have twenty years."
Use of *to be* to express hunger, thirst, etc. "I am thirsty."	Spanish uses *to have;* hence, "I have hunger"; "I have thirst."
English negative imperative: "Don't run!"	Spanish does not have the auxiliary *do;* hence, "No run!"
Questions with *do, does,* and *did:* "Does this man work?"	No auxiliaries exist in Spanish. Tendency is to say: "This man works?" or "Works this man?"
Indefinite article used in front of noun identifying occupation: "She is a nurse."	Spanish does not use the indefinite article; hence, "She is nurse."

The following English-Spanish language differences cause particular problems.

English often uses the single phonological feature of voiced vs. voiceless sounds (e.g., *z* vs. *s*) to distinguish spoken words. For example: race-raise; lacy-lazy; niece-knees; seal-zeal; price-prize. This difference in sound is never the sole feature to separate meanings in Spanish.

English uses the phonological difference between *n* and *ng* to distinguish meanings while Spanish does not. For example: ran-rang; sin-sing; kin-king; thin-thing; fan-fang; ban-bang.

The Spanish speaker learning English must learn many new consonant sounds. *Sh* in *shine* and *wh* in *when*.

While Spanish uses only five vowel sounds, English uses many more *to distinguish meanings*. Practice is necessary for the Spanish-speaking person to develop auditory discrimination of such pairs as the following: heat-hit; met-mate; tap-tape; look-luck; pin-pine; hat-hot; sheep-ship; mit-meet; eat-it; late-let; bed-bad; fool-full; coat-caught; caught-cut.

Distinguishing between some consonant sounds can cause trouble too: pig-big; pig-pick; thank-sank; then-den; place-plays. Also, clusters like *ts* in *hats; lpt* in *helped; lkt* in *talked*.

Modifiers do *not* follow the noun in English:

The blue sky, not *the sky blue*.
The juicy apples, not *the apples juicy*.
The bus station is not the same as *the station bus*.
The pocket watch is not the same as *the watch pocket*.

Word order in sentences has more flexibility in Spanish than in English. For example, any of the following Spanish sentences is correct, but only one of the literally translated English.

Ayer vine aquí.	Yesterday I came here.
Aquí vine ayer.	Here I came yesterday.
Vine ayer aquí.	I came yesterday here.
Ayer aquí vine.	Yesterday here I came.

The irregularity of some words causes difficulty after children learn to generalize from regular forms: I *teared* the paper. I *throwed* the ball. I *dood* it.

Intonation and stress are very important in conveying meanings:

Which book did *you* buy?
Which book *did* you buy?
Which book did you *buy?*
Are *you* going back to school this fall?
Are you going back to school *this* fall?
Are you going *back to school* this fall?

Programs that teach English as a second language in the United States have been based generally upon contrastive analysis of Spanish and English. Weaver has pointed out that this bias does not fit the needs of the Indian child. The points of contrast between English and Indian languages that cause most difficulty are not at all like the English-Spanish contrasts. The difficulties that Navajo children, for example, are most likely to encounter are:

1. Distinction of number.
2. Expression of possession.
3. Application of adjective to noun.
4. Distinction of gender.
5. Usage of subject and object.
6. Usage of definite and indefinite articles.
7. Usage of definite and indefinite pronouns.
8. Usage of correct verb inflections.
9. Usage of negative questions.[24]

Indian languages need the same contrastive study with respect to English as European languages have had so that educators can improve English language instruction for Indian people.

"Linguistic" Reading Programs

By 1968 three or four sets of so-called "linguistic readers" were published. They were based on the general principle that the spelling patterns of new words introduced to beginning readers must be rigidly controlled. The decoding process was thus emphasized to the exclusion of teaching reading as a meaningful process. These books have nothing to offer the classroom teacher of reading. They contradict any first grade teacher's efforts to encourage good oral language and expanded usage in conversations and to enlarge vocabulary and attention span by reading good stories to children. These books offer as a lesson only uninteresting, artificial bits of text containing, for example, no vowel except short *a*. Few teachers could motivate much interest in "day-after-day" reading of such passages as this:

A cat sat.
A fat cat sat.
A cat had a hat.
A man had a cat.
A cat had a fat rat.

A remedial reading clinician once used such books in individual tutoring situations with youngsters to encourage them to read either silently or orally. At the next session many children asked if they could please have a different book to read.

Loban[25] and Strickland[26] have helped teachers to understand how the English language is used by children for whom it is the first language. The fact that only a few basic patterns are used in ordinary conversations provides a basis for English language practice that will help other children learn it as a second language. Similarly the sentence word order of children's oral usage probably should be carried over into written material used for teaching reading. Reading comprehension should be greater in materials that utilize high frequency sentence patterns from oral language structure than in materials using unusual or unfamiliar types of sentence patterns.

Survival Skills

If the newly-arrived child knows no English, the first thing that must concern her teacher is that she learn enough survival language to make her days tolerable with the least possible tension and frustration. Survival language includes phrases used in greeting peers and adults and in offering the child assistance in making her adjustments to the classroom, and in understanding the simple directions that will be used regularly in the classroom. A small group of teachers expecting non-English-speaking enrollees would do well to work together to build a list of phrases or oral language expressions that have priority in learning survival skills. A few examples are:

What's your name?
Welcome to our class.
May I go to the restroom?
It's time for lunch.
Please come with me.
Do it this way.
Please sit here.
Listen carefully.

Learning survival language will be accelerated with appropriate "tours" of different areas of the school plant. Such a tour, or tours, can emphasize important locations within the building: the restrooms, the principal's office, the cafeteria, the music room, and permissible entrances and exits.

Teachers with no previous opportunity to learn how to teach English as a second language can try to remember guidelines like the following:[27]

1. Be patient. It will take time for some non-English-speaking students to feel "ready" or "brave" enough to try to use English spontaneously.
2. Try to allow the non-English-speaking student to speak when *he or she* is ready.
3. Don't worry about accent. Worry only about being able to understand.
4. Collect visual materials—tiny objects from toy stores, hardware stores, drug stores, and garage sales. Collect pictures from all available sources.
5. Use gestures and all possible nonverbal means of communication to make sure the students understand what they are to do.
6. Stay optimistic. Smile a lot and be genuine.
7. Don't settle for yes-no answers. The ultimate goal is to get *verb forms* used in comprehensible sentences.
8. Encourage "risk-taking." Reward children for trying to use the language in meaningful ways.
9. The classroom should be a place where lots of talking is "legal" and encouraged. *Quiet* rooms do not extend children's ability to generate their own language.
10. Rooms with one or two children learning English as a second language are becoming more and more common all over the country. You might like to get enrolled in a university class in which you can take a course in how to teach it.

Peer Tutoring

In order to give the non-English-speaking student maximum opportunity to hear and practice English, the teacher will probably find that the other children in the classroom are among the best resources. Peer teachers will adjust to elementary levels of language use, will demand understanding on the part of the new student, and will focus intently on the goal of successful communication. With a few pointers from the teacher and an understanding of flexible use of the environment, peer tutors should be able to engage the new student in many hands-on activities in, near, or outside the classroom that will require his purposeful use of English.

1. *Playing catch.* The peer tutor tosses the ball to the new student. While the ball is in the air, she says, "Catch!" The tutor uses gestures and motions for the new student to return the ball. As she

returns it, the tutor says, "Throw it back to me." When she catches the ball, she may ad-lib different expressions such as: "Thanks," or "That's right," or "A good toss."

2. *Carrying messages to other rooms or to the principal's office.* The tutor needs to use such expressions as: "Let's go to the principal's office," or "We're going to Mr. Bell's room," or "We have a message to deliver."

3. *Working jigsaw puzzles together.* The tutor can model: "Can you find this piece?" "Please hand me that piece," "Will that piece fit in over here?"

Peer tutoring accomplishes several objectives: (1) it uses language that is needed in the everyday operation of the class in its natural environment; (2) it maximizes the amount of time that the new student must *listen and respond* to one other person using English; and (3) it puts the emphasis on learning in a satisfying, affective environment that should generate its own motivation and reward for learning.

Peer tutoring should also be used to extend learning for the English-speaking students. After a few successful lessons with the new student learning English, he should be encouraged to reverse the process and try to teach his tutors a few words of his native language. Thus there is the faint hope that the fluent English speaker will become interested in the other language and may even acquire some skill with it.

Teaching Reading to the Bilingual Child

Perez writes:

> The reading process is founded on oral language experiences which the child brings to school from home, and when these experiences have occurred in Spanish rather than in English, they are of little value for English reading. For these children, an effective instructional program in reading must begin with an expansion of oral English skills.[28]

Perez cautions us that while unilingual English-speaking children may progress from spoken to written language fairly quickly, children for whom English is a second language may require a much longer period of mastering fluent oral English before forging ahead in the reading program.

Perez assembled packets of language exercises to use with boys and girls who entered third grade reading at about primer level. The packets provided lessons using simple analogies, idiomatic expressions, compound words, synonyms, antonyms, multiple meanings, and words associated in pairs. There were also rhymes, poems, competitive games, and some sentence pattern practice. The three teachers who used these packets got very good results after only one semester of the school year. Perez concluded that these kinds of oral language lessons need to be continued through the sixth grade with Mexican-American students learning English as a second language.[29]

Because every "regular" classroom teacher today must be prepared to accommodate children who do not speak English, every teacher must be prepared to work effectively with these children. Gonzales suggests three very significant areas in which the teacher can be prepared to work:[30]

1. *Survival skills.* What are the minimal language expressions that the child must be able to use in order to function in the classroom? Some examples: "Hello." "My name is _____ ." "What is your name?" "Do you need to go to the restroom?" "Please come with me." "Do it this way." "Listen carefully." Gonzales suggests that a small group of teachers can compose a common list of such expressions and then try to find ways to make the new students understand them.

2. *Peer tutoring.* The teacher's richest resource for help in working intensively with speakers of other languages is the children in the class. It is easy for one seven-year-old to talk with another in *highly nonverbal ways* if they are playing ball together, dusting the blackboard erasers, carrying a note to the principal's office, or working a puzzle. Then, there are many picture books that can be used to "talk about" the contents of the book.

   Peer tutoring must also include, at times, providing for the student who knows a different language to have some opportunity to teach it to the fluent English speaker. Affective values will be learned by both students.

3. *Suggestions to the teacher.* Teachers must remember to accommodate every attempt when the non-English-speaking student is willing to try to respond. Make an extra effort to be patient; accept the accents in language attempts; use gestures and make nonverbal language count; be pleasant; use the native language of the child if you know it; accept the meaning of the child's words and not the "current grammar"; encourage the non-English speaker to be a risk-taker and respond.

When Children Fail to Respond

Failing to answer is one of the most obvious ways in which children fail to meet a teacher's demand. Unfortunately, this reveals little. The child may not have heard the question, may not have understood some part of it, may not know that an answer is expected, may not feel like answering, or may genuinely not know the answer. It is the teacher's task to find out which of these caused the problem by using an appropriately varied question to encourage a more easily analyzed answer. Usually, there are indications in the child's behavior of what the problem might be. As an example, imagine that the teacher asks, "Why doesn't this brick roll?" and the child does not answer. If the child makes no response at all, looking at neither the brick nor the teacher, then one might suppose that the child did not hear the question. Repeating the question would probably be worthwhile in this case, perhaps calling the child by name and being sure of getting attention,

"Look, John, why doesn't this brick roll?" There may be something in the question that John doesn't understand, and this can be checked. Does he know what *roll* means, for example; is it perfectly clear which brick he is being asked about?[31]

TESOL Text Materials

Following is a selected list of texts available to teachers for teaching English as a second language:

Boggs, Ralph, and Robert Dixon. *English Step by Step with Pictures.* New ed. New York: Regents, 1980. Grades four through twelve.

English Language Services, Inc. *English This Way.* 12 vols. New York: Macmillan, 1963–65. Tapes available.

English Language Services, Inc. *The New English 900.* 6 vols. New York: Macmillan, 1973.

Evans, A. J., and Marilyn Palmer. *Writing About Pictures: Using Pictures to Develop Language and Writing Skills.* 6 vols. New York: Teachers College Press, 1982. For elementary grades.

Hall, Eugene J. *English Self-Taught, Books 1–12.* New York: Regents, 1974–76. Cassette tapes available.

Hall, Eugene J. *Practical Conversation in English, Books I and II.* New York: Regents, 1981.

Lado, Robert. *English Series: A Complete Course in English as a Second Language.* 6 vols. New York: Regents, 1977–80.

Mellgren, Lars, and Michael Walker. *New Horizons in English.* 6 vols. Reading, Mass.: Addison-Wesley, 1973–74.

National Council of Teachers of English. *English for Today.* 6 vols. New York: McGraw-Hill, 1973–76.

Taylor, Grant. *Practicing American English.* New York: McGraw-Hill, 1962.

Materials for Bilingual Schools

Schools interested in finding text materials for elementary school classes will be able to find an adequate supply. Since the passage of funding for the Bilingual Education Act, more than a hundred federally funded programs in bilingual education have been in progress. The large majority have been Spanish-English bilingual, although more than twenty different native American languages were used in 1973–74 in developing Indian language-English bilingual programs. Anyone seeking sources of available materials could address inquiries to:

Center for Applied Linguistics
1611 N. Kent Street
Arlington, Virginia 22209

U.S. Commission on Civil Rights
Washington, D.C. 20425

Materials Acquisition Project
2950 National Avenue
San Diego, California 92120

Dissemination Center for Bilingual Bicultural Education
6504 Tracor Lane
Austin, Texas 78721

Motivation to Learn a New Language

Learning language seems to require stimulation from others and considerable reinforcement (feedback) from others. Consider the following:[32]

1. *Stimulation.* Young children are literally surrounded by it. Parents, other adults, siblings, the TV, the radio, and the record player. The language youngsters hear will be, it is hoped, the natural language of a wide variety of speakers.

2. *Identification.* Young children identify with the adult who gives them the intensive care that they need. Identification with the adult leads to a strong motivation to imitate what the adult does.

3. *External reinforcement.* The caring adults are very likely to reward young children for their language attempts. The more adults or older siblings in the environment, the more the child is praised, asked to say a new word again, and given tangible rewards for "trying to talk."

4. *Conveying information.* Very early, children are trying to ask for their needs to be met and to communicate information about their environment. Children's insatiable curiosity can frustrate the parent who tires of "What's that?" or "Why?"

5. *Self-reinforcement.* Children start talking to themselves by verbalizing the rhythm of adult speech, using much repetition.

The Integrated Day

The teaching of the English language cannot be carried on as if English were an isolated subject in the curriculum. Instead, the learning of English must be a part of the everyday experiences and activities of boys and girls. Everyday experiences must be the source of "language lessons" to give practice with the language and to clarify what is going on normally in their lives.

Using the new language in interesting and purposeful ways provides the motivation for children to learn oral and written English. They sense actual needs, rather than deciding that they are being made to learn simply for the sake of learning. New vocabulary and new verb forms must be related to the experiences of the children, and the language patterns must be appropriate to the way children talk about those experiences. There is opportunity during the school day to provide short and varied drills to reinforce meaningful language that needs to be learned.

The teacher should provide frequent review to make sure that students have opportunities to hear themselves learning the new language. The teacher must generate new and innovative applications for the language in social situations, activities, and other school experiences. English-as-a-second-language (ESL) lessons can be "constructed" out of the social studies lesson, the health lesson, or the art lesson.

Understanding Bilingual Education Legislation

In 1967, a Senate bill was introduced as an amendment to the Elementary and Secondary Education Act of 1965. It provided for bilingual education in the schools that would:

1. Incorporate the teaching of the native language of the child.
2. Incorporate the teaching of English as a second language.
3. Develop programs that would teach native-speaking children a knowledge of and pride in their ancestral language and culture.
4. Encourage schools to employ teachers who could use the native language of the child.
5. Establish closer ties between the school and the home.

The bill was tied to a poverty context, but it provided for making schools open institutions that would build on the cultural strengths of students, reinforce the languages the children already knew, and build personal identification and stronger egos into the objectives of the school program. For millions of children in the public schools, the bill, which eventually became the Bilingual Education Act, promised greater opportunity to participate in the "open" society. The bill became law in 1967 with financial support authorized for fiscal year 1969.

The Bilingual Education Act recognized the following needs:[33]

1. There are large numbers of children of limited English proficiency.
2. Many of these children have a cultural heritage that differs from that of English-speaking persons.
3. A primary means by which a child learns is through the use of that child's language and cultural heritage.
4. Therefore, large numbers of children of limited English language proficiency have educational needs that can be met by the use of bilingual educational methods and techniques.
5. In addition, children of limited English proficiency and children whose primary language is English benefit through the fullest utilization of multiple language and cultural resources.
6. Children of limited English proficiency have a high dropout rate and low median years of education.
7. Research and evaluation capabilities in the field of bilingual education need to be strengthened.

Therefore Congress, to insure equal educational opportunities for all children, encouraged the establishment and operation of programs using bilingual educational practices, techniques, and methods, and provided financial assistance to enable schools to offer such programs.

The 1974 amendments to the Bilingual Education Act of 1967 broadened the definition of students included under the act, using the term "limited English-speaking ability." The 1978 amendments modified the term to "limited English proficiency." Eligibility of students to be included in the 1978 amendments included those "who cannot read, write, or understand English at the level appropriate for their age and grade." Limited English proficiency refers to individuals not born in the U.S., those whose native language is not English, those who come from environments where languages other than English are dominant, and American Indian and Alaskan native students whose native language and environment have had a significant impact on their level of English language proficiency.[34]

Summary

. . . There is general agreement all over the educational world that the child should begin his education in his mother tongue or . . . the language he most easily understands.

. . . we are not producing bilingual school children and we never shall, as long as the second language is *not* used as an instrument of expression and *not* merely as a subject to be learned for an examination. In other words, the second language must be used as a medium in the school.[35]

Thompson and Hamalainen stated:

In the ever shrinking world the attainment of goals of communication and understanding among its people is imperative if we are to live in peace and security. It is an obvious fact known to almost everyone that we are only one day's distance from every place in the world. Not only are we this close to each other in time, but in increasing numbers we are establishing contact with each other.[36]

The United States government, aware of the importance of foreign languages to the national interest, enacted pertinent legislation to provide support for research and training. The National Defense Education Act (NDEA) of August 1958 in its Title VI promoted the study of foreign languages and the quality of instruction. NDEA has provided more schools and colleges with the opportunity to teach foreign languages more effectively than any other measure in recent years.

The focus on foreign language study has shown that learning a second language is very difficult. The learner must follow many of the same steps children take in learning their native language. However, adult learners experience much interference from previously learned speaking and reading and writing habits. Yet, they must learn to hear and to discriminate the significant sounds of that new language as used by its speakers. Learners must produce sound units that are new and, therefore, difficult because these sounds are not found in the structure of their native language. Since learners are fluent and at ease in the use of their native tongue, there are additional barriers to overcome: feelings of awkwardness, of inhibition, and limitations in language expression.

The communication explosion presents promises and problems. While it makes the world one village, technology alone cannot bring about human understanding. Knowledge of one or more foreign languages has become a practical necessity.[37]

Teaching reading in English to the bilingual child will not differ as a process if the child has an opportunity to master the sound system of the English language before he or she is expected to learn to read and write it. Teachers need to understand and appreciate the cultural background of the child, the cognitive learning processes for all children, some of the phonemic and syntactical differences between their language and the child's, the present-day methods of teaching the reading and writing skills and the contribution of linguistics to this process, and the problems of vocabulary expansion for the second-language student. In addition, where children already understand the sound system of another language, opportunity should be found for them to retain and develop it. If large numbers of children have a common *other* language, a successful bilingual school has deep significance to the community and to the larger society.

For Further Reading

Cargill-Power, Carol. "Approaches to Improving the Reading Skill of the Bilingual Student." *NABE Journal* 4 (Spring 1980): 93–99.

Crymes, Ruth. "Current Trends in ESL Instruction." *TESOL Newsletter* 14 (August 1980): 1–4.

Herrell, Ileana C., and James M. Herrell. "Affective and Cognitive Aspects of Bilingualism." *NABE Journal* 4 (Spring 1980): 81–92.

Lado, Robert, "Developmental Reading in Two Languages." *NABE Journal* 6 (Winter/Spring 1981–82): 99–110.

Ruddell, Robert B. "Nonstandard Dialects and Second Language Learning: The Instructional Program." In *Reading Language Instruction: Innovative Practices,* pp. 263–89. Englewood Cliffs, N.J.: Prentice-Hall, 1974.

Santiago, Ramón L. "The Future of ESL and Bilingual Education in the Next Decade." *TESOL Newsletter* 16 (June 1982): 1-4.

Savage, John F., ed. *Linguistics for Teachers: Selected Materials.* Chicago: Science Research Associates, 1973.

Yandell, Maurine, and Miles V. Zintz. "Some Difficulties which Indian Children Encounter with Idioms in Reading." *The Reading Teacher* 14 (March 1961): 256–59.

Zintz, Miles V. "Teaching the Linguistically and Culturally Different Child." In *Corrective Reading,* 4th ed., pp. 315–47. Dubuque, Iowa: Wm. C. Brown, 1977.

———. *What Classroom Teachers Should Know About Bilingual Education.* ED 028 427. ERIC TESOL. 1969.

Notes

1. Alexander Frazier, ed., *Educating the Children of the Poor* (Washington, D.C.: Assn. for Supervision and Curriculum Development, National Education Assn., 1968).

2. Eskimo term for white person. Derived from Russian word *cossack.*

3. Lee H. Salisbury, "Teaching English to Alaska Natives," *Journal of American Indian Education* 6 (January 1967): 4–5.

4. Evelyn Evvard and George C. Mitchell, "Sally, Dick and Jane at Lukachukai," *Journal of American Indian Education* 5 (May 1966): 5.

5. William Madson, *The Mexican-American South Texas* (New York: Holt, Rinehart and Winston, 1964), p. 106.

6. Robert Hall, *Linguistics and Your Language* (Garden City, N.Y.: Doubleday, 1960), p. 193.

7. Dora V. Smith, *Communication: The Miracle of Shared Living* (New York: Macmillan, 1955), p. 51.

8. Miles V. Zintz, *Education Across Cultures* (Dubuque, Iowa: Kendall/Hunt, 1969), p. 28.

9. Ricardo L. Garcia, *Teaching in a Pluralistic Society: Concepts, Models, Strategies* (New York: Harper & Row, 1982), p. 126.

10. Miles V. Zintz, "Cultural Aspects of Bilingualism," in *Vistas in Reading,* ed. J. Allen Figurel (Eleventh Annual International Reading Assn. Proceedings, 1967), p. 357.

11. R. E. Davies, *Bilingualism in Wales* (Capetown, South Africa: Juta, 1954), p. 14.

12. Ibid., pp. 17, 90.

13. Elizabeth Peal and Wallace Lambert, "The Relationship of Bilingualism to Intelligence," *Psychological Monographs: General and Applied,* No. 76: 1–23 (Washington: American Psychological Association, 1962).

14. Mabel Richardson, "An Evaluation of Certain Aspects of the Academic Achievement of Elementary Pupils in a Bilingual Program," (Coral Gables, Florida: Graduate School, University of Miami, 1968).

15. Nancy Modiano, "A Comparative Study of Two Approaches to the Teaching of Reading in the National Language," New York University School of Education, 1966.

16. Paul Rosier and Lillian Vorik, "Rock Point Community School: An Example of a Navajo-English Bilingual Elementary Program," *TESOL Quarterly,* 13 (September 1978): 263–69.

17. Kathy Gales, et al., "Academic Achievement in the Milingimbi Bilingual Education Program," *TESOL Quarterly* 15 (September 1981): 297–314.
18. Ibid., p. 309.
19. Carolyn Graham, *Jazz Chants for Children* (New York: Oxford University Press, 1979).
20. Mary Finocchiaro, *Teaching Children Foreign Languages* (New York: McGraw-Hill, 1964), pp. 26–28.
21. Louise Binder Scott and J. J. Thompson, *Talking Time,* 2d ed. (New York: McGraw-Hill, 1966), p. 327.
22. Eric H. Lenneberg, *Biological Foundations of Language* (New York: John Wiley and Sons, 1967) pp. 291–92.
23. Board of Education of the City of New York, *Teaching English As a New Language to Adults,* Curriculum Bulletin No. 5, 1963–1964 series (Publications Sales Office, 110 Livingston Street, Brooklyn, N.Y.: Board of Education of the City of New York), pp. 7–9.
24. Yvonne Weaver, "A Closer Look at TESL on the Reservation," *Journal of American Indian Education* 6 (January 1967): 28.
25. Walter Loban, *The Language of Elementary School Children* (Champaign, Ill.: National Council of Teachers of English, NCTE Research Report, No. 1, 1963).
26. Ruth Strickland, *The Language of Elementary School Children: Its Relationship to the Language of Reading Textbooks and the Quality of Reading of Selected Children* (Bloomington, Ind.: Indiana University Bulletin of the School of Education 38, No. 4, 1962).
27. Phillip C. Gonzales, "How to Begin Language Instruction for Non-English Speaking Students," *Language Arts* 58 (February 1981): 175–80.
28. Eustolia Perez, "Oral Language Competence Improves Reading Skills of Mexican American Third Graders," *The Reading Teacher* 35 (October 1981): 24.
29. Ibid., pp. 24–27.
30. Gonzales, "Language Instruction for Non-English Speaking Students," pp. 175–80.
31. Sara Meadows, Janet Philps, Angela Simkiss, and Asher Cashdan, "Matching the Child's Level: One Aspect of a British Preschool Intervention Study," in *Applied Linguistics and Reading,* ed. Robert E. Shafer (Newark, Del.: International Reading Assn., 1979).
32. Arthur Wingfield, E. Hugh Rudorf, and Richard T. Graham, "Why Should the Child Want to Learn to Read?" in Shafer, *Applied Linguistics,* pp. 26–28.
33. National Clearinghouse for Bilingual Education, *The Bilingual Education Act* (1500 Wilson Boulevard, Suite 802, Rosslyn, Va. 22209: National Clearinghouse for Bilingual Education, 1979).
34. Arnold H. Leibowitz, *The Bilingual Education Act: A Legislative Analysis* (National Clearinghouse for Bilingual Education, 1980), pp. 17–18.
35. T. J. Haarhoff, "Introduction," in *The Bilingual School* by E. G. Malherbe (Capetown, South Africa: Juta, 1946), pp. 5, 8.
36. Elizabeth Thompson and Arthur Hamalainen, "Foreign Language Teaching in the Elementary Schools," in *An Examination of Current Practices* (Washington, D.C.: Association for Supervision and Curriculum Development, National Education Association, 1958), p. 9.
37. Dolores Gonzales, "Auditory Discrimination of Spanish Phonemes" (Ed. D. dissertation, University of Pennsylvania, 1967), pp. 4–5.

Teaching Reading to Children Who Speak Nonstandard English

A Cognitive Map: Teaching Reading to Children Who Speak Nonstandard English

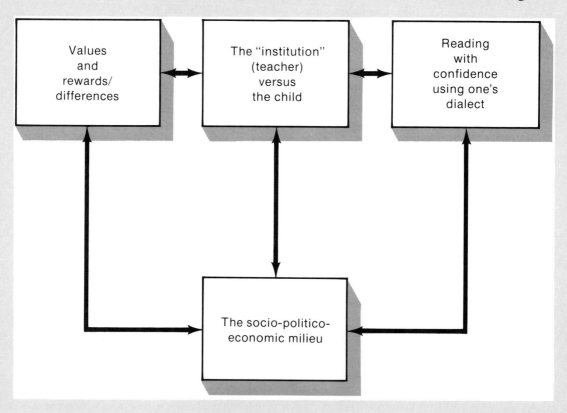

16

Guide Questions

1. What are the values and rewards for the child living in the culture of poverty? Consider the socio-politico-economic milieu of the community.

2. How are nonstandard dialect and poverty related?

3. What often happens to this child when he or she comes in conflict with the school?

4. How would you work with language so that nonstandard speakers in your classroom have a fair chance to learn to read?

Terminology

Black English

culture of poverty

dialect

dialectology

inferior versus different

nonstandard English

standard English

Some years ago a kindergarten teacher in an inner-city kindergarten wanted to develop some feeling about the importance of George Washington and Abraham Lincoln during the month of February. On Lincoln's birthday, the concept that Mr. Lincoln had been president of the United States was discussed and his picture was displayed. The comment was made that Mr. Kennedy was now president of our country.

Mark asked: "Why Lincoln not president now?"

Teacher: "Mr. Lincoln is dead now."

Mark persisted: "Why he dead?"

The teacher realized that these children knew something of the reality of life and that shooting was not uncommon in the neighborhood, so she said, "A man shot him."

The kindergartners looked big-eyed at the teacher and asked, "Who?" "Why?"

Mark said, unbelieving, "He shot him dead?"

Mr. Booth was discussed briefly as a man who thought some of the things President Lincoln had done were not right and that he had become mentally ill and committed the act of violence.

Mark continued all day to go and look at the picture of President Lincoln and repeat to himself, "He shot him dead." He took the teacher's hand and led her to the picture several times and said, "That good man. He shot him dead."

The teacher responded calmly, "Yes, Mark, he shot him dead."

Mark responded, "That good Mr. Lincoln. [Pause.] Bastard!"[1]

Any kindergarten teacher distressed with the vivid way Mark characterized John Wilkes Booth must first understand why "bastard" is the word that Mark brings easily to the conscious level. If he has heard it often at home or near home, should she tell Mark it is "bad" language or "wrong" for him to say it? How soon should Mark learn there is one language spoken at school and another at home? If the teacher wishes to encourage Mark to use language, to expand language, and to evaluate through language, she must start where he is with the language he has.

There are three parts to the discussion in this chapter:

1. People who live with values and needs not recognized by the school.
2. Conflicts between the institution of the school and the child who has an incompatible lifestyle.
3. Reading standard English in one's own dialect with confidence.

The Culture of Poverty

Among the fifty million people in the United States who fit into the classification of poor, Lewis estimates that perhaps one-fifth, or ten million, live in a "culture of poverty." The largest numbers of this group are made up of Negroes, Puerto Ricans, Mexicans, American Indians, and Southern poor whites.[2]

The hard-core poor in the United States are said to live in a culture of poverty. The *culture of poverty,* in this sense, indicates that they are caught in a vicious circle—with no solution to meeting even minimum economic needs. The individual who grows up in the culture of poverty develops attitudes of fatalism, helplessness, and inferiority. Such a person's primary concerns are immediate, and a strong present-time orientation is characteristic of his or her behavior. With a weak ego structure, the person has little disposition to defer personal gratification or to think about the future.[3]

Miller has characterized the hard-core lower class in our country as being primarily female-based households as the basic child-rearing unit and as having "serial monogamy" mating as the primary marriage pattern.[4]

> The lower-class Negro family pattern commonly consists of a female dominated household, with either the mother or the grandmother acting as the mainstay of the family unit. The husband, if present, is often an ineffective family leader. The boy growing up in a Negro family frequently perceives his father as a person with a low-status job, who is regarded with indifference or varying degrees of hostility by members of the out-group. In short, the lower-class Negro adult male is seldom regarded as a worthwhile masculine model for the boy to emulate.[5]

Harrington has described the insoluble economic problems that keep the poverty cycle operating:

> Here is one of the most familiar forms of the vicious circle of poverty. The poor get sick more than anyone else in the society. That is because they live in slums, jammed together under unhygienic conditions; they have inadequate diets, and cannot get decent medical care. When they become sick, they are sick longer than any other group in the society. Because they are sick more often and longer than anyone else, they lose wages and work, and find it difficult to hold a steady job. And because of this, they cannot pay for good housing, for a nutritious diet, for doctors. At any given point in the circle, particularly when there is a major illness, their prospect is to move to an even lower level and to begin the cycle, round and round, toward even more suffering.[6]

After describing how the family structure of the poor is different from that of the rest of society, Harrington went on to contrast the attitudes of the middle class and the urban poor toward the city policeman:

> For the middle-class, the police protect property, give directions, and help old ladies. For the urban poor, the police are those who arrest you. In almost any slum there is a vast conspiracy against the forces of law and order. If someone approaches asking for a person, no one there will have heard of him, even if he lives next door. The outsider is a "cop," bill collector, investigator (and in the Negro ghetto, most dramatically, he is "the Man").[7]

People in the culture of poverty talk about the middle-class values as if they accept them, but, in day-to-day living, they fail to live by most of them. Poverty forces them to buy small quantities of goods at high prices, to pawn personal goods often, and to pay usurious rates of interest on bits of borrowed money.

All children learn very early in life, in the home, about help from adults, security with adults, trust of others, and the extent to which life is pleasant or painful. Communication develops early too. Words, intonation, gesture, inhibitions, listening with care, or withdrawing are all learned as children observe and experience how they are valued in the family and how they are to value others—both peers and adults.

> One mother, speaking of a previous Parents Association meeting, said, "In that there meeting the principal and all the teachers called us dopes—poor slobs that don't know what our kids are getting from school." To which the principal immediately countered: "Why, Mrs. _____ , you know very well that no one said anything of the kind in that meeting," and the mother in question replied, "Maybe you didn't say it, but that's what the atmosphere said." However correct or incorrect this parent was in her perception, it is clear that communication between her and the professional staff would be difficult.[8]

Conflicts in values between the lower-class child and the middle-class teacher are *inevitable*. The concepts of authority, education, religion, goals, society, delinquency, time orientation, violence, sex, and money are viewed very differently by the middle-class teacher and the families of the inner-city poor.

The civil rights movement of the 1960's centered attention on the inequities of the public school system. Closer scrutiny of then-current educational practices revealed considerable prejudice and bias with respect to the culturally different. Biases were evident in the textbooks, in the tests themselves, in grading standards, and in the verbal and nonverbal interaction between adult and child.

Since many parents are reluctant to come to school until they know and trust the people there, it is necessary for the school to go to the parents. Visiting in the homes gives each teacher an opportunity to see a child in the family setting. Parents are usually convinced that the teacher is interested in learning ways to work successfully with their child. Such visits need to be made when there are no problems needing solutions. Schools should do everything possible to help parents help their children learn in school. Even though parents look to the school with hope, many are fearful and confused by it. Principals who wish to bring about change are often baffled by what seems to them to be teacher indifference.

Many of the undesirable characteristics of the poor of Appalachia are common to the inner-city poor. Scarnato reported from Appalachia:

> A few years ago, a public spirited group of doctors in Kanawha County, in which the state capitol is located, gave a physical and psychiatric examination to some 329 welfare clients listed as totally disabled, and they found no cases of conscious malingering and found that strong and conscious feelings of inferiority and guilt were resulting in depressive apathy and serious physical illness. The result of their findings was summed up in the graphic phrase, "Idleness is a disease."[9]

Urban ghettos are a world incomprehensible to many beginning middle-class teachers who may be selected to teach there. Hilliard found that for millions of the hard-core poor in Chicago, their ghetto segregated them, unemployment was very high, and many, many adults lacked adequate literacy skills for even unskilled employment. Lost in a feeling of hopelessness, discriminated against in many subtle ways, and without resources to climb out of the deep rut that entombs them, these people have no way to become sufficiently integrated into the mores and culture of the middle class. Yet, Hilliard found also that when these people were offered literacy education, their response as a group was enthusiastic, their attendance was excellent, their personal appearance indicated a strong desire to conform, and the adult education classes had few discipline problems.[10]

The Child in the Inner-City School

Ausubel considered the motivational aspects of learning as an integral part of the real life learning situation:

> Doing without being interested in what one is doing results in relatively little permanent learning, since it is reasonable to suppose that only those materials can be meaningfully incorporated on a long-term basis into an individual's structure of knowledge that are relevant to areas of concern in his psychological field. Learners who have little need to know and understand quite naturally expend little learning effort; manifest an insufficiently meaningful learning set; fail to develop precise meanings, to reconcile new ideas with existing concepts, and to formulate new propositions in their own words; and do not devote enough time and energy to practice and review. Material is therefore never sufficiently consolidated to form an adequate foundation for sequential learning.[11]

Motivation to learn is derived generally from a child's natural curiosity and predisposition to explore, to manipulate, and to cope with the environment. Theoretically, meaningful school learning, when successful, furnishes its own reward.

Teachers should never completely give up the idea that if children achieve adequate success in the learning situation, the success will in turn generate motivation. This is most apt to happen when teachers are able to generate contagious excitement and enthusiasm about the subjects they teach, and when they are people with whom the learners can identify.

Because lower-class students often have an anti-intellectual and pragmatic attitude toward the academic purposes of the school, it may be much harder for the teacher to motivate them. For this reason, such intrinsic motivation is even *more* necessary for inner-city children than for middle-class children. For the motivation to be intrinsic to the learning probably requires that rewards be more immediate and experiences be more concrete.

McCreary observed:

> Early in the school careers of many socially disadvantaged youths, teachers notice an eagerness, a very great responsiveness to new experiences and especially to the kindness, personal attention, and assistance that some teachers give. Some children come to school very early in the morning, because they like the teacher and the warmth, physical and personal, that they find in the classroom. Some want to stay on after school to help the teacher or to talk with her. But for far too many, the early responsiveness to affection and to learning is destroyed by experiences of failure. Teachers need to find ways to strengthen and maintain the initial enthusiasm for school characteristic of many disadvantaged children by providing continuing opportunities for success and recognition.[12]

Levy studied elementary education at Harvard and did student teaching in a middle-class school in Lexington, Mass. Then she wrote of her experience as a fourth grade teacher in Harlem:

> What impressed me most was the fact that my children (9–10 years old) are already cynical and disillusioned about school, themselves, and life-in-general. They are hostile, rebellious, and bitter. Some belong to gangs, some sniff glue, and some even have police records. They are hyperactive and are constantly in motion. . . .[13]
>
> Most teachers . . . grow up in and are trained to work in a middle-class environment. Working in a Negro slum school is in many ways like going to a foreign country. The values, interests, goals, experiences, and even language of the children are quite different and often in conflict with the middle-class oriented school and its teachers.[14]

Levy emphasized two points in teacher education:

> . . . need to train teachers to be able to deal with an attempt to overcome their own "culture shock" and "culture bias" . . . need to be prepared to deal with parents who may be illiterate or partly illiterate, concerned but helpless, or hostile and abusive.[15]

Deutsch, studying underprivileged children in New York City, found that early in life these children develop a "negative self-image." His observers recorded derogatory remarks made by teachers toward individual children:

The most frequent such remark was to call a child "stupid," and as a result, the teacher, and through the teacher, the school played a role in reinforcing the negative self-image of the child, and contributed a negative reason for learning.[16]

Bettelheim suggested that occasionally teachers misread children's behavior and do not really understand the deep-seated feelings children have. He counseled teachers to take seriously the remarks of the hurt child:

> If a child says to you, "I hate your ugly white face," you are certainly going to be bothered unless you don't take the child seriously. . . . If we don't take a person's nasty remarks seriously, that means that we really don't take him seriously. It implies, "You're irresponsible, no good, of no account." Because if a person is of any account, then it seems to me that we must take seriously what he says.[17]

Henry, in an article called "White People's Time, Colored People's Time," said:

> Poor children often come to school unfed, after wretched nights torn by screaming, fighting, bed-wetting; often they cannot sleep because of cold and rats. They come to class hungry, sleepy, and emotionally upset. To start routine schoolwork effectively at once is impossible.[18]

To attempt, constructively, to meet this problem, he suggested:

> Their teachers should breakfast with them at school. The school should, of course, furnish the food, perhaps out of government surplus. School breakfast would accomplish two things: it would feed hungry children, otherwise unable to concentrate adequately on their work; and it would bring teacher and pupil together in an informal and friendly atmosphere, associated with satisfaction, before the strain of classroom constriction and peer-group pressures dictate that teacher become an enemy. It is essential, therefore, that the teacher be present.[19]

A program like this suggested by Dr. Henry in Kansas City brought about immediate and sharp improvement in attendance, behavior, and in schoolwork. The more the teachers know about the emotional management of these children, the better.

The President's 1969 message to Congress on the Economic Opportunity Act emphasized the importance of providing intellectual stimulation during the early years to enable children of the inner-city poor to interact with middle-class children when in the public school:

> We have learned . . . that environment has its greatest impact on the development of intelligence when that development is proceeding most rapidly—that is, in those earliest years. . . . So crucial is the matter of early growth that we must make a national commitment to providing all American children an opportunity for healthful and stimulating development during the first five years of life.[20]

Sociocultural Problems in the School That Cause Failure

The school has been aware for decades that large numbers of minority group children—blacks, Latins, Indians—fail or become severely retarded educationally as they are promoted through the public schools. Expenditures for additional instruction materials and for small-group remedial teaching have not solved the problem.

> . . . we find minority schools almost morbidly preoccupied with the early identification of deficits and handicaps rather than the identification of individual patterns of skills. Similarly, a substantial amount of school time and resources is spent in the discovery of these assumed deficits rather than in the establishment of standards of competence and the creation of the types of supportive and challenging learning environments capable of enhancing the learning of the minority child.[21]

McDermott has argued that the cleavage between the teacher, with one set of values and behaviors, and the minority child, with a quite different set of values and behaviors, may actually be contributing to the school failure. McDermott attributed this failure to something he called "the politics of everyday life." By that term he meant that the patterns of attention or inattention, of motivation to learn or resistance to learning, and of feeling "with the teacher" or "against the teacher" are actually a child's rational adaptation to the subtle messages transferred from teacher to child all day in the classroom. Support versus antagonism, trust versus deference, respect versus anxiety, and success versus failure—all are learned responses in a mutually misunderstanding social atmosphere. In such an atmosphere the student can learn how not to see—or, more specifically, how not to look in order not to see.[22] Taro Yashima writes about Chibi (Crow Boy);

> He was always at the end of the line, always at the foot of the class, a forlorn little tag-along. Soon Chibi began to make his eyes cross-eyed, so that he was able not to see whatever he did not want to see.[23]

In this politics of everyday life, minority children may learn how *not* to read; *not* to attend to printed information. Once the teacher treats the child as inadequate, the child will find the teacher oppressive. Once the child finds the teacher to be oppressive, the child will start to behave inadequately. Once behaviors become dichotomized, as two opposing forces in the school, the student can take sides by attending or by not attending. Those who attend learn to read; those who do not attend do not learn to read.[24]

Language and Concept Development that Improve Literacy

Inner-city children may have gone to school at age six without ever having had their mothers sing them traditional lullabies and with no knowledge of nursery rhymes. Similarly, they may not have been told any of the fairy stories or folklore of their country. They may have taken few trips. Deutsch found many children had not been farther than two miles from home even in downtown New York City. They may well be children of a minority group, sent to inferior schools, taught by indifferent teachers. As early as age six, they had been isolated from many rich experiences that other children their age had enjoyed. Their isolation may have been caused by poverty, meagerness of intellectual resources at home, or the incapacity, illiteracy, or indifference of the adults with whom they have lived.

Brooks recommended:

1. Standard English should and can be taught successfully as though it were a second language to children who speak nonstandard English as a result of cultural differences or cultural deprivation.
2. If standard English is taught as a second language, it is not necessary to insist that the child reject entirely the other or "first" language.[25]

Language serves different purposes for lower-class, inner-city children. For them, language controls others more than it conveys information. They learn to respond because the speaker is a figure of authority. Verbal interchange is apt to be an order, request, or threat expressed in a single word, an idiomatic expression, or a short sentence.

This language is considered substandard by middle-class employers and frequently by middle-class schools and teachers. It might better be considered *non-*standard or a dialect of English. Dialectology, "the study of dialects, especially as they differ socially and geographically,"[26] provides teachers with insights and perspectives about the nonstandard language of many of their students. Norms for language development and use begin in the "socioeconomic and ideological dominance relations in a society, and the social values of groups, which produce distinct varieties. . . ."[27] Dialects are viewed as different from the standard language rather than as deficient,[28] for they are effective ways for children to communicate at home and with their friends. Effective communication *is* the primary goal of language.

Children may be encouraged to use their own dialect for personal communication. However, if disadvantaged children are to have a fair chance in our mobile society, they must learn standard English for use in school and on the job.[29] They become bidialectal, to fit into the two-language communities in which they hold membership.

After hearing the case of eleven low-income black children in Michigan, a judge ruled that black children's self-confidence and ability to learn standard English were being undermined by the negative attitudes held by the classroom teachers toward the home language of the child.[30] At the present time, we have all the evidence we need to state that black children are not linguistically inadequate, nor do they need to be cognitively uneducated. According to Baratz and Baratz, the language of black children

> is a fully developed, highly structured system that is more than adequate for aiding in abstract thinking.[31]

According to Bryen, Hartman, and Tait, young black children

> develop syntactic rules for pluralization, negation, possession, third person indicative, and past tense as readily as do white children who speak some version of standard English.[32]

The linguistic system of "Black English" is as sophisticated, regular, and governed by rules as other languages.

There must be more coordinated effort among schools, local governments, and other social and civic agencies. School faculties must carry out academic studies of the impact of social-class differences on students and teachers. These studies need to be done community by community. And there must be direct teaching aimed at changing attitudes and self-concepts for the students, for the teachers, and for the parents.[33]

Teaching strategies should follow three basic guidelines: (1) initial teaching should be geared to the learner's state of readiness, (2) it should provide the necessary foundation for successful sequential learning, (3) it should provide structured learning materials that will facilitate efficient sequenced learning.[34] Such a teaching plan demands that all subject matter that learners cannot economically assimilate at their present level of academic functioning be eliminated. One of the Philadelphia programs provides for an on-school-time, in-service training program for teachers. While the teachers are attending in-service sessions, their classes participate in a carefully planned program of storytelling, literature films, filmstrips, and recordings. Library books have been provided to support the special literature program. This program has been very effective in raising reading achievement levels.[35]

Bloom reports three characteristics of successful learning experiences: cognitive entry behaviors, affective entry characteristics, and quality of instruction.[36] These characteristics of mastery learning, similar to the guidelines just mentioned, would describe educational settings in which children from nonstandard language backgrounds would have a fair chance of being successful in school.

The Junior High School 43 Project in New York City was designed as a comprehensive approach to effective education of culturally different children. It provided the following services: systematic guidance and counseling; clinical services when indicated; a cultural enrichment program that included trips to the theater, museums, opera, college campuses; a parent-education program; and a systematic supplementary remedial program in reading, mathematics, and languages.[37]

When teachers have a low expectation level for their children's learning, the children seldom exceed that expectation. The process may well represent a self-fulfilling prophecy.

Acceptance of the child is of vital importance. It is based on a firm belief that the child is capable of self-determination. It seems to be a respect for the child's ability to be a thinking, independent, constructive human being.[38]

When a teacher respects the dignity of a child, whether or not he be six or sixteen, and treats the child with understanding, kindliness, and constructive help, she is developing in him an ability to look within himself for the answers to his problems, and to become responsible for himself as an independent individual in his own right.

Possibly the greatest contribution that educators can make to the younger generation is the type of guidance that places the emphasis on self-initiative and transmits to the young people by living example the fact that each individual is responsible for himself. In the final analysis, it is the ability to think constructively and independently that marks the educated man. Growth is a gradual process. It cannot be hurried. It comes from within the individual and cannot be imposed by force from without.

It is the relationship that exists between the teacher and her pupils that is the important thing. The teacher's responses must meet the real needs of the children and not just the material needs—reading, writing, arithmetic.[39]

Our inner-city schools contain thousands of culturally different boys and girls who are innately bright. The schools must identify those individuals and challenge and stimulate them so that they will be sure to overcome the shackles of poverty and keep alive their intellectual curiosity. Perhaps these highly intelligent students have been the most neglected in our system of mass education. Stimulation for them in enriched programs in language, social studies, and general science early in the elementary school may keep them motivated to succeed in the intellectual life.[40]

Teaching Reading to Children Who Speak Nonstandard English

The language model that a person has always used in communications with other people should not be considered a substandard version of school language. It is *neither wrong nor substandard.* It is a different dialect of the language. Every dialect is a complete, systematic, functioning language that is correct for the speaker who uses it at certain times, in certain places, and under certain circumstances.

The language that the child learns before coming to school is a valuable personal possession. Likewise, the people about whom the child cares most are not to be labeled *incorrect* or *inferior* because they do not use the language of the school.

For many of the children who speak "Black English," motivating learning in the classroom is probably the most crucial need. If teachers can become strong motivators, boys and girls will exercise greater learning drive. Here are a few suggestions that have worked with other teachers:

1. The best way to reflect both the language and the experience of a child is to *record them as he or she brings them* to the classroom.
2. The closer the language of the material in the book matches the language the child would customarily use, the easier the reading task will be, especially for beginning readers.
3. When a child's nonstandard language is intact, systematic, and organized, and the child's experiences are known, these are the strengths he most needs in learning to read.
4. But after the child has read his own stories, in his own dialect, there is probably no need for the creation of specific dialect materials for wide-scale use in teaching beginning reading to speakers of nonstandard dialects. Of course, we need to use trade books such as *Stevie*[41] and *Train Ride,*[42] which reflect the everyday nonstandard language of their characters. Such books are fun to read or listen to but are not meant to serve as basal readers. Pilon provides a short list of such books. She further discusses working with *is* and *are* and the inflectional endings *s* and *ed* and provides specific methodology for the teacher and lists of materials to use with children.[43]

    Seymour provides numerous exercises to help the nonstandard language user with consonant clusters, tense and person markers, and plurals and possessives.[44]

Baratz does not accept the idea that there is no need for dialect-specific materials in basal readers. She wrote in the early '70s that school use of dialect readers was "an idea whose time has not yet come," but she believed that it would come in the future.[45]

5. Reading is not *really* "talk written down." Notice, for example:

The "Sounds" We Speak	The Words We Write
Itzabook.	It is a book.
nooshooz	new shoes
plejeleejens	pledge allegiance
Juwannago?	Do you want to go?

6. Some children remain apparently nonverbal despite instruction in the standard language. The nonverbal behavior may be quite misleading and not representative of the child's actual abilities. Day reported a study of five Samoan or Hawaii Creole English-speaking children labeled as nonverbal.[46] Placed in a special setting loosely structured in terms of teacher demands, with a small group, and in a supportive and accepting classroom climate, the children soon began talking freely. The researcher concluded that teachers cannot always judge that a child has not learned from language instruction programs because little talking is done. Special environments may be necessary to get these children talking, and once talking begins, the teacher's verbal behavior has little impact on the amount of language the children produce or what they talk about.

7. It will be a good idea to model reading behavior by reading aloud to the boys and girls every day. This reading material must be interesting and relevant, must include principal characters from the black population, and, hopefully, will use both standard English and some Black English expressions.

8. Search out parents and friends in the neighborhood who can come to the school and either talk with the boys and girls or demonstrate some skill of interest to the class.

9. Probably most important is to enable children to pursue those interests that they already exhibit and to encourage them to use language to clarify thinking and extend meanings. Accept the language of the child as long as he or she communicates, and plan for its improvement and extension over a long period of time.

The root of the problem is not in the nonstandard English itself. Rather, the problem is embodied in the attitudes expressed about it by teachers and other adults.

Teachers should:

1. Teach standard English as a second language to those students who have habituated an oral nonstandard language pattern.

2. Use nonstandard dialect in written form for beginning reading. If the teacher begins the reading program with a language-experience approach, this should be no problem.

By planning interesting activities and modeling language in meaningful settings, the teacher can encourage language growth in children with limited English proficiency.

3. Be sure that the speakers understand clearly that there are two variations of the same language. Their pronunciation "fits" the written-down language if the teacher emphasizes understanding. Labov wrote:

> There is no reason to believe that any nonstandard vernacular is in itself an obstacle to learning. The chief problem is ignorance of language on the part of all concerned. . . . Teachers are being told to ignore the language of Negro children as unworthy of attention and useless for learning. They are being taught to hear every utterance of the child as evidence of his mental inferiority. As linguists, we are unanimous in condemning this view as bad observation, bad theory, and bad practice.[47]

There is abundant evidence that traditional teaching of "language" to speakers of nonstandard dialects of English has been ineffective. Most culturally different students leave school after twelve years still using the nonstandard variety of English they were using when they came to school. Many teachers *still* project the attitude that the language used by the nonstandard speaker is inferior and that all nonstandard dialects are *substandard*.

Sherk analyzed the language produced by five-year-olds in Kansas City and reported:

> Language is a very personal thing. Pupils whose language is always criticized soon come to feel that it is themselves that are being criticized, and this reflects on their parents, their neighbors, and their whole world. Because teachers refuse to accept their words, pupils feel they are not accepted as persons. In turn, pupils reject their teachers, and thereby in effect they reject school language, textbook language, and the language of the larger society.[48]

A Rationale for the Teacher

Standard English is a language system. So is nonstandard English. Nonstandard English has features that deviate from standard English in systematic and predictable ways. Nonstandard English provides a functional, efficient, and satisfying means of communication among its users, just as does standard English among its users.

Here are some points to remember when working with children who speak a nonstandard dialect of English:

1. No dialect of English is inferior to any other.
2. Negative attitudes about children's speech can affect teacher expectations of student performance. There is evidence to suggest that too many teachers still possess such negative attitudes.
3. Dialect differences must be understood if teaching is to be effective. Teachers can master some of the major phonological, syntactical, and lexical attributes of the dialect.
4. Classroom teachers would do well to cultivate their own abilities to converse with and listen to the boys and girls they teach. The children can teach the adults a great deal about the dialect if teachers become good observers.
5. Teachers can become more accepting of both "school" and "out-of-school" registers of language used by the students they teach. Such flexibility will foster greater trust.
6. Children should have ample opportunity to use both their own dialect and the standard English of the school. As they mature and are properly motivated by learning, they will sense the need to know well both dialects of the language.

Black English Features

Black English can generally be distinguished by the following features:

Initial consonants are usually standard except *th*, which is *d*.
A few initial consonant clusters are altered: *stream* for *scream*.
R's are generally omitted: *guard* becomes *god*.

L's are frequently omitted: *tall* becomes *toe; help* becomes *hep; fault* becomes *fought.*

M and *n* are expressed as nasalized preceding vowels: *ram* and *ran* sound alike.

Final consonant clusters are simplified: *past* becomes *pass; bites* becomes *bite; nest* becomes *nes.*

The consonant cluster *sk* becomes *ks: ask* becomes *aks.*

Final consonants may be weak or missing: *ba* may represent *bat, bad,* or *bag.*

Final voiced *th* may be sounded *v: breathe* becomes *breav;* final voiceless *th* may be sounded *f: breath* may become *breaf.*

Before *m* and *n,* the vowels *e* and *i* may be pronounced the same: *Pen = pin; ten = tin.*

Dorothy Seymour has listed a few of the grammatical forms that teachers will find to be typical of Black English.[49]

Grammar	Standard English	Black English
1. Verb usage		
Present tense	He runs.	He run.
Present progressive	He is running.	He run.
Past tense, irreg.	He took it.	He taken it.
Past perf., irreg.	He has taken it.	He have took it.
Future	I will do it, or I am going to do it.	I'm a do it.
Present habitual	He is (always, usually) doing it.	He be doing it.
Past habitual	He (always) used to do it.	He been doing it.
2. Negation	I don't have any.	I don't got none.
	He hasn't walked.	He ain't walked.
3. Question	How did he fix that?	How he fix that?
Indirect question	I asked if he fixed that.	I asked (aksed) did he fix that.
4. Treatment of subject	My brother is here.	My brother, he here.
5. Noun plural	those books; men	them book; mens
6. Pronouns	We have to go.	Us got to go.
7. Possessive	Jim's hat	Jim hat
	The hallway of Jim's family's building	Jim and them hallway

Working with bilingual Native American and Spanish-speaking children was discussed in chapter 15. However, some children who are Native Americans or Spanish are actually native speakers of English. Even though they speak English, they may hear a Native American language or Spanish spoken around them; others may have contact with the ancestral language only through the English of their parents or grandparents, who in turn heard the language spoken.

Wolfram examines the characteristics of English spoken by Native Americans who to one degree or another have had contact with their native language.[50] While the causes may vary, many different linguistic groups utilize similar English constructions and forms. These Native American groups seem to use English in ways dissimilar to "other non-mainstream varieties of English."[51]

Wolfram reports that Native Americans who learned a native language before they learned English tend to reduce consonant clusters at the ends of words.[52] This is a more marked characteristic in speakers of languages that do not permit consonant clusters at the ends of words. It was also reported that unmarked tenses tend to characterize English as spoken by Native Americans; included would be *s, ed,* and *ing* endings, as well as modals, *be* verbs, and *have* and *do* in verb phrases. Certain kinds of problems with the formation of negatives were also reported.

Dulay and Burt report a study of eight hundred Hispanic children described as *limited English proficient* children.[53] They found that many of the children who were underachieving in English language skills spoke little or no Spanish, and they reported several other studies that resulted in similar findings. They noted that language dominance can mean relative proficiency, but that even the greater proficiency in one language is often inadequate for meeting communication needs. Teachers need to be aware of this and to help children develop competence in at least one language, probably the school language. Surely this competence can be developed best in experience-rich classrooms that encourage intense use of oral English for as long as needed before stress on written language is begun.

Summary

Teachers of students who habitually use nonstandard English must study and accept the children's language and, in due course, help them to use both nonstandard and standard English effectively. Some of the generalizations upon which this statement is based are:

1. There is such a thing as Black English. Black English and standard English differ phonologically and syntactically. They also differ in vocabulary.
2. Generally, in the past, nonstandard English was rejected. However, insistence by teachers on the use of only standard English has not led to satisfactory achievement.

3. A child brings to school at least six years of life experience, which embody the cultural, social, economic, and other values the child has acquired.

4. Rather than deny any value of the nonstandard language, teachers must encourage students to use it in positive ways to help them develop self-esteem.

5. Teachers must be sensitive when communicating with pupils so they do not convey a nonaccepting attitude toward the language the child speaks. The teacher must also be keenly sensitive to nonverbal clues.

6. Students speaking a nonstandard English dialect have a well-structured, sophisticated language and vocabulary that is suited to their everyday needs. They must never be looked upon as having *no* language or an inferior language.

7. In itself, speaking nonstandard English is not detrimental to learning how to read. A child with a nonstandard dialect is likely to have the *same capacity to learn* to read as a user of a middle-class standard dialect.

8. Of course, the standard dialect must be taught, and it should be learned. Even though there is nothing inherently *wrong* or *bad* about using a nonstandard dialect, there will be times when it will be detrimental to the person who cannot use standard English (prevent one from getting a job, for example).

For Further Reading

Bryen, Diane N., Cheryl Hartman, and Pearl Tait. *Variant English.* Columbus, Ohio: Charles E. Merrill, 1978.

Cazden, Courtney, Vera John, and Dell Hymes. *Functions of Language in the Classroom.* New York: Teachers College Press, 1972.

Garcia, Ricardo L. *Teaching in a Pluralistic Society: Concepts, Models, Strategies.* New York: Harper & Row, 1982.

Hymes, Dell. *Language in Education: Ethnolinguistic Essays.* Washington, D.C.: Center for Applied Linguistics, 1980.

Johns, Jerry L. "What Do Inner City Children Prefer to Read?" *The Reading Teacher* 26 (February 1973):462–67.

Johnson, Kenneth. "Teaching Mainstream American English." *Journal of Black Studies* 9 (June 1979): 411–22.

Laffey, James L., and Roger Shuy. *Language Differences: Do They Interfere?* Newark, Del.: International Reading Assn., 1973.

McDermott, Ray P. "Achieving School Failure: An Anthropological Approach to Literacy and Social Stratification." In *Theoretical Models and Processes of Reading,* 2d ed., ed. Harry Singer and Robert Ruddell, pp. 389–428. Newark, Del.: International Reading Assn., 1976.

McDermott, Ray P. "The Ethnography of Speaking and Reading." In *Linguistic Theory: What Can It Say about Reading?* ed. Roger Shuy, pp. 153–85. Newark, Del.: International Reading Assn., 1977.

McDermott, Ray P. "Social Relations as Contexts for Learning in School." *Harvard Educational Review* 47 (May 1977): 498–513.

Meier, Terry Ryan, and Courtney B. Cazden. "A Focus on Oral Language and Writing from a Multicultural Perspective." *Language Arts* 59 (May 1982): 504–12.

Myers, Hector F. "Mental Health and the Black Child." *Young Children* 34 (May 1979): pp. 25–31.

Padak, Nancy D. "The Language and Educational Needs of Children Who Speak Black English." *The Reading Teacher* 35 (November 1981):144–51.

Shuy, Roger, ed. *Linguistic Theory: What Can It Say About Reading?* Newark, Del.: International Reading Assn., 1977.

Smith, R. B. "Sociological Aspects of Black English Dialects in the United States." In *Language and Society,* ed. William C. McCormack and Stephen A. Wurm. New York: Mouton, 1979.

Spolsky, Bernard. "Sociolinguistics of Literacy, Bilingual Education, and Tesol." *TESOL Quarterly* 16 (June 1982): 141–51.

Wolfram, Walt. "The Nature of Nonstandard Dialect Divergence." In *Linguistics for Teachers: Selected Readings,* ed. John F. Savage. Chicago: Science Research Associates, 1973.

Wolfram, Walt. "Sociolinguistic Alternatives in Teaching Reading to Nonstandard Speakers." In Savage, *Linguistics for Teachers,* 1973.

Yellin, David. "The Black English Controversy: Implications from the Ann Arbor Case." *Journal of Reading* 24 (November 1980): 150–54.

Zintz, Miles V. *Corrective Reading,* 4th ed. Dubuque, Iowa.: William. C. Brown, 1981. Especially chapter 14, "Teaching The Linguistically and Culturally Different Child," pp. 315–47.

Notes

1. This episode was contributed by Dr. Catherine Loughlin, Professor of Education, University of New Mexico.
2. Oscar Lewis, "The Culture of Poverty," *Scientific American* 215 (October 1966):25.
3. Ibid., pp. 19–25.
4. Walter B. Miller, "Lower-Class Culture as a Generating Milieu of Gang Delinquency," *Journal of Social Issues* (1958).
5. Israel Woronoff, "Negro Male Identification Problems and the Education Process," *Journal of Educational Sociology* (September 1962); reprinted in *Understanding the Educational Problems of the Disadvantaged Learner,* ed. Staten W. Webster (San Francisco: Chandler, 1966), pp. 293–95.
6. Michael Harrington, "The Invisible Land," reprinted in Webster, *The Disadvantaged Learner,* p. 17.
7. Ibid., p. 18.
8. John Niemeyer, "Some Guidelines to Desirable Elementary School Reorganization," in Webster, *The Disadvantaged Learner,* p. 394.
9. Sam A. Scarnato, "The Disadvantaged of Appalachia," a presentation made at a meeting of a special language study committee of the National Council of Teachers of English, Champaign, Illinois, July 1968.
10. Raymond M. Hilliard, "Massive Attack on Illiteracy," *American Library Association Bulletin* 57 (1963):1034–38.
11. David P. Ausubel, "A Teaching Strategy for Culturally Deprived Pupils: Cognitive and Motivational Considerations," *The School Review* 71 (Winter 1963):457.

12. Eugene McCreary, "Some Positive Characteristics of Disadvantaged Learners and Their Implications for Education," in Webster, *The Disadvantaged Learner*, pp. 51–52.

13. Betty Levy, "An Urban Teacher Speaks Out," in Webster, *The Disadvantaged Learner*, p. 430.

14. Ibid., p. 434.

15. Ibid., p. 435.

16. Martin Deutsch, *Minority Group and Class Status as Related to Social and Personality Factors in Scholastic Achievement*, Monograph No. 2 (Ithaca, N.Y.: Society for Applied Anthropology, Cornell University, 1960), p. 26.

17. Bruno Bettelheim, "Teaching the Disadvantaged," *NEA Journal* (September 1965).

18. Jules Henry, "White People's Time, Colored People's Time," in Webster, *The Disadvantaged Learner*, p. 190.

19. Ibid.

20. From the president's message to Congress on the Economic Opportunity Act, *A News Summary of the War on Poverty*, Office of Economic Opportunity, 24 February 1969.

21. Hector F. Myers, "Mental Health and the Black Child," *Young Children* 34 (May 1979): 27.

22. Ray P. McDermott, "Achieving School Failure: An Anthropological Approach to Literacy and Social Stratification," in *Theoretical Models and Processes of Reading*, 2d ed., ed. Harry Singer and Robert Ruddell (Newark, Del.: International Reading Assn., 1976), pp. 389–428; Ray P. McDermott, "The Ethnography of Speaking and Reading," in *Linguistic Theory: What Can It Say About Reading?* ed. Roger Shuy (Newark, Del.: International Reading Assn., 1977), pp. 153–85.

23. Taro Yashima, *Crow Boy* (New York: The Viking Press, 1955).

24. McDermott, "Achieving School Failure," and "Speaking and Reading."

25. Charlotte K. Brooks, "Some Approaches to Teaching English as a Second Language," in *Non-Standard Speech and the Teaching of English*, ed. William A. Stewart (Washington, D.C.: Center for Applied Linguistics, 1964).

26. Mario Pei, *Glossary of Linguistic Terminology* (New York: Columbia University Press, 1966), p. 68.

27. Norbert Dittmar, *Sociolinguistics* (London: Edward Arnold, 1976), p. 111.

28. Walt Wolfram, "The Nature of Nonstandard Dialect Divergence," in John F. Savage, *Linguistics for Teachers: Selected Readings* (Chicago: Science Research Associates, 1973), pp. 68–78.

29. Ellen Newman, "An Experiment in Oral Language," in Webster, *The Disadvantaged Learner*, p. 570.

30. Nancy Padak, "The Language and Educational Needs of Children Who Speak Black English," *The Reading Teacher* 35 (November 1981): 145.

31. Stephen Baratz and Joan Baratz, "Early Childhood Intervention: The Social Science Base of Institutional Racism," *Harvard Educational Review* 40:36.

32. Diane Bryen, Cheryl Hartman, and Pearl Tait, *Variant English: An Introduction to Language Variation* (Columbus, Ohio: Charles E. Merrill, 1978).

33. Delmo Della-Dora, "The Culturally Disadvantaged: Educational Implications of Certain Social-Cultural Phenomena," in *Education and Social Crisis: Perspectives on Teaching Disadvantaged Youth*, ed. Everett T. Keach, et al. (New York: Wiley, 1967), pp. 279–80.

34. David P. Ausubel, "A Teaching Strategy for Culturally Deprived Pupils: Cognitive and Motivational Considerations," *The School Review* 71 (Winter 1963):454–55.
35. Ibid., pp. 329–30.
36. Benjamin Bloom, *Human Characteristics and School Learning.* (New York: McGraw-Hill, 1976).
37. Kenneth B. Clark, "Educational Stimulation of Racially Disadvantaged Children," in Keach et al., *Education and Social Crisis,* p. 308.
38. Virginia Mae Axline, *Play Therapy* (Boston: Houghton Mifflin, 1969), p. 21.
39. Ibid., pp. 75–76.
40. Staten W. Webster, ed., *Educating the Disadvantaged Learner* (San Francisco: Chandler, 1966), pp. 580–81.
41. John Steptoe, *Stevie* (New York: Harper & Row, 1969).
42. John Steptoe, *Train Ride* (New York: Harper & Row, 1971).
43. Barbara Pilon, "Culturally Divergent Children and Creative Language Activities," in *Language Differences: Do They Interfere?* ed. James L. Laffey and Roger Shuy (Newark, Del.: International Reading Assn., 1973), pp. 129–45.
44. Dorothy Seymour, "Neutralizing the Effect of the Non-Standard Dialect," in Laffey and Shuy, *Language Differences,* pp. 149–60.
45. Joan Baratz, "The Relationship of Black English to Reading: A Review of Research," in Laffey and Shuy, *Language Differences,* p. 110.
46. Richard R. Day, "Silence and the ESL Child," *TESOL Quarterly* 15 (March 1981): 35–39.
47. William Labov, "Logic of Nonstandard English," in *Language, Society, and Education: A Profile of Black English,* ed. Johanna S. DeStefano (Worthington, Ohio: Charles A. Jones, 1973), p. 43.
48. John K. Sherk, Jr., "Psychological Principles in a Strategy for Teaching the Reading of a Standard Dialect," in *Reading: Process and Pedagogy,* 19th Yearbook, ed. George B. Shick and Merrill M. May (Milwaukee: National Reading Conference, 1970), p. 291.
49. Dorothy Seymour, "Black English in the Classroom," *Today's Education* 62 (February 1973): 63–64.
50. W. Wolfram, "Dynamic Dimensions of Language Influence: The Case of American Indian English," in *Language: Social Psychological Perspectives,* ed. Howard Giles, W. Peter Robinson, and Philip M. Smith (New York: Pergamon, 1980), 377–88.
51. Ibid., p. 387.
52. Ibid., pp. 383–87.
53. Heidi Dulay and Marina Burt, "The Relative Proficiency of Limited English Proficient Students," *NABE Journal* 4 (Spring 1980): 1–23.

Exceptional Children and Reading Instruction

A Cognitive Map: Exceptional Children and Reading Instruction

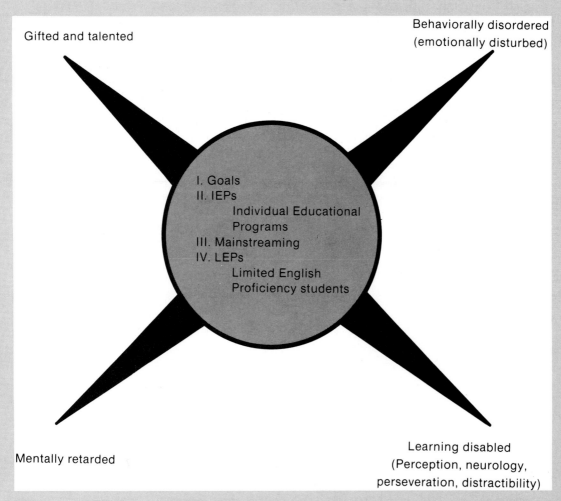

Gifted and talented

Behaviorally disordered
(emotionally disturbed)

I. Goals
II. IEPs
　　Individual Educational
　　Programs
III. Mainstreaming
IV. LEPs
　　Limited English
　　Proficiency students

Mentally retarded

Learning disabled
(Perception, neurology,
perseveration, distractibility)

17

Guide Questions

1. Compare the educational goals for special students to the goals for regular students.

2. What would an IEP be like?

3. How would you, as a teacher, plan for mainstreaming some children in your classroom?

4. What are the important principles of providing suitable education for the gifted? How would you organize reading instruction?

5. What is the regular teacher's responsibility in providing education for the mentally retarded?

6. What is meant by the term *learning disability,* and how can learning disabled children be helped in the regular classroom?

7. What can the regular teacher do for a child who demonstrates the signs of emotional disturbance?

Terminology

aggression

distractibility

exceptional children

gifted

hyperactivity

IEP

learning disability

least restrictive environment

mainstreaming

mental retardation

neurological handicap

perceptual handicap

perseveration

withdrawal

Any teacher who has spent a few years in elementary school classrooms is well aware from firsthand experience that there are in all heterogeneously grouped classes a few rapid learners, a few more who are above-average learners, a larger group of middle achievers, a smaller number of below-average achievers, and a few with learning difficulties. Occasionally, the teacher has one whom he or she considers a *very* rapid learner or a *very* slow learner. While the limitations of intelligence tests are well known, one can accept without qualification the inevitable range of abilities that must be dealt with in any classroom (see chapter 2).

If the teacher is going to take into account the basic principle that the longer children attend school, the greater will become the spread of differences in almost any selected ability, then some adaptations must be made in the program to make it fit both the rapid learner and the slow learner. The differences are not *in kinds* of learning, but, rather, *in degree* of children's accomplishments.

Therefore, the general suggestions offered throughout this book for a developmental reading program apply to the atypical students as well as to the majority of the class.

Exceptional children have been assigned to categories in an effort to provide the best services for their needs. State departments of education, legislative and judicial bodies, experts in the fields, and medical personnel have helped to establish these divisions. The categories often include gifted children, learning disabled, behaviorally disordered, mentally handicapped (mentally retarded), physically handicapped, visually and/or auditorily impaired, speech handicapped, and neurologically impaired. A great deal of literature is available in each of these areas, and the teacher will profit greatly from specialized courses devoted to methods of teaching exceptional children. This chapter will discuss the instructional needs of students in the first four categories: gifted, learning disabled, behaviorally disordered, and mentally handicapped.

Goals

Classifying some children as having learning or behavior deviations has led to problems in the development of adequate school programs for them.[1]

1. Children so classified are often victimized by the stigma associated with the label.
2. Assigning a label suggests that all the children given that label conform to a stereotyped behavioral expectation.
3. Some children who are labeled and placed in special programs may not really need a special education program.
4. Some children have been misplaced or misclassified.
5. Sometimes decisions for assigning children to special programs have been made without adequate data, without legal basis, and without parental involvement.

From Theory to Practice 17.1
Spending Time in a Special Education Classroom

Arrange with your instructor to visit a special education classroom for one of the exceptionalities discussed in this chapter. You will need to stay for at least two hours.

While in the classroom, note how the teacher works with the children, the kinds of materials and lessons used, and the ways in which the teacher responds to the children. Spend some time observing a single child—what the child does, the language used, and how the child responds to instruction. Take careful notes of actual behaviors of the child.

Back in your class, share the experience with other students. There should be much to share and discuss if each has observed a special education classroom.

Public Law 94–142 has clarified several general concepts that all teachers must accept and work very hard to implement:[2]

1. All children can learn.
2. Education is that continuous, developmental process by which individuals learn to cope and to function within their environment.
3. Children with handicaps *may* participate in all programs and activities provided by the schools.
4. Every handicapped child *will be* provided a free appropriate education at no additional expense to the parents or guardian.
5. Diagnosis and evaluation will provide for those children who have different languages and cultures so they will not be discriminated against.
6. To the maximum extent possible, handicapped children will be educated with children who are not handicapped. All children will be provided an optimal learning environment.
7. Handicapped children are *children* first; second, they are children with special learning needs.

With these concepts in mind, the goals for children with special needs become apparent. All teachers must work to see that these youngsters, along with all others, are helped to achieve to the limits of their abilities. They must have the opportunities to develop themselves physically, mentally, creatively, and emotionally as far as they are capable of going.

Individualized Education Program (IEP)

The individualized education program (IEP), required by law for all exceptional children, is a detailed statement of the educational services that will be provided to *a specific child*. Thus, for every exceptional child who needs a specialized program, an IEP will be developed. The IEP will include long- and short-term goals, instructional objectives, and needed materials and services. It is the product of planning by the school personnel, including the teacher, and the parents, and the child where possible and desirable. The IEP can be an extremely useful tool in the education of each child if it is developed thoughtfully and with sound educational principles in mind.

Mainstreaming

Public Law 94–142 specifies that each child will be educated in the least restrictive environment. The intent of this requirement is to keep exceptional children with normal children as much of the time as is congruous with their educational progress.

One response to this requirement has been *mainstreaming*. In mainstreaming, the child spends as much of the time in a regular classroom as is deemed desirable. Some children may have their skill subjects with a special teacher in the morning, for example, and spend the afternoon in the regular classroom. Others may be out of the regular classroom for a few minutes or not at all, while others may spend only a few minutes a day in the classroom with normal children. The decision to mainstream or not, and if so for how long each day, is individually determined, based on the needs of the child.

Ten teaching strategies that have been successfully used to accommodate the exceptional child in the regular classroom are presented here. Of course, each child must have his or her IEP, but the following suggestions will serve well for general reference:

1. Establish a warm and accepting atmosphere.
2. Help all the students develop an accepting attitude toward the handicapped.
3. Work closely with other teachers.
4. Make your classroom less physically restrictive.
5. Plan success experiences.
6. Take advantage of individual strengths.
7. Set up effective testing procedures.
8. Spice up your lesson plans.
9. Communicate with the parents of your mainstreamed students.
10. Take a little of the pressure off yourself.[3]

Education of the Intellectually Gifted

The goals of education for the able learners, the gifted, are the same as for all children: self-realization, human relationships, economic efficiency, and civic responsibility. For the gifted, greater emphasis may be given to creativity, use of abstract intelligence, critical reading and thinking, growth toward communal versus individual values, and opportunities to experience leadership and develop leadership qualities.

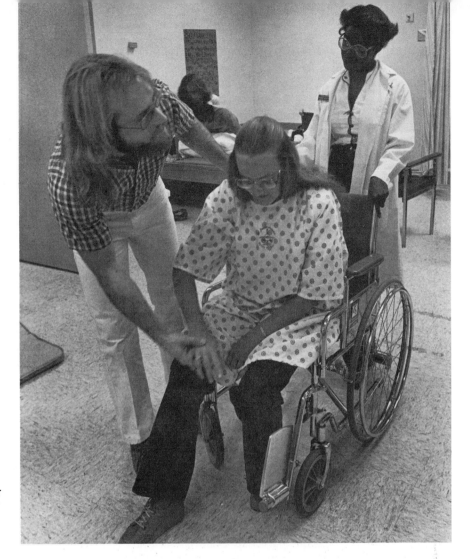

Teachers in regular classrooms need to develop strategies for working with mainstreamed students in their classrooms.

Teachers desperately need to help the general citizenry understand that equality of opportunity in education does not mean identical opportunities for all children of the same chronological age in a community. Gifted children may begin the school year in September with most of the knowledge and skills that other children in the same classroom will acquire during the course of the school year. If the year is to be constructively used, the gifted children too must be challenged to grow. They do not need to do the exercises that many other children do just to demonstrate that *they can do them*. Teachers have inventories, checklists, pretests, and unit tests of skills and abilities that they can administer to find out which children already have the skills. Those children can spend their time on enriching activities that make use of the skills in evaluative and creative ways. It is imperative that teachers have many different activities for the children in a class. There is no other way that each individual can have a challenging job to "dig into."

Most schools accept the recommendation that some combination of moderate acceleration and enrichment will produce the best results in the education of gifted children. Each child must have activities that enrich for him or her. Acceleration makes it possible for a child to finish elementary school in five years instead of six; junior high school in two years instead of three; and/or senior high school in two years instead of three. It is better for some children than for others. Similarly, acceleration of two years may be more appropriate for some children than acceleration of one year would be for others.

Acceleration should evolve from staffing conferences at which principal, teacher, psychologist, and parent sit down together to review the case. Information should be available from the school social worker, school nurse, and school physician if it is contributory to the case.

If the so-called normal child spends twelve years going through the public school with its present academic bent, the slow learner should be privileged to spend thirteen years or more, and the gifted ought to be permitted to spend eleven or fewer years. Terman wrote in 1954 about the issue of educational acceleration for the gifted:

> It seems that the schools are more opposed to acceleration now than they were thirty years ago. The lockstep seems to have become more and more the fashion, notwithstanding the fact that practically everyone who has investigated the subject is against it.[4]

In his follow-up studies of 1,500 gifted students, Terman found that 29 percent graduated from high school by age 16½.[5] This group constituted his "accelerated" group. Compared to the remainder (ages 16½ to 18½ at graduation), they made better grades in college, were more apt to complete undergraduate work, and were more apt to go on to graduate school.

The major concern in the school for the gifted child should be to free the child to learn. If schools are able to provide adequate learning experiences, the gifted child will be challenged without respect to acceleration, enrichment, or segregation per se. Children must be *free* to learn outside the classroom, *free* to acquire information apart from formal teacher-pupil efforts, and *free* to work in small groups with good teacher-pupil planning but little teacher supervision. Providing learning experiences for children does not mean necessarily that the child even comes to school to learn—the school may make the experiences available somewhere else.

One of the greatest obstacles to better education of children may be faulty communication between parents and teachers. Parents may be poor communicators, and therefore teachers should go more than halfway. Teachers generally do not communicate nearly well enough with parents, even though they are supposedly prepared, ready, and anxious to do so.

It is especially important that teachers, in their desire to help gifted children, not use certain words that may arouse strong sentiments and negative notions. If teachers are to be challenged about whether they will "enrich," "accelerate," *or* "segregate," they will get nowhere. Maybe schools need to discard these words that have been misused and misapplied so teachers can think clearly about *all the ways* they can bring adequate learning experiences to children. Probably they best meet the needs of gifted children in the elementary school by individual combinations of accelerating, segregating and *always* enriching.

Teachers' attitudes vary. Some ignore high-ability children and try to teach them as if they were average. Others do nothing *special* to help them and rationalize that in a large class one can't. Some teachers give extra time to slow learners and rationalize that gifted children will take care of themselves.

Havighurst and De Haan reported a case study of a gifted boy in a junior high school social studies class. As his special report, he chose to work alone on a study of national highway construction because the topic was in the news at that time.

An office of a large highway engineering company was located in the city. This company was working on projects in several states and had many books on materials, surveys, machinery, and cost estimates. As James began to develop his project of designing a system of highways, the teacher made appointments for him to go to the offices of the engineers and to laboratories. Soon he was making his own appointments. Sometimes he was gone from her class for as long as two weeks at a time, visiting these offices, making appointments with the engineers, consulting with them, and taking pictures of their models of highways.

He learned how to make maps and drawings on sheets of clear plastic that would overlay each other. He compiled data from the maps, describing how various cities and regions would be affected by the highway plan.

When the time came to make his report, he had a table piled with material and notebooks filled with figures and charts. He used an opaque projector to present his material. The report was a masterpiece. Later he made a report to the regional meeting of the engineers of the company where he had obtained so much help.[6]

The authors point out that the significant aspect of the boy's experience is that the office staff of engineers was an invaluable resource in that community to help this boy in his project in the social studies. In another community, it may not be engineers but rather other specialists who can, in their way, be as helpful to other gifted children.

Havighurst has also stated:

Thinking, then, of the unusual child as the talented child, I suggest that we speak of four areas of talent. We have found this useful in our work: first, the area of intellectual talent—a child with high intelligence or high I.Q.; second, the area of artistic talent—talent in music, drawing or dramatics, and so on; third, the area of social leadership—this is something we sometimes do not think of as a talent, but certainly in our society a gift for social leadership is an important and precious thing; and, fourth, something which I cannot define so clearly but I like to call "creative intelligence" or the ability to find new ways of doing things and solving problems. . . .

The principal factor within the individual which affects the supply of talent is motivation. Motivation is necessary to the development of intellectual or artistic talent—the motivation being a desire to seek training and willingness to sacrifice other desires while undergoing training. Lack of motivation appears to be more powerful than lack of money in reducing the supply of talent.[7]

Pintner reminds school personnel:

Educators at all levels of instruction must divest themselves of the belief that gifted students can get along by themselves and that it is undemocratic to give them special education suited to their particular needs. And we must also dispel the fear sometimes expressed that the gifted may become selfish through too much consideration, for "it is precisely this group of individuals of great ability who, in the long run and as a group, will be the least selfish, the least likely to monopolize the good things in this world, and by their inventions and discoveries, by their creative work in the arts, by their contributions to government and social reform, by their activities in all fields, will in the future help humanity in its groping struggle upward toward a better civilization."[8]

The teacher is the most important factor in the classroom success of the gifted child:

Teachers of gifted children should display unusual sensitivity in recognizing the potentialities of such pupils; they should maintain a balance between individual and group work in the classroom; they should help pupils solve problems and resolve conflicts; they should aid pupils in mastering the knowledge needed for understanding themselves and the world; and they should display a sincere interest which will inspire confidence.[9]

"Young children can be bored by the school work offered to them. One first grader spoke sharply to his teacher, 'Take that pusillanimous primer away!' One can imagine how that teacher warmed up to him!"[10]

Zettel reported in 1979 that twenty-one states had state-level plans for the education of their gifted and talented students and that twenty-one more states were in the planning stage.[11] In 1980, Mitchell and Erickson reported that thirty-two states responded to inquiries indicating some type of service was available for the gifted.[12] Still, however, most of the country's gifted children are the direct responsibility of teachers in regular classrooms. In fact, almost every year each teacher has one or two gifted children enrolled in his or her class. Often these children have not previously been identified formally or informally.

Objectives

Many of the objectives of reading instruction for the gifted are essentially the same as for the regular child. Gifted children do not always learn to read before coming to school and need basic instruction in reading. However, they will usually move through any instructional program with greater ease and rapidity than their regular classmates. As a consequence of the accelerated learning rate, additional objectives are necessary. They might include: (1) gaining proficiency in the techniques of reading and refining these skills in each successive year, (2) learning how to use books for study projects: outlining, summarizing, and reporting on information gained from reading, (3) exploring the wide world of reading, discovering the best books for every possible purpose and the books of special interest to the individual reader, (4) learning how to use the facilities of the school library, and (5) becoming acquainted with the best literature and learning to appreciate the value of reading great books.[13]

Nelson and Cleland list the following implications for the teacher of the intellectually gifted child:[14]

1. The teacher must possess an understanding of self.
2. The teacher must possess an understanding of giftedness.
3. The teacher should be a facilitator of learning rather than a director of learning.
4. The teacher must provide challenge rather than pressure.
5. The teacher must be as concerned with the process of learning as with the product of learning.
6. The teacher must provide feedback rather than judgment.
7. The teacher must provide alternate learning strategies.
8. The teacher must provide a classroom climate which promotes self-esteem and offers safety for creative and cognitive risk-taking.

Cassidy provides additional ideas for managing the reading program of the gifted.[15]

Inquiry reading gives an opportunity to apply one's reading skill in a practical situation. Inquiry reading utilizes a problem approach to learning and enables students to research independently topics of particular interest to them.[16]

He quotes Stauffer as setting four requirements to enable students to work best:

1. A definite focus on a specific problem.
2. Freedom to select data: physical freedom to select from a wide range of media and intellectual freedom to process their data as they see fit.
3. A multimedia center that is as well stocked as possible.
4. Opportunity to share creatively what they have gathered and to learn to be attentive listeners to what others share.

Cassidy further suggests that the reading inquiry activity is a "continuing" one and may be planned with students somewhat like this:

First week: (1) define inquiry, (2) establish requirements, (3) probe areas of interest, (4) formulate questions to be researched, (5) discuss resources, (6) review interview procedures if interviews will be used, (7) discuss sharing activities, and (8) draw up a contract with each student that sets deadlines for completion.

Second and third weeks: (1) review notetaking, (2) locate references, (3) keep note cards or folders, (4) interact with other students to share successes and problems, (5) hold individual conferences, and (6) help the student visualize ways to communicate the information he or she has gained.

Fourth week: (1) complete the project, (2) have a dress rehearsal of the planned report, (3) present the report to an outside audience, (4) teacher and student evaluate the project together with the contract before them.

Inquiry reading makes "reading to learn" a reality for those who have already "learned to read."[17]

The Bright Child Who Must Learn English as a Second Language

Many, many of our schoolchildren today are blessed with a bountiful amount of innate intelligence and learning ability, and so demonstrate on tests that do not involve heavy use of English. Yet in school, such children are almost completely unable to function if the school uses some language other than their own.

In many parts of the United States, schools have done untold psychological damage to boys and girls, first by devaluing their first language, and second by causing children to suspect that the school devalues them and, in turn, their families. If the school denies children the right to speak their own language, they can only conclude that it must be inferior—or at least that the teachers think it is inferior. If their language is no good and it is the only language their parents and whole extended family can use, they can only conclude that they must all be inferior. Such ego destruction can do serious harm to children as they progress through the school.

Native American students in college often have difficulties with the English language. One group of such students entering college expressed need for help in all the following areas: reading skills, vocabulary development, written and oral expression, spelling, taking notes, taking examinations, listening to lectures, and effective studying.

One student wrote about his reading problem in this way:

> Looking back to my high school days, I find that the ACADEMIC course that caused the UTMOST agony was English. It was my belief that English was an *insurmountable obstacle;* but after a lengthy discussion with my English tutor, Mr. Charles, who is also a philosopher, I was enlighten [*sic*] that my belief was false. He said that English can be mastered if a student is willing to persistently and diligently works [*sic*] at it. . . . The principle [*sic*] cause of slow reading is lip reading of which I am guilty. To become an efficient reader, I must overcome this impediment. This I did by placing a pencil between my teeth.[18]

In a tutoring-counseling program on the university campus, a number of Native American students were given the *Wechsler Adult Intelligence Scale.* Almost invariably, there were large discrepancies between the performance scale and the verbal scale. A performance IQ score of 120 and a verbal IQ score of 80 for the same person was not an uncommon result. The low verbal score was attributable in large part to the language, culture, and experience barrier faced by the student.

Such nonsuccess stories testify to the failure of the schools and the teachers, *not* of the students.

A success story, on the other hand, would be more like the following. It is presented here to emphasize the importance of planned, sequenced lessons in order to prevent frustration and failure in learning a second language.

> Edna was a thirteen-year-old Japanese girl transplanted suddenly and unexpectedly to a city in the American southwest to live with her uncle's family and attend school. Edna was very bright and spoke Japanese expertly but had heard very little English as spoken by native speakers. She had studied only a few isolated words. This young lady found herself in a junior high school attending eighth grade classes in mathematics, American history, general science, and English grammar and literature— all taught only in English.

Edna's aunt was perplexed that the school had no provision for meeting this problem. Her own difficulty using and understanding English was partly illustrated by an early telephone call with Edna's new language clinician when she was explaining how she was trying to make the young lady feel at home. She said she was "trying to break out the ice."

Edna was enrolled in the remedial reading clinic to study English as a second language. She reported to her school daily at 8:30 A.M. and left at 10:00 to catch a city bus to the reading clinic. Her tutors at the clinic were relatively unskilled in techniques for teaching English as a second language. Their formal education had prepared them to teach developmental reading skills remedially. However, they used the principles of teaching English as a second language (TESOL) as described in chapter 15, and helped Edna develop oral language ability to reproduce the language she heard. Her teachers quickly taught her the common utterances used in casual conversation. Every day for several weeks she practiced all the previously studied questions and answers and substitution drills and added new ones. The most common sentence structures were taught, modeled, repeated, drilled, and reviewed and, because Edna was a very bright girl and living in an environment where remembering the work had such high reward value, she quickly mastered the material.

Special attention was devoted to the common prepositions, verb tenses, homonyms, antonyms, synonyms, and personal pronouns. Dictation of simple sentences was begun early about subject matter to be presented in Edna's history and literature classes. Edna attended her tutoring sessions from early December until the following August.

Humorous moments occasionally broke the sometimes tense feelings Edna had because she wished she could learn English much faster than was humanly possible. One day early in the spring, when Edna was responding to elementary antonyms in English, her tutor gave the stimulus word *noisy*. She looked puzzled, and the tutor said, "The class is very noisy today." Edna's eyes lighted up, and she said in a loud voice, "Shut up!"

The Mentally Retarded Child

John is nine and a half years old. He entered kindergarten at five and a half and after several weeks of observation of his intellectual and language immaturity, his kindergarten teacher had referred him to the school psychologist for an evaluation. There were no physical findings in his medical evaluation to indicate lack of development. His muscle tone, vision, hearing, motor coordination, and reflexes all seemed to be within the normal limits for a five-year-old. However, the individual intelligence test was administered and yielded a mental age of three years and nine months although he was five years and nine months at the time of testing. He was permitted to repeat kindergarten at age six and a half and to spend two years in the first grade. At nine and a half, he has been placed in second grade.

If he is not placed in a special classroom and mainstreamed part of his school day, individual arrangements are needed that best accommodate his developing intellectual powers, his physical growth, and his emotional and social needs. Creative ways may be found, such as having some lessons in a particular classroom, engaging in less academic subjects with his age group, and spending time in a neighborhood setting where he could learn a skill he particularly desires. The major concept is not that a pattern be followed for all these special children, but that an education program be designed to meet their needs and interests.

When John was retested by the psychologist at a chronological age of nine years and seven months, the results showed his mental age to be only six years and three months. He comes from an "average" family with two girls ages seven and six who are doing well in school. Even though John is not quite as large as many boys nine and a half, he is one of the largest in his class of seven- and eight-year-olds. His physical skills in active play approximate those of second and third grade children. John is reasonably well accepted in the group, but he needs a great deal of help to adjust socially: not to laugh too much, not to pester the other children, and not to put his hands on the others.

Since John will spend the year in the regular class, there are a few cautions the teacher must remember. He or she will try never to think or say aloud: "He doesn't really belong here; he ought to be in a room for the retarded." The teacher will realize that John is only one other different individual in a whole class of different individuals who each need planned, specific objectives. The teacher's attitude about differences is contagious and, for this reason, of primary importance.

The objectives for John's school year include his learning both social behaviors and academic behaviors. The general objectives are to help John in the following ways:

1. Adjust to other members of the group.
2. Extend reading readiness and develop beginning reading abilities.
3. Learn habits of good health and safety.
4. Develop personal habits of cleanliness, grooming, and neatness.
5. Learn about his immediate environment.
6. Build language and quantitative concepts.
7. Learn habits of punctuality, orderliness, and following directions.

The teacher's objectives in language arts with respect to John are the following:

1. Use more oral than written language.
2. Give much instruction in following directions.
3. Extend his ability to listen with understanding.
4. Help him develop skills in beginning reading.
5. Provide practice reading with another child at a level commensurate with his mental age and understanding in order to get repetition on basic sight words.
6. Teach him to read signs, labels, and brief explanations.

With John's motor coordination, he will be able to write anything he can read. Motivating him to do very well with manuscript writing will be one possible place where John can excel in the class. In the unit work of the class, there will be activities associated with the content in which John should be able to participate with small groups. Generalizations in science, social studies, health, and safety that are explained in class may be understood to some degree by all members of the class.

The appreciations—music, art, physical education, and literature—are all areas where John can participate to some degree with the others. The teacher will be able to accept different levels of performance in the same activity.

The most important thing is that in a group of thirty John will not be *the only one* who is different, and the difference is a matter of degree, not kind. He may be more different in some respects than in others, but no two are alike.

The classroom teacher must be alert to the appearance of *slow learners* in the class. If such children can be identified early, their programs can be planned in terms of their functioning levels of ability so that the time in school will be used constructively even though they do not attain the achievement norms for the class. It is likewise extremely important for the teacher to know who slow learners *are not*. They *are not* children who learned another language as their first language and enroll in school as so-called bilinguals with a severe English language handicap. They *are not* children who have speech, hearing, or vision problems or neurological impairment or minimal brain dysfunction, which may or may not have been diagnosed. They *are not* children whose primary problems in school stem from emotional, social, or other personality difficulties. However, any child who is a slow learner may *also* have any of these problems concomitantly. Diagnosis should reveal a child's primary problem, and it should have the attention of the special educator before the secondary problems can be adequately addressed.

Slow learners are students whose general learning ability, as measured by individual intelligence tests, is below average. Slow learners have a degree of mental retardation which, to date, is believed to be a permanent handicap for which they must make the best possible adjustment. Regular classroom teachers, from time to time, will find mentally retarded boys and girls in their classrooms.

In individual cases, it may be better for such a child to remain with the *regular* class instead of being enrolled in a class for *slow learners* or a class for the *educable mentally retarded*.

The curriculum goals for the mentally handicapped child are theoretically the same as for any child: self-realization, learning proper human relationships, achieving economic efficiency, and assuming civic responsibility. The behavioral goals of self-discipline, self-development, and self-actualization are most important. A life-experience curriculum will help the learner to learn about physical and mental health, useful knowledge and skills, and worthwhile use of leisure time, and to gain some sense of the interdependence of individuals. A life-experience curriculum teaches such values, knowledge, skills, and abilities through units built around (1) home and family life; (2) the community, its helpers and its resources; and (3) expanding concepts about the community to the city, the state, and the nation. Activities other than reading from textbooks are utilized as much as possible to enrich these concepts for slow learners.

Functional learning for the slow learner includes tasks in everyday living: filling out an application blank; being able to use telephone directories, road maps, travel schedules, street guides, restaurant menus; understanding written directions of various sorts, radio and TV program schedules, classified ads, and various types of catalogs.

The life-experience approach to teaching mentally retarded children is primarily concerned with helping them understand and cope with practical problems of living that will persist all through life. Such problems include understanding and using money, understanding and making efficient use of time, developing skills for all kinds of interaction with people, and learning prevocational skills from as early an age as possible.

The following generalizations are believed to be true of most slow learners:

1. They are satisfied to continue doing work that is repetitive.
2. They need more drill and practice and are more apt to enjoy it.
3. They need careful guidance in all assignments; goals need to be fairly immediate and carefully explained.
4. They need more help with planning in the form of specific directions to follow, ego support, and close supervision to see that the directions are carried out.
5. They need success experiences and opportunities to do things they can do well (e.g., handwriting).
6. They have trouble when assignments are abstract, when abstract reasoning is required, or when evaluation "beyond the book" is under discussion.

For slow learners in regular classes, teachers need to remember the following:

1. Formal reading and using reading as a thinking process must be developed in proportion to the extent of mental retardation. A child of six with an IQ of 85 is more like a five-year-old than a six-year-old. An eight-year-old with an IQ of 75 is more like a six-year-old

than an eight-year-old. While children at all these ages can profit from any language and concept development experiences that they can understand, expecting them to move to the complex, abstract process of reading should come much later. When children have sufficient language and understanding of concepts and can verbalize freely, they will be ready to move toward the more formal activities of reading and writing. However, when children are provided with compensatory training, increases in mental age—and therefore, by definition, IQ—are sometimes greater than one might expect.

2. The way reading is taught to slow-learning children is very similar to the way it is taught to normal children. However, there are differences. When the child is ready for reading, overlearning the core of basic sight words is important. Slow learners must have all the time they need to master them. This necessitates more books, more stories, and more language-experience reading at the appropriate level before progressing to more difficult levels. And a structured, systematic phonics and spelling program may be indicated. The Hegge-Kirk-Kirk *Remedial Reading Drills* were first prepared for mentally retarded boys.[19] If a child growing at the normal rate requires one year at the second grade level of difficulty, a mentally retarded child whose growth rate is approximately two-thirds that of a normal child needs perhaps one-third year more time to grow through the same quantity of learning. He is not fundamentally different; he just grows more slowly.

3. The teacher can take advantage of the student's acceptance of repetition and monotony. Stories can be reread for different purposes. The student needs few purposes at one time under any circumstances. So he may reread to learn something he missed the first time. Beyond reading to find out what happened in the story, he may practice reading aloud so he can record his *best* reading on the tape recorder. Every rereading provides additional practice on the basic sight words he needs to overlearn.

4. Teachers will probably encourage more oral reading with slow learners.

5. Teachers must give much help in making directions clear in preparation for independent seatwork before leaving slow learners to work on their own.

6. Concrete experiences are more valuable than abstract ones. The reader is referred to Dale's "Cone of Experience" in chapter 2. Pictures, objects, drawings, cartoons, and photographs all help to make words more meaningful.

Slow learners, as a group, may exhibit behavior caused by repeated experiences of failure in the classroom, poor motivation, dislike for school, compensations for academic failure, and dropping out of school. Poor health and poor home conditions may be more prevalent among slow learners because of socio-economic factors in their lives. It is logical that slow learners need a greater number of years of compulsory school attendance than normal if they learn at a slower pace. For too long, schools operated on a contradictory principle: that because slow learners were retarded, their formal education was terminated as soon as they passed the age for compulsory attendance.

Schools must anticipate and hasten the day when *all* children will be provided for according to their individual talents. Then there need be *no* forgotten children. Today, however, Rose's experience pointedly suggests she has been forgotten:

Rose was an *unfortunate* retarded child who was assigned to a special room half-days and to a regular class the other half. One day a university student appeared to administer a test to Rose. When he asked for Rose in the special class, he was told she was in another classroom nearby. When he asked there for Rose, he was told there was no one there by that name. He returned to the school office and asked again. Upon returning to the same classroom and stating that the office records indicated that she should be there in the afternoon, the teacher thought a moment, then said, "Oh, that must be her over there. She just sits in the corner."

The Learning Disabled

The National Joint Committee on Learning Disabilities recommends the following definition of learning disabilities:

Learning disability is a generic term that refers to a heterogeneous group of disorders manifested by significant difficulties in the acquisition and use of listening, speaking, reading, writing, reasoning, or mathematical abilities. These disorders are intrinsic to the individual and presumed to be due to central nervous system dysfunction.

Even though a learning disability may occur concomitantly with other handicapping conditions (e.g., sensory impairment, mental retardation, social and emotional disturbance) or environmental influences (e.g., cultural differences, insufficient/inappropriate instruction, psychogenic factors), it is not the direct result of those conditions or influences.[20]

Children have many problems that affect their ability to read. These problems can be physical, emotional, or cultural. Most often there is a combination of factors. Perceptual and neurological disorders are often misunderstood by the average teacher. What is probably the most frequent cause of learning difficulties, although it is perhaps the least widely recognized of all, is a disturbance of perceptual abilities—visual perception, auditory perception, kinesthetic perception, or a combination of these.

Perceptual Handicaps

Learning disability refers to those children of any age who demonstrate a substantial deficiency in a particular aspect of academic achievement because of perceptual or perceptual-motor handicaps, regardless of etiology or other contributing factors. The term *perceptual* as it is used here relates to those mental (neurological) processes through which the child acquired his basic alphabets of sounds and forms. The term *perceptual handicap* refers to inadequate ability in such areas as the following: recognizing fine differences between auditory and visual discriminating features underlying the sounds used in speech and the orthographic forms used in reading; retaining and recalling those discriminated sounds and forms sequentially, both in short- and long-term memory; ordering the sounds and forms sequentially, both in sensory and motor acts . . .; distinguishing figure-ground relationships . . .; recognizing spatial and temporal orientations; obtaining closure . . .; integrating intersensory information . . .; relating what is perceived to specific motor functions.[21]

Frostig has divided visual perception into five parts:

1. Deficiency in visual-motor coordination results in difficulty in cutting, pasting, drawing, and in learning how to write. The child also displays clumsiness, and even dressing himself can be difficult.

2. Deficiency in perceptual constancy results in inadequate recognition of the adaptation to the environment. The child may learn to recognize a number, letter, or word in one particular form or context but fail to recognize it when seen in a different manner. Learning to read or work with symbols in any way poses many problems.

3. Deficiency in perception of position in space results in difficulty in understanding what is meant by the words up and down, in and out, before and behind, etc. Difficulty becomes apparent in academic tasks—letters, words, phrases, numbers, and pictures appear distorted and confusing. The child may be able to pronounce the sounds *p a t* in "pat," but then, when blending them together, they may come out "tap." The child may perceive *b* as *d, p* as *q, saw* as *was,* and *24* as *42.* This makes it difficult if not impossible to learn to read, write, spell, or to do arithmetic without special teaching.

4. Deficiency in perception of spatial relationships leads to many difficulties in academic learning. They may make impossible the proper perception of the sequence of letters in a word, remembering the sequences of processes involved in long division or understanding graphs.

5. Disability in perception of figure-ground is characterized by inattentive and disorganized behavior, inability to shift attention from one stimulus to another, inability to stay within lines or to form letters correctly, inability to find the place on a page, or words in the dictionary, inability to solve familiar problems on the crowded page in a workbook. Children with such difficulties literally cannot find anything, even when it is right in front of their noses.[22]

Schools need to be prepared to adjust their curricula to enable students to demonstrate their abilities in the most positive way. Learning-disabled students who cannot read fast enough or write correct spellings need to be allowed to use alternative ways to demonstrate their achievements. They could be allowed to respond orally instead of in writing, by, for example, telling answers to questions via a tape recorder instead of writing them. They could tape a teacher's class periods instead of trying to take notes. They could listen to a tutor read aloud just as a blind student would. They could work with another student as a pair, in a "buddy system." All of these techniques may help disabled learners keep up with their age mates.[23]

Cox has presented case histories of two young adults whose school failure as children would today be diagnosed as learning disability. She discusses their rehabilitation in adulthood, when their problems were finally diagnosed. Their success offers much hope for similar students who have not yet been recognized. Cox discusses the need for such techniques as those listed previously and the psychological needs of those who have experienced repeated failure.[24]

Kirk and Elkins observed Child Service Demonstration Centers for Learning Disabilities in twenty-one different states. In reviewing the provisions for 3,000 children, they found that: (1) most were enrolled in the lower elementary grades; (2) the ratio of boys to girls was three to one; (3) about two-thirds were rated as reading problems; (4) they were educationally retarded; (5) they were more retarded in reading and spelling than in arithmetic; and (6) assigning children to the resource room was the most commonly used method of delivering services.

On the basis of their observations that 80 percent of the time emphasis was on remedial reading but that deficiencies in spelling and arithmetic were also often given as reasons for assigning children to the resource room, Kirk and Elkins questioned whether underachievement in these three subjects can be considered specific learning disabilities.[25] They concluded that often what was being dealt with was not specific learning disabilities, but rather a *general learning problem* such as found in slow learners or children from environments unlike that expected by the middle-class school.

Lack of school learning opportunities, poor instruction, poor motivation for learning, or poor school attendance are all valid concepts, but they should not be confused with the concept of specific learning disabilities.

Neurological Handicaps

Jill, in the fifth grade, was one of the children who had not made adequate progress in developmental reading despite a great deal of special attention from her teachers and some additional tutoring with a competent clinician during the summer following third grade. Although she was a bright child, her instructional level of reading was only middle-third grade. While she had never repeated a grade, her classroom teachers had observed her carefully and forwarded their observations. From year to year, written anecdotes for her cumulative folder more strongly underscored teacher dissatisfaction with her progress. The teachers noted that after tutoring following third grade, Jill had overcome many of her problems of reversals and confusions. Jill's teachers, in a shared decision, concluded that the basic problem was an emotional instability exhibited at school in a very short attention span, inability to concentrate, and general lack of efficient organization. They reasoned that her father's manner of discipline might be excessively rigid and authoritarian while the mother was too indecisive and used a laissez-faire attitude. Since the father traveled and was away from home at times, this could cause the child to be mixed up about which pattern of values and behaviors to follow. Fortunately, the teachers conveyed, as tactfully as possible, their thoughts to the parents, who insisted on further clinical study.

The Wechsler Intelligence Scale for Children confirmed an above-average IQ reported on a previous group test, the *California Test of Mental Maturity*. However, an especially low score on the block-design test in the performance scale was judged to be clinically significant, and a *Bender-Gestalt Visual Motor Test* was administered. This instrument revealed a tendency for the child to rotate her drawings by ninety degrees when she reproduced drawings from a set of dots on cards—sufficient evidence to recommend a complete neurological examination.

The neurologist discovered an unusual neurological problem. While Jill had never demonstrated any overt symptoms of epilepsy or other convulsive disorder, her electroencephalogram indicated the brain wave pattern of a person with some form of *petit mal* or *grand mal*. The neurologist explained to the parents and the reading therapist that this positive finding might account for the short attention span, flighty behavior, and resultant poor progress in school. After a few weeks of establishing the appropriate anticonvulsant drug therapy, Jill's behavior did change noticeably. Her progress in the reading clinic was rapid, and she was more *conforming and competent* in the regular classroom.

This case study shows how crucial are competent diagnosis and treatment. The implications of not having such a thorough examination and diagnosis are many. Dangerous, unfounded "blaming" assumptions can cause parents to say, "If teachers would only . . .," or teachers to say, "The parents are inconsistent in their discipline, so . . ." Jill's problem also emphasizes that even the most competent classroom teacher, teaching all of the developmental skills of reading in the most commendable way, will probably experience failure in a situation where organic disorders are the primary cause of learning disability.

The following description is a synthesized sketch of a typical hyperactive child:

> Charles was nine years old when first seen, and the chief complaint was that he was doing badly in school. He vomited a lot as a baby, banged his head and rocked in his bed for hours, and cried much more than his sister. He walked at eleven months, talked first at two-and-a-half years, did not talk in sentences until four. Always very active, he has broken a bed and a trampoline and wears out the double knees in his jeans before the second washing. At age five, he was constantly turning off the furnace and water heater. He does not learn from punishment, is afraid of nothing, wanders from home and gets lost, dashes into the street without looking. He never completes projects at home and never finishes work at school. Hard to get to bed at night, he takes two hours or more to go to sleep and gets up at six A.M. Neighbors "live in quiet terror" because he has run water into their basements through the hose, ridden his bicycle over their gardens, and blocked their sewers. He fights all the time with the neighborhood children and has no friends. In school he is "creative" in

avoiding work, he hides his books, eats crayons, tears papers, and pokes the other children. Every teacher reports that she has to stand over him to get him to do any work. Though bright, he has had to repeat second grade twice and is now in a special school.[26]

Suggestions for Teaching the Neurologically Impaired Child

There are some general principles to enhance instruction for neurologically impaired children:

1. The classes should be small.
2. The room should contain a minimum of distracting stimuli.
3. Activities must be paced at the child's capacity for sustained participation with frequent periods of guided and supervised large-muscle play, such as bicycle riding or running.
4. The children should be permitted to leave the classroom and run about the playground to release mounting tensions.
5. Group discipline must be firm, and clearly defined limits must be set.
6. Children must not be permitted to experience failure regularly or habitually. Success will build self-esteem and enhance the child's ability to try harder the next time.

But it is clear that teachers must be prepared to deal with many kinds of behaviors in the classroom beyond what is characteristic of the normal child. Some specific suggestions about how to handle particular kinds of behavior are offered below.

Hyperactivity and Distractibility

The child may be seated at the front of the room in order to separate him or her as far as possible from classmates without isolation from the group. The room decoration should be minimal, perhaps limited to one wall or area. A quiet corner completely devoid of distracting stimuli where the child can sit when he is particularly excited or irritable may help. Special worksheets that contain small amounts of material and omit extraneous illustrations or designs may help the child learn to pay attention. The teacher should keep his or her appearance plain and should avoid wearing nonessential jewelry.

Some youngsters develop hysterical reactions to stressful situations. The alert teacher tries to anticipate such situations and prevent them as much as possible.

Hyperactive children require a teacher with patience and sympathetic understanding of their problems. This teacher will provide materials which will help slow down and channel their random motor movements. The children will be able to construct many of their own learning devices through such activities as cutting, pasting, and sorting. When purposefully engaged, these children tend to become calmer. Calmer behavior leads to gradually improved attention, increased success experiences, and greater interest in the acquisition of academic skills.

Use of drugs to make it possible for a child to control impulsive behavior or attention to a topic for longer periods of time is now a controversial subject. Divoky discusses the negative aspects in an article entitled "Toward a Nation of Sedated Children,"[27] to which there is an excellent, reasoned reply in the letters to the editor in the October 1973 issue of *Learning.*[28]

Perseveration

To help the child overcome perseveration, the teacher can vary the ongoing task with one that is completely different or provide new materials to encourage the child to change responses. At the same time, the child can be encouraged to *branch out* by generalizing from the first task. These boys and girls must be specifically taught to do these things.

In making shifts of attention from one type of work to another, the teacher must be aware of the child's difficulties in such shifting and help by waiting for the child's attention. The teacher can ask specifically if the child is following or can move closer and put a hand lightly on the child's shoulder or can help put away material or get new materials ready.

Meticulousness

Keep the learning assignment short with a time limit. This requires careful diagnosis of functioning levels, including attention span, to be sure that the task is an appropriate one. The teacher may be able to encourage attending and interacting by using the operant-conditioning technique. Tangible rewards for completion of simple tasks under conditions previously agreed upon are sometimes helpful in establishing the pattern of behavior the teacher desires. Oral work should be emphasized in preference to written, but at all times overstimulation and failure should be avoided in oral as well as written expression.

Withdrawal Tendencies

Be sympathetic. Include the child as a part of the group. Any attempt at group socialization must be carefully controlled by the teacher. It is advantageous to recognize those children with a high social quotient or ability to adapt to differences in behavior. The teacher then manipulates the situation so that communication takes place. For example, "John and Billy, will you please put these notices in their envelopes?" The teacher should always try to use visual, tactile, and auditory devices to help the student learn.

Difficulty with Abstraction

Concepts must be broken down into isolated, compartmentalized learning. Concrete representations of numbers, letters, and color cues, for example, are helpful in securing insight. Keying new tasks to what the child is capable of performing will help insure that his responses will be more consistently correct. In self-tutoring activities, the correct answer should be immediately available. Overlearning is important. Responses need to become automatic after insight is achieved. Separate bits of knowledge should chain upon each other in sequential steps until whole concepts are learned.

Probably this common language disorder of children prevents them from perceiving and/or accurately recording the symbols of the printed page. They cannot interpret written language in the way unaffected children can. Certain remedial approaches are very effective with these children. Many exercises in proper discrimination of left-right direction will be helpful for those who display letter and word reversals. Shapes and sizes must be perceived. The child will benefit by being taught to look for letter details within a word.

Tactual experiences with letter contours can be gained through using wooden letters upon which sandpaper surfaces are pasted. The child's memory for letter shapes is thus reinforced through the sense of touch. Tracing the word also reinforces memory through the use of muscle or kinesthetic sense. Through writing, tactual, and kinesthetic experiences, he becomes aware of letter details.

Another effective teaching method is to present a word with one or two letters left out. As the child fills in blanks and finds that she is right, she is forced to become aware of the missing details.

Children with Emotional Disturbances

Hewett has found that emotionally disturbed children are usually not ready for "formal" instruction in which skill mastery is the primary objective. He lists *five* readiness levels prerequisite to skill mastery. They are ability to: (1) pay attention, (2) respond to others in learning situations, (3) respond to instructions or follow directions, (4) explore the environment meaningfully, and (5) get along with others and value social approval. Beyond these readiness levels, the school expects (6) mastery of skills and (7) achievement (see table 17.1). Hewett summarized these seven tasks in relation to the child's difficulties with each, the educational goal, types of learner rewards, and the amount of teacher involvement in structuring child behavior.[29]

Letting Angry Feelings Come Out

When the standards others have set for children do not match their own natural way of growing up in their own good time, conflicts will result. "No, no!" "You're a big girl now." "Give that to your little sister!" "I'm not going to let go of you until you apologize to your grandmother!" Many remarks like that will cause anger and resentment and hostility to build up in the child. These moments of "bad feelings" against another child or an adult must not be pushed deep down inside; they need to come out.

If children try to let their feelings come out in drawings or paintings, teachers must not say, "Oh, don't paint such an unhappy picture. Start again and make a nice one."[30] Children could also pound nails, hit punching bags, and tackle dummies to work out some of these feelings. A child may spank a doll, put it in an oven, be willing to burn it up, try to flush it down the toilet, stomp on it, or otherwise try to mutilate it. Teachers should keep as neutral as possible and not say, "Oh! the nice dolly. You must be nice to it."[31] The neutral response to the child's expressions of "I hate it" is "You don't like the doll [or whoever the doll represents at the moment] very well today, do you?"[32]

Table 17.1 Description of educational tasks.

	Readiness Skills						
	Attention	Response	Order	Exploratory	Social	Mastery	Achievement
Child's Problem	Inattention due to withdrawal or resistance	Lack of involvement and unwillingness to respond in learning situations	Inability to follow directions	Incomplete or inaccurate knowledge of environment	Failure to value social approval or disapproval	Deficits in basic adaptive and school skills not in keeping with IQ	Lack of self-motivation for learning
Educational Goal	Get child to pay attention to teacher and task	Get child to respond to tasks he likes and which offer promise of success	Get child to complete tasks with specific starting points and steps leading to a conclusion	Increase child's efficiency as an explorer and get him involved in multisensory exploration of his environment	Get child to work for teacher and peer group approval and to avoid their disapproval	Remediation of basic skill deficiencies	Development of interest in acquiring knowledge
Learner Reward	Provided by tangible rewards (e.g., food, money, tokens)	Provided by gaining social attention	Provided through task completion	Provided by sensory stimulation	Provided by social approval	Provided through task accuracy	Provided through intellectual task success
Teacher Involvement	Minimal	Still limited	Emphasized	Emphasized	Based on standards of social appropriateness	Based on curriculum assignments	Minimal

Adapted from Frank N. Hewett, "Educational Engineering with Emotionally Disturbed Children," *Exceptional Children* 33 (March 1967):461. Used with permission.

Asquith, Donaher, and Barton have described one emotionally disturbed little girl as follows:

> She is hyperactive, interrupts, cries easily, has temper tantrums and is utterly unpredictable from one moment to another. Recently she climbed on top of her desk and screamed and threw books, crayons, and paper all over the room.[33]

If a class has a student who obviously is emotionally disturbed, it is the teacher's responsibility to assist the remaining students in a subtle manner to accept the defiant child as part of the group. The term "individual differences" in educational jargon does not apply only to academic work. Just as children differ in academic ability, they also differ in the background experiences that cause each one to respond to situations in a unique manner. Therefore, each child must be accepted, with weaknesses as well as strong points, as a person having worth and dignity as a human being. The teacher has the responsibility of encouraging individuality insofar as any one child's behavior does not impinge on the rights of others.

According to national figures, in a class of thirty-five students, the teacher can expect, on the average, from two to five students to show symptoms of some sort of exceptionality. How these exceptional children are handled depends on the teacher's educational background and personal maturity.

The teacher must not only be able to recognize deviant behavior, but also should try to discover the cause. Emotional disturbance is generally expressed by the following four types of behavior: aggression, anxiety, withdrawal, and bizarre behavior. For each type, certain distress signals are given below and appropriate teacher responses suggested.

Aggression

Aggression manifests itself in temper tantrums, bullying, teasing, destroying property of others, being physically abusive to other children, interrupting and disrupting classroom routine, stealing, or lying.

To help the children with certain of these behaviors, the teacher may respond in any of the following ways:

1. Have a corner set aside that is neutral and nondistracting.
2. Separate the child from the group during periods of active aggressive behavior.
3. Be accepting but firm; be matter-of-fact, businesslike, and *fair*.
4. Anticipate aggressive behavior and help the child regain control or select alternate behavior.
5. Set up minimum standards of expected behavior *with* the child, then when corrective measures are taken, the child knows it is his or her own standard that has been violated.
6. Provide acceptable outlets for tensions that build up aggression: modeling clay, punching bags, nondestructible toys.

Anxiety   The anxious child cries easily, is timid, is afraid to tackle new tasks, is overanxious about grades, cannot accept less than his or her understanding of your standards.

To help the child who is anxious, the teacher should respond as follows:

1. Maintain warm rapport with the child.
2. Help the child build self-confidence based on successes.
3. Reassure but do not coddle the child.
4. Help the child minimize stress over grades.
5. Be able to discipline in a kind way, but be firm.
6. Do not allow the child to become overly dependent on a teacher for security.
7. Maintain a sense of proportion by businesslike friendliness.
8. Ask for responses in class when you know the child will be successful.

Withdrawal   The withdrawing child daydreams, prefers to be alone, does not seek the company of anyone, has few friends, maybe only one with whom he or she can feel intimacy. To help the child who withdraws, the teacher can respond as follows:

1. Bring the child into class activities when he or she is able to handle it emotionally.
2. Make sure that class activities are varied between quiet and active work.
3. Help the child develop interest in school work by varying teaching techniques to include games, giving the child responsibility in group projects, and calling on the child to respond when you know he or she can be successful.

Suggestions for the Classroom Teacher

1. The child with deviant abilities should be kept in the regular classroom as much as possible, even if for only a few minutes at a time. The use of programmed materials, paced at the child's performance level, is recommended for some children. Some teachers have successfully used the rebus technique in easy reading.
2. There should be a movable screen in the classroom that can be used to partition off a corner or other working space in order to shut out unwanted stimuli. This is carefully interpreted to the child as a way to make it easy for him or her to work; it is *not a punishment*. The teacher can explain that "Some people need a quiet place where they won't be disturbed if they are to get anything done."
3. The teacher must become skilled in sizing up children's moods early in the day. A child who is upset and having a bad day should be kept in the teacher's line of vision all day long. On bad days the teacher should make a special effort to support the child by any of the following behaviors carried out casually:
   a. close physical proximity;
   b. gentle massage of the shoulder and neck muscles as the teacher passes the child's desk (if the child permits);

From Theory to Practice 17.3
Reading About a Special Area

Each teacher needs to be informed about the education of exceptional children. The information you have obtained from this chapter is simply a beginning for your studies in this area.

Read a book or several articles concerning *one* of the exceptionalities discussed in this chapter. Suggestions for readings may be found in "For Further Reading," or you may use your library catalog to find other sources.

After you have done your reading, prepare a report of your findings and conclusions. If all students were to duplicate their reports and give copies to each other, each would have a fine resource as you move to the classroom.

    c. talk to the child, even if he or she doesn't respond;
    d. set reasonable limits and hold firmly to them;
    e. check the child's medical record or ask the mother's permission to talk with the child's family doctor.

Channels of communication are very important so that everyone who may have useful information has a way to share it with others who badly need it. Teacher, principal, family doctor, school nurse, social worker, parents, neurologist, school psychologist, and, if indicated, psychiatrist—all need to share information, even though they may not have learned to "talk the same language." It is necessary for them all to exchange ideas and learn how to work together.

Summary

Although Roger is eleven years old *chronologically,* the teacher must not expect him to be eleven *behaviorally*—or *academically.* He may not even seem to be eleven *physically,* although he is most apt to approximate the norm in this respect. Roger may be *eight* behaviorally, or eight academically. What teachers must be able to do is to see through the eleven-year-old exterior and see the eight-year-old inside and work from there. This has been called X-ray vision—to look through the structure to see the *real* child inside.

For the bright child, the problem is comparable. An eleven-year-old exterior can harbor a fifteen-year-old problem-solver. The intellectually gifted child is apt to have a social age above but approximating his chronological age. As emphasized, a bright child who must function in a second language needs technical help to succeed in school.

Special problems of children who are neurologically handicapped or emotionally disturbed have been reviewed in this chapter. It is apparent that most beginning teachers will need expert help when working with children having these problems. With patience and calmness, many teachers are able to help such children function in regular classes by tailoring their program to fit specific needs.

Although not discussed in this chapter, it is extremely important for the teacher to develop the ability to recognize his or her own emotional needs as well as the child's emotional needs and to be able to separate the two.

For Further Reading

Abeson, Alan, and Jeffrey Zettel. "The End of the Quiet Revolution: The Education for All Handicapped Children Act of 1975." *Exceptional Children* 44 (October 1977): 114–28.

Bender, Lauretta. *A Visual Motor Gestalt Test and Its Clinical Use.* New York: American Orthopsychiatric Assn., 1938.

Charles, C. M. *Individualizing Instruction.* 2d ed. St. Louis: C.V. Mosby, 1980.

Gonzales, Eloy, and Leroy Ortiz. "Bilingualism and Special Education: Social Policy and Education Related to Linguistically and Culturally Different Groups." *Journal of Learning Disabilities* 10 (June/July 1977): 331–38.

Harris, A. J. *A Casebook on Reading Disability.* New York: David McKay, 1970.

Jenkins, J. R., and L. M. Jenkins. *Cross-Age and Peer Tutoring: Help for Children with Learning Problems.* Reston, Va.: Council for Exceptional Children, 1981.

Jones, R. L., ed. *Mainstreaming and the Minority Child.* Reston, Va.: Council for Exceptional Children, 1976.

Jordan, June B. *Teacher, Please Don't Close the Door: The Exceptional Child in the Mainstream.* Reston, Va.: Council for Exceptional Children, 1976.

Kroth, Roger. *Communicating with Parents of Exceptional Children.* Denver: Love Publishing, 1975.

Kroth, Roger, and Richard Simpson. *Parent Conferences as a Teaching Strategy.* Denver: Love Publishing, 1977.

Loughlin, Catherine, and Joseph H. Suina. "Supporting Children with Special Needs." Chapter 9 in *The Learning Environment: An Instructional Strategy,* pp. 208-31. New York: Teachers College Press, 1982.

Lowenthal, Barbara. "IEP: Purposes and Implications." *Young Children* 35 (November 1979): 28–32.

Reynolds, Maynard, and Jack W. Birch. *Teaching Exceptional Children in All America's Schools: A First Course for Teachers and Principals,* Rev. ed. Reston, Va.: Council for Exceptional Children, 1982.

Gifted Children and Reading

Divoky, Diane. "Room 13: Roni Howard's Oasis for Kids." *Learning* 6 (Aug./Sept. 1977): 76–85.

Gallagher, James John. *Teaching the Gifted Child,* 2d ed. Boston: Allyn & Bacon, 1975.

Hauck, Barbara, and Maurice Freehill. *The Gifted: Case Studies.* Dubuque, Iowa: Wm. C. Brown, 1972.

Labuda, Michael, ed. *Creative Reading for Gifted Learners: A Design for Excellence.* Newark: International Reading Assn., 1974.

Renzulli, Joseph S., and Linda H. Smith. "Two Approaches to Identification of Gifted Students." *Exceptional Children* 43 (May 1977): 512–18.

Renzulli, Joseph S., and E. P. Stoddard, eds. *Gifted and Talented Education in Perspective*. Reston, Va.: Council for Exceptional Children, 1980.

Rowe, Ernest Ras. "Creative Writing and the Gifted Child." *Exceptional Children* 34 (December 1967): 279–82.

Stanley, Julian C., Wm. C. George, and Cecelia H. Solano. *The Gifted and the Creative: A Fifty-Year Perspective*. Baltimore: Johns Hopkins University Press, 1977.

Syphers, Dorothy F. *Gifted and Talented Children: Practical Programming for Teachers and Principals*. Reston, Va.: Council for Exceptional Children, 1972.

Torrance, Ellis Paul. *Discovery and Nurturance of Giftedness in the Culturally Different*. Reston, Va.: Council for Exceptional Children, 1977.

Trezise, Robert L. "Teaching Reading to the Gifted." *Language Arts* 54 (November/December 1977): 920–24.

Slow Learners and Reading

Benyon, Sheila D. *Intensive Programming for Slow Learners*. Columbus, Ohio: Charles E. Merrill, 1968.

Gardner, Wm. I. "Social and Emotional Adjustment of Mildly Retarded Children and Adolescents." *Exceptional Children* 33 (October 1966): 97–106.

Guthrie, Frances M., and Patricia Cunningham. "Teaching Decoding Skills to Educable Mentally Handicapped Children." *The Reading Teacher* 35 (February 1982): 554–59.

Kephart, Newell C. *The Slow Learner in the Classroom*. Columbus, Ohio: Charles E. Merrill, 1970.

Kirk, Samuel, Sister Joanne Marie Kliebhan, and Janet W. Lerner. *Teaching Reading to Slow and Disabled Learners*. Boston: Houghton Mifflin, 1978.

Learning Disabilities and Reading

Book, Robert M. "Predicting Reading Failure: A Screening Battery for Kindergarten Children." *Journal of Learning Disabilities* 7 (January 1974): 43–47.

Cruickshank, Wm. M. "Myths and Realities in Learning Disabilities." *Journal of Learning Disabilities* 10 (January 1977): 51–58.

Divoky, Diane. "Screening: The Grand Delusion." *Learning* 5 (March 1977): 34.

Gearhart, Bill. *Learning Disabilities: Educational Strategies,* 2d ed. St. Louis: C.V. Mosby, 1977.

Hartman, Nancy C., and Robert Hartman. "Perceptual Handicap or Reading Disability." *The Reading Teacher* 26 (April 1973): 684–95.

Johnson, D. J., and H. R. Myklebust. *Learning Disabilities: Educational Principles and Practices*. New York: Grune & Stratton, 1967.

Kirk, Samuel A., and John Elkins. "Characteristics of Children Enrolled in the Child Service Demonstration Centers." *Journal of Learning Disabilities* 8 (December 1975): 630–36.

The Emotionally Disturbed Child and Reading

Axline, Virginia. *Dibs: In Search of Self—Personality Development in Play Therapy*. Boston: Houghton Mifflin, 1964.

———. *Play Therapy*. Boston: Houghton Mifflin, 1969.

Baruch, Dorothy. *New Ways in Discipline*. New York: McGraw-Hill, 1949.

Gallagher, Patricia A. "Structuring Academic Tasks for Emotionally Disturbed Boys." *Exceptional Children* 38 (May 1972): 711–20.

Hewett, Frank M. *The Emotionally Disturbed Child in the Classroom.* Boston: Allyn & Bacon, 1968.

Long, Nicholas, ed. *Conflict in the Classroom.* Belmont, Calif.: Wadsworth, 1971.

Newcomer, P. L. *Understanding and Teaching Emotionally Disturbed Children.* Boston: Allyn & Bacon, 1980.

Tift, Katharine. "The Disturbed Child in the Classroom." *NEA Journal* 57 (March 1968): 12–14.

Zintz, Miles V. *Corrective Reading,* 4th ed., pp. 173–78. Dubuque, Iowa: Wm. C. Brown, 1981.

Notes

1. Alan Abeson and Jeffrey Zettel, "The End of the Quiet Revolution: The Education for All Handicapped Children Act of 1975," *Exceptional Children* 44 (October 1977): 114–28.

2. Ibid., pp. 122–28.

3. "Mainstreaming Minimanual: Ten Steps to Success." *Instructor* 91 (March 1982): 63–66.

4. Lewis M. Terman, "The Discovery and Encouragement of Exceptional Talent," *The American Psychologist* 9 (June 1954).

5. Terman used the Stanford-Binet IQ score of 140 as a criterion of giftedness.

6. Robert F. DeHaan and Robert J. Havighurst, *Educating Gifted Children* (Chicago: The University of Chicago Press, 1957), p. 151. They recommended that qualities of leadership and special abilities also be evaluated. They believed that the top 15 to 20 percent of the population should be considered talented and that a lower IQ score, perhaps 120, would be sufficient to identify this group.

7. Robert J. Havighurst, Virgil M. Rogers, and Paul Witty, "Are the Community and the School Failing the Unusual Child?" University of Chicago Round Table, 27 April 1952, cited in Helen M. Robinson, *Promoting Maximal Reading Growth Among Able Learners* (Chicago: University of Chicago Press, 1954), pp. 29–30.

8. Rudolph Pintner, "Superior Ability," *Teachers College Record* 42 (February 1941): 419, as cited in Paul Witty, ed., *The Gifted Child* (Boston: D.C. Heath, 1951), p. 275.

9. Louise Krueger et al., "Administrative Problems in Educating Gifted Children," in Witty, *The Gifted Child,* p. 266.

10. Witty, *The Gifted Child,* p. 151.

11. Jeffrey Zettel, "State Provisions for Educating the Gifted and Talented," in *The Gifted and the Talented,* Seventy-eighth Yearbook of the National Society for the Study of Education, Part I, ed. A. Harry Passow (Chicago: University of Chicago Press, 1979), p. 7.

12. Patricia B. Mitchell and Donald K. Erickson, "The Education of Gifted and Talented Children: A Status Report," in *Gifted and Talented Education in Perspective,* ed. Joseph S. Renzulli and Elizabeth P. Stoddard (Reston, Va.: The Council for Exceptional Children, 1980), p. 210.

13. Gertrude H. Hildreth, *Introduction to the Gifted* (New York: McGraw-Hill, 1966), p. 217.

14. Joan B. Nelson and Donald L. Cleland, "The Role of the Teacher of Gifted and Creative Children," in *Reading for the Gifted and the Creative Student,* ed. Paul A. Witty (Newark, Del.: International Reading Assn., 1971), pp. 48–54.

15. Jack Cassidy, "Inquiry Reading for the Gifted," *The Reading Teacher* 35 (October 1981): 17–21.
16. Ibid., p. 17.
17. Ibid., p. 21.
18. Miles V. Zintz and Joyce Morris, "Tutoring Counseling Program for Indian Students" (Albuquerque: The College of Education, University of New Mexico, 1962, mimeographed), p. 13.
19. T. Hegge, S. Kirk, and W. Kirk, *Remedial Reading Drills* (Ann Arbor, Mich.: George Wahr, 1955).
20. "U.S. National Joint Committee on Learning Disabilities Urges Revised Definition of LD," *The Reading Teacher* 35 (November 1981): 135.
21. N. Hobbs, ed., *Issues in the Classification of Children,* Vol. I (San Francisco: Jossey-Bass, 1975), p. 306.
22. Marianne Frostig, *Administration and Scoring Manual, Developmental Test of Visual Perception* (Palo Alto, Calif.: Consulting Psychologists Press, 1966), p. 5.
23. Frances B. DeWitt, "Tear off the Label: the Older Student and SLD," *Academic Therapy* 13 (September 1977): 69–78.
24. Sheralyn Cox, "The Learning-Disabled Adult," *Academic Therapy* 13 (September 1977): 79–86.
25. Samuel A. Kirk and John Elkins, "Characteristics of Children Enrolled in the Child Service Demonstration Centers," *Journal of Learning Disabilities* 8 (December 1975): 630, 636.
26. Roger Signor, "Hyperactive Children," *News Bulletin Quarterly* 37 (Winter 1967): 19 describes the work of Dr. Mark A. Stewart, Professor of Child Psychiatry, Washington University School of Medicine, St. Louis.
27. Diane Divoky, "Toward a Nation of Sedated Children," *Learning* 1 (March 1973): 7–13.
28. Avrum L. Katcher, M.D., letter to the editor, *Learning* 2 (October 1973): 8.
29. Frank M. Hewett, "Educational Engineering with Emotionally Disturbed Children," *Exceptional Children* 33 (March 1967): 461.
30. James Hymes, *Understanding Your Child* (Englewood Cliffs, N.J.: Prentice-Hall, 1952), p. 147.
31. Ibid., p. 149.
32. Virginia Axline's case study *Dibs* describes dramatically how one little boy's personality was restored to good mental health through play therapy. Virginia Axline, *Dibs* (Boston: Houghton Mifflin, 1967).
33. Melrose Asquith, Mrs. Robert Donaher, and Clifford Barton, "I Have an Emotionally Disturbed Child in My Classroom," *Grade Teacher* 85 (April 1968): 77–80.

Evaluation in the Reading Program

Part 6

Part 6 is composed of chapters that relate in various ways to evaluation in the reading program. Chapter 18, "Corrective Reading," addresses the problems the teacher faces when some of the children are having more than average difficulty in making satisfactory progress in learning to read and enjoying reading. Suggestions are given for fitting the daily schedule and classroom tasks to the needs of the children, diagnostic and instructional techniques are suggested for working with readers in need of special help, and a list of high-interest, low-vocabulary materials is provided.

Chapter 19 provides teachers with evaluation tools, both formal and informal, to help them evaluate the reading program. Several common standardized tests are discussed, along with ways to implement informal assessments, such as examining oral and written language samples, keeping anecdotal records, conducting interest inventories, and assessing interpersonal relationships among class members.

Chapter 20 is not only the synthesizing chapter of the book, but also the chapter that stresses the need for diagnostic teachers of reading. The teaching of reading should be diagnostic in nature, so that instruction fits the needs of the learner, no matter what the level of achievement may be. Teachers should also diagnose their own knowledge about the reading process, reading instruction, classroom attitudes toward reading, diagnostic teaching, and adapting instruction to the needs of individuals.

Corrective Reading

A Cognitive Map: Corrective Reading

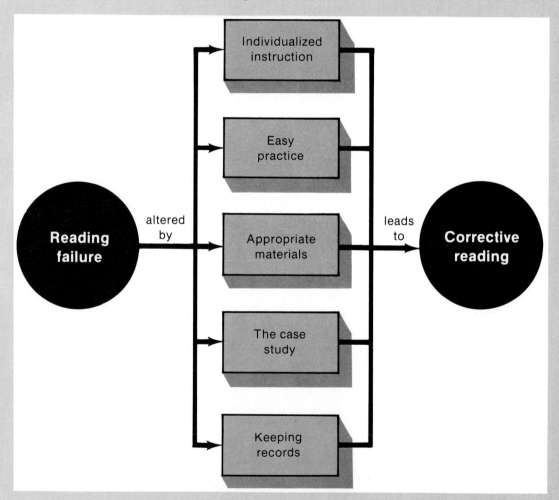

18

Guide Questions

1. What are the major characteristics of children who are failing in reading?

2. How does one individualize instruction?

3. What are some materials that you feel would provide suitable easy reading practice?

4. How would you go about completing a case study? Why?

5. Why are records on the progress of a disabled reader important?

6. What is corrective reading?

Terminology

case study

conventions about print

corrective reading

directional sense

easy reading materials

individualized instruction

interest inventory

reading failure

record keeping

Holt has suggested that the expectations of the school and the efforts of boys and girls are not directed toward the same goals:

> When I started, I thought that some people were just born smarter than others and that not much could be done about it. This seems to be the official line of most of the psychologists. It isn't hard to believe, if all your contacts are with students in the classroom or the psychological testing room. But, if you live at a small school, seeing students in class, in the dorms, in their private lives, at their recreations, sports, and manual work, you can't escape the conclusion that some people are much smarter part of the time than they are at other times. Why? Why should a boy or girl, who under some circumstances is willingly observant, imaginative, analytical, in a word, intelligent, come into the classroom and, as if by magic, turn into a complete dolt?[1]

When Carolyn came for instruction in remedial reading, she made it quite evident that she thought neither the teachers' efforts nor the school program were designed to help her.

Carolyn's mother called and asked if her daughter, age fourteen and finishing the eighth grade, might have an evaluation of her reading skills. It was the final week of school late in May, and an appointment was made for early June.

Carolyn came for testing in an obviously belligerent mood. Her mother brought her and waited for her during the testing, and this was an obvious irritation for Carolyn.

Carolyn explained to the clinician that she was stupid. When the clinician raised some doubt about it, Carolyn said, "Just ask all the teachers over at junior high, they'll all tell you I'm stupid." The clinician presented a brief list of polysyllabic words to be pronounced and divided in syllables, and Carolyn commented, "O.K., so you can see how stupid I really am."

When she defined the vocabulary words in the Stanford-Binet test and earned an "average adult" score on that subtest, the clinician used this bit of evidence to say that she was apparently doing as well as the average on that particular test. At this, Carolyn said acidly, "So that's an intelligence test! I've had those at junior high, too, and the counselor there told me I was stupid."

Later the young lady revealed that, not only was she stupid, but she was also huge. She thought she was as big as a horse. She was a large-boned fourteen-year-old, taller and heavier than the average girl in her class.

On the reading survey test, she scored at beginning fifth grade on vocabulary, speed, and comprehension. This was no surprise to Carolyn and she let it be known that she understood that the clinician was collecting further evidence of her inadequacy.

Carolyn's summer program included one lesson a week, during which she studied spelling, phonic and structural analysis, and syllabication and wrote paragraphs about topics of her choice. In addition, she came twice a week to complete, independently, exercises from the *SRA Junior Reading for Understanding Laboratory*. She began with card No. 17, at beginning fifth grade level. At this level she was successful, and completed two cards at each level until she reached beginning sixth grade level in about two weeks. When she read the table of grade placement values in the teacher's guidebook, she began to appear much more confident. By the end of eight weeks, she was ready for cards at beginning ninth grade level and appeared confident that she would be able to do her reading work in the fall.

Her summer program had been well planned apart from the reading lessons, too, and she had enjoyed short courses at the YWCA in cheerleading, drama, and charm. In addition, she was an excellent swimmer and participated as a member of a girls' swimming team.

Why Do Children Fail?

It may be well to look first at some erroneous reasons given for why children fail. Although they are often cited, the following are *not* reasons why so many children fail in reading.

1. It is *not* because teachers do *not* teach phonics in the elementary schools today. In the lessons on word-attack skills, specific techniques are presented in all teacher's guides.
2. It is *not* because teachers do not know how to teach reading. If a teacher in a busy, crowded classroom teaches 85 percent of her class to read successfully in terms of their potential ability to achieve, it is unfair to look at the small percentage of children who fail to progress and place all the blame on the teacher. Might it not be much more logical to say that the overcrowded conditions of the classrooms may be a primary cause?
3. It is *not* because schools are progressive and permit anarchy in their classrooms. Sufficient standard test data are available today to prove convincingly that groups of children today read better than comparable groups did at any time in the past. Further, there is evidence to show that children who are taught in classrooms where *activity* work, teacher-pupil planning, and student responsibility are encouraged read better, on the average, than children taught in more formally organized classrooms.
4. It is *not* because too little time is devoted to the 3 Rs. Visits to classrooms would soon show one that teachers still devote much time to the 3Rs—in fact, they may spend *too much time* working on routine, unmotivating, monotonous lessons in an attempt to help children learn the 3 Rs.
5. It is *not* because parents won't cooperate with the schools. Although there are a few situations where teachers and parents are incompatible, parent-teacher conferences help immeasurably to clarify the problems of children in school.

While none of these five causes should be used as a general reason for our problems, it is true that any one of them may be a primary contributing factor in individual cases.

Does the Child "Fit" the Work Schedule?

The main causes for children failing to learn to read are related to the traditional organization of schools. A school that puts children into classes where *standards* have been defined arbitrarily in terms of grade placement automatically labels as failures all children who do not measure up. All children are expected to come to school when they are six and be enrolled in the first grade. All parents are strongly pressured by the mores of their community to see that their children fit a normal pattern.

The organized school works far too hard trying to make everybody alike—and conform to a preconceived stereotype—rather than encouraging real individuality. Even when schools give lip service to the idea of accepting individuality, they often work against it in practice. Teachers are habituated to a deeply entrenched practice of teaching *books* rather than teaching *children* to read books.

The continuing effort to make *every* first grader read first grade readers, *every* second grader read second grade readers, and *every* third grader read third grade readers will never work. Teachers should have children read for regular classes only those books that are appropriate for their instructional level. (Instructional level is that level at which a child fails to pronounce correctly no more than five words in reading a passage of one hundred words and can answer questions to show that at least 75 percent of the ideas are understood (see chapter 4).

Teachers who do not hold stringently to this standard and who allow children to work in basal readers that are too difficult keep the children struggling at their frustration levels. Children can do little more than memorize statements and parrot facts when they are kept reading at this level.

Teachers, generally, have not followed an application of our knowledge of the psychology of individual differences to its logical conclusion. One hears from teachers and administrators, "What are you going to do when they get to the fourth grade?" "What will they do when they get to seventh grade?" or "How about when they come to high school at ninth grade?"

One accepts the situation as he or she finds it. Two basic principles about learning apply here: (1) the spread of mental ability in any grade is going to increase as children go through school; and (2) no child can read a more difficult book until he or she can read an easier one. If these two principles are accepted, there is no alternative to starting where the child is. Rejecting or not knowing these principles, a few teachers have said, "But I'm a sixth grade teacher and I don't know anything about phonics," or "I'm an upper grade teacher and I don't know how to teach primary reading," or "I teach seventh grade and they're supposed to learn that in the lower grades."

Teachers need to remember that in their classes children exhibit different levels of understanding. Level of understanding is determined by degree of intelligence and previous experiences either firsthand or vicarious. Children may understand a concept very well; or they may understand some things about the concept; or they may have only a vague idea of what the concept is about. It helps little to try to clarify concepts in children's thinking if their chief concern is remembering facts to give back to a teacher. Teachers can best help to clarify concepts by seeing that the same concept is dealt with in many ways, and by using the concept in problems related to the child's life experience.

Finally, many schools do not have an overall school policy that gives teachers confidence in what they do in one calendar year. Overall policy gives continuity to the school program from grade to grade. Present-day school programs must recognize the necessity of teaching reading all the way through the secondary school and having a cumulative record available for each child so that each teacher has access to all the helpful information compiled by the child's previous teachers.

Does the Work Schedule "Fit" the Child?

Causes of reading failure will be met only by:

1. *Doing* something about individual differences. This means doing something about them *all day long*. A child who reads at the fourth grade level much of the year while in the sixth grade probably should spell fourth grade spelling words and read books no more difficult than fourth grade reader level for factual information in all the content subjects. It means accepting careful measures of readiness for reading before putting all children into a formal reading program in first grade. It means that educators must stop expecting all children in a class to learn the same thing, in the same amount of time, with the same amount of practice.

   The sixth grader who reads more adequately at fourth grade level can read and write about all the same topics studied by other sixth graders if the teacher and the librarian search out collateral reading that is appropriate.

2. Knowing how to use information about children and where to get it, such as cumulative records, which should include:
   a. Intelligence test records
   b. Health records
   c. Reading record of books previously read
   d. Summaries of personal conferences with child, parent, or other professionals
   e. Standardized tests of achievement

3. Having an accepted school policy that the school faculty is willing to put into effect. The school program should be well enough understood by each teacher to provide a sense of security. Overall school policies should accept these basic principles:
   a. The school exists solely to help children. This means that no child is a misfit. They *all* belong.
   b. Since no two children are alike, the teacher must start to help each child "where the child is." This means that each teacher must feel secure in knowing that each succeeding teacher will also accept the wide range of differences in a class when they are promoted.

c. Every teacher is a reading teacher. Children must be taught how to read all the different kinds of material with which they are confronted: extensive reading, intensive reading, reading to evaluate critically, reading to remember details, and recreational reading are some of the types.

d. An accepting, analytical approach will be followed to solve existing problems. An open-mindedness and "pooling of ideas" should occur when teacher, principal, and special services representatives discuss a child with a problem. No one should feel insecure in asking for help with children who present difficult problems.

4. Special services departments include people who are able to analyze problems in the areas of: remedial reading, behavior, mental retardation or acceleration, physical handicaps, speech correction, and speech improvement. When a child's problem has been studied and a case study has been prepared, a round table discussion should include as many people as are concerned with the case and will implement the findings. Any or all of the following people should participate in such a discussion: teachers, parents, principal, school guidance counselor, school social worker, school nurse, school psychologist, school doctor, visiting teacher, and special therapists.

5. Having adequate *materials of instruction.* Schools need adequate materials of all sorts for teacher use (books, magazines, pamphlets, charts, maps, pictures, films, filmstrips, models, workbooks).

6. The best practice in reporting a child's progress to his parents is some kind of two-way communication. There must be some time and some way that the teacher can discuss "face-to-face" with the parents the progress in academic work and social development the child is making. The parents can say in the same "face-to-face" situation to the teacher what they are thinking, and then, in this same conversational atmosphere, they can work out any semantic differences. While they may not agree, at least they have a greater degree of understanding of each other's opinions. Sometimes, such a conversation gives them much mutual support.

In summary, then, here are six suggestions for meeting the problems of reading failure:

1. Recognize and meet individual differences.
2. Know how to obtain and use information about children.
3. Establish a school policy that is effective from the first year through senior high school.
4. Utilize special services and special personnel in studying about children.
5. Provide adequate materials of instruction.
6. Work cooperatively with parents.

**Individualized
Instruction**

If teachers are to combat reading failure, they must find out what each child
knows about comprehension and word recognition, about print and how print
works, and about attitudes toward reading, books, and school. With enough information in each of these areas and with the support of the home, the teacher
is in a position to individualize instruction in order to give the child the best
possible opportunity to overcome the reading problems and to begin to experience
success in schoolwork.

Many useful ideas for assessing comprehension abilities have already been
presented in chapter 10 and will not be repeated here. The informal reading inventory and the cloze procedure are particularly useful comprehension assessment tools.

Word-recognition assessment and teaching strategies were presented in
chapter 9. Only two further assessments are presented here.

Measuring
Abilities in
Phonics and
Structural Analysis

The teacher can informally test how well children in a reading group can identify
the initial, medial, and final sounds in words by merely asking:

What is the first sound you hear in *book, toy, forest, party, kitchen,
candy* (either k or c)?
What are the first two letters in these words *fright, snake, skate, scales*
(either sk or sc), *praise, dwelling?*
What is the middle sound you hear in *cabbage, forest, balloon, reading,
practice?*
What is the vowel that this word begins with: *Indian, olives, elephant,
umbrella, apple?*

The teacher needs, however, a more standard measure of which phonic elements a child knows and does not know. There are some inventories available to the teacher for this purpose.

The *Inventory of Phonetic Skills* is one of these.[2] The inventories are developed for end of grade one, end of grade two, and end of grade three and are called Test One, Test Two, and Test Three. They sample the phonic and structural elements that have been taught in the Houghton Mifflin Reading Program through each respective grade level. Test Two includes seven subtests: initial consonant sounds, final consonant sounds, structural elements, vowel elements, initial consonant sounds (more difficult), structural elements (more difficult), and vowel elements (more difficult). Test Two is reproduced in part in figure 18.1. A teacher's guide contains the rationale for the test, directions for administering and scoring, and suggestions for reteaching items a child misses.

As another source, most series of readers provide at each achievement level adequate tests of the phonic and structural elements taught.

Several subtests of the *Silent Reading Diagnostic Tests*[3] are also useful for analyzing phonic and structural errors in children's reading test performances. They provide for identifying initial, medial, and final errors in word-recognition; locating visual elements in words; syllabication; locating root words; hearing beginning sounds; hearing rhyming words; and identifying letter sounds.

Directional Sense on the Page — Left-to-Right Orientation

Another factor that seems to underlie some reading failures is lack of knowledge of the conventions about print. Many of these conventions center around directional sense. Children may be confused about which direction English print is read, how to make the return sweep at the end of the line, where the front of the book is, how to scan words from left to right, how to read from top to bottom, and the meanings of such words as *first* and *last*. Marie Clay's *Early Detection of Reading Difficulties* is in part an assessment of these conventions about print.[4]

The arbitrary necessity for reading from left-to-right on the line of print is a learned behavior needed in our culture—although not in all cultures. A number of children have difficulties with this orientation when they come to school, and the difficulty varies in intensity from one child to another. Teachers must have some techniques for helping children overcome their confusion.

Children may reverse whole words: *was* for *saw; ten* for *net.* They may reverse some of the letters inside words: *form* for *from; left* for *felt; tired* for *tried.* Or, they may reverse only one letter: *pig* for *dig; put* for *but; way* for *may.*

It is common for the so-called dyslexic child to have imperfect directional sense—to confuse left and right and up and down. As a result, the child is likely to reverse letters and words, or syllables within words: *b* becomes *d, p* becomes *q; saw* may be written as *was, left* as *felt, on* as *no,* and *sorrow* as *sowro.* Numbers may be similarly reversed, with *42* substituted for *24.* Up and down confusion leads a child to write *M* for *W* and *d* for *p.* All children up to about age six may have a few difficulties of this kind, but the so-called dyslexic child's reversals are far more numerous and persist much longer.[5]

Figure 18.1

Inventory of Phonetic Skills, Test Two, Houghton Mifflin, 1972.

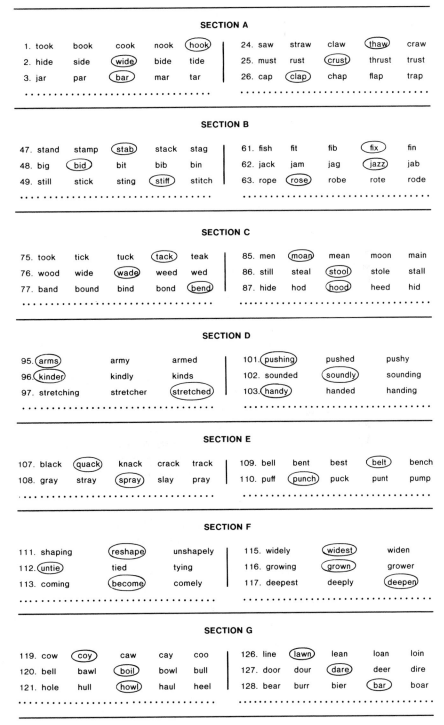

SECTION A

1. took	book	cook	nook	(hook)	24. saw	straw	claw	(thaw)	craw
2. hide	side	(wide)	bide	tide	25. must	rust	(crust)	thrust	trust
3. jar	par	(bar)	mar	tar	26. cap	(clap)	chap	flap	trap

SECTION B

47. stand	stamp	(stab)	stack	stag	61. fish	fit	fib	(fix)	fin
48. big	(bid)	bit	bib	bin	62. jack	jam	jag	(jazz)	jab
49. still	stick	sting	(stiff)	stitch	63. rope	(rose)	robe	rote	rode

SECTION C

75. took	tick	tuck	(tack)	teak	85. men	(moan)	mean	moon	main
76. wood	wide	(wade)	weed	wed	86. still	steal	(stool)	stole	stall
77. band	bound	bind	bond	(bend)	87. hide	hod	(hood)	heed	hid

SECTION D

95. (arms)	army	armed	101. (pushing)	pushed	pushy
96. (kinder)	kindly	kinds	102. sounded	(soundly)	sounding
97. stretching	stretcher	(stretched)	103. (handy)	handed	handing

SECTION E

| 107. black | (quack) | knack | crack | track | 109. bell | bent | best | (belt) | bench |
| 108. gray | stray | (spray) | slay | pray | 110. puff | (punch) | puck | punt | pump |

SECTION F

111. shaping	(reshape)	unshapely	115. widely	(widest)	widen
112. (untie)	tied	tying	116. growing	(grown)	grower
113. coming	(become)	comely	117. deepest	deeply	(deepen)

SECTION G

119. cow	(coy)	caw	cay	coo	126. line	(lawn)	lean	loan	loin
120. bell	bawl	(boil)	bowl	bull	127. door	dour	(dare)	deer	dire
121. hole	hull	(howl)	haul	heel	128. bear	burr	bier	(bar)	boar

The teacher will utilize any device that will help a child remember always to begin on the left until the habit has been established. Some techniques for teaching directional sense are: uncovering words from left to right; coloring the first letter of a word green and the last letter red; repeatedly moving the hand left-to-right under lines of print when reading with the boys and girls; comparing two words already confused, like *was* and *saw,* to call attention to how they are alike and how they are different. A teacher who knows that a child has such a problem will avoid teaching two words at the same time that are often confused. For example, if the word *left* is being used in reading, the word *felt* should be avoided in writing until emphasis on remembering the word *left* has caused it to be fixed in the child's memory. The teacher will find lists of suggestions in Harris and Sipay[6] and Zintz.[7]

Ellingson reports in her book *The Shadow Children:*

> A favorite anecdote among the group I have worked with concerns a boy who, after painstaking care, finally learned the composite parts of the word "until," but still could not "pull" the word instantly from memory when he tried to read it. Finally, he said to his teacher, "If I could just *see* an 'until,' I know I could remember it." What was necessary to complete the boy's mastery of the word was an associative method. The boy was instructed to draw, from within himself, his idea of the word— to make a picture to go with a sentence using the word. The boy then carefully drew a picture of a herd of cows, pastureland, a fence with a gate, and a farmhouse in the distance, with the cows going through the gate toward the farmhouse. He then wrote his sentence, "I will wait until the cows come home." For this boy, with this word, "until the cows come home" provided the needed association and visual memory that firmly "set" it in his mind. From then on, whenever he came across the word, no matter how different or complicated the context, he could look at it and say, "Oh, yes, that's until—until the cows come home." This achievement is not inconsequential. The child had used all of his avenues of learning—then added association and was able to read, write, spell, and comprehend the word "until."[8]

| Interest and Attitude Inventories | No assessment of reading problems is complete without some type of interest and attitude inventory. With the knowledge from such an inventory, the teacher can select materials and develop language experience themes that build on what the reader already knows or is interested in experiencing. This information helps the teacher to individualize further; note that individualization does not necessarily mean that the child will work alone. Interest inventories may help the teacher group together children who have common interests and needs. |

Further information on interest inventories may be found in chapter 14, "Developing Permanent Reading Habits."

Easy Practice While it is difficult for the teacher to find time, it is necessary for each child to have as much oral reading practice as possible. Children who do not have mastery over the sight words must read them over and over and over in interesting stories until they do know them. Other children can be pupil-teachers if the teacher plans carefully how children can read in pairs. Older brothers and sisters who read well can be very helpful in listening to a child read. Placing the tape recorder in a quiet corner and stationing one child with it who knows how to operate it makes it possible for children to go there for three or five-minute intervals to record their oral reading. The teacher can then evaluate the results after school or with the child at an appropriate time.

"Grandparent groups" are organized in many communities to work in classrooms at a variety of tasks. One of the best contributions they can make is to read to children and listen to children read to them. The child gets a significant amount of word recognition and oral reading practice and the "grandparent" and child both get the satisfaction of sharing together.

Reading in Phrases

To help children overcome word-by-word reading, practice on reading phrases may help them anticipate endings of prepositional phrases. Such phrases as the following might be used for motivated flash card drill:

On Phrases	*In* Phrases	*To* Phrases
on the house	in a minute	to the river
on the hilltop	in a hurry	to the house
on the mountainside	in the basket	to the window
on the far side	in her pocketbook	to the candy store

Materials for Easy Practice

Other sources of easy reading practice are predictable books, books written by children for each other, books prepared by the teacher using words the teacher knows the children should practice, collections of dictated stories bound and placed in the reading corner, books of former "door signs," books of signs, labels, and sentences gathered from the environment, signs and notices in the classrooms, and books the teacher has read enough times that the children can predict the words they do not recognize independently.

Appropriate Materials

The following list of books should be especially useful to reading teachers in their corrective and remedial work. The high interest appeal of the subjects motivates children and the low vocabulary level used keeps them from becoming discouraged.

American Adventure Series. Lexington, Mass.: D. C. Heath. About twenty titles ranging in difficulty from second through sixth grade.

Animal Adventure Series. Westchester, Ill.: Benefic Press. Preprimary to grade 3. Record or cassette available for each book.

Beginner Books Series. New York: Random House. Dozens of titles of first and second grade levels of difficulty.

Checkered Flag Series. Menlo Park, Calif.: Addison-Wesley. Four books especially designed to appeal to older boys with severe reading handicaps.

Childhood of Famous Americans Series. Indianapolis, Ind.: Bobbs-Merrill. More than 100 titles with vocabulary controlled to about fourth grade level.

The Clyde Bulla Books. New York: Thomas Y. Crowell.

Contact. Prepared by the editors of Scholastic Scope. Englewood Cliffs, N.J.: Scholastic Book Services.

Cowboy Sam Series. Westchester, Ill.: Benefic Press. Ten titles ranging in difficulty from preprimer to third grade level.

Dan Frontier Series. Westchester, Ill.: Benefic Press. Ten titles ranging in difficulty from preprimer to third grade level.

Deep Sea Adventure Series. Menlo Park, Calif.: Addison-Wesley. Eight books ranging in difficulty from high first to low fifth grade level.

The Dolch Four-Step Reading Program. Champaign, Ill.: Garrard.

Easy Reading Book Bags. Chicago: Children's Press.

Easy Reader Wonder Books. New York: Wonder-Treasure Books. Inexpensive editions with vocabularies controlled to between 100 and 200 words.

Follett Beginning to Read Series. Chicago: Follett. Some preprimer level, first grade level, second grade level, and third grade level.

Interesting Reading Series. Chicago: Follett. Ten titles written for older boys and girls with vocabulary controlled to about third grade reading level.

Jim Forest Reading Series. Menlo Park, Calif.: Addison-Wesley. Six books ranging in difficulty from first grade to third grade.

Landmark Books. New York: Random House. More than 100 titles ranging in difficulty from fourth grade through ninth grade level.

Monster Books. Los Angeles: Bowmar/Noble. Strong appeal for reluctant readers; also available in Spanish.

Morgan Bay Mysteries. Menlo Park, Calif.: Addison-Wesley. Eight mystery stories written at about independent third grade reading level.

Our Animal Story Books Series. Lexington, Mass.: D. C. Heath. Preprimer level vocabulary.

Pioneer Series. Westchester, Ill.: Benefic Press. Many titles with vocabulary controlled to about third grade reading level.

Read-by-Yourself Books. Boston: Houghton Mifflin.

Reading Incentive Program. Los Angeles: Bowmar/Noble.

Sailor Jack Series. Westchester, Ill.: Benefic Press. Ten titles ranging in difficulty from preprimer to third grade level.

Signal Books. Garden City, New York: Doubleday. Ten titles in the series with reader level controlled to about fourth grade level.

Simplified Classics. Glenview, Ill.: Scott, Foresman. Many children's classics rewritten at about fourth grade level of difficulty.

Target Today Series. Westchester, Ill.: Benefic Press. Four books with teachers' manuals, pupils' editions, activity books, and participation and involvement kits.

Venture Books. Leland Jacobs and John McInnes, consultants. Champaign, Ill.: Garrard.

Wild Life Adventure Series. Menlo Park, Calif.: Addison-Wesley. Stories of wild animals written with about fourth or fifth grade reading level of difficulty.

Yearling Individualized Reading Program. Los Angeles: Bowmar/Noble.

Bamman, Henry, et al. *Kaleidoscope Readers.* Menlo Park, Calif.: Addison-Wesley. Paperback story and workbook-type exercises for the elementary grades.

Bushman, John D., Marvin Laser, and Cherry Tom. *Scope: Reading I,* and *Scope: Reading II.* New York: Harper & Row. Short articles and stories of interest to older students.

Crosher, C. R. *Pacemaker Story Books.* Belmont, Calif.: Fearon-Pitman. Short paperback books with high interest appeal for older students.

Darby, Jean. *The Time Machine Series*. Menlo Park, Calif.: Addison-Wesley. Science interest for intermediate grades but vocabulary control for first through third grades.

Granite, Harvey, et al. *Houghton Mifflin Action Series*. Boston: Houghton Mifflin.

Hillert, Margaret. *Follett Just Beginning to Read Books*. Chicago: Follett.

Martin, Bill, ed. *The Owl Books*. New York: Holt, Rinehart & Winston.

Martin, Bill, and Peggy Brogan. *The Sounds of Language Readers*. New York: Holt, Rinehart & Winston.

McCall, Edith. *Button Family Adventure Series*. Westchester, Ill.: Benefic Press. Twelve titles ranging in difficulty from preprimer to third grade level.

Rambeau, John and Nancy. *Better Reading Series*. Oklahoma City: Educational Guidelines Co., A Division of the Economy Co.

Sheldon, William, et al. *Breakthrough*. Boston: Allyn & Bacon. Easy reading paperback books for junior and senior high pupils.

Warner, Gertrude. *The Box Car Children Books*. Glenview, Ill.: Scott Foresman.

The Case Study

The child who is not succeeding in reading should be studied carefully to obtain the data for the individualized program needed to promote growth in language and reading. The most systematic way to study the child and plan for instruction is called the *case study*. It embodies the entire approach to the child—the gathering of appropriate data on the pupil's history and current status, the synthesis and interpretation of the data, the recommendations, individualized instruction, and periodic reevaluations alternated with instruction.

Case studies, properly done, take time and should be the responsibility of the support personnel in the school as well as the child's classroom teacher. However, the time is well spent when it provides a studied and systematic approach to reading instruction.

Figure 18.2 provides a model of the case study as a way to assess the child's abilities and needs and to plan for instruction. Five types of information should go into the case history. (1) There should be a parent interview concerning family background, significance of reading success in the family, and probable causes for reading failure. (2) A medical examination should include evaluation of the child's visual and hearing acuity and general health. The family doctor will make referrals to specialists when neurological problems, problems of basal metabolism, or convulsive disorders are present. (3) A psychological evaluation will include both tests of general intelligence and structured or unstructured personality tests. (4) A school history will reveal grades, attendance, persistent problems, teachers' evaluations, and work habits. (5) Guidance information will describe the child's motivation, aptitude, and level of aspiration.

This body of information gathered in the case history must be studied and analyzed by the school psychologist or the school social worker. In turn, it must be interpreted to the pupil, the parents, and the pupil's teacher and principal.

Basic to analyzing problems of specific learning disabilities are four areas of diagnosis:

1. Possible genetic findings. If one or both parents of a child had serious learning problems in school, or if the child has uncles or aunts or brothers or sisters who never learned to read, the possibility that such a trait is inherited gains credibility.
2. The diagnostician will eliminate as many causal factors as possible, such as: emotional disturbance; perceptual defects; low intelligence; poor reading instruction; poor motivation. When such understood factors are known *not* to be related to a child's problem, professionals must search for more adequate answers.
3. The diagnostician examines clues or indications, sometimes referred to medically as *soft signs:* low subtest scores on block design or object assembly on the *Wechsler Intelligence Scale for Children;* mild but not definitive electroencephalogram abnormalities; lack of cerebral dominance; inefficient eye movements in reading.
4. Do specific teaching methods produce positive results? If techniques help these children, then the clinician categorizes the child's problem with greater confidence.

A teacher can keep a progress report on children having corrective reading instruction by completing a summary of an informal reading analysis at intervals throughout the school year. A suggested form is presented in figure 18.3.

Figures 18.4, 18.5, and 18.6 show some suggested forms for keeping records of progress for individuals or small groups. A teacher could adapt them to 5-by-8-inch index cards or loose-leaf notebook sheets.

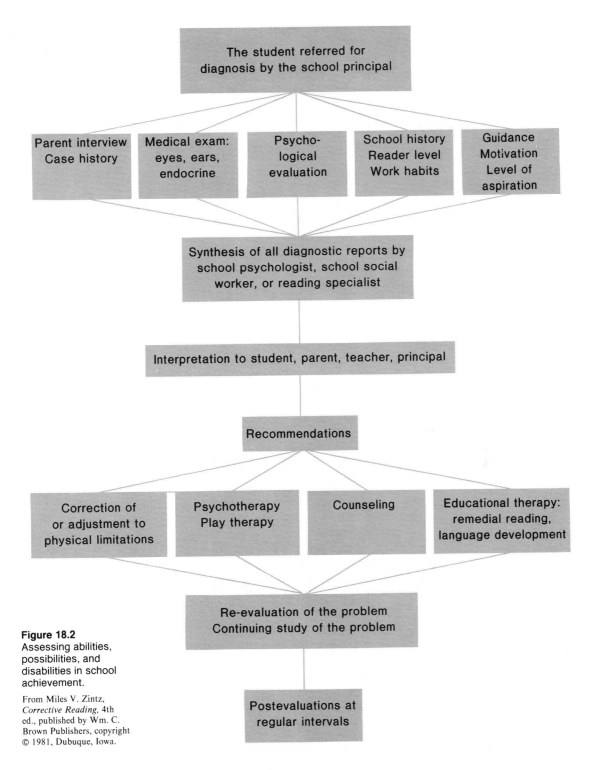

Figure 18.2
Assessing abilities, possibilities, and disabilities in school achievement.

From Miles V. Zintz, *Corrective Reading,* 4th ed., published by Wm. C. Brown Publishers, copyright © 1981, Dubuque, Iowa.

Figure 18.3
Summary of informal
reading analysis.

Teacher (Clinician) _____ Date _____

Student _____ C. A. _____ Grade _____ Date _____

I. Reader level found in a series of readers

    A. Oral reading

Level of book	Total words	Total errors	Percent of error	Percent of accuracy	Suitability of level of difficulty

    B. Silent reading

Level of book	No. of words	Time in sec.	Rate of reading	Percent of comprehension	Suitability of level of difficulty

    C. Capacity level for material read to student

_____

_____

_____

II. Analysis of errors on sight word test (Dolch, San Diego, Slosson, etc.)

Initial errors (most commonly made)	Medial errors (grade level indicated)	Final errors (comments)

III. Other word perception abilities

    Does student always recognize compound words? _____

    Errors in any area of phonics survey: _____

    At what grade level can student spell (60 percent correct before study)? _____

    Does student have reversals and confusions? _____ What kinds?

_____

_____

IV. Summary

    Instructional level of reading: _____

    Plans for reading progress: _____

_____

Name (last name first)	Date	Grade in school
Parent or guardian	School	Attended kindergarten?
Home address	Home telephone number	Grades repeated
Estimated capacity level	Intelligence level (individual or group test?)	Date of birth
Reading instructional level	Knowledge of phonics	Grade level of spelling
Vision	Hearing	Motor coordination
School absences last year	Socio-economic status	Number of siblings
Report from parents	Report from family doctor	
Specific plans for beginning work	Report from previous teacher	

Figure 18.4
Initial summary of information about the child who has a reading disability.

Name (last name first)	Date	Grade in school
Standardized reading test	Date given	Results (grade placement)
Standardized reading test	Date given	Results (grade placement)
(1) IRI (material used)	(1) Date of IRI	Instructional level
(2) IRI (material used)	(2) Date of IRI	Instructional level
(3) IRI (material used)	(3) Date of IRI	Instructional level

Notes: _____

Interest inventory findings

Personality data

Figure 18.5
Record of reading progress throughout the school year.

Name	Date	Grade in school
Name of book or program:	Beginning date:	Finishing date:

Figure 18.6
Books and materials used for the reading program.

From Theory to Practice 18.3
Reviewing a Case Study

Visit with a classroom teacher, a guidance counselor, or a special education teacher to find out how a case study is developed in that school. Find out what kind of data are obtained, who participates in the case study, how the data are analyzed and interpreted, and how curriculum evolves from the earlier steps in the process.

Perhaps you will be shown or given some of the forms that are used. It is even possible that you might sit in on one or more meetings as a case study is developed.

Be prepared to share your experiences with class members and your instructor. Collectively, you should be able to share a variety of ways in which case studies are developed.

Corrective reading is the instruction provided by the regular classroom teacher during the school day to help individual children overcome whatever stumbling blocks prevent them from achieving appropriate developmental skills in reading. Children who need more time and practice to master a basic sight vocabulary, to develop auditory discrimination of the phonemes of the English language, and to learn to read fluently enough to read entertainingly to others are in need of additional learning time to master the missing mechanical skills. Of course, adequate comprehension of material read must also be considered. Children who fail to comprehend may or may not have adequate word-recognition skills.

To distinguish corrective from remedial instruction is only to indicate that the extra effort to help the child is made by the classroom teacher within the framework of the regular teaching day rather than by a remedial reading clinician who teaches the child at a special time outside the classroom. While no clear-cut distinction can be made between what is remedial and what is corrective, the latter term helps us to think specifically about ways the classroom teacher can function *all day long* as a teacher of children with skill deficiencies.

We can hope that corrective reading cases will not be severely complicated by emotional or neurological problems or language deficits, but they very well may be. Hopefully, if the philosophy of teaching throughout the elementary school has been a diagnostic one, many of these problems will have been identified early and deep-seated emotional problems averted.

With early identification, teachers need to emphasize ways in which children learn best, try to strengthen learning styles that are weak, and provide a systematic program of sequenced instruction of skills over as long a period of time as is indicated.

Summary

Following are some principles of corrective reading for the classroom teacher:

1. Corrective reading instruction must be based on a diagnosis of the reading problem, and the instruction must be directed to supplying the missing skills in the developmental sequence.
2. Corrective reading instruction must begin at the level where the child will be successful in whatever he or she does. The maxim "Nothing succeeds like success" is still true.
3. The teacher and the child both need to feel, and to express this feeling, that it is *all right* for the child to begin *where he or she is* and progress from there.
4. Corrective reading instruction teaches the missing skills but takes care to see that all skills needed for successful reading are developed.
5. The key element in corrective reading, as in any teaching of reading, is meaningful practice. The learner must put all the reading skills to work in meaningful situations.
6. Corrective reading materials must be selected both to teach skills and to cultivate the student's interests and aptitudes.

7. In corrective reading, one should build on strengths. If one avenue to learning produces better results, use it.
8. In developmental reading, corrective or otherwise, there is a sequence in levels of difficulty, and the child moves from the simple to the complex.
9. The student must grow toward independence. Long-range goals should include preparing the student for longer and longer periods of independent seatwork without direct supervision.
10. Records must be kept to indicate progress, regression, or change in both the cognitive and the affective areas.

For each child with reading difficulties, the teacher must be prepared to measure the following: (1) instructional level of reading using the IRI; (2) knowledge of basic sight words using an instrument like the *Dolch Basic Sight Word Test* or *Fry's Instant Words* as a recall test; (3) ability to use the phonic and structural skills commensurate with the child's instructional reader level, moving progressively from initial consonant sounds to consonant blend sounds, most elementary suffixes (s, ed, ing), short and long vowel sounds, variant vowel sounds, roots, prefixes, and suffixes; and (4) ability to administer and evaluate performance on cloze tests and to utilize the data in instruction.

These four measures will be sufficient to avoid assigning children work at their frustration level. Preventing this frustration will greatly reduce concomitant emotional problems in children.

For Further Reading

Bond, Guy L., Miles A. Tinker, and Barbara B. Wasson. *Reading Difficulties: Their Diagnosis and Correction.* 4th ed. Englewood Cliffs, N.J.: Prentice-Hall, 1979.

Clay, Marie. *The Early Detection of Reading Difficulties: A Diagnostic Survey with Recovery Procedures.* 2d ed. Auckland, New Zealand: Heinemann, 1979.

Harris, Albert. "What Is New in Remedial Reading?" *The Reading Teacher* 34 (January 1981): 405–10.

Harris, Albert, and Edward R. Sipay. *How to Increase Reading Ability.* 7th ed. New York: Longman, 1980.

Kennedy, Eddie C. *Classroom Approaches to Remedial Reading.* 2d ed. Itasca, Ill.: F.E. Peacock, 1977.

La Pray, Margaret. *On-The-Spot Reading Diagnosis File.* West Nyack, N.Y.: Center for Applied Research in Education, 1978.

McGinnis, Dorothy J., and Dorothy E. Smith. *Analyzing and Treating Reading Problems.* New York: Macmillan, 1982.

Noble, Eleanor F. "Self-Selection: A Remedial Strategy for Readers with a Limited Vocabulary." *The Reading Teacher* 34 (January 1981): 386–88.

Rubin, Dorothy. *Diagnosis and Correction in Reading Instruction.* New York: Holt, Rinehart and Winston, 1982.

Silvaroli, Nicholas. *Classroom Reading Inventory.* 4th ed. Dubuque, Iowa: Wm. C. Brown, 1979.

Wilson, Robert M. *Diagnostic and Remedial Reading, For Classroom and Clinic.* 3d ed. Columbus, Ohio: Charles E. Merrill, 1977.

Zintz, Miles V. *Corrective Reading.* 4th ed. Dubuque, Iowa: Wm. C. Brown, 1981.

Notes

1. John Holt, *How Children Fail* (New York: Harper & Row, 1964), p. 5.
2. *The Inventory of Phonetic Skills,* Tests One, Two, and Three (Boston: Houghton Mifflin, 1972).
3. Guy L. Bond, Theodore Clymer, and Cyril J. Hoyt, *Silent Reading Diagnostic Tests* (Chicago: Lyons and Carnahan, 1970).
4. Marie M. Clay, *The Early Detection of Reading Difficulties: A Diagnostic Survey with Recovery Procedures* (Auckland, New Zealand: Heinemann, 1979).
5. Careth Ellingson and James Cass, "Teaching the Dyslexic Child," *Saturday Review,* 16 April, 1966.
6. Albert Harris and E. R. Sipay, *How To Increase Reading Ability,* 6th ed. (New York: David McKay, 1975), p. 414.
7. Miles V. Zintz, *Corrective Reading,* 3d ed. (Dubuque, Iowa: Wm. C. Brown, 1977), pp. 104–5.
8. Careth Ellingson, *The Shadow Children, A Book About Children's Learning Disorders* (Chicago: Topaz Books, 1967), pp. 89–90.

Evaluation in the Reading Program

A Cognitive Map: Evaluation in the Reading Program

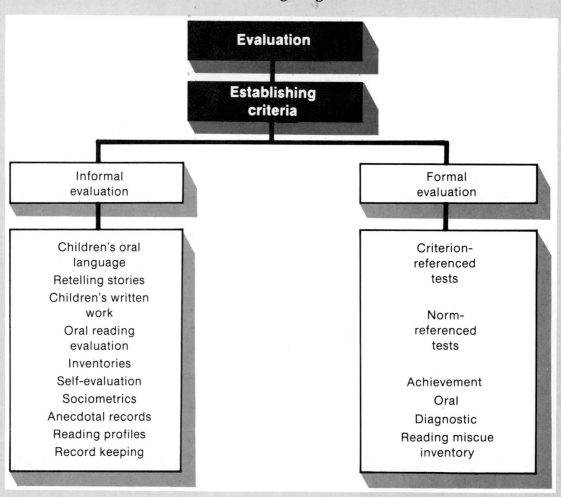

19

Guide Questions

1. Describe the different informal assessment instruments. How would you integrate them into your teaching of reading?

2. Compare criterion-referenced and norm-referenced tests.

3. What do test makers mean by percentiles, grade scores, and stanines?

4. What are the convenient categories of reading tests?

Terminology

anecdotal record

anticipate meaning

criterion-referenced test

diagnostic reading test

formal evaluation

grade score

informal evaluation

norm-referenced test

oral reading test

percentile

raw score

reading achievement test

reading miscue inventory

reading profile

self-evaluation

sociogram

stanine

story structure (grammar)

text

utterance

Ongoing evaluation of how efficiently the teacher is teaching and how effectively the child is learning is essential to any successful reading program. Through evaluation, the teacher does not only determine the extent to which objectives have been met. Evaluation also identifies the need for corrective and remedial teaching and the extent of review and reinforcement that should be included in the reading program.

Evaluation will be both *formal*, as in the use of standardized measures of achievement, and *informal*, as in the use of subjective judgment, opinions of both students and teacher, and records kept of desired behaviors registered in knowledge, attitudes, and skills. Informal evaluation measures especially involve much more than testing cognitive learning and achievement of specific study skills. Records of the types of library books read during the year are good sources for evaluation of growth of interests. A good way for the teacher to evaluate growth in interpretive abilities and verbal fluency is to have scheduled periods with groups of six to eight students to discuss books or stories read.

There are three steps in evaluation:[1]

1. Formulation of objectives to be used. These objectives must be defined clearly in terms of specific behaviors to be achieved.
2. Identification of sources of evidence. Evaluation in the reading program requires information from several sources.
   a. Standardized reading tests would be used as well as tests provided by publishers of graded series of readers, to be administered as each book is finished, or semiformal tests such as those provided by *My Weekly Reader* or the *Student Record Book* of the SRA laboratories.
   b. Written work of the children may be summaries of stories they have read, original essays, or answers to questions.
   c. Oral work may include, besides the child reading aloud to the teacher and to groups of children, tape recorded samples of the child reading aloud early in the year compared with samples from later in the year. A tape recorder may also be used to record the child talking about the books and stories read.
   d. The informal checklists used to evaluate individual children from time to time with respect to accuracy in oral reading, attitudes toward reading, and efficiency in silent reading should be included.
   e. Sociometric tests by which the teacher evaluates the extent of personal interaction in the group should be included.
   f. Anecdotal records should be filed chronologically throughout the year to help the teacher judge progress or lack of it in the child's total growth.

g. Children should contribute self-evaluations, which help show how successful or profitable they feel their school year has been to them.

h. Teachers' evaluations of both cognitive and affective growth are useful.

i. Profiles that evaluate many skills and abilities will also be useful.

3. Interpretation of results. Final results must be interpreted in terms of behavioral objectives established initially. If the reading program has been based on a prescribed set of behavioral objectives from the beginning, in which the teacher has already defined the behavior to be expected if the objectives are met, then final evaluation will be very specific and will have been built into the reading program.

Informal Evaluation

Every teacher needs a variety of informal ways to assess the child's ability with language, reading, and writing. Also needed are strategies for identifying interests, attitudes, and values as they relate to reading growth.

Children's Oral Language

The relationships between children's oral language abilities and their learning to read and write have been both confused and confusing. Most of the studies of phoneme acquisition, length of utterances, grammatical structures, and vocabulary have failed to yield consistent correlations with reading and writing achievement. Yet, the conviction still exists that oral and written language skills are related.

Studies of how children learn about stories and learn to tell stories have been particularly helpful in moving toward an understanding of the relationships between oral and written language. The elements of stories develop over several years and have their genesis and nourishment in the rich and happy experiences of being read to and told stories.

> The extent to which these conventions are recognized and used by children can be taken, to a certain extent, as an indication of the degree to which stories have begun the long march from the child's initial recognition that a story is in some way different from other uses of language, to the final firmly established recognition of a story as a mode of communication. . . .[2]

Reading has been characterized as a predictive process. An understanding of how stories "work" will provide readers with valuable information in making appropriate predictions. Children who are aware of the parts of stories and of how transitions and connections are made between these parts have an excellent chance of comprehending what has been written and how it has been expressed.

Other writers have discussed the differences between utterance and text and how children cope with these differences to capitalize on the similarities. When children learn to talk, they also learn how "to conventionalize more and more of the meaning in the speech signal."[3] Moving to written language means taking a giant step toward further abstraction and conventionalization. Olson writes:

From Theory to Practice 19.1
Studying Children's Storytelling

The child's mastery of story structure seems to be an important element in the reading process. Teachers should devote much time to reading and telling stories and letting children do likewise. Teachers should also learn to analyze a child's storytelling performance.

Ask a child to tell you a story. You may ask him or her to work from a wordless picture book, an interesting picture, or from some personal experience. Tape the child's efforts.

Bring your tape to your class to share with two or three other students. Listen for the parts of the story and for how the child connects the parts or moves from one part to another. Does the story make sense without having the picture book or picture in front of you? (This means you are concerned with the clarity of expression and its content independence.) Identify the vocabulary that lends interest and clarity to the story. Does the child tell a story or simply name objects or events?

If three or more people listen to that many stories, you will begin to get a sense of the range of ability in the development of a child's sense of story.

The relations between utterances and texts become acute when children are first confronted with printed books . . . children are familiar with using the spoken utterance as one cue among others. Children come to school . . . only to be confronted with an exemplar of written text, the reader, which is an autonomous representation of meaning. Ideally, the printed reader depends on no cues other than linguistic cues; it represents no intentions other than those represented in the text; it is addressed to no one in particular; its author is essentially anonymous; and its meaning is precisely that represented by the sentence meaning. . . . Children familiar with the use of textlike language through hearing printed stories obviously confront less of a hurdle than those for whom both reading and that form of language are novel.[4]

Hearing many stories, then, has at least two important purposes: (1) to find out the structures of stories and (2) to sense the formality and abstractness of text as compared to utterance.

The teacher would do well to spend time each school day reading and telling stories to children. Children should also have opportunities to tell stories so that they may grow in their understanding of how the elements of stories combine into wholes. As teachers listen to their students tell stories, they can gain important insights into the children's understanding of story structures.

The teacher should have books and materials in the classroom that facilitate storytelling and reading. Books of many kinds are appropriate. Wordless picture books may be particularly helpful if children are encouraged to spin tales based on them. Tape recorders encourage children to preserve their stories. (Teachers may analyze them later in an effort to understand children's concepts of stories.) Action figures, such as zoo or farm animal sets, collections of human figures, doll houses, farms, and villages may all stimulate storytelling. "Show and tell" times can be beneficial if they are made into storytelling sessions.

Children's Written Work

There are several means by which the classroom teacher can obtain written expression from children that conveys how well they read, how well they can think about and use what they read, and also how they feel about the material read and how they feel about the job of reading.

Teachers often obtain from children early in the year an original paragraph describing a summer vacation incident. Since children usually need to be helped to delineate specifics and describe them in concrete terms, teachers should help them delimit their topic and *not use* such global titles as "What I Did Last Summer" or "My Summer Vacation."

More valid information about children's reading-related writing abilities may be obtained by asking them to write about an interesting picture. The teacher might say, "Write the best *story* you can about this picture." The directions suggest that you do not want a list or a description; however, do not discuss or plan the story with them.

While the teacher may want to note the children's uses of writing mechanics, it is their attempts to structure their stories that will be more directly related to reading instruction. Some children will only name objects in the picture, describe it, or grasp fleeting scraps of the plot. For example, one child recorded about a picture of a movie being filmed:

> This picture here, it is a film about a winter storm. Seems to me like the boy and the girl are trying to get home or they are lost. . . .

Then the child lapsed back into naming other people and objects in the picture.

Other children may be able to record parts or all of a story, showing a better grasp of the grammar of a story. Finally, some children may be able to relate stories containing great detail, while at the same time demonstrating a relative mastery of the mechanics of writing. Westby relates the ability to create a story to the ability to comprehend stories when she writes:

> The child's comprehension of a story is based upon the story he has read or heard, not the story the adult thinks the child has read or heard. That is, a child's comprehension of a story is dependent upon the child's interpretation of the story. Story comprehension, as measured by adult standards, is only possible when a child has a narrative schema for stories.[5]

Children can only write or tell stories for which they have the necessary schema. Children who cannot demonstrate this knowledge are likely to have difficulty understanding stories in their readers. They will be limited in their ability to predict what is apt to be coming next, since they do not know what *should* happen next in a story.

Writing a summarizing paragraph about a lesson is a difficult assignment in the elementary school. Boys and girls need help and guidance in arriving at the main point with two or three supporting details. They may write paragraphs that follow the suggestion in chapter 10 about understanding the anatomy of a paragraph.

When the primary objective is for the young child to express an idea on paper, the teacher should accept the idea and not judge accuracy in mechanics harshly. After the ideas are on paper, they can be edited as seems necessary to the teacher.

Figure 19.1 shows two book reports written by a fourth grade girl after she had read the books and discussed them with her remedial reading teacher. The child is expressing ideas. If teachers insist primarily on capital letters, periods, and margins and indentations, they may get carefully presented paragraphs without ideas.

The Oral Reading of Children

There are three major reasons why teaching oral reading in the elementary school classroom is important. The first is its usefulness as a testing or evaluation instrument. In the primary grades on a day-to-day basis, the child must read aloud so the teacher knows how successful the child is in learning to anticipate meaning and master all the basic sight words that must be learned in order to read anything. In the higher grades, there must also be testing of oral reading ability. Samples of each child's oral reading will help the teacher evaluate how well the child reads so that a reading improvement program can be mapped out with the child. Taping such individual oral-reading samples can be very useful in parent conferences, too, because they allow the parents to listen and consider how well and at what grade level their child reads orally. A tape recording of children's reading carried from year to year provides a valid record of reading growth.

The second reason oral reading in a classroom is important is that it allows pleasurable sharing of interesting passages and motivates the reading of good books, thereby firmly establishing the belief that books are treasures of interesting information to be shared and enjoyed. If a teacher is a good oral reader (see chapter 13), the boys and girls can be easily motivated to share interesting anecdotes, jokes, witticisms, and informational materials that add documentary evidence to formal classroom argumentation and debate on issues.

The third reason why oral reading should be taught is that it may help someone present evidence to prove a point, to settle an argument, or to show that a line of reasoning is supported by authorities.

The latter two uses of oral reading are audience situations wherein only the reader has the information being shared. It will be well for the teacher to use the informal reading inventory to get initial levels of oral reading, to measure progress for any students with special needs, and to get final measures.

Figure 19.1
Book reports prepared by a fourth grade girl in her special reading class.

Walter Farley, *Little Black, A Pony* (New York: Beginner Books, Random House, copyright © 1961); and Edith McCall, *Butternut Bill and the Big Pumpkin* (Chicago: Beckley Cardy, Benefic Press).

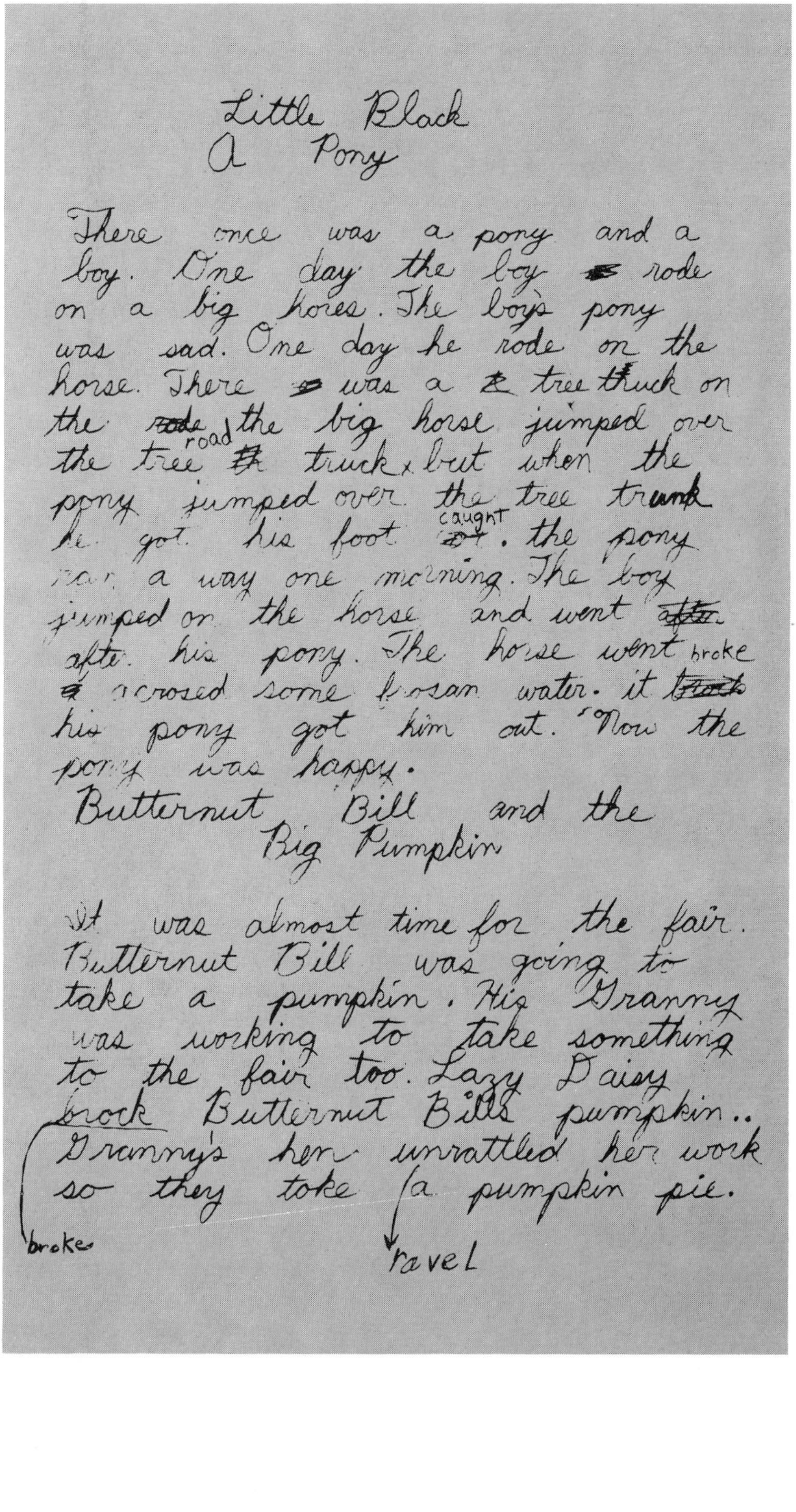

Little Black
A Pony

There once was a pony and a boy. One day the boy rode on a big hores. The boy's pony was sad. One day he rode on the horse. There was a tree thuck on the ~~rode~~ road the big horse jumped over the tree truck but when the pony jumped over the tree trunk he got his foot caught. the pony ran a way one morning. The boy jumped on the horse and went ~~after~~ after his pony. The horse went acrosed some frosan water. it broke his pony got him out. Now the pony was happy.

Butternut Bill and the Big Pumpkin

It was almost time for the fair. Butternut Bill was going to take a pumpkin. His Granny was working to take something to the fair too. Lazy Daisy brock Butternut Bills pumpkin.. Granny's hen unrattled her work so they toke a pumpkin pie.

broke

ravel

**Inventories:
Checklists and
Questionnaires**

Teachers should be continually learning more and more about the boys and girls they teach. How well or how poorly they perform in reading must be seen in relation to the home environment in which they live, the emotional stability of the adults in their lives, the socioeconomic level of the home, the *pressures* on a child for academic success, and other pressures of day-to-day living. At the same time, every day the teacher must make decisions about each child. In the affective domain, the concerns with respect to a child are:

How does the teacher feel about George?
How does George feel about the teacher?
How does George feel about himself in relation to all other people?
How do George's parents feel about George?
How do the other children in the room feel about George?

In the cognitive domain, the concerns are:

How well does George perform on a standardized reading test?
How well can he read aloud?
How well can he read silently?
How well does he retain what he reads?

The teacher can prepare a checklist of behavioral items that will help answer the preceding questions to some degree. The following items might constitute a checklist of reading behaviors for the classroom teacher. Any checklist can be edited or extended as the teacher uses it.

Does the child:
Read with understanding?
Apply phonics skills?
Read independently?
Finish assignments?
Read well orally?
Use independent study time efficiently?
Follow directions?
Understand reading assignments?
Pronounce new words efficiently?
Work well in small groups?
Bring in new information from outside of school?
Become embarrassed in front of class?
Read in too soft a voice to be heard?
Miss little words (basic sight words)?
Read in a monotone?

**Children's Self-
Evaluations**

Self-evaluation should guide children in developing self-direction. Helping children learn to analyze their own strengths and weaknesses, successes and failures, means helping them to improve their skills in problem-solving. Thus they develop the ability to set purposes and evaluate end results, which represents mature behavior.

Children need guidance to learn how to evaluate themselves. Checklists, charts, and development of work standards can provide this guidance. Children can, with the help of the teacher, prepare their own guidelines for improving study and work habits. The following questions illustrate what such guidelines would be:

Do I do my own work?
Do I finish whatever I begin?
Do I listen to directions?
Do I return materials I have used?
Do I work quietly without asking too many questions?

Teachers'
Informal
Evaluations

Teachers could check on their own behavior in teaching reading by asking themselves such questions as the following:

Do I introduce new words and new concepts in order to teach their meanings?
Do I provide for review and reinforcement after initial teaching?
Do I have informal reading inventory results to show that each child is reading at a level where he or she understands at least 75 percent of the ideas in the materials and makes no more than five uncorrected errors in 100 consecutive words?
When teaching a directed reading lesson, do I have too many interruptions from children working independently? If so, is the material that the children are studying too difficult?
Do any children still need a marker when reading? If so, is there a justifiable reason for it?
Do any children still move their lips when reading silently?
Do my boys and girls see purpose in their work, and is the climate a constructive one?

Other Informal Evaluation Techniques

For too long, teachers have thought of evaluation only as measurement of cognitive growth. When a unit of work was finished, the test should determine whether the child had absorbed all the facts the teacher had emphasized. There are many other ways, of course, by which a teacher can estimate permanent cognitive learning.

More important, however, is the effort to measure growth in affective behavior. Teachers need to be doing the following also:

Developing appropriate leadership-followership qualities.
Identifying children who are always on the periphery in social situations.
Finding out how a child feels about success or lack of it.
Utilizing teacher judgment about both the cognitive and affective changes in child behavior necessary in the present-day school.

Sociometrics

A sociogram is a chart showing the social interaction among the members of a group at a given time. An example is shown in figure 19.2. Sociograms help the teacher to visualize social status of the members of the group. By constructing a sociogram, a teacher can determine cliques, most popular children, isolates, and leaders. Restructuring the room environment through such activities as assigning a leader to work with an isolate on a worthwhile project, the teacher may be able to effect a real change in children's behavior over a period of time. Teachers do not discuss the results of the sociogram with the boys and girls; they never indicate who is the reject, the isolate, or the most popular. Neither do they naïvely urge popular children to be nice to neglected ones. There are many sources of specific information about how to construct the sociogram. Two such sources are:

Welton, David A., and John T. Mallan. *Children and Their World: Strategies for Teaching Social Studies,* 2d ed., pp. 321–23. Boston: Houghton Mifflin, 1981.
Zintz, Miles V. *Corrective Reading,* 4th ed., pp. 169–72. Dubuque, Iowa: Wm. C. Brown, 1981.

Anecdotal Records

Anecdotal records are brief descriptions of specific instances of a child's behavior; they are *not* superficial comments made about a child by a teacher. An anecdotal record may be made more meaningful by quotes from the child. Well thought-out anecdotal records become very helpful when the teacher holds parent-teacher conferences. Anecdotal records begin to have value as soon as the teacher has recorded enough specific behaviors so that patterns of behavior begin to become evident. (See figure 19.3.)

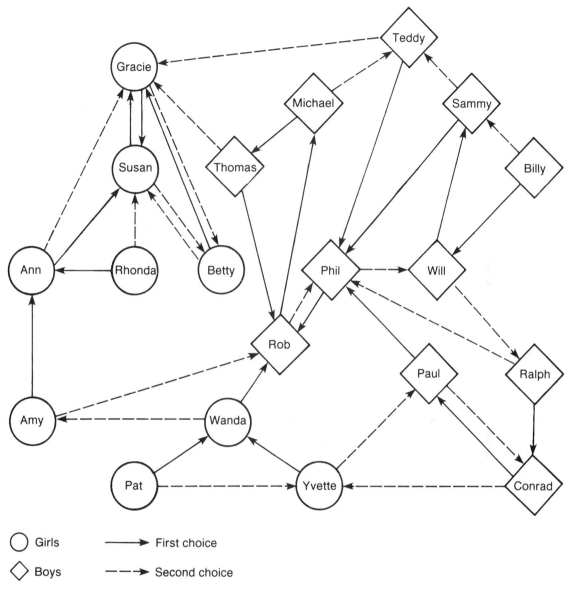

Girls

Boys

First choice

Second choice

Figure 19.2
Sociogram of second
grade class showing
first and second
choices for friends.
Popular children and
isolates are clearly
identified.

Sept 14 Robin completed workbook assignment (two pages) today. First time she has done complete assignment on time.

Sept. 17 Robin brought a newspaper clipping about State Fair from home. Asked for help with 4 words while reading it to herself. Read it without help to her reading group.

Sept. 19 Robin completed independent seatwork and spent 20 min. pasting three clippings about State Fair on sheets of paper. Robin said her uncle had won a "best of breed" ribbon for a sheep he entered.

Sept. 20 Robin asked if she could make a book about State Fair. Started writing as soon as she bound some sheets together. Worked at desk by herself.

Sept. 21 Robin spent independent work time drawing illustrations for her Fair book. Told aide she wanted only drawings — did not want to color. Asked aide to "go over" her writing. Got upset when Ann found some spellings to correct. Put work on shelf and played a game.

Sept. 24 Robin told me she would finish book on State Fair. Corrected spelling errors and pasted in newspaper clippings. Painted front cover and labeled title in caps. Asked if she could put it in room library.

Reading a Profile	A profile is any type of graphic aid that portrays many measures of knowledge, skills, and abilities so that the observer can see in one picture at a quick glance any student's strengths and weaknesses or high, average, and low scores. By observing which scores are above and which below the median, the teacher can quickly see how strengths compare to weaknesses.

The profiles of two fifteen-year-old eighth graders are presented in figures 19.4 and 19.5. One has a mental age of only nine years, six months, while the other has a mental age equal to his chronological age. The one with normal intelligence is a nonreader *but* with sufficient capacity to read at grade level. The other has a fourth grade reader level, which is approximately equal to his level of mental ability. The second student is not retarded in reading since he is reading as well as his mental ability indicates. It is clear that the reading teacher needs two entirely different programs for these two students. One student needs an intense rehabilitation program, while the other needs an adapted reading program that will provide efficient teaching of skills at the level he can read with understanding.

Informal Record Keeping	Busy classroom teachers need ways of keeping records that are as concise and simple as possible. Each one will develop a technique for keeping notes, anecdotes, and needed information to make it as useful as possible. Figure 19.6 has been prepared to show how a teacher might summarize on one sheet of paper some of the important data about individual children. If results of individual intelligence tests are available, that information might be included. If an intelligence test has been administered to all the children at one time by the classroom teacher, the probability of the results being invalid for the lower half of the class is so great that the teacher might indicate on the summary only broad categories, such as "high," "above average," "average," "below average."

Formal Evaluation	Formal evaluation includes both criterion-referenced and norm-referenced tests. Both varieties of formal assessments are useful for teachers and other professional educators, but they should never become the sole basis for decisions about instruction. They should always be combined with informal assessment, and the results of both used for making decisions.

Criterion-Referenced Testing	Interest in criterion-referenced testing is related to the ever-increasing emphasis on accountability, on performance-contracting, and on the principle that a child must master one level of learning before being advanced to the next level.

Programmed instruction, when competently done so that the student is almost sure to be able to move from each frame to the next and continue to make a very high percentage of correct responses, is criterion-referenced for mastery of knowledge about some unit of content or sequence of information.

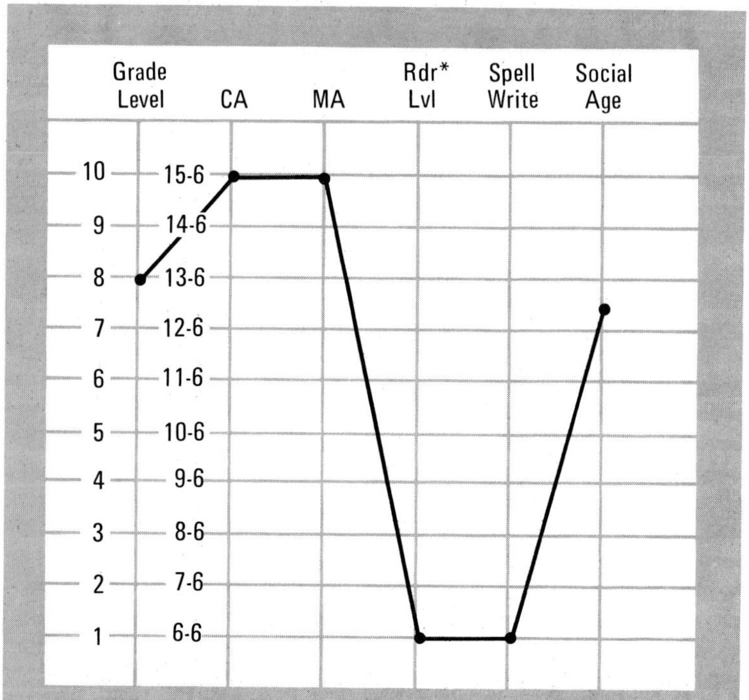

Figure 19.4
This eighth grade student tests completely normal intellectually and is severely retarded educationally.

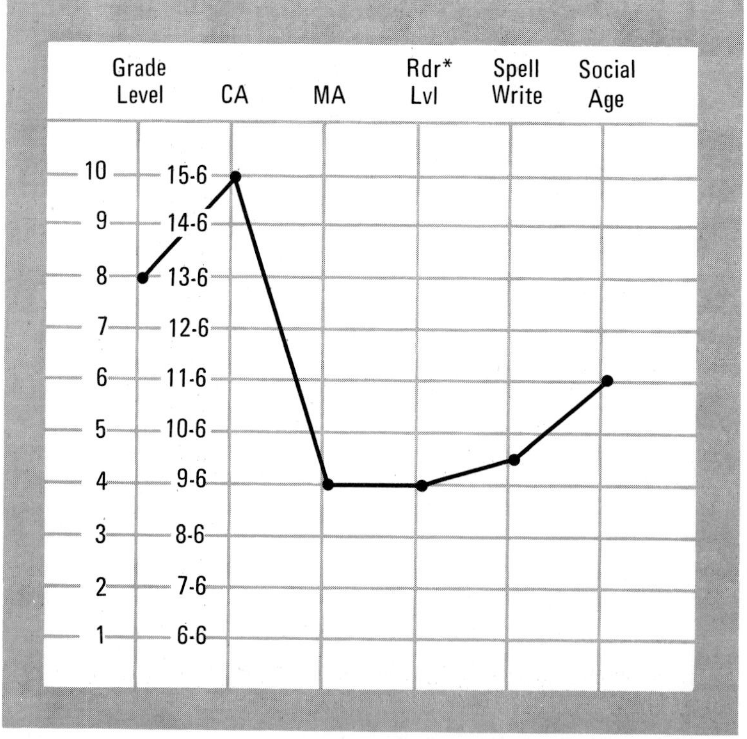

Figure 19.5
Profile of a fifteen-year-old eighth grade student whose tests show a mental age about equal to the student's reading and writing levels. If the tests are accurate, the student is mentally retarded but not educationally retarded.

Figure 19.6
Summary of
information about
reading for each child
in my class.

Name of child	IRI Oral Reading	IRI Silent Reading	IRI Capacity Level	Standardized Reading Test[1]	Phonic Skills[2]	Vocabulary Sight Words	Vocabulary Standard Tests[3]	Spelling Ability[4]	Other Information
1.									
2.									
3.									
4.									
5.									
6.									
7.									
8.									
9.									
10.									
11.									
12.									

1. Name of test _____
2. Name of test _____
3. Name of test _____
4. How determined _____

The principle of teaching reading for mastery at successively more difficult levels is excellent. But whether new criterion-referenced tests can actually measure mastery at specific levels is something else. In reading, it is very difficult to set specific goals to be achieved in a specific sequence within a hierarchy. As a child's reading base widens and she gets beyond the need to laboriously figure out what the words are, her progress will not be measurably comparable to that of her peers.[6] Self-motivation and self-teaching will do more for the child's growth in reading than formal instruction. Therefore, there is not much basis for criteria that assign grade levels to reading material.

An argument sometimes advanced for criterion-referenced testing is that each student competes only with himself or herself and will not be unfavorably compared with others. This argument is not entirely valid, however, since no test can be independent of a context. For example, what is appropriate for fourth grade? Or, *at what level* should the boys and girls be able to define the words in a vocabulary list?

Further problems with criterion-referenced testing arise because psychological and environmental factors that influence a child's success in academic learning are ignored. Such factors are: Does the child feel that the content is relevant to his needs? What is the quality of teaching? What is the child's learning aptitude? Ransom cautions that performance objectives must take into account what we know about learning theory; the complete range of learning to read, liking to read, and reading to learn; the child's reaction to print with thought and feeling; and peer group, cross-age, and child-adult interaction in manipulating ideas.[7]

Criterion-referenced tests can provide information that teachers need for both guiding pupil learning and evaluating their own work. If teachers have clearly defined the behavioral objectives desired according to the criteria established, then theoretically success in achieving the objectives can be measured.

Norm-Referenced Reading Tests

A test becomes standardized by administering it to a large number of subjects of given age and grade status so that the examiner can determine the *expected* performance of boys and girls under given circumstances. Such a test is a norm-referenced test. Results of such a test are most easily interpreted in percentile ranks.

A child's percentile rank is determined by the percentage of the total number of children who took the test who perform less well than that child. For example, if 1,000 children in fifth grade complete a given reading test and they are rank-ordered by score, the 500th ranking person is in the fiftieth percentile. Naturally the scores of fifth graders will tend to cluster around an average score. This means that the difference between the 40th and 60th percentiles may be a very small number of raw score points. However, the differences in raw score points between given percentiles are likely to get greater at high and low extremes of the distribution. The 70th percentile represents the raw score below which 70 percent of the students scored, the second percentile is the level below which only 2 percent of all the students in a given grade scored, and the 99th percentile is the level below which 99 percent of the children scored.

It is especially important for the classroom teacher to find out which students can perform in the upper third of the distribution, which perform in the middle third, and which perform in the lower third on standardized tests. With this information, the teacher can begin to accumulate many kinds of informal diagnostic information to try to provide instruction in reading skills that will be challenging but not too difficult. In a fifth grade class, for example, the teacher should expect to find one or two children performing at seventh or eighth grade level in reading ability and one or two performing at no better than first or second grade level. (See chapter 2.) Administering an individual oral reading test to a child would provide the teacher with some much-needed information for planning the child's work for the year. This is why it is so important for the teacher to do informal reading inventories as early in the school year as possible. (See chapter 4.) For those few boys and girls with many reading deficiencies, the teacher may wish to administer standardized oral reading tests as pre- and post-tests in order to measure progress during the school year.

The raw scores on norm-referenced tests may sometimes be converted to grade scores. Grade scores will appear as decimal figures, for example, 3.6 or 11.3. The numeral to the left of the decimal point refers to the grade, while the one to the right indicates the month of school. Therefore, 3.6 means third grade, sixth month. The grade score 3.6 is interpreted to mean that it is derived from the mean raw score of that portion of the norm group that is in the sixth month of third grade. Grade scores are often misinterpreted. Sometimes it is assumed that the first grader earning the 3.6 grade score can read as well as a child in the last half of third grade. Undoubtedly the child is a good reader, but he or she is not often ready to read the content of a third reader. Grade scores are not consistent across tests and textbooks. A grade score of 3.6 on a specific standardized reading test does not coincide with a particular set of readers. In fact, the grade score may be equivalent to a frustration level score, and placement on its basis would result in a poor instructional experience for the child. Finally, some schools want all children to score above grade level. This is not a reasonable or even possible expectation, since a grade score is an average or mean score, which, by definition, implies that half of the children will score above it and half below. School systems should work to provide learning environments in which each child can make optimum progress rather than struggle to get all children at or above grade level.

The third type of score often reported for norm-referenced tests is the stanine. A stanine is a standard score; the word itself means standard nine-point scale. All raw scores are assigned to some point on the nine-point scale. Points 1, 2, and 3 contain the lowest scores, points 4, 5, and 6 represent the middle range of scores, and points 7, 8, and 9 represent the highest scores. Since each point represents a range of raw scores, there is less danger of over-representing small differences in children's performances. Stanines are now the most common way of reporting reading test scores.

Reading Achievement Tests	Norm-referenced tests of reading abilities can be divided into several categories. One category could be labeled as reading achievement tests. The *Botel Reading Inventory* uses word-recognition and word-opposites tests to help teachers place students at appropriate levels of difficulty. The *Nelson Reading Skills Test* permits teachers to place students based on vocabulary and paragraph comprehension scores; some diagnostic information is also available to the teacher. The *Gates-MacGinitie Reading Tests* are carefully graduated in difficulty levels and can be used with separate answer sheets to allow much easier scoring by teachers. A test summary sheet is shown in figure 19.7.

Oral Reading Tests

Many teachers find oral reading tests to be valuable in learning more about the reading behaviors of their students, particularly the poorer readers in the class. The *Gilmore Oral Reading Test* is one of the easiest of such tests to administer. It can be completed with a child in fifteen to twenty minutes and yields a grade placement score for accuracy in mechanics, a grade placement score in comprehension, and a rating for rate of reading (see figure 19.8). The *Basic Achievement Skills Individual Screener (BASIS)*, in addition to an assessment of math, spelling, and writing skills, provides an evaluation of a young child's readiness skills. It also assesses the older child's ability to read paragraphs and fill in cloze blanks with acceptable responses. The passages range from primer through grade eight. Figure 19.9 shows a summary of a child's work in reading and spelling on the *BASIS*.

Diagnostic Reading Tests

The *Durrell Analysis of Reading Difficulty*, Third Edition, contains many subtests to facilitate the teacher's diagnosis of children's reading difficulties. The profile chart (see figure 19.10) allows the teacher to plot scores on the different subtests from grades one through six. The profile chart makes identification of strengths and areas for growth relatively easy. The *Silent Reading Diagnostic Tests*, grades 2 through 6, provide the teacher with very useful diagnostic information and results that can be presented concisely on a profile provided in the test booklet (see figure 19.11).

The following list contains selected oral and written standardized reading tests, including those just described.

Individually Administered Reading Tests

Basic Achievement Skills Individual Screener (BASIS). Tests arithmetic, spelling, and writing skills in addition to reading readiness, word recognition, sentence recognition, and paragraph reading combined items. New York: Harcourt Brace Jovanovich, 1982.

Botel Reading Inventory. Tests word recognition, word opposites, spelling placement, and phonic ability. Chicago: Follett, 1970.

Durrell Analysis of Reading Difficulty. 3d ed. Tests oral and silent reading, listening comprehension, spelling, and various aspects of word recognition and analysis. A comprehensive and rather complex test to administer. New York: Harcourt Brace Jovanovich, 1980.

Gilmore Oral Reading Test. Ten reading paragraphs of increasing difficulty. Yields separate accuracy of reading mechanics and level of comprehension scores. New York: Harcourt, Brace and World, 1968.

Figure 19.7
While Ivan is in the sixth grade, he has performed above the eighth grade level on the four measures of the *Gates-MacGinitie Reading Test.*

Reproduced from *Gates-MacGinitie Reading Tests,* Primary C., Form 17. Copyright © 1964 by Teachers College Press, Columbia University, New York. Reproduced by permission.

Name _Ivan_
    (LAST)   (FIRST)

Birth date _____ Boy **X** Girl _____
    (MONTH, DAY, YEAR)

Grade _6th grade_ Testing date _5-9-1968_

Teacher _____

School _Buena Vista_

City _____

GATES — MACGINITIE READING TESTS

SURVEY D, FORM 3

Speed & Accuracy
Vocabulary
Comprehension

☐ ☐ ☐   ☐ ☐ ☐ ☐ ☐ ☐

TEACHERS COLLEGE PRESS
TEACHERS COLLEGE
COLUMBIA UNIVERSITY
NEW YORK

To the Teacher:
BE SURE to follow the directions in the Manual (included in each test package) when giving these tests. The directions will tell you how to explain the tests and how to work the sample items with the students. Allow the exact time specified in the Manual.

DIRECTIONS: Read sample paragraph S 1. Under it are four words. Find the word that best answers the question.

> **S1.** Mary pulled and tried to turn the knob. She could not turn it. It was a cold day to be locked outside. What was Mary trying to open?
>
> box   bag   (door)   safe

The word **door** is the best answer to the question. Draw a line under the word **door**.

Now read paragraph S2. Find the word below the paragraph that best completes the paragraph, and draw a line under it.

> **S2.** The huge animals walked slowly, swinging their trunks from side to side. They had big floppy ears and long white tusks. These animals were
>
> tigers   deer   lions   (elephants)

The word **elephants** best completes paragraph S2. You should have drawn a line under the word **elephants**.

On the next two pages are more paragraphs like these samples. When you are asked to turn the page, read each paragraph and find the word below it that best answers the question or completes the paragraph. Draw a line under the best word. Mark only *one* word for each paragraph. Do the paragraphs in the order in which they are numbered: 1, 2, 3, etc. If you can't answer a question, go on to the next one. Work as fast as you can without making errors.

	SPEED & ACCURACY		VOCABULARY	COMPREHENSION
	Number attempted	Number right	Number right	Number right
Raw score	24	23	39	47
Standard score	52	53	57	57
Percentile score	58	62	76	76
Grade score	8.1	8.9	8.4	9.5

© 1964 by Teachers College, Columbia University
Printed in U.S.A.

10   9   8   7   6   5   4   3

Figure 19.8
The back page of the revised *Gilmore Oral Reading Test* provides for a summary of a fourth grade student's performance.

From John V. Gilmore and Eunice C. Gilmore, *Gilmore Oral Reading Test*, copyright © 1968 by Harcourt, Brace & World. Reproduced by special permission.

NAME _Susan_

TEST SUMMARY

Form C

PARA-GRAPH	ACCURACY		COMPREHENSION	RATE	
	ERRORS	10 MINUS NO. ERRORS	NO. RIGHT (OR CREDITED)	WORDS IN ¶	TIME IN SEC.
1		10	5	24	
2		10	5	45	
3	1	9	4	50	20
4	4	6	4	73	25
5	9	1	2	103	45
6	9	1	1	117	50
7	10	0	1	127	60
8			0	161	
9			0	181	
10			0	253	
	ACC. SCORE (TOT. "10 MINUS NO. ERRORS" COLUMN)	37	COMP. SCORE (TOT. NO. RIGHT OR CREDITED) 22	(1) NO. WORDS READ*	470
				(2) TIME IN SEC.*	200
STANINE		5	5	(1) ÷ (2)	2.4 X 60
GRADE EQUIV.		5.3	4.1	RATE SCORE (WPM)	144
RATING	Average		Average	Fast	

*Do **not** count "ceiling" paragraph or paragraphs below "basal."

COMMENTS:

Figure 19.9
Summary page of *Basic Achievement Skills Individual Screener (BASIS)* provides grade and age scores and grade-referenced placements.

Reproduced by permission from the Basic Achievement Skills Individual Screener Record Form. Standardization edition, copyright © 1982 by Harcourt Brace Jovanovich, Inc. All rights reserved.

Name: _____ Last _____ Bill _____ First _____ MI

School: _____

Teacher: _____

Examiner: _____ Code: _____ Sex: _____

Grade: **6**

Date of Testing: **12** Yr / **6** Mo / Day

Date of Birth: **12** Yr / **2** Mo / Day

Age at Testing: **12** Yr / Mo / Day

SUMMARY SCORES

	Grade Scores			Total Raw Score	Age Scores			Grade-Referenced Placement
	GE	S	PR		PR	S	AE	
READING								**5**
MATHEMATICS								
SPELLING								**3**

Writing Sample Used:

Grade _____

Below Average	Average	Above Average

(circle one)

BASIS

READING TALLY

Cluster Grade	No. Right	Base Score
READINESS		
Letter Ident.		0
Visual Disc.		4
BEGINNING READING		
Word Rdg.		8
Sentence Rdg.		12
PASSAGES		
P-1		16
P-2		18
P-3		20
(1-1)	**3**	(**22**)
1-2	**1**	25
2	**3**	28
3	**5**	34
4	**6**	40
5	**3**	46
6	**0**	52
7		58
8		64
Total No. Right	**26** +	**22**
TOTAL RAW SCORE	**48**	

MATHEMATICS TALLY

Cluster Grade	No. Right	Base Score
Readiness		0
1		6
2		14
3		22
4		30
5		38
6		46
7		54
8		62
Total No. Right		+
TOTAL RAW SCORE		

SPELLING TALLY

Cluster Grade	No. Right	Base Score
(1)	**5**	(**0**)
2	**5**	6
3	**4**	12
4		18
5		24
6		30
7		36
8		42
Total No. Right	**14** +	**0**
TOTAL RAW SCORE	**14**	

DIRECTIONS FOR TALLYING AND SCORING

Read these instructions before completing the above Tally charts and the box for Summary Scores. More detailed instructions can be found in the Manual.

1. Follow carefully the scoring directions for each test as described in the Manual, and indicate on each item in the Record Form whether it is correct or incorrect.

2. For each test, determine the *lowest* grade-referenced cluster administered. Circle this Cluster Grade on the Tally charts.

3. Circle the Base Score in the same row as the circled Cluster Grade. Record this Base Score at the bottom of the "Base Score" column to the right of the " + ".

4. For each grade-referenced cluster administered, count the number of items the student answered correctly, obtaining this information from the appropriate Record Form page. Then, opposite the appropriate cluster in the Tally chart, enter each count in the "No. Right" column.

5. Add the entries in the "No. Right" column and enter the sum at the bottom of the column in the "Total No. Right" row (to the left of the " + "). Add this number to the Base Score and write the sum in the "Total Raw Score" line. Copy this Total Raw Score into the "Total Raw Score" column of the "Summary Scores" above.

6. See the Manual for converting Total Raw Scores into Grade or Age Scores.

Figure 19.10
The cover page of the *Durrell Analysis of Reading Difficulty* provides a useful profile of data concerning a child's achievement and possible potential.

Reproduced by permission from the Durrell Analysis of Reading Difficulty Individual Record Booklet. Copyright © 1980, 1955, 1937 by Harcourt Brace Jovanovich, Inc. All rights reserved.

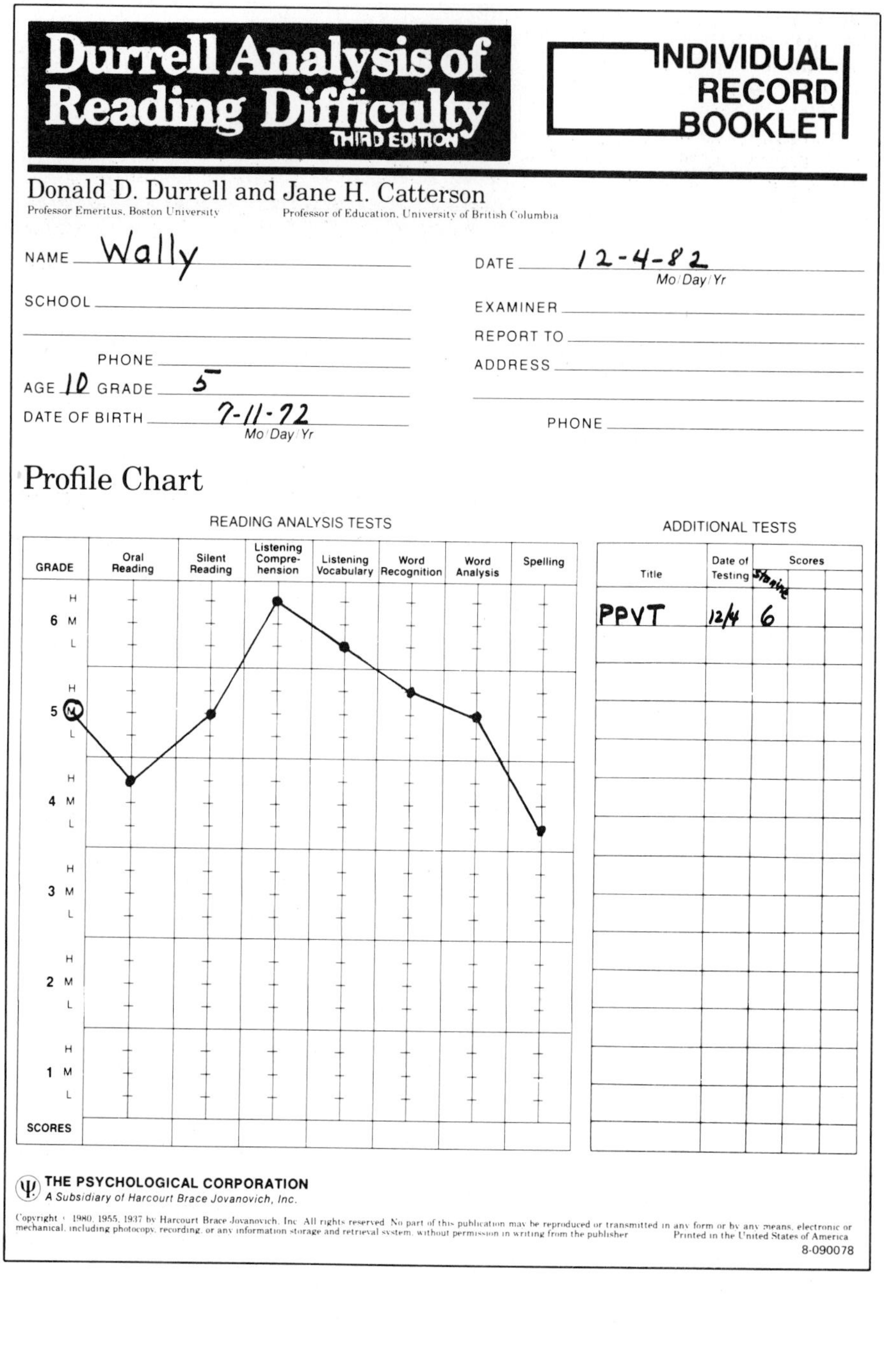

Durrell Analysis of Reading Difficulty
THIRD EDITION

INDIVIDUAL RECORD BOOKLET

Donald D. Durrell and Jane H. Catterson
Professor Emeritus, Boston University — Professor of Education, University of British Columbia

NAME Wally
SCHOOL
PHONE
AGE 10 GRADE 5
DATE OF BIRTH 7-11-72 (Mo/Day/Yr)

DATE 12-4-82 (Mo/Day/Yr)
EXAMINER
REPORT TO
ADDRESS
PHONE

Profile Chart

ADDITIONAL TESTS

Title	Date of Testing	Scores (Stanine)		
PPVT	12/4	6		

THE PSYCHOLOGICAL CORPORATION
A Subsidiary of Harcourt Brace Jovanovich, Inc.

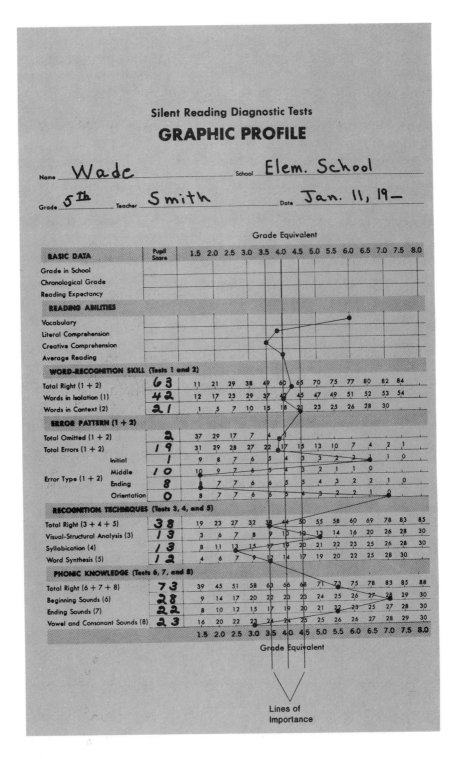

Silent Reading Diagnostic Tests

GRAPHIC PROFILE

Name **Wade**   School **Elem. School**

Grade **5th**   Teacher **Smith**   Date **Jan. 11, 19—**

Standardized Silent Reading Tests	*California Reading Achievement Tests.* Separate tests for lower primary, primary, elementary, junior high, and advanced grades. Tests vocabulary and comprehension. New York: McGraw-Hill, 1970.
	Gates-MacGinitie Reading Tests. Tests vocabulary and comprehension in primary grades; vocabulary, comprehension, and speed in upper grades. Primary A: Grade 1; Primary B: Grade 2; Primary C: Grade 3; Survey D: Grade 4, 5, 6; and Survey E: Grade 7, 8, 9. May be machine or hand scored. New York: Teachers College Press, 1965.
	Iowa Tests of Basic Skills. The reading test may be obtained separately from the battery in a reusable booklet. Tests paragraph comprehension and vocabulary. Boston: Houghton Mifflin, 1973.
	Nelson Reading Skills Test. For Grades 3–9. Timed. Eight minutes vocabulary; twenty-five minutes paragraph comprehension. Boston: Houghton Mifflin, 1977.
	Silent Reading Diagnostic Tests. Tests word recognition, left-to-right orientation, syllabication, root words, auditory discrimination, and word synthesis. Provides profile for each child. Chicago: Rand McNally, 1970.

The Reading Miscue Inventory

The reading miscue inventory is another measure of the accuracy with which a child reads a passage orally.[8] It provides an opportunity to study the "match" or the "mismatch" between the exact wording in the test and the language used by the reader in reproducing that text orally. A miscue is the term used to describe those oral responses that differ from the phrasing in the text. The use of the miscue inventory allows the teacher to make the very important distinction between reading miscues that preserve meaning and should be overlooked and miscues that represent the traditional "inability to read well" examined in the informal reading inventory discussed previously. In fact, use of such tools as the miscue inventory offers some understanding of how the process of reading works. It shows, for example, that beginning readers who have strong motivation for interpreting sentence structure and sentence meaning in what they read may be deterred and badly taught by teachers who emphasize the phonic or "sounding out" approaches to word identification. It seems clear that if emphasis were placed on extracting meaning rather than on pronunciation of words, fewer reading problems would develop.

> The *Reading Miscue Inventory* provides a view of a student's reading performance that is very different from the ones provided by the traditional standardized reading tests or by informal reading inventories. During the oral reading, the student receives no external help; he must rely on his own strategies. His miscues are evaluated to see if he makes appropriate use of syntactic and semantic information. The results of the inventory register the reader's strengths and give information about ineffective and inefficient uses of strategies. It also provides the teacher with information about causes and quality of miscues.[9]

Both the informal reading inventory and reading miscue inventory serve useful purposes for the teacher. It is important to recognize that the two assessments, which in some ways seem similar, serve different needs and have different applications for the teacher. The former provides a means of identifying different

From Theory to Practice 19.3
Administering a Formal Reading Test

Your instructor will identify a formal reading test to be administered. Study the administration manual carefully to learn exactly what you must do and say. This is important since these behaviors are required for the administering of such tests.

Administer the test to one child of appropriate age and reading ability. After you have scored the test, bring it to your class. Join with a small group to analyze your test and the tests others have brought. This analysis should lead to some recommendations for curriculum for the children in question. (Note that tests and the giving of tests have *no* value if the information obtained is not used to improve the quality of the child's school experience.)

reading levels, of comparing oral and silent performances, of studying responses to comprehension questions, of observing attitudes and other reading behaviors, and of studying to some degree the reader's reading strategies. The latter provides for in-depth study of a child's reading strategies and his or her use of different kinds of linguistic information, such as semantic and syntactic clues.

Summary

Evaluation of reading abilities is an important part of the reading program. Teachers should utilize many informal strategies, such as oral and written language evaluations, sociograms, interest inventories, and anecdotal records. Informal techniques may be supplemented and strengthened with the application of information derived from formal tests when developing instructional plans. Teachers should be aware of the various kinds of scores that may be used to report achievement. It is important to know and to be able to use reading tests in at least three categories—achievement tests oral reading tests, and diagnostic tests.

For Further Reading

Applebee, Arthur. "A Sense of Story." *Theory Into Practice* 16 (December 1977): 342–47.

Baumann, James F., and Jennifer A. Stevenson. "Understanding Standardized Reading Achievement Test Scores." *The Reading Teacher* 35 (March 1982): 648–54.

Baumann, James F., and Jennifer A. Stevenson. "Using Scores from Standardized Reading Achievement Tests." *The Reading Teacher* 35 (February 1982): 528–32.

Gillet, Jean Wallace, and Charles Temple. *Understanding Reading Problems*. Boston: Little, Brown, 1982.

Greenhalgh, Carol, and Donna Townsend. "Evaluating Students' Writing Holistically—An Alternative Approach." *Language Arts* 58 (October 1981): 811–22.

McConaughy, Stephanie H. "Using Story Structure in the Classroom." *Language Arts* 57 (February 1980): 157–65.

McGinnis, Dorothy J., and Dorothy E. Smith. "Informal Assessment of Reading Performance," "Standardized Tests," and "Observation and Interview." Chapters 6–8 in *Analyzing and Treating Reading Problems*. New York: Macmillan, 1982.

Rauch, Sidney J. "A Checklist for the Evaluation of Reading Programs," *The Reading Teacher* 21 (March 1968): 519–22.

Rubin, Dorothy. "Instruments and Techniques for the Assessment and Diagnosis of Reading Performance." Part 3 in *Diagnosis and Correction in Reading Instruction,* pp. 99–178. New York: Holt, Rinehart and Winston, 1982.

Schell, Leo M., and Robert E. Jennings. "Test Review: Durrell Analysis of Reading Difficulty (3d edition)." *The Reading Teacher* 35 (November 1981): 204–10.

Notes

1. Joseph Crescimbeni, "The Need for Diagnostic Evaluation," *Education* 88 (November–December 1967): 161.

2. Arthur Applebee, *The Child's Concept of Story* (Chicago: University of Chicago Press, 1978), p. 36.

3. David R. Olson, "From Utterance to Text: The Basis of Language in Speech and Writing," in Maryanne Wolf, Mark K. McQuillan, and Eugene Radwin, *Thought and Language/Language and Reading,* p. 102 (Cambridge, Mass.: Harvard Educational Review, 1980).

4. Ibid., p. 103.

5. Carol Westby, "Children's Narrative Development—Cognitive and Linguistic Aspects" (Prepared for the Conference on Language, Learning, and Reading Disabilities: A New Decade, 22–23 May 1980).

6. Frank Smith, *Understanding Reading* (New York: Holt, Rinehart and Winston, 1971), p. 162.

7. Grace Ransom, "Criterion Referenced Tests—Let the Buyer Beware," *The Reading Teacher* 26 (December 1972): 282–85. *See also* George A. Prescott, "Criterion Referenced Test Interpretation in Reading," *The Reading Teacher* 24 (January 1971): 347–54, reprinted in *Elementary Reading Instruction: Selected Materials,* 2d ed., ed. Althea Beery, Thomas C. Barrett, and William R. Powell (Boston: Allyn & Bacon, 1974), pp. 605–13.

8. Yetta Goodman and Carolyn Burke, *Reading Miscue Inventory: Procedure for Diagnosis and Evaluation* (New York: Macmillan, 1972).

9. Yetta Goodman and Dorothy J. Watson, "A Reading Program to Live With: Focus on Comprehension," *Language Arts* 54 (November/December 1977): 868–79.

Teaching Reading in Proper Perspective

20

A Cognitive Map: Teaching Reading in Proper Perspective

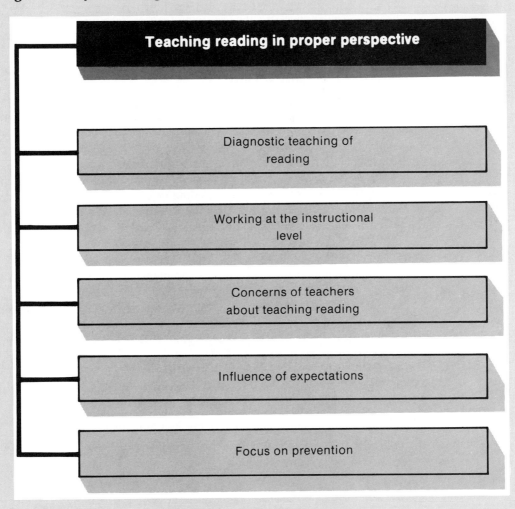

Teaching reading in proper perspective

Diagnostic teaching of reading

Working at the instructional level

Concerns of teachers about teaching reading

Influence of expectations

Focus on prevention

Throughout the text, we have emphasized the extent of differences in children's learning. All the principles of learning that cause boys and girls to become more different rather than more alike as they progress through school are in direct contradiction to the organization by chronological age level and the inflexible patterns deeply embedded in schools today. Having copies of the same textbook for every child in the class is just the opposite of a flexible pattern to encourage teachers to provide for many levels of ability within the class. What is the classroom teacher to do?

A suggestion was made in chapter 5 that inexperienced teachers might rely more heavily than experienced teachers on basal readers and their corresponding manuals to keep several reading groups progressing in the sequential development of reading skills. Experienced teachers will feel more confident about working with individualized reading programs and language-experience types of reading and writing. However, they too will rely on organized, sequenced basal-reader lessons for some children.

In perspective, how can the classroom teacher keep up with each child in the room if nearly all are doing different things? Is the atmosphere one of noise and chaos? How will the principal react to this?

Probably the teacher will not wish to keep up with ten or more separate reading groups day after day if they are all in basal reading series and are dependent upon the teacher for guidance. Yet, with some well-planned lessons that include individualized reading for those who really want to read and individualized work-type lessons for those who need planned, guided seatwork, most of the children can work independently for much of an hour that the teacher may have scheduled for reading in the daily program.

Two of the classroom teacher's most valuable tools for diagnostic teaching in primary reading are the informal reading inventory, as discussed in chapter 4, and the use of cloze exercises to insure anticipation of meaning and understanding of sentence structure.

Diagnostic Teaching of Reading

Diagnostic teaching of reading requires acceptance and application of the following principles:

1. Children are indivisible entities.
2. No learning takes place without a motive. If something isn't important *to the child,* it won't be learned very efficiently.
3. There is *no necessary relationship* between level of intelligence and being a disabled reader.
4. Differences within a group become greater as children progress through elementary school.
5. Each child has his or her own optimal time for learning.
6. No two children can learn the same thing in the same amount of time with the same amount of practice.
7. No child is inherently lazy. If a child acts that way, there has to be a reason.

8. Almost everything that is learned must be reviewed from time to time or it will be forgotten.
9. When an objective is stated behaviorally for a child, the teacher can determine whether the objective is achieved.

Not all teachers accept these principles, but all recognize that there are problems in applying them in their day-to-day work. Some examples of teacher behavior are discussed here.

A second grade teacher showed the following duplicated letter to her student teacher early in the school year and explained that the second graders were *too far behind* in reading.

Dear Parent:
The attached list of 175 words was taught last year in first grade. In second grade, your child will be expected to know them. Please see that your child knows all of these words so that he or she can do the work in the second grade.

> Your child's teacher
> Mary Smith

Did all children learn 175, and only 175, service words in first grade? Does forgetting during the summer constitute any problem? Is second grade only for people who have already learned to recognize the 175 words? Or can a child be in second grade and know very few sight words?

If Miss Smith has the *usual* heterogeneous group of thirty children about seven years old, she should expect to find the full range of differences in intellectual, psychological, physical, and social growth usually found in children at this age. Such children became *more different* in first grade, *not more alike*. How they grew in emotional stability and independence varied in relation to how each set of parents applied "individual" quantities and combinations of overindulgence, acceptance, rejection, neglect, punishment, or tender loving care. For the teacher to assume that parents can or will teach their child a basic sight vocabulary implies that their know-how in methodology is equal to that of the teacher. This is occasionally true! However, the letter tells parents nothing about how to proceed; nothing about being sure that learning the words is a meaningful, rewarding kind of experience for the child; nothing about the psychological danger of trying to coerce a child into learning.

A teacher teaching diagnostically in second grade would find out early in the year how many of the 175 sight words each child knew and then arrange for different subgroups to start their reading experiences with materials that took account of how many words they already knew. Some children might learn best with more auditory work to help them hear phonic elements in words. Others might benefit more from practice in writing sentences containing words they have learned. Some might do better with more oral reading practice. And still others might need special attention directed to letters or words often confused (*b* and *d, n* and *m, was* and *saw, and* and *said*). The teacher should also expect the children to show varying degrees of emotional, social, and intellectual maturity. And, as a professional, the teacher will probably know how to accomplish this job better than most parents.

The fact that a student teacher received the "letter to parents" from her supervisor indicates to the young student teacher that such a letter is supposed to represent *good* teaching practice. An example of better teaching practice would be the following:

A teacher, knowing that children need a great deal of easy reading practice to become good readers, would do well to ask young children to carry home their textbooks *after* they have learned *all* the new words. The teacher would hope that the mothers or fathers would be good listeners and encourage their children in oral reading practice. But because parents are *not* oriented in teaching methodology, the teacher would send a letter like the following to the parents:

Dear Parent:

Bill has read all of *Peanuts, the Pony*[1] at school and knows all the new words. Of course, he needs much practice to become a good reader. Will you please listen attentively while he reads aloud for you so you can enjoy the story together? After he has read for you, please sign your name below and let *Bill* return the letter to me.

Thank you for your kind cooperation,
Miss Smith

Bill has read *Peanuts, the Pony* aloud, and we enjoyed it together.

Parent _____

Working at the Instructional Level

Mrs. Walker has been a sixth grade teacher for many years. She has many pictures, which she has beautifully arranged on bulletin boards many times. Her room is clean, efficient, and very quiet. She organizes the work of her student teacher so that the student teacher will learn to perform exactly the way Mrs. Walker performs.

In a culturally deprived, low socioeconomic area of the city, Mrs. Walker has grouped her twenty-seven sixth graders into three reading groups. About one-third read from a first-semester fifth grade reader; another third read from a first-semester fourth reader; and the final third read from a first-semester second reader. This last group includes children with many types of reading problems, each of whom needs carefully tailored individual planning. What they get each day, however, are superficially motivated, directed reading lessons that follow the manual written for second graders.

Paradoxically, each week for spelling class all three groups study the same list of words in *My Word Study Book,* Book Six. Perhaps more than half the class would not know the meanings of these words and cannot pronounce them. The most serious result from the mental health point of view is the destruction of ego and devaluation of self when the teacher asks, "How many perfect papers?" after the Friday test and then looks approvingly at the two or three children who always raise their hands. When all those who fail are admonished to study harder or to write each word ten times, it is apparent that this teacher does not follow the practice of teaching diagnostically. No child has a *need* for any

Figure 20.1
The many faces of
reading.

spelling words he or she cannot *pronounce and use* in writing. The level of difficulty in spelling that a child is asked to master can hardly be greater than the child's ability to read.

In this same sixth grade, all students used the regular sixth grade arithmetic textbook, and every day *all* tried to learn the same mathematics skills in the same amount of time with the same amount of practice.

Grouping children according to their instructional reading levels makes it possible to provide study activities all day long that the child can do successfully. This is one of the advantages of the self-contained classroom.

Perhaps one way to emphasize the extent of differences in the self-contained classroom is to talk about "The Many Faces of Reading." Figure 20.1 depicts some of the many different attitudes toward reading found in the classroom. All classroom teachers teaching heterogeneous groups of boys and girls are sure to have had at one time or another a child who comes from a foreign language background, a fearful child, a child who is already convinced that he or she can't learn, a child who is emotionally disturbed and cannot think logically about immediate problems, a child who thinks that right-to-left direction is as appropriate for reading as is left-to-right, or a child who uses all kinds of excuses when the words are difficult but doesn't want to admit it. Then there are children who always know all the words, who have read many interesting stories before they get to the class, who delight in good reading ("Gee, that's a neat story!"), and who overwork the expression "I'm so bored!" A few children have been told emphatically that they have never been taught phonics and that is the reason they are not good readers. With this mixture, the teacher must find constructive ways to group students within the class, ways to identify and develop leadership for groups, and varied activities to make reading fun to do.

Concerns of Teachers about the Teaching of Reading

Teaching reading diagnostically requires both ability and judgment on the part of the teacher. Following are many questions for which teachers need answers. They are typical of many other questions teachers can ask themselves.

1. How will I organize my room for reading in the fall when school starts?
2. How can I get some kind of grouping established early in the year?
3. How will I explain to parents or other teachers what I am doing?
4. What will my basic organization be: basal reader, individualized reading, or language-experience?
5. What will each child be reading at his or her instructional level all the rest of the school day?
6. How can I make sure children are not expected to write and spell words they cannot read?
7. How will I make a daily lesson plan that incorporates everything (including independent seatwork to last long periods of time)?
8. What reading plans do I make for those who do almost all reading at grade level or above? those in a normal distribution in the achievement range? those whose achievement is below grade level?
9. How have I made reading just *one* of the parts of a language arts curriculum?
10. How do I teach diagnostically those who speak nonstandard English?
11. How do I first teach English to the student for whom English is a foreign language, the culturally different child?
12. If I accept and respect the course of study as a guide for what to teach in a given class, how will I adapt it for each child's achievement?
13. The child *never* just all of a sudden "catches on" to reading. If children want to do well, to follow the principles of growing toward maturity, how can I find out what is wrong in case of trouble?

14. No teacher can know all the answers. There has to be support from many disciplines. How can I find answers outside the classroom?
15. How can I make sure the child has a good year *in my room* and let next year take care of itself?
16. What will I tell parents who ask, "Does the school teach phonics?"
17. How does the school provide programmed material for independent seatwork? What materials?
18. What is dyslexia? How can I help the child who has it?
19. When should a child repeat a grade in the elementary school?

Some teachers still feel that regardless of what a child has learned or has failed to learn, a book of the grade level to which the child is assigned is what must be used.[2] Such an attitude could hardly be less productive or more inefficient.

English says:

> . . . the textbook in its present form is outdated, expensive, and inefficient. The assumptions underlying its present usage are false; they do not explain or foster learning in depth or promote student inquiry. . . . The removal of legal straitjackets [textbooks] will provide the freedom necessary to arrive at modern education in a time when "modern" is woefully out of date.[3]

Soghomonian, in a response to English, says:

> There are good and bad textbooks, easy-to-read ones, and hard-to-understand ones. But the major fault, the core of the problem, is not the text *per se,* but that too many teachers have made the text an icon. Therein lies the monster. The text is not protoplasm; the teacher is. The classroom text is inert, as is any tool. It hardly seems fair to criticize the tool and not the operator.[4]

Influence of Expectations

Do a teacher's expectations about a pupil's performance affect that performance? The answer is *yes*. Rosenthal and Jacobson[5] found that when teachers in an elementary school were told that certain children would do especially well, those children—even though they were picked at random—showed significantly greater gains than did others during the school year. This effect of expectation was greater at the primary than at the intermediate levels.

Subjective teacher descriptions of the same designated children at the end of the year rated them as having better chances of success, being significantly more interesting and curious, and being somewhat more adjusted and affectionate.

Two questions follow: (1) How much does a teacher's attitude toward a child influence how successfully the child learns to read? (2) How much do teachers' favorable or unfavorable expectations of individual children influence the results of educational research done by the teachers?

Coopersmith[6] studied behavior patterns in a group of boys, ages ten to twelve, in order to evaluate qualities that build self-confidence and feelings of personal worth. Expectation of success, motivation to achieve, initiative, and dealing with anxieties are behaviors necessary for developing self-esteem. Coopersmith found that a boy's behavior was significantly related to the opinion he had of himself.

High self-esteem is associated with academic or social success, confidence, optimism, originality, and having parents who are generally strict and consistent in enforcing rules. Low self-esteem is related to being convinced of inferiority, fear of social encounters, self-consciousness, sensitivity to criticism, lack of confidence, remaining in the shadows, and listening rather than participating.

The relationship between self-esteem and level of aspiration needs to be studied and evaluated carefully. If Coopersmith's study is valid, the crucial role of primary teachers is underscored and reemphasized. The young child who experiences personal failure during the first two or three years of school may be fitting into a behavior pattern of low self-esteem with all the negative behavior that this suggests.

Winne, Woodlands, and Wong studied the self-concepts of sixty children classified as learning disabled, normal, or gifted. They found that on academic subtests, normal and gifted children had stronger self-concepts than learning disabled children. On physical and social subtests, learning disabled children seemed to exceed gifted children in self-concept. The researchers concluded that though there seems to be a relationship between self-concept and achievement, the details of that relationship are very complex and may function differently with different categories of children.[7]

Focus on Prevention

Early identification of learning difficulties in school could prevent much of the painful correction that now takes place in remedial teaching situations. As was emphasized in the chapter on readiness, the basic idea in evaluation before formal reading should be to study the child's status in school with respect to physical, intellectual, emotional, and social readiness for the complex task of learning to read. Formal reading instruction should be carefully delayed for the child who is immature and can profit from prereading development in any of these four major areas.

For each school day, the teacher plans experiences that will help each child's growth in learning. In a supportive learning environment, each child takes from those experiences that which is meaningful. The teacher must resist the notion that each child will learn and perform exactly as the adult has planned. Ignoring the fact that the child has learned in accordance with personal needs and abilities and focusing only on the fact that the child did not learn what the teacher wanted are twin traps that may lead the teacher to see failure when growth has actually taken place.

If the teacher notes that the child is not growing and learning and that, in fact, the child seems alienated from the learning environment, the teacher must act immediately. He or she should examine the classroom environment. Is there material from which the child can profit? Are there potential learning experiences that the child perceives as being available? It is important to view the classroom environment as the child would see it, not as the teacher would want the child to see it.

If the environment is judged to be supportive, the next step is for the teacher to examine himself or herself. Are the interpersonal communications satisfying and effective? Am I making myself a helpful, stimulating, and supportive resource? Does the child feel I can be counted on whether things go well or poorly? If no problem seems to surface in this area, the study of the child must begin in earnest, for failure symptoms must be turned to success signs quickly. Otherwise, the child will begin to see the school as a hopeless place from which nothing good can be expected and in which continuing to try is not justified. At that point, helping the child becomes a complex problem.

When failure symptoms first appear, the alert teacher searches for ways to redirect the child's efforts so that he or she will experience success. Strengthening an area of weakness prepares the child for continuous growth.

Diagnostic teaching is the technique whereby each child is taught the specific skills not yet mastered, but which must be learned before he or she can go on to more difficult learning.

Diagnostic teaching begins with attention to one child and that child's range of competencies, concerns, enthusiasms, self-concept, learning style, aspirations, and personal way of learning. Learning for each child is a highly personal experience.

Dorris M. Lee reminds us:

Diagnostic teaching employs procedures that are based on the findings of experience and research about children and learning, those that can be effective in attaining the goals of the school, and those that recognize unique personal values.[8]

Olsen and Kelley both emphasize special needs of lower-class children in school. Olsen says:

We have yet to face the fact that lower-class children are socialized in ways that are quite different from those of the middle-class. We have yet to take full account of the differing value patterns, attitudes, and beliefs with which the lower-class child comes to school. The child brings the reality of his own life into the classroom, and to be effective, the school must admit that reality. I suggest that the central challenge that the slum child presents to the school is not only the disadvantages that he brings with him. His challenge to us is much more profound than this. His ambitions, his hopes, his desires, his attitudes toward authority, education, success, and school, his fears, his habits, his hates—in short, his basic orientation toward life—are, in many ways, so different from ours that we do not understand him nor does he understand us.[9]

And Kelley reminds us:

The child born and raised in a lower-class setting derives his perceptions and values, attitudes and habits of living in a cultural setting that teaches, rewards, and reinforces his way of life. His way of perceiving, behaving, and becoming is distinctly different from the school culture.[10]

The profession needs teachers with the determination that Hunt described in Aunt Cordelia when she explains why she must continue to teach the rural school near her farm:

Aunt Cordelia didn't really have to teach for a livelihood; the income from the farm was sufficient for her needs, and the modest salary she received for each month of the school year was not the incentive which brought her back to her desk year after year. Her reason for teaching was actually the belief that no one else would do the work quite as well, would understand the backgrounds of these children whose parents she had taught when she was young. There was never a doubt in Aunt Cordelia's mind but that *her* teaching was the best to be had, and she would have felt that she was denying something beyond price to the handful of country children who sat in her classroom if she allowed a younger or a less dedicated woman to take over.[11]

Finally, there is Francie, who finds the magic and experiences what all good teachers dream of for their students.

Betty Smith, in *A Tree Grows in Brooklyn,* describes Francie's first year in school. Although she has begun to feel that much of the school day is grim, she is greatly enamored of the music teacher and the art teacher who each come once a week to the classroom. Then Francie discovers the *magic* of reading:

Oh, MAGIC HOUR when a child first knows it can read printed words! For quite a while, Francie had been spelling out letters, sounding them and then putting the sounds together to mean a word. But one day, she looked at a page and the word "mouse" had instantaneous meaning. She looked at the word and the picture of a gray mouse scampered through her mind. She looked further and when she saw "horse," she heard him pawing the ground and saw the sun glint on his glossy coat. The word "running" hit her suddenly and she breathed hard as though running herself. The barrier between the individual sound of each letter and the whole meaning of the word was removed and the printed word meant a thing at one quick glance. She read a few pages rapidly and almost became ill with excitement. She wanted to shout it out. She could read! She could read!

From that time on, the world was hers for the reading. She would never be lonely again, never miss the lack of intimate friends. Books became her friends and there was one for every mood. There was poetry for quiet companionship. There was adventure when she tired of quiet hours. There would be love stories when she came into adolescence, and when she wanted to feel a closeness to someone she could read a biography. On that day when she first knew she could read, she made a vow to read one book a day as long as she lived.[12]

For Further Reading

Ashton-Warner, Sylvia. *Teacher.* New York: Simon & Schuster, 1963.

Austin, Mary C., and Coleman Morrison. *The Torch Lighters, Tomorrow's Teachers of Reading.* Cambridge, Mass.: Harvard University Press, 1961.

Bush, Clifford, and Mildred H. Huebner. "Challenging Every Reader." In *Strategies for Reading in the Elementary School,* 2d ed., pp. 363–89. New York: Macmillan, 1979.

Daniels, Steven. *How Two Gerbils, Twenty Goldfish, Two Hundred Games, Two Thousand Books and I Taught Them How to Read.* Philadelphia: Westminster Press, 1971.

Gonzales, Phillip. "What's Wrong with the Basal Reader Approach to Language Development?" *The Reading Teacher* 33 (March 1980): 668–73.

Herndon, James. *How to Survive in Your Native Land.* New York: Bantam Books, 1971.

———. *The Way It Spozed to Be.* New York: Simon & Schuster, 1965.

Holt, John. *What Do I Do Monday?* New York: Dell, 1970.

Huck, Charlotte. "Literature as the Content of Reading." *Theory Into Practice* 16 (December 1977): 363–71.

International Reading Assn., P.O. Box 695, Newark, Del. 19711.

    a. Proceedings of the Annual Convention.

    b. *The Reading Teacher,* eight issues per year.

    c. *The Journal of Reading,* eight issues per year.

    d. *The Reading Research Quarterly.*

    e. *Perspectives in Reading.*

Kohl, Herbert. *36 Children.* New York: New American Library, 1967.

Otto, Jean. "The New Debate in Reading." *The Reading Teacher* 36 (October 1982): 14–18.

Postman, Neil, and Charles Weingartner. *The Schoolbook.* New York: Delacorte Press, 1973.

Rogers, Vincent, ed. *Teaching in the British Primary School.* London: Macmillan, 1970.

Shannon, Patrick. "Some Subjective Reasons for Teachers' Reliance on Commercial Reading Materials." *The Reading Teacher* 35 (May 1982): 884–89.

Soghomonian, Sam. "The Textbook—Tarnished Tool for Teachers?" *Phi Delta Kappan* 48 (April 1967): 395–96.

Notes

1. Preprimer, *Our Animal Story Series* (Boston: D. C. Heath, various dates).

2. Madeline C. Hunter, "You—as a Diagnostician," *The Instructor* 76 (February 1967): 31, 126.

3. Fenwick English, "The Textbook—Procrustean Bed of Learning," *Phi Delta Kappan* 48 (April 1967): 395.

4. Sam Soghomonian, "The Textbook—Tarnished Tool for Teachers?" *Phi Delta Kappan* 48 (April 1967): 395.

5. "Science and the Citizen," *Scientific American* 217 (November 1967): 54. Reported from Robert Rosenthal and Lenore Jacobson, "Self-Fulfilling Prophecies," *Psychological Reports* 19, no. 1 (1966): 115–18.

6. Stanley Coopersmith, "Studies in Self Esteem," *Scientific American* 218 (February 1968): 96–102.

7. Philip H. Winne, Margaret J. Woodlands, and Bernice Y. L. Wong, "Comparability of Self-Concept Among Learning Disabled, Normal, and Gifted Students," *Journal of Learning Disabilities* 15 (October 1982): 470–75.

8. Dorris M. Lee, *Diagnostic Teaching* (Washington, D.C.: National Education Assn., 1966).

9. James Olsen, "Challenge of the Poor to the Schools," *Phi Delta Kappan* 47 (October 1965): 79.

10. Earl C. Kelley, *Perceiving, Behaving, Becoming, A New Focus on Education* (Washington, D.C.: National Education Assn., 1962).

11. Irene Hunt, *Up a Road Slowly* (Chicago: Follett, 1966), p. 21.

12. Betty Smith, *A Tree Grows in Brooklyn* (New York: Harper & Row, 1943), p. 128.

Appendix 1

Books in Which American Indians Are Principal Characters

Characters in children's fictional literature provide an important avenue for student self-identification. When literature is used for the purpose of building self-image, it is essential that the characterizations in the stories selected portray a reasonably accurate and positive image with which the reader can identify.

American Indians are used quite extensively as storybook characters in children's literature. Unfortunately, many of the characterizations are inaccurate or portray a negative, stereotyped image. It is important that teachers and librarians carefully preview reading materials before making them available to children.

The following bibliography includes some of the better books using American Indians as characters. The Indian tribe represented and the reading level of the book are indicated in each case. Those books that are starred are especially recommended for classroom use.

Juanita O. Cata
Chief, Division of Education
Bureau of Indian Affairs, Albuquerque Area Office

Agle, Nan Hayden. *Makon and the Dauphin*. New York: Charles Scribner's Sons, 1961. (Woodland; intermediate)

Agnew, Edith J. *Nezbah's Lamb*. New York: Friendship Press, 1954. (Navajo; primary)

Armer, Laura Adams. *Waterless Mountain*. New York: David McKay, 1931. (Navajo; upper)

Baker, Betty. *And One Was a Wooden Indian*. New York: Macmillan, 1970. (Apache/Papago; intermediate)

———. *Killer-Of-Death*. New York: Harper & Row, 1963. (Apache; upper)

———. *Little Runner of the Longhouse*. New York: Harper & Row, 1962. (Iroquois; primary)

————. *The Shaman's Last Raid*. New York: Harper & Row, 1963. (Apache; intermediate)

*————. *Walk the World's Rim*. New York: Harper & Row, 1965. (Southwest; upper)

Balch, Glenn. *Horse of Two Colors*. New York: Thomas Y. Crowell, 1969. (Nez Percé; intermediate)

————. *Indian Paint*. New York: Scholastic Book Services, 1962. (Plains; intermediate)

*Bannon, Laura. *When the Moon Is New*. Chicago: Albert Whitman, 1953. (Seminole; intermediate)

Baylor, Byrd. *Before You Came This Way*. New York: E. P. Dutton, 1969. (Anasazi; primary)

*————. *Hawk, I'm Your Brother*. New York: Scribners, 1976. (Southwest; primary)

Beatie, Bernadine. *Little Turtle*. Chicago: Scott, Foresman, 1971. (Hopi; intermediate)

Beatty, Hetty Burlingame. *Little Owl Indian*. Boston: Houghton Mifflin, 1951. (Iroquois; primary)

Behn, Harry. *The Painted Cave*. New York: Harcourt Brace Jovanovich, 1957. (Southwest; intermediate)

Bleeker, Sonia. *The Crow Indians: Hunters of the Northern Plains*. New York: William Morrow, 1953. (Crow; intermediate)

————. *The Navajo*. New York: William Morrow, 1958. (Navajo; intermediate)

*Buff, Mary, and Conrad Buff. *Hah-Nee*. Boston: Houghton Mifflin, 1965. (Anasazi; intermediate)

————. *An Indian Boy Before the White Man Came*. Los Angeles: Ward Ritchie Press, 1966. (California; intermediate)

Bulla, Clyde Robert. *Eagle Feather*. New York: Thomas Y. Crowell, 1963. (Navajo; intermediate)

*————. *Indian Hill*. New York: Thomas Y. Crowell, 1963. (Navajo; intermediate)

————. *Pocahontas and the Strangers*. New York: T.Y. Crowell, 1971. (intermediate)

*Bulla, Clyde R., and Michael Syson. *Conquista!* New York: T. Y. Crowell, 1978. (primary)

Carlson, Vada, and Gary Witherspoon. *Black Mountain Boy*. Chinle, Ariz.: Rough Rock Demonstration School, Navajo Curriculum Center, 1974. (Navajo; intermediate)

*Chandler, Edna Walker. *Charley Brave*. Chicago: Albert Whitman, 1962. (Sioux; intermediate)

Christense, Cardell Dano. *Buffalo Kill*. New York: Archway, n.d. (Blackfoot; intermediate)

*Clark, Ann Nolan. *Brave Against the Enemy*. Haskell Institute: U.S. Indian Service Press, 1944. (Sioux; intermediate)

————. *The Desert People*. New York: Viking Press, 1962. (Papago; primary)

————. *In My Mother's House*. New York: Viking Press, 1972. (Pueblo; intermediate)

————. *Little Boy of Three Names*. Haskell: Bureau of Indian Affairs, Haskell Press, 1959. (Pueblo; intermediate)

————. *Little Navajo Bluebird*. New York: Viking Press, 1943. (Navajo; intermediate)

—. *Little Navajo Herder.* Haskell: U.S. Indian Service Press, 1951. (Navajo; intermediate)

—. *Summer Is for Growing.* New York: Farrar, Straus & Giroux, 1968. (Southwest; intermediate)

*—. *Sun Journey.* Washington, D.C.: Government Printing Office, 1945. (Zuni; intermediate)

*Clymer, Eleanor. *The Spider, the Cave, and the Pottery Bowl.* New York: Atheneum, 1971. (Hopi; intermediate)

Cossi, Olga. *Fire Mate.* Independence, Mo.: Independence Press, 1977.

*DeHuff, Elizabeth. *Blue Wings Flying.* Reading, Mass.: Addison-Wesley, 1977. (primary)

Dodge, Carol. *Kine-U.* Washington, D.C.: U.S. Office of Education, 1971. (Menominee; primary)

*Dodge, Nanabah Chee. *Morning Arrow.* New York: Lothrop, 1975. (Navajo; primary)

Embree, Margaret. *Shadi.* New York: Holiday House, 1971. (upper)

*Fall, Thomas. *Ordeal of Running Standing.* New York: Bantam, 1971. (Kiowa; upper)

Feague, Mildred H. *The Little Indian and the Angel.* Chicago: Children's Press, 1970. (Navajo; primary)

*Friskey, Margaret. *Indian Two Feet and His Eagle Feather.* Chicago: Children's Press, 1967. (primary)

—. *Indian Two Feet and His Horse.* Chicago: Children's Press, 1959. (Plains; primary)

*—. *Indian Two Feet and the Grizzly Bear.* Chicago: Children's Press, 1974. (primary)

George, Jean Craighead. *Julie of the Wolves.* New York: Harper & Row, 1972. (Eskimo; intermediate)

*Goble, Paul. *The Girl Who Loved Wild Horses.* New York: Bradbury Press, 1978. (primary)

*Goble, Paul, and Dorothy Goble. *Lone Bull's Horse Raid.* New York: Bradbury Press, 1973. (Ogalala Sioux; intermediate)

Hale, Janet Campbell. *The Owl's Song.* New York: Avon Books, 1976. (Couer d'Alene; upper)

*Harris, Christie. *Forbidden Frontier.* New York: Atheneum, 1968. (Haida)

—. *Raven's Cry.* New York: Atheneum, 1966. (Haida; upper)

Harris, Marilyn. *Hatter Fox.* New York: Random House, 1973. (Navajo; upper)

*Harvey, James O. *Beyond the Gorge of Shadows.* New York: Lothrup, Lee & Shepard, 1965. (Anasazi; intermediate)

Hoffine, Lyla. *The Eagle Feather Prize.* New York: David McKay, 1962. (Sioux; upper)

*—. *Jennie's Mandan Bowl.* New York: Longman, Green, 1960. (Mandan; intermediate)

Holling, Clancy. *The Book of Indians.* New York: Platt & Munk, 1962. (mixed; intermediate)

*Hood, Flora. *Pink Puppy.* New York: G. P. Putnam's Sons, 1966. (Cherokee; primary)

*—. *Something for the Medicine Man.* Chicago: Melmont Publishers, 1962. (Cherokee; intermediate)

James, Harry C. *Ovada: An Indian Boy of the Grand Canyon.* Los Angeles: Ward Ritchie Press, 1969. (Havasupi; intermediate)

Katz, Jane B., ed. *Let Me Be a Free Man: A Documentary of Indian Resistance.* Minneapolis: Lerner, 1975. (leadership; upper)

Kendall, Lace (A. Stoutenburg). *The Mud Ponies.* New York: Coward-McCann, 1963. (Pawnee; intermediate)

LaFarge, Oliver. *Cochise of Arizona.* New York: E. P. Dutton, 1953. (Apache; intermediate)

Lampman, Evelyn Sibley. *Cayuse Courage.* New York: Harcourt Brace Jovanovich, 1970. (Cayuse; upper)

*Lauritzen, Jonreed. *The Ordeal of the Young Hunter.* Boston: Little, Brown, 1954. (Navajo; upper)

Leech, Joey, and Zane Spencer. *Bright Fawn and Me.* New York: Harper & Row, 1979. (primary)

Marriott, Alice. *Indian Annie: Kiowa Captive.* New York: David McKay, 1965. (Kiowa/Choctaw; intermediate)

Meigs, Cornelia. *The Willow Whistle.* New York: Macmillan, 1931. (Sioux; upper)

Miles, Miska. *Annie and the Old One.* Boston: Little, Brown, 1971. (Navajo; primary)

*Momaday, Natachee Scott. *Owl in the Cedar Tree.* Flagstaff, Ariz.: Northland Press, 1975. (Navajo; primary)

*———. *A Visit to Grandmother.* Gallup, N.M.: McKinley County Public Schools, 1975.

Moon, Grace. *One Little Indian.* Rev. ed. Chicago: Albert Whitman, 1967. (Navajo; intermediate)

*Mulcahy, Lucille. *Fire on Big Lonesome.* Chicago: Elk Grove Press, 1967. (Zuni; intermediate)

Nelson, Mary Carroll. *Michael Naranjo: The Story of an American Indian.* Minneapolis: Dillon Press, 1975. (Pueblo; upper)

O'Dell, Scott. *Island of the Blue Dolphins.* Boston: Houghton Mifflin, 1960. (California; upper)

*———. *Sing Down the Moon.* Boston: Houghton Mifflin, 1970. (Navajo; upper)

*———. *Zia.* Boston: Houghton Mifflin, 1976. (California; upper)

Penny, Grace J. *Moki.* New York: Avon, 1973. (Cheyenne; intermediate)

Randall, Janet. *The Buffalo Box.* New York: David McKay, 1969. (Nez Percé; intermediate)

*Redhouse, Gloria. *A Present for Bahe.* Blanding, Utah: Blanding Indian Education Center, 1971.

Reit, Seymour. *Child of the Navajos.* New York: Dodd, Mead, 1971. (Navajo; primary/intermediate)

*Robinson, Marileta. *Mr. Goat's Good Bad Idea.* New York: Crowell, 1979. (Navajo)

*Rockwood, Joyce. *Long Man's Song.* New York: Holt, Rinehart and Winston, 1975. (Cherokee; upper)

Schweitzer, Byrd Bayler. *One Small Blue Bead.* New York: Macmillan, 1965. (Southwest; primary)

Searcy, Margaret. *Ikwa of the Temple Mounds.* Montgomery: University of Alabama Press, 1974. (Prehistoric; primary)

Selden, Alice, and Carol Dodge. *One Menominee Boy.* Washington, D.C.: U.S. Office of Education, 1971. (Menominee; intermediate)

Smucker, Barbara C. *Wigwam in the City.* New York: E. P. Dutton, 1966. (Chippewa, intermediate)

*Sneve, Virginia Driving Hawk. *Chichi Hoohoo Bogyman.* New York: Holiday House, 1975. (intermediate)

*———. *High Elk's Treasure.* New York: Holiday House, 1972. (intermediate)

*———. *Jimmy Yellowhawk.* New York: Holiday House, 1972. (Sioux; intermediate)

*Sobol, Rose. *Woman Chief.* New York: Dial Press, 1976. (Crow; intermediate)

*Steiner, Stan. *The Last Horse.* New York: Macmillan, 1961. (Navajo; intermediate)

Supree, Burton, and Ann Rose. *Bear's Heart: Scenes from the Life of a Cheyenne Artist of One Hundred Years Ago with Pictures by Himself.* Philadelphia: Lippincott, 1977. (Plains; upper)

Thompson, Eileen. *The Blue Stone Mystery.* New York: Abelard-Schuman, 1963. (Pueblo; intermediate)

Waltrip, Lela, and Rufus Waltrip. *Quiet Boy.* New York: David McKay, 1961. (Navajo; intermediate)

Warren, Mary P. *Walk in My Moccasins.* Philadelphia: Westminster Press, 1966. (Sioux; intermediate)

Witter, Evelyn. *Clawfoot.* Minneapolis: Lerner Publications, 1976. (Sioux; primary)

*Especially recommended for classroom use.

Appendix 2

The Informal Reading Inventory

Every teacher should know how to administer and interpret the informal reading inventory. Early efforts at both giving and interpreting the informal reading inventory should probably be done with the help of someone skilled in its use. There are also excellent publications and journal articles that will offer further insights.

Even though teachers may know how to give the informal reading inventory and use the results, they are often concerned about what test to use. Some teachers turn to commercial inventories; others use those provided by basal series. Neither type is appropriate for most readers, since they are prepared for readers in general. The better inventories are prepared by teachers for their own students. One way to find suitable passages is to search the writings of the children. The passages selected can be edited (only as much as absolutely necessary), questions can be developed, and all passages can be graded and duplicated. The result is a useful, appropriate informal reading inventory. The teacher knows that the passages are relevant because they were created by the children. The children will be pleased to see their writings used for such an important purpose.

This appendix contains an informal reading inventory based on children's writing. The stories in this inventory come from the efforts of two groups of Indian children and their teachers, and are relevant for these groups. They may or may not be suitable for other readers. They serve as an example of what one or more teachers and a group of children can do to provide a suitable reading assessment.

If this assessment were to be used with children, it would be important to prepare the preprimer, primer, first reader, and second reader levels on the primary typewriter for ease of reading by young children. The other levels could be prepared on a regular typewriter. If teachers prepare informal reading inventories from their own sources, they should also have the lower-level passages prepared in large print for the sake of young readers.

Preprimer Level (oral)

Nelda's Pets

19 words
20 syllables
4 sentences

Motivating statement: This is a story about a child and some pets. Let's find out who the child is and what pets she has.

Nelda has a cat and a dog.
The dog is big.
The cat is big.
They run and jump.

Questions

1. Who was the child in the story? (Nelda)
2. What pets did she have? (cat, dog)
3. Show me how big a big dog might be. (no one correct response)
4. What did the two pets do? (run, jump)

Summary

Word Recognition

No. Miscues _____

% Accuracy _____

Level _____

Comprehension

No. Errors _____

% Accuracy _____

Level _____

Overall Level _____

(Independent; Instructional; Frustration)

Preprimer Level (silent)

The Dogs

23 words
24 syllables
5 sentences

Motivating statement: This is a story about some dogs. Let's find out what they are like.

Here are the dogs.
The dogs are black and white.
One dog is big.
One dog is little.
The dogs can run fast.

Questions

1. How many dogs were in the story? (two)
2. What did the dogs do? (run fast)
3. If you drew a picture of these dogs, what crayons would you need to color the dogs' pictures? (black, white)
4. What is another word you could use to tell about a dog being small? (little)

Summary

Comprehension

    No. Errors _____

    % Accuracy _____

    Level _____

    (Independent; Instructional; Frustration)

Primer Level (oral)

The Rodeo

23 words
27 syllables
 3 sentences

Motivating statement: Going to a rodeo is fun. Let's read about some children who went to the rodeo.

Pat and Jim ran to the rodeo.
Jim is crying because he fell off the horse.
Pat looked at Dad ride the bull.

Questions

1. Who rode the bull? (Dad)
2. Why did Jim cry? (fell off horse)
3. In the story, how many children went to the rodeo? (two)
4. What word did you read that told you the two boys were in a hurry to get to the rodeo? (ran)

Summary

Word Recognition

    No. Miscues _____

    % Accuracy _____

    Level _____

Comprehension

    No. Errors _____

    % Accuracy _____

    Level _____

Overall Level _____

    (Independent; Instructional; Frustration)

Primer Level (silent)

On the Bus

Motivating statement: This is a story about two friends. Let's find out what they are doing.

Pat's friend is Kay.
Pat ran to the bus.
Kay is in the bus.
They are sitting and looking at something.
It is a house.

25 words
28 syllables
5 sentences

Questions

1. Who was on the bus first? (Kay)
2. Where were the girls when they looked at something? (on the bus)
3. What did the girls see out of the bus window? (a house)
4. How do we know Pat was in a hurry to get to the bus? (she ran)

Summary

Comprehension

No. Errors ———————————————

% Accuracy ———————————————

Level ———————————————

(Independent; Instructional; Frustration)

First Reader Level (oral)

Motivating statement: This is a story about the space shuttle. Watching the space shuttle on TV is exciting. I wonder how the men on it felt?

The Space Shuttle

The space shuttle went up last Monday.
Two men went up in it.
They looked around the world.
They worked, ate food, and slept.
They stayed in space eight days.
The space shuttle came down this morning at 9:00 A.M.
I want to go up in space.

47 words
53 syllables
7 sentences

Questions

1. When did the writer say the space shuttle went up? (last Monday)
2. Who went up in the space shuttle? (two men)
3. What did the men do while they were in space? (worked, ate, slept)
4. How does the writer tell you he or she thinks the shuttle travels very fast? (in eight days they looked around the world)

Summary

Word Recognition

No. Miscues ———————————————

% Accuracy ———————————————

Level ———————————————

Comprehension

No. Errors ———————————————

% Accuracy ———————————————

Level ———————————————

Overall Level ———————————————

(Independent; Instructional; Frustration)

First Reader Level (silent)

Working and Playing

Motivating statement: This is the story about what one child's family does in the springtime. Let's read to see what they do.

I like the green grass and green trees.
I like birds and the pretty sun.
I like to plant corn and wheat.
We all go back up the mountain.
We herd sheep, and we will plant at the corn field.
We can see your horses go down to the water well.
We can play in the green grass and ride our horses.

62 words
66 syllables
7 sentences

Questions

1. The child said two things become green in the spring. What were they? (grass, trees)
2. What did they plant? (corn, wheat)
3. Why do you think the writer liked spring? (answers will vary, but should fit story)
4. Did all the horses in the story belong to the family of the child telling the story? (No) Why not? (referred to some as "your horses")

Summary
Comprehension
No. Errors _____
% Accuracy _____
Level _____
(Independent; Instructional; Frustration)

Second Reader Level (oral)

Our Beautiful Car

Motivating statement: This is a story about a family's car. You can decide if it is a good car.

Our beautiful car is red and gold. It is a small 1982 pickup. It is a Dodge Ram and it runs fast. My mother drives it to town and everywhere else she wants to go. We have lots of roads that get very muddy when it rains. And when it is winter, the roads are muddy much of the time. The pickup needs to be washed off and cleaned up a lot of the time.

Our car needs gas, oil, and water in order to run. You have to check on the oil, the gas, and the water before you drive it. Sometimes I put the gas in the gas tank myself and I put water in the radiator.

Our car is for traveling to wherever you want to go. People drive it and it helps them do their work. It is also great for racing on the road or on the highway.

Questions

1. What kind of car did the child write about? (1982 Dodge Ram pickup)
2. Tell what you do to "check the oil and gas." (answers will vary)
3. Who seems to drive this car a lot? (mom)
4. What did the writer say the car needed to run on? (gas, oil, water)

152 words
182 syllables
13 sentences

Summary

Word Recognition

No. Miscues _____

% Accuracy _____

Level _____

Comprehension

No. Errors _____

% Accuracy _____

Level _____

Overall Level _____

(Independent; Instructional; Frustration)

**Second Reader
Level (silent)**

What I Do
Each Day

Motivating statement: This is a story about a child's day. As you read, you will be able to compare it with your own day.

I get up early each school day so I can catch the school bus at 8:30. First, when I get to school I write in my journal. Then I go to breakfast.

With my teacher, we have reading and Navajo language first. In reading I work in level 17 in our reading series. Then we have mathematics. Before lunch we have reading again. After lunch I start my work again. Then there is recess and P.E. After that I eat a snack.

Then I go home. At home I clean the house. Then my parents come home from work. Together, we make a good dinner. Afterwards, I wash the dishes. Then I do my homework. When I finish my homework, I watch TV until ten o'clock when I go to bed.

131 words
171 syllables
16 sentences

Questions

1. How do we know this child lives far from school? (must ride a bus)
2. When does the child have P.E.? (after noon)
3. What chores does the child do at home? (clean house, cook, wash dishes)
4. Do you have any classes or subjects in school that this child does not have? What are they?
   (answers will vary, but should fit story)

Summary

Comprehension

    No. Errors _____

    % Accuracy _____

    Level _____

    (Independent; Instructional; Frustration)

Third Reader Level (oral)

Problems with Friends

198 words
226 syllables
15 sentences

Motivating statement: Have your friends ever been angry with you? This story is about someone who had such a problem.

One day at school, when I was trying to talk with my friends, they wouldn't talk back to me. I even tried to be nice to them, but it didn't work. Then, later, when I was going to eat my lunch, I saw all my friends and went toward them. Just when I was going to sit down by them, they moved away and sat somewhere else. So I had to eat alone. After school when I was walking home, they came up to me and said that I had told a lie about them. I tried to tell them that I hadn't. They didn't believe me. While we were standing there, I saw a girl who looked scared. I told her to come over. She did, and I said that she was the one who had told a lie about them. She didn't say anything so I knew she was the one who told the lie. Then I just walked on to the dormitory where I live. The next morning when I was walking to class, my friends called to me and said that they were sorry. So I was glad to go walking around with them.

Questions

1. What happened when the child went to school? (friends wouldn't speak to the child)
2. Who was the person who told the lie? (girl)
3. What does "believe" mean in the sentence "they didn't believe me"? (trust)
4. Why did the writer think the girl had told a lie? (she acted scared)
5. What would you have done if your friends wouldn't talk to you? (answers will vary)

Summary

Word Recognition

    No. Miscues _____

    % Accuracy _____

    Level _____

Comprehension

    No. Errors _____

    % Accuracy _____

    Level _____

Overall Level _____

    (Independent; Instructional; Frustration)

**Third Reader
Level (silent)**

Motivating statement: This is a story about a very special pet. Let's read to see what kind of pet it was and why it was very special.

My Dog, Snappy

My dog is a very special friend. Her name is Snappy. I named her that because Snappy is an unusual name in our neighborhood. Snappy has been with us for more than five years now. She is black and has fuzzy hair that covers her eyes.

Now, she has only one eye to see with. She lost her right eye when my aunt ran into her with a car. My aunt didn't mean to hurt Snappy. It is just that Snappy is too friendly. She was so happy to see my aunt coming that she got in the way of the car. My aunt felt just sick over hurting Snappy. We took the dog to an animal hospital and carried along the eye that she had lost. The veterinarian thought he could save Snappy's eye, but he found out it couldn't be done.

My sister and I felt sad because Snappy lost one eye. But even though Snappy has only one eye, she is still as happy as she can be. She plays with us and watches our home while we are at school. Snappy is my very special friend.

190 words
235 syllables
17 sentences

Questions
1. Who is Snappy? (a dog)
2. How did Snappy lose her eye? (was run into by aunt of writer)
3. What do we mean when we say "neighborhood?" (answers will vary)
4. What did the animal doctor try to do? (replace the eye)
5. What does Snappy do for the family? (plays with them and watches house)

Summary
Comprehension
No. Errors _____

% Accuracy _____

Level _____

(Independent; Instructional; Frustration)

**Fourth Reader
Level (oral)**

Motivating statement: This is a story about a mother who weaves rugs. The writer is telling about watching her.

Weaving a Rug

When my mother weaves a Navajo rug, I like to watch her. But I don't want her to know that I am watching her while she is working. She says that she makes more mistakes in making design counts when someone is watching her. I have heard her counting the strings before she puts the yarn through. She makes designs in the rugs. Sometimes I wonder how many numbers she has counted when she finishes a rug. My mother thinks of many different patterns for a Navajo rug.

Questions

1. What is a design? (answers will vary)
2. Why do you think it bothers the mother that someone watches her as she weaves? (makes her nervous; makes more mistakes)
3. What does *design count* mean? (answers will vary)
4. What did the writer sometimes wonder about while watching? (how many numbers the mother counted)

Summary

Word Recognition

No. Miscues _____

% Accuracy _____

Level _____

Comprehension

No. Errors _____

% Accuracy _____

Level _____

Overall Level _____

(Independent; Instructional; Frustration)

Fourth Reader Level (silent)

Motivating statement: This is a story about herding sheep in the summer. Let's find out what happened.

Herding Sheep for Grandmother

Last summer my dog and I went to my grandmother's house to stay with her for about a week. While we were there, I herded sheep for my grandmother. First, I let the sheep out of the corral in the morning. We herded them to the forest, and in the evening about 4 o'clock we herded them back to my grandmother's house. When I counted the sheep, there were five sheep missing. I told my dog to go find them. He left, and in a few minutes I heard the dog barking. I ran outside, and there he was chasing the five sheep back. It is easy to like a dog who can do that. It was fun to herd the sheep.

Questions

1. What did the writer do while he stayed at his grandmother's house? (herded sheep)
2. Who found the sheep? (the dog)
3. What kinds of things would you see in a forest? (answers will vary; should include trees, various plants, animals)
4. Why do you think the boy likes his dog? (answers should relate to the dog's ability to herd sheep)

Summary
Comprehension
   No. Errors _____

   % Accuracy _____

   Level _____

   (Independent; Instructional; Frustration)

Fifth Reader Level (oral)

Motivating statement: Has anyone in your family ever hunted a deer? This is a story about a boy and his family and what they did with their deer.

Deer Hunting

My two brothers, my father and I went hunting. We hunted in the southern part of the Zuni Reservation. I saw two huge deer. My brother shot one, and my father shot the other one.

   We took the deer home to skin them, cut their bodies open and removed the stomach and liver. We ate the liver with onions for dinner. When we finished eating, we went back to cut off the hoofs of the deer so they could be used for the dancer's rattles. We cut the meat into thin, flat pieces and hung it on a long wire to dry. When the meat was completely dry, we stored it to eat later. The remaining meat we gave to our neighbors.

122 words
154 syllables
10 sentences

Questions
   1. Where did the men find the deer? (southern Zuni)
   2. Which part of the deer did they eat first? (liver)
   3. What were the deer hooves used for? (dancer's rattles)
   4. What did they do with the flat pieces of meat? (hung on a wire to dry)
   5. What does the word *remaining* mean? (left over)

Summary
Word Recognition
   No. Miscues _____

   % Accuracy _____

   Level _____

Comprehension
   No. Errors _____

   % Accuracy _____

   Level _____

Overall Level _____
   (Independent; Instructional; Frustration)

Fifth Reader Level (silent)

Motivating statement: How do you spend your summer vacation? This is a story about a girl who spent her vacation with her grandmother.

Living with Grandmother

Last summer I was left alone with my eighty-five-year-old grandmother. Every day was a day of hard work for me. I would get up early in the morning to let the sheep out of the gate and water the flowers that were blooming and our tall green corn. The corn was almost ripe to harvest but it needed some more water. And this was what I did every morning. There was no problem to it when Mom and Dad left to go back to town. Every day was lonely for me, and Grandma would be cleaning the house while I was out chopping wood so we could cook our chili stew.

One evening when it was almost sundown, I was walking through the woods. I heard every single noise of the birds singing in the treetops. This made my day come alive, and I wasn't lonely at all. Then I put the sheep back in the corral and fastened the gate. The sun was finally going down when I went back to the house. I had been gone almost all day, and Grandmother was sewing her new black velvet blouse she got at the trading post. She asked me if I was hungry, and I told her I was starving. She laughed at my reply, and finally I sat down and stuffed myself. Oh, how good that mutton stew was! I never wanted to get through eating.

239 words
296 syllables
16 sentences

Questions

1. Name two chores that the girl did every morning. (watered flowers and tall corn)
2. Why did the girl chop wood? (for fire for chili stew)
3. What was the grandmother doing when the girl got home? (making a velvet blouse)
4. What does velvet mean? (type of fabric)
5. Did the girl like mutton stew? (yes) How do you know? (said it was good; never wanted to get through eating)

Summary
Comprehension

No. Errors _____

% Accuracy _____

Level _____

(Independent; Instructional; Frustration)

Sixth Reader Level (oral)

Motivating statement: This story was written by someone who might like to be a teacher someday. Let's read to find out what the writer thinks a teacher does.

If I Were a Teacher

If I were a teacher at Tohatchi Boarding School, I would like to teach music and art classes and maybe piano, too. But if I couldn't teach music, art, and piano, I would like to teach the eighth grade. I would require students to stay in the classroom unless it was time for classes to change or break time. But even when break time came, I'd ask them to keep the noise down so they wouldn't disturb the other classes. I would try to make them learn lots of things. I would allow them to go outside for ten minutes to get fresh air. And about their classwork, I would want all children to finish their lessons by the end of the class hour. And about their homework, I would expect them to finish it by the next day and turn it in. But on Fridays, they could have free time or watch movies.

155 words
191 syllables
9 sentences

Questions

1. If the writer couldn't teach art or music, what grade did the person want to teach? (eighth grade)
2. Would you want to be in that person's classroom? (yes, no) Why? (answers will vary, but should represent the facts in the story)
3. Why would students be told to *keep the noise down?* (so they would not disturb others)
4. In what ways would Fridays be different? (free time and movies all day)
5. What does the word *expect* mean? (to think something is going to happen)

Summary

Word Recognition

No. Miscues _____

% Accuracy _____

Level _____

Comprehension

No. Errors _____

% Accuracy _____

Level _____

Overall Level _____

(Independent; Instructional; Frustration)

Sixth Reader Level (silent)

Motivating statement: Many children live away from home in dorms during the school year. This story was written by someone living in a dorm.

Dormitory Life

I will tell you about living in my dormitory. These days dormitory living is sometimes boring. In much of your free time, all you have to do is sit and watch television or play games. When you are staying at school over the weekend, it is especially tiresome when all your friends go home. All I can think of is running away or calling my parents and asking them to check me out. On weekdays you can always have fun being with your friends and doing your work. Friends are very special to each other. Having lots of friends can be very special, and all you think of is being together all year.

My dormitory is large, and it is well-equipped to meet our needs. But I really dislike some of the dormitory aides who can become very angry with us girls. They can always take things away from you that don't belong to them, but then you have to work for them in order to get your own things back. Naturally, I am very unhappy when I have to do that.

Questions

1. How did the writer say it often felt to stay in the dorm? (boring)
2. Who gets mad at the girls? (aides)
3. Compare how you feel about friends with how the writer felt about her friends. (answers will vary, but should be consistent with the story)
4. Do you feel the aides acted correctly when a girl would do something that angered them? (yes, no) Why? (answers will vary, but should be consistent with the story)
5. What is meant by a *special* friend? (answers will vary, but should suggest best friend or closest or oldest friend)

Summary
Comprehension

No. Errors _____

% Accuracy _____

Level _____

(Independent; Instructional; Frustration)

Seventh Reader Level (oral)

Autumn in Zuni

Motivating statement: This is a story about what happens in Zuni as fall comes.

Autumn has come to the village of the Zuni people. The first sign of cold has hit the corn fields, and the leaves on the trees are turning into pretty colors. A sudden change of color of the landscape, and the animals begin to fatten up for the cold days ahead. The wool on the sheep is beginning to thicken.

The apples and all the other delicious fruits are beginning to ripen. The days are getting shorter, and the nights longer. The feeling of autumn is in the air, cold nights and frosty early mornings.

Deer hunting time will soon be here. The deer are fat this year, because of an abundant supply of food this past summer. Much rain brought a lot of food, as well as floods.

Snow will come when the leaves have all blown away and the trees stand bare. Yes, autumn is here, and winter is right around the corner. Snow will come!

Questions

1. What changes does the writer say take place in fall? (leaves turn color; animals fatten up; wool on sheep thickens; fruit ripens; days get shorter and nights longer; cooler air)
2. What does the writer say caused the deer to be fat? (abundant food supply)
3. Why do you think the writer is especially concerned with the deer being fat? (used for food)
4. What will come when the trees stand bare? (snow)
5. What things must be part of the Zuni landscape, based on the writer's story? (village, animals, fruit trees, trees, corn fields, sheep, deer)

Summary

Word Recognition

No. Miscues _____

% Accuracy _____

Level _____

Comprehension

No. Errors _____

% Accuracy _____

Level _____

Overall Level _____

(Independent; Instructional; Frustration)

Seventh Reader Level (silent)

Shalako

Motivating statement: Shalako is a very important time of year at Zuni. This is one person's experiences about Shalako one year.

Last year we had Shalako at our house. We started to build the Shalako house around June or July. It took a lot of money and manpower to build the house. I usually came home on weekends to help, since I was working in the Forest Service. Sometimes a lot of men would come, and sometimes no one would come to help. When school began in September, I helped the men in the afternoon. Finally, two days before the Shalako arrived, the house was finished.

One day before they came, I butchered a lot of sheep that needed to be stewed in order to feed the people and the Shalako. I was really tired that night after I butchered those sheep.

Then the Shalako came to the house and danced all night. I went to sleep. The next afternoon I woke up. I didn't even see the Shalako leave.

Well, this year they are coming to another house to bless it. Every year they come to different houses, and sometimes there will be two Shalakos in one house.

180 words
236 syllables
15 sentences

Questions

1. When did the building of the Shalako house begin? (June or July)
2. What did it take to build it? (money/manpower)
3. Why couldn't the author spend all his time helping build the house? (in summer worked for the Forest Service; in fall went to school)
4. What else needed to be done before the Shalako arrived? (butcher and prepare sheep)
5. When the Shalako came, how do we know the boy was tired? (slept until afternoon; did not see the Shalako leave)

Summary

Comprehension

    No. Errors _____

    % Accuracy _____

    Level _____

    (Independent; Instructional; Frustration)

High School Level (oral)

Motivating statement: This is a story about helicopters and the excitement people feel when seeing them for the first time at close range. Read the story to see what the purpose of the helicopters was.

Operation Mudlift

Though it appeared as if they were coming from nowhere, the helicopters descended from the sky. Two enormous pairs of propellers rotated and shook the dry earth and made tumbleweeds turn. We could hear the sound a great distance away.

Spectators watched with their hair and hats flying in the wind. In the early twilight, the dust fiercely swept over the highway and tumbleweeds.

Onlookers waited curiously to see the men in green emerge from the huge helicopters. They came out brave and strong and ready. They were Anglo.

The rotors began to turn like a silent river until it comes to a lake. The silence was interrupted by a truck backing up to each helicopter. The growing crowd was gathering and talking.

Tirelessly, volunteers put hay into the helicopters. The people knew they must help, because other people needed their help to survive.

141 words
212 syllables
13 sentences

Questions

1. What was stirring up the dust and tumbleweeds? (turning of helicopter rotors)
2. Who were the *men in green?* (men in helicopters)
3. At what time of day was the action taking place? (twilight)
4. Why had the helicopters come? (to take hay and perhaps other supplies to people needing them)

Summary

Word Recognition

    No. Miscues _____

    % Accuracy _____

    Level _____

Comprehension

    No. Errors _____

    % Accuracy _____

    Level _____

Overall Level _____

    (Independent; Instructional; Frustration)

High School Level (silent)

Operation Mudlift, continued

Motivating statement: This passage continues the story of the helicopters and the excitement they created.

Reporters running around with their cameras; students browsing here and there; kids anxiously hoping to go on the helicopters; crowds buzzing with anticipation; and automobiles scattered around like carts in a shopping center parking lot are just a few events at the airlift.

Now, at last, they are ready to take off. The helicopters begin to lift themselves with a sound that is so loud that the clouds seem like they are being driven away. Dust is everywhere, and the tumbleweeds are dancing. Their rhythm rocks the earth; suddenly they take off like giant birds. People linger and follow them with their eyes until they disappear into the darkening mountain pass.

Far out on the Reservation, stranded families look out anxiously from their windows, like little rabbits from their dens. The glittering snow and deep mud alternately cover the earth.

The livestock are out in the cold and the mud, with frost biting their coats. Cold and hungry, they stand waiting for a taste of green hay.

Stranded families are greeted by the helicopter volunteers who give them food, hay, coal, and medical supplies and attention. After getting their supplies, the families are relieved and say good-bye with friendly smiles.

200 words
299 syllables
12 sentences

Questions

1. Why were the people so excited? (the helicopters being there; the emergency; all the activity)
2. How did the land and sky look as the helicopters took off? (clouds moving; dust and tumbleweeds moving)
3. What does *browse* mean in the first sentence of the passage? (look around)
4. Why were the helicopters needed? (to help stranded families)
5. Compare a stranded family's feelings before and after the helicopter left. (before—anxious; after—thankful and relieved)

Summary
Comprehension

No. Errors _____

% Accuracy _____

Level _____

(Independent; Instructional; Frustration)

Bibliography

Abrahams, Roger D., and Rudolph C. Troike. *Language and Cultural Diversity in American Education.* Englewood Cliffs, N.J.: Prentice-Hall, 1972.

Alexander, J. Estill, ed. *Teaching Reading.* Boston: Little, Brown, 1979.

Aukerman, Robert C. *Approaches to Beginning Reading.* New York: Wiley, 1971.

————. *Basal Reader Approach to Reading.* New York: Wiley, 1981.

Aukerman, Robert C., and Louise Aukerman. *How Do I Teach Reading?* New York: Wiley, 1981.

Aulls, Mark W. *Developing Readers in Today's Elementary School.* Boston: Allyn & Bacon, 1982.

Baratz, Joan C., and Roger W. Shuy. *Teaching Black Children to Read.* Washington, D.C.: Institute for Applied Linguistics, 1969.

Bond, Guy L., Miles A. Tinker, and Barbara Wasson. *Reading Difficulties: Their Diagnosis and Correction.* 4th ed. Englewood Cliffs, N.J.: Prentice-Hall, 1979.

Bowren, Fay F., and Miles V. Zintz. *Teaching Reading in Adult Basic Education.* Dubuque, Iowa: Wm. C. Brown, 1977.

Brunner, Joseph F., and John J. Campbell. *Participating in Secondary Reading: A Practical Approach.* Englewood Cliffs, N.J.: Prentice-Hall, 1978.

Burmeister, Lou. *Reading Strategies for Secondary School Teachers.* 2d ed. Reading, Mass.: Addison-Wesley, 1978.

————. *Words: From Print to Meaning: Classroom Activities for Building Sight Vocabulary, for Using Context Clues, Morphology and Phonics.* Reading, Mass.: Addison-Wesley, 1975.

Burns, Paul C., and Betty D. Roe. *Teaching Reading in Today's Elementary Schools.* 2d ed. Chicago: Rand McNally, 1980.

Burron, Arnold, and Amos Claybaugh. *Basic Concepts in Reading Instruction: A Programmed Approach.* 2d ed. Columbus: Charles E. Merrill, 1977.

Bush, Clifford L., and Mildred H. Huebner. *Strategies for Reading in the Elementary School.* 2d ed. New York: Macmillan, 1979.

Butler, Dorothy, and Marie Clay. *Reading Begins at Home.* Auckland, New Zealand: Heinemann, 1979.

Cazden, Courtney B., Vera John, and Dell Hymes, eds. *Functions of Language in the Classroom.* New York: Teachers College Press, 1972.

Clay, Marie. *Reading: The Patterning of Complex Behaviour*. London: Heinemann, 1973.

Clinard, Linda. *The Reading Triangle*. Farmington Hills, Mich.: Focus, 1981.

Coody, Betty, and David Nelson. *Teaching Elementary Language Arts: A Literature Approach*. Belmont, Calif.: Wadsworth, 1982.

Cunningham, Patricia, Sharon V. Arthur, and James W. Cunningham. *Classroom Reading Instruction, K–5, Alternative Approaches*. Lexington, Mass.: D.C. Heath, 1977.

Dallman, Martha, et al. *The Teaching of Reading*. 6th ed. New York: Holt, Rinehart and Winston, 1982.

Dechant, Emerald V. *Improving the Teaching of Reading*, 3d ed. Englewood Cliffs, N.J.: Prentice-Hall, 1982.

DeStefano, Johanna. *Language, the Learner, and the School*. New York: Wiley, 1978.

Dillner, Martha H., and Joanne P. Olson. *Personalized Reading Instruction in Middle, Junior and Senior High Schools*. 2d ed. New York: Macmillan, 1982.

Downing, John. *Reading and Reasoning*. New York: Springer-Verlag, 1979.

———. *The Initial Teaching Alphabet Explained and Illustrated*. New York: Macmillan, 1964.

Drew, Clifford J., Michael L. Hardman, and Harry P. Bluhm, eds. *Mental Retardation: Social and Educational Perspectives*. St. Louis: C.V. Mosby, 1977.

Duffy, Gerald, and George B. Sherman. *Systematic Reading Instruction*. 2d ed. New York: Harper & Row, 1977.

Durkin, Dolores. *Teaching Them to Read*. 3d ed. Boston: Allyn & Bacon, 1978.

———. *Strategies for Identifying Words: A Workbook for Teachers and Those Preparing to Teach*. 2d ed. Boston: Allyn & Bacon, 1980.

Ekwall, Eldon. *Diagnosis and Remediation of the Disabled Reader*. Boston: Allyn & Bacon, 1976.

———. *Locating and Correcting Reading Difficulties*. 3d ed. Columbus: Charles E. Merrill, 1981.

Fader, Daniel. *The New Hooked on Books*. New York: Berkley Books, 1976.

Fernald, Grace. *Remedial Techniques in Basic School Subjects*. New York: McGraw-Hill, 1971.

Flood, James E., and Diane Lapp. *Language/Reading Instruction for the Young Child*. New York: Macmillan, 1981.

Fry, Edward. *Elementary Reading Instruction*. New York: McGraw-Hill, 1977.

Furth, Hans G. *Piaget for Teachers*. Englewood Cliffs, N.J.: Prentice-Hall, 1970.

Gallant, Ruth. *Handbook in Corrective Reading*. 2d ed. Columbus: Charles E. Merrill, 1978.

Gearheart, B. R. *Learning Disabilities: Educational Strategies*. 3d ed. St. Louis: C.V. Mosby, 1981.

Graves, Donald H. *Writing: Teachers and Children at Work*. Exeter, N.H.: Heinemann, 1982.

Gray, W. S. *On Their Own in Reading*. 2d ed. Chicago: Scott, Foresman, 1960.

Guszak, Frank J. *Diagnostic Reading Instruction in the Elementary School*. 2d ed. New York: Harper & Row, 1978.

Hafner, Lawrence E. *Developmental Reading in Middle and Secondary Schools: Foundations, Strategies, and Skills for Teaching*. New York: Macmillan, 1977.

———. *Teaching Reading to Children*. New York: Macmillan, 1982.

Hall, Maryanne. *Teaching Reading as a Language Experience.* 3d ed. Columbus: Charles E. Merrill, 1981.

Harris, Albert J., and Edward R. Sipay. *How to Teach Reading: A Competency-Based Program.* New York: Longman, 1978.

————. *How to Increase Reading Ability.* 7th ed. New York: David McKay, 1980.

Harris, Albert J., and Edward R. Sipay, eds. *Readings on Reading Instruction.* 2d ed. New York: David McKay, 1972.

Harris, Larry A., and Carl B. Smith. *Reading Instruction: A Handbook.* 3d ed. New York: Holt, Rinehart and Winston, 1980.

Heilman, Arthur. *Phonics in Proper Perspective.* 4th ed. Columbus: Charles E. Merrill, 1981.

Heilman, Arthur, William H. Rupley, and Timothy R. Blair. *Principles and Practices of Teaching Reading.* 5th ed. Columbus: Charles E. Merrill, 1981.

Herber, Harold L. *Teaching Reading in Content Areas.* 2d ed. Englewood Cliffs, N.J.: Prentice-Hall, 1978.

Herr, Selma. *Learning Activities for Reading.* 4th ed. Dubuque, Iowa: Wm. C. Brown, 1982.

Hillerich, Robert L. *Reading Fundamentals for Preschool and Primary Children.* Columbus: Charles E. Merrill, 1977.

Hittleman, Daniel R. *Developmental Reading: A Psycholinguistic Perspective.* Chicago: Rand McNally, 1978.

Hodges, Richard E., and Hugh Rudorf. *Language and Learning to Read.* Boston: Houghton Mifflin, 1972.

Holdaway, Don. *Foundations of Literacy.* Sidney, Australia: Ashton Scholastic, 1979.

Huey, Edmund Burke. *Psychology and Pedagogy of Reading.* New York: Macmillan, 1908; Cambridge, Mass.: M.I.T. Press, 1968.

International Reading Assn., Box 695, Newark, Del. 19711.
    Perspectives in Reading
    Proceedings of the Annual Convention
    Reading Aids
    Annotated Bibliographies
    IRA + ERIC/CRIER
    The Reading Teacher
    Journal of Reading
    The Reading Research Quarterly

Jansky, Jeannette, and Katrina De Hirsch. *Preventing Reading Failure: Prediction, Diagnosis, Intervention.* New York: Harper & Row, 1972.

Karlin, Robert. *Teaching Elementary Reading: Principles and Strategies.* 3d ed. New York: Harcourt Brace Jovanovich, 1980.

Kean, John M., and Carl Personke. *The Language Arts: Teaching and Learning in the Elementary School.* New York: St. Martin's Press, 1976.

Kennedy, Eddie C. *Classroom Approaches to Remedial Reading.* 2d ed. Itasca, Ill.: F.E. Peacock, 1977.

————. *Methods in Teaching Developmental Reading.* 2d ed. Itasca, Ill.: F.E. Peacock, 1981.

Labuda, Michael, ed. *Creative Reading for Gifted Learners: A Design for Excellence.* Newark, Del.: International Reading Assn., 1974.

LaPray, Margaret. *Teaching Children to Become Independent Readers.* New York: Center for Applied Research in Education, 1972.

Lee, Dorris M., and Joseph B. Rubin. *Children and Language: Reading and Writing, Talking and Listening.* Belmont, Calif.: Wadsworth, 1979.

Lee, Dorris M., and Roach Van Allen. *Learning to Read Through Experience.* 2d ed. New York: Appleton-Century-Crofts, 1963.

Long, Nicholas J., William C. Morse, and Ruth G. Newman. *Conflict in the Classroom: The Education of Emotionally Disturbed Children.* 4th ed. Belmont, Calif.: Wadsworth, 1980.

Lundsteen, Sara W. *Children Learn to Communicate: Language Arts Through Creative Problem-Solving.* Englewood Cliffs, N.J.: Prentice-Hall, 1976.

McCracken, Robert A., and Marlene J. McCracken. *Reading Is Only the Tiger's Tail.* San Rafael, Calif.: Leswing Press, 1972.

McCracken, Marlene, and Robert McCracken. *Reading, Writing and Language: A Practical Guide for Primary Teachers.* Winnipeg, Manitoba: Peguis Publishers, 1979.

Malmstrom, Jean. *Understanding Language: A Primer for the Language Arts Teacher.* New York: St. Martin's Press, 1977.

Mangieri, John N., Lois Bader, and James E. Walker. *Elementary Reading: A Comprehensive Approach.* New York: McGraw-Hill, 1982.

Mason, George E. *A Primer on Teaching Reading.* Itasca, Ill.: F.E. Peacock, 1981.

Mazurkiewicz, Albert J. *Teaching About Phonics.* New York: St. Martin's Press, 1976.

Moffett, James. *A Student-Centered Language Arts Curriculum, K–6.* Boston: Houghton Mifflin, 1976.

Natchez, Gladys, and Florence Roswell. *Reading Disability: A Human Approach.* 3d ed. New York: Basic Books, 1980.

Olson, Joanne P., and Martha H. Dillner. *Learning to Teach Reading in the Elementary School, Utilizing a Competency-Based Instructional System.* 2d ed. New York: Macmillan, 1982.

Pearson, P. D., and D. D. Johnson. *Teaching Reading Comprehension.* New York: Holt, Rinehart and Winston, 1978.

Piercey, Dorothy. *Reading Activities in the Content Areas: An Ideabook for Middle and Secondary Schools.* 2d ed. Boston: Allyn & Bacon, 1982.

Quandt, Ivan J. *Teaching Reading: A Human Process.* Chicago: Rand McNally, 1977.

Ransom, Grayce. *Preparing to Teach Reading.* Boston: Little, Brown, 1978.

Robinson, H. Alan. *Teaching Reading and Study Strategies: The Content Areas.* 2d ed. Boston: Allyn & Bacon, 1978.

Ruddell, Robert B. *Reading Language Instruction: Innovative Practices.* Englewood Cliffs, N.J.: Prentice-Hall, 1974.

Russell, David, Etta Karp, and Anne Marie Mueser. *Reading Aids Through the Grades.* 4th rev. ed. New York: Teachers College Press, 1981.

Savage, John F., ed. *Linguistics for Teachers, Selected Readings.* Chicago: Science Research Associates, 1973.

Savage, John F., and Jean F. Mooney. *Teaching Reading to Children with Special Needs.* Boston: Allyn & Bacon, 1978.

Schubert, Delwyn G., and Theodore L. Torgerson. *Improving the Reading Program.* 5th ed. Dubuque, Iowa: Wm. C. Brown, 1980.

Smith, Frank. *Reading Without Nonsense.* New York: Teachers College Press, 1979.

———. *Understanding Reading, A Psycholinguistic Analysis of Reading and Learning to Read.* 3d ed. New York: Holt, Rinehart and Winston, 1982.

Smith, Frank, ed. *Psycholinguistics and Reading.* New York: Holt, Rinehart and Winston, 1973.

Smith, Nila Banton. *American Reading Instruction.* Newark, Del.: International Reading Assn., 1965.

Smith, Nila B., and H. Alan Robinson. *Reading Instruction for Today's Children.* 2d ed. Englewood Cliffs, N.J.: Prentice-Hall, 1980.

Smith, Richard J., and Thomas C. Barrett. *Teaching Reading in the Middle Grades.* 2d ed. Reading, Mass.: Addison-Wesley, 1979.

Smith, Richard J., and Dale D. Johnson. *Teaching Children to Read.* 2d ed. Reading, Mass.: Addison-Wesley, 1980.

Spache, Evelyn. *Reading Activities for Child Involvement.* 3d ed. Boston: Allyn & Bacon, 1981.

Spache, George. *Diagnosing and Correcting Reading Disabilities.* Boston: Allyn & Bacon, 1976.

Spiro, Rand J., Bertram C. Bruce, and William F. Brewer, eds. *Theoretical Issues in Reading Comprehension: Perspectives from Cognitive Psychology, Linguistics, Artificial Intelligence, and Education.* Hillsdale, N.J.: Lawrence Erlbaum Associates, 1980.

Stauffer, Russell G. *Directing the Reading-Thinking Process.* New York: Harper & Row, 1975.

———. *The Language-Experience Approach to the Teaching of Reading.* 2d ed. New York: Harper & Row, 1980.

Temple, Charles A., Ruth Nathan, and Nancy Burris. *The Beginnings of Writing.* Newton, Mass.: Allyn & Bacon, 1982.

Thonis, Eleanor Wall. *Literacy for America's Spanish-speaking Children.* Newark, Del.: International Reading Assn., 1976.

Tinker, Miles A. *Preparing Your Child for School.* New York: McGraw-Hill, 1976.

Tinker, Miles A., and Constance McCullough. *Teaching Elementary Reading.* 4th ed. Englewood Cliffs, N.J.: Prentice-Hall, 1975.

Tonjes, Marian J., and Miles V. Zintz. *Teaching Reading/Thinking/Study Skills in Content Classrooms.* Dubuque, Iowa: Wm. C. Brown, 1981.

Vacca, Richard T. *Content Area Reading.* Boston: Little, Brown, 1981.

Valett, Robert E. *Developing Cognitive Abilities: Teaching Children to Think.* St. Louis: C.V. Mosby, 1978.

Veatch, Jeannette, et al. *Key Words to Reading: The Language Experience Approach Begins.* 2d ed. Columbus: Charles E. Merrill, 1979.

Wilson, Robert M., and Maryanne Hall. *Programmed Word Attack for Teachers.* 3d ed. Columbus: Charles E. Merrill, 1979.

Zintz, Miles V. *Corrective Reading.* 4th ed. Dubuque, Iowa: Wm. C. Brown, 1981.

Name Index

Subject Index

C

Caldecott medal, 193, 429
California Reading Test, 121, 576
California Test of Mental Maturity, 517
Canterbury Tales, 69
capacity level, 28, 31, 93, 94, 111
card catalog, 328, 330, 420, 421
case reports
  Carolyn, 532–33
  Edna, 508–9
  Ernesto, 5–6
  Jack, 4–5
  Jill, 516–17
  John, 510
  Mark, 478
  Susan, 370
case study, 531, 543–45
cassette recorder, 187
categorizing, 304
catharsis, 415, 431
cause-effect, 381–82
causes of failure, 533–36
censorship, 19
chaining, 30
characteristics of language, 66
Charlotte's Web, 57, 302
charts, 337, 341, 352
checklists, 554, 560
child-centered learning, 143
children out of school, 18
child-teacher interaction, 359
Choosing Shoes, 118
clarifying responses, 56
classification, in discourse, 299
classifying, 127, 132
classroom environment, 208–9
classroom management, 30, 34, 181, 200, 212
closed questions, 42
closed syllables, 270
close proximity, 201
cloze, 82, 284–85, 316–21, 550, 580
  scoring, 316
  as teaching technique, 321
  tests, 316–20
clues
  configuration, 236, 244–45
  context, 71, 235, 257–60, 371
  picture, 235
Clymer-Barrett Prereading Battery, 131
cognition, 48, 51, 287
cognitive behavior, 208
cognitive domain, 28, 29, 31, 48–49, 56, 560
cognitive strategies, 14
cognitive structure, 75

color blindness, 121
combining forms, 70, 71, 342, 344, 350
communication skills, 23
communicative relationships, 207
comparing word meanings, 259
competition, 39
compound words, 71, 268, 270, 467
comprehension, 49, 66, 93, 400
  in cognitive domain, 56
  creative, 314
  defined, 14
  in determining reading level, 94
  evaluative, 315
  in the IRI, 104–5
  literal, 304
  requirements for, 291
  skills of, 284–86
computer instruction, 141, 174
computer research, 330–31
concept development, 125
concepts, 29, 290, 370, 534
  formation of, 30, 44, 50, 51–53, 343
  interrelation of, 371
  in language development, 217
  in reading, 77, 257, 328, 375, 519
Concepts About Print Assessment, 134, 135
conceptualization, 42, 44, 51, 52
concrete experience, 43, 45, 46
concrete operations, 51, 53, 136
conditions of learning, 37
cone of experience, 29, 42, 43, 44, 513
conference, parent-teacher, 215
configuration clues, 236, 244–45
confirming, 10
conformity, 391
connotative meaning, 288, 289
consonant, 79, 80, 85
consonant blends, 38
consonant clusters, 255, 261, 271
consonant digraph, 84, 262
consonant spellings, 264
consonant-vowel-consonant (CVC) generalization, 262
content methodology, 45
context, 81, 285, 286
context clues, 71, 235, 257–60, 371
context reader, 399, 410
contrastive analysis, 440, 443, 461–64
contrived experience, 43
conventional grade competence, 34, 36
conventions about print, 531, 538
convergent thinking, 285, 302
coping strategies, 280
corpus of speech, 74
corrections, 108
corrective reading, 166, 167, 168, 193, 529, 530–31, 549
Council on Interracial Books for Children, 388

creative comprehension, 314–15
creative reading, 31
creative writing, 195
creativity, 502
criterion-referenced tests, 553, 565–68
critical reading, 31, 312–13, 315, 368–69, 372, 382–91
  elements in, 392–93
  environment for, 392
  skills, 392–93
  teaching of, 368, 391–93
critical thinking, 293–94
criticism, 391
cross-age grouping, 193
cross-cultural communication, 446
cultural acceptance, 444
cultural conflicts, 444
cultural determinism, 84
cultural differences, 18, 444
cultural pluralism, 387
cultural understanding, 442–44
culture of poverty, 477, 478–81
cumulative records, 100, 184, 222
curve of forgetting, 47, 48
curve of normal distribution, 29, 31, 32
curve of retention, 48

D

Death Be Not Proud, 58
decoding, 7–8, 44, 79, 174, 292, 464
deep structure, 65, 81, 84, 294
deletions, 297
denotative meanings, 288, 289
derived forms, 84
descenders, 244
description, 299
descriptive linguistics, 66
developmental reading skills, 96
Dewey Decimal System, 330, 420
diacritical marks, 84
diagnostic reading tests, 553, 570
diagnostic teaching, xvii, xxi, 113, 440, 529, 580, 584, 587
diagrams, 352
dialect of English, 476, 491
dialectology, 477, 485
dialects, 68, 82, 84, 142
dictionary, 273, 274, 276, 332, 371
differences
  achievement, 189, 191
  boys vs. girls in reading, 191
  individual, 21, 188
  sex, 189–91
differentiation, 310, 311
digraphs, 84, 262
diphthong, 84
directed reading lessons, 186
  steps in, 158–60

instructional level of, 91, 92, 93
recreational, 23, 161
and self-concept, 6
skills of, 22
tasks in, 22
reading achievement tests, 92, 570
reading analysis summary, 546
reading charts, 153
reading clinic, 191
reading corner, 416
reading efficiency, 358
reading failure, 530, 531
causes, 535–36
overcoming, 536
parent-teacher communication
about, 536
school standards, 534
special services, 536
reading games, 195, 255, 277–78
reading groups, 186, 580, 582
reading habits, 414, 416
reading materials
environmental print, 541
predictable books, 541
reading miscue, 553
Reading Miscue Inventory, 576
reading models, 7, 14
reading practice, 541
reading process, 66, 92, 142, 169, 576
reading profile, 553, 565, 566
reading readiness tests, 130
reading retardation, 111
Ready Steps, 133, 137
Real Mother Goose, The, 119
reasoning, 286
rebus, 85, 141, 154, 155, 170, 173
record keeping, 280, 417, 531, 544,
546–48, 565
record of skills taught, 280
recreational reading, 23, 161
redundancy, 65, 83, 86
reference books, 328, 329, 332
reference points, 369, 375
reinforcement, 54, 328, 376, 470
relationships, the 4th R, 216
remedial readers, 441, 549
remembering, rules for, 48
repetition, 91, 107, 108
report cards, 217, 228, 229
research and writing method, 154, 166
retarded child, 440
reversals, 102, 132, 133, 538
review, 30, 47
rewards, 41, 42, 60
rhyming words, 243
rhythm, 85
Right to Read, 16
roleplaying, 45, 218, 221
roots, 84, 268
root word, 79

S

sampling, 10
San Diego Quick Assessment, 99
Sand Test, 134, 135
Scale for Determining Reader Level,
102
scheduling reading instruction, 185
schemata, 85, 285, 292, 557
schema theory, 284, 285, 287–89
Scholastic Book Service, 436
school culture, 588
school failure, 17, 19, 20, 132
school-home cooperation, 217
school language, 73
school and middle-class values, 446
school policy, 535, 536
schwa, 262
seatwork
constructive, 187
independent, 186, 197
segregation of gifted, 504
self-concept, 39, 411, 482, 486, 586
self-evaluation in reading, 161, 560
self-fulfilling prophecy, 487, 585, 586
self-motivation, 161
self-pacing, 161
self-selection, 161
semantic cue, 85, 440
semantic processing, xix
semantics, 9, 65, 70–71, 76–77, 85, 86
sense of story, 557
sensorimotor period, 51
sentence patterns, 70, 465
sentence transformation, 70
sequencing, 305, 379, 380
service words, 79, 156, 248–50, 255,
581
sex differences, 183, 189–91
shared oral reading, 160
sight words, 13, 80, 145, 235
lists of, 156
in reading programs, 76–77
teaching, 243, 247–55
signal learning, 30
silent letters, 79, 80, 262
silent reading, 400, 401
guided, 107, 160, 184
Silent Reading Diagnostic Test, 538,
575
simile, 346
skills approach, 7, 9
slang expressions, 68, 70, 71
Slosson Oral Reading Test, 101
slow learners, 511
Snellen Chart, 121
socialized speech, 75
social maturity, 117, 133
social problems, 17, 20
socioeconomic status, 35

sociogram, 553, 554, 562, 563
sociolinguistics, 65, 66, 85, 86
Socratic method, 383
software, 276–77
Sounder, 58
sound-symbol correspondence, 7
spaced review, 328
Spanish vocabulary, 349
specialized vocabulary, 342
speech
egocentric, 75
handicapped, 500
speech problem, 35
speed of comprehension, 326, 356, 357
speed of reading, 371
spelling, 22, 80, 81, 263
SQ3R, 369, 378–79
standard deviation, 32, 33
standard English, 142, 477, 485, 491,
494
standardized reading test, 31, 92, 529
standardized silent reading tests, 576
standard references, 416, 437
stereotypes, 369, 388–90
stimulus response, 30
Stones, 134
Stone word list, 156, 249–50, 256
stories
read to children, 556
told to children, 556
story grammar, 557
story method, 235, 240–41
story-telling ability, 555–56
stress, 70, 85, 272
generalizations, 273
structural analysis skills, 144, 233, 241,
244, 261, 267–73, 537
structured overview, xviii, 368, 369,
371–74
structure words, 79, 343
student-teacher interaction, 205–8
study guide, 362–65
three levels of, 364
studying a lesson, steps to follow, 377
study skills, 326, 372
study skills, interpretation, 372
location, 372
organization, 372
problem solving, 372
reading rate, 372
vocabulary, 372
substitution, 91, 106, 108
success experiences, 39, 41–42, 43, 60
suffixes, 70, 71, 84, 268, 350
summaries, written, 339, 341
supplementary reading, 161
suprasegmentals, 65, 70, 71, 85
surface structure, 81, 85, 294